"This book is a breakthrough for the study of
has uncovered much new evidence and has lev
of Aceh to reveal hidden aspects of the nationa
an original argument on why the mass murder .... ue understood as a genocide.
Her book is not an ordinary contribution to the field of Indonesian history – it is a
game-changer."

—John Roosa, University of British Columbia, Canada

"It seems impossible to overstate the significance of Jess Melvin's monumental,
heartbreaking work. Not only does she make a devastating argument that Indonesia's
mass killings constitute genocide under international law, she took a simple yet
fateful step in the history of scholarship on Indonesia: she walked into a military
archive and asked for their records. That nobody had done this before attests to
the formidable courage it required. She analyzes thousands of pages of hitherto
secret documents with patient attention to detail and unflinching moral clarity. The
result transforms our understanding of Indonesian history, identity, and politics.
Beautifully written, endlessly important, Jess Melvin has authored one of the great
studies of genocide, anywhere. Period."

—Joshua Oppenheimer, Academy Award–nominated director,
The Act of Killing (2012) and *The Look of Silence* (2014), Denmark

"Melvin's book is a dramatic breakthrough in our understanding of the Indonesian
killings of 1965–66. She taps new archival sources to demonstrate powerfully
that the Indonesian military was deeply engaged in planning and carrying out
the murder of Indonesian communists. In the process, the military manipulated
domestic and international public opinion to conceal its role in political genocide."

—Robert Cribb, Australian National University, Australia

The Army and the Indonesian Genocide

For the past half-century, the Indonesian military has depicted the 1965–66 killings, which resulted in the murder of approximately one million unarmed civilians, as the outcome of a spontaneous uprising. This formulation not only denied military agency behind the killings, it also denied that the killings could ever be understood as a centralised, nation-wide campaign.

Using documents from the former Indonesian Intelligence Agency's archives in Banda Aceh, this book shatters the Indonesian government's official propaganda account of the mass killings and proves the military's agency behind those events. This book tells the story of the 3,000 pages of top-secret documents that comprise the Indonesian genocide files. Drawing upon these orders and records, along with the previously unheard stories of 70 survivors, perpetrators and other eyewitness of the genocide in Aceh province, it reconstructs, for the first time, a detailed narrative of the killings using the military's own accounts of these events. This book makes the case that the 1965–66 killings can be understood as a case of genocide, as defined by the 1948 Genocide Convention.

The first book to reconstruct a detailed narrative of the genocide using the army's own records of these events, it will be of interest to students and academics in the field of Southeast Asian studies, history, politics, the Cold War, political violence and comparative genocide.

Jess Melvin is Rice Faculty Fellow in Southeast Asia Studies and Postdoctoral Associate in Genocide Studies at the Whitney and Betty MacMillan Center for International and Area Studies at Yale University.

Rethinking Southeast Asia

Edited by Duncan McCargo
University of Leeds, UK

For a full list of titles in this series, please visit www.routledge.com

Southeast Asia is a dynamic and rapidly changing region which continues to defy predictions and challenge formulaic understandings. This series publishes cutting-edge work on the region, providing a venue for books that are readable, topical, interdisciplinary and critical of conventional views. It aims to communicate the energy, contestations and ambiguities that make Southeast Asia both consistently fascinating and sometimes potentially disturbing.

Some titles in the series address the needs of students and teachers, published in simultaneous in hardback and paperback, including:

Rethinking Vietnam
Duncan McCargo

Rethinking Southeast Asia is also a forum for innovative new research intended for a more specialist readership. Titles are published initially in hardback.

Studies of the Weatherhead East Asian Institute, Columbia University

The Studies of the Weatherhead East Asian Institute of Columbia University were inaugurated in 1962 to bring to a wider public the results of significant new research on modern and contemporary East Asia.

A Study of the Weatherhead East Asian Institute
Columbia University

Mechanics of Mass Murder, © Alit Ambara, 2017.

The Army and the Indonesian Genocide

Mechanics of Mass Murder

Jess Melvin

Routledge
Taylor & Francis Group

LONDON AND NEW YORK

First published 2018 by Routledge

2 Park Square, Milton Park, Abingdon, Oxfordshire OX14 4RN
711 Third Avenue, New York, NY 10017

Routledge is an imprint of the Taylor & Francis Group, an informa business

First issued in paperback 2018

British Library Cataloguing-in-Publication Data
A catalogue record for this book is available from the British Library

Library of Congress Cataloging-in-Publication Data
Names: Melvin, Jess, author.
Title: The army and the Indonesian genocide : mechanics of mass murder/
   Jess Melvin.
Description: New York : Routledge, 2018. | Series: Rethinking Southeast
   Asia; 15 | Includes bibliographical references and index.
Identifiers: LCCN 2017047047 | ISBN 9781138574694 (hardback) |
   ISBN 9781351273329 (ebook)
Subjects: LCSH: Indonesia—History—Coup d'âetat, 1965. | Genocide—
   Indonesia—Nanggroe Aceh Darussalam. | Political atrocities—
   Indonesia—Nanggroe Aceh Darussalam. | Indonesia—Armed
   Forces—Political activity.
Classification: LCC DS644.32 .M45 2018 | DDC 959.803/5—dc23
LC record available at https://lccn.loc.gov/2017047047

ISBN: 978-1-138-57469-4 (hbk)
ISBN: 978-1-138-34797-7 (pbk)

Typeset in Times
by Apex CoVantage, LLC

In memory of the victims of 1965.
And with love to Munawar and Mirah Jugi.

Contents

Illustrations

Maps

Figures

Tables

Acknowledgements

This book would not have been possible without the assistance and support of a great number of people.

First, I would like to thank each of my interviewees in Aceh, Medan, West Sumatra, Jakarta and Hong Kong, many of whom must unfortunately remain anonymous. Thank you for welcoming me into your homes and for sharing your often-painful experiences with me. This is your story. I hope I have done your memories justice.

This book grew out of my doctoral thesis. I will be forever grateful to my three PhD supervisors at the University of Melbourne: Kate McGregor, Tim Lindsey and Steve Welch, for their many suggestions, support and patience. I would additionally like to thank Ben Kiernan and David Simon for sponsoring my time at Yale University, where I substantially revised the original thesis into its current form as a Postdoctoral Associate with the Yale Genocide Studies Program. I am also grateful to Duncan McCargo, Dorothea Schaefter and Lily Brown at Routledge for seeing this project through its final stages.

I am indebted to all the people who helped me during my fieldwork in Indonesia and Hong Kong. I would especially like to thank Yasmin Shabri and Farhan Miswar for transcribing the interviews found in this book. I would also like to thank Azhari Aiyub and Reza Idria at Tikar Pandan; Bang Idal at LBH; Nurul Kamal and Irin Caisarina at the Aceh Institute; Rusdi Sufi, Bang Alkaf, Saiful Mahdi, Kak Ayu, Arabiyani Iya and *semua kawan-kawan* in Banda Aceh; Zulfadlie Kawom and Mun in North Aceh; Ida Nursdia and Zulhelmi Ridwan in West Aceh; Diyus Hanafi and Zamzami Mohammad in East Aceh; Deni, Heri and Pang Edi in South Aceh; Mustawalad Blang and Ibrahim Kadir in Central Aceh; Casper and family in Medan; Kak Nova in Jakarta; Chan Chung Tak and members of the Sumatra Fraternity in Hong Kong; staff at the Ali Hasjmy Library, the Pustaka Wilayah, Arsip, Pusdok, ICAIOS, Isa Sulaiman and LBH libraries and archives in Banda Aceh; as well as staff at the Waspada Arsip in Medan.

My sincere thanks to David Chandler for his expert editing magic and to the other brave souls who have read through sections of this book in its various stages: Ed Aspinall, Tendayi Bloom, Daniele Botti, Robert Cribb, Harold Crouch, Thomas Kehoe, Ben Kiernan, Duncan McCargo, Dirk Moses, Annie Pohlman, Geoffrey Robinson, Thomas Rogers, John Roosa and Kathryn Smithies. Your suggestions have been invaluable.

I am deeply grateful to Robert Cribb for creating the book's maps. I would also like to thank: Charles Coppel, Vannessa Hearman, Max Lane, Michael Leigh, Joshua Oppenheimer, Helen Pausacker, Jemma Purdey, Anthony Reid, Djin Siauw, Brad Simpson, Jim Siegel, Sri Lestari Wahyuningroem, Saskia Wieringa, Faizah Zakaria and Hui Yew-Foong, with a special thank you to Douglas Kammen for sending me the Complete Yearly Report that became so central to this book.

My heartfelt thanks to my families in Melbourne and Banda Aceh for supporting me throughout what at times seemed to be a never-ending project.

Finally, my deepest thanks and love to Munawar and Mirah Jugi, who joined me on every step of this journey. Mirah, who toddled through my first interviews at 23 months, is this year 10 years old.

New Haven, Connecticut July 2017

***

This research was made possible through the financial assistance of the Melbourne University Human Rights Scholarship, Prue Torney Award, PhD Fieldwork Grant Scheme and Gilbert Postdoctoral Fellowship.

It was also made possible thanks to the MacMillan Centre at Yale University.

Sections of material presented in chapter 1 of this book were first published in, Jess Melvin, 'Mechanics of Mass Murder: A Case for Understanding the Indonesian Killings as Genocide', *Journal of Genocide Research*, Vol. 19, No. 4, 2017.

Sections of material presented in chapter 6 of this book were first published in, Jess Melvin, 'Why Not Genocide? Anti-Chinese Violence in Aceh, 1965–66', *Journal of Current Southeast Asian Affairs*, Vol. 3, 2013.

This book evolved from the author's doctoral thesis, which won the 2016 Asian Studies Association of Australia President's Prize.

Note on translations and pseudonyms

All translations are my own unless otherwise specified. When providing original Indonesian quotations to accompany translations, I have maintained the typography and capitalisation used in the original document to help maintain the integrity of these citations.

Prior to 1972, 'j' was written as 'dj'; 'y' as 'j'; 'c' as 'tj'; 'u' as 'oe'; 'ny' as 'nj'; 'sy' as 'sj'; and 'kh' as 'ch'. According to this typography, 'Aceh' was written as 'Atjeh'; 'Jakarta' as 'Djakarta'; 'Syamsuddin' as 'Sjamsuddin'; 'Sukarno' as 'Soekarno'; 'Rakyat' as 'Rakjat' and 'Akhir' as 'Achir'.

The interviews presented in this book, along with the many that did not make it into the final draft, have been taped and transcribed in their original Indonesian or Acehnese. Although each of my interviewees signed release forms granting permission for the use of their names in this research, I have made the decision to use pseudonyms to protect the identities of survivors and eyewitnesses. The names of perpetrators, government and military officials, individuals who have since died, and individuals who have already been named publically in relations to the events of 1965–66, have been retained.

Acronyms and glossary

Abang, bang Indonesian term of address for 'older brother'
ABRI, Angkatan Bersenjata Republik Indonesia Indonesian Armed Forces
AKRI, Angkatan Kepolisian Republik Indonesia Indonesian Police Force
Algojo Executioner
Amanat Mandate
Ampera, Amanat Penderitaan Rakyat Mandate of the People's Suffering
Angkatan '45 'Generation of '45', a reference to the generation of Indonesians
   who fought during the national revolution
Ansor From the Arabic '*al-ansar*', 'followers of the Prophet', a youth organisation
   affiliated to the Nahdlatul Ulama (NU)
Asosiasi Huakiau Association of Overseas Chinese

Bang See, 'Abang'
Bapak Father, 'Mr' or 'Sir'
Baperki, Badan Permusyawaratan Kewarganegaraan Indonesia Consulta-
   tive Body for Indonesian Citizenship
Batak An ethnic group from North Sumatra
Berdikari, 'Berdiri di atas kaki sendiri' lit. 'Standing on ones feet', self-reliance
BKR, Badan Keamanan Rakyat People's Security Agency
Brimob, Brigade Mobile Mobile Police Brigade
BTI, Barisan Tani Indonesia Indonesian Peasants' Front
Bupati Regent, District Head

Camat Subdistrict Head
CC, Comite Central Central leadership body of the PKI
CDB, Comite Daerah Besar Provincial Headquarters of the PKI
Cek Acehnese term of address for 'uncle' or 'aunty'
CGMI, Consentrasi Gerakan Mahasiswa Indonesia Unified Movement of
   Indonesian Students
CPM, Corps Polisi Militer Military Police
CSS, Comite Subseksi Sub-Section Committee of the PKI
Cut Bang Acehnese term of address for 'youngest older brother'

Daerah Province

Dan Jonif, Komandan Batalion Infantri Infantry Battalion Commander

Dan Resort Militer, Komandan Resort Militer Subregional Military Commander

Dan Sekhan, Komandan Sektor Pertahanan Defence Sector Commander

Dandim, Komandan Distrik Militer District Military Commander

Darul Islam 'Abode of Islam', name of the armed rebel movement that fought in Aceh between 1953 and 1962 and elsewhere in Indonesia between 1948 and 1965

Dejah, Deputi MKN/KASAD Wilajah, Deputi Menteri Keamanan Nasional/ Kepala Staf Angkatan Darat Wilajah Regional Deputy to the National Minister for Security/Army Chief of Staff

Dewan Revolusi Indonesia Indonesian Revolution Council

Didong A form of traditional sung poetry from Central Aceh

DI/TII See, *Darul Islam*

DKA, Djawatan Kereta Api Railway Bureau

DPR, Dewan Perwakilan Rakyat People's Representative Council, Indonesia's Legislative assembly

DPR-GR, Dewan Perwakilan Rakyat –Gotong Royong People's Representative Council – Gotong Royong Cabinet, the Guided Democracy–era replacement for the DPR

DPRD Tingkat I, Dewan Perwakilan Rakyat Daerah Tingkat I Level I Regional People's Representative Council, Level I Provincial Government, Provincial Government

DPRD Tingkat II, Dewan Perwakilan Rakyat Daerah Tingkat II Level II Regional People's Representative Council (District level), Level II Provincial Government, District Government

DPRD-GR Tingkat I, Dewan Perwakilan Rakyat Daerah – Gotong Royong Tingkat I Level I Regional People's Representative Council – Gotong Royong Cabinet, the Guided Democracy–era replacement for the Level I Regional People's Representative Council, Level I Provincial Government, Provincial Government

DPRD-GR Tingkat II, Dewan Perwakilan Rakyat Daerah – Gotong Royong Tingat II Level II Regional People's Representative Council – Gotong Royong Cabinet, the Guided Democracy–era replacement for Level II Regional People's Representative Council, Level II Provincial Government, District Government

Dwikora, Dwi Komando Rakyat 'People's Double Command'

Dwitunggal Hind. lit. 'two-in-one'

Fatwa Islamic legal opinion

Front Nasional National Front

Front Pembela Pancasila Pancasila Defence Front

Front Pembela Pantja Sila Daerah Tk II Level II Pantja Sila Defence Front

Front Pemuda Pembela Pantjasila Pancasila Defence Youth Front

G30S   See *Gerakan 30 September*

GAM, Gerakan Aceh Merdeka   Free Aceh Movement

Ganyang Malaysia   Crush Malaysia

Gasbindo, Gabungan Serikat Buruh Indonesia   Amalgamated Indonesian Islamic Labour Federation

Gayo   An ethnic group from Central Aceh

Gerakan 30 September (G30S)   30 September Movement

Gerakan Massa Ummat Jang Bertuhan Untuk Mempertahankan Pantjasila   Movement of Believers for the Defence of Pancasila

Gerakan Pemuda Marhaenis   Marhaenist Youth Movement, a socialist Youth Movement associated with Sukarno

Gerwani, Gerakan Wanita Indonesia   Indonesian Women's Movement

Gestapu, Gerakan September Tiga Puluh   30 September Movement, an acronym for the 30 September Movement used by the military and its allies to create an association with the Nazi Gestpo

Gestok, Gerakan Satu Oktober   First of October Movement, the acronym given to the 30 September Movement by Sukarno

GMNI, Gerakan Mahasiswa Nasional Indonesia   Indonesian National Student Movement

Gotong Royong   'Mutual self-help'

GPTP, Gabubungan Perkumpulan Tionghoa Perantauan   Federation of Overseas Chinese

Hanra, Pertahanan Rakyat   People's Defence, village-level paramilitary units under the command of the Puterpra

Hansip, Pertahanan Sipil   Civilian Defence, village-level paramilitary units under the command of the Puterpra

HMI, Himpunan Mahasiswa Islam   Islamic Students Association

HSI, Himpunan Sardjana Indonesia   Association of Indonesian Scholars

IP-KI, Ikatan Pendukung Kemerdekaan Indonesia   League of Supporters of Indonesian Independence

IPPI, Ikatan Pemuda Peladjar Indonesia   Association of Indonesian High School Students

Jaga malam   Night patrol

Jihad   Holy war

Jon, Batalion   Battalion

Jon-Inf, Batalion Infanteri   Infantry Battalion

Ka Sub Sie, Kepala Sub Provinsie   Subdistrict Level Committee Head

Kabupaten   District

Kafir   Non-believer

Kafir harbi   A non-believer whom it is permitted to kill

KAMI, Kesatuan Aksi Mahasiswa Indonesia   Indonesian Students Action Front

Kamp konsentrasi Concentration camp

Kampung Village

KAP-Gestapu, Komando Aksi Pengganyangan Gerakan Tiga Puluh September Action Front to Crush the 30 September Movement

KAPI, Kesatuan Aksi Pelajar Indonesia Indonesian School Students Action Front

KAPPI, Kesatuan Aksi Pemuda Pelajar Indonesia Indonesian Youth and School Students Action Front

Kas Kogam, Kepala Staff Kogam Kogam Head of Staff

Kasdam-I, Kepala Staf Komando Daerah Militer-I Head of Staff of the Aceh Military Region Command

Kebal Invulnerability

Kecamatan Subdistrict

Kima, Kompi Markas lit. (Mil.) Barracks Company, a military company tied to a particular post or barracks

Koanda, Komando Antar Daerah Inter-Provincial Military Command

Kodahan, Komando Daerah Pertahanan Defence Region Command

Kodahan 'A', Komando Daerah Pertahanan 'A' Defence Region Command 'A' (Aceh)

Kodam, Komando Daerah Militer Regional Military Command

Kodim, Komando Distrik Militer District Military Command

Kogam, Komando Ganyang Malaysia Ganyang Malaysia Command

Kohanda, Komando Pertahanan Daerah Regional Defence Command

Kohanda 'A', Komando Pertahanan Daerah 'A' Regional Defence Command 'A' (Aceh)

Kolaga, Komando Mandala Siaga Mandala Vigilance Command

Komando Aksi Pemuda Youth Action Front

Komando Aksi Action Front

Komando Mandala Satu First Mandala Command

Komnas HAM, Komisi Nasional Hak Asasi Manusia National Human Rights Commission

Kontras, Komisi untuk Orang Hilang dan Korban Kekerasan Commission for the Disappeared and Victims of Violence

Kopkamtib, Komando Operasi Pemulihan dan Ketertiban Operational Command for the Restoration of Security and Order

Koramil, Komando Rayon Militer Military Precinct Command

Korem, Komando Resort Militer Military Resort Command

Kosekhan, Komando Sektor Pertahanan Defence Sector Command

Kostrad, Komando Strategis Angkatan Darat Army Strategic Reserve Command

Kosubdahan, Komando Sub-Daerah Tahanan Defence Region Sub-Command

KOTI, Komando Operasi Tertinggi Supreme Operations Command

Kuala Skodam, Staf Komando Daerah Militer Kodam Staff

Laksus, Pelaksana Khusus Daerah lit. 'Special Regional Director', internal security, military intelligence

LEKRA, Lembaga Kebudayaan Rakyat Institute of People's Culture

Mandala Satu   First Mandala, Mandala I

Manipol/USDEK, Manifesto Politik/Undang-Undang Dasar 1945, Sosialisme Indonesia, Demokrasi Terpimpin, Ekonomi Terpimpin dan Kepribadian Indonesia   Political manifesto [based on] the 1945 Constitution, Indonesian Socialism, Guided Democracy, Guided Economy and Indonesian Identity; the political manifesto of Guided Democracy

Marhaen   a term coined by Sukarno to refer to a category of poor Indonesians who were oppressed by capitalism and imperialism, but who were not part of the traditional peasant or proletarian classes as they were small landowners and owned a few tools

Masjumi, Majilis Sjuro Muslimin Indonesia   Consultative Council of Indonesian Muslims

Men/Pangad, Menteri/Panglima Angkatan Darat   Minister and Commander of the Armed Forces

Minang   An ethnic group from West Sumatra

MPR, Majelis Permusyawaratan Rakyat   People's Consultative Council

MPRS, Majelis Permusyawaratan Rakyat Sementara   Provisional People's Consultative Council

Muhammadiyah   'Followers of Muhammad', a modernist Islamic organisation

Mukim   Residency; a subdivision of a subdistrict in Aceh

Musyawarah Alim-Ulama Sedaerah Istimewa Aceh   Ulama Council for Aceh Special Region

Nasakom, 'Nasionalisme, Agama, Komunisme'   'Nationalism, Religion, Communism', a Guided Democracy–era doctrine that officially recognised the role of these three major political tendencies in Indonesian political life

Nekolim, 'Neo-Kolonialisme, Kolonialisme, Imperialisme'   'Neo-Colonialism, Colonialism, Imperialism', 'Neo-Colonialist, Colonialist, Imperialist', a term coined by Sukarno during the Guided Democracy period

NKRI, Negara Kesatuan Republik Indonesia   Unitary State of the Republic of Indonesia, the official name of the Republic of Indonesia

NU, Nahdlatul Ulama   'Revival of the Islamic Scholars', a traditionalist Islamic group

Oknum   lit. 'element', a member of an organisation or movement

Operasi Singgalang   Singgalang Operation

Pagar betis   'Fence of legs', a counter-insurgency encirclement strategy used by the Indonesian military

Pak   See, 'Bapak'

Pak Cik   Acehnese for term of address for 'uncle'

Panca Sila: The five principles of the Indonesian state, as first articulated by Sukarno   belief in Almighty God, humanity that is just and civilised, the unity of Indonesia, democracy guided by the wisdom of representative deliberation and social justice for all Indonesians

Pangad, Panglima Angkatan Darat   Commander in Chief of the Armed Forces

Pangdahan, Panglima Daerah Pertahanan   Defence Region Commander

Pangdahan 'A', Panglima Daerah Pertahanan 'A'   Defence Region Commander 'A' (Aceh)

Pangdam, Panglima Daerah Militer   Regional Military Commander

Pangkoanda, Panglima Komando Antar Daerah   Inter-Provincial Military Commander

Panglatu, Panglima Mandala Satu   First Mandala Commander

Panglima Tertinggi   Supreme Commander of the Armed Forces

Pantja Tunggal   'Five in One'

Pantjasila   See *Panca Sila*

Parkindo, Partai Kristen Indonesia   Indonesian Christian Party

Partai Katolik   Catholic Party

Partai Komunis Indonesia   The Indonesian Communist Party

Partindo, Partai Indonesia   Indonesia Party

PBR, Pemimpin Besar Revolution   Great Leader of the Revolution, an official title used by Sukarno

Pembela Pantja Sila Daerah Tk II   Level II Pantja Sila Defence

Pembela Rakyat   People's Defence, the name of a military-sponsored death squad in South Aceh

Pemuda   Youth

Pemuda Alwasliyah   Alwasliyah Youth

Pemuda Ansor   Ansor Youth, a youth wing of Ansor

Pemuda Kristen Indonesia   Indonesian Christian Youth

Pemuda Marhaenis   Marhaenist Youth, otherwise referred to as the Marhaenist Youth Movement (*Gerakan Pemuda Marhaenis*)

Pemuda Muhammadijah   Muhammadijah Youth, a youth group affiliated to Muhammadijah

Pemuda Muslimin Indonesia   Indonesian Muslim Youth

Pemuda Pancasila   Pancasila Youth

Pemuda PUSA   All-Aceh Association of Islamic Scholars Youth, see PUSA

Pemuda Rakyat   People's Youth

Pendahan, Penerangan Daerah Pertahanan   Defence Region Information Officer

Pendopo   Open audience hall

Pepelrada, Penguasa Pelaksanaan Dwikra Daerah   Regional Authority to Implement Dwikora

Peperda, Penguasa Perang Daerah   Regional War Authority

Perbum, Persatuan Buruh Minyak   Oil Workers Union

Perhimi, Perhimpunan Mahasiswa Indonesia   Indonesian University Students' Association

Perti, Persatuan Tarbyiah Islamiyah   Islamic Education Association

Perwira Konsinjir Kodahan   Assigned Kodahan Officers, officers placed on alert under the Kodahan command

Perwira Siaga   'Alert Officers'

PI Perti, Partai Islam Persatuan Tarbyiah Islamiyah   Islamic Education Association Islamic Party
PII, Peladjar Islam Indonesia   Islamic Students of Indonesia
PJM, Paduka Jang Mulia   Your Excellency, an official title used by Sukarno
PKI   See *Partai Komunis Indonesia*
PM   See *Polisi Militer*
PMI, Pemuda Muslim Indonesia   Indonesian Muslim Youth
PNI, Partai Nasional Indonesia   Indonesian National Party
Pomdam, Polisi Militer Daerah Militer   Military Police
Pramuka, [Gerakan] Praja Muda Karana   Indonesia's Scouting Organisation
PRRI/Permesta, Pemerintah Revolusioner Republik Indonesia/Piagam Perjuangan Semesta Alam   Revolutionary Government of the Republic of Indonesia/Universal Struggle Charter
PSII, Partai Sarekat Islam Indonesia   Indonesian Islamic Union Party
PUSA, Persatuan Ulama Seluruh Aceh   All-Aceh Association of Islamic Scholars
Puskesmas, Pusat Kesehatan Masyarakat   Community health clinic
Puterpra, Perwira Urusan Teritorial dan Perlawanan Rakyat   Territorial Affairs and People's Resistance Officer
Putri Alwasliyah   Daughters of Alwasliyah
Putri Muhammadijah   Daughters of Muhammadiyah, a women's group affiliated with Muhammadiyah

Rakyat Bersenjata   Armed civilians
Rakyat Pejuang   People's Resistance
Rentjong   A traditional Acehnese dagger used both ceremonially and in warfare
Resort   District-level military or police command
Rindam, Resimen Induk Kodam   Main Regiment of a particular Kodam
RPKAD, Resimen Para Komando Angkatan Darat   Indonesian Special Forces
RRI, Radio Republik Indonesia   Indonesian Republic Radio, Indonesia's national radio broadcaster
Ruang Yudha   War Room

SABUPRI, Sarekat Buruh Perkebunan Republik Indonesia   *Plantation Workers Union of the Republic of Indonesia*
Sarbuksi, Sarekat Buruh Kehutanan Seluruh Indonesia   All Indonesia Forest Workers Union
Sarekat Islam Merah   Red Islamic League
Sarekat Islam Putih   White Islamic League
SBKA, Serikat Buruh Kereta Api   Railway Workers Union
Sholat   Muslim prayer
SI, Sarekat Islam   Islamic Union
SI-AD, Sekolah Inteligen-Angkatan Darat   Military Intelligence School
Sie Komite, Seksi Komite   Section-level Committee
Skodam, Staff Komando Daerah Militer   Kodam Staff

SOBSI, Serikat Organisasi Buruh Seluruh Indonesia All-Indonesia Workers' Organisation Union

SOKSI, Sentral Organisasi Karyawan Socialis Indonesia Union of Indonesian Socialist Karyawan Organisation (an umbrella organisation for anticommunist trade unions)

Subdahan, Sub-Daerah Pertahanan Defence Region Sub-Command

Sub Sie Komite, Sub Provinsie Komite Sub-District Committee

Supersemar, Surat Perintah Sebelas Maret 'Order of March Eleventh'

Syariat Islam Islamic Law

Tengku (Tgk.) An Acehnese term of address used for Islamic leaders, usually ulama

Teuku (T.) A term of address used in Aceh for men from uleebalang (noble) families. In Malaysia, 'Tunku'

Teungku See *Tengku*

Tjatur Tunggal 'Four in one'

Tjentjang (cincang) 'To cut up' (mince)

TKKB, Tentara Komunis Kalimantan West Kalimantan Communist Army

TKR, Tentara Keamanan Rakyat People's Defence Army

TNI, Tentara Nasional Indonesia Indonesian National Army

TRI, Tentara Republik Indonesia Army of the Republic of Indonesia

Tri Ubaya Cakti lit. 'Three Sacred Promises'

Trikora, Tri Komando Rakyat People's Triple Command

Tritura,Tri Tuntutan Rakyat 'Three Demands of the People'

Ulama Islamic religious scholar, often translated as 'cleric'

Uleebalang Traditional Acehnese aristocracy

Wakil Deputy

Wali Kota City mayor

Wedana Subdistrict chief

WH: Wilayatul Hisbah Syariat Police

WNA, Warga Negara Asing Foreign citizen

WNI, Warga Negara Indonesia Indonesian citizen

WMD, 'Wajib Darurat Militer' 'Mandatory Military Emergency', a civilian milita group in Central Aceh

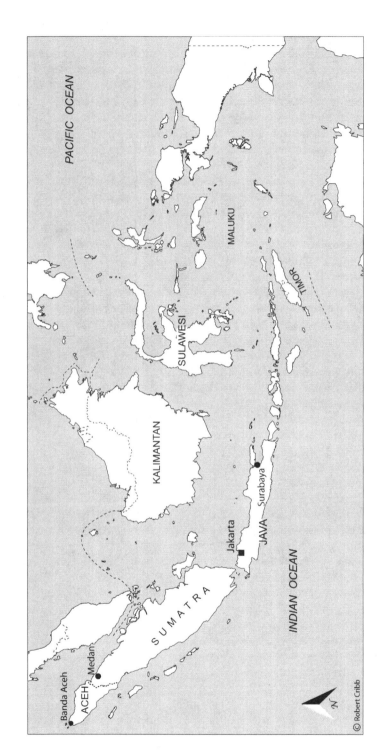

Map 1 Map of Indonesia showing Aceh province

© Robert Cribb

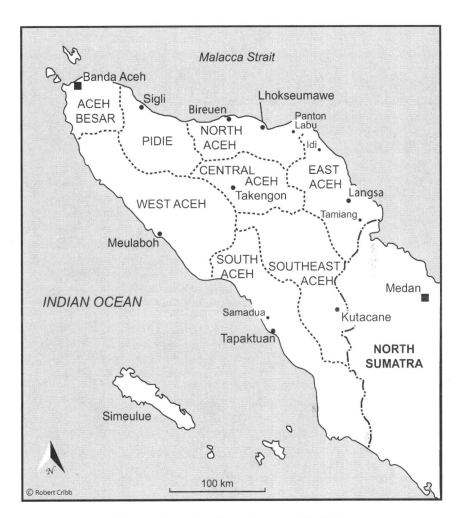

Map 2 Map of Aceh showing district borders as they existed in 1965

Introduction

The Indonesian genocide files

On a hot afternoon in 2010, I returned home from the former Indonesian Intelligence Agency's archives in Banda Aceh with a heavy cardboard box filled with photocopied documents. I did not yet know it, but the documents that I held in my hands would soon definitively shatter the Indonesian government's official propaganda account of the 1965–66 mass killings and prove the military's agency behind those events. I have called these documents the Indonesian genocide files.

For the past half-century, the Indonesian military has depicted the killings, which resulted in the murder of approximately one million unarmed civilians, as the outcome of a "spontaneous" uprising by "the people".[1] This formulation not only denied military agency behind the killings. It also denied that the killings could ever be understood as a centralised, nation-wide campaign.

That was not, however, how the Indonesian military understood the killings internally at the time. Throughout the 3,000 pages of top-secret documents that comprise the Indonesian genocide files, the military describes the killings as an "Annihilation Operation" (*Operasi Penumpasan*),[2] which it launched with the stated intention to "annihilate down to the roots" (*menumpas sampai ke akar-akarnja*)[3] its major political rival, the Indonesian Communist Party.

The armed forces implemented this Operation after seizing control of the Indonesian state on the morning of 1 October 1965. They ordered civilians to participate in the campaign from 4 October[4] and established a 'War Room' on 14 October with the stated intention to "carry out non-conventional warfare . . . [to] succeed in annihilating [the military's target group] together with the people".[5] The killings, it can now be proven, were implemented as deliberate state policy.

The use of the term genocide to describe these events has long been contested. This book makes the case that the 1965–66 killings can be understood as a case of genocide, as defined by the 1948 Genocide Convention. In chapter 1, I argue that key orders and records found within the Indonesian genocide files are able to prove the military possessed and acted upon a clear "intent to destroy, in whole or in part, a national, ethnic, racial or religious group, as such" and that these events thus meet the legal definition of genocide.

This book tells the story of the Indonesian genocide files. Drawing upon these orders and records, along with the previously unheard stories of 70 survivors, perpetrators and other eyewitness of the genocide in Aceh province, it reconstructs, for the first time, a detailed narrative of the killings using the military's own accounts of these events.

Sacred Pancasila Day

During the still cool morning of 1 October 2015, on the fiftieth anniversary of the genocide, Indonesia's President, Joko "Jokowi" Widodo, stood before rows of soldiers dressed in parade uniform in the capital, Jakarta.[6] The purpose of the event, known as Sacred Pancasila Day,[7] was not to commemorate the victims of the genocide, but rather to remember the trigger event that, in official narratives, overwrites and displaces the killings.

According to this official narrative, 1 October 1965 marks the day the Indonesian Communist Party (PKI: *Partai Komunis Indonesia*) launched an "abortive coup" against the Indonesian state through a front organisation named the 30 September Movement (G30S: *Gerakan Tigapuluh September*). The story of the actions of the 30 September Movement is complicated because it contains elements of truth as well as complete fabrications that were used in the psychological warfare operation launched by the military against Indonesia's population during the aftermath of 1 October.

More ink has been spilled trying to explain the actions of the 30 September Movement than on the genocide itself. Here I do not intend to retell this story in full.[8] Several key points are nonetheless vital to understand how the military leadership justified its attack against members of the PKI and the much larger group of people who would eventually fall victim to the military's genocidal policies.

Before dawn on 1 October 1965, a group of mostly middle-ranking military officers calling itself the 30 September Movement kidnapped six key superior officers, members of the Indonesian Armed Forces High Command, including the Commander of the Indonesian Armed Forces, General Ahmad Yani, and a lieutenant who was apparently kidnapped in a case of mistaken identity for the Army Chief of Staff, Abdul Haris Nasution.[9] The middle-ranking officers who carried out this kidnapping operation were in close contact with the PKI's Chairman, D.N. Aidit, and his secret Special Bureau, but Aidit did not inform his other colleagues in the PKI leadership or membership of the operation.

The kidnapped generals were accused by the 30 September Movement of plotting a CIA-backed coup against Indonesia's popular and self-avowed Marxist President Sukarno. During the course of the operation three of the generals, including Yani, were killed in their homes. The surviving generals and lieutenant, along with the bodies of the three murdered generals, were then transported to Halim Airbase on the outskirts of Jakarta. Aidit was there at the time. Upon arrival, the generals are alleged to have been sadistically tortured and humiliated by communist women; their penises cut off and eyes gouged out as the women engaged in a mass orgy.[10] The generals and lieutenant were then murdered and their bodies dumped down a disused well next to the Airbase in an area known as the 'Crocodile Hole' (*Lubang Buaya*).

Following these killings, the military explained, the PKI, through the 30 September Movement, had attempted to spark a national uprising and "people's war"[11] through a series of radio messages. This uprising was reported to include a plan to massacre the PKI's political rivals. Supporting this claim, the military declared it had discovered pre-dug graves throughout the country.[12] Specifically, it was said, the communists planned to murder pious Muslims, who were accused of blocking the PKI's land reform campaign.[13] Within days, the military began to report the PKI and its supporters had begun to murder Muslims.[14]

In response to this alleged communist plot, the military claims it stepped in to "restore the peace" after overseeing the surrender of the 30 September Movement's visible members during the morning of 2 October. It launched this campaign under the leadership of Major General Suharto, who, as the Army's Strategic Reserve (*Kostrad*) Commander, had not been targeted by the 30 September Movement.[15] Upon hearing of the PKI's planned atrocities, "the people" are said to have "spontaneously" risen up in anger against the "inhuman" and "atheist" (*atheis, anti-tuhan*) communists. "These tensions", the official narrative explains, then "exploded into communal clashes resulting in bloodbaths in certain areas of Indonesia",[16] as civilians set about butchering their former neighbours with machetes until the military stepped in to stop the violence.

The killings are thus depicted as the result of horizontal, religiously inspired violence, sparked by the population's response to PKI atrocities. The military had saved the nation from the "communists". It had also saved the nation from itself.

This account is a gross and deliberate distortion of the truth. While it is true a group calling itself the 30 September Movement kidnapped and murdered six generals and a lieutenant during the early hours of 1 October, before declaring its intention to replace the Indonesian government, the actions of this group had no connection to the PKI as a mass organisation, or to the much larger group that was eventually targeted for annihilation by the military. The generals were not mutilated.[17] Nor did the PKI dig mass graves or begin to kill Muslims.[18] These stories were cynical propaganda fabrications intended to justify the military's own seizure of power.

Rather, records of diplomatic cables between the United States State Department and its diplomatic officials in Jakarta reveal the Indonesian military leadership had been deliberately waiting for a "pretext" event that could be blamed on the PKI, its major political rival, and used to orchestrate the military's own coup against Sukarno.[19] This coup, military informants had explained, "would be handled in such a way as to preserve Sukarno's leadership intact".[20] It was to be a coup that would not appear to be a coup. It was also to be a coup that would rely on the mass mobilisation of the population.

New evidence presented in chapter 2 of this book will show that the military's preparations to seize power during the lead-up to 1 October were much more extensive than it has previously been possible to demonstrate. While there is no evidence the military pre-planned the genocide *per se*, the order to carry out systematic mass killings evolved, chapters 3 to 6 will show, between 1 and 14 October. The military had deliberately established structures that would allow it to internally implement martial law once it decided to initiate its seizure of state power. It had also engaged in extensive militia and paramilitary training that would enable it to conduct such an operation.

The military, the Indonesian genocide files show, officially coordinated these preparations on Sumatra, one of Indonesia's main islands, from April 1965 through a military campaign labelled 'Operation Berdikari'. It would then activate this Operation during the morning of 1 October, at a time when the military was still ostensibly deciding how to react to the actions of the 30 September Movement. The activation of this Operation entailed the implementation of martial law throughout Sumatra and the activation of a new military command structure in Aceh known as the Defence Region Command (Kohanda: *Komando Pertahanan Daerah*). It would be through this new military command structure that the military would implement the genocide.

Evidence presented in chapter 3 shows that the military leadership pre-emptively treated the 30 September Movement as a coup attempt. Although the 30 September Movement did not declare its intention to replace the government until 2pm during the afternoon of 1 October,[21] the military leadership, in its internal correspondence, had that morning already begun to describe the 30 September Movement as a coup movement. But until 2pm, the 30 September Movement described its actions as an "internal" military affair aimed at alerting Sukarno to the generals' alleged plan to launch their own coup.

It is at this point that the story of the 30 September Movement often becomes unnecessarily complicated. This is because, in an attempt to highlight the military's subsequent genocidal attack against the PKI and other individuals who would become caught up in this violence, it is tempting to downplay the actions of the 30 September Movement or to dismiss the military's claim that the PKI had been involved in its actions. The 30 September Movement did kidnap and murder six key members of the military leadership, though there is no evidence the generals were mutilated, either before or after death.

There is also evidence PKI Chairman D.N. Aidit and the PKI's clandestine Special Bureau were aware of the plans of the 30 September Movement and that Aidit, as noted, was present at Halim Airbase on 1 October. There is not, however, any evidence that Aidit or the Special Bureau communicated their knowledge of the Movement's plans to the PKI Central Committee or other parts of their mass organisation either on or before 1 October. Nor is there any evidence that anyone attempted to mobilise the PKI as a mass organisation in support of the actions of the Movement either on or before 1 October.[22] This silence and inaction effectively left the PKI in the dark about the Movement and open to attack. It was, however, consistent with Aidit's apparent belief that the 30 September Movement was an internal military action.[23]

The leadership of the 30 September Movement consisted of five men. Three were mid-level military officers. Lieutenant Colonel Untung, the Movement's head, was a battalion commander in the Palace Guard; Colonel Abdul Latief was a member of the Jakarta Regional Military Command; and Major Soejono was a member of the Halim Air Force base guard. The two other members of the Movement's leadership were Sjam and Pono, both of whom are believed to have been linked to the PKI's Special Bureau, a secret underground organisation that answered exclusively to Aidit, not to the PKI Central Committee or the party membership.

It appears the initial intention of this group was not to murder the generals, but rather to bring them before Sukarno, who, it was hoped, would use the opportunity to expose the military leadership's plans to launch a coup and replace the generals with individuals who were loyal to him. Political kidnappings were not without precedent in Indonesia. Sukarno himself had been kidnapped by revolutionary youths in 1945, when he had appeared to backtrack on his promise to issue a declaration of Indonesian independence. He was not harmed by his captors and, upon being released, issued his now famous 17 August proclamation, while his captors were treated as national heroes.[24] After the killings, however, such an ending was no longer possible for the Movement.

Pointing to this failure of logic in the Movement's actions, scholars have proposed the Movement did not plan to murder the generals and that the killings appear to have occurred in the heat of the moment when several generals resisted arrest.[25] This development then left the Movement scrambling to come up with an alternative plan. It was at this late point (at 2pm on 1 October) that the Movement announced its intention to replace the government with a body called the Indonesian Revolution Council (*Dewan Revolusi Indonesia*), which it explained would "constitute the source of all authority" in Indonesia until elections could be held.[26] No national elections had been held since 1955.

When the membership of the Indonesian Revolution Council was then announced at 2.05pm over the national radio station, *Radio Republik Indonesia* (RRI), which had been seized during the morning of 1 October by the Movement, no mention was made of what Sukarno's role would be within this new body.[27] It is these later announcements that are touted as evidence by the military that the Movement intended to launch a coup.[28] The general murkiness of the 30 September Movement's actions coupled with Aidit and the PKI Special Bureau's involvement in these events made the actions of the 30 September Movement an ideal pretext event for the military. It is hard to imagine the military could have come up with a more perfect sequence of events if it had tried. Some scholars have even suggested Suharto was secretly behind the Movement.[29] Others have suggested he simply had personal foreknowledge of the actions of the 30 September Movement.[30] It was this foreknowledge, it is argued, that allowed him to respond to the Movement so quickly and with such clarity of vision.

This book proposes that the military leadership was actively preparing to seize state power during the lead-up to 1 October 1965. My argument does not require Suharto to have had specific foreknowledge of the actions of the 30 September Movement, though he may have had. He and the surviving military leadership responded so quickly and with such clarity of thought because it had already been training to launch a territorial warfare campaign aimed at seizing state power that was to be framed as a response to just such a PKI provocation. The murder of the generals, which pushed the actions of the 30 September Movement outside the realm of accepted political behaviour, undoubtedly enabled the military to launch a much more aggressive attack than may otherwise have been possible.

The extreme nature of the Movement's actions has also meant that some scholars have felt compelled to try to downplay the role of Aidit and the PKI's Special

Bureau as if their involvement may in some way lessen the military's culpability for the subsequent genocide. The question that should be asked is not whether the PKI leadership was completely innocent of involvement in the actions of the 30 September Movement, but whether the military's response to this event was proportionate and justifiable. Given the killings of nearly a million people, the answer to this second question must certainly be in the negative.

The murder of up to one million unarmed civilians in a deliberate and systematic campaign to destroy not only the PKI as a mass organisation but also a much broader group of civilians that had no organisational affiliation to the PKI whatsoever, targeted purely because of their alleged "association" with the PKI, is manifestly disproportionate to the actions of the 30 September Movement. Any claim of self-defence is completely without merit. What happened was a crime that must be assessed separately from the actions of the 30 September Movement.

Yet, far beyond justifying the genocide, the military's official propaganda account of the actions of the 30 September Movement has almost totally displaced and overwritten the genocide as an event. In 1969, Suharto, by then President, opened a giant monument to the dead generals at *Lubang Buaya*. The site includes seven life-sized bronze statues of the dead generals and lieutenant. They stand atop a bronze frieze that depicts a revisionist re-telling of Indonesia's post-colonial history, through which the PKI is portrayed as an instigator of chaos and evil.[31] This portrayal was a sharp repudiation of Sukarno's recognition that for him at least communism constituted an indispensable stream within the variety of Indonesian political thought. Also depicted in the frieze are images of the communist women alleged to have mutilated the generals, shown dancing naked around a man stuffing a body down a well. Suharto, for his part, emerges from this image as a strongman and saviour who was able to restore order and reunify the nation.

Towering over the monument stands a giant *garuda*, a mythical eagle-like bird, which, since the time of the 1945–49 Indonesian revolution, has come to embody the Indonesian state. Over its chest sits a shield portraying the five principles of Indonesian nationalism, known as the *Pancasila* (lit. five principles): belief in God, humanity, national unity, democracy and social justice. First enunciated by President Sukarno in 1945, *Pancasila* was adopted and sacralised by the New Order military regime. The purpose of this symbolism is to project the authority of the Indonesian state onto the military's propaganda version of events. The story of the military's crushing of the PKI is the foundation myth of the post-Sukarno Indonesian state.

It is at this site that the Sacred Pancasila Day ceremony is held on an annual basis. The story of the murdered generals overwrites and displaces the story of the genocide. Not once do we see the scenes of military-sponsored death squads executing civilians at military-controlled killing sites. Nor do we see the steady stream of trucks transporting victims to these killings sites from military-controlled jails under the cover of darkness or the mass rallies where the military ordered civilians to kill or be killed, which remain so vivid in the memories of eyewitnesses of this period. The victims of the genocide, if they are mentioned at all, are blamed for having brought their fate upon themselves. This perverse victim-blaming continues to this day.

When Jokowi was asked by waiting reporters at the conclusion of the formal fiftieth-anniversary Sacred Pancasila Day ceremony whether he intended to issue an apology to victims and survivors of the genocide, he broke into a broad smile before replying he had "no thoughts about apologising".[32]

The West's best news for years in Asia

If it seems remarkable that the Indonesian state continues to justify the killings, it should be remembered that Suharto's rise to power on the back of the killings was openly celebrated in the West. The destruction of the "communist threat" in Indonesia was considered a major strategic victory that helped to turn the tide of the Cold War in Southeast Asia. Suharto's rise, *TIME* magazine explained just after the worst of the killings had ended, was "the West's best news for years in Asia".[33]

Since the end of the Second World War, the Unites States had sought to increase its influence over Southeast Asia. In early 1965, the United States media was preoccupied with the war in Vietnam. The United States government, however, considered the sprawling archipelago nation of Indonesia to be of at least equal strategic importance to the whole of Indochina.[34] Indonesia, then the sixth most populous country in the world, lies across key sea-lanes through which the United States Navy passes. These sea-lanes are also some of the world's busiest commercial routes. Blessed with abundant raw materials, Indonesia was a major supplier of oil, tin and rubber and the site of significant American economic interests.[35]

Indonesia was also home to the largest communist party in the world outside of the USSR and China. In August 1965, the PKI boasted a membership of 3.5 million people.[36] When members of the PKI's affiliated organisations were also taken into account, adjusted to account for duplication of membership, the PKI and its affiliated organisations had a following approaching 20 million.[37] In addition to being highly active, Indonesia's communist movement was embraced by Indonesia's popular and self-proclaimed Marxist President Sukarno, who had declared communism to be a key element of Indonesian nationalism in 1961. As the PKI's influence grew, the United States government became increasingly concerned that Indonesia would become a new southern front for communist expansion should the PKI succeed in coming to power, a situation that could draw the United States into a second Vietnam-type war that it could ill afford. As such, the US committed itself to supporting all domestic attempts within Indonesia to crush the PKI before it could come to power. As we shall see, the US would also play a major, covert, role in supporting and facilitating the genocide.

This concern with Indonesia's internal affairs was not new. Since the mid-1950s, the United States government had repeatedly attempted to implement regime change in Indonesia. This covert campaign had included the transfer of one million dollars to Indonesia's main Islamist party Masjumi during the 1955 general election,[38] in an attempt to counteract support for Sukarno's Indonesian National Party (PNI: *Partai National Indonesia*) and the growing PKI. After the vote resulted in a tie, the Eisenhower administration threw its support behind a series of regional rebellions on Indonesia's Outer Islands in 1958, where rebels were supplied with military equipment and a number of B-26 bombers.[39] It was hoped that the rebellions, which were supported by Masjumi and key Indonesian military leaders who were dissatisfied with the trajectory in which Sukarno was taking the nation, would result in the breaking up of Indonesia. This plan was dramatically exposed, however, when Allen Pope, an American CIA operative who was piloting one of the bombers, was shot down by the Indonesian Air Force. This incident led to an even further deterioration of relations between the two countries.

The Kennedy administration demonstrated a more accommodative approach when it attempted to appease Sukarno in 1962 by supporting Indonesia's claim to the territory of Dutch New Guinea or West Irian (*Irian Barat*), today divided into the two provinces of Papua and West Papua. West Irian was the final territory claimed by the Dutch East Indies to remain under Dutch control and held a special place in Indonesia's nationalist rhetoric. US-sponsored talks led to the signing of the 'New York Agreement' between the Netherlands and Indonesia in August 1962. Under the terms of this agreement, Indonesia was to be awarded control over West Irian after a brief transitional period that was to be overseen by the United Nations, with the provision that Indonesia should facilitate an election on self-determination in the territory before the end of 1969.[40] Sukarno was pleased with this development and approved a series of American loans, which the Kennedy administration hoped could be used to leverage US influence over the President, who was courting Soviet and Chinese overtures at this time.[41] In addition to supplying financial support, the United States provided specialist military training to Indonesian military officers, many of whom were sent to Fort Leavenworth in Kansas.

This brief honeymoon period ended abruptly when Sukarno announced his opposition to the formation of an independent Malaysia (including former Malaya and former British possessions on the island of Borneo), in January 1963, on the grounds that the new nation would remain under British political control and function as a neo-colonial force in the region. Britain had granted independence to peninsular Malaya in 1957, in the hope of retaining its military base in Singapore, which it considered critical to its ability to maintain its naval presence in the 'Far East' and to honour its security commitments to the American-led Southeast Asia Treaty Organisation (SEATO) and for the defence of Australia and New Zealand.[42] In 1963, the territories of Sarawak and Sabah, which shared a border with Indonesia's provinces on the island of Borneo/Kalimantan, were incorporated into the new Malaysian federation. Sukarno subsequently threw his support behind the 'Crush Malaysia' (*Ganyang Malaysia*) campaign, resulting in low-level border skirmishes that, by August 1964, threatened to escalate into full-scale war.[43] In a further sign of deepening tensions, Indonesia withdrew from the United Nations in January 1965 after Malaysia was admitted as a member of the United Nations Security Council.

In the face of growing anti-Western demonstrations throughout Indonesia, including the storming of the US consulate in Medan in February 1965 and other attacks against American government buildings in Jakarta in March, the Johnson administration adopted what it called a "low-posture policy".[44] This policy entailed the withdrawal of most embassy personnel and the dramatic reduction of United States' visibility, while the remaining American officials would quietly keep contact with "the constructive elements of strength in Indonesia" and try to give these elements "the most favourable conditions for confrontation [with the PKI]".[45] The United States, in other words, would reduce its visible presence within Indonesia in order to encourage an internal showdown against the communists, as soon as a suitable opportunity arose. As outlined above, the United States government was aware and supportive of the Indonesian military leadership's intention to wait for a suitable pretext for launching this campaign such that the military could preserve Sukarno's leadership while justifying its seizure of power as a reaction to PKI provocation.

Such a tactic would have the benefit of providing the military with a free rein to crush the PKI while acknowledging the immense popularity that Sukarno continued to enjoy. The United States Ambassador to Indonesia, Howard Jones (1958- April 1965), further speculated at a closed-door meeting of State Department officials in the Philippines in March 1965 that: "From our viewpoint . . . an unsuccessful coup attempt by the PKI" would be the ideal pretext to "start the reversal of political trends in Indonesia".[46] This assessment appears to have been adopted by United States officials at this time. The United States government and its friends in the Indonesian military leadership spent the next few months "waiting for some sort of dramatic action from the PKI that would provide a justification for repressing it".[47]

This opportunity presented itself on the morning of 1 October.

The United States consulate in Medan, North Sumatra, initially appears to have been caught off-guard by the actions of the 30 September Movement. Before dawn, the consulate staff began to send telegrams to the State Department asking for further information about whether a coup was underway.[48] The United States government, however, was quick to extend its support to Suharto and to stress its preference for decisive action. In a significant show of public support for the new emerging regime, the new United States Ambassador to Indonesia, Marshall Green (June 1965–1969), attended a mass funeral for the murdered generals on 5 October in Jakarta.

During the first week of October, the US embassy and policy makers in Washington were concerned that the military leadership "would not take full advantage of the opportunity to attack the PKI" but would instead settle for "only limited action" against those "directly involved in the murder of the generals".[49] This was despite "repeated" assurances to army generals since early 1965 "that the United States would support them if they moved against the PKI" and despite the military leadership having already begun to move publically against the PKI.[50] On 5 October, the same day as the mass funeral in the capital, US Ambassador Green cabled Washington to propose that he once again "indicate clearly to key people in army such as Nasution and Suharto our desire to be of assistance where we can".[51] This proposal received the support of the State Department. As this book will show, however, the United States had no reason to worry about the resoluteness of the military's intentions.

The exact role played by the United States in the genocide remains unclear, as US government archives relating to Indonesia from the period remain sealed.[52] It is known, however, that at a minimum, in addition to openly celebrating Suharto's rise to power, the United States supplied money and communications equipment to the Indonesia military that facilitated the killings;[53] gave fifty million rupiah to the military-sponsored KAP-Gestapu death squad;[54] and provided the names of thousands of PKI leaders to the military, who may have used this information to hunt down and kill those identified.[55] The United States, Britain and Australia additionally played an active role in "black propaganda operations" in Indonesia during the genocide, including broadcasting clandestine radio broadcasts into the country.[56] These broadcasts repeated Indonesian military propaganda as part of a psychological warfare campaign to discredit the PKI and encourage support for the killings.

This propaganda campaign was also extended to domestic audiences in the West. In Australia, where extensive news media surveys from the time of the genocide have been conducted, the accusation that the PKI had carried out an abortive coup was repeated uncritically while the mass killings themselves received very little media coverage or coverage that was "grossly distorted".[57] Reports of the genocide did not make headlines; the number of dead was systematically under-reported, while the killings were largely reported as "agentless". When agency was attributed to the killings, "Moslem extremists" and "students", rather than the military, were usually the ones identified.[58]

Racism also permeated reporting of the killings. NBC reporter Ted Yeates, in a 1967 special report into Suharto's "decisive victory" in "our war in Asia", depicted Indonesians as monkey who had performed the genocide as the continuation of an ancient "passion play".[59] Cutting between footage of Sukarno and Suharto and a performance of *kecak* dance in Bali, in which participants percussively chant "*cak*" and move their arms to depict a battle from the Ramayana, Yeates compares Sukarno to the "monster king" Rahwana and Suharto to the "good king" Rama, while comparing the Indonesian people to Rahwana and Rama's "rival armies of monkeys".[60]

The concept of "amok", one of the few Indo-Malay words to make its way into the English language, was also often employed to describe the killings.[61] According to this racist colonial-era trope, Indonesians were depicted as naturally "submissive" to authority but as also possessing the propensity to erupt into murderous violence if provoked by religious leaders or "alien" political provocateurs, such as the PKI, who were alleged to have disrupted the "harmony" of traditional village life. In this way, the killings were explained to Western audiences as "an unavoidable tragedy".[62]

This pattern of minimisation and gross misrepresentation of the violence in Western media reporting of the genocide mirrored public statements by Western political leaders at the time. President Johnson, United States Secretary of State Dean Rusk and Ambassador Marshall Green refused to comment publicly on the killings.[63] In justifying this silence, they cynically claimed information about the number of people killed was too sketchy to justify public comment, while suggesting that condemning the killings could have constituted "interference" in Indonesian domestic affairs.[64] It is clear this coordinated policy of silence was intended to deflect attention from the events in Indonesia and the United States' own role in supporting the killings.

Australian Prime Minister Harold Holt was less guarded in his public comments. In mid-1966, on a visit to New York, Holt remarked: "With 500,000 to one million communist sympathisers knocked off, I think it's safe to say a reorientation had taken place."[65] His remarks, stunning in their callousness, were not only a frank admission of conditions in Indonesia, but a declaration of implied approval for the killings. Despite being published in the *New York Times*, Holt's comments were ignored by the Australian media. Richard Tanter has proposed this media silence was a deliberate attempt, either imposed or self-imposed, to "protect" readers from the reality that the Australian government was supporting a "holocaust" in Indonesia.[66]

The United Nations also failed to condemn the killings. Instead of launching an investigation into what was happening, the United Nations welcomed overtures by Indonesia's new post-genocide Foreign Minister, Adam Malik, for Indonesia to re-join the international organisation, before re-admitting Indonesia on 28 September 1966 without debate.[67] At that time, the violence in Indonesia was ongoing. Indeed, neither the United Nations 1965 or 1966 official Yearbook makes any reference to the killings, noting only Indonesia's aggression against Malaysia prior to the killings and Indonesia's subsequent return to the organisation.[68] This lack of concern for the unfolding humanitarian crisis in Indonesia is deeply troubling. Suharto was an important pro-West ally and the United Nations would close its eyes to human rights abuses in Indonesia throughout the long three decades of the New Order regime.[69] The international community, it appears, was determined to ignore the killings entirely or to treat the victims as unavoidable Cold War collateral damage.

Investigating the Indonesian genocide

Academia, for its part, has also historically shown a reluctance to characterise the killings as the result of a centralised military campaign. The first academic accounts of the killings essentially repeated the military's own propaganda version. In a classic account of the killings that is still viewed as a standard text in some universities today, Ulf Sundhaussen, in his 1982 study, *The Road to Power*, explained that although:

> [t]he simplest way of explaining the mass killing is to charge the Army with having used its near-monopoly of the means of violence to kill the communists. . . . It would be difficult to prove that the massacre was planned by Soeharto and the officers supporting him, or even to argue that they stood in any way to gain from it.[70]

Indeed, Sundhaussen continued, the military acted to limit the killings, which were primarily carried out by "Muslims" and "villagers", whom the military were unable to "stop".[71] The PKI itself, Sundhaussen claims, was ultimately to blame for the genocide, as a result of its political campaigns before 1 October 1965, which had "eradicated the harmony in the community". "It is this reckless breaking-up of community accord by the communists," Sundhaussen explained, "which must be primarily regarded as the cause for the indiscriminate mass slaughter in 1965/6."

In the case of Aceh, Sundhaussen proposed:

> Violent mass action against the PKI first began in Aceh. When rumours reached that area that Muslims had been killed by communists in Jogjakarta, Acehnese in a frenzy of *jihad* (holy war) set out to kill all communists in Aceh. . . . In Aceh General Ishak Djuarsa attempted to limit the mass slaughter.[72]

Sudhaussen thus depicted the genocide as the result of spontaneous, religious-inspired popular violence, with the military acting to bring this violence to an end.

Harold Crouch presented a somewhat different analysis in his classic 1978 study, *The Army and Politics in Indonesia*. In this study, Crouch cautiously suggested that the military may not have initiated the genocide, but seized the chance to work with others to conduct it, explaining:

> While it is not clear that the army leaders intended that the post coup massacres should reach the ferocity experienced in areas like East Java, Bali and Aceh, they no doubt consciously exploited the opportunity provided by the coup attempt to liquidate the PKI leadership. In rural areas of Java and elsewhere, army officers coordinated with members of anti-Communist civilian organisations to murder several hundred thousand PKI activists. . . .[73]

The genocide is thus depicted by Crouch as having begun spontaneously and as not being entirely under the control of the military. Rather, Crouch describes the relationship between the military and civilian anti-Communist organisations during the killings as being based on shared goals and mutual assistance rather than on a chain of command relationship. As for the scope of the killings, he suggested they were limited to PKI cadres only.

In the case of Aceh, Crouch observed:

> The first full-scale massacre of PKI supporters broke out in Aceh in the first part of October. Although the PKI in Aceh was very small, the Muslim leaders in Indonesia's most strongly Islamic province regarded it as a threat to Islam, and its largely non-Acehnese following became the target of what amounted to a holy war of extermination. Although the army commander, Brigadier General Ishak Djuarsa, reportedly "tried to limit the killing to only the cadres," many of his troops apparently shared the outlook of the religious leaders.[74]

Here, Crouch describes the killings as the result of spontaneous, religiously inspired violence, while the military is portrayed as having acted to bring the violence to an end.

This account is likewise mirrored in Robert Cribb's 1991 account of the killings in the province. Cribb observes:

> In strongly Muslim Aceh, where the PKI's support was miniscule and largely confined to the towns, cadres and their families are reported to have been

eliminated swiftly in early October. We know little more, but the fact that Aceh's history contains a number of instances of the rapid and ruthless elimination of political opponents when the opportunity presented itself makes this brief account plausible.[75]

As with the two above accounts, Robert Cribb presents the killings in Aceh as the result of spontaneous religious violence. He also adds a dash of cultural determinism, suggesting that "Aceh's history" reveals a propensity towards violence. This explanation is perplexing considering Cribb's pertinent criticisms of the use of "amok" theory to explain the violence.[76] Indeed, Sundhaussen's explanation that the "Acehnese" erupted into a "frenzy of *jihad*" and Cribb's more secular explanation that Acehnese had a historical propensity to unleash murderous violence against their political opponents reflect stereotypical tropes of Acehnese as "fanatical Muslims" that have existed since colonial times.[77] These tropes, this book will show, were consciously exploited by the military during the time of the genocide.

To the casual reader, the consensus found within these three accounts may appear to strengthen their veracity. This apparent consensus, however, is deeply problematic. Indeed, as far as Aceh is concerned, all three accounts are drawn from the same source: a single interview with the architect of the genocide in the province, Brigadier General Ishak Djuarsa. As an examination of the footnotes of these studies reveals, Crouch drew his original quote from Sundhaussen's 1971 PhD dissertation, who drew his information from an interview with Djuarsa, while Cribb in turn has referenced Crouch.[78] The sum of our understanding of the genocide in Aceh in these three studies rests on an interview with the very person who, as will be shown throughout this book, is perhaps most accountable for the genocide in that province.

I do not intend to criticise these early studies unfairly. In the 1970s, 80s and 90s, when these accounts were written, limited sources were available against which military propaganda accounts could be compared. It was often difficult for researchers to travel outside Indonesia's major cities without a military chaperone. It was also impossible to access internal military documents of the type found in this book.

It is not the case, however, that no alternative sources were available. Academic contemporaries of Sundhaussen and Crouch led by Benedict Anderson, Ruth McVey and Rex Mortimer were highly critical of the military's propaganda account. Indeed, both Anderson and McVey were banned from Indonesia for writing a critical analysis of the 30 September Movement and the military's reaction in 1966, known as the 'Cornell Paper'. In this report they argued that the military's attack had been offensive and "*quite separate*" from the 30 September Movement's activities.[79] Mortimer, for his part, explained:

There was no immediate, spontaneous explosion of violence; indeed, the first outbursts seem to have occurred only after the army had despatched reliable units to areas where the feelings of the populace, played upon by dramatizations of the murders of the fallen generals and a campaign to pin responsibility on the PKI, could be given full reign.[80]

These accounts were, however, largely sidelined. The banning of Anderson and McVey from Indonesia was held up as a warning, while Mortimer, a self-declared Marxist, was dismissed as being "partisan".[81]

The idea that the genocide was the result of spontaneous violence has also been contradicted by eyewitness accounts of the killings, which began to trickle and then flood out of Indonesia from the 1990s. These eyewitness accounts have often formed the backbone of newer studies of the killings. Beginning with Cribb's pioneering work to tell the stories of victims through his 1991 edited collection, *The Indonesian Killings of 1965–1966: Studies from Java and Bali*, these newer studies have generally been structured as regional studies and have provided scholars with critical insights into particular aspects of the military's initiation and implementation of the genocide. Early examples of such studies focused on the role of the military's Para-Commando Regiment (RPKAD: *Resimen Para Komando Angkatan Darat*) in leading the outbreak of violence in Java and Bali,[82] as well as on the role of the military in conducting large-scale arrest campaigns leading to the systematic execution of these detainees at military-controlled killing sites.[83]

These accounts led some scholars to criticise the understanding that the genocide occurred as the result of spontaneous violence. Geoffrey Robinson, writing in 1995, observed, "The victimization and the physical annihilation of the PKI were *not* simply or even primarily the consequences of a spontaneous or natural religious impulse".[84] Instead, Robinson proposed, the massacre was the result of a military campaign led by Suharto, who had orchestrated a "countercoup" in the wake of the actions of the 30 September Movement.[85]

The question of whether or not the genocide was the result of a deliberate and centralised military campaign, however, remained an open debate. Cribb, for example, suggested in 2002 that while:

> [t]here is a powerful argument that the killings came about as a deliberate and massive act of political assassination carried out by Suharto and his allies in the army against their rival for power, the PKI. . . . The main objection to this explanation is that it does not seem to account for the scale of the killings. . . . The Indonesian army could have achieved its primary goal of destroying the PKI as a political force with a much smaller death toll. If the killings were solely a matter of military agency, one has to believe that Suharto wanted mass violence for the sake of its terrifying effect and to bloody the hands of as many people as possible in order to ensure that they would never be able to swing back to the PKI if political circumstances changed.[86]

If Cribb seems to be ruling out the later interpretation, we must infer that the very scale of the genocide, the fact that it was nation-wide and that it was able to generate such a large death toll is, here, to be taken not as proof of the centralised and coordinated nature of the campaign, but rather, paradoxically, as evidence of

its spontaneity and decentralisation. Likewise, the examples of military coordination that have been uncovered through regional studies have not always been
explained as evidence of the centralised and coordinated nature of the campaign,
but rather as evidence of "regional variation", an ambiguous concept that side-
steps this paradox at the heart of national interpretations of the 1965–66 events.[87]
After all, even a nationally coordinated, centrally organised campaign might still
be expected to show *some* degree of "regional variation".

For many years the main difficulty in proving whether there was military agency
behind the genocide has been the lack of documentary evidence with which to
counter the military's own account of what happened. Indeed, until the discovery
of the Indonesian genocide files in 2010, it was seriously debated whether the
military had kept records or even issued orders during the time of the genocide.[88]

This difficulty in accessing military records has not prevented major strides
being made in research in recent years. Indeed, it could be said that research
into the genocide is currently undergoing a renaissance.[89] This process has been
focused around the fiftieth anniversary of the genocide and has been largely driven
by the runaway success of Joshua Oppenheimer's award winning 2012 documentary film, *The Act of Killing*, which depicts some of the civilian perpetrators
of the genocide boasting about their participation in the killings and the killers'
relationship to the Indonesian state.[90] This film has dealt a spectacular blow the
military's official propaganda account of the killings. Likewise, Oppenheimer's
second (2014) film, *The Look of Silence*, which presents the killings through the
eyes of the brother of a man killed by members of a military-sponsored death
squad in rural North Sumatra, has shone a bright light on the continued impunity
enjoyed by perpetrators of the genocide.[91]

The international attention generated by Oppenheimer's films, both nominated
for an Academy Award, has spurred unprecedented interest in the genocide and
led to an array of civil society initiatives, including the International People's
Tribunal for 1965, which convened a non-legally binding investigation into the
killings in the Hague in 2015.[92] It has also sparked a variety of official responses
by the Indonesian government aimed at damage control.

In April 2016, the Indonesian government convened a 'National Symposium on
the 1965 Tragedy'.[93] Billed as a means for victims and civil society representatives to meet with the government, hopes for change were quickly squashed when
Indonesia's then Coordinating Minister for Political, Legal and Security Affairs,
Luhut Pandjaitan, who provided opening remarks for the Symposium, cast doubt
on the existence of mass graves, while reiterating the government's refusal to
issue an apology to victims of the genocide.[94] "We will not apologise," he stated
before explaining, "We are not that stupid. We know what we did and it was the
right thing to do for the nation."[95]

Luhut then issued a rather unusual challenge at a press conference following
the Symposium:

> We don't have any evidence now that a [large] number of people got killed
> back in 1965 . . . Some people say 80,000 or 400,000 [people were killed],

[but] we don't have any evidence of that . . . I challenge some of the media, if you can show us where the mass graves are, we are more than happy to look.[96]

I would like to present this book as evidence not only of the existence of mass graves, but as evidence the Indonesian state is fully aware that the genocide was implemented as deliberate state policy.

Discovery of the Indonesian genocide files

My interest in the topic of the '1965–66 mass killings', as they are commonly referred to in Western literature, was initially borne out of a desire to better understand the more recent separatist conflict in Aceh. This interest grew as I realised that patterns in military violence seen in Aceh during the conflict often drew their origin from the 1965–66 period.

Between 1976 and 2005, Aceh was locked in a bitter separatist war. This conflict officially began on 4 December 1976, when Hasan di Tiro, a descendant of a prominent *ulama* (Islamic scholar), originally from Pidie in North Aceh, declared Aceh's independence. He portrayed his struggle to be a continuation of both Aceh's *Darul Islam* (Abode of Islam) rebellion (1953–62) and its holy war against the Dutch (1873–1914) (see chapter 2). Just as important to Tiro's decision to lead an armed rebellion against the Indonesian state was his failure to secure a pipeline contract with the new Mobil Oil gas plant that was being built in Lhokseumawe, North Aceh, when he was outbid by Bechtel. Nonetheless, Tiro's message of anger against the central government struck a chord. Aceh was, and remains to this day, one of Indonesia's poorest provinces and numerous young men soon began to join Tiro in the mountains. In a vicious cycle, the Indonesian military treated Aceh's civilian population as potential combatants, which, in turn, spurred support for the separatists. It is believed that approximately 15,000 people, mostly civilians, were killed as a result of the conflict.

In 2003 the military intensified the conflict. This followed a swell in popular support within Aceh for independence. The pro-democracy movement that had been the driving force behind the fall of the New Order regime in 1998 had morphed into a pro-referendum movement in Aceh by 1999. At one point, approximately 500,000 of Aceh's 4.2 million people had converged on Banda Aceh to demand a vote on whether Aceh should "join or separate" from Indonesia. Police had thrown off their uniforms and abandoned their posts. The military, however, had regained the upper hand and launched a brutal attack against both the separatists, known as the Free Aceh Movement (GAM: *Gerakan Aceh Merdeka*), and civilian activists.

In addition to employing a territorial warfare strategy of the type used in 1965–66, the military also relied heavily upon the use of civilian militia groups and mandatory "night watch" (*jaga malam*) campaigns.[97] In Aceh's rural villages (*kampung*), the military would travel from *kampung* to *kampung* searching for suspected GAM militants. Individuals who were accused of being "GAM", or who were accused of having connections to the organisation, could be shot on sight. In Aceh's towns, the military pursued civilian activists. Many of these activists, mostly university-age students, were rounded up, interrogated and tortured. Others were "disappeared" and their mutilated bodies later discovered. The public display of bodies was a common sight. Then, with no end to the conflict in sight, the war was short-circuited by a freak act of nature.

During the early hours of 24 December 2004, an Indian Ocean tsunami sent 30-meter-tall black waves over the province. The devastation was apocalyptic. Approximately 170,000 people in Aceh were killed and 504,518 were made homeless.[98] Entire villages and subdistricts were destroyed. In some places the ground was swept clear. Dotted concrete foundations were the only evidence that houses had once stood in the area. In other places, the debris of smashed buildings made roads unpassable. The tsunami stopped the worst of the fighting. It did not stop the military from brutalising suspected separatists, many of whom had descended from Aceh's hilly interior to search for loved ones.

I first travelled to Aceh six weeks after the tsunami. At the time I was a second-year undergraduate student researching the conflict in Aceh. Prior to the tsunami, Aceh had been closed to foreigners and it was not known how long Aceh's borders would remain open. My plan was to interview student activists involved in Aceh's pro-referendum movement and GAM fighters. In addition to carrying out these interviews, I volunteered with a local NGO distributing food aid to tsunami victims. Later I would work for the Aceh Monitoring Mission, which oversaw the 15 August 2005 peace deal between GAM and the central government, as well as for the Indonesian government's tsunami Rehabilitation and Reconstruction Board.

In February 2005, bodies were still being fished from the sea and food was scarce. The war, meanwhile, continued to grind on. At night I could hear gunfire. During the day, I passed though apparently endless military roadblocks and saw tanks and armoured vehicles snake through the streets. At all times people were careful about what they said, speaking in whispers and looking out the corner of their eyes, fearful that a wrong word or gesture might place them under suspicion. It is a testament to the brutality of the conflict that many people I spoke to described the tsunami as a blessing in disguise. These experiences formed a snapshot in my mind of a society gripped by fear and military terror. It would be to these scenes that my mind would often wander as I read accounts of military actions in 1965.

To begin with, I assumed that the brevity with which the topic of the genocide was treated in the literature was a reflection of the fact that we already knew so much about these events. It was when I decided to investigate what had happened in Aceh in 1965 – something that I thought could be resolved by a quick visit to the library – that I was faced with the realisation that only a handful of paragraphs could be found in the literature regarding the killings in the province and that, in fact, very little was known about the killings as a *national* event. It was from this initial investigation that I embarked on the research that would eventually result in this book.

During my research I conducted three fieldwork trips: the first in early 2009, the second in late 2010 and early 2011, and the third between mid-2011 and early 2012. During these trips I met with former members of the PKI, family members of people who had been killed during the genocide, former military personnel, government officials and members of the civilian militias and death squads who had participated in the genocide. I also met with other eyewitnesses who were able to recall the killings. In total, I conducted over seventy interviews in Banda Aceh, North Aceh, East Aceh, Central Aceh, West Aceh, South Aceh, Medan, West Sumatra, Jakarta and Hong Kong.

I located my interviewees by means of a referral method, whereby I would travel to a specific location and establish contact with human rights activists or other local contacts who were aware of older members in the community linked to the events of 1965–66. I would then meet these potential interviewees, who would often refer me on to others. This method was adopted as a result of the continued sensitivity with which the killings are still viewed in Aceh. The 1965 genocide remains a much more sensitive topic than the recent separatist struggle in the province. Thus while former members of the Free Aceh Movement and other survivors and participants in the recent separatist struggle often speak proudly of their actions, people considered to be associated with the PKI retain a sense of stigma even fifty years after the event. There is no official registered network of survivors or perpetrators of the genocide in Aceh. The interviews presented in this book represent the largest collection of oral history testimony to be collected on the topic in Aceh.

The interview process was a humbling experience. Many of the survivors I met had never spoken publicly about their experiences. Some wept, and all spoke with a steely determination. Most have attempted to keep their status as survivors secret, for fear of continued intimidation and harassment. As they told me about loved ones who had been murdered it struck me as unbelievably tragic that even to this day they have not been able to mourn publicly. Many continue to express bewilderment about why their lives were so suddenly and irrevocably turned upside down. Suppression of information about the genocide has also meant that survivors are often confused about whether or not their own experiences are unique. One of the most common questions I was asked was whether the killings had been similar in other areas. It may well be that the social taboo surrounding discussion of the genocide has helped preserve the integrity of their testimony.

Speaking with perpetrators was a surreal experience. While villagers who had been forced to participate in the killings were often reluctant to speak about their experiences, former death squad leaders spoke openly and boastfully about their actions. They considered themselves national heroes. Their greatest regret was that they had not received more recognition for their actions. As I sat drinking tea with such men I quickly discovered that so long as I kept my opinions to myself, they were more than happy to speak openly to me. They believed, or at least told themselves, that what they had done was right. I also came to realise, as so many have before me, quite disconcertingly at first, the humanness of such individuals. They were not monsters. They spoke to me politely and in some cases even kindly. I can only imagine the fear they must have once inspired and the horror that they have seen and implemented, but today they are grandfathers, hoping to tell their stories before it is too late. This realisation does not minimise their crimes. It did, however, make me see that even in the most extreme of circumstances people like to externalise evil: it is something that we like to think that only our enemies can do. Such thinking makes it only too easy for great wrongs to be committed in our name.

During the course of my fieldwork I also conducted extensive archival research. After discovering with great disappointment that all pre-2004 newspapers in Aceh had been destroyed by the tsunami, which had inundated the offices of Aceh's daily newspaper *Serambi Indonesia*, parts of the Aceh Information and Documentation Centre and the Aceh Provincial Library. I was fortunate to discover the Ali Hasjmy Library, originally the personal collection of Ali Hasjmy, Aceh's Governor between 1957 and 1964, and its extensive collection of public government records and rare memoirs stretching back to the time of the national revolution.

I was also able to collect many public government documents and statistics from the Aceh Provincial Library, the Aceh Information and Documentation Centre[99] and the Aceh Statistics Bureau, and to search the collections at the Banda Aceh Legal Aid Organisation (LBH – Banda Aceh), the International Centre for Aceh and Indian Ocean Studies (ICAIOS), Tikar Pandan, the Aceh Institute and Isa Sulaiman libraries. I am most grateful to the archivists at these institutions who graciously allowed me to spend days poring through their collections. It was only at the Medan-based *Waspada* newspaper, which reported on and sold newspapers in Aceh throughout the 1960s, that I felt restricted in my ability to enjoy unhindered access to these collections. Having been invited to return the next day to begin my research, I was sadly told on my return that their collection of newspapers from 1965 had mysteriously "disappeared".

My first major breakthrough came in early 2010, when Indonesia researcher Douglas Kammen sent me a scanned copy of a document that would change the course of my research.[100] This scanned 250-page typescript document was entitled the 'Complete Yearly Report for Kodam-I/Kohanda Atjeh for the Year 1965'. It had been produced by the Aceh Military Command and signed by Aceh's Military Commander, Brigadier General Mohammad Ishak Djuarsa (1 October 1964–1 April 1967). This document had never previously been cited. Similar reports have yet to be discovered elsewhere in Indonesia. Tellingly it included a comprehensive eighty-nine-page report by Djuarsa detailing the military's "annihilation campaign" against the PKI in the province. It is undoubtedly authentic.

This report also includes a remarkable collection of "attachments", including a "death map" recording the number of "dead PKI elements" (*oknum PKI jang mati*), and a flow chart labelled 'Result of the Annihilation of Gestok during 1965 in Kodam-I/Atjeh', plotting these deaths to demonstrate graphically which of Aceh's districts had higher death counts. The attachments also include: various military organisational charts and tables detailing the military chains of command in operation in the province at the time, stretching from the provincial down to the district, subdistrict and village levels; tables detailing the number of military personnel in each district and the number of arms they had been distributed; as

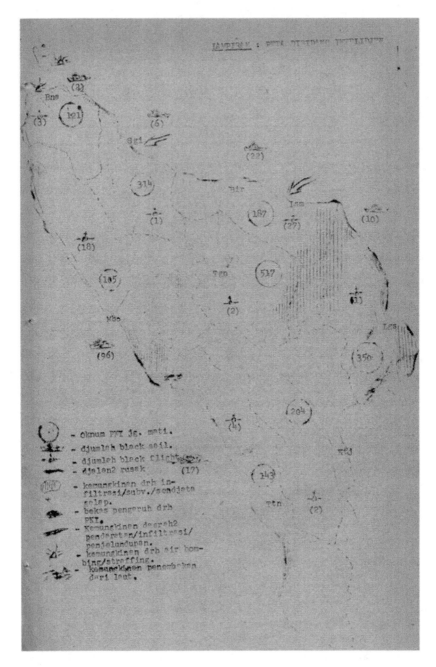

Figure 0.1 Death map: 'Attachment: Intelligence map'. Circled numbers show "Dead PKI
elements".

KRONOLOGIS ... J. H. N2 J. N8 B KRUKUN. N
... 30 ... ...
... .H-I/.AJ H

NR : TNGG.L :	U R I N - N ... J I K
1 : 1 OKT.'65 :	a. Diterima berita d..i Men/Pangad tentang adanja gerak-an Coup dibawah pimpinan Letkol Untung.
	b. Diterima berita dari Panglatu tentang adanja peristi-wa Dewan jenderal di Djakarta dengan meng-instruksi-kan :
	1. Tetap tenang ditempat masing
	2. Djalankan tugas sebagaimana biasa
	3. Djaga disiplin pasukan se-baik2nja
	4. Menunggu perintah/instruksi selandjutnja dari Pang latu.
	c. Berdasarkan instruksi tersebut telah di-instruksikan-kepada kesatuan bawahan dengan radiogram Pangdahan".." nomor Notekilat-5/Kos/65 10020100 dan instruksi nomor T.K.No/G-1/1001180/65.
2 : 3 OKT.'65	Djam 07.30 wib di Idie .tjeh Timur telah terdjadi demons trasi tanpa idzin dan dapat digagalkan/dibubarkan, namun demikian para demonstrasi sempat mengrusakkan baberapa - toko.
3 : 4 OKT.'65 :	Djam 20.00 wib telah diadakan rapat dipendopo Gubernuran jang dihadiri oleh Pantja Tunggal Tk-I dan Staf Kodahan-".." serta Pantja Tunggal Tk-II .tjeh Beser/Kotapradja - Banda .tjeh, untuk membitjarakan dan menentukan sikap serta melakukan penilaian keadaan jang berhubungan de - ngan gerakan 30 September.
	Pada djam 23.00 wib dilandjutkan rapat Staf Kodahan ".."-di aula Skodam-I dan mengeluarkan instruksi Pepelrada no mor TOK-3/Kilat/1005000, djuga kawat utjapan belasungka-wa dari Pangdahan ".." kepada PJM PR SIDEN.
4 : 5 OKT.'65 :	Djam 12.00 wib Kasdam-I memberikan briefing chusus kepa-da anggota Skodam-I, tentang kedjadian2 Gerakan 30 Sep-tember. Masing2 djawatan melandjutkan kepada bawah anja-untuk mentjegah timbulnja salah pengertian tentang situ-asi jang dihadapi. Sedjak tanggal 5 Oktober 1965 dimana-mana telah dilakukan sembahjang gaib oleh kaum Muslimin. Perasaan2 anti PKI su'ah sangat meluas dan dapat dibukti kan dengan adanja pamplet2, spanduk2, tjoretan2 dan teri akan2.
5 : 6 OKT.'65 :	a. Djam 11.00 wib rapat Parpol bersama Front Nasional - Tingkat-I dan Pantja Tunggal Tingkat-I mengeluarkan - pernjataan a.l. :
	1. Tuntutan 7 Parpol kepada Pepelrada untuk membubar-kan PKI dan Ormasnja.
	2. Keputusan bersama terbentuknja Front Pantjasila.
	3. Mengutuk Gerakan 30 September
	4. Pernjataan Pantja Tunggal morah .tjeh.
	b. Djam 16.00 di Banda .tjeh telah terdjadi demonstrasi-oleh Parpol PKI beserta Ormasnja, bergerak dari arah-setui menudju ke Pendopo dan diterima oleh Pantja - Tunggal Tk-I Daista .tjeh, dengan pernjataan menuntut pembubaran Parpol PKI. Kemudian para demonstrasi ber-keliling kota sambil mengumpulkan slogan dan pamflet2 PKI jang berada/dipasang disimpang-simpang djalan ser ta membakarnja.

Bersambung kehalaman-2-

Figure 0.2 First page of the Military Chronology: 'Chronology of events related to the 30 September Movement in Kodam-I/Aceh Province'.

well as the number of civilian militia members at the disposal of each of these military detachments at the time of the genocide. The report additionally includes a twenty-one-page 'Chronology of events related to the 30 September Movement in Kodam-I/Aceh Province', which provides an hour-by-hour account of events between 1 October and 22 December.

Reading this document, I began to believe for the first time that it would be possible to create an accurate chronological narrative of the genocide in the province based on the military's own account of events – a first for the killings nationally. The Complete Yearly Report also made it possible to cross-check the information I had been hearing in my interviews and to begin to move from the flexible timespans of hearsay to establish certain facts.

My second major breakthrough occurred in late 2010 when I decided to search the Aceh Government Library and Archives, the site of the former Indonesian Intelligence Agency's archives in Banda Aceh. Armed with the knowledge that documents had indeed been produced during the killings, I entered the Archives and requested permission at the front desk to access its catalogues. Direct shelf access to the documents was not possible, but I was able to request a collection of seventeen files based on their titles, unsure whether the information in them would be of any use. The titles of these files were obscure, ranging from 'Proceedings of the Special Meeting of the West Aceh Level II Provincial Government on 11 October 1965 to discuss the affair that has named itself G.30.S/PKI',[101] to 'Report of the Regent and District Head T. Ramli Angkasah in leading the District Government in North Aceh',[102] to 'Former Civil Servants that have been involved in the G30S PKI in Aceh Besar'.[103]

When I had first requested to view the files, I had been hopeful that I might be given a handful of documents. When I was subsequently presented with a box containing over 3,000 pages of photocopied classified documents I could not believe my luck.[104] These documents, combined with the Complete Yearly Report, are by far the most detailed collection of documents ever recovered from the time of the Indonesian genocide. They fundamentally change what is knowable in terms of both chronology and accountability. They were, as one of my colleagues observed, not just a proverbial smoking gun but a "smoking arsenal".

The most important of these documents is the 'Proceedings of the Special Meeting of the West Aceh Level II Provinical Provincial Government on 11 October 1965 to discuss the affair that has named itself G.30.S/PKI' file, which I will hereafter refer to as the 'Chain of Command documents bundle'. This bundle contains eight documents, collectively twenty-one pages in length, that were collated by the West Aceh Level II Provincial Government. It includes executive orders produced in Banda Aceh initiating the genocide in the province. Another significant file within the collection relates to the establishment of death squads in Aceh. This file includes the founding document of the East Aceh Pantja Sila Defence Front death squad, as well as a document produced by the East Aceh Level II Provincial Government endorsing the establishment of this death squad and pledging the state's full support and material assistance for its activities. Another bundle of documents records the campaign of anti-Chinese violence that broke out in the province in April 1966. These documents provide the first documentary evidence that systematic race-based killings did occur in Aceh during the genocide. Other documents record the military's campaign at the district and subdistrict levels in Banda Aceh, North Aceh, East Aceh, West Aceh, South Aceh and Central Aceh. There is also a large collection of documents that record the subsequent purge of the civil service throughout the province.

It is these documents, together with the information drawn from my interviews with survivors, perpetrators and other eyewitnesses of the genocide, that form the basis of this book.

Notes

1 *40 Hari Kegagalan 'G.30.S': 1 Oktober–10 November 1965* (Jakarta: Staf Angkatan Bersendjata, Pusat Sedjarah Angkatan Bersendjata, 1965), p. 111.
2 *Laporan Tahunan Lengkap Kodam-I/Kohanda Atjeh, Tahun 1965* (Banda Aceh: Kodam-I Banda Aceh, 1 February 1966), p. 17.
3 The earliest known use of this phrase occurred at midnight on 1 October 1965. See below.
4 'Pengumuman: Peng. No. Istimewa P.T.', *Banda Aceh*, 4 October 1965.
5 *Laporan Tahunan Lengkap*, pp. 17, 85.
6 TVRI live broadcast, 'Upacara Hari Kesaktian Kesaktian Pancasila 2015', 1 October 2015. Available online: https://youtu.be/Hcu01ZJJo_4 [Accessed on 20 October 2016].
7 '*Pancasila*', lit. 'five principles', is the name given to the five guiding principles of Indonesian nationalism first enunciated by Sukarno in 1945. These principles – belief in God, humanity, national unity, democracy and social justice – are vague in nature and were adopted and sacralised by the New Order regime.
8 Others have already done this. See, in particular, John Roosa, *Pretext for Mass Murder: The 30th September Movement & Suharto's Coup D'Etat in Indonesia* (Madison: The University of Wisconsin Press, 2006).
9 The remaining kidnapped generals and lieutenant were Major General S. Parman, Major General Mas Tirtodarmo, Major General R. Suprapto, Brigadier General Soetojo Siswomihardjo, General Donald Ishak Panjaitan and Lieutenant Pierre Tandean.
10 See, for example, 'Treachery of the G30S/PKI' (*Pengkianatan G30S/PKI*), the official propaganda film produced by the Indonesian government. *Pengkhianatan G30S/PKI*, directed by Arifin C. Noer (Jakarta: Produksi Film Negara, 1984).
11 Nugroho Notosusanto and Ismail Saleh, *The Coup Attempt of the "September 30 Movement" in Indonesia* (Jakarta: P.T. Pembimbing Masa-Djakarta, 1968), p. 65.
12 John Roosa, *Pretext for Mass Murder*, p. 26.
13 See, for example, the opening scenes of 'Treachery of the G30S/PKI'; *40 Hari Kegagalan 'G.30.S': 1 Oktober- 10 November 1965*, p. 103.
14 See, for example, 'Chronologis Kedjadian2 jang Berhubungan dengan Gerakan 30 September Didaerah Kodam-I/Atjeh', p. 2, in Kodam-I Banda Atjeh, *Laporan Tahunan Lengkap Kodam-I/Kohanda Atjeh, Tahun 1965* (Jakarta: Staf Angkatan Bersendjata, Pusat Sedjarah Angkatan Bersendjata, 1965); also, Nugroho Notosusanto and Ismail Saleh, *The Coup Attempt*, p. 65.
15 Some have proposed Suharto was not attacked because he was the ultimate "*dalang*" (puppet master) behind the Movement. See, for example, Wilem Frederik Wertheim, 'Whose Plot? New Light on the 1965 Events', *Journal of Contemporary Asia*, Vol. 9, No. 2 (1979), pp. 197–215. While this is possible, I do not think his subsequent actions are reliant on such an interpretation.

16 Nugroho Notosusanto and Ismail Saleh, *The Coup Attempt*, p. 77.
17 Benedict Anderson, 'How Did the Generals Die?', *Indonesia*, Vol. 43 (April 1987).
18 Seymour Topping, 'Slaughter of Reds Gives Indonesia a Grim Legacy', *New York Times*, 24 August 1966, pp. 1, 16.
19 John Roosa, *Pretext for Mass Murder*, p. 31.
20 *Ibid.*, p. 189.
21 'Decree No. 1 on the Establishment of the Indonesia Revolution Council', in 'Selected Documents Relating to the "September 30th Movement" and Its Epilogue', *Indonesia*, Vol. 1 (April 1966), p. 136.
22 Aidit did not, for example, issue a radio announcement, despite the 30 September Movement occupying the national RRI (*Radio Republik Indonesia*) radio station in Merdeka Square, Jakarta, until 6pm on 1 October. Nor did the PKI issue a call to arms in its national daily newspaper, *The People's Daily* (*Harian Rakjat*), which printed its 2 October issue during the afternoon of 1 October. Instead, the newspaper characterised the actions of the 30 September Movement as an internal military affair.
23 John Roosa, *Pretext for Mass Murder*, pp. 174–175, 215–216.
24 Benedict Anderson, *Java in a Time of Revolution: Occupation and Resistance, 1944–1946* (Jakarta: Equinox Publishing, 2006, originally 1972), p. 74. Chaerul Saleh, who helped to lead the kidnapping action, for example, became a close confidant of Sukarno and in 1965 was third deputy prime minister.
25 John Roosa, *Pretext for Mass Murder*, pp. 217–218.
26 'Decree No. 1 on the Establishment of the Indonesian Revolution Council', in 'Selected Documents', pp. 136–137.
27 'Decision No. 1 Concerning the Composition of the Indonesian Revolution Council', in 'Selected Documents', pp. 137–138.
28 While it may appear to be hair-splitting in the face of the Movement's actions in killing the generals, the Movement initially described its actions as a means of protecting Sukarno. The Movement's failure to repeat its earlier pledge of loyalty to Sukarno at 2pm appears to have been a tactical error as it further alienated potential pro-Sukarno allies while making it even easier for the military leadership to justify responding with force to the Movement.
29 Wilem Frederik Wertheim, 'Whose Plot? New Light on the 1965 Events'.
30 Mary S. Zurbuchen, 'History, Memory and the "1965 Incident"', *Asian Survey*, Vol. 42, Issue. 4 (2002), p. 566.
31 John Roosa, *Pretext for Mass Murder*, p. 8.
32 Berita Satu, 'Hari Kesaktian Pancasila Jokowi Bertindak Sebagai Inspektur Upacara', 1 October 1965. Available online: https://www.youtube.com/watch?v=LBgLH2iucRg [Accessed on 20 October 2016].
33 'Indonesia: Vengeance With a Smile', *Time*, 15 July 1966.
34 Jaechun Kim, 'U.S. Covert Action in Indonesia in the 1960s: Assessing the Motives and Consequences', *Journal of International and Area Studies*, Vol. 9, No. 2, (2002), pp. 64–66.
35 *Ibid.*
36 Rex Mortimer, *Indonesian Communism Under Sukarno: Ideology and Politics, 1959–1965* (Jakarta: Equinox Publishing, 2006, originally 1974), p. 366.
37 *Ibid.*, p. 367.
38 Joseph Barkholder Smith, *Portrait of a Cold Warrior* (New York: C.P. Putnam's Sons, 1976), p. 215. Barkholder Smith, a former CIA operative who was head of the CIA's Indonesia desk at the time, describes Masjumi as "progressive Moslems".
39 Audrey Kahin and George McTurnan Kahin, *Subversion as Foreign Policy: The Secret Eisenhower and Dulles Debacle* (Washington: University of Washington Press, 1997), p. 170.
40 The problematic nature of this transfer and the subsequent injustices suffered by the people of West Papua have been well documented. Richard Chauvel, *Essays on West Papua, Volume 1* (Clayton: Centre of Southeast Asian Studies, Monash Asia Institute, Monash University, 2003).

41 Bradley Simpson, 'International Dimensions of the 1965–68 Violence in Indonesia', in Douglas Kammen and Katherine McGregor (eds.), *The Contours of Mass Violence in Indonesia, 1965–68* (Singapore: NUS Press, 2012), p. 52.

42 David Easter, *Britain and the Confrontation with Indonesia: 1960–66* (London: Tauris Academic Studies, 2004), p. 141.

43 Easter proposes that the desire to prevent such a war (which could have become a second Vietnam) was one of the major reasons the US, Britain and Australia pushed so hard for the Indonesian generals to take action against Sukarno. *Ibid.*, p. 90.

44 Jaechun Kim, 'U.S. Covert Action in Indonesia', pp. 66–67.

45 Cited in, David Easter, *Britain and the Confrontation with Indonesia*, p. 137.

46 John Roosa, *Pretext for Mass Murder*, p. 190.

47 *Ibid.*, p. 191.

48 'Incoming telegram' to the US Department of State, 1 October 1965, p. 1. Cited in US Department of State, *Foreign Relations of the United States, 1964–1968: Volume XXVI, Indonesia; Malaysia-Singapore; Philippines* (Washington DC: Government Printing Office, 2001).

49 John Roosa, *Pretext for Mass Murder*, p. 194.

50 *Ibid.*, p. 193.

51 US embassy in Jakarta to US Department of State, 5 October 196[5]. Cited in, John Roosa, *Pretext for Mass Murder*, p. 194.

52 In mid-2017 the National Archives and Records Administration in Maryland announced it would soon be declassifying US embassy files from Jakarta produced between 1963 and 1965 due to public interest in the files. The National Security Archive plans to scan these files and make them available to the public in late 2017.

53 In late 1965, the United States supplied the Indonesian military with state-of-the-art mobile radios, flown in from the Clark Air Base in the Philippines. An antenna was also given to the Army Strategic Reserve Command (Kostrad). *Ibid.*, p. 194.

54 Telegram from US Ambassador Green to US State Department, 2 December 1965 in US Department of State, *Foreign Relations of the United States, 1964–1968*. The KAP-Gestapu (*Komando Aksi Pengganyangan Gerakan Tiga Puluh September:* Action Front for the Crushing of the 30 September Movement) was established in Jakarta on 2 October under the direction of Brigadier General Sutjipto. Harold Crouch, *The Army and Politics in Indonesia* (Jakarta: Equinox Publishing, 2007, originally 1978), p. 141.

55 Kathy Kadane, 'U.S. Officials' Lists Aided Indonesian Bloodbath in 60s', *The Washington Post*, 21 May 1990.

56 Voice of America, the BBC and Radio Australia were involved in this campaign. David Easter, *Britain and the Confrontation*, pp. 168–169; also, Marlene Millott, 'Australia's Role in the 1965–66 Communist Massacres in Indonesia', *Australian Institute of International Affairs*, 30 September 2015. Available online: www.internationalaffairs.org.au/australian_outlook/australias-role-in-the-1965-66-communist-massacres-in-indonesia/.

57 Richard Tanter, 'Witness Denied', *Inside Indonesia*, Vol. 71 (July–September 2002). See also, Ross Tapsell, 'Australian Reporting of the Indonesian Killings: The Media and the "First Rough Draft of History"', *Australian Journal of Politics & History*, Vol. 54, No. 2 (June 2008).

58 Ross Tapsell, 'Australian Reporting', pp. 216–221.

59 The relevant extract of the report, narrated by Yeates, reads as follows: "Indonesia's present turmoil, conflict and power struggle is not altogether new. The Balinese *kecak*, a kind of Hindu passion play, illustrates vividly complex and alien struggles going on today. Here the priest blesses the participants, one hundred men representing rival armies of monkeys, one good, the other evil, each convinced they are in the right." The report proceeds to cut between images of men performing the *kecak* dance, in which participants percussively chant "*cak*" and move their arms to depict a battle from the Ramayana, and contemporary news footage from Indonesia. "Today's real battle between the forces of good and evil," Yeates

continues, "rages in the streets. They [anti-Sukarno demonstrators] demand social reform and political freedom. Their cry is not 'down with America' or 'Yankee go home', what they are demanding in effect is 'down with the communists', 'Yankee come back'. The garish leader of the forces of evil is a monster king called Rahwana." Footage is shown of a man dressed as the monster king Rahwana, cheered by his army of monkeys, and then swiftly shifts to an image of Sukarno. "President Sukarno, with flamboyance and arrogance, led Indonesia to liberation in 1945 after 350 years of Dutch rule." The camera cuts again to an image of Rahwana and then back to Sukarno. "He also let his nation fall under communist influence, into bankruptcy and chaos. The good king, portrayed by a girl, is named Rama." An image of a girl dressed as Rama is shown. "Rama, with the help of his army, tries to save the country and destroy the evil forces of Rahwana. Today it is General Suharto and his army that crushed the communist coup." The camera cuts to an image of Suharto. "It is General Suharto who leads the effort to remove President Sukarno." NBC News Special, 'Indonesia: The Troubled Victory', originally aired 19 February 1967. Available online: www.nbcuniversalarchives.com/nbcuni/clip/51A08495_s01.do.

60 *Ibid.*

61 The concept of "running amok", originally a term used to refer to the redemption of honour by an individual or group of soldiers by means of frenzied violence, resulting in the death of the "amokker", was misappropriated by Europeans, who used the term to explain what they perceived as sudden "irrational" outbursts of violence by colonised peoples in Indonesia. Robert Cribb, 'Problems in the Historiography of the Killings in Indonesia', in Robert Cribb (ed.), *The Indonesian Killings of 1965–1966: Studies From Java and Bali* (Clayton, Victoria: Centre of Southeast Asian Studies, Monash University, 1991), p. 33.

62 Geoffrey Robinson, *The Dark Side of Paradise: Political Violence in Bali* (Ithaca, NY: Cornell University, 1995), p. 303.

63 Arnold C. Brackman, *The Communist Collapse in Indonesia* (New York: W.W. Norton & Company, 1969), p. 122. Green was less guarded in his 1990 memoir, where he blamed the PKI for bringing the genocide upon itself. "In the last analysis," Green explained, ". . . the bloodbath visited on Indonesia can largely be attributed to the fact that communism, with its atheism and talk of class warfare, was abhorrent to the way of life of rural Indonesia." Marshall Green, *Indonesia: Crisis and Transformation, 1965–1968* (Washington: The Compass Press, 1990), pp. 59–60.

64 Arnold C. Brackman, *The Communist Collapse in Indonesia*, p. 122.

65 Henry Raymont, 'Holt Says U.S. Actions Protect All Non-Red Asia', *New York Times*, 6 July 1966, cited in Richard Tanter, 'Witness Denied: The Australian Response to the Indonesian Holocaust, 1965–66', Paper prepared for the International Conference on Indonesia and the World in 1965, Goethe Institute, Jakarta, 18–21 January 2011. Available online: http://nautilus.org/wp-content/uploads/2011/12/Witness-Denied.pdf.

66 Richard Tanter, 'Witness Denied', p. 31.

67 'Yearbook of the United Nations: 1966', Office of Public Information, United Nations, New York, 1965, p. 208.

68 'Yearbook of the United Nations: 1965', Office of Public Information, United Nations, New York, 1965, p. 194; also, 'Yearbook of the United Nations: 1966', pp. 207–208.

69 In 1969, for example, United Nations Secretary General, U Thant, "saw no reason to undermine the West's policy of encouraging and supporting the anti-communist President Suharto" when it became clear the new regime had no intention of honouring its commitments to facilitate a vote on self-determination in West Irian in 1969. John Saltford, *The United Nations and the Indonesian Takeover of West Papua, 1962–1969: The Anatomy of Betrayal* (New York: RoutledgeCurzon, 2003), p. 170. The United Nations has also been criticised for its failure to prevent Indonesia's invasion and occupation of East Timor in 1975.

70 Ulf Sundhaussen, *The Road to Power: Indonesian Military Politics, 1945–1967* (Kuala Lumpur: Oxford University Press, 1982), p. 218.

71 *Ibid.*, pp. 218–219.

72 *Ibid.*, pp. 214, 218.

73 Harold Crouch, *The Army and Politics in Indonesia*, p. 135.

74 *Ibid.*, pp. 142–143.

75 Robert Cribb, 'Introduction', in Robert Cribb (ed.), *The Indonesian Killings*, p. 23.

76 Robert Cribb, 'Problems in the Historiography of the Killings in Indonesia', in Robert Cribb (ed.), *The Indonesian Killings*, p. 33.

77 For a discussion of the development of this stereotype and its use up to the time of the recent separatist struggle in Aceh, see, Elizabeth F. Drexler, *Aceh, Indonesia: Securing the Insecure State* (Philadelphia, PA: University of Pennsylvania Press, 2008), pp. 60, 75, 83, 106. Such stereotypical tropes have not been limited to Aceh. In the case of Bali, Geoffrey Robinson has convincingly demolished the trope of "the Balinese" as possessing a unique and "exotic" character featuring inexplicable shifts between extreme submissiveness and frenzied violence. Geoffrey Robinson, *The Dark Side of Paradise*.

78 Harold Crouch, *The Army and Politics in Indonesia*, p. 143, n. 14; Ulf Sundhaussen, 'The Political Orientation and Political Involvement of the Indonesian Officer Corps, 1945–1966: The Siliwangi Division and the Army Headquarters', PhD thesis, Monash University, 1971, p. 630; Robert Cribb, 'Introduction', in Robert Cribb (ed.), *The Indonesian Killings*, p. 23, n. 44.

79 Emphasis in original. This report was initially meant to be an internal document but was later leaked. Benedict Anderson and Ruth McVey, *A Preliminary Analysis of the October 1, 1965 Coup in Indonesia* (Ithaca and New York: Cornell University Southeast Asia Program, 1971), p. 63. Rex Mortimer, 'The Downfall of Indonesian Communism', *The Socialist Register*, Vol. 6 (1969), p. 213. A similar analysis was proposed by Noam Chomsky and Edward Herman. See, Noam Chomsky and Edward S. Herman, *The Washington Connection and Third World Fascism: The Political Economy of Human Rights, Volume I* (Boston: South End Press, 1979), p. 207.

80 Rex Mortimer, 'The Downfall of Indonesian Communism', p. 213.

81 See, for example, Justus M. van der Kroef, 'Review: *Indonesian Communism Under Sukarno*', *Journal of Asian History*, Vol. 9, Issue 2 (1975), pp. 193–194. In this review van der Kroef describes Mortimer's analysis as "decidedly lacking in objectivity". He dismisses Mortimer's discussion of Suharto's potential role in the coup as "highly tenuous", p. 193. The re-writing of the history of the Indonesian genocide will require a sober disengagement from Cold War narratives and a perhaps uncomfortable acknowledgement that these classic accounts often came perilously close to becoming an uncritical repetition of military propaganda.

82 See, for example, Michael van Langenberg, 'Gestapu and State Power in Indonesia', in Robert Cribb (ed.), *The Indonesian Killings*, pp. 49, 57. For a more recent accounts of the role of the RPKAD in the killing, see David Jenkins and Douglas Kammen, 'The Army Para-commando Regiment and the Reign of Terror in Central Java and Bali', in Douglas Kammen and Katharine McGregor (eds.), *The Contours of Mass Violence in Indonesia*, pp. 75–103. Also, Leslie Dwyer and Degung Santikarma, '"When the World Turned to Chaos": 1965 and Its Aftermath in Bali, Indonesia', in Robert Gellately and Ben Kiernan (eds.), *The Spectre of Genocide: Mass Murder in Historical Perspective* (New York: Cambridge University Press, 2003), pp. 289–306.

83 An early account of this process in Aceh can be found in John R. Bowen, *Sumatran Politics and Poetics: Gayo History, 1900–1989* (New Haven: Yale University Press, 1991), p. 7. For more recent accounts, see: for Java, Vannessa Hearman, 'Dismantling the "Fortress": East Java and the Transition to Suharto's New Order Regime (1965–68)', PhD thesis, The University of Melbourne, 2012, pp. 93–94; for Bali, Geoffrey Robinson, *The Dark Side of Paradise*, p. 297; for North Sumatra, Joshua Oppenheimer, 'Show of Force: Film, Ghosts and Genres of Historical Performance

in the Indonesian Genocide', PhD thesis, University of the Arts London, 2004, p. 98; for South Sulawesi, Taufik Ahmad, 'South Sulawesi: The Military, Prison Camps and Forced Labour', in Douglas Kammen and Katharine McGregor (eds.), *The Contours of Mass Violence in Indonesia*, pp. 156–181. The best sustained narrative describing how killings were implemented at military-controlled killing sites, as told by former death squad members who participated in the killings, can be found in, *Snake River*, directed by Joshua Oppenheimer, 2004. This film has not been publically released but was submitted as part of Oppeneheimer's PhD thesis, 'Show of Force'.

84 Emphasis in original. Geoffrey Robinson, *The Dark Side of Paradise*, p. 279.

85 *Ibid.* This argument was also supported by Saskia Wieringa, who, writing in the same year, explained how military-fabricated stories about members of the left-wing women's organisation Gerwani (*Gerakan Wanita Indonesia*: Indonesian Women's Movement) participating in sadistic and sexualised acts against the generals murdered by the 30 September Movement at *Lubang Buaya* had been used to justify the killings. Saskia Wieringa, 'The Politicization of Gender Relations in Indonesia: The Indonesian Women's Movement and Gerwani Until the New Order State', PhD thesis, The University of Amsterdam, 1995.

86 Robert Cribb, 'Unresolved Problems in the Indonesian Killings of 1965–1966', *Asian Survey*, Vol. 42, No. 4 (July–August 2002), pp. 551–552.

87 The concept of "regional variation" appears to stem from Robert Cribb's assessment that the "ferocity [of the killings] seems to have been a product of local factors". Robert Cribb (ed.), *The Indonesian Killings*, p. 23. This concept has resulted in a tendency to describe the killings as a series of inter-related but separate events that occurred in each province. This approach was used by Crouch and Sundhaussen, who provide brief overviews of the killings in several provinces. Harold Crouch, *The Army and Politics in Indonesia*, pp. 143–154; and, Ulf Sundhaussen, *The Road to Power*, pp. 214–219. The two major national studies of the killings, Robert Cribb (ed.), *The Indonesian Killings*; and Douglas Kammen and Katharine McGregor (eds.), *The Contours of Mass Violence in Indonesia*, meanwhile, present the killings as a series of regional studies without providing an overall analysis of these studies.

88 Harold Crouch, for example, proposed in 1978: "Suharto did not send formal, written orders instructing [regional military commanders] on how to deal with the PKI." Harold Crouch, *The Army and Politics in Indonesia*, pp. 141–142. Robert Cribb has likewise echoed this sentiment, stating: "There is no evidence of systematic records being kept of the killings." Robert Cribb, 'Political Genocides in Postcolonial Asia', in Donald Bloxham and Anthony Dirk Moses (eds.), *The Oxford Handbook of Genocide Studies* (Oxford and New York: Oxford University Press, 2010), p. 453.

89 Much of this new research is being carried out by researchers in Indonesia. See, for example: Roberto Hutabarat (ed.), *Melawan Lupa: Narasi-narasi Komunitas Taman 65 Bali* (Bali: Taman 65 Press, 2012); Putu Oka Sukanta (ed.), *Sulawesi Bersaksi: Tuturan Penyintas Tragedi 1965* (Jakarta: Lembaga Kreativitas Kemanusiaan, 2013); Baskara T. Wardaya (ed.), *Truth Will Out: Indonesian Accounts of the 1965 Mass Violence* (Clayton: Monash University Publishing, 2013); Putu Oka Sukanta (ed.), *Breaking the Silence: Survivors Speak About 1965–66 Violence in Indonesia* (Clayton: Monash University Publishing, 2014); Kurniawan (ed.), *Pengakuan Algojo 1965: Investigasi Tempo Perihal Pembantaian 1965* (Jakarta: Tempo Publishing, 2014); Mery Kolimon, Liliya Wetangterah and Karen Campbell-Nelson (eds.), *Forbidden Memories: Women's Experiences of 1965 in Eastern Indonesia* (Clayton: Monash University Publishing, 2015).

90 *The Act of Killing*, directed by Joshua Oppenheimer (Denmark: Final Cut for Real, 2012).

91 *The Look of Silence*, directed by Joshua Oppenheimer (Denmark: Final Cur for Real, 2014).

92 I was fortunate to contribute to the International People's Tribunal's Final Report. The Final Report of the International People's Tribunal is available online: www. tribunal1965.org/final-report-of-the-ipt-1965/.

93 '1965 Symposium Indonesia's Way to Face Its Dark Past', *The Jakarta Post*, 19 April 2016. Available online: www.thejakartapost.com/news/2016/04/19/1965-symposium-indonesias-way-to-face-its-dark-past.html.

94 See, for example, 'Simposium Nasional Tragedi 1965: Sebuah Jalan Menuju Rekonsiliasi', *Kompas*, 20 April 2016. Available online: http://nasional.kompas.com/read/2016/04/20/09320701/Simposium.Nasional.Tragedi.1965.Sebuah.Jalan. Menuju.Rekonsiliasi?page=all.

95 Cited in, Jess Melvin, 'Symposium on Indonesia's 1965 Genocide Opens Pandora's Box', *New Mandala*, 9 May 2016. Available online: www.newmandala.org/symposium-on-indonesias-1965-genocide-opens-pandoras-box/.

96 *Ibid.*

97 See, for example, 'Aceh Dibawah Darurat Militer: Dibalik Perang Rahasia', *Human Rights Watch*, Vol. 15, No. 10 (December 2003).

98 Shannon Doocy et al., 'Tsunami Mortality in Aceh Province, Indonesia', *Bulletin of the World Health Organization*, Vol. 85, No. 2 (February 2007), p. 1. Available online: www.who.int/bulletin/volumes/85/4/06-033308.pdf.

99 The collections at these two institutions were only partially destroyed by the tsunami.

100 My sincere thanks to Douglas Kammen for sending me this document, which apparently mysteriously appeared at The Royal Institute of Southeast Asian and Caribbean Studies (KITLV) to be scanned as part of the Aceh Digital Library project. Initiated by KITLV as a response to the destruction of Aceh's library and archive collections during the tsunami, the Aceh Digital Library project digitised a major part of the literature on Aceh that is kept in the KITLV Library. It may never be known exactly why this document was given to KITLV. It is my suspicion that it was inadvertently included in a mass collection of printed material from a government archive in Aceh. No other 'Complete Yearly Report' produced by the Aceh military command can be found in the collection, though multiple yearly reports relating to various government departments produced during the 1960s and 1970s have been included, such as the 'Complete Yearly Report' of Aceh's Department of Education and Culture for the year 1970. The Complete Yearly Report produced by the Aceh military command is undoubtedly authentic. Orders and details found in the report can also be found in the documents I independently recovered from the Aceh Government Library and Archives in 2010. It is hard to understand why the Aceh government would possess and treat as authentic such self-incriminating documents if they are not, in fact, genuine. Likewise, orders and details contained in both of these sources have been independently confirmed by my interviewees, including both survivors and perpetrators.

101 'Risalah Sidang Istimewa DPRD Gotong Royong Daerah Tingkat II Aceh Barat tanggal 11 October 1965 dengan acara pembahasan peristiwa apa yang dinamakan dirinya G.30.S/PKI', Meulaboh, West Aceh, 11 October 1965.

102 'Laporan Bupati Kepala Daerah T. Ramli Angkasah dalam memimpin Pemerintahan Kabupaten Aceh Utara mulai April 1965 s/d Mei 1966 disampaikan dalam Sidang Paripurna ke 1/1966 DPRD-GR Kabupaten Aceh Utara di Lhokseumawe tanggal 15 Juni 1965', Lhokseumawe, North Aceh, 15 June 196[6].

103 'Bekas PNS yg terlibat G30S PKI Aceh Besar', No. 222/24, *Daftar Kendali Peminjam Arsip*.

104 I was given each of the files I had requested. I do not know if the files were reviewed before being released to me. I paid for photocopying costs. I cannot remember the exact amount, but it was not significantly different to the amount I would usually be asked to pay for photocopying at archives in Aceh.

1 Why genocide?

Since the 1965–66 killings, Indonesian and foreign commentators have debated the appropriate language with which to label them. The scale of the killings – believed to have claimed up to a million lives – along with their killers' stated aim to "exterminate down to the roots" (*menumpas sampai ke akar-akarnya*) an unarmed civilian group have led many to ask whether the 1965–66 killings constitute a case of genocide. For those who wish to use the term, the motivation has often been twofold: to provide an analytical tool with which to understand the killings as an event and to underline their criminal nature.

Genocide as a concept has a very specific origin. The term was first coined in 1943, by Raphael Lemkin, the Polish-Jewish lawyer, for his book on Nazi imperialism, *Axis Rule in Occupied Europe*.[1] Derived from the Greek word for people – *genos* – and the Latin suffix – *cide* – for murder, the term was intended to capture the idea of the "murder of a people".[2] This act, epitomised by the state-sponsored liquidation of European Jews and other national minority groups during the Nazi Holocaust, was believed to be especially egregious because it not only destroyed individuals, but eradicated entire peoples.[3]

The term was not, however, meant to apply only to the Nazi Holocaust. Lemkin described the murder of Armenians in 1915 as another example of genocide.[4] Meanwhile, the introduction of the term into international law through the 1948 Genocide Convention was intended to establish a framework through which future cases of genocide could be identified and their perpetrators brought to account.

Genocide, as a legal term, also possesses a more specific meaning. Genocide, according to the 1948 Genocide Convention, is the act of attacking members of a particular target group with the intent to destroy this target group "as such".[5] This targeting occurs outside a situation in which such targeting might be described as a reasonable use of force, as in the context of a security operation, although such targeting may well be portrayed as an act of self-defense.[6] Meanwhile, a target group of genocide must constitute a stable group within society that can be described as a "national, ethnic, racial or religious group".[7] The members of a political organisation cannot, as such, be the target of genocide, though political affiliation may well overlap with such a sociocultural group.[8] For a particular event to be described as genocide, these two key requirements relating to intent and identity of the target group must be met.

In the case of the 1965–66 killings, it has been unclear whether these two requirements could be established. This ambiguity has been caused, in large part, by the severe shortage of information available with which to make this assessment. Throughout the New Order period, the Indonesian government retained obsessive control over its official propaganda narrative of events, while making independent research both difficult and potentially dangerous.[9] Since the fall of the New Order in 1998, the limited success of Indonesia's democratisation process has meant this official propaganda narrative has remained potent.[10] Specifically, until the discovery of the Indonesian genocide files, it has not been possible to prove military intent behind the killings. Likewise, it has remained difficult to prove exactly how victims of the killings were identified, as the precise manner in which they were targeted remained unclear.

This evidentiary lacuna has not stopped Indonesian and foreign commentators from using the available information to describe the 1965–66 killings as a case of genocide. Since the early 1980s, there has been general consensus among genocide scholars that the 1965–66 killings constitute a case of genocide in its general sense.

This chapter reviews how the term has been used and interpreted in Indonesia before turning to an overview of how genocide studies scholars have applied the genocide concept to the Indonesian case. It then presents an overview of the new information now available with which to address this evidence problem. The chapter argues that this new evidence meets the key concerns raised by genocide scholars to confirm the early assumption that the 1965–66 killings can be understood as a case of genocide according to both its sociological (non-legal) and legal definitions.

How has the term been used and interpreted in Indonesia?

Within Indonesia, it was dangerous to publicly criticise official narratives of the 1965–66 killings until the fall of Suharto in 1998. The first uses of the term "genocide" to describe the killings within Indonesia coincide with the radical period of reform (*reformasi*) that accompanied the fall of the dictatorship. *Reformasi* was characterised by sharp political criticism of Suharto and the New Order regime. Newspapers ran front-page exposés of Suharto's economic and political crimes, including "investigations" into Suharto's alleged role in "G30S/PKI", which had brought the New Order regime to power.[11] As the country transitioned to democracy, there was an expectation within Indonesian civil society that Suharto and other key officials would soon be arrested and put on trial.[12]

One of the earliest uses of the term "genocide" to describe the killings within Indonesia can be found in a fictional "trial" of Suharto, published in 1999 by Wimanjaya K. Liotohe.[13] Through this text, Liotohe, who had been arrested and interrogated in 1994 for alleging Suharto had been behind the 30 September Movement[14] – the abortive coup movement used as a pretext by the military to launch its attack against the PKI during the morning of 1 October 1965 – accused Suharto of "carrying out mass killings against his own people (genocide) outside a situation of war".[15] The military, he explains, "armed" and "incited" civilian groups "in order to carry out a holy war (*perang suci*)" against "*kafir*", with the intent to "terrorize" the population into accepting Suharto's new "fascist-military" regime.[16] He also links the 1965–66 killings with other atrocities committed by the Indonesian military throughout the New Order period, including in East Timor, West Papua and Aceh, which he describes as "genocidal".[17] His use of the term is centered on both apportioning accountability for the killings and pointing to the asymmetric nature of the killings.

In 2002, Indonesian historian Bonnie Triyana would also describe the 1965–66 killings as genocide. After explaining Suharto seized "de facto" control of the state on 1 October 1965, Triyana proposes the military became the "main supporter" of the killings in Indonesia's provinces.[18] These killings, he explains, were portrayed within the community as an extension of local tensions over land and religion, but did not begin in Purwodadi, Central Java, where he conducted his research, until "the military [became] directly involved".[19] In using the term genocide to describe the killings, Triyana adopts Helen Fein's 1993 definition (discussed below), to propose "genocide . . . is a strategic kind of killing, not just caused by hate or revenge, towards a racial, ethnic or political group to eliminate the [perceived] threat from this group to the validity of the power of the killers".[20] Triyana thus proposes that it is the strategic nature of the military's killing campaign, targeted at the elimination of a particular group, which is decisive in his adoption of the term genocide.

The idea that the Indonesian state should be held accountable for the 1965–66 killings gathered momentum during the early *reformasi* period. This understanding translated into real legal and political changes. Restrictions placed on former political prisoners were eased. Indonesia became a signatory to numerous human rights conventions it had previously abstained from. In 2000, a law was passed to establish a Human Rights Court to resolve gross violations of human rights, including genocide and crimes against humanity.[21] Four years later, in 2004, a new law was passed concerning the establishment of a Truth and Reconciliation Commission, specifically to deal with gross human rights violations in the nation's past.[22] While, in a symbolic breakthrough, school curriculums were adjusted in to remove "PKI" from "G30S/PKI", the official name used as shorthand to refer to the events of 1 October 1965 that laid blame squarely on the PKI. These advances, however, did not go unchallenged.

From the mid-2000s, the winds of *reformasi* began to falter. The government, having churned through four successive presidents since the fall of Suharto by 2004, began to see talk about digging up the past as potentially destabilising. Meanwhile, the military, still smarting from its forced removal from East Timor in 1999, was keen to reassert its right to use force to resolve growing separatist struggles in Aceh and West Papua. In late 2006, Indonesia's Constitutional Court overturned the 2004 law establishing a Truth and Reconciliation Commission as unconstitutional,[23] while in 2007 the use of the term "G30S/PKI" in school teaching materials was reasserted. In March of that year, Indonesia's Attorney General would go so far as to order the burning of 14 offending school history textbooks.[24] It was within these conditions that old propaganda narratives of the killings began to reassert themselves.

Tensions began to develop between the increasingly articulated understanding that the military was responsible for the 1965–66 killings and New Order–era propaganda accounts. This tension is neatly captured in the introduction to Husnu Mufid's 2008 book *Epilogue to the G30S/PKI Coup D'état: Who Was Resisting Who?* Here it is asked by the book's editor: "Is it true the mass actions against the PKI and the killings of its members and supporters were the result of 'spontaneous' actions, or were they, indeed, carried out with the 'blessing' of the military?"[25] Mufid responds by repeating, almost verbatim, the military's original propaganda version of events: "When, in the regions, rumors were heard that Muslims had been killed in Yogyakarta by the communists, the Acehnese, who were enveloped in an overflowing mood of *jihad* (*diliputi suasana jihad yang meluap-luap*), began to take action to kill all communists in Aceh."[26] This impulsive violence, Mufid alleges, then spread spontaneously to other provinces throughout Indonesia.

Many of the books published during this period that support this new reactionary stance did not attempt to engage with new accounts of the killings. They certainly did not engage with the issue of whether the killings should be understood as a case of genocide.[27] In many cases the killings are ignored completely, as attention was turned, once again, to the actions of the 30 September Movement and the alleged duplicity of the PKI.[28] Meanwhile, government and civil society attempts to rehabilitate victims of the killings were condemned and ridiculed, while the victimhood of survivors was called into question. As one author explained: "It is indeed ironic, they [the PKI] are the ones who carried out 'killings' against the generals, yet it is they who feel they are the victims."[29] Once again, the actions of the 30 September Movement were being used to overwrite and displace the military's killing campaign.

This backlash proved hard to counter. The biggest challenge for those wishing to counter these new reactionary accounts was the lack of documentary evidence with which to disprove them. Rather than focus on the then almost impossible task of proving military accountability for the killings, new progressive accounts, which often took the form of collections of survivors' accounts, began to describe the 1965–66 killings as a "tragedy".[30] This new term was a recognition that, as powerful and important as these new progressive accounts were, agency behind the killings was once again heavily contested.[31]

The question of whether or not the 1965–66 killings should be understood as a case of genocide would re-emerge in 2012. In July of that year, Indonesia's National Human Rights Commission (Komnas HAM) presented the results of its four-year exploratory investigation into whether or not gross human rights, including genocide and crimes against humanity, had occurred during the "1965/1965 Affair".[32] The report used Indonesia's 2000 Human Rights Court Act as the basis for its investigation, which adopts the 1948 Genocide Convention's definition of genocide.[33]

Despite intimidation aimed at halting investigations,[34] this remarkable report argues that the killings were a "result of government policy at the time to implement the annihilation of members and sympathizers of the . . . PKI".[35] It named

Suharto, as the commander of the internal security agency (Pangkopkamtib), and all regional military commanders active between 1965 and 1978, as requiring investigation for command responsibility for the violence. A long list of military and police personnel, prison and detention center staff, village heads, civilian defense unit members and members of civilian militias are named as having been specifically identified by witnesses in the six regions covered by the report as requiring investigation as direct perpetrators of the violence.

Interestingly, the report did not present evidence that genocide had occurred in 1965–66. Rather, it limited its findings to presenting evidence that crimes against humanity, including killings, extermination, slavery, eviction or forced removals, arbitrary removal of people's right to freedom, torture, rape, persecution and forced disappearances had occurred.[36] The reason for this omission is not given in the report. It is possible the issue was considered to be too politically divisive.[37]

The report was rejected in November 2012 by Indonesia's Attorney General, Basrief Arief, despite the report's recommendation that the "1965/1966 Affair" be immediately referred for further investigation. The reason given for this rejection was that "[t]he evidence Komnas has gathered was insufficient to justify an official investigation".[38] In light of the serious findings made by the report, this rejection must be interpreted as a politically motivated attempt to stall further investigation.[39] The investigation remains stalled to this day. This legal impasse has not, however, stopped debate within civil society over how the killings should be interpreted.

Since 2013, the use of the term genocide to describe the killings has become increasingly popular in Indonesia. The adoption of the term has coincided with the ballooning success of Joshua Oppenheimer's documentary film *The Act of Killing* (2012), which was first screened in Indonesia in December 2012. Oppenheimer, as will be discussed below, openly described the killings as a genocide in his public statements.[40] This description was intended to highlight not only the scope of the killings, but also to draw attention to the intentional and state-sanctioned nature of the killings.

The international attention and recognition generated by the media-hype surrounding the film and its partner, *The Look of Silence* (2014), combined with the fast approaching fiftieth anniversary of the killings and other newly published research into the killings,[41] helped to open up new public space within Indonesia. Most importantly, the film was instrumental in breaking public taboos surrounding the identification of the perpetrators of the killings. The term began to become normalised and has appeared in the title of art exhibits,[42] front-page magazine articles[43] and online think pieces.[44] Meanwhile, a new spike in use of the term accompanied the International People's Tribunal for 1965 (IPT-65), held in The Hague in November 2015. The IPT-65's Final Report found it possible that genocide had been perpetrated against Indonesia's Chinese community during the 1965–66 killings, in part based on the research presented in chapter 7 of this book.[45] This non–legally binding people's tribunal heard testimony from survivors and researchers of the killings and received significant media coverage within Indonesia.[46] As during the early *reformasi* period, the term was once again being used to highlight the intentional nature of the killings and to demand an acknowledgement of its still silenced victims.

The 1965–66 killings within the field of genocide studies

Internationally, the first uses of the term genocide to describe the 1965–66 killings can be found from the late 1970s. One such early example can be found in the speeches and essays of Siauw Giok Tjhan, written between 1978 and 1981 in the Netherlands.[47] Siauw had been a member of Indonesia's national parliament and the head of Baperki[48] before he was arrested and imprisoned for thirteen years following 1 October 1965.

Writing from the safety of exile, he described the horrific conditions he had endured as a political prisoner. Suharto, he explained, had "implemented a policy of mass murder by refusing food to thousands of prisoners".[49] This policy, he proposed, was crueler than the Nazis' use of poison gas to exterminate prisoners and equated to "a genocide" that "should be condemned by the world". His use of the term was focused on bringing international attention to events in Indonesia by drawing historical parallels to the then well known horrors of the Nazi Holocaust.

A similar comparison between the 1965–66 killings and the Nazi Holocaust was made by Noam Chomsky and Edward S. Herman in 1979, who were not genocide scholars, but rather writing in the capacity of political commentators. They describe Suharto's campaign to "clean out" the PKI as a "final solution" and the killings, which they assert were led by the military, as a "holocaust".[50] The reason why so little is known about the 1965–66 killings, unlike the Holocaust, they suggest, is because the killings received the full support of the West and were, in effect, seen as a "constructive bloodbath".[51] The question of whether or not a particular case of genocidal mass killings is acknowledged as a case of genocide, they remind us, is not a purely dispassionate one.[52]

The sheer scale of the killings has, however, made them difficult to ignore. The use of comparison between different genocidal events has been a feature of genocide studies since its earliest days during the post–Second World War period.[53] This comparative approach has often involved, especially since the late 1970s, the comparison of particular instances of genocidal violence against generic definitions or themes in order to better understand the parameters of the phenomenon.[54] The 1965–66 killings were presented in one of the very first such compilations: Leo Kuper's *Genocide: It's Political Use in the Twentieth Century*, published in 1981.

Kuper dismisses official Indonesian accounts that the killings occurred as a result of spontaneous horizontal violence in response to the actions of the 30 September Movement. "The 'people's revenge'," he explains, as the killings had been described by a key military chief, Admiral Sudomo (who had estimated half a million "actual or suspected Communists" were killed between 1965 and 1966), "was not the spontaneous independent mass action the phrase suggests."[55] "On the contrary," he proposes, "the army engaged actively in the operation, participating directly in the massacres, and indirectly by organizing and arming civilian killers." The killings, he suggests, should be considered a potential case of genocide due to their large scale and their deliberate nature.

The major hurdle in recognising the 1965–66 killings a case of genocide, he explains, is the exclusion of "political groups" from protection under the 1948 Genocide Convention.[56] He proposes, however, that: "In the slaughter of the Communists, the criterion of past affiliation had a finality and immutability quite comparable to massacre by virtue of race and it was based on a similar imposition of collective responsibility."[57] The killings, moreover, transcended the boundaries of inter-political group conflict by additionally drawing upon "class" and "religious" differences between victims and perpetrators.[58] Ethnicity was also a factor, as evidenced by the killing of "Chinese merchants and their families".[59] He thus proposes the 1965–66 killings should be considered as a case of genocide under the Convention.

"[T]he major distinction," he explains, between the 1965–66 killings and classic "racial or ethnic massacres" was that they "did not extend to the same extent to family members."[60] This caveat is no longer applicable. There is now extensive evidence that family members, including children, of alleged communists were regularly killed during the 1965–66 killings (chapter 6). There is also an understanding that the deliberate "murder of young men, heads of families and community leaders" from a particular target group, as occurred during the Armenian genocide, can be understood as genocidal in intent.[61]

The 1965–66 killings were also included in Frank Chalk and Kurt Jonassohn's classic study, *The History and Sociology of Genocide: Analyses and Case Studies*, published in 1990. They describe the 1965–66 killings as a case of genocide, while noting the killings were "encouraged" by the military, with the intention of bringing about regime change in Indonesia through the use of terror.[62] They also observe that: "While this genocide was directed at a political party," and thus did not, at face value, conform to the legal definition of genocide, "it had curious overtones of an ethnic, religious, and economic character."[63] The main obstacle to the inclusion of the 1965–66 killings within the canon of comparative genocide studies, they propose, was the "great deal of conflicting information available" at the time relating to how the killings were implemented.[64]

This "conflicting information", based on the differences between official Indonesian propaganda accounts and other eyewitness accounts of the killings, coupled with the general scarcity of detailed information available with which to explain exactly how the killings had been implemented, was a major challenge for genocide studies scholars. This became particularly apparent when scholars attempted to prove the military had initiated and implemented the killings as part of a deliberate national campaign with the aim of destroying its target group (intent to destroy) and the manner in which this target group was identified for destruction (identity of the target group). In 1991, Samuel Totten described the 1965–66 killings as one of the "least documented . . . genocidal acts" of the twentieth century.[65] This shortage of information, which would characterise research into the killings for close to fifty years, can be traced back to the evidence problem faced by Indonesia researchers.

The evidence problem

Early accounts of the 1965–66 period written by Indonesia researchers focused on attempting to understand the actions and motives of the 30 September Movement, rather than on the killings themselves.[66] The question of whether the PKI had been responsible for the Movement would not be resolved until 2006, with the publication of John Roosa's *Pretext for Mass Murder*.[67] Meanwhile, key studies of the 1965–66 period struggled to explain the role the military had played in the killings, how the killings had been implemented and the process by which victims had been targeted. This confusion was caused by the near blackout of information available with which to counter the military's own propaganda accounts.

Lucien Rey, writing in 1966, proposed the military had "encouraged" armed mobs "to take advantage of [the] anti-PKI climate" during the aftermath of 1 October 1965.[68] "The technique," he explains, "has been for the army to enter a village, force the headman to give names of all PKI members and sympathizers, round them up and then let the extremist right-wing Muslim and Christian mobs know when they were to be released. As they came out of the jail they are chopped up with billhooks and machetes." This technique was indeed used by the military (chapter 6). What this explanation does not explain, because it was not known, is that this was but the tip of military accountability for the killings.

In 1971, Ruth McVey and Benedict Anderson described the killings as "a systematic campaign to uproot the Communist Party".[69] "The Army," they explain, "clearly intended to destroy the party root and branch."[70] They refrain, however, from providing an analysis of how this campaign was implemented, beyond explaining that: "the PKI was rapidly rounded up and destroyed" with the assistance of military-trained vigilante groups – how this campaign was led and by what method it was implemented is not explained.[71] Similarly, in 1974, Rex Mortimer explained the military leadership understood the failure of the 30 September Movement as "their opportunity to destroy once and for all" the PKI and its affiliated organisation.[72] He proposes: "Word was passed to Moslem and anti-Communist groups . . . on 7 October that a sweep of the Communists should begin; thereupon mobs in Djakarta began to destroy and burn PKI buildings and houses. In the following days . . . the razzia extended to the shops, homes, and persons of Indonesians of Chinese descent." It was not yet known that the military had ordered an annihilation campaign against the 30 September Movement from 1 October and that civilian participation had been ordered, and not merely encouraged, from 4 October (chapter 3).

This uncertainty was further complicated by studies that uncritically repeated military propaganda accounts to present the killings as a result of spontaneous horizontal violence. In 1978, Harold Crouch suggested the military may not have initiated the killings, but instead seized upon the opportunity they presented "to liquidate the PKI leadership".[73] While, in 1982, Ulf Sundhaussen proposed the killings had been initiated by "Muslims" and "villagers", whom the military were unable to "stop".[74]

This sense of doubt over how the killings were implemented and by whom was repeated into the 2000s. In 2002, Robert Cribb questioned whether the genocide was the result of a deliberate and centralised military campaign.[75] In 2010 it was still believed there was "no evidence" of systematic records being kept of the killings.[76] This is not to fault these early studies. It would remain impossible to definitively dispel the military's claim of non-responsibility for the killings until the discovery of the Indonesian genocide files. This shortage of information acted to severely restrict the ability of researchers to analyze the nature of the violence perpetrated during the 1965–66 killings.

Genocide studies scholars generally responded to this shortage of information by either referring to the 1965–66 killings as a potential or borderline case of genocide,[77] or by ignoring the case entirely.[78] A smaller number of scholars argued that the 1965–66 killings should not be understood as a case of genocide because, they reasoned, evidence did not exist to suggest victims of the killings consti-tuted a protected group under the Convention.[79] A debate, meanwhile, would develop between those who believed the 1965–66 should be understood as a case of genocide over how the genocide concept could be applied using the informa-tion available.

Working with the information available: two key approaches

Two key approaches emerged within this debate. The first sought to explain how the Convention could be applied to the Indonesian case, while the second sought to produce a new definition of genocide. Both ultimately saw the military's intent to destroy the PKI as the foundation for characterising the Indonesian case as genocide.

The first approach has often been interpreted as an attempt to work around the exclusion of political groups from protection under the Convention.[80] This has not, however, always been the case. As outlined above, in 1981, Leo Kuper had proposed the military's target group had possessed the characteristics of a racial group. This position was echoed by Frank Chalk and Kurt Jonassohn in 1991, when they had proposed the killings possessed "overtones of an ethnic, religious, and economic character".

This line of argument would be taken up by Robert Cribb in 2001. Since this time, Cribb has been the leading proponent of the argument that the 1965–66 killings can be understood as a case of genocide as defined by the Convention. The Indonesian case, he argued, could, in fact, "shed light on the phenomenon of genocide", by demonstrating the problematic nature of the artificial distinction made between concepts of race, ethnicity, national identity and political identity within mainstream interpretations of the Convention.[81] Traditional understand-ings of race, ethnic identity and national identity as "fixed" and "immutable", he argues, are no longer supported by contemporary "constructionist" understand-ings of these identities.[82] This understanding, he continues, is able to provide a "firm bridge between 'classical' ethnic genocide and political genocide", by dem-onstrating the similarities between the two forms of identity.

Specifically, in the case of Indonesia, he agues that the category of "national groups", as defined as a protected group under the Convention, could be expanded to include ideologically constituted national groups. He explains, "The nature of Indonesian national identity shows with unusual clarity how political cleansing can also be ethnic cleansing."[83] To support this argument, Cribb provides a detailed overview of the historical development of Indonesian national identity as the embodiment of three distinct "nations of intent", or "expressions" of this identity.[84] These three "expressions" – identified as "communist", "Islamist" and "developmentalist" – were not just differentiated from each other by cultural, social and ideological antagonisms but also overlaid with economic and class hostilities.[85]

From the 1950s, Cribb argues, Indonesia underwent a process of political "pillarization" that solidified and institutionalised these three competing expressions of Indonesian national identity.[86] Sukarno had sought to control these groups through his rhetoric of national unity, while the groups themselves, dominated under Guided Democracy by competition between the communist group (led by the PKI) and developmentalist group (led by the military), attempted to outmaneuver each other. The 1965–66 killings, Cribb proposes, were an opportunistic attempt by the military to permanently eliminate its major political rival by destroying not just the PKI as a political organisation, but Indonesia's communist group in "a successful exercise in national obliteration".[87] He thus proposes Indonesia's communist group can potentially be understood as a protected group under the Convention while also providing a deep historical analysis of inter-group conflict within Indonesia.

This argument was taken a step further by the IPT-65, which proposed that the "Indonesian national group" became the target of genocide because the Indonesian national group had been wiped out "in part".[88] The IPT-65 thus proposed that victims of the 1965–66 killings constituted a protected group under the Convention as members of the Indonesian national group. A similar approach has also been adopted by Daniel Feierstein in the case of Argentina to explain the repressive events that took place in that country between 1974 and 1983.[89]

This approach has been treated with caution by legal scholars of genocide, however. International law expert, William Schabas, for example, explains that: "Confusing mass killing of the members of the perpetrators' own group with genocide is inconsistent with the purpose of Convention, which was to protect national minorities from crimes based on ethnic hatred."[90] International law establishes the Convention does not apply to members of a national group who are targeted by members of the same national or ethnic group – a phenomenon sometimes referred to as "auto-genocide".

This was not Cribb's position. Cribb's explanation suggests that it was Indonesia's "communist group", rather than the "Indonesian national group" as a whole that became the target of the military's annihilation campaign. This "communist group", he argues, constituted a quasi-ethnic group as its own ideologically constituted national group or subnational group. That the military explicitly identified Indonesia's communist group (*kaum komunis*) to be the target of its annihilation campaign is supported by evidence found within the Indonesian genocide files.[91]

On the other side of the debate, Helen Fein led the attempt to free the 1965–66 killings from the confines of the Convention. In 1993, she suggested that genocide should be defined by the intent of a perpetrator group to physically destroy an unarmed "collectivity", regardless of how this group is identified.[92] Genocides, she explained, are implemented to achieve political aims. In the case of Indonesia, the killings enacted a "counter-revolution [that] reoriented class relations in Indonesia [and] assured continuing military domination by removing communist and populist challenges".[93] This interpretation highlights the strategic nature of genocidal violence and focuses on the intentions of the perpetrator group, while seeking to escape the narrow confines of the Convention.

This position was adopted by Joshua Oppenheimer in 2004, when he explained that Helen Fein's definition of genocide "encompasses both the seemingly religious-racial-ethnic Nazi genocides as well as the 1965–66 Indonesian politicide".[94] He believes understanding the similarities between the Holocaust and the 1965–66 killings should take precedence over semantics based discussions over the nature of the PKI as a target group. Beyond describing perpetrators of the 1965–66 killings as Nazis and "SS officers",[95] he explains that both the Indonesian killings and the Nazi Holocaust were state-driven and sustained through "banal (if not ordinary) bureaucracies".[96] He thus urges that understanding the process by which a state is able to transform itself into a killing machine capable of dispensing mass death against its own population should be just as important to scholars as understanding the process by which a target group is identified by perpetrators of genocide.

These two major schools of thought for understanding the 1965–66 killings as a case of genocide can be seen as complementing each other. Fein and Oppenheimer stress the strategic[97] and state-led nature of the killings[98] while removing themselves from debate over whether or not the victims of the killings constitute a protected group under the Convention. While Kuper, Chalk, Jonassohn and Cribb highlight military leadership of the killings, while proposing that the military's target group extended beyond the confines of a political party to affect a broader group within Indonesian society that might conceivably be understood as a protected group under the Convention.

The main difficulty faced by these two schools of thought has remained the serious shortage of documentary evidence available with which to prove the military had initiated and implemented the killings as part of a deliberate and systematic national campaign. This "evidence problem" has created an impasse based on the shortage of evidence rather than on the existence of contradictory evidence. In essence, genocide scholars have been open to interpreting the 1965–66 killings as a case of genocide but have not had the evidence necessary to confirm this finding. In turn, Indonesia researchers have taken this open finding as evidence that the 1965–66 killings cannot easily be understood as a case of genocide. This impasse can now quite simply be resolved through the reevaluation of these earlier assessments in light of the new information that now exists.

Below I present an overview of the new information that is now available regarding evidence of military intent to destroy "in whole or in part" its target group during the 1965–66 killings and the manner in which this target group was identified by the military, before reflecting on whether victims of the 1965–66 killings can be understood as a protected group under the Convention.

Evidence of intent

Before the discovery of the Indonesian genocide files, it was difficult to prove military agency behind the killings. Public military propaganda issued during the time of the killings showed the military supported the extermination of the PKI but did not prove the military had ordered the killings. An example of such military-produced propaganda can be found in a cartoon published in the military-controlled newspaper *Angkatan Bersedjata*, on 8 October 1965. In this cartoon, labelled 'Exterminate [them] down to the roots!' (*Tumpas terus sampai ke-akar2nja!*), a man, wearing a traditional *peci* hat (a symbol of both Indonesian and Islamic identity), and a shirt inscribed with words "[t]he people and the armed forces" (*Rakjat dan ABRI*), is seen violently striking a tree trunk with an axe.[99] The trunk reads "G.30.S", while the tree's roots spell "PKI". The image shows the man kicking aside the severed trunk as he strikes at the roots. This is clear incitement to "exterminate" the 30 September Movement and the PKI as a broader target group. The hesitation of some scholars to describe the military's campaign as genocidal lay in part in the fact that although it was clear the military possessed the conscious desire to see this target group destroyed, it could not be proven that the military had directly ordered the killing of this target group, let alone directly coordinated a killing campaign intended to facilitate the physical destruction of this target group. Indeed, as I have mentioned, it was seriously debated whether the military had even issued orders during the time of the genocide.

The Indonesian genocide files provide evidence that, from at least midnight on 1 October 1965, in the words of Sumatra's Inter-Regional Military Commander: "all members of the Armed Forces" had been "ordered" to "completely annihilate" the "30 September Movement" (described in this order as a counter-revolution), "down to the roots" (chapter 3).[100] Meanwhile, it can also now be proven that the military leadership described this campaign as an "operation to annihilate GESTOK [another name for the 30 September Movement]".[101] This operation, Aceh's Military Commander explains, was launched on 1 October 1965 and was known internally within the military as 'Operation Berdikari'. The stated intent of this Operation was to physically destroy the military's target group.

That the terms "exterminate" and "annihilate" were not meant metaphorically by the military leadership can be seen in its actions following 1 October. After ordering civilians on 4 October to "assist" the military "in every attempt to completely annihilate the Counter Revolutionary Thirtieth of September Movement along with its Lackeys",[102] Aceh's Military Commander embarked on a coordination tour of the province from 7 October (chapter 4).[103] During this tour he met with local military and government leaders and held public mass meetings where he explicitly ordered civilians to "kill" people considered to be associated with the PKI. At these meetings civilians were told that if they did not help the military to hunt down and "exterminate" this target group "down to the roots" they themselves would be "punished" by the military.[104] Meanwhile, other documents discovered as part of the Indonesian genocide files show that the military mobilised and armed thousands of paramilitary members to participate in Operation Berdikari.[105]

The military also sponsored the establishment of death squads, which were provided with material support to "assist" the military to carry out its annihilation campaign.[106] These military-sponsored death squads led to a series of public killings in the province between 7 and 13 October (chapter 5). The military supported these killings and recorded their progression on flow charts and a "death map".[107] In tandem with this public killing campaign, death squad members also participated in an extrajudicial "arrest" campaign, during which time a large number of targeted individuals were abducted and subsequently "surrendered" to the military. These individuals were then held in military-controlled jails and "concentration camps", resulting in a large detainee population being created in the province.

From 14 October the military began to implement a systematic killing campaign intended to destroy this detainee population (chapter 6). On this date, Aceh's Military Commander issued an 'Instruction' establishing the creation of a "War Room" intended to "enable" the military leadership to "carryout NON-CONVENTIONAL war" to "succeed in annihilating" its target group.[108] From this time, the military began to play a direct role in the killings in Aceh. Targeted individuals, who had been hunted down and extra-judicially "arrested" and detained in military-controlled jails and "concentration camps" during the first two weeks of the military's Operation, were now transported to a network of military-controlled killing sites. Each night truckloads of detainees were sent to these sites where they were killed, either directly by the military or by its para-military and civilian proxies. The purpose of this killing campaign was to systematically exterminate this detainee population.

In some areas, such as Central Aceh, this destruction was almost total. According to eyewitness accounts from this district, only one man survived the military's arrest and kill campaign. In Banda Aceh, meanwhile, it is believed only one member of the Aceh PKI's leadership structure survived. In all districts in Aceh it is extremely difficult to find survivors. The killings in Aceh appear to have been particularly intense and achieved the near complete physical destruction of the military's target group. It has been estimated that between 3,000 and 10,000 individuals were killed in the province as a result of this campaign.[109] In other provinces of Indonesia, larger numbers of survivors can be found.[110] Indeed, in the months following the most intense wave of killings during the immediate aftermath of 1 October, the military facilitated large-scale, long-term incarceration programs throughout other areas of Indonesia that could be viewed as detention centres and labour camps, rather than as kill-camps.[111]

These detention centres and labour camps housed hundreds of thousands of individuals who were considered to be less dangerous than the military's primary target group. According to a national detainee classification system that was implemented nationally in Indonesia from December 1966, a full year after the end of the military's systematic killing campaign in Aceh and after the worst of the killings nationally, such prisoners were classified as 'Category B' and 'Category C' prisoners.[112] Many of these individuals were later released back into the community after years of torture and abuse, where they continued to face systematic discrimination.[113]

The existence of this long-term detention program, however, does not detract from the military's intent to destroy its primary target group. The systematic mass killings that characterise the 1965–66 killings in Indonesia form a distinct phase within the military's broader campaign to seize state power. The period of systematic mass killings in late 1965 and early 1966 should be understood as the genocide proper.

The military's target group

The identification of the military's target group is complicated by the multiple names given to this group. Military records show this group was initially identified on 1 October as "this counter-revolution",[114] before being identified, from 4 October, as "that which calls itself the '30 September Movement'".[115] From 6 October, meanwhile, this group was linked explicitly with "the PKI and the Organisations under its banner".[116]

A formal list of "affiliated" organisations was signed by Suharto on 31 May 1966. This list included organisations officially affiliated to the PKI, such as: the PKI's youth organisation, People's Youth (*Pemuda Rakyat*); its peasant organisation, the Indonesian Peasant's Front (BTI: *Barisan Tani Indonesia*); its workers union, the All-Indonesia Workers' Union (SOBSI: *Serikat Organisasi Buruh Seluruh Indonesia*) and its cultural organisation, the Institute of People's Culture (LEKRA: *Lembaga Kebudayaan Rakyat*).[117] This list additionally included organisations that were not officially affiliated with the PKI, but which shared a similar political vision for Indonesia, including the Indonesian Women's Movement (Gerwani: *Gerakan Wanita Indonesia*) and the Consultative Body for Indonesian Citizenship (Baperki: *Badan Permusyawaratan Kewarganegaraan Indonesia*), a mass organisation for Chinese Indonesians who identified as pro-communist.

This evolution in the naming of the military's target group is consistent with the understanding that the military had planned to induce a showdown with the PKI, its major political rival, since at least January 1965,[118] and that this attack was intended to appear as a defensive move in reaction to an appropriate pretext that could be blamed on that party. The actions of the 30 September Movement provided this pretext and, as such, the military conflated the "30 September Movement" with the "PKI" when naming its target group. As the military's extended list of "affiliated" organisations demonstrates, however, it was not only the organisational membership of the PKI that was targeted.

In this context, the label "PKI" was used to refer to both the PKI cadre and members of these "affiliated organisations" (see Table 1.1 below). It was also used to refer to family members of the PKI cadre and the families of members of these "affiliated organisations". It was additionally used to refer to friends and associates of these individuals as well as to certain village populations and, at certain times and places, to Indonesia's ethnic Chinese community. It is thus clear the military's target group was a lot broader than the organisational membership of the PKI. Indeed, it included a much broader cross-section of individuals who were connected by a combination of familial ties, non-familial business or community

Table 1.1 Table of the military's target group, identified collectively by the military as "PKI"

ties, cultural ties, perceived shared socio-political identity, ethnic identity and perceived shared religious identity.

This broad target group was also collectively identified as "the communist group" (*kaum komunis*),[119] "counterrevolutionaries", "unbelievers" (*kafir, tidak beragama*) and "atheists" (*atheis, anti-tuhan*). These collective labels were intended to project the idea that this target group was internally cohesive and possessed a shared belief structure and self-identity. Its members were additionally often collectively described as "traitors" (*pengkhianat*), "inhuman" (*biadab*), "devils" (*iblis*), "dogs" (*asu*) and, in the case of women, as "whores" (*pelacur*).

The actual connection of such targeted individuals to the actions of the 30 September Movement, the official justification for the military's targeting of this group, was thus rendered secondary to the idea that such individuals should be targeted because of *who* they were alleged to be once the military's attack against this group commenced. According to such logic, each of these labels became conflated: "PKI" meant "communist" meant "traitor"; "PKI" meant "counterrevolutionary" meant "inhuman"; "PKI" meant "*kafir*" meant "devil"; "PKI" meant "atheist" meant "dog"; and vice versa. This meant that a family member of a PKI cadre or member of an "affiliated organisation", or a friend or associate of such an individual, could find themselves labelled "PKI" and targeted as such. This was also the case for individuals with no connection to either the PKI or its "affiliated organisations" who found themselves living in a village with a PKI Village Head, or for a member of Indonesia's ethnic Chinese community, who may or may not consider themselves sympathetic to the PKI. Meanwhile, such targeted individuals, commonly accused of being a member of this target group through mere allegation or association, once identified as such, had no formal means of appealing this designation.

A protected group?

Victims of the 1965–66 killings were targeted for destruction based on their alleged identity as "communists". They were also targeted for destruction based on their alleged identity as "atheists" (*atheis, anti-tuhan*) and "unbelievers" (*kafir, tidak beragama*). Indeed, as new data gathered during my research reveals, outlined in further detail below, this would be a major way in which the killings were justified at the time, both by the military in its public announcements and by civilian participants.

This aspect of the military's targeting of the PKI has, to date, remained largely unexplored. The reluctance to explore whether targeted individuals were identified as atheists has been, in large part, due to the perceived sensitivity of the topic.[120] Atheism is not recognised by the Indonesian state.[121] Meanwhile, survivors are often anxious to distance themselves from the accusation that they are "atheist", both because of this legal requirement and because they consider themselves to be practicing Muslims (or Hindus or Christians).[122]

Jurisprudence exists to suggest an atheist group can be accepted as a "religious group" under the Convention. The ICTR, in the case of *Akayesu*, defined a religious group as "one whose members share the same religion, denomination or mode of worship".[123] This definition, legal scholars Matthew Lippman and David Nersessian argue, encompasses atheistic groups. Lippman, for example, argues: "Religious groups encompass both theistic, non-theistic, and atheistic communities which are united by a single spiritual ideal."[124] For his part, Nersessian proposes: "The concept of religious groups should be sufficiently flexible to include atheists and other non-theists targeted for genocide, based either on their internal 'beliefs' or their functional 'mode of worship' (not worshipping at all)."[125]

The argument that the PKI should be understood as a religious group is further strengthened by the understanding that this group considered itself to be a theistic group "united by a single spiritual ideal", as per Lippman's definition. As will be outlined in chapter 2, Indonesia's communist movement emerged during the 1920s as an offshoot of the Dutch East Indies' pan-Islamic anti-colonial movement. From this time, the majority of PKI members and adherents of Indonesian communism identified both with Marxism and "Red Islam": a distinct stream of Islam articulated by the "Red Haji", Haji Mohammad Misbach, who preached that Islam and communism were compatible.

It is thus possible to argue that victims of the 1965–66 killings were, in part, identified for destruction as a religious group, both because this is how the military identified this group (as "atheists") and because this is how this group self-identified (as adherents of "Red Islam").

Meanwhile, in the case of ethnic Chinese victims of the 1965–66 mass killings, this group was, in certain times and in certain places, additionally targeted for destruction based on their alleged ethnic and racial identity. An analysis of how this targeting occurred can be found in chapter 7.[126] Similarly, as per Cribb's argument, it is possible to argue that victims of the 1965–66 killings were targeted as members of an ideologically constituted national or subnational group as part of Indonesia's communist group.

When presented in conjunction with the clear evidence that the military both possessed and acted upon an intent to destroy this group(s) "as such", the 1965–66 killings can be understood as a case of genocide under the Convention.[127] It is certainly clear the military's target group extended beyond the members of a political organisation. The following section presents new information regarding military manipulation of religion during the time of the genocide gathered during research for this book.

Military manipulation of religion during the time of the genocide

The military leadership deliberately encouraged an understanding that the killings should be interpreted in religious terms. This understanding was encouraged through a military-led black propaganda campaign at the time of the killings, when false accounts of PKI attacks against Muslims were circulated to stimulate fear within the community. On 7 October, for example, the military in Aceh reported that an "anonymous letter" had been "discovered", allegedly sent from the PKI to government and political leaders in Banda Aceh, which stated: "we will carry-out revenge against Islamic Youth".[128] It was also reported by the military on the same day that "rumours have been spread" that a religious boarding school (*asrama*) in Yogyakarta, named after the Acehnese hero Tjut Njak Dien, had been attacked by the "30 September Movement" and its religious leader and several students murdered. The next day on 8 October, meanwhile, it was reported by the military that "several letters of appeal" had been "found" announcing that the "30 September Movement along with the PKI" had "killed" an unspecified number of male and female Acehnese students in Yogyakarta and "Muslims" in Java. No records of these attacks, which would have been a propaganda coup for the military had they occurred, exist in military (or any other) accounts of the post–1 October period in Java.[129]

Another example of a different type of false military report alleging PKI plans to murder Muslims was recorded by the military on 28 October in Aceh. On this date it was alleged by the military that two "unknown individuals" armed with machetes had approached a store owned by an Islamic religious scholar (*ulama*) in northern Aceh with the intention of carrying out a "revenge killing" against *ulama* in the province.[130] Fortunately, the report continues, the military "happened" to be patrolling the area at the time and, as such, the alleged attack was able to be stopped. This report is similar to information I was given by one of my interviewees, a prominent *ulama* in North Aceh, Abu Panton, who recalled how he and other Muslim youth at his religious boarding school (*pesantren*) were warned by the military that the PKI would "attack" their *pesantren* if they did not defend themselves.[131] It can be assumed that this warning was based on a fabricated threat. As this book will outline, there is no evidence the PKI mobilised any significant resistance to the military's attack from 1 October and indeed, the majority of the PKI cadre in Aceh had already been killed by 28 October. Rather than representing a real threat in the community, it appears such military reports were a deliberate attempt to spread fear in the community and to encourage the impression that the killings should be understood in religious terms.

Military-controlled newspapers published during the time of the killings also attempted to portray the violence as having been religiously inspired. Geoffrey Robinson has observed that from the first week of October, "the press was thick with references to the 'holy task' of the Army and its civilian allies in destroying the PKI".[132] One such reference, Robinson explains, includes an article published on 8 October in the national military-controlled newspaper *Angkatan Bersendjata*. This article, he proposes: "appeared to be calling for a 'holy war'" when it explained: "The sword cannot be met by the Koran . . . but must be met by the sword. The Koran itself says that whoever opposes you should be opposed as they oppose you."[133] On 14 October, meanwhile, *Angkatan Bersendjata* editorialised: "God is with us because we are on the path that is right and that He has set for us."[134]

The military also propagated this understanding at public meetings it organised in Aceh, where civilians were ordered to "assist" the military in its killing campaign. On 7 October in Takengon in Central Aceh, for example, Aceh's Military Commander, Ishak Djuarsa, is reported to have announced at one such meeting: "The PKI are *kafir*" before ordering civilians to "kill" the PKI under the threat that anyone who did not comply would themselves be "punish[ed]".[135]

In addition, the military mobilised Islamist parties and Islamist youth to help form the frontline of its attack against the PKI. Members of the HMI (*Himpunan Mahasiswa Islam*) and PII (*Pelajar Islam Indonesia*) Islamist youth organisations (which had been the unofficial youth organisations of the modernist Islamist party Masjumi before it had been banned by Sukarno in 1960 for its support of the United States–backed regional rebellions in the late 1950s),[136] this book will show, played an especially prominent role in the military-sponsored death squads that assisted the military to hunt down, torture and murder individuals and especially students alleged to be involved with the PKI.[137]

Meanwhile, on 19 December, Sumatra's Inter-Regional Military Commander, Ahmad Mokoginta, who played a central role in coordinating the military's Annihilation Operation in Sumatra, including Aceh, publicly endorsed a *fatwa* issued by Aceh's Ulama Council (*Musyawarah Alim-Ulama Sedaerah Istimewa Aceh*) (Aceh's peak state-affiliated Islamic body[138]) in front of Banda Aceh's Grand Mosque. This *fatwa* declared the PKI to be "*kafir harbi*" (unbelievers whom it was permitted to kill).[139] Issued, as it were, by Aceh's peak Islamic organisation, in front of Aceh's most holy site, with the endorsement of the military leadership, this order was especially devastating. Acehnese historians Rusdi Sufi and M. Mudir Azis, in a government-sponsored history of the province, have explained that this *fatwa* helped to provide the military's campaign with "moral legitimation".[140] This *fatwa* was used to justify the killings and appears to have been intended to help ease the conscience of civilians who had been ordered to participate in the killings.

The military also sought to depict the killings as the result of religious violence in its post-genocide propaganda. The opening scenes of the official propaganda film *Treachery of the G30S/PKI* (*Pengkhianatan G30S/PKI*), produced by Suharto's New Order regime in 1984 as required viewing for all Indonesian school children until the fall of the regime in 1998, depicts an incident that was alleged to have demonstrated PKI hostility towards Islam. In the scene, set in Kanigoro, East Java in January 1965, a mob of PKI and Indonesian Peasants' Front (BTI) members, brandishing sickles and other farm implements, attack a group of worshipers praying in a mosque.[141] The PKI and BTI members are then shown murdering the mosque's spiritual leader (*kiai*) and desecrating Islam's 'Holy Book', the Qu'ran. This depiction of events, Indonesian historian Asvi Warman Adam has observed, was a gross misrepresentation of actual historical events.[142] According to Adam, during the incident a group of PKI youth entered a school run by the Islamist youth organisation PII, which had ties to the banned Masjumi party. The PKI intruders then accused the PII of opposing Sukarno's Land Reform campaign and marched several PII members to the local police station.[143] This incident highlighted the severity of inter-group political and social conflict during the lead-up to the killings; it was not, however, an example of fatal religious-inspired violence, as the Indonesian state sought to depict in its propaganda film of the incident.

Multiple examples of the military's annihilation campaign being justified in religious terms also emerged in my interviews throughout the province. In Banda Aceh, Let Bugeh, a former death squad leader and member of the Islamist youth organisation HMI, told me: "[the PKI] didn't recognise God".[144] Dahlan Sulaiman, another former death squad leader and member of the Islamist youth organisation PII, explained: "They were atheists." "They were anti-God, they didn't carry out God's orders, or [the orders] of any religion." "[The killings were] an opportunity to fight against atheism, to fight against people who were anti-God, who, all this time, had tormented us."[145] Meanwhile, Zainal Abidin, a former Subdistrict Head, who detained victims in his government office prior to their transportation to military-controlled killing sites, proposed the killings had occurred because: "They [the PKI] didn't believe in religion."[146]

In North Aceh, "Sjam", a civilian perpetrator, who in 1965 was a small-scale metal worker, suggested the killings had occurred because the PKI were "*kafir*".[147] "Hamid", a civilian perpetrator, who in 1965 was a peasant and prayer leader who participated in night watch duty and who witnessed killings at military-controlled killings, also told me: "The PKI had no religion."[148] While, "Arief", a travelling theatre performer who had close ties to the PKI's cultural group, LEKRA, who had survived by going into hiding, explained the killings by stating: "They [the PKI] didn't want to accept God." "The PKI's mission was to eradicate religion in Aceh."[149]

In Central Aceh, "Abdullah", a civilian perpetrator who had been a member of *Darul Islam* in the district but who in 1965 was a school teacher, told me: "[It was said] they have to be killed because they have no God."[150] Meanwhile, as mentioned above, the sole known survivor of the military's detention and kill campaign in Central Aceh, Ibrahim Kadir, recalled how Aceh's Military Commander had announced at a mass meeting where civilians had been ordered to "assist" the military: "The PKI are *kafir*. They killed the generals, they killed the *ulama*."[151]

In West Aceh, T.M. Yatim, a government official, explained that non-Muslims were the real targets: "If they couldn't recall the confession of faith, it meant they were PKI and could be killed."[152] In South Aceh, "Oesman", a former school teacher who was an eyewitness to the killings, proposed: "The PKI was anti-religion, the PKI had no religion."[153] While, in East Aceh, "Saifuddin", a peasant who was an eyewitness to the killings, recalled: "People said the communists had no God."[154] Meanwhile, "Ibrahim", a law graduate, who was also an eyewitness to the killings, explained to me: "It was said, if the communists win, Islam will be abolished."[155]

I was originally confused when I heard my interviewees describe the killings as being the result of religiously inspired violence. This was because it was so abundantly clear from the other information these same interviewees had told me that the military was responsible and that the killings were not the result of horizontal violence. It would appear, however, that this characterisation of the violence played an important propagandistic role that was deliberately encouraged and manipulated by the military.

The military's depiction of the genocide as the result of religiously inspired violence was a deliberate strategy. The purpose of this strategy was to dehumanise the victims of the military's attack and to justify the killings. This dehumanisation process functioned by depicting the PKI and its affiliated organisations as being beyond the "community of belief" to which this group had belonged before 1 October. By being labelled an "atheist", an individual was ostracised from the Islamic community. They were also declared to be an enemy, whom it was obligatory to kill (*kafir harbi*). This terminology brought back memories in Aceh of the vicious holy war that had been fought against the Dutch and encouraged the notion that the PKI was not only a political threat, but a threat to the very existence of Acehnese and Indonesian identity. Such logic also appears to have been used nationally. When the PKI was officially banned in 1966, the official justification given was that the PKI was not compatible with Indonesia's official state ideology *Pancasila*,[156] specifically, because "the teachings of Communism . . . are incompatible with the principles . . . of the Indonesian nation which [include] belief in God".[157]

This dehumanisation process appears to have been an important means by which civilians, who had been ordered by the military to participate in the killings, were able to justify their participation in the violence to themselves as they were forced to turn on their former neighbours. This strategy also made it very difficult for the population to enunciate any opposition to the killings without being seen as "anti-God" themselves. Meanwhile, perhaps most importantly, through falsely depicting the genocide as the result of horizontal conflict, the military disguised its own central role behind the killings. It is significant to note, however, as this book will show, that never once did the military justify the killings in religious terms in its own internal correspondence. Internally, the military did not see the killings as a holy war. Rather, it understood that it could manipulate religion in order to achieve its political goals.

Towards a political understanding of genocide

Based on the above evidence, there are good grounds for reevaluating whether the 1965–66 killings can be understood as a case of genocide under the 1948 Genocide Convention. The importance of the Convention as a key means through which access to the international legal system can be achieved cannot be underestimated. It is through an application of the Convention that a charge of genocide can be made and perpetrators of such crimes brought to account. The Convention and the legal definition of genocide it contains is not, however, the only means by which the 1965–66 killings can be understood as genocide.

Debates surrounding the inclusion of the 1965–66 killings as a case of genocide under the Convention expose two key limitations of the current legal definition of genocide. The first limitation is that groups subjected to an otherwise identical process of extermination, but not explicitly listed under the law, are not protected under the Convention. Gay victims of the Holocaust, for example, who were killed alongside Jewish victims in the gas chambers of Auschwitz, are excluded from protection under the law if a literalist reading is employed.[158] There is no morally justifiable reason for such an exclusion.[159]

A similarly illustrative case can be found in the case of the Cambodian genocide. While ethnic Vietnamese, Cham, Chinese and Thai victims of the Khmer Rouge are recognised as victims of genocide, ethnic Khmer victims – who share the same ethnic identity as their perpetrators – and who were killed based on their assigned identity as "class enemies", are not.[160] This is despite this second group of victims enduring the same forced work, starvation and systematic killing campaigns faced by the first and constituting a larger number of the overall deaths.[161] Explained as a desire to remain faithful to the letter of the law,[162] this exclusion also appears to be unjustifiable. A similar inconsistency can be seen in the explicit exclusion of political groups from protection under the Convention.[163]

The second limitation of the Convention is that by basing its definition of genocide on how target groups are identified, this definition, beyond allowing perpetrators to effectively self-define the violence they perpetrate, does not facilitate an understanding of why such violence occurs. The current legal definition of genocide fails to explain that genocidal violence cannot easily erupt without the active endorsement and facilitation of a state or state-like body with the resources and reach to implement such a campaign.[164]

In the case of Indonesia, the observation of patterns in the killings both within individual provinces and throughout Indonesia's ultimately diverse and far-flung regions, reported since the earliest eyewitness reports of the killings, was a strong indicator of the likelihood of central coordination behind the genocide. Here I do not intend to present a pre-determinist argument. It was not inevitable that the kind of empirical evidence presented in this book would be found. Nor is it necessarily the case that genocidal violence is always reliant upon the central coordination of a state or state-like body.[165] The exact methods ultimately used by the Indonesian military to initiate and implement the genocide are unique and could not be known in any detail prior to the discovery and analysis of the military's own internal records of these events. Indeed, the specific details of how this organisation took place at the local level in provinces other than Aceh remains open to debate, though the general contours of this organisation can now be proven. A theoretical understanding of genocide as a social phenomenon must nevertheless take structural and organisational factors into account.

A growing body of scholars have advocated for a political understanding of genocidal violence. Jennifer Balint, for example, in examining what makes genocide and other forms of mass harm directed at civilian populations unique, has argued it is through an understanding of the role of the state or state-like body behind such violence that the mechanisms through which such violence is actually implemented can be understood.[166]

Of particular interest to this study, Balint has also highlighted the connection between genocide and war, describing genocide as "a form of war . . . fought against the state's own citizens, resulting in their ultimate disenfranchisement".[167] In doing so, Balint builds on the work of Martin Shaw, who argues that "the links between war and genocide are not simply external or causal, but are *internal* to the character of genocide . . . genocide can best be understood as *a form of war in which social groups are the enemies*".[168] As will be outlined in chapter 6, it would appear this is precisely how the Indonesian military perceived its genocidal attack against Indonesia's communist group. What this political explanation of genocidal violence explains, which the current legal definition of genocide cannot, is that this violence had an ultimate purpose, namely to secure the seizure of state power.[169]

Hannah Arendt, in her classic study, *Eichmann in Jerusalem: A Report on the Banality of Evil*, also pointed to the political causes of genocide, describing the genocidal state as a "bureaucracy of murder".[170] She identifies several important factors that were necessary for the implementation of the Nazi Holocaust, including the use of legal frameworks to normalise the actions of a criminal state; the mobilisation of the state and its resources to implement its genocidal policies; compartmentalisation of steps undertaken by individual perpetrators to reduce feelings of individual responsibility amongst perpetrators; the graduation of violence used in the pursuance of these policies;[171] the use of "winged words" to shield perpetrators and the population at large from the reality of violence; and the use of a "grand narrative" to allow perpetrators to feel as if they were part of something "heroic".[172] All these factors, as this book will show, can also be identified in the case of the Indonesian genocide in Aceh.

Balint, Shaw and Arendt's analyses help to identify and explain the actual mechanics behind mass murder – that is, the structural means through which large-scale mass violence can be initiated and implemented. From a classificatory perspective, these analyses are more satisfying than the taxonomical and semantics-based debate that often accompanies debate over the current legal definition of genocide.

A political understanding of genocidal violence demands that we ultimately recognise genocide as a political crime.[173] Genocide is an intentional and coordinated process that can only be initiated if sufficient political will and ability to exercise hegemony over state power is present to mobilise a particular society to this end. Conversely, perpetrators of genocidal violence are brought to account only if sufficient political will exists to see through such a process.[174]

A strong case can be made for applying the Genocide Convention to the Indonesian killings. The Indonesian military's intentional and centralised campaign to initiate and implement the physical annihilation of the PKI and all those associated with it also clearly fits within broader sociological understandings of genocidal violence. Genocide as a concept is not perfect. Even so, it remains an important tool to bring perpetrators of systematic state-sponsored mass murder to account. For this reason, I use the term "genocide" in both its legal and sociological sense to describe the events depicted throughout this book.

Notes

1 Anthony Dirk Moses, 'Raphael Lemkin, Culture, and the Concept of Genocide', in Donald Bloxham and Anthony Dirk Moses (eds.), *The Oxford Handbook of Genocide Studies* (Oxford: Oxford University Press, 2010), pp. 19–41.

2 Paul Boghossian, 'The Concept of Genocide', *Journal of Genocide Research*, Vol. 12, No. 1–2 (March–June 2010), p. 70. The term *"genos"* can also be translated as "tribe", "nation" and "class". Steve Fenton, *Ethnicity* (Malden, MA: Polity Press, 2010), p. 12. Many competing definitions can be found that build upon Lemkin's basic formulation. See, Frank Chalk and Kurt Jonassohn, *The History and Sociology of Genocide*: *Analyses and Case Studies* (New Haven: Yale University Press, 1990), pp. 8–11.

3 The origins of the concept of genocide can also be found in the "social ontology of 'groupism' prevalent in the Eastern European context in which Lemkin was raised [and in] the Western legal tradition of international law critical of conquest, exploitative occupations, aggressive wars that target civilians". Anthony Dirk Moses, 'Raphael Lemkin, Culture, and the Concept of Genocide', p. 22.

4 Michael Bazyler, *Holocaust, Genocide and the Law: A Quest for Justice in the Post-Holocaust World* (Oxford: Oxford University Press, 2016), pp. 33–34.

5 'Convention on the Prevention and Punishment of the Crime of Genocide', Adopted by the General Assembly of the United Nations on 9 December 1948. The term "as such" conveys the special intent (*dolus specialis*) requirement of the crime.

6 Martin Shaw, *War & Genocide: Organized Killing in Modern Society* (Cambridge: Polity Press, 2003), pp. 34–53.

7 'Convention on the Prevention and Punishment of the Crime of Genocide'.

8 Robert Cribb, 'Political Genocides in Postcolonial Asia', in Donald Bloxham and Anthony Dirk Moses (eds.), *The Oxford Handbook of Genocide Studies*, pp. 445–465; Beth van Schaack, 'The Crime of Political Genocide: Repairing the Genocide Convention's Blind Spot', *The Yale Law Journal*, Vol. 106, No. 7 (May 1997), pp. 2259–2291.

9 For Indonesians, the consequences could be fatal. Foreign Indonesia researchers could be denied entry to the country if they challenged official military narratives.

10 Vedi Hadiz, 'The Left and Indonesia's 1960s: The Politics of Remembering and Forgetting', *Inter-Asia Cultural Studies*, Vol. 7, No. 4 (2006), pp. 555–556.

11 For example, 'Usut Peran Soeharto Dalam G30S/PKI', *Sinar Reformasi* (n.d.), also, 'Soeharto Gembong PKI', *Harian Batavia*, 5 March 1999, reproduced in Wimanjaya W. Liotohe, *Mengadili Diktator Suharto in Absentia: Pengadilan Rakyat Semesta-Pengrata* (Jakarta: n.p. [self-published], 1999), pp. 9, 47; 'Dari Mana Datangnya Harta Keluarga', *D&R*, 6 June 1998.

12 Donald K. Emmerson, *Indonesia Beyond Suharto: Polity, Economy, Society, Transition* (New York: M.E. Sharpe, 1999), p. 297. An overview of civil society initiatives seeking legal redress for the 1965–66 killings can be found in Sri Lestari Wahyuningroem, 'Seducing for Truth and Justice: Civil Society Initiatives for the 1965 Mass Violence in Indonesia', *Journal of Current Southeast Asian Affairs*, Vol. 3 (2013), pp. 115–142.

13 Wimanjaya W. Liotohe, *Mengadili Diktator Suharto in Absentia: Pengadilan Rakyat Semesta-Pengrata* (Jakarta: n.p. [self-published], 1999).

14 Wimanjaya W. Liotohe, a writer and Protestant teacher of religion, was interrogated by police in April 1994 for his self-published book *Prima Dosa* (Prime Sin). The book

was banned in January 1994. Network of Concerned Historians, *Annual Report 1998*, p. 10. Available online: www.concernedhistorians.org/ar/98.pdf.

15 Wimanjaya W. Liotohe, *Mengadili Diktator Suharto in Absentia*, p. 18.

16 *Ibid.*, p. 16.

17 *Ibid.*, pp. 72–75.

18 Bonnie Triyana, 'Konspirasi dan Genosida: Kemunculan Orde Baru dan Pembunuhan Massal', first presented in Yogyakarta, 17 October 2002, p. 2.

19 *Ibid.*, p. 3.

20 *Ibid.*, p. 4.

21 Undang-Undang Republik Indonesia Nomor 26, Tahun 2000, Tentang Pengadilan Hak Asasi Manusia, p. 3. Available online: www.dpr.go.id/dokjdih/document/uu/UU_2000_26.pdf.

22 Undang-Undang Republik Indonesia Nomor 27, Tahun 2004, Tentang Komisi Kebenaran dan Rekonsiliasi. Available online: www.dpr.go.id/dokjdih/document/uu/28.pdf.

23 Michael Sung, 'Indonesia Court Overturns Law Creating Truth and Reconciliation Commission', *Jurist*, 8 December 2006. Available online: www.jurist.org/paperchase/2006/12/indonesia-court-overturns-law-creating.php.

24 Paige Johnson Tan, 'Teaching and Remembering', *Inside Indonesia*, 4 May 2008. Available online: http://www.insideindonesia.org/teaching-and-remembering

25 Husnu Mufid, *Epilog Kudeta G30S/PKI: Siapa Melawan Siapa?* (Surabaya: JP Books, 2008).

26 *Ibid.*, p. 28.

27 An example of resistance to this reactionary turn can be found in a paper presented by Indonesian historian Asvi Warman Adam in late 2007 in the Philippines. Through this paper, 'The Master Narrative Challenged: Dominant Histories and Emerging Narratives', he proposes "the events of 1965–66" can be considered an "act of genocide". This is because, he explains, the killings resulted in the destruction of a group "with a certain ideology", while the killings also acted to "intimidate the rest of the community into submitting to the authorities". His explanation of how the killings occurred is less clear. The military, he proposes, "is suspected of playing a role in motivating the masses to commit violence". But, the killings "were not carried out systematically", and were a "natural consequence" and "simply a reaction" to "social conflict that had already developed at the time". This explanation demonstrates the dilemma faced by scholars wishing to question official narratives in the absence of hard evidence of military agency behind the killings. Asvi Warman Adam, 'The History of Violence and the State in Indonesia', *CRISE Working Paper*, No. 54 (June 2008), pp. 1, 11, 8.

28 See, for example, Aco Manafe, *Teperpu: Pengkianatan PKI pada Tahun 1965 dan Proses Hukum bagi Para Pelakunya* (Jakarta: Pustaka Sinar Harapan); Firos Fauzan, *Civil War ala PKI 1965 Menyingkap Dewan Revolusi PKI* (Jakarta: Accelerate Foundation, 2011); Herman Dwi Sucipto, *Kontroversi G30S* (Yogyakarta: Palapa, 2013).

29 Firos Fauzan, *Civil War ala PKI 1965*, p. vi.

30 Mardiya Chamim (ed.), *Saatnya Korban Bicara: 'Menata Derap Merajut Langkah'* (Jakarta: Yayasan TIPFA, 2009); Putu Oka Sukanta (ed.), *Memecah Pembisuan: Tuturan penyintas tragedy '65-'66* (Jakarta: Lembaga Kreatifitas Kemanusiaan, 2011); Baskara T. Wardaya et al., *Suara di Balik Prahara: Berbagi Narasi tentang Tragedi '65* (Yogyakarta: Galang Press, 2011).

31 Progressive counter-histories were produced during this time to counter military propaganda interpretations of the 30 September Movement, but understandings of how the killings had been technically implemented remained sketchy. See, for example, Asvi Warman Adam, *1965: Orang-orang di Balik Tragedi* (Yogyakarta: Galang Press, 2009); Sukmawati Sukarno, *Creeping Coup D'état Mayjen Suharto* (Yogyakarta: Media Pressindo, 2011); Bernd Schaeffer and Baskara T. Wardaya, *1965: Indonesia dan Dunia* (Jakarta: Gramedia Pustaka Utama, 2013).

32 Nur Kholis, 'Statement by Komnas HAM on the Results of Its Investigations into Grave Violations of Human Rights During the Events of 1965–1966', 23 July 2012; 'Tim Ad Hoc Penyelidikan Pelanggaran HAM yang Berat Peristiwa 1965–1966', *Laporan Akhir Tim Ad Hoc Penyelidikan Pelanggaran HAM yang Berat Peristiwa 1965–1966 ('Laporan Akir '65')*, Komnas HAM, Jakarta, 5 May 2012.

33 'Undang-Undang Republik Indonesia Nomor 26 Tahun 2000 Tentang Pengadilan Hak Asasi Manusia', in *Buku Saku Hak Asasi Manusia* (Banda Aceh: Koalisi NGO HAM Aceh, 2004). This law states that gross violations of human rights that occurred prior to the coming onto force of the Act shall be heard and ruled on by an ad hoc Human Rights Court.

34 'Derailed: Transitional Justice in Indonesia Since the Fall of Soeharto', A Joint Report By the International Center for Transitional Justice and Kontras, March 2011, p. 35. Available online: www.ictj.org/sites/default/files/ICTJ-Kontras-Indonesia-Derailed-Report-2011-English_0.pdf.

35 '*Laporan Akhir '65*', p. 1.

36 *Ibid.*, pp. 848–851.

37 The report did not present original research into whether Indonesia's Chinese community was targeted during the killings. Nor did it consider whether the victims of the killings, who, it notes, were labelled and targeted as "atheists", should be considered as constituting a protected religious group. *Ibid.*, pp. 182, 185–189.

38 Rangga Prakoso, 'AGO Rejects Komnas HAM Report on 1965 Massacres', *Jakarta Globe*, 10 November 2012. Available online: http://jakartaglobe.id/archive/ago-rejects-komnas-ham-report-on-1965-massacres/.

39 Jess Melvin, 'Film Exposes Wounds of Denial of 1965 Violence', *The Jakarta Post*, 30 September 2014. Available online: www.thejakartapost.com/news/2014/09/30/film-exposes-wounds-denial-1965-violence.html.

40 See, for example, Joshua Oppenheimer, 'Director's Statement', *The Act of Killing* official website. Available online: http://theactofkilling.com/statements/.

41 An overview of this new research is given in the Introduction.

42 In 2014, Indonesian artist Dadang Christanto produced an exhibition on the topic of the killings titled '1965–66 Genocide'. Louise Martin-Chew, 'Preview: Dadang Christanto', 13 July 2016. Available online: http://artguide.com.au/dadang-christanto.

43 In 2015, *Bhinneka* magazine published a front-page article to commemorate 'Half a Century Since the '65 Genocide' and held an essay competition on the same topic. 'Setengah Abad Genosida '65', *Bhinneka*, October 2015.

44 See, for example, Iqra Anugrah, 'Genosida* 1965: Tragedi Kemanusiaan dan Serangan atas Perjuangan Kelas', *IndoProgress*, 9 October 2015. Available online: https://indoprogress.com/2015/10/genosida-1965-tragedi-kemanusiaan-dan-serangan-atas-perjuangan-kelas/. Anugrah explains: "I use the term genocide for two reasons. *First*, new research, especially Jess Melvin's research (2013) indicates that the 1965 Mass Killings, in addition to being politically motivated (anti-communist) were also ethnically motivated (anti-Chinese), at least in several areas, such as Aceh. *Second*, I agree with Joshua Oppenheimer that, as far as I know, there is no better term to describe such a large scale humanitarian tragedy than genocide." Examples of online groups include: 'genosida1965wordpress.wordpress.com'; 'ypkp1965.org'; 'Keluarga Tragedi '65'; and 'Taman 65'.

45 The report notes: "Jess Melvin's research in Aceh has uncovered events of mass killings of Chinese in that province, which indicates that members of the Chinese community were targeted through three distinct waves of violence. Melvin has proposed that the violence that occurred against the Chinese community in Aceh at this time can and should be classified as genocide. Further investigation is required to determine whether this qualification can be made." 'Final Report of the IPT 1965: Findings and Documents of the IPT 1965', 20 July 2016.

46 See, for example, Rohmatin Bonasir, 'IPT Den Haag "bantu internasionalisi" kasus 1965', *BBC Indonesia*, 12 November 2015. Available online: www.bbc.com/indonesia/berita_indonesia/2015/11/151112_indonesia_sidang65_diplomasi; 'Siapa Menjadi Korban?',

SindoNews, 13 November 2015. Available online: https://nasional.sindonews.com/read/1061164/16/siapa-menjadi-korban-1447358868; Syahrul Ansyari, 'IPT 1965: Indonesia Bersalah Atas Kejahatan Kemanusiaan', *Viva*, 20 July 2016. Available online: www.viva.co.id/berita/nasional/799010-ipt-1965-indonesia-bersalah-atas-kejahatan-kemanusiaan.

47 Siauw Giok Tjhan, *G30S dan Kejahatan Negara* (Bandung: Ultimus, 2015). The book is a collection of speeches and essays written by Siauw during his time in exile in the Netherlands (1978–81).

48 Baperki (*Badan Permusyawaratan Kewarganegaraan Indonesia*: Consultative Body for Indonesian Citizenship), a mass organisation for Chinese Indonesians who identified as pro-communist.

49 *Ibid.*, p. 95.

50 Noam Chomsky and Edward S. Herman, *The Washington Connection and Third World Fascism: The Political Economy of Human Rights, Volume I* (Boston: South End Press, 1979), p. 235.

51 *Ibid.*, p. 247.

52 The United States government, through the Central Intelligence Agency, would actively promote the idea that blame for the 1965–66 violence should be projected on to the PKI. 'Indonesia 1965: the coup that backfired', Central Intelligence Agency, Washington, 1968.

53 This comparative approach began with Raphael Lemkin, who first coined the term genocide. Donald Bloxham and Anthony Dirk Moses, 'Editor's Introduction', in Donald Bloxham and Anthony Dirk Moses (eds.), *The Oxford Handbook of Genocide Studies*, p. 2.

54 *Ibid.*

55 Leo Kuper, *Genocide: Its Political Use in the Twentieth Century* (New Haven: Yale University Press, 1981), pp. 152–153.

56 *Ibid.*, p. 138.

57 *Ibid.*, p. 154.

58 *Ibid.*

59 *Ibid.*, p. 153.

60 *Ibid.*, p. 154.

61 The resultant disintegration of the group's social structure can lead to its destruction through absorption into the general population. Richard L. Rubenstein, 'Jihad and Genocide: The Case of the Armenians', in Steven Leonard Jacobs (ed.), *Confronting Genocide: Judaism, Christianity, Islam* (Lanham, MD: Lexington Books, 2009), p. 134. In the case of Indonesia, surviving family members also faced systematic state-sanctioned discrimination for over thirty years. Children were excluded from education, while adults were excluded from employment in the government, civil service and military. They were also compelled to report regularly to the state and carry specially marked ID cards. This discrimination often condemned survivors to inter-generational poverty.

62 *Ibid.*, pp. 381, 35.

63 *Ibid.*, p. 382.

64 Frank Chalk and Kurt Jonasshon, *The History and Sociology of Genocide: Analyses and Case Studies* (New Haven: Yale University Press, 1990), p. 35.

65 Israel W. Charny (ed.), *Genocide: A Critical Bibliographic Review, Volume Two* (New York: Facts on File, 1991), p. 331.

66 See, for example, Lucien Rey, 'Dossier of the Indonesian Drama', *New Left Review*, Issue I/36, 1 April 1966; Ruth McVey and Benedict Anderson, *A Preliminary Analysis of the October 1, 1965 Coup in Indonesia* (Ithaca and New York: Modern Indonesia Project, Cornell University, 1971).

67 As discussed in the Introduction to this book, John Roosa explained the 30 September Movement was used as a "pretext" by the military to launch its long anticipated attack against the PKI. Details surrounding the military's planning for this attack would not be known until the discovery of the Indonesian genocide files (chapter 2).

68 Lucien Rey, 'Dossier of the Indonesian Drama', p. 35.

69 Ruth McVey and Benedict Anderson, *A Preliminary Analysis of the October 1*, p. 60.

70 *Ibid.*, p. 62.

71 They explain: "In the cities the PKI was rapidly rounded up and destroyed. In the countryside the process took a little longer, but followed essentially the same course. The struggle was completely one-sided . . . Moreover the Army immediately began training and arming vigilante bands of Nationalist and Islamic youths to scour the villages for those suspected of Communist sympathies." *Ibid.*, p. 63.

72 Rex Mortimer, *Indonesian Communism Under Sukarno: Ideology and Politics, 1959–1965* (Jakarta: Equinox Publishing, 2006, originally 1974), p. 389.

73 Harold Crouch, *The Army and Politics in Indonesia* (Jakarta: Equinox Publishing, 2007, originally 1978), p. 135.

74 Ulf Sundhaussen, *The Road to Power: Indonesian Military Politics, 1945–1967* (Kuala Lumpur: Oxford University Press, 1982), pp. 218–219.

75 Robert Cribb, 'Unresolved Problems in the Indonesian Killings of 1965–1966', *Asian Survey*, Vol. 42, No. 4 (July–August 2002), pp. 551–552.

76 Robert Cribb, 'Political Genocides in Postcolonial Asia', in Donald Bloxham and Anthony Dirk Moses (eds.), *The Oxford Handbook of Genocide Studies* (Oxford and New York: Oxford University Press, 2010), p. 453.

77 Leo Kuper, *Genocide: Its Political Use in the Twentieth Century*; Israel W. Charney (ed.), *Genocide: A Critical Bibliographic Review, Volume One* (New York: Facts on File, 1988), the book references the 1965–66 killings in a bibliography of potential cases of genocide but provides no further information beyond stating that not enough is known about the case (pp. 55, 331); Frank Chalk and Kurt Jonasshon, *The History and Sociology of Genocide*; Helen Fein (ed.), *Genocide Watch* (New Haven: Yale University Press, 1992), the book described the 1965–66 killings as a "genocide" that falls outside the "restrictive specifications" of the 1948 Genocide Convention because "social, political, economic" groups do not qualify as protected groups, p. 18; Samuel Totten, William S. Parsons and Israel W. Charny's 1997 (first 1995) edited collection, *Century of Genocide: Eyewitness Accounts and Critical Views* (New York: Garland, 1997, originally 1995). A full chapter in this study, written by Robert Cribb, is devoted to the 1965–66 killings (discussed further below).

78 See, for example, Jack Nusan Porter (ed.), *Genocide and Human Rights: A Global Anthology* (Washington: University Press of America, 1982), the book interestingly includes a chapter on East Timor, pp. 238–243; Israel W. Charny (ed.), *Genocide: A Critical Bibliographic Review, Volume Two* (New York: Facts on File, 1991); Samuel Totten and William S. Parsons (eds.), *Centuries of Genocide: Essays and Eyewitness Accounts* (New York: Routledge, 1997) (republished in 2004, 2009 and 2013), this book also includes a chapter on East Timor; and Samantha Power, *"A Problem From Hell": America and the Age of Genocide* (New York: Basic Books, 2002).

79 Ben Kiernan, writing in 2003, for example, argued that the 1965–66 killings were "not genocide" because they did not meet the legal definition of the term. The reason for this, he explains, is because: "[t]he number of ethnic Chinese killed . . . was comparatively small and limited to two regions of the country", while the majority of victims shared the same ethnic identity as their perpetrators. Ben Kiernan, 'Twentieth-Century Genocides: Underlying Ideological Themes From Armenia to East Timor', in Robert Gellately and Ben Kiernan (eds.), *The Specter of Genocide: Mass Murder in Historical Perspective* (Cambridge: Cambridge University Press), p. 46.

80 See, for example, Annie Pohlman, 'Incitement to Genocide Against a Political Group: The Anti-Communist Killings in Indonesia', *PORTAL Journal of Multidisciplinary International Studies*, Vol. 11, No. 1 (January 2014).

81 Robert Cribb, 'Genocide in Indonesia, 1965–1966', *Journal of Genocide Research*, Vol. 3, No. 2 (2001), p. 221.

82 *Ibid.*, pp. 221–222.

83 *Ibid.*, p. 222.

84 *Ibid.*, p. 226.

85 *Ibid.*, p. 227.

86 *Ibid.*, p. 228.

87 *Ibid.*, p. 237.

88 'Final Report of the IPT 1965'.

89 See, for example, Daniel Feierstein, 'Political Violence in Argentine and Its Genocidal Characteristics', *Journal of Genocide Research*, Vol. 8, No. 2 (June 2006), pp. 149–169.

90 William A. Schabas, *Genocide in International Law: The Crimes of Crimes*, 1st ed. (Cambridge: Cambridge University Press, 2000), p. 119.

91 See, for example, 'Panitia Aksi Gerakan Massa Ummat Bertuhan untuk Mempertahankan Pantjasila', Idi, East Aceh, 14 October 1965.

92 Helen Fein, 'Revolutionary and Antirevolutionary Genocides: A Comparison of State Murders in Democratic Kampuchea, 1975 to 1979, and in Indonesia, 1965 to 1966', *Comparative Studies in Society and History*, Vol. 35, No. 4 (October 1993), p. 789.

93 *Ibid.*, p. 801.

94 Joshua Lincoln Oppenheimer, 'Show of Force: Film, Ghosts and Genres of Historical Performance in the Indonesian Genocide', PhD thesis, University of the Arts, London, 2004, p. 2.

95 '"The Act of Killing": New Film Shows U.S.-Backed Indonesian Death Squad Leaders Re-enacting Massacre', Interview with Joshua Oppenheimer, *Democracy Now*, 19 July 2013. Available online: www.democracynow.org/2013/7/19/the_act_of_killing_new_film.

96 Joshua Lincoln Oppenheimer, 'Show of Force', p. 161.

97 On the strategic logic of killing, see, Benjamin A. Valentino, *Final Solutions: Mass Killing and Genocide in the 20th Century* (Ithaca: Cornell University Press, 2004).

98 See also, Ernst Fraenkel, *The Dual State: A Contribution to the Theory of Dictatorship* (Oxford: Oxford University Press, 2017, originally 1941).

99 *Angkatan Bersendjata*, 8 October 1965, p. 1.

100 'Tetap tenang dan penuh kewaspadaan terhadap setiap anasir jang merusak dan ingin menghantjurkan Pantjasila-Revolusi-Negara dan Bangsa Kita, baik dari luar maupun dari dalam', in Letdjen A.J. Mokoginta (ed.), *Koleksi Pidato2/Kebidjaksanaan Panglima Antar Daerah Sumatra* (Medan: Koanda Sumatera, 1966), p. 152.

101 *Laporan Tahunan Lengkap Kodam-I/Kohanda Atjeh, Tahun 1965* (Banda Aceh: Kodam-I Banda Aceh, 1 February 1966), pp. 16–17.

102 'Pengumuman: Peng. No. Istimewa P.T.', Banda Aceh, 4 October 1965.

103 See Chapter Three.

104 Interview with Ibrahim Kadir, Takengon, Central Aceh, 7 February 2009, p. 7. Interview with "Latifah" (a pseudonym), Banda Aceh, 15 February 2009, p. 2.

105 'Daftar: Kekuatan ABRI Hansip/Hanra/Sukwan di Kohanda Atjeh', in *Laporan Tahunan Lengkap Kodam-I/Kohanda Atjeh, Tahun 1965* (Banda Aceh: Kodam-I Banda Aceh, 1 February 1966), p. 2.

106 'Pernjataan: No. 12/Pernj/Dprd/1965', Langsa, East Aceh, 28 October 1965, p. 1.

107 See, 'Death Map'.

108 *Laporan Tahunan Lengkap*, p. 17.

109 John R. Bowen proposes 3,000 people were killed in Aceh in 1965–66. John R. Bowen, *Sumatran Politics and Poetics: Gayo History, 1900–1989* (New Haven: Yale University Press, 1991), p. 272. Rusdi Sufi proposes the same figure. Rusdi Sufi, *Pernak-Pernik Sejarah Aceh* (Banda Aceh: Badan Arsip dan Perpustakaan Aceh, 2009), p. 194. Sumatra's Inter-Regional Military Commander, Ahmad Mokoginta, told the American Consul in Medan, North Sumatra, on 25 December 1965 that 6,000 people had been killed in Aceh. Cited in, Yen-ling Tsai and Douglas Kammen, 'Anti-communist Violence and Ethnic Chinese in Medan, North Sumatra', in Douglas Kammen and Katherine McGregor (eds.), *The Contours of Mass*

Violence in Indonesia, 1965–68 (Singapore: NUS Press, 2012), p. 139. I have estimated up to 10,000 people were killed in Aceh during the killings based on military reporting that 1,941 people were killed in Aceh during the phase of public killings in the province (7–13 October). Jess Melvin, 'Documenting Genocide', *Inside Indonesia*, 30 September 2015. Available online: www.insideindonesia.org/documenting-genocide. A more accurate estimate is not possible without extensive forensic research.

110 It is estimated approximately 580,000 political prisoners were arrested between 1965 and the end of 1975. Justus M. van der Kroef, 'Indonesia's Political Prisoners', *Pacific Affairs*, Vol. 49, No. 4 (1976), p. 1.

111 The largest number of these detention centres and labour camps was on Java. Such centres were also established in Sumatra (but not, to my knowledge, in Aceh), Kalimantan, Sulawesi, Maluku, West Irian and, most infamously, on Buru Island. 'Map of Detention Centres Across Indonesia', ca. 1976. Available online: http://intersections.anu.edu.au/issue10/pohlman.html.

112 'Category A' prisoners were those who were to be killed. 'Presidential Instruction No. 9/KOGAM/5/1966', cited in, Justus M. van der Kroef, 'Indonesia's Political Prisoners', p. 628.

113 The majority of political prisoners arrested between 1965 and the end of 1975 were released by the early 1970s. Justus M. van der Kroef, 'Indonesia's Political Prisoners', p. 625.

114 'Tetap tenang dan penuh kewaspadaan', p. 152.

115 The concept of 'Pantja Azimat Revolusi' was proposed by Sukarno in June 1965. The five 'talismans' or 'charms' include the Indonesian ideological concepts of Nasakom, Pancasila, the Political Manifesto, Trisakti and Berdikari. See, Sukarno's Independence Day Speech on 17 August 1965, in *Antara*, 17 August 1965.

116 'Keputusan Bersama: No. Ist. II/Pol/Kpts/1965', Banda Aceh, 6 October 1965, p. 1.

117 'Keputusan Presiden No. 85/KOGAM/1966', in Alex Dinuth (ed.), *Dokumen Terpilih Sekitar G.30.S/PKI* (Jakarta: Intermasa, 1997), pp. 190–194. This document lists each of these organisations as part of a longer four-page list naming "organisations that share the principles of/are protected by/sheltered by the PKI" (*organisasi yang seazas/berlindung/bernaung di bawah PKI*). This is the official list of organisations deemed by the military to be "affiliated" with the PKI.

118 John Roosa, *Pretext for Mass Murder: The 30th September Movement & Suharto's Coup D'Etat in Indonesia* (Madison: The University of Wisconsin Press, 2006), p. 189.

119 See, for example, 'Panitia Aksi Gerakan Massa Ummat Bertuhan untuk Mempertahankan Pantjasila', Idi, East Aceh, 14 October 1965.

120 Literature exploring the targeting of religious groups in the context of genocide remains scarce. In part, this is due to the perceived sensitivity of the topic. Doris L. Bergen explains: "Scholars hesitate to write about religion and the perpetration of extreme violence from within their own tradition, they are also often reluctant to venture into the faiths of others." 'Religion and Genocide: A Historiographical Survey', in Dan Stone (ed.), *The Historiography of Genocide* (Basingstoke: Palgrave Macmillan, 2008), p. 198. Key studies on the topic include: Leo Kuper, 'Theological Warrants for Genocide', *Terrorism and Political Violence*, Vol. 2, No. 3 (1990), pp. 351–379; Omer Bartov and Phyllis Mack (eds.), *In God's Name: Genocide and Religion in the Twentieth Century* (New York: Berghahn Books, 2001); Steven Leonard Jacobs, *Confronting Genocide: Judaism, Christianity, Islam* (Plymouth: Lexington Books, 2009).

121 While it is not illegal to hold atheist thoughts in Indonesia *per se*, it is illegal to express these thoughts publicly under religious blasphemy laws. The banning of atheistic expression is traced to the Indonesian constitution, which recognizes "belief in the Almighty God" as the basis of the Indonesian state. The condemnation of atheism

became institutionalized under the New Order period and was linked to the 1966 banning of the PKI and "Marxism-Leninism". Ismail Hasani, 'The Decreasing Space for Non-Religious Expression in Indonesia: The Case of Atheism', in Tim Lindsey and Helen Pausacker (eds.), *Religion, Law and Intolerance in Indonesia* (London and New York: Routledge, 2016), pp. 197–210.

122 In 2010, 87.2% of Indonesians identified as Muslim; 9.9% as Christian; 1.7% a Hindu; and 1% as Buddhist. In Aceh, approximately 98% of the population identify as Muslim.

123 'The Prosecutor Versus Jean-Paul Akayesu', International Criminal Tribunal for Rwanda, 2 September 1998, paragraph 515, p. 210.

124 Matthew Lippman, 'The 1948 Convention on the Prevention and Punishment of the Crime of Genocide: Forty-Five Years Later', *Temple International and Comparative Law Journal*, Vol. 8 (1994), p. 1.

125 David Nersessian, *Genocide and Political Groups* (Oxford: Oxford University Press, 2010), p. 24.

126 In addition to the attacks on Indonesia's ethnic Chinese population, this could also apply to Aceh's Javanese community, who were collectively treated with suspicion and, in some cases, attacked as a group.

127 The killings can also be understood as a case of extermination. This definition does not, however, capture the military's intention to destroy this group "as such". The Indonesian military has previously been found to have committed the crime of extermination. In 2005, the United Nations found the Indonesian military committed the crime of extermination during its brutal occupation of East Timor (1975–1999). Sian Powell, 'UN Verdict on East Timor', *The Australian*, 19 January 2006.

128 'Chronologis Kedjadian2 jang Berhubungan dengan Gerakan 30 September Didaerah Kodam-I/Atjeh', p. 2.

129 See, for example, *40 Hari Kegagalan 'G.30.S'*, pp. 115–118.

130 'Chronologis', p. 12.

131 Interview with Tengku H. Ibrahim Bardan "Abu Panton", Panton Labu, North Aceh, 18 December 2011.

132 Geoffrey Robinson, *The Dark Side of Paradise: Political Violence in Bali* (Ithaca: Cornell University Press, 1995), p. 281.

133 *Angkatan Bersendjata*, 8 October 1965. Cited in Geoffrey Robinson, *The Dark Side of Paradise*, p. 281.

134 *Angkatan Bersendjata*, 14 October 1965. Cited in Geoffrey Robinson, *The Dark Side of Paradise*, p. 281.

135 My interview with Ibrahim Kadir, Takengon, Central Aceh, 7 February 2009, p. 5.

136 Robert W. Hefner, *Civil Islam: Muslims and Democratization in Indonesia* (Princeton: Princeton University Press, 2000), p. 47.

137 One such military-sponsored death squad, which was established on 14 October in East Aceh, was given the religiously inspired named 'Action Committee of the Movement of Believers for the Defence of Pancasila' (*Panitia Aksi Gerakan Massa Ummat Jang Bertuhan Untuk Mempertahankan Pancasila*). This particular group consisted of traditionalist Islamist parties, the NU, PSII and Perti and members of the Indonesian Nationalist Party (PNI). See, 'Panitia Aksi Gerakan Massa Ummat Jang Bertuhan Untuk Mempertahankan Pantjasila', Idi, East Aceh, 14 October 1965.

138 Aceh's Ulama Council is one of the oldest state-affiliated bodies of its kind in Indonesia. It would later serve as a model for the national *Majelis Ulama Indonesia* (MUI). R. Michael Feener, *Shari'a and Social Engineering: The Implementation of Islamic Law in Contemporary Aceh, Indonesia* (Oxford: Oxford University Press, 2013), p. cxxxvi.

139 'Keputusan-keputusan Musyawarah Alim-Ulama Sedaerah Istimewa Aceh', Presidium Musyawarah, 18 December 1965, reproduced in, H. Said Abubakar, *Berjuang Untuk daerah: Otonomi Hak Azazi Insani* (Banda Aceh: Yayasan Nagasakti, 1995), pp. 161–165.

140 Rusdi Sufi and M. Munir Aziz, *Peristiwa PKI di Aceh: Sejarah Kelam Konflik Ideolo-gis di Serambi Mekkah* (Banda Aceh: CV. Boebon Jaya, 2008), p. 129.
141 *Pengkhianatan G30S/PKI*, directed by Arifin C. Noer (Indonesia: PPFN, 1984).
142 Asvi Warman Adam, *Pelurusan Sejarah Indonesia* (Jakarta: Tride, 2004), p. 23.
143 *Ibid.* Also, Robert Hefner, *Civil Islam*, p. 54.
144 Interview with Let Bugeh, Banda Aceh, 17 January 2010, p. 1.
145 Interview with Dahlan Sulaiman, Banda Aceh, 29 December 2011, pp. 15, 11, 35.
146 Interview with Zainal Abidin, Banda Aceh, 14 February 2009, p. 11.
147 Interview with "Sjam" (a pseudonym), North Aceh, 19 December 2011, p. 8.
148 Interview with "Hamid" (a pseudonym), North Aceh, 19 December 2011, p. 18.
149 Interview with "Arief" (a pseudonym), North Aceh, 5 February, 2009, pp. 5, 16.
150 Interview with "Abdullah" (a pseudonym), Central Aceh, 9 February 2009, p. 9.
151 Interview with Ibrahim Kadir, Central Aceh, 7 February 2009, p. 5.
152 Interview with TM Yatim, West Aceh, 3 December 2011, p. 22.
153 Interview with "Oesman" (a pseudonym), South Aceh, 6 December 2011, p. 16.
154 Interview with "Saifuddin" (a pseudonym), East Aceh, 11 December 2011, p. 11.
155 Interview with "Ibrahim" (a pseudonym), East Aceh, 18 December 2011, p. 18.
156 'PKI Sebagai Organisasi Terlarang: Keputusan Presiden/Panglima Tertinggi Bersendjata Republik Indonesia/Mandataris MPRS/Pemimpin Besar Revolusi No. 1/3/1966', signed by Suharto, 12 March 1966, in Alex Dinuth (ed.), *Dokumen Terpilih*, pp. 168–169.
157 'Penjelasan Ketetapan Majelis Permusyawaratan Rakyat Sementara Republik Indo-nesia, No. XX/MPRS/1966', in Alex Dinuth (ed.), *Dokumen Terpilih*, p. 223.
158 An account of the targeting of gay men and women during the Holocaust can be found in, Gunter Grau (ed.), *Hidden Holocaust? Gay and Lesbian Persecution in Germany 1933–45* (Chicago: Fitzroy Dearborn Publishers, 1995).
159 Many have written on these issues. See, for example, William A. Schabas, *Geno-cide in International Law: The Crime of Crimes*, 1st ed. (Cambridge: Cambridge University Press, 2000), pp. 102–150; David Nersessian, *Genocide and Political Groups*; Beth van Schaack, 'The Crime of Political Genocide: Repairing the Geno-cide Convention's Blind Spot', *The Yale Law Journal*, Vol. 106, Issue. 7 (1997), pp. 2259–2291.
160 David Chandler, *Voices From S-21: Terror and History in Pol Pot's Secret Prison* (Berkeley and Los Angeles: University of California Press, 1999), p. vii.
161 Ben Kiernan, 'The Cambodian Genocide, 1975–1979', in Samuel Totten and William S. Parsons (eds.), *Century of Genocide: Critical Essays and Eyewitness Accounts* (New York: Routledge, 2009), p. 348; see also, Ben Kiernan, *The Pol Pot Regime: Race, Power and Genocide in Cambodia Under the Khmer Rouge, 1975–79* (New Haven: Yale University Press, 1996).
162 The Extraordinary Chambers in the Courts of Cambodia have, to date, only tried charges of genocide in relation to the killing of members of the Vietnamese, Cham and Khmer Krom ethnic groups. See, www.eccc.gov.kh/en.
163 The exclusion of political groups from the list of groups protected by the law was a result of political compromise between signatories to the Convention. For a discus-sion of this process, see, Steven R. Ratner, Jason S. Abrams and James L. Bischoff, *Accountability for Human Rights Atrocities in International Law: Beyond the Nurem-berg Legacy* (New York: Oxford University Press), p. 44. Legal expert Beth van Schaack has argued: "no legal principal can justify" this exclusion, while observ-ing this exclusion leads to "arbitrary justice". She has observed that the exclusion of political groups from protection under the Convention has led to a "blind spot" under the law. This exclusion, she proposes, contravenes peremptory norms regard-ing the crime of genocide. Specifically, she argues, the *jus cogens* (common law) prohibition on genocide, as expressed in a variety of sources, predates the drafting of the Genocide Convention and provides broader protections than the Convention itself. In international law these is no hierarchy of sources. Both custom and treaty possess equal rank. This means, van Schaack explains, that the deliberate exclusion

of political groups from the Convention "is without legal force to the extent that it is inconsistent with the *jus cogens* prohibition of genocide". If van Schaack is correct, the exclusion of political groups from protection under the law is not just morally unjustifiable, it may also be legally indefensible. Beth van Schaack, 'The Crime of Political Genocide', pp. 2259, 2261–2262, 2290.

164 Benedict Anderson, for example, has observed that, "domestic mass murder on a large scale is always the work of the state". Benedict Anderson, 'Impunity and Reenactment: Reflections on the 1965 Massacre in Indonesia and Its Legacy', *The Asia-Pacific Journal*, Vol. 11, Issue 15, No. 4 (14 April 2013), p. 1. Jacques Semelin, meanwhile, has explained how "massacre can only spread on a grand scale if a central authority more or less overtly encourages it". Jacques Semelin, *Purify and Destroy: The Political Uses of Massacre and Genocide* (New York: Columbia University Press, 2007), p. 167.

165 Genocidal frontier violence may be one example of non-centralised genocidal violence. Such violence certainly takes a different form to the type described in this book. Genocidal frontier violence is often linked to land acquisition, in addition to ideals of racial purity, see Ben Kiernan, *Blood and Soil: A World History of Genocide and Extermination From Sparta to Darfur* (New Haven: Yale University Press, 2008), pp. 165–168. It may also occur over a much longer time frame. Frontier violence in Australia, to provide one example, occurred over a 140-year period and as the result of multiple campaigns and events. The debate over agency behind genocidal frontier violence in Australia nonetheless possesses similarities with debates over agency behind the 1965–66 Indonesian killings. In short, it is also debated whether genocidal frontier violence in Australia was "spontaneous", locally directed or state-led. Thomas Rogers and Stephen Bain, 'Genocide and Frontier Violence in Australia', *Journal of Genocide Research*, Vol. 18, No. 1 (2016), p. 85.

166 Jennifer Balint, *Genocide, State Crime and the Law: In the Name of the State* (Abingdon and New York: Routledge, 2012), p. 14.

167 *Ibid.*, p. 24.

168 Martin Shaw, *War and Genocide: Organised Killing in Modern Society* (Oxford: Blackwell, 2003), pp. 44–45.

169 Daniel Feierstein has described "the ultimate purpose of genocide" as "not the destruction of a group as such but the transformation of society as a whole". The terror of genocide, he explains, is "used as an instrument of social transformation". Daniel Feierstein, 'The Concept of Genocide and the Partial Destruction of the National Group', *Logos*, Winter 2012. Available online: http://logosjournal.com/2012/winter_feierstein/.

170 Hannah Arendt, *Eichmann in Jerusalem: A Report on the Banality of Evil* (New York: Penguin Books, 2006, originally 1963), pp. 116, 289.

171 Hannah Arendt identifies three main phases within the Nazis' campaign: expulsion, concentration and killing. *Ibid.*, pp. 56–111.

172 *Ibid.*, pp. 48, 85–86, 89–90, 105–106, 149, 293–294.

173 Discussion with Dirk Moses, 25 June 2017. See his *The Problems of Genocide* (Cambridge: Cambridge University Press, forthcoming).

174 A classic example of a genocide that has never been brought to account due to lack of political will is the genocide of indigenous Australians at the time of British colonisation. See Anthony Dirk Moses (ed.), *Genocide and Settler Society: Frontier Violence and Stolen Indigenous Children in Australian History* (New York: Berghahn Books, 2004).

2 The struggle for the Indonesian state

In 1965 Indonesia was at a crossroads. The Cold War was at its height in Southeast Asia and it appeared to many observers to be only a matter of time before the PKI would come to power. The Indonesian military, however, was determined to halt the PKI's rise and place the Indonesian state under its own direction.[1] A major challenge for researchers investigating the events of 1 October 1965 and the subsequent genocide has been the difficulty in pinpointing exactly how the military was able to coordinate its attack against the PKI. This is because while it has been observed that Suharto's response to the actions of the 30 September Movement "suggests preparation",[2] the nature of this preparation has not previously been known beyond its broadest contours.

National military command structures

The Indonesian military had extensive access to the organs of the Indonesian state. Since the time of the national revolution the military had experimented with several organisational structures.[3] The commonality between these structures and the underlying ideology that conceived of them was the idea that the military should not exist separately from civilian society, but, rather, that it should remain intimately and permanently integrated within all levels of Indonesian society. This concept, which emerged as a legacy of the Indonesian military's origins as a guerrilla army in the crucible of the Indonesian revolution, was articulated by Abdul Haris Nasution, who had fought during the revolution as an idealistic young solider and who later rose to become the Indonesian military's chief architect. In 1953, Nasution explained that modern warfare must be fought as a "total people's war", in which all layers of society were to be mobilised in order to "destroy" the enemy.[4] The greatest short-term threat the Indonesian military faced after independence, Nasution argued, consisted of internal challenges to domestic security, and as such, particular attention should be placed on preparing for a counter-guerrilla insurgency.[5] This notion lay at the heart of the organisation of the military's command structures.

In 1957, the Indonesian military adopted a command structure organised into sixteen Regional Military Commands (Kodam: *Komando Daerah Militer*), to coincide with Indonesia's provincial boundaries. At the top was the Supreme

Commander of the Armed Forces (*Panglima Tertinggi*), a position held by Sukarno as President. Immediately below the Supreme Commander was the Commander in Chief of the Armed Forces (Pangad: *Panglima Angkatan Darat*) (a position held on the morning of 1 October 1965 by Lieutenant General Ahmad Yani until he was killed by the 30 September Movement).[6]

A network of military commanders existed beneath the Pangad at the inter-provincial, provincial, district and subdistrict levels. Each of Indonesia's provincial- (*daerah*) level Regional Military Commands (*Kodam: Komando Daerah Militer*) was headed by a Regional Military Commander (*Pangdam: Panglima Daerah Militer*). These were, in turn, coordinated at the inter-provincial level by an Inter-Provincial Military Commander (*Pangkoanda: Panglima Komando Antar Daerah*).

Beneath the provincial level, each of Aceh's[7] district- (*kabupaten*) level District Military Commands (*Kodim: Komando Distrik Militer*) was headed by a District Military Commander (*Dandim: Komandan Komando Distrik Militer*), while at the subdistrict (*kecamatan*) level there existed a network of Territorial Affairs and People's Resistance Officer (*Puterpra: Perwira Urusan Teritorial dan Perlawanan Rakyat*) units.[8] These Kodam-affiliated military command structures were additionally responsible for various troops, including multiple infantry battalions,[9] while the Puterpra were tasked with training and indoctrinating village-level Civilian Defence (*Hansip: Pertahanan Sipil*) and People's Defence (*Hanra: Pertahanan Rakyat*) paramilitary units.[10] Meanwhile, two Inter-District Military Resort Commands (*Korem: Komando Resort Militer*) coordinated, respectively, the east coast and central highlands Kodim and the west coast and southeast coast Kodim in Aceh.

The Indonesian military through its national command structures was thus able to extend its influence down to the village level. This, however, was not the limit of the military's reach into Indonesian society. The military command structure had been established to parallel the regional civilian bureaucracies[11] and, in addition to military roles, the provincial-level Pangdam and district-level Dandim also held positions in Indonesia's 'Level I' Provincial Government (DPRD: *Dewan Perwakilan Rakyat Daerah*) and 'Level II' Provincial Government (DPRD Tingkat II) respectively. Military representatives were also appointed to the National Front (*Front Nasional*)[12] bodies established by Sukarno in 1960 as a means of allowing political parties increased participation in the political process after the suspension of national elections in 1957 following the declaration of Guided Democracy.[13]

A shifting balance of power

The early 1960s was a period of intense political competition in Indonesia that would eventually crystallise into a struggle for the Indonesian state among the military leadership, Sukarno and the PKI. Between 1960 and 30 September 1965, the balance of power among these three forces would shift from a position initially favourable to the military, to one that appeared to favour the PKI. Harold Crouch has identified three main stages in this power struggle. Between 1960 and 1962, the balance of power was stable.[14] Sukarno and the military shared the balance of power "founded on a mutual awareness that one could not easily do away with the other".[15] The organisational and armed strength of the military was something that Sukarno could not ignore, while the military was forced to accept Sukarno's authority as President, which gave the regime and the military's role an "aura of legitimacy it would not have without him". Although Sukarno had worked with the military to reduce the strength of the political parties through the implementation of Guided Democracy, he recognised the PKI as an integral component of Indonesian political life, as epitomised through the 'Nasakom' (*Nasionalisme, Agama, Komunisme*: 'Nationalism, Religion, Communism') doctrine, which, announced in 1961, was intended to officially recognise the role of these three major tendencies in Indonesian political life.[16] Sukarno also drew upon the organisational strength of the PKI to act as a counterweight to the military.

By the early 1960s, the PKI had a membership of 1.5 million, not including members of its affiliated organisations.[17] The PKI's national leadership was headed by Chairman D.N. Aidit, who led the Party's national secretariat (*Comite Central*). Party secretariats also existed at the provincial, regional centre, district, subdistrict and village levels.[18] Its largest bases at this time were on Java and Sumatra.[19] Since the early 1950s it had also expanded to Bali, Madura, Sulawesi and Kalimantan. In these places, it had a strong base among city workers, estate labourers and squatters on forestry land.

From 1959 the Party made a concerted effort to expand its base within the peasantry.[20] Inspired by developments in China, PKI cadres were sent into villages as part of what was called a 'Go Down' (*Turba: Turun ke Basis*) movement designed to both better educate Party cadres and introduce local populations to the Party's policies and programs.[21] At the local level in such rural areas, the PKI competed with the PNI (*Partai Nasional Indonesia*: Indonesian National Party), which had been established in Jakarta in 1927 under the leadership of Sukarno, the NU (*Nahdlatul Ulama*: 'Revival of the Islamic Scholars'), a traditionalist Islamic group and, until 1960, Masjumi (*Majilis Sjuro Muslimin Indonesia*: Consultative Council of Indonesian Muslims) a modernist Islamic party, which, founded in November 1945, was banned in 1960 by Sukarno for supporting the Darul Islam and PRRI/Permesta regional rebellions.[22]

Party discipline and education was less strong within the PKI than in comparable communist parties. This was, in large part, due to the United National Front policy adopted by the Party.[23] This policy, which was based on the Party's analysis that the Indonesian working class and peasantry was not yet prepared for open class struggle, advocated for mass action and organisation with all progressive nationalist forces. This policy allowed the PKI to attract new followers around the country and led to significant electoral gains. In the 1955 general election, the PKI had garnered 16.4% of the vote, making it the fourth most popular political party nationally.[24] Yet, between 1957 and 1959, the Party's leadership would vote to overthrow parliamentary democracy.[25] The subsequent enactment of Guided Democracy effectively blocked the PKI's democratic road to power and made the Party's influence contingent on its ability to champion Sukarno's policies.

Rex Mortimer has observed that one reason the PKI was prepared to suppress its own interests in this way was because it did not see itself in an antagonistic position to Sukarno and his government.[26] As a proud participant in Indonesia's national revolution it considered itself to be a protector and heir of the Indonesian revolution. This meant that while it wished to consolidate its own influence with the ultimate aim of coming to power, its "experiences had prepared [the Party] for a struggle *within*, not for one *against*, the constituted Republic".[27]

The PKI was also sensitive to the accusation that it had "stabbed the revolution in the back" in 1948 during the Madiun Affair, when, during the height of the war of independence a series of clashes between pro-communist militias and Republican forces had occurred.[28] Republican forces had depicted the situation as the beginning of a communist insurrection and pro-communist forces had been forcibly put down. Most of the Party's leadership lost their lives at that time, while Aidit, a junior member of the Party's Central Committee, had fled to Singapore, before returning to Indonesia in the mid-1950s. In supporting Guided Democracy, the PKI hoped it could demonstrate its patriotism, while, in return, earning Sukarno's protection.[29] The PKI wanted to one one day seize state power, but there is no indication the Party expected to achieve this goal in the near future.

In 1956, the PKI had endorsed a "peaceful road to socialism".[30] This does not mean it was unaware of the threat posed by the military. By proving itself the most loyal and most pro-nationalist party, it hoped any attack against it would be seen as an attack against Sukarno and the national interest. The PKI also advocated for educational training within the armed forces, in the hope that officers could also be won over to its position and the military captured from within. From May 1965, such education began through a Sukarno-sponsored Nasakomisation campaign.[31] There are indications that by the eve of 1 October 1965 this strategy was showing some success.[32]

The military leadership, however, was also busy consolidating itself. In 1961, a new military chain of command, known as KOTI (*Komando Operasi Tertinggi*: Supreme Operation Command), was established in Sumatra, Kalimantan, Sulawesi and eastern Indonesia to coordinate the West Irian campaign, aimed at forcing the Netherlands to cede control over the last territory formerly held by the Dutch East Indies.[33] Sukarno benefitted from the West Irian campaign by using it to articulate a popular and unifying program that drew upon anti-colonial sentiment and focused attention beyond the horizon of Indonesia's troubled domestic and economic affairs.

The military leadership, meanwhile, benefitted from the campaign by using it as a justification for the continued implementation of martial law, which had been implemented in 1958, when a 'State of War' (*Keadaan Perang*) had been declared in response to a series of regional rebellions, including the Darul Islam rebellion in Aceh (1953–62), West Java (1948–62) and South Sulawesi (1953–65) and the PRRI/Permesta rebellions in West Sumatra and Sulawesi (1958–61). The military also used the West Irian campaign as a means to cement their position at the centre of the nation's political life.

Between 1962 and 1964, the military began to lose ground in its relationship with Sukarno and the PKI.[34] This shift began with the end of the West Irian campaign in August 1962, when, with the support of the US, it was decided that authority for the administration of West Irian would be immediately transferred from the Dutch to the United Nations, with a referendum to be held to determine the fate of the territory.[35]

The conclusion of the West Irian campaign weakened the military's justification for maintaining martial law and this situation was only exacerbated by the end of the regional rebellions during the same year. The military leadership began to fear that its influence would be rolled back, while the PKI feared that the settling of the conflict could lead to closer relations between Indonesia and the West, especially the US, which had began offering generous "development" loans to the Indonesian military.[36] The question of what sort of a state Indonesia would become was once again open for negotiation as it had been during the period immediately after the national revolution.

Sukarno, for his part, took the opportunity to move against Nasution, using Yani, then one of Nasution's deputies, to help manoeuvre the General out of his powerful position as Chief of Staff into a relatively powerless, though still influential, role as Minister for Defence and Security.[37] This "betrayal" of Nasution by Yani would cause a rift in the national military leadership that would weaken the military's position.[38]

In the meantime, Sukarno once again began to look for a unifying campaign to unite Indonesia's political elite. The 'Crush Malaysia' (*Ganyang Malaysia*) campaign came to fulfil this role. Sukarno had originally signalled no interest in opposing the formation of an independent Malaysia.[39] This was in contrast to the PKI, which publicly argued that the new nation would act as a puppet for British imperialism in the region. From September 1963, however, Sukarno threw his support behind the *Ganyang Malaysia* campaign, seeing it as a means to reclaim the spirit of national unity that had been generated by the West Irian campaign.

The PKI supported Sukarno's new-found enthusiasm, but the military leadership opposed it, worried that it would damage its close relationship with the US military, which, beyond offering economic aid, was also engaged in training the cream of the Indonesian military's officer corps.[40] Both Mokoginta and Djuarsa were trained during this time at the US Command and General Staff College at Fort Leavenworth in Kansas. Mokoginta would emerge as a distinguished figure in the national military leadership, alongside Nasution and Yani. This led to him becoming known as Yani's "right hand man" in Sumatra.[41]

As Sukarno's support for the *Ganyang Malaysia* campaign wore on, however, the military leadership came to realise that it could use the situation to its own advantage to strengthen military command structures and intensify civilian militia training under the auspices of preparing for a potential (but highly unlikely)[42] invasion across the Malacca Strait. This new-found enthusiasm would eventually allow the military to oversee the implementation of Sukarno's new Dwikora campaign, which, as will be outlined below, would be used by the military leadership to allow for the effective re-implementation of martial law without martial law having to be officially declared. This campaign would have particular significance for Aceh due to the province's physical proximity to the Malay Peninsula.

In 1964–65, meanwhile, the balance of power in Indonesia began to shift in the PKI's favour.[43] As the *Ganyang Malaysia* campaign gathered momentum so too did anti-US sentiment. The US embassy and cultural centres were attacked, while US-made films were banned and US-owned plantations were occupied and taken over, including in Aceh's neighbouring province, North Sumatra.[44] The PKI went on the offensive and, of most concern to the military, initiated training of civilian militia groups under the cover of the *Ganyang Malaysia* campaign in Jakarta and the provinces, including Aceh.[45] When, on 17 August 1965, Sukarno used a speech to declare that he had publicly adopted the PKI's call for the arming of a 'Fifth Force' (*Angkatan Kelima*) or People's Army,[46] conceived of as an auxiliary service to be made up of armed workers and peasants that would exist parallel to the army, air force, navy and police force,[47] the military began making contingency plans for moving against Sukarno and the PKI as soon as the opportunity presented itself.

Sukarno's support for the creation of a 'Fifth Force', no matter how rhetorical, was a red line the military leadership was not willing to cross. It appears his announcement acted as a trigger for the military to abandon its previous policy of waiting for Sukarno to "step off stage" before initiating its own takeover of government.[48] As we have seen in the Introduction, the possibility of the military launching a pre-emptive seizure of power while Sukarno remained in office had been discussed since at least January 1965. At this time, General Parman, a key leader of the military leadership, who would later be killed by the 30 September Movement, met with a US embassy representative to discuss the military's "specific plans for takeover of government".[49]

US Ambassador Howard Jones would later report to the US State Department that is was the belief of the military leadership that should the military decide to launch its coup while Sukarno remained in power, it would be best if the military could appear to be acting in a defensive manner.[50] The ideal scenario for such a move, Jones explained, would be an abortive coup action that could be blamed on the PKI.[51] Such a move would also preferably preserve Sukarno's leadership, at least officially, intact. It was to be a coup, John Roosa has observed, "that would not appear to be a coup".[52]

In April, the military leadership had held a conference in Bandung. This conference, which was attended by Suharto, who would attend as a member of a 'Coordination Group Steering Committee', and by Mokoginta, who would attend as 'Head of the Revolutionary War Doctrine Group',[53] upheld Nasution's concept of 'Territorial Warfare' and the internal guerrilla war strategy that this concept advocated through a doctrine that it named '*Tri Ubaya Cakti*' (lit. 'Three Sacred Promises').[54]

The military were still unwilling to move openly against the PKI because of Sukarno's broad popularity and his support of the Party. It had already decided, however, that its major concern was not whether it should move against the PKI and seize state power for itself, but rather when and how it might initiate this takeover.

Between 1960 and 1965, the PKI and its affiliated organisations had experienced a steady increase in popularity. By August 1965, 27 million Indonesians had joined the PKI and its affiliated organisations. This growing popularity was a result of both the Party's strident anti-imperialism, which was fully embraced by Sukarno, as well as its long-term advocacy on behalf of the peasantry and other poorer sections of Indonesian society. The PKI's vision for a future based on radical egalitarianism would become especially attractive during early 1965 as food shortages and inflation raged.[55]

The Party's antagonisms with the military were also growing. Sukarno and the PKI's anti-imperialism threatened the military's warm relationship with the US.[56] The military had also grown increasingly economically powerful throughout the late 1950s, as it came to operate nationalised businesses throughout the country.[57] These new economic interests provided the military leadership with an added incentive to maintain the status quo.

The PKI, for its part, had also grown gradually radical in its pursuit of land reform. Since the early 1960s, its 'Go Down' program had developed into support for land seizures and other "unilateral actions" (*aksi sepihak*).[58] This land reform campaign, which received the blessing of Sukarno, created tensions with local rural elites, who feared having their land taken from them. In an attempt to keep land from peasants, elites began to transfer their landholdings to local *pesantren*, and, in Bali, to local Hindu temples.[59] This phenomenon allowed the PKI's land reform campaign to be depicted by its adversaries as an attack against religion and forged an alliance between these elites and the military. It also played upon deep ideological schisms within Indonesian political thought which had first emerged in the 1920s.

Members of the PKI and its affiliated organisations did not self-identify as atheist. Instead, they overwhelmingly described themselves as Muslim, or, in non-Muslim majority areas, as Hindu or Christian. Indeed, the Indonesian communist movement had first emerged during the 1920s from the same Islamic nationalist movement that gave rise to Indonesia's modernist Islamist movement, the Islamic Union (SI: *Sarekat Islam*).[60]

Founded in 1912, the Islamic Union (*Sarekat Islam*) was the Dutch East Indies' first modern political organisation for native rights and quickly drew a mass following.[61] First established to defend the interests of Muslim merchants against Chinese rivals, the organisation originally relied heavily on Islamic appeals. As the organisation grew, the organisation became divided between those who remained committed to Islamist politics and those who were attracted to the ideas of Marxism and secular nationalism.[62]

In 1921, *Sarekat Islam* split between its two major factions, the 'White Islamic League' (*Sarekat Islam Putih*), whose members formed the modernist Indonesian Islamic Union Party (PSII: *Partai Sarekat Islam Indonesia*) and the 'Red Islamic League' (*Sarekat Islam Merah*), whose members identified as Marxist and who would come to form the Indonesian Communist Party (PKI).[63]

This split was not based on irreconcilable theological differences. The two groups disagreed on the role of Islam in the political sphere, but neither rejected Islam as a belief system. Rather, the split was based on differences in strategy about the best way to build a strong nationalist movement. The White Islamic

League faction advocated on behalf of concentrating the League's membership base among the middle-class traders and explicitly Islamic organisations that had formed the organisation's original core membership base, while encouraging cooperating with the colonial regime to strengthen the national movement.[64] The Red Islamic League faction, meanwhile, advocated organising all layers of Indonesian society, including working-class labour, peasant, cultural and women's organisations, to grow the League as a mass political organisation explicitly opposed to Dutch colonial rule.[65]

The appeal of communism to the Red Islamic League faction lay in its strong liberationist traditions and its advocacy on behalf of the poor. As Ruth McVey has suggested, the group's acceptance of an explicitly Marxist-Leninist ideology lay in Marxism-Leninism's "apparent ability to trump imperialist Europe's claim to be the true possessor of the science of modernity".[66]

The Red Islamic League faction was not opposed to Islam and included deeply pious Muslims amongst its membership. Indeed, the Red Islamic League encouraged a partnership between Islam and communism. Haji Mohammad Misbach, a key national leader of the Red Islamic League faction and an *ulama* from Surakarta, Central Java, argued in 1925:

> Those comrades amongst us who identify as communist, but who share ideas about the disappearance of Islam, I am brave enough to say they are not true communists, or they do not yet understand the position of communism . . . conversely, those who identify as Muslim, but do not agree with communism, I am brave enough to say they are not real Muslims, or do not yet truly understand the position of Islam.[67]

This tradition was continued by the PKI, which, as an organisation, was at pains to explain that it did not see "Islam" as the problem faced by Indonesian society. It was nonetheless openly antagonistic towards what it described as 'Islamic capitalism' and had singled out H.O.S. Tjokroaminoto, the leader of the White Islamic League, as an enemy of the people and true Islam.[68] The military would skilfully exploit this social rift from 1 October 1965.

The primary material basis for antagonism between the PKI and the military leadership, however, was the Party's attempt to disrupt the military's monopoly over armed force. Sukarno's support for the creation of a 'Fifth Force' in August 1965 helped to shift its plans to seize state power to the next stage. Nasution's concept of Territorial Warfare would become the blueprint for this attack, which would be launched through the framework of Dwikora under the guise of the *Ganyang Malaysia* campaign.

Dwikora and the Mandala Satu Command

On 3 May 1964, Sukarno had announced his concept of *Dwikora* ('People's Double Command'), which called for the intensification of the Indonesian revolution and the *Ganyang Malaysia* campaign, as well as for the mobilisation and training of 21 million volunteers to support the *Ganyang Malaysia* campaign.[69] These concepts were subsequently formalised in September through a piece of legislation entitled 'Decision to Increase the Implementation of Dwikora'.[70] This legislation provided for the establishment of a new military chain of command to oversee this campaign, which was granted broad and sweeping powers akin to Indonesia's existing State of Military Emergency[71] and State of War legislation.[72]

Sukarno's apparent intention was to use this legislation to curtail the military's powers by placing his own allies in control of this command and to provide a counterbalance to the military's monopoly on arms by providing basic arms training to civilians. The military leadership, however, also appears to have sensed the opportunities that this legislation presented for it to launch its own attack against the PKI, so long as it was able to wrest control over the campaign. It therefore chose to support the implementation of Dwikora. This led to the odd situation from April 1965, when Dwikora was first implemented through the activation of the KOTI command, whereby the military leadership publicly committed itself to preparing for an armed conflict with Malaysia, while it secretly went about sabotaging military actions related to this campaign.[73] This disguised power play would produce the structures that would eventually be used by the military to launch its attack against the PKI.

In October 1964, a new military chain of command, the Mandala Vigilance Command (Kolaga: *Komando Mandala Siaga*), was established parallel to the Kodam command under the KOTI command. The purpose of this new command was to coordinate and direct all military activities related to the *Ganyang Malaysia* campaign in Sumatra and Kalimantan, due to the physical proximity of these two provinces to Malaysia.[74] The military leadership conceived of this new command as a means to prevent any further escalation of the *Ganyang Malaysia* campaign while additionally expanding the military leadership's power in the affected provinces by granting the KOTI/Kolaga leadership with authority over all troops within its area of command.[75]

In concession to Sukarno, this new command was placed under the command of Air Marshal Omar Dhani (who was pro-Sukarno and who would later be implicated in the 30 September Movement), with Suharto appointed as First Deputy Commander from 1 January 1965.[76] As outlined in chapter 3, in addition to seizing the position of Commander in Chief of the Armed Forces (Pangad) during the morning of 1 October 1965, Suharto would also seize command of the KOTI/Kolaga command. In Sumatra this new command was known as the First Mandala (*Mandala Satu*) Command, while in Kalimantan it was known as the Second Mandala (*Mandala Dua*) Command.[77]

The Mandala Satu Command in Sumatra was headed by a Mandala Satu Commander (*Panglatu*: *Panglima Mandala Satu*), a position held by Mokoginta, who was also the Inter-Provincial Military Commander (Pangkoanda) for Sumatra under the Kodam command structure.[78] Under the Panglatu in Sumatra, meanwhile, there existed a network of Regional Authorities for the Implementation of Dwikora (*Pepelrada*: *Penguasa Pelaksanaan Dwikora Daerah*) responsible for territories corresponding with the Kodam. In Aceh this position was held by

Djuarsa, Aceh's Regional Military Commander.[79] The Pepelrada had sweeping powers, including the right to seize property, impose curfews, search people and their belongings, ban people from living in or leaving certain areas, temporarily exile people, require civilians to assist in the implementation of Dwikora, and arrest and detain people for up to thirty days without charge.[80] These powers mirrored those possessed by Regional War Authorities (*Peperda: Penguasa Perang Daerah*) under national State of Military Emergency and State of War legislation. They were a realisation of the military's ambition to "create a situation of Martial Law rule without Martial Law", which PKI Chairman D.N. Aidit had prophesised in 1963.[81]

The main difference between these emergency laws and those possessed by the Panglatu and Pepelrada was that while a State of Military Emergency and State of War could only be declared by the President/Supreme Commander of the Armed Forces,[82] Dwikora was implemented internally through the KOTI command, allowing the military to internally impose de facto martial law conditions without having to seek permission from Sukarno.[83] This difference would become crucial to the military's ability to act autonomously from 1 October 1965. The Panglatu and Pepelrada also possessed the additional freedom of being limited only by what was "considered necessary" (*dianggap perlu*) for the "implementation of Dwikora".[84]

The provincial-level Pepelrada, like the provincial-level Pangdam (Regional Military Commander) under the Kodam command structure, also had access to civilian government. At the provincial level, the Pepelrada were "required to deliberate" with the Provincial Pantja Tunggal.[85] The *Pantja Tunggal* ('Five in One') had been established in March 1964 as a modification of the original *Tjatur Tunggal* ('Four in One'); the top executive board at a provincial or district level, which incorporated both military and civilian representatives. This new body added a representative from the *Front Nasional* to the original four members of Military Commander, Chief Prosecutor, Police Chief and Provincial Governor. A modification which, according to Ulf Sundhaussen, was meant as a means for "communists and leftists", who often came to hold this position, to act as a "counterweight" to the army officers in the provinces.[86] Once Dwikora was enacted in response to a military threat, this book will show, the Pantja Tunggal acted to subsume the provincial government under military control.

Military preparations to seize state power in Sumatra

In March 1965, the Mandala Satu Command began to engage in a training exercise under the direction of Mokoginta, acting in his capacity as Panglatu (Mandala Satu Commander), that it named the '*Operasi Singgalang*'.[87] This Operation, which was carried out in each Kodam in every province in Sumatra, entailed the mobilisation of "all members of the Armed Forces and all layers of society, consisting of People's Resistance (*Rakjat Pedjuang*) [and] Armed Civilians (*Rakjat Bersendjata*)", along with Hansip units, for "an entire month with complete seriousness and full of the spirit of struggle".[88] The Operation was a dry run to test the preparedness of provincial military and paramilitary units to respond to a call to mobilise, described by the military as a theoretical invasion by Malaysia.

Amir Hasan Nast, a former member of the military-sponsored Action Command (*Komando Aksi*) death squad that was active in North Sumatra after 1 October 1965, has described his participation in the Operasi Singgalang as a Hansip (Civilian Defence) paramilitary member in Simpang Matapao, North Sumatra, explaining how:

> At the time of Operasi Singgalang Hansip members were ordered every morning to deliver by motorbike SECRET REPORTS to the Operation Centre in Kotari Subdistrict, and once we were asked to deliver food supplies with members of Buterpra [*Puterpra*: subdistrict level Territorial Affairs and People's Resistance Officer units] . . .[89]

Mokoginta, in a speech in Medan on 23 March 1965, described the Operasi Singgalang as being:

> Extremely successful in providing the Nation and the People with confidence about the capabilities of our Nation to make Dwikora's destruction of the Nekolim ['*Neo-Kolonialism, Kolonialisme, Imperialisme*': 'Neo-Colonialist, Colonialist, Imperialist'][90] Malaysia Project a success.
>
> In addition, the highly successful Operasi Singgalang was also a manifestation of the Nation's lack of fear when confronting the actions of the Nekolim and its lackeys, both now and in the future.[91]

The Operasi Singgalang thus appears to have been a means for the military to involve civilians in its own preparations to move against the PKI once the opportunity presented itself. It was also an attempt to neutralise Sukarno's call to mobilise 21 million volunteers to support the *Ganyang Malaysia* campaign, which the military leadership feared would become the nucleus of Sukarno's projected 'Fifth Force' People's Army, by allowing the military to maintain its own ideological leadership over this training process.

The Operasi Singgalang additionally appears to have been a means for the military to inaugurate an additional military command structure that it would subsequently use to initiate and implement the genocide, suggesting an even higher level of preparation behind the military's subsequent attack than it has previously been possible to demonstrate. Djuarsa, for example, through the 'Complete Yearly Report', described the Operasi Singgalang accordingly:

1   Between January and March 1965 the "SINGGALANG" manoeuvre was carried out, and really demonstrated the activities of the Armed Forces and the Civilian Government. Meanwhile, since April 1965 up until today [1 February 1966, the date the report was signed], the "BERDIKARI" [*Berdiri di atas kaki sendiri*: 'standing on ones own feet'] Operation [*Operasi Berdikari*][92] has been carried out, in which not only the Armed Forces and the Civilian Government participated, but also the entire society joined in the attempt to prepare the potential of the territorial defence of ATJEH. . . .

3   On 1 August KODAM-I/Iskandarmuda was inaugurated as Defence Region Command 'A' [Kodahan 'A': *Komando Daerah Pertahanan 'A'*]. In connection with the formation of the organisation for the defence of the Defence Region Command 'A' with Letter of Decision 'A', Decision Number-3/8/1965 on [25 August 1965], explaining that the organisation of the leadership and implementation for Aceh defence region has already begun. The integration of the four Armed Forces [Military, Police, Navy and Air Force] is already materialising better, with the result that [these four Armed Forces] are working together more smoothly, and with greater efficiency in the framework of defence than previously. At the same time as the formation of the KODAHAN 'A', 2 KOSUBDAHAN [*Komando Sub-Daerah Pertahanan*: Defence Region Sub-Command] and 8 KOSEKHAN [*Komando Sektor Pertahanan*: Defence Sector Command] were also formed,[93] and since October 1965 the name of KODAHAN 'A' has been changed to become KOHANDA "ATJEH", as short for KOMANDO PERTAHANAN DAERAH "ATJEH" [Regional Defence Command for 'Atjeh'].[94]

Djuarsa thus describes Operasi Singgalang as a full mobilisation of the "entire society" in Aceh to test its preparedness to assist the military in the task of "territorial defence" (a military concept designed by Nasution, conceived as an anti-guerrilla campaign carried out at the village level to obliterate an internal enemy). He also explains how a new military command structure, the Defence Region Command (Kodahan), was established to compliment this preparation exactly two months before the military launched its seizure of state power. The name of this command structure was subsequently changed to the Regional Defence Command (Kohanda: *Komando Pertahanan Daerah*) on 1 October, the day the military leadership launched its seizure of state power. New territorial command structures were also established at the inter-district (Kosubdahan) and district levels (Kosekhan) to mimic the regular Kodam command but under the autonomous command of the KOTI command.[95] It would be through this new command structure that the military would ultimately initiate and implement the genocide in Aceh. It named this campaign 'Operasi Berdikari'. Djuarsa explains:

2   Since 1 October 1965, the Plan for Operation "Berdikari" has been activated [*telah dikeluarkan Rentjana Operasi "Berdikari"*], which included a determination regarding the outlines of policy for the ACEH DEFENCE REGION COMMAND as related to the territorial defence of ACEH. The realisation of these Operation Plans are still at the level of preparation, [including] a determination of tasks and consignment, a determination of strategic targets and sites of resistance, a determination of strengths etc. . . .

7   Since the occurrence of the GESTOK affair on 1 October 1965, **the entire strength of KOHANDA "ATJEH" has been mobilised to achieve the success of the operation to annihilate GESTOK** [*dikerahkan untuk melantjarkan operasi penumpasan GESTOK*]. This operation has been weighted towards intelligence and territorial operations actions. This Operation has

already been a brilliant success [*telah mentjapai hasil jang gemilang*] such that within a short period the attention and potential of KOHANDA "ATJEH" has already been able to return to its main focus, the NEKOLIM.[96]

This extraordinary statement, the first of its kind to be recovered, is the most explicit admission produced by the Indonesian military leadership that it used the structures it had ostensibly established as part of the *Ganyang Malaysia* campaign to launch its genocidal campaign against the PKI. Operasi Singgalang can thus be understood as a preparation by the military for its subsequent attack against the PKI. This is because even if it is not accepted that the military leadership understood the potential of these preparations from their inception in terms of their potential future use (despite Djuarsa's explanation that the Operation that implemented the genocide was established two months prior to the initiation of the military's attack against the PKI and that this Operation was subsequently "activated" [*dikeluarkan*, lit. 'issued'] on 1 October, when the military leadership was ostensibly still deciding how to react) it is impossible to escape the fact that, from 1 October, these preparations *were* used by the military leadership to initiate and implement the genocide in Aceh. The military considered this campaign to be a "brilliant success".[97]

The Acehnese elite and its relationship with the military leadership

Before turning to the events of 1 October, this section will focus on specific conditions in Aceh, in order to shed light on some of the peculiarities of what happened later in the province. This is because although the genocide must ultimately be understood as a national event, these peculiarities help explain why killings may have broken out first in Aceh, and why the military was able to secure the support of Aceh's elite so quickly.

The relationship between the post-independence Acehnese elite and the military leadership has always been fraught. Throughout the recent separatist struggle in the province many excellent studies by Indonesian and foreign scholars were devoted to probing the Free Aceh Movement's demand for an independent state of Aceh, a claim which was presented as based on Aceh's unique history as an independent sultanate which fought a fierce holy war of resistance against Dutch occupation (1873–1914) and the subsequent Darul Islam rebellion in the province (1953–62). This scholarship has largely overlooked the period immediately prior to the genocide and the genocide itself, before skipping to the outbreak of the recent separatist struggle (1976–2005).[98] This situation has tended to highlight the 'uniqueness' of Aceh's past and the points of difference between the post-independence Acehnese elite and Indonesian central government.

In order to understand the relationship between the post-independence Acehnese elite and the national military leadership in 1965–66, however, it is necessary to also understand the rapprochement between these two forces.

Aceh's post-independence elite first began to crystallise during the late 1930s around the province's most prominent modernist Islamist leader, Daud Beureu'eh, an *ulama* who in 1939 formed the All-Aceh Association of Islamic Scholars (PUSA: *Persatuan Ulama Seluruh Aceh*).[99] PUSA claimed its spiritual legacy from Aceh's holy war, when the Dutch had launched a particularly violent colonisation of the former sultanate and relentlessly pursued *ulama*-led resistance.[100] Through PUSA, Beureu'eh advocated a radical anti-colonial, spiritual and educational renaissance in the province and personally led and participated in social betterment programs, such as the construction of a new irrigation channel in northern Aceh, built using volunteer labour.[101] This approach made Beureu'eh and PUSA genuinely popular in the province, especially in the Acehnese heartlands.

PUSA's popularity was further heightened by the Dutch regime's spurning of this new leadership in favour of Aceh's *uleebalang*, a traditional hereditary elite who were granted official positions within the colonial bureaucracy and paid generous stipends for their support.[102] This co-option made Aceh's *uleebalang* hugely unpopular and has led to a tendency for historians and political scientists to view Acehnese politics through the optic of historical rivalry between *ulama* and *uleebalang*, an analysis which works for the early colonial period, but became less relevant as PUSA came to represent not only Aceh's religious elite, but an emerging regional elite with economic and governmental ambitions.[103] This new elite, as with the anti-colonial movement nationally, was ideologically heterogeneous, and included leaders such as Teungku Husin Al Mudjahid, the founding leader of PUSA's youth wing PUSA Youth (*Pemuda PUSA*) (formed in 1940), who would align himself with the PKI following the declaration of Indonesian independence.[104]

In early 1942, the Acehnese elite around Beureu'eh openly encouraged Japan to occupy Aceh.[105] The PKI, meanwhile, vehemently opposed the occupation. This divergence split the nationalist movement in Aceh, as occurred throughout the Indies at this time.[106] The Japanese forces, however, were initially wary of Beureu'eh and PUSA's popularity, and chose, as the Dutch had done, to govern through Aceh's *uleebalang*. As the *uleebalang* increasingly became the target of popular frustration, in large part due to their appointed role of mobilising civilians to participate in Japanese-led forced labour campaigns, the Japanese came to rely upon Beureu'eh and PUSA to mobilise the population.[107] During this time the Acehnese elite around Beureu'eh became vocal supporters of the Japanese regime, making appeals for enthusiastic compliance with Japanese demands.[108] This support, which coincided with growing frustrations within the population towards the occupation and a growing threat of famine as 35–40% of rice fields in the province lay untended as a result of the forced labour campaigns,[109] acted to tarnish the popularity of this new leadership.[110]

By the end of the war, Beureu'eh and those around him had been largely discredited. They were quiet at the time of the declaration of Indonesian independence in the province.[111] Support for the Republic in Aceh had nonetheless been strong, with Sukarno describing the province in 1948 as a "flame of the revolution" (*obor revolusi*).[112] In recognition of his leadership role, Beureu'eh was subsequently appointed Military Governor of Aceh.

In 1946, Aceh was one of five regions in Indonesia to experience social revolution.[113] Social revolutionary forces in Aceh were in part led by Xarim MS and

Nathar Zainudin, PKI leaders who had helped to lead the social revolution in East Sumatra.[114] This movement in Aceh called for the redistribution of arms surrendered by the Japanese and land controlled by the *uleebalang*, and resulted in the killing of many *uleebalang* families.[115] It gained critical momentum when Al Mudjahid, the leader of Pemuda PUSA, joined the revolutionary forces, splitting PUSA's membership and polarising the province.[116] This polarisation was subsequently formalised though the formation of a 'Banda Aceh Front', centred around Beureu'eh, which was happy to see the *uleebalang* divested of its power but concerned that its own privileges would soon come under attack, and a 'Langsa Front', centred around Al Mudjahid and Aceh's social revolutionary forces that were allied with the PKI-led social revolution in East Sumatra.[117]

This process starkly exposed two competing leaderships within Aceh: one Islamist and provincialist in outlook, the other secular, leftist and pan-Indonesianist. The confrontation between these two Fronts reached its height in March 1946 when Al Mudjahid marched on Banda Aceh to demand that Beureu'eh step down as Aceh's Military Governor.[118] Perhaps surprisingly, this growing polarisation, which threatened to escalate into open conflict, was resolved when the Central Government prioritised stability over ideological difference to back Beureu'eh and the Banda Aceh Front, reaffirming Beureu'eh as Aceh's Military Governor,[119] even though Al Mudjahid and the Langsa Front arguably held an ideological outlook closer to that of the central government.

This cosy relationship between the central government and the Acehnese elite, however, did not last long. In January 1951 Aceh had its provincial status revoked and was merged with East Sumatra into the single province of North Sumatra. Aceh had been granted provincial status in 1949 by the interim Republican government, which, based in West Sumatra, had been sympathetic to Acehnese aspirations. Unlike much of Indonesia, including much of Java and East Sumatra, Aceh was not recolonised by the Dutch and had operated semi-autonomously throughout the national revolution as a 'military region' (*daerah militer*). This situation was considered unacceptable by the new Republican government, which sought to establish centralised control over the regions. Beureu'eh resigned his post in protest and declared that Aceh had joined the Darul Islam rebellion.[120] In response, the central government launched a brutal attack against Beureu'eh's rebel forces. The Darul Islam rebellion, however, drew widespread sympathy from the civilian population in Aceh. One reason for this was the military's brutal crackdown in the province, which included a series of military-led massacres of civilians in Aceh Besar in early 1955.[121] Even nationalist leaders such as Ali Hasjmy, Aceh's Governor (1957–64), who had been one of Sukarno's greatest supporters at the time of the national revolution,[122] expressed his sympathy for the rebellion, offering to act as a negotiator between the two sides.

The stated grievance of the Acehnese elite was that Aceh had been promised by the central government, and in particular by Sukarno, that it could implement a form of Islamic law (*Syariat Islam*). This was proven to be a false promise when Aceh had its provincial status revoked.[123] Beyond the question of ideological conviction, the removal of provincial status removed the Acehnese elite's access to the mechanisms of government, forcing its members to compete with the larger and more industrialised elite in Medan. This grievance was expressed through growing concern about, and distrust of Sukarno and the central government.[124] To the Acehnese elite, the PKI and PNI epitomised everything that was wrong with the central government, due to the association of the parties with the central government's programs and their open animosity towards Darul Islam.[125]

It appears that this antagonism may have led to acts of violence during this period. Nazaruddin Sjamsuddin, for example, has explained how Darul Islam fighters established "a kidnapping and killing group in every company" to "deal with this section of the population".[126] The extent of violence targeted against the PKI during this period is unknown. It appears, however, that the PKI was targeted due to its association, either real or perceived, with Sukarno and politics in Jakarta, rather than any specific programmatic principle held by the PKI. These tensions were no doubt exacerbated by PKI and PNI support for the 1960 banning of Masjumi, Indonesia's second largest political party and the largest political party in Aceh, because of its support for the regional rebellions. In 1956, in Aceh's first election following its re-emergence as a province, Masjumi won twenty-three seats in Aceh's provincial government.[127] This was twice as many as all the other parties combined. The PKI, by comparison, at this time held one seat, the same as the PNI. Following Masjumi's banning, this electoral space was taken up by other Islamist parties, including Perti, which came to hold six seats, NU and PSII, which came to hold two seats each, while the PKI and PNI and gained one extra seat each.[128]

The national military leadership under Nasution would come to play a personal role in bringing the Darul Islam rebellion to an end. In a sign of good faith, Nasution had sent Lieutenant General Muhammad Jasin, who, though ethnically Javanese, had spent part of his childhood in Sabang on Aceh's Weh Island, to facilitate negotiations. Jasin achieved widespread success in convincing Darul Islam fighters, including, finally, Beureu'eh himself to come down from the mountains. Central to the peace agreement was the promise that Aceh would have its status as a province returned and be allowed to implement a limited form of regional autonomy. It was also agreed that an amnesty would be granted to former Darul Islam fighters, who were to be re-integrated into the national military structure.[129] It was thus to the national military leadership and not Sukarno to whom former rebels now found themselves indebted. In recognition of his achievement, Jasin was appointed as Aceh's Military Commander (10 November 1960–1 October 1963). Sukarno's policies, meanwhile, remained unpopular in the province.[130]

Following the amnesty, many former Darul Islam fighters were incorporated into the national military structure. The Aceh military command's official 'Complete Yearly Report' has recorded that 2,497 former Darul Islam fighters joined the national military in the province at this time, constituting a substantial 38% of the province's 6,282-person active military force.[131] These former Darul Islam fighters, the Report explains, were "extremely difficult to supervise [but] easily influenced".[132]

With the end of the Darul Islam rebellion, the national military leadership was able to strategically befriend the Acehnese elite. This alliance was centred around the two groups' shared dislike for Sukarno and the PKI, and based on a sense of gratitude and obligation of behalf of former members of the Darul Islam, who owed their freedom and rehabilitation to the national military leadership. Meanwhile, as we shall see, the Darul Islam itself ceased to exist as an independent organisation.

Growth of the PKI in Aceh

The PKI first emerged in Aceh during the 1920s and followed a similar pattern in its growth to other provinces in Indonesia.[133] Initially spreading to the province from transmigrant plantation workers and unionised railway workers,[134] the PKI had become a "respectable player" in the province by the 1940s.[135] From the late 1950s, "Coan" (the pseudonym of a PKI cadre active in Medan, North Sumatra, who often travelled to Aceh for Party business), has recalled, the PKI in Aceh, as elsewhere in Indonesia, had a strategy to "turn red" (*memerahkan*) the government by encouraging its members to take up government offices. As Coan has explained:

> After Aceh became a province [again], there was an attempt to get PKI cadre, those in the government, to become officials (*pejabat*) and move to Aceh – an example of this, the head of the judiciary in North Aceh, they were PKI. In this way they [the PKI in Aceh], hoped to build a mass party of the type [built by] Lenin.[136]

By 1965, the PKI in Aceh had succeeded in having two of its members, PKI Vice-Secretary in Aceh Thaib Adamy and Njak Ismail elected to Aceh's provincial government. Adamy was first elected in 1956. He used this position to speak out against what he saw as the military's unfairly accommodating treatment of ex–Darul Islam combatants.[137] He was also critical of an attempt in 1962 by Aceh's then Governor Ali Hasjmy to implement aspects of Islamic law in the province at the request of Aceh's Military Commander Muhammad Jasin. This request was the fulfilment of a promise made to Beureu'eh during negotiations to end the Darul Islam rebellion.[138] Adamy accused Hasjmy and Jasin of attempting to bypass the normal democratic process and the PKI, through its national newspaper, helped to turn the affair into a national scandal.[139] This approach won the PKI in Aceh new supporters. It also won it new enemies, including within the military, after Jasin was replaced by Lieutenant Colonel Njak Adam Kamil as Military Commander – a humiliation the military leadership blamed on the PKI.

The PKI in Aceh, however, appears to have made a grave strategic error in 1964 when it used its position in the provincial government to support the ousting of Governor Ali Hasjmy, a firm supporter of Sukarno, in favour of Aceh's then Military Commander Nyak Adam Kamil. This process was a major, though little remembered, event in the province.[140] The US embassy in Jakarta, for example, described on 18 March 1964 the ousting of Hasjmy as "a PKI victory" and "a significant one also . . . the effectiveness of PKI power has now been demonstrated even in the citadel of opposition [Aceh]".[141] It was, however, a short-sighted victory, as it meant the position of Military Commander was left vacant: a position which was subsequently filled by the ardently anti-communist Ishak Djuarsa.[142]

Also of great significance to the outcome of the military's coup in Aceh was the military's ability to make use of the province's Pantja Tunggal bodies, which existed at both the provincial and district levels through its newly increased presence in civilian government in the province. In 1965 in Aceh, the Pantja Tunggal was overwhelmingly weighted in favour of anti-communist forces. Aceh's Military Commander Ishak Djuarsa was an avid anti-communist who had been trained at Fort Leavenworth in the United States. Aceh's Chief Prosecutor Harip Harahap had become famous for jailing PKI Vice-Secretary in Aceh Thaib Adamy in 1964 on trumped-up charges of "causing a security disturbance and insult to the government".[143] While Aceh's Governor Njak Adam Kamil, who, although believed by the PKI itself to be sympathetic to the Party, in part because of his history of friendly communication with the organisation prior to 1 October,[144] would go on to play a key role in the military's attack against the PKI by effectively freezing Aceh's provincial government and placing it under military control. Meanwhile, Aceh's Police Chief S. Samsuri Mertojoso, about whom little is known other than that he had been stationed in East Java during the time of the national revolution, when he had fought the Dutch as a Mobile Brigade commander in Malang,[145] would also come to play a leading role in the genocide in the province. While the position of *Front Nasional* representative was held by T. Ibrahim, a member of Aceh's provincial government, who is described in government documents as a member of the "Islamic group" (*Golongan Islam*), which had supported the 1962 attempt by Hasjmy and Jasin to implement Islamic law in the province.[146]

Early 1965 was a period of rapid growth for the PKI in Aceh. Indeed, *Harian Rakjat*, the PKI's national newspaper, carried thirty-seven articles with Aceh-related titles between February and September 1965, compared with one article in 1962, five in 1963 and fifteen in 1964. These articles paid particular attention to listing the many new PKI[147] and PKI-affiliated branches, including new branches of the Indonesian Peasants' Front (BTI: *Barisan Tani Indonesia*);[148] All-Indonesia Workers' Organisation Union (SOBSI: *Serikat Organisasi Buruh Seluruh Indonesia*);[149] Indonesian Women's Movement (Gerwani: *Gerakan Wanita Indonesia*);[150] People's Youth (*Pemuda Rakjat*);[151] and the PKI's cultural organisation, the Institute of People's Culture (LEKRA: *Lembaga Kebudayaan Rakyat*), which were established throughout the province at this time.[152] These newspaper articles support my interviewees' claims that these organisations could be found in each of Aceh's districts by 1965. The PKI appears to have been genuinely popular in Aceh during this period. Eyewitness accounts of how the PKI was perceived in the province during this period can be found at the end of the chapter.

Buoyed by this success, the PKI became increasingly vocal in its opposition to the remnants of the Darul Islam in the province. On 1 March, for example, *Harian Rakjat* publicised PKI support for the banning of the Darul Islam[153] as well as, more generally, the prohibition in Aceh of "religious sermons that ruin the unity of Nasakom and [that] are Communist phobic".[154] It also renewed its support for a government instruction to "clean ex-elements" (*membersihkan elemen2*) of the organisation from "all levels of the villages".[155] This instruction had first been announced by the Minister of Internal Affairs in 1964, but *Harian Rakjat*'s provocative reopening of the issue in early 1965 appears to have been aimed at launching a scare campaign against the organisation, with the PKI expressing frustration that "it turns out that many [former members of the Darul Islam rebellion] are still being protected [within the villages]".[156] It also announced that the new "major campaign" of the PKI in East Aceh was to "clean" (*bersihkan*) "ex [Darul Islam] members from the civilian defence units (*Hansip*)". This language was clearly provocative and intensified feelings that a showdown between the two groups would occur. It also exposed the PKI to great risk, insofar as the Party remained unarmed and unable to counter any possible violent retaliation. However, while it should be acknowledged the PKI helped to develop such rhetoric, which can also be found in the government's own rhetoric at this time, and which would later find an echo in military rhetoric during the time of the genocide, it is critical to make the point that only the military implemented this rhetoric through a program of killings.

The PKI in Aceh in 1965 projected an exuberant sense of optimism and began to flaunt its growth. In June 1965, the party held a large celebration in Banda Aceh to mark the forty-fifth anniversary of its founding. This would be the PKI's final big event in Aceh. As *Harian Rakjat* reported:

> The town changed its face. On every corner and [word unclear] great posters were displayed, the streets were adorned with red banners, and everybody spoke about the People's Struggle, about the absolute essentialness of the unity of Nasakom, about the rabidness of US led imperialism, about the peasants, about the work that must be done, yes – about revolution . . . the communist-phobic reactionaries were burning with fear . . . the Red and White [the Indonesian flag] and the Hammer and Sickle flew from every height.[157]

Anti-communist forces in Banda Aceh were disturbed by the PKI's rapid advance. They were not, however, paralysed and "burning in fear". On 30 May, before the anniversary celebrations, Aceh's Governor Njak Adam Kamil (who, as Kodam Chief of Staff had assisted Jasin to bring the Darul Islam rebellion to an end) issued a veiled caution at a public meeting at the sports stadium in Banda Aceh, said to have been attended by approximately 10,000 people.[158] He expressed his "hope that the PKI would remember its ability to work with the other groups that have also led the Indonesian [national] revolution" and reminded the PKI in Aceh that "the revolution cannot be completed by just one group". Most importantly, the military leadership was also actively moving behind the scenes to secure its control over the military command and other structural means of exercising power that were available in the province.

Civilian militias in Aceh prior to 1 October

The training of civilian militias in Aceh, formulated as part of the Dwikora campaign, had begun in 1964. This training involved high school students, university students and volunteers from the general population drawn from nationalist, Islamist and communist groups. The military's campaign to train high school students has been described by Dahlan Sulaiman, who in 1965 was a member of the PII (*Pelajar Islam Indonesia*: Indonesian Islamic Students Organisation) in his final year of senior high school, who would serve as a death squad leader during the genocide:[159]

> I joined the secondary student youth regiment called the Malem Dagang Regiment [in 1964], he [Malem Dagang] was a famous leader of education in Aceh. . . . It had a battalion, like in the military and we were fitted out, first we were recruited and trained as military (*dilatih sebagai militer*) by the military at the military education centre [at Mata le Greater Aceh, 9km from the centre of Banda Aceh].
>
> The education there was exactly like that given to the military, beginning from the most basic, lining up and standing to attention, discipline training, physical training, combat training, learning the way to shoot, to attack, to defend yourself, until you could graduate, when we were armed . . . with real [weapons]. At the time, first I was given a long rifle, because I was a member, then, after a second round of training, I became a troop leader and I was given a pistol. . . . Lots of us were trained, all school kids at that time, those in class two and class three of SMA [junior high school] were trained, university students . . . [were also] trained . . . in Banda Aceh there were four [university student regiments] . . . so there was a great lot [trained], but they received basic training, there weren't so many who made it through the [full] three levels. But they weren't conscripted or forced, it was just those who wanted to and whoever volunteered.[160]

This training was militaristic and involved the use of real weapons. Zainuddin Hamid, or 'Let Bugeh' as he is commonly known, a member of the Islamic University Students Association (HMI: *Himpunan Mahasiswa Islam*), who participated in training with the University Students Regiment (*Resimen Mahasiswa*) and who would also serve as a death squad member during the genocide, has recalled how he was involved in training under the coordination of Aceh's Military Commander in Banda Aceh in the name of preparing for the *Ganyang Malasysia* campaign. "Because we practiced, we were given weapons [by Kodam] . . . [we] were taught how to shoot and everything," explains Bugeh.[161]

It was not only anti-communist groups, however, that were involved in this training. At a national level the PKI also supported the training and arming of civilian militias, though for vastly different ends. The PKI supported the *Ganyang Malysia* campaign for ideological reasons. It also supported militia training for strategic purposes. In line with Sukarno's announcement in May 1964 that 21 million volunteers should be mobilised and trained to support the *Ganyang Malaysia* campaign, the Banda Aceh branch of SOBSI pledged its support on 6 March 1965 for "15 thousand workers and peasants to be armed to destroy 'Malaysia'".[162] It is known that some of this training took place in Aceh. Asan, the sole surviving member of the PKI's Central Committee in Banda Aceh, who today lives in

Hong Kong, has recalled the PKI-affiliated youth organisation Pemuda Rakyat engaged in training in the province involving "drills" (*latihan berbaris*) as part of the *Ganyang Malaysia* campaign, though he stresses that this training did not involve weapons.[163] Bugeh has independently supported Asan's statement, recalling: "They [the PKI] engaged in lots of training. But, according to what we know, it never got out that they had weapons, yeah. They did engage in drills and use wooden guns."[164]

Sulaiman also corroborates that the PKI was involved in training, including joint-training with his own group,[165] before adding, "but whether they were being got ready for the movement that they were meant to be in [the *Ganyang Malaysia* campaign], it goes without saying, no".

The insinuation here by Sulaiman is that the PKI was, in fact, planning to launch its own bid for state power, and that, as a result, the military's subsequent attack against the PKI should be seen as defensive rather than offensive in nature. Whether or not the PKI in Aceh trained with real weapons can be neither proved nor disproved. It is clear, however, that both the PKI and the military were using the *Ganyang Malaysia* campaign as a disguised power play. Tensions were high and an intensive mobilisation of society was occurring, perhaps unparalleled since the period of the national revolution, ostensibly in preparation for confrontation with a common and external enemy.

When training, Sulaiman explains, both communist and non-communist groups were able to put their differences aside: "In the training [we could work together] because we all had the same target planted in us all [the Free Irian and Crush Malaysia campaigns], there was no conflict between us."[166]

Sulaiman, however, has also described a growing sense of confrontation between communist and non-communist groups in the province, including at his school, which at times resulted in non-fatal physical conflict. Sulaiman explains:

> At that time school children [who were] organised into parties or non-party [affiliated organisations] like the PII which were independent and non-communist, when they went to school they not only took books in their bags, but also equipment (*perlengkapan*) to defend themselves with every day, because there would definitely be fights between school children who were communist and who had joined the PPI, the Indonesian School Students Union (*Persatuan Pelajar Indonesia*) or *Pemuda Rakyat*, it would always happen. The teachers were also like that.[167]

Such fights, though significant, were largely symbolic in nature. I have yet to come across evidence that more serious violence occurred during this period. The atmosphere was tense. The province was not, however, spiralling into communal violence.

Other examples of growing confrontation between the PKI and non-communist groups in the province include the claim by Bugeh that the PKI in Aceh provoked Muslims by claiming that God was a "lie".[168] This claim has been supported by Coan, who has explained that an "extremist faction" emerged within the PKI in Aceh that was "open about dialectical historical materialism" and which would demand proof that God existed.[169] This was not, however, the widespread position of the PKI in Aceh – indeed, as will be discussed further below, the majority of its members considered themselves to be practicing Muslims, following in Indonesia's long tradition of Islamic communism. There is no evidence PKI members were ostracised from their communities, let alone threatened with violence prior to 1 October, on account of their spiritual beliefs. Both communist and non-communist groups, despite holding divergent political beliefs, belonged to Aceh's Islamic community.

It would appear Sukarno hoped such joint-training would smooth antagonisms between communist and anti-communist groups by providing them with a shared external enemy. Yet, despite the possible short-term advantages of such training, its most significant legacy was the training and arming of a new generation of Indonesian youths for violent conflict, crucial preparation upon which the military's subsequent attack against the PKI relied. Indeed, as we shall see, many of those who were trained by the military during this period would later spring into action as the shock troops of the new military regime, working under the coordination of their old training commanders in the military to lead the initial propaganda assault against the PKI in Aceh, before participating in the hunting-down and killing of suspected communists.

Conditions in Aceh's districts prior to 1 October 1965

The following section provides an overview of conditions in Aceh's districts prior to 1 October 1965, as recalled by my interviewees. In addition to providing insight into conditions in Aceh's districts prior to 1 October 1965, this overview provides a preview to the structure of this book, which takes a chronological and multi-site approach, with each chapter focusing first on Banda Aceh, before turning its attention to each of Aceh's remaining districts in turn.

I asked each of my interviewees what they remembered about life in their village or town before the outbreak of the genocide. I questioned them about what they remembered about the activities of the PKI and its relationship with other organisations in the province. I also asked them whether it was former Darul Islam fighters who had attacked the PKI. In doing so, I hoped to discover whether Aceh had, in fact, been teetering on the brink of communal violence during the lead-up to 1 October as a result of an essential antagonism between the PKI and the province's particularly strong brand of Islam. As discussed in the Introduction, Harold Crouch has proposed the killings in Aceh "amounted to a holy war of extermination" because "Muslim leaders in Indonesia's most Islamic province [Aceh] regarded [the PKI] as a threat to Islam".[170] Ulf Sundhaussen, meanwhile, has proposed the killings in Aceh were primarily carried out by "Muslims" and "villagers" whom the military were unable to "stop".[171]

North Aceh

North Aceh,[172] along with Banda Aceh, is the spiritual heartland of Acehnese history and culture. Strategically situated at the northern tip of the Malacca Strait, the area hosts the oldest archaeological evidence of royal conversion to Islam in Southeast Asia, dated 1211, at Lamri (Lamuri), near present-day Banda Aceh.[173] It is also the site of the Samudra Pasai Sultanate, located near present-day Lhokseumawe, which emerged during the thirteenth century. More recently, North Aceh became a site of resistance during the Dutch-Aceh War, as it did again during the Darul Islam rebellion and recent separatist conflict. In 1965, as today, its population is overwhelmingly rural and engaged in small-scale fishing, wet rice cultivation and market garden farming.[174]

Hamid was born in rural North Aceh.[175] He moved around as a child, before settling in Lhokseumawe, where he lives today. In 1965, he worked as small-scale metalworker, crafting machetes and knives. He has recalled the PKI did not have a large base in the town.[176] He does, however, remember that in Muara Satu sub-district, 12 km away, a man named Saman Syahlia Bunta had joined the PKI and formed a popular traditional Acehnese *seudati* dance troupe.[177] He also recalls at least three other people from Sawang, Tengoh *kampung* and Cot Seurani, 30 km west of Lhoseumawe, who joined the PKI during this period, suggesting that even in the heart of former Darul Islam territory the Party was able to find recruits.

The most important political event in the district prior to 1 October 1965, Hamid recalls, had been the formal admission of former Darul Islam fighters into the national military. "On 4 May 1964," Hamid explains:

> DI/TII people had been merged (*disatukan*) with RI [the Republic of Indonesia], so DI/TII people had been billeted, in this area, they had been billeted in Lhokseumawe in the People's Meeting Hall building, for several months, until the end of September, at the end of that there were some who returned to their *kampung*, and some that had become members of the [national] military.[178]

Those who joined the military, Hamid continues, "were taken to Padang Tiji near Sigli, where they underwent training . . . military training . . . to be used as an elite force within the military".[179] There were no ideological requirements, Hamid has explained, for ex-Darul Islam fighters to be accepted by the military, only "exceptions based on physical fitness or illness". This was because "they had all already returned to the Republic of Indonesia".

"Tjoet", was born in approximately 1950 in "Kampung X",[180] North Aceh.[181] She does not know the exact year she was born.[182] When she was seven years old she began primary school. In 1964, when she was thirteen or fourteen years old, she married "Hasan", a coffee shop worker and the PKI Treasurer for Kampung X, with whom she had a child.[183]

According to Tjoet, she did not know her husband was a member of the PKI until after arrests began in the *kampung* in the aftermath of 1 October.[184] At this time, PKI had only just begun to establish itself in Kampung X.[185] Tjoet recalls the PKI had been involved in distributing and promising material assistance to families in the *kampung*. This assistance, which was part of the PKI's national program to win village support for the Party, included the distribution of "hoes, fertiliser and rice".[186]

Tjoet has proposed people in Kampung X were told during the PKI's recruitment campaign:

> The 'I' in PKI stood for 'Islam' [i.e. that the Indonesian Communist Party was called the 'Islamic Communist Party'], and if people wanted to join the organisation they were told they had to be able to pray (*sholat*). If they couldn't pray, they couldn't join the PKI.[187]

A variation of this story is often told by survivors from the period and appears intended to stress the "innocence" of the teller of the story by suggesting they were not "aware" of the "true" nature of the PKI. The PKI was demonised as "*kafir*" during the time of the genocide and Tjoet's story should most likely be understood as a survival mechanism adopted over the years. It also expresses her desire to remain identified as a member of the Islamic community. Tjoet does, however, stress that there "were no tensions between the people and the PKI" during the lead-up to 1 October.[188] As Tjoet's companion "Zahara", who sat next to Tjoet throughout the interview explains, "There was no problem because the PKI people were part of the *kampung*, we all fasted and said evening prayers together."[189]

"Jamil" was born around 1940 in Kampung X, where he lives today.[190] His father was a fisherman. As a child, Jamil completed three years of primary school before studying the Qur'an at the district mosque. When he was between twelve and fifteen, he began working as a fisherman.[191] After he sold his catch in the evening, he would sit at the local coffee shop where his brother-in-law Hasan (Tjoet's husband), the PKI Treasurer for Kampung X, worked. It was at this coffee shop that he says he came into contact with the PKI. "They told us," Jamil recalls:

> that they would help us, [they would] give us hoes, give us rice, give us cigarettes, give us spending money (*peng sirap*). That is what they said. In the meantime, they didn't tell me that [because I had accepted these promises of assistance] I would be put down as a member [of the PKI].[192]

Jamil was subsequently listed as a member of the PKI by Hasan without his knowledge.[193] Jamil does not believe this was done with any intention of causing him trouble, but rather because Hasan considered it to be such a non-issue that he did not tell Jamil until after arrests began in the district after 1 October 1965. "It wasn't just me who had my name written down", Jamil explains, "there were a lot of us . . . I was his relative, so he just put my name down . . . if it hadn't turned into a big issue [from 1 October] maybe I would have never known."[194] Jamil does not feel animosity towards Hasan, explaining how it was Hasan who told him that he was being hunted by the military after 1 October and that he should run away to save himself. This information would ultimately save his life.[195] There was no relationship, Jamil has explained, between the Darul Islam and "what happened to the PKI" in Kampung X.[196]

Central Aceh

Central Aceh is located in Aceh's highlands at the start of the Bukit Barisan mountain range that traverses Sumatra. The district is relatively isolated, as travellers are required to pass along a narrow, winding mountainside road to reach the area. Takengon, Central Aceh's main town, sits beside a large inland lake, Lake Laut Tawar (*Danau Laut Tawar*). The area is home to the Gayo ethnic group, who constitute a majority of the district's inhabitants. It is also home to a substantial Javanese community, many of whom first travelled to the area as coolie labourers during the colonial period to work on coffee and sugar cane plantations.[197] In 1965, as today, its population was overwhelmingly rural and engaged in fresh water fishing, wet rice cultivation, market garden farming and work on the area's sugar and coffee plantations, some of which now supply the Starbucks coffee chain.

Ibrahim Kadir was born in 1942 in Takengon, Central Aceh.[198] In 1965, Kadir was a primary school teacher and *didong* (a form of traditional sung poetry from Central Aceh) performer. He was not a member of the PKI. He has recalled, however, that the PKI was popular in the region. It had members who were teachers, peasants, teachers, civil servants, artists and even members of the military in the district.[199]

These people appear to have been quite well known and respected in the local community. Kadir, for example, explains how two PKI-affiliated teachers, Daud and a man affectionately referred to as "Teacher Rama" (*Guru Rama*), had managed to develop a following of supportive teachers.[200] The PKI in Central Aceh had also established a *didong* group, while within the local military command, the PKI had managed to recruit a soldier who held the rank of Corporal.[201]

The PKI's largest membership groups in the district, Kadir remembers, were peasants who worked in the rice fields and market gardens and plantation workers who worked in the sugar cane plantations.[202] PKI members in Central Aceh, Kadir has explained, were mainly Gayonese, the dominant ethnic group in Central Aceh, as well as the relatives of transmigrant Javanese, with several Acehnese, Batak[203] and Minang[204] members.[205]

Kadir has described the increased political polarisation in the district following the Darul Islam rebellion. At this time, he explains, it became possible to identify different *kampung* as either "PKI *kampung*", such as Nosar *kampung* and Kebayakan *kampung*, which mainly consisted of transmigrant Javanese families, some of whom had joined the PKI before leaving for Sumatra, and "Darul Islam *kampung*", such as Kenawat *kampung*, where the population was said to have helped supply food to Darul Islam fighters during the rebellion.[206]

Central Aceh had become a staging post for the military during the Darul Islam rebellion, and Kadir has explained how a government-sponsored civilian militia group called the "WMD", which he explains stood for "Mandatory Military Emergency" (*Wajib Darurat Militer*),[207] had been established and given "training by the military"[208] during the time of the rebellion to assist the military to fight Darul Islam forces, in an apparent reversal of the tactic used by the military in 1965. The existence of such a group would seem to establish that the use of civilian militias was a routine tactic of the military during the 1950s and 1960s, used to serve the ultimate goal of furthering the military's strategic objectives.

The WMD in Central Aceh, Kadir has explained, became associated with the PKI[209] and this association may well have fostered a sense of "historical animosity"[210] among former supporters of the Darul Islam in the district, who felt that the military's subsequent turn against the PKI allowed them a chance to seek revenge. Kadir is adamant, however, that it was the military and not former members of Darul Islam who initiated and led the attack against the PKI in 1965.[211]

"Latifah" was born in 1939 in Central Aceh.[212] Her parents were members of Muhammaddiyah[213] and she attended a Muhammadiyah school. In 1965, Latifah was a young mother and wife to "Said", a policeman from South Tapanuli, North Aceh, living in Takengon, Central Aceh. Said would later be accused of being associated with the PKI.[214]

Supporting the notion that Central Aceh was already in a state of semi-mobilisation prior to 1 October, Latifah has described how prior to 1 October police men and women in the district "were involved in drill training" as part of the civilian militia training program described earlier in this chapter.[215] "We were trained," Latifah explained, "to pull apart and assemble guns, I don't know what for. After it happened [the events of 1 October 1965], there was not even a squeak . . . about what would happen."[216]

Latifah does not, however, recall there being any specific tensions between political parties in the district prior to 1 October 1965.[217]

Abdullah was born in the late 1930s in Keunawat *kampung* in Central Aceh (described by Kadir as a Darul Islam *kampung*).[218] He had been an active member of Darul Islam, during which time he fought as a member of the Ilyas Lube Fifth Regiment in Central Aceh.[219] Abdullah claims he "did not feel angry" with the PKI when he was a member of Darul Islam.[220] "The DI/TII did their own thing, and the PKI did their own thing, they were separate," he has recalled.

Following the peace deal between Darul Islam and the central government, Abdullah withdrew from politics and became a teacher.[221] It was only under the instruction of the military, he has insisted (as will be detailed in chapter 6), that he was coerced into acting as an executioner for the military.[222] Abdullah's insistence that he did not willingly participate in the killings may be an attempt to deny responsibility for his actions. As will be shown, however, his position is markedly different from members of non–Darul Islam-affiliated civilian death squads, who appear to have participated in the genocide out of ideological conviction.

West Aceh

West Aceh was once one of the world's largest pepper-growing areas and sailing ships from around the world would come to its port to trade in the precious spice.[223] Today, the district is isolated. During the 1960s it could take a day's travel from Banda Aceh to reach the area despite being closer than Lhokseumawe, which could be reached in several hours by train. The region is best understood as an extension of the Acehnese heartland and was a strong, if small, base of resistance during the Dutch-Aceh War, Darul Islam rebellion and the recent separatist conflict. It is also very religiously conservative. In 2009, the district made international headlines when a local official banned women from wearing tight pants.[224] Today, as in 1965, its population is engaged in small-scale fishing, wet rice cultivation and market garden farming.

T.M. Yatim was born in the 1930s in rural West Aceh.[225] His father had been a respected travelling teacher who had taught along Aceh's west coast, but he had died when Yatim was a baby ('Yatim' means 'orphan').[226] Yatim began school at a Dutch-language school.[227] After the Dutch fled in 1942, Yatim attended a Japanese-language school in Bukittinggi, West Sumatra. After graduating, Yatim returned to West Aceh, where he began to work for the new Republican government.

In 1965 Yatim was Assistant District Chief for Johan Pahlawan, 10 km north of Meulaboh.[228] He recalls that during the early 1960s conditions in West Aceh "were the same" as elsewhere in Aceh.[229] Under Guided Democracy, Yatim explains, "everything was guided". This included the West Aceh provincial government operating only semi-democratically. The West Aceh provincial government, Yatim has recalled, "directly selected a representative from the military". It also had a veto over elections for the position of *bupati* (regent).

The PKI had members in Meulaboh. "They were only a few," Yatim has explained, "but they had the strongest discipline and were able to withstand attacks."[230] As an example of their discipline and lack of pretention, Yatim has recalled how "they would eat anything, [and say] 'wah, we are not picky like you [big politicians], we are happy to just eat grated coconut'[231] ... it was impressive". "They were very good at capturing the hearts of the people," Yatim explains.[232] They were also adept at using government campaigns to their own advantage. Once, Yatim recalls:

> We, as part of the government, were building an organisation for the people (*sebuah organisasi rakyat*) . . . this is an example, I said to Sidik [a PKI member] I would go [to a particular area], and before we could get there the PKI would go, they would sit with the people. They were leaders, they mobilised the people, they would ask for assistance [from the government], they would ask for hoes, they would know [what was needed in the community]. When the government was going to distribute the hoes, they would know in advance, then they would go to the *kampung* and ask, even though we already had plans to distribute them . . . [then] they would come with the people from the *kampung* [to make it look as if it was their presence that had resulted in the hoes being distributed]. Oh my, they were very shrewd. They were really extraordinary, very quick-moving.[233]

This competition did not cause ill will with the government, Yatim claims, though he recalls some PKI leaders began to grow arrogant (*tidak mau bergaul*) as a result of their successes, allegedly refusing, for example, to recognise Yatim when they met in Banda Aceh.[234]

During the 1950s, Yatim explained, the main conflict in the district had been between the central government and the Darul Islam. This conflict was subsequently resolved by "the Acehnese themselves" when Daud Beureu'eh had come down from the mountains and encouraged ex-fighters to join the military.[235] Yatim, who attended the signing of the peace agreement between Darul Islam and the central government in Kutaradja [Banda Aceh], was impressed by the handling of the peace agreement as facilitated by Aceh's then Military Commander M. Jasin.

South Aceh

South Aceh is an extremely isolated area. Its main town, Tapaktuan, is a beautiful seaside town near Aceh's border with North Sumatra that feels far from both Banda Aceh and Medan. Today, children still ride pushbikes in large groups to school. The area is also home to an interesting syncretic belief system: it hosts both the footprint and alleged gravesite of a giant ('Tapak Tuan' means 'Giant Footprint'), which is treated as a holy site.[236] South Aceh can be understood as a transition area. On its western edge sits Labuan Haji, a port town, where pilgrims would historically leave for the 'Holy Lands' and which today remains the site of several prestigious religious boarding schools. The district's eastern areas, meanwhile, back on to large plantation areas once controlled by the Dutch from East Sumatra.[237] Its population is engaged in small-scale fishing, wet rice cultivation and farming in large market and forest gardens.

Oesman was born during the 1940s in Tapaktuan, South Aceh.[238] After completing primary school, he attended high school in Banda Aceh during the time of the Darul Islam rebellion. In 1960, he returned to South Aceh, where he began working as a junior high school teacher in Tapaktuan.[239] Ten years later he would become a principal.[240]

Oesman has recalled there was no pronounced conflict between political parties in the district prior to 1 October 1965.[241] "The PKI here," he has explained:

> was one of the bigger parties here along with the PNI.[242] Because [the PKI was big], the Pemuda Rakyat was also big, and next the BTI. We are an agrarian country; by indoctrinating the peasants they [the PKI] were able to increase their impact. They would go into the villages while the TNI (*Tentara Nasional Indonesia*: Indonesian National Army, the military) was a bit elitist (*sedikit agak elit*) and would mainly stay in the town, [so] they operated at different political levels. But the PKI was pro-people, by guiding the people through the BTI, they went in through different lines, but there was never any conflict between the different parties. They just promoted their own ideas, they were all spreading their ideas, each trying to gain as much influence as possible. . . . [t]here was LEKRA here . . . BTI was here, Pemuda Rakyat was here . . . the one that was the biggest was the peasant organisation, the BTI.[243]

Oesman presents an image of the PKI competing peacefully alongside other political parties in the district for influence, and gaining popularity in part because its members were willing to speak out on behalf of the ongoing hardships faced by the peasant population. The PKI, Oesman explains, was also in political completion with the military, which he describes as performing a political role in the district.

The PKI had yet to implement any major programs in the district, but, Oesman has recalled, its members would tell people how the Party would increase the living standards of the peasants.[244] The PKI also promised:

> There would be tractors distributed and things like that, but it was still at the stage of words. . . . They were based at their office in Merdeka Street, in the main street. . . . They would hold meet and greets, also activities, LEKRA, for example, would hold plays and music. It wasn't yet clear what their ultimate intentions were . . . they were just trying to gain the interest of the people first.[245]

It was only after 1 October, Oseman explains, that people in Tapaktuan started to hear negative things about the PKI. One such story was about the 'Bandar Betsy Affair'[246] on the Bandar Betsy plantation in Simalungun, in North Sumatra.[247]

"Hamzah" was born during the 1940s in South Aceh.[248] In 1965, he was working in the Subdistrict Office in Labuan Haji, 46 km northwest from the district capital of Tapaktuan. Hamzah has recalled how "the PKI was indeed strong" in South Aceh prior to 1 October 1965. The PKI had "strong proselytising abilities",[249] he has explained, and was able to respond to the poor economic situation of peasants in the *kampung*.

The PKI was also involved in distributing farming equipment to attract peasants to the Party and its affiliated organisations. "The economic situation of people in the *kampung* was too low," Hamzah recalls. "Just by being given a hoe, people could be persuaded to join [the PKI]."[250]

Support for Darul Islam, Hamzah recalls, had also been strong in Labuan Haji, but this had not caused tensions with the PKI.[251] Support for Darul Islam, Hamzah explains, had been based on opposition to Aceh's integration with North Sumatra rather than on anti-PKI ideology.[252] Meanwhile, the agreement between Darul Islam and the military leadership had been successful in resolving conflict in the district, with former Darul Islam fighters in South Aceh joining either the national military or the civil service. "After the Lam Teh Agreement (*Ikrar Lam Teh*) [signed by the Darul Islam leadership and the military leadership]," Hamzah explains, "the Darul Islam didn't exist anymore."

"Ali" was born during the late 1940s in Sama Dua, 12 km northwest of Tapaktuan.[253] His parents were peasants. Ali attended primary school in Sama Dua before working as a peasant farmer. He has recalled how "there were a lot" of PKI members in Sama Dua.[254] Sama Dua is said to have been a PKI hot spot. Indeed, Ali recalls a PKI cadre named Yono was sent into the *kampung* by the PKI leadership in Banda Aceh to help organise potential members in the subdistrict.

It is not known why this poor farming area, located between the coast and the base of fertile mountain market gardens that stretch into the Leuser mountain range, became a PKI hot spot, though this may have been influenced by historical factors. At the time of the Indonesian national revolution, Bakongan, 65 km from Tapaktuan and also in South Aceh, had become famous as a bastion of Republican resistance. The leadership of this resistance had been influenced by the PKI.[255] The neighbouring district of Southeast Aceh, meanwhile, had been a plantation area controlled by the Dutch directly from Medan, which could have helped to bolster labour activism in the district. It may be that this legacy helped to encourage support for the PKI in South Aceh during the 1960s.

The PKI, however, was not the only popular party in Sama Dua. Prior to 1 October 1965, Ali has explained, the PKI had been in stiff competition with the PNI. The two parties, as during the period of the Darul Islam rebellion, were often considered to have similar viewpoints and competed with one another for members.[256] This competitiveness does not appear, however, to have led to any violence between the two groups in Sama Dua. As Ali has observed, "the PKI was a big party and so was the PNI",[257] but the security situation in Sama Dua had been "safe enough".[258]

East Aceh

East Aceh is another transition area. Idi Rayeuk, on East Aceh's western edge, is the final frontier of the Acehnese heartland. Eastern East Aceh, meanwhile, has its own unique character and is home to Aceh's largest plantations, which were established during the colonial period to produce rubber and tobacco for sale on the world market.[259] These plantations were administered directly from East Sumatra and this commercial relationship with Medan continued after independence. Eastern East Aceh is also home to Aceh's largest Javanese community. Many of the original members of this community first came to the area as coolie labourers to work on the plantations and later established villages where Javanese is still spoken. Today these plantation areas have been expanded and produce palm oil. East Aceh has also been the site of active oil fields since the colonial period.[260] In addition to supporting the plantation and oil economy, East Aceh's population in 1965 was engaged in small-scale fishing, wet rice cultivation and market garden farming.

Saifuddin was born in 1940 in East Aceh's coastal peasant-based Idi subdistrict.[261] Both of his parents were peasants. He completed three years of schooling at the local Islamic primary school before also beginning work as a peasant.[262] During the period preceding 1 October, Saifuddin has observed the PKI "didn't have a base, but it did have leaders" in Idi.[263] The Party was particularly successful, Saifuddin has recalled, in recruiting plantation workers and railway workers in the district. "It wasn't clear what the PKI's intentions were," Saifuddin has explained, "[but] what was said was 'if you want to join with us, you will be given gifts (*diberikan hadiah*) . . . that is what interested people here, the poor people, that is why people became interested."[264]

There were nine members of the PKI in Saifuddin's *kampung*.[265] These men and women, Saifuddin recalls, "were given positions" in their workplaces "because they had become Communists". "If someone joined," Saifuddin has explained, "they had to be given a position [such as by becoming a union official], and that's how they had their voices heard." This was especially the case in the subdistrict's market gardens.

The PKI had an established base in the subdistrict's market gardens and plantations during the time of the Darul Islam rebellion, Saifuddin has explained, but "no one", including the PKI had been "brave enough to fight against Darul Islam" in Idi at this time.[266] Rather, Saifuddin has recalled, members of the Darul Islam and members of the PKI had chosen to keep their distance from one another, with the PKI keeping to the "town and plantations", which were patrolled by pro-government security guards.

The divide between political orientation in the towns and rural areas in Idi continued to the time of the *Ganyang Malaysia* campaign. "People in the towns", Saifuddin has explained, "agreed" with the *Ganyang Malaysia* campaign, while "people in the *kampung* didn't understand".[267] Idi has traditionally had a strong relationship with Malaysia, with traders conducting business over the Malacca Strait since pre-colonial times,[268] and this fostered antipathy to actions seen as damaging to this relationship among sections of the population who had not been convinced of the broader nationalist and anti-imperialist objectives of the campaign.[269]

"Taufik" was born in 1937 in Blengkunang, Central Java.[270] During the period of Dutch rule, his father had been a coolie transport agent who sent coolie labourers throughout the archipelago, including to Kalimantan and Sumatra. He had also sent coolie labourers to the Dutch South American colony of Suriname. This work made his father wealthy. When Taufik was still young, just before the outbreak of the Second World War, his family had moved to Deli, North Sumatra, a major coolie hub.

Shortly after the outbreak of the war, Taufik's father died and Taufik fled with his mother and sisters to "Village 1"[271] in Tamiang, East Aceh, Aceh's main plantation area, just inside the Acehnese side of the border with North Sumatra, to avoid his being enlisted in the Japanese army.[272] Taufik attended primary school in Village 1 from 1948, before also completing middle and senior school. He then travelled to Medan, North Sumatra, where he completed a law degree at the North Sumatra Islamic University.[273] Upon graduation, he returned to Village 1, where he saw the end of the Darul Islam rebellion and where he was living in 1965.

Taufik has recalled there were "no PKI members" in Village 1, but there were many in neighbouring "Village 2",[274] which was considered to be a "PKI village" because the Village Head, "Pak Rusdi", was a member of the Party.[275] Village 1, meanwhile, was considered to be a "PNI village" because of its Village Head's affiliation.[276] The PKI, Taufik explains, had spread into the district from nearby, previously Dutch-owned, plantation areas such as the Kebon Serang Jaya plantation.[277]

The PKI had also been strong in Village 2, where it had distributed hoes and other farming equipment to peasants and plantation workers.[278] Besides this activity, Taufik continues, the PKI was very popular, with people "continually joining" its affiliated plantation workers union SABUPRI (*Sarekat Buruh Perkebunan*

Republik Indonesia: Plantation Workers Union of the Republic of Indonesia). This occurred, Taufik has explained:

> because it [the PKI] would fight for better wages . . . [and] so the rice rations [distributed to plantation workers as part-payment for their labour[279]] would be better . . . so they weren't given poor quality rice.[280]

The BTI, Gerwani, LEKRA and Pemuda Rakyat also had a strong presence in the district.[281] Indeed, it was not unusual for plantation worker families in the district to have been members of the PKI and its affiliated organisations since the 1940s.[282]

Taufik recalls the PKI's largest rival in East Aceh had been Masjumi, whose members the PKI had liked to taunt. "The PKI would quarrel (*bertengkar*) with Masjumi" and sing a provocative song in Javanese as part of a shadow play that they would stage in the village. The words of this song, Taufik remembers, were:

> The Majumi Party is going to be hooked on the hammer and sickle [the PKI's emblem], *ginjal-ginjal* [this would appear to be a reference to '*genjer-genjer*', the chorus in a song made popular by the PKI about the 'genjer' plant, a food eaten by the poor], they want a beating, they are going to be hooked on the hammer and sickle, *ginjal-ginjal*. (*Partai Masjumi mau digantol sama palu-arit 'kan ginjal-ginal mau dipukul, mau di gantol sama palu arit 'kan ginjal-ginjal.*)[283]

"This would scare people", Taufik has explained, and children from Village 1 were banned from listening to this song and from going to watch the shadow play.[284] It was "provocation" he continues, but did not escalate into physical confrontation. Masjumi, after all, had been banned in 1960 by Sukarno because of its support for the PRRI and Darul Islam rebellions and was in no position to fight back. Villagers in Village 1, Taufik has explained, had also been wary of the Darul Islam.

Villagers in Village 1, Taufik has recalled "did not support DI/TII".[285] This was because they already considered themselves to be Muslim and resented the Darul Islam telling them that they were not pious enough. Villagers had also become "scared" when Darul Islam fighters would come into the village in the middle of the night and "stick notices up on the prayer house, at the mosque", calling for the population "to be religious".[286] The notices at the mosque had the effect of making "people pray more", but this was "primarily because they were scared".

As descendants of Javanese coolie labourers and transmigrants, Taufik has explained, the population in Village 1 felt they were being intimidated by the Darul Islam. "It's like this", he continues:

> we were living in Aceh . . . but . . . we were not Acehnese, we were from Java. This was Aceh. If we already had a house, if we already had a market garden, if we were told to leave by Darul Islam people, now, we'd really lose out, wouldn't we![287]

This statement suggests that opposition to the PKI, in East Aceh at least, did not automatically translate into sympathy for the Darul Islam. Darul Islam fighters identified the Javanese community in Tamiang, East Aceh, primarily by its ethnic, rather than religious, identity.

"Aminah" was born around 1950 in Village 2.[288] Her parents were originally from Java and had come to Aceh as coolie labourers. When Aminah was twelve she had had joined the PKI's cultural organisation LEKRA because she loved to play music and LEKRA had been the most vibrant cultural organisation in the village.[289] Many of her friends had also joined.[290] Aminah recalls, "We were asked if we wanted to join in to dance, to learn to sing, to just come along, children are happy to have lots of friends." To begin with the orchestra had not "belonged to the PKI", she continues, "the orchestra was just part of normal entertainment in the *kampung*, but because the PKI [were the most involved], it became associated [with the PKI]".[291] The leader of the orchestra was a man named "Pak Joesoef",[292] who was also a leader of the PKI in the village. She would later marry "Karim" (below). The couple settled in Village 2, where they live to this day.

Karim was born in the late 1940s in Village 1 in Tamiang, East Aceh.[293] His parents were originally from Jakarta and had travelled to Aceh as coolie labourers. His father died when he was still a child. After completing three years of primary school, he travelled to Medan in 1962, where he attempted to join the military police, in the hope of joining the *Ganyang Malaysia* campaign.[294] Karim's mother, however, forbade him to join as five of his younger siblings were still living at home and she feared losing him.

Karim and Aminah have explained the PKI had a large presence in Village 2. In addition to running cultural activities, the PKI leadership in the village sent their most promising new recruits to a PKI cadre school in Banda Aceh.[295] Karim recalls that the Village Head, "Pak Rusdi", as well as the PKI's secretary in the village, "Pak Saleh", along with two other men and "Djoened", a youth leader, had attended this cadre school.[296] When Djoened had returned, he had brought a uniform and "emblems" (*atribut*) of the Party's logo, which he proudly wore in the village.[297] Karim had also been invited to attend the cadre school and had wanted to go but his mother, who was now ill, had again asked him not to go.[298]

Village 2 and Village 1 had engaged in inter-village rivalry, but this was not, Karim insists, as a result of ideological differences. Rather, Karim has described how male youths from the two villages competed over "girls" and the brands of clothes and cigarettes that they were able to afford, without this competition extending to serious violence or open antagonism over political affiliation.[299] Those who worked on the plantations, Karim recalls, had more disposable income and as a result were able to buy expensive "*trelin* brand" clothing and "*wemble* cigarettes", provoking jealousy in their neighbours.[300] "Yeah, like often happens", Karim has explained:

> the problem of youth. It would be this little problem or that little problem . . . sometimes we would get into fights, sometimes we had been drinking alcohol, then we'd get angry, but it wasn't more than that, it wasn't a fight over politics.[301]

Karim has, however, described antagonism during this period between PKI members and members of the Pemuda Pancasila,[302] the paramilitary youth organisation established by Nasution in 1955, whose members were often employed to work as security guards on military-controlled plantations that had been nationalised during the late 1950s.[303] Djoened, the PKI youth leader from Village 1, Karim recalls, would goad members of the Pemuda Pancasila, singing out, "if the Pemuda Pancasila come, we will hit them", causing Karim to laugh.[304] The PKI felt confident in its popularity, and the situation in the village, Karim has recalled, was "safe enough".[305]

***

The above accounts illustrate that each of Aceh's districts possessed subtle socioeconomic differences. These would later be reflected in patterns in the violence in the province, though the genocide must ultimately be understood as a national event. To be sure, the situation in Aceh prior to 1 October was tense. These accounts do not, however, suggest that Aceh was teetering on the brink of communal violence. The PKI was a growing presence in the province and was engaged in heated competition with other political forces in Aceh's districts. It did not, however, breach the norms of what was acceptable behaviour for political parties at that time. Indeed, the PKI appears to have drawn respect even from its critics, who could see the success it was having in mobilising local populations around the ideas of social justice.

Despite this growing PKI influence, however, it is also clear that the military was the strongest structural entity in the province, with its command structures stretching right down to the village level. While both the PKI and military may have imagined a future without the other, only the military had the capacity to make this wish a reality. Since 1945, the struggle for the Indonesian state had been ongoing. From early 1965, the national military leadership had begun to actively prepare to seize state power in order to settle this struggle once and for all. This included preparations in Aceh at the provincial and district levels.

Through its control over Aceh's Pantja Tunggal bodies, the Aceh military command could subsume civilian government in the province under its control. It also possessed new de facto martial law powers through the Mandala Satu Command and the Kohanda Command structures that it could call into effect without first needing to seek permission from the President under Indonesia's new Dwikora legislation. It had trialled these new powers through Operasi Singgalang and was training civilian militia groups in the province under the guise of preparing for a confrontation with Malaysia. In fact, the military leadership was activey waiting for an event that could be used as a pretext to move against the PKI and seize control of the Indonesian state. As will be shown in chapter 3, these command structures were activated by the military during the morning of 1 October and were subsequently used to initiate and implement the genocide in Aceh.

There is no evidence of the PKI being rejected in Aceh prior to the outbreak of the genocide on religious grounds. The characterisation of the PKI as "atheist" was largely a product of military propaganda during the time of the genocide.

Having grown out of Indonesia's socialist-Islamic tradition, the PKI saw no contradiction in embracing both a Marxist and Muslim identity. Although some PKI members identified as atheist, the majority of PKI members in Aceh were Muslims and engaged in varying levels of religious activity within their local communities, from daily prayer to the fast.

The Darul Islam, meanwhile, was no longer an independent force and does not appear to have been considered a rival of the PKI. Although in certain areas where the PKI had been strong, such as in Central and East Aceh, there had been a history of conflict between the two groups, this conflict appears to have been mediated by the two groups' relationships with the central government and military leadership at the time. This would also be the case during the genocide.

The Acehnese elite enjoyed a strong relationship with the military leadership during the period immediately leading up to 1 October. It was this relationship, rather than its relationship with Sukarno, that had led to the conclusion of the Darul Islam rebellion in the province. The Acehnese elite and the national military leadership both disliked Sukarno and had no reason to prop up his diminishing power in the aftermath of 1 October, except in so far as this would safeguard and legitimate the military's desires. The Acehnese elite preferred the military leadership to Sukarno and the PKI. The Acehnese elite also owed the military leadership a debt of gratitude for supporting its bid for Aceh to be re-formed as an independent province, as well as for granting former Darul Islam fighters amnesty and the opportunity to be re-integrated within the national military. It is likely that the Acehnese elite and former Darul Islam fighters felt compelled to assist the military to demonstrate their loyalty to the new military regime as a means of preserving these gains.

It is also apparent that the PKI was gaining strength in Aceh during this period, and was considered to be an organic political force in the province by most political actors. The PKI made some tactical errors in Aceh, such as when it campaigned to remove Ali Hasjmy as Governor, and in its failure to gain a broader base of support in the province. Such over-confidence was presumably a result of the security the Party leadership felt as an institutional component of Aceh's provincial government and due to the growing support it felt it was receiving from Sukarno. This sense of security helps to explain the Party's self-assurance before 1 October and its lack of preparedness to defend itself in the event of an attack by its political enemies. Yet, although regional dynamics played a role in determining the manner in which local forces were prepared to react from 1 October, this, by itself, does not explain how and why the genocide erupted in the province. These issues can only be understood if we interpret the military's attack as a national campaign emanating from Jakarta.

Notes

1   Throughout this book I use the term 'military' to refer to both the Indonesian army and military police, unless otherwise specified. Historically, Indonesia's Air Force and Navy, along with sections of the military police in East Java, were considered by the army leadership to be more sympathetic to Sukarno. (Harold Crouch, *The Army and Politics in Indonesia* [Jakarta: Equinox Publishing, 2007, originally 1978], p. 189). On 4 October, Suharto would accuse the Air Force of being involved in the 30

September Movement. I have yet to discover specific references to the actions of the Air Force or Navy in Aceh during the time of the genocide. I prefer to use the term 'military' instead of the more restrictive 'army' because I think it best captures the use of these terms in Aceh. In Aceh, the 'Ground Forces' (*Angkatan Darat*: Army) is popularly referred to as '*militer*' ('*militer*' can be translated as either 'military' or 'army'). Meanwhile, in the military documents cited in this book, the 'Army' commonly refers to itself as 'ABRI', the 'Armed Forces of the Republic of Indonesia', i.e. the 'military'.

2 John Roosa, *Pretext for Mass Murder: The 30th September Movement & Suharto's Coup D'Etat in Indonesia* (Madison: The University of Wisconsin Press, 2006), p. 221.

3 Ulf Sundhaussen has observed the earliest of these structures, the 'People's Security Agency' (BKR: *Badan Keamanan Rakyat*), established on 22 August 1945, and the 'People's Security Army' (TKR: *Tentara Keamanan Rakyat*), established on 5 October 1945, "existed largely on paper only", before the establishment of the Army of the Republic of Indonesia (TRI: *Tentara Republik Indonesia*) on 24 January 1946, which had operational control over ten divisions. In 1950, the military command was restructured according to the 'Territorial Concept', which reduced the number of military command divisions to seven Military Territories (*Tentara dan Territorium*). Between 1957 and 1959 the military command was again restructured into sixteen Regional Military Commands (Kodam: *Komando Daerah Militer*). Ulf Sundhaussen, *The Road to Power: Indonesian Military Politics, 1945–1967* (Kuala Lumpur: Oxford University Press, 1982), pp. 7, 9–10, 58.

4 Abdul Haris Nasution, *Fundamentals of Guerrilla Warfare* (New York: Frederick A. Praeger, 1965, originally 1953), p. 11.

5 *Ibid.*, p. 99. Through this text Nasution makes references to the Madiun Affair of 1948 in East Java, which was blamed on the PKI by the military, and the Darul Islam rebellion that began in West Java during the same year. His analysis was later applied to the regional rebellions of the 1950s and early 1960s.

6 Yani replaced Nasution as Commander in Chief of the Armed Forces in May 1964 after Sukarno became concerned Nasution was growing too powerful. See Ulf Sundhaussen, *The Road to Power*, pp. 164–165.

7 Some variation exists in the province-level military command structures. This information is valid for Aceh in 1965.

8 Today the position of the 'Puterpra' is held by a Military Precinct Command (Koramil: *Komando Rayon Militer*) Commander (Danramil).

9 A list of the various troops under the command of the Pangdam in Aceh between October and December 1965 stretches to eight pages. 'Daftar Dislokasi Pasukan Oktober/Nobember/Desember '65', pp. 1–8, in *Laporan Tahunan Lengkap Kodam-I/Kohanda Atjeh, Tahun 1965* (Banda Aceh: Kodam-I Banda Aceh, 1 February 1966).

10 A list of the numerical strength of Hansip and Hanra units in each of Aceh's districts is attached to the Complete Yearly Report. According to these figures, 148,167 civilians in the province were active Hansip/Hanra members during the time of the genocide (11.9% of Aceh's total population). In 1965, Aceh's population was 1,774,160. 'Daftar Kekuatan ABRI Hansip/Hanra/Sukwan Di Kohanda Atjeh', pp. 1–3, in *Laporan Tahunan Lengkap Kodam-I/Kohanda Atjeh, Tahun 1965* (Banda Aceh: Kodam-I Banda Aceh, 1 February 1966); also, 'Tabel: 4.5.2. Penduduk Daerah Istimewa Atjeh Tahun 1961–1970', in *Atjeh Dalam Angka 1970* (Banda Aceh: Badan Perentjanaan Pembangunan Atjeh, 1971).

11 See, David Jenkins, *Suharto and His Generals: Indonesian Military Politics, 1975–1983* (Ithaca, NY: Cornell Modern Indonesia Project, Southeast Asia Program, Cornell University, 1984), p. 46.

12 The *Front Nasional* was established in Jakarta in August 1960 by Sukarno with *Manipol/USDEK* [the Political Manifesto of Guided Democracy] as its program. It included all political parties and organisations and was headed by Sukarno. The military held eleven out of its seventy-three national Executive Board positions. The

Front Nasional was established at the provincial level in April 1961, with the military chairing nine out of seventeen provincial branches. Ulf Sundhaussen, *The Road to Power*, p. 152. Ishak Djuarsa, through the 'Complete Yearly Report', would describe the *Front Nasional*'s role during the time of the genocide as a "tool to achieve unity" and as a means to "mobilise the people". 'Complete Yearly Report', p. 12.

13 Guided Democracy was officially declared by Sukarno on 5 July 1959 with the support of the military leadership. Guided Democracy reinstated the 1945 Constitution and gave greater power to the President and the Cabinet. After the reintroduction of the 1945 constitution, provisional bodies, including the Provisional People's Consultative Council (MPRS: *Majelis Permusyawaratan Rakyat Sementara*) and the People's Representative Council – Gotong Royong Cabinet (DPR-GR: *Dewan Perwakilan Rakyat Gotong Royong*) were created to carry out the functions of the People's Consultative Council (MPR: *Majelis Permusyawaratan Rakyat*: People's Consultative Council) and the People's Representative Council (DPR: *Dewan Perwakilan Rakyat*) until elections could be held. Harold Crouch, *The Army and Politics in Indonesia*, p. 47. Free and fair elections would not be held until after the fall of the New Order regime.

14 *Ibid.*, p. 45.

15 *Ibid.*, p. 46.

16 An extended explanation of the meaning of Nasakom can be found in, Sukarno, *Persatuan Total Dengan Poros Nasakom* (Jakarta: Departemen Penerangan, 1962).

17 Rex Mortimer, *Indonesian Communism Under Sukarno: Ideology and Politics, 1959–1965* (Jakarta: Equinox Publishing, 2006, originally 1974), p. 68.

18 'Lampiran Keputusan Presiden/Panglima Tertinggi Angkatan Bersenjata Republik Indonesia/Panglima Besar Komando Ganyang Malaysia No. 85/KOGAM/1966', in Alex Dinuth (ed.), *Dokumen Terpilih Sekitar G.30.S/PKI* (Jakarta: Intermasa, 1997), p. 190.

19 *Ibid.*, p. 49.

20 Robert Hefner, *Civil Islam: Muslims and Democratization in Indonesia* (Princeton: Princeton University Press, 2000), p. 51.

21 Rex Mortimer, *Indonesian Communism Under Sukarno*, p. 278.

22 A history of the PRRI/Permesta (*Pemerintah Revolusioner Republik Indonesia/Piagam Perjuangan Semesta Alam*: Revolutionary Government of the Republic of Indonesia/Universal Struggle Charter) rebellions can be found in Audrey Kahin, *Rebellion to Integration: West Sumatra and the Indonesian Polity* (Amsterdam: Amsterdam University Press, 1999).

23 *Ibid.*, p. 47.

24 Herbert Feith, *The Decline of Constitutional Democracy in Indonesia* (Jakarta: Equinox Publishing, 2007, originally 1962), p. 434.

25 Rex Mortimer, *Indonesian Communism Under Sukarno*, p. 68.

26 *Ibid.*, p. 58.

27 Emphasis in original. *Ibid.*

28 *Ibid.*, p. 38.

29 Sensitivity to this issue would also appear to be one of the reasons the PKI did not arm itself during the lead-up to 1965. It was not until an external enemy presented itself – as occurred during the *Ganyang Malaysia* campaign – that it felt it could justify embarking on arms training.

30 Rex Mortimer, *Indonesian Communism Under Sukarno*, p. 172.

31 The PKI described this campaign as "Nasakomisation in all fields". See, Harold Crouch, *The Army and Politics in Indonesia*, pp. 87–88.

32 Rex Mortimer, *Indonesian Communism Under Sukarno*, p. 383.

33 On 17 August 1961 Sukarno declared West Irian (*Irian Barat*) should be "returned" to Indonesia, using military force if necessary. On 19 December 1961 Sukarno established the People's Triple Command (Trikora: *Tri Komando Rakyat*) to prepare to militarily seize the territory. The Supreme Command for the Liberation of West Irian

(KOTI: *Komando Tertinggi Pembebasan Irian Barat*) was established under the direct leadership of Sukarno to coordinate this campaign, while its operational command was coordinated through an Area Command for the Liberation of West Irian (*Komando Mandala Pembebasan Irian Barat*), established on 11 January 1962, under the direction of Major General Suharto. Ulf Sundhaussen, *The Road to Power*, pp. 155–156.

34 *Ibid.*, p. 51.

35 This culminated in the transfer of sovereignty over West Irian to Indonesia on 1 May 1963.

36 Bradley Simpson, *Economists With Guns: Authoritarian Development and U.S.-Indonesian Relations, 1960–1968* (Stanford, CA: Stanford University Press, 2008), pp. 48, 76–77.

37 Harold Crouch, *The Military and Politics in Indonesia* (Jakarta: Equinox Publishing, 2007, originally 1978), pp. 52–53.

38 *Ibid.*, p. 54.

39 *Ibid.*, pp. 56–57.

40 For a detailed account of the US role in training the military leadership, see Bryan Evans III, 'The Influence of the United States Army on the Development of the Indonesian Army (1954–1964)', *Indonesia*, Vol. 47 (April 1989), pp. 25–48.

41 Mokoginta had previously served as head of the military's Armed Forces Staff and Command School (SESKOAD: *Sekolah Staf dan Komando Angkatan Darat*). Bryan Evans III, 'The Influence of the United States Army on the Development of the Indonesian Army (1954–1964)', p. 28.

42 As mentioned earlier, neither the British or Indonesian militaries wished the confrontation to escalate into open warfare.

43 Harold Crouch, *The Military and Politics in Indonesia*, p. 62.

44 Loren Ryter, 'Scalpers and Destroyers: Pemuda Pancasila in Medan in the 1960's', originally presented at the 1999 AAS Conference in San Diego, 10 March 2000, pp. 35–42.

45 A rare photograph in *Life* magazine shows PKI-affiliated Gerwani (*Gerakan Wanita Indonesia*: Indonesian Women's Movement) members conducting a drill in Jakarta carrying rifles as part of the *Ganyang Malaysia* campaign. Image available online: http://pramukanewss.blogspot.com.au/2013/06/ganjang-malaysia-dengan-angkatan-kelima.html. In Jakarta, PKI-affiliated People's Youth (*Pemdua Rakyat*) members participated in training at Lubang Buaya. Saskia E. Wieringa, 'The Birth of the New Order State in Indonesia: Sexual Politics and Nationalism', *Journal of Women's History*, Vol. 15, No. 1 (2003), p. 78.

46 By way of signalling his depth of support for this proposal Sukarno claimed the idea for a Fifth Force had been his own. Rex Mortimer, *Indonesian Communism Under Sukarno*, p. 384.

47 The formation of a 'Fifth Force' was first publically proposed by PKI Chairman D.N. Aidit in January 1965. Harold Crouch, *The Army and Politics in Indonesia*, p. 87.

48 John Roosa, *Pretext for Mass Murder*, p. 189.

49 *Ibid.*

50 *Ibid.*

51 *Ibid.*, pp. 189–191.

52 *Ibid.*

53 'Doktrin Perdjuangan TNI "Tri Ubaya Cakti": Buku Induk', Hasil Seminar Angkatan Darat, Tgl. 2 s/d 9 April 1965 (Bandung: Departemen Angkatan Darat, 1965), pp. 55, 58.

54 The three "promises" were 'Basic National Security', 'Civil Action' and 'Development'. 'Doktrin Perdjuangan TNI "Tri Ubaya Cakti" ', p. 13.

55 *Ibid.*, pp. 267–268.

56 *Ibid.*, p. 268.

57 Harold Crouch, *The Army and Politics in Indonesia*, pp. 38–39.

58 Robert Hefner, *Civil Islam*, p. 52; see also, Rex Mortimer, *Indonesian Communism Under Sukarno*, pp. 277–278.
59 Robert Hefner, *Civil Islam*, p. 53.
60 Ruth McVey, *The Rise of Indonesian Communism* (Ithaca, New York: Cornell University Press, 1965), pp. 10–12.
61 *Ibid.*, pp. 8–11.
62 Takashi Shiraishi, *An Age in Motion: Popular Radicalism in Java, 1912–1926* (Ithaca, New York: Cornell University Press, 1990), p. 217; Ruth McVey, *The Rise of Indonesian Communism*, pp. 19–22.
63 Takashi Shiraishi, *An Age in Motion*, pp. 217, 225–231.
64 Barbara S. Harvey, 'Diplomacy and Armed Struggle in the Indonesian National Revolution: Choice and Constraint in Comparative Perspective', in Daniel S. Lev and Ruth McVey (eds.), *Making Indonesia: Essays on Modern Indonesia in Honour of George McT. Kahin* (Ithaca, New York: Cornell University, 1996), p. 71.
65 *Ibid.*, p. 72.
66 Ruth McVey, 'Teaching Modernity: The PKI as an Educational Institution', *Indonesia*, Vol. 50, 25th Anniversary Edition (October 1990), p. 6.
67 *Medan Moeslimin*, 5 Djoemadilakhir Dal 1343, 1 Djanuari 1925, Tahun XI, No. 1. Cited in Djohan Effendi, *Pembaruan Tanpa Membongkar Tradisi* (Jakarta: Penerbit Buku Kompas, 2010), p. 42.
68 Misbach described the Sarekat Islam Putih as a group that "falsely profess Islam". "To be sure," he continues, "they always make a show of their Islamness, but actually it is only on their lips. To be sure, they perform the precepts of the religion of Islam, but they pick and choose from those precepts that suit their desire . . . Put bluntly, they oppose or defy the demands of God . . . and rather fear and love the will of Satan – that Satan whose evil influence is apparent in this pregnant age in [the system of] Capitalism." Takashi Shiraishi, *An Age in Motion*, pp. 285–286.
69 Ulf Sundhaussen, *The Road to Power*, p. 186.
70 'Keputusan Peningkat Pelaksanaan Dwikora' Keppres/Plm Tert. ABRI/KOTI/KOTOE No. 52/KOTI tahun 1964; mb 14 September 1964, in Muhono (ed.), *Ketetapan MPRS dan Peraturan Negara jang Penting bagi Anggauta Angkatan Bersendjata* (Jakarta: Tentara Nasional Indonesia, 1966), p. 1244.
71 'Keadaan Darurat Militer', Bab III, 'Keadaan Bahaya', Perpu 2/1959; LN 1959–139; TLN 1908 (sdu. dg. Perpu 52/1960–170), in *Himpunan Peraturan Perundangan-Undangan RI* (Jakarta: Ichtiar Baru van Hoeve, n.d.), pp. 455–457.
72 'Keadaan Perang', Bab IV, 'Keadaan Bahaya', Perpu 2/1959; LN 1959–139; TLN 1908 (sdu. dg. Perpu 52/1960–170), in *Himpunan Peraturan Perundangan-Undangan RI*, pp. 457–459.
73 Harold Crouch, *The Military and Politics in Indonesia*, pp. 69–72.
74 *Ibid.*, p. 187.
75 *Ibid.*, p. 71.
76 *Ibid.*, pp. 187–188.
77 Marwati Djoened Poesponegoro and Nugroho Notosusanto, *Sejarah Nasional Indonesia VI: Zaman Jepang dan Zaman Republik Indonesia* (Jakarta: Balai Pustaka, 2008), p. 466.
78 Letdjen A.J. Mokoginta, *Koleksi Pidato2/Kebidjaksanaan Panglima Daerah Sumatra* (Medan: Koanda Sumatera, 1966).
79 It is not known how common it was in other provinces under the Kolaga command in Sumatra and Kalimantan for the Pangdam to also hold the position of Pepelrada prior to 1 October 1965. The appointment of Omar Dhani as original Kolaga Commander suggests that an attempt was made by Sukarno to appoint armed forces personnel more aligned to his own political outlook to this command. Mokoginta, meanwhile, a key member of the military leadership, would have preferred to appoint commanders considered aligned to the military leadership. The appointment of Djuarsa to the

position of Pepelrada provided the military leadership in Aceh with military powers unprecedented outside of times of war.

80 'Keputusan Peningkat Pelaksanaan Dwikora', pp. 1244–1247.

81 Ulf Sundhaussen, *The Road to Power*, p. 176.

82 'Keadaan Bahaya', Perpu 2/1959; LN 1959–139; TLN 1908 (sdu. dg. Perpu 52/1960–170), in *Himpunan Peraturan Perundangan-Undangan RI*, p. 452.

83 'Keputusan Peningkat Pelaksanaan Dwikora', p. 1244. As described below, the power possessed by the Mandala Satu Commander in Sumatra would be demonstrated through the implementation of Operasi Singgalang in March 1965.

84 *Ibid.*, p. 1246.

85 *Ibid.*, p. 1245.

86 Ulf Sundhaussen, *The Road to Power*, pp. 185–186.

87 Mount Singgalang is a picturesque twin volcanic mountain adjacent to Mount Tandikat that overlooks Bukittinggi, West Sumatra. In late 1948, Bukittinggi became the bastion of the Republican government following the collapse of the Republic's capital in Java.

88 Emphasis in original. 'Operasi Singgalang: Mentjapai suksus jang gemilang' Medan, 23 Maret 1965, in Letdjen A.J. Mokoginta, *Koleksi Pidato2/Kebidjaksanaan Panglima Daerah Sumatra*, p. 72.

89 Amir Hasan Nast BA, *Embun Berdarah* (self-published, undated manuscript, in author's possession), p. 5.

90 A term first coined by Sukarno during the Guided Democracy period. A discussion of Sukarno's use of the term 'Nekolim' can be found in Ulf Sundhaussen, *The Road to Power*, p. 154.

91 'Operasi Singgalang: Mentjapai suksus jang gemilang', p. 72.

92 'Berdikari' was a term used by Sukarno to promote Indonesian self-reliance. His 17 August 1965 Independence Day speech, for example, was entitled 'The Year of Self-Reliance' (*Tahun Berdikari*). Operasi Bedikari was not related to the 'Berdikari Operation Command' (*Komando Operasi Berdikari*), as declared on 2 September 1965 via Presidential Decree, which was a plan oriented towards the establishment of a leadership body to oversee Sukarno's economic plans. Operasi Berdikari, by contrast, was a military operation activated on 1 October 1965 in Aceh that was specifically linked to the establishment of the Aceh Defence Region Command and the "territorial defence of Aceh" (see p. 47).

93 The eight Kosekhan (*Komando Sektor Pertahanan*: Defence Sector Command) in Aceh mirrored the administrative *daerah* (district) units under the Kodam chain of command. The eight Kosekhan followed the same basic territorial boundaries as Aceh's districts and were named as the Greater Aceh, Pidie, West Aceh, South Aceh, North Aceh, East Aceh, Central Aceh and Southeast Aceh Kosekhan. The west coast Kosekhan in West Aceh and South Aceh were coordinated by a Kosubdahan (*Komando Sub-Daerah Pertahanan*: Defence Region Sub-Command) named the Teuku Umar Kosubdahan, while the Kosekhan on the north coast and in the highlands region in North Aceh, East Aceh, Central Aceh and Southeast Aceh were coordinated by a Kosubdahan named the Lilawangsa Kosubdahan. See, 'Peta Bagian Daerah Kohanda Atjeh', in *Laporan Tahunan Lengkap Kodam-I/Kohanda Atjeh, Tahun 1965* (Banda Aceh: Kodam-I Banda Aceh, 1 February 1966). As detailed in the opening to this chapter, each Kosekhan had jurisdiction over extensive military, police and 'Hansip/Hanra' personnel. See, 'Komando Antar Daerah Pertahanan Sum[atra] Komando Pertahanan Daerah Atjeh', in *Laporan Tahunan Lengkap.*

94 *Laporan Tahunan Lengkap*, pp. 16–17.

95 The reason for this name change is not known, it would seem to indicate the activation of the military's 'Operasi Berdikari'.

96 *Laporan Tahunan Lengkap Kodam-I/Kohanda Atjeh, Tahun 1965* (Banda Aceh: Kodam-I Banda Aceh, 1 February 1966), pp. 16–17.

97 *Ibid.*
98 For example, Otto Syamsuddin Ishak, *Dari Maaf ke Panik Aceh: Sebuah Sketsa Sosiologi – Politik* (Jakarta: Lambaga Studi Pers dan Pembangunan, 2000), p. xv; M. Hamdan Basyar (ed.), *Aceh Baru: Tantangan Perdamaian dan Reintegrasi* (Jakarta: Pustaka Pelajar dengan Pusat Penelitian Politik LIPI, 2008), p. 5; and Harry Kawilarang, *Aceh dari Sultan Iskandar Muda ke Helsinki* (Banda Aceh: Bandar Publishing, 2008), p. 157. Indeed, to date, only one book has been produced on the topic of the genocide in Aceh: Rusdi Sufi and M. Munir Aziz, *Peristiwa PKI di Aceh: Sejarah Kelam Konflik Ideologis di Serambi Mekkah* (Banda Aceh: C.V. Boebon Jaya, 2008, originally 2006). Unfortunately, Sufi and Aziz's study is better understood as a survey of the genocide nationally in Indonesia, with only six pages in the book specifically referring to what happened in Aceh. Through this study, the authors problematically explain agency behind the violence by proposing, "it was the people, with that terrible force that they have (*dengan kekuatan yang dahsyat itu*), that acted to resist and destroy their enemy, that is, the PKI and its lackeys" (p. 126), thus mirroring military propaganda accounts of the events.
99 For an analysis of the emergence of PUSA, see James Siegel, *The Rope of God* (Berkeley, CA: University of California, 1969).
100 Anthony Reid, 'Colonial Transformation: A Bitter Legacy', in Anthony Reid (ed.), *Verandah of Violence: The Background to the Aceh Problem* (Singapore: Singapore University Press, 2006), p. 100.
101 James Siegel, *The Rope of God*, pp. 61–67, 98–133.
102 Aceh's *uleebalang* pre-dated the Acehnese Sultanate, when they ruled over small independent statelets. Kenneth R. Hall, 'Upstream and Downstream Unification in Southeast Asia's First Islamic Polity: The Changing Sense of Community in the Fifteenth Century *Hikayat Raja-Raja Pasai* Court Chronicle', *Journal of the Economic and Social History of the Orient*, Vol. 44, No. 2 (2001), pp. 198–229. In response to the growth of the Achenese Sultanate, the *uleebalang* entered into a power-sharing relationship with the new state, similar to the *raja* in neighbouring East Sumatra and in peninsular Malaya. By the time of the Aceh War, the *uleebalang* appear to have drawn their power from control of trade over the Malacca Strait and the capital outlays required to establish new market gardens to grow Aceh's primary export crop, pepper (by 1822 Aceh produced an estimated half of the world's supply of pepper). Two classic studies on the role of the *uleebalang* are C. Snouck Hurgronje, *The Achehnese* (Leyden: E. J. Brill Publishers, 1906); and James Siegel, *The Rope of God*.
103 Nazaruddin Sjamsuddin calls this new non-*ulama* group loyal to the *ulama* leadership "*zuama*". Nazaruddin Sjamsuddin, *The Republican Revolt: A Study of Acehnese Rebellion* (Singapore: Institute of Southeast Asian Studies, 1985).
104 Teungku Husin Mudjahid, who would come to be known as Teungku Husin Al Mudjahid ("the hero"), was born in around 1910 in Idi, East Aceh. He later helped to lead Aceh's social revolution, which was, in part, inspired by the PKI-led social revolution in neighbouring East Sumatra. Due to his association with the PKI, Al Mudjahid is seen as a deeply ambiguous figure in Aceh. Nazaruddin Sjamsuddin, for example, calls him "opportunistic" (Nazaruddin Sjamsuddin, *The Republican Revolt*, p. 186). This ambiguity appears to be based on the apparent ease with which he was able to traverse Aceh's major political divide, though this would actually appear to point to the original convergence between these two political streams in the province.
105 On the Japanese period, see Anthony Reid, *The Blood of the People: Revolution and the End of Traditional Rule in Northern Sumatra* (Kuala Lumpur and New York: Oxford University Press, 1979), pp. 84–90, 104–147.
106 An account of this period in Java can be found in Anton Lucas, *Local Opposition and Underground Resistance to the Japanese in Java, 1942–1945* (Clayton, Victoria: Centre of Southeast Asian Studies, Monash University, 1986). See also, Rex Mortimer, *Indonesian Communism Under Sukarno*, pp. 30–33.

107 Anthony Reid, *The Blood of the People*, pp. 125–126.
108 Nazaruddin Sjamsuddin, *The Republican Revolt*, p. 23.
109 Anthony Reid, *The Blood of the People*, p. 149.
110 *Ibid.*, pp. 127, 137.
111 "Insider" (a pseudonym of S.M. Amin) has explained, "There was a mood of 'passivity' and a mood of 'fatalism'." Insider, *Atjeh Sepintas Lalu* (Jakarta: Fa Archapada, 1950), pp. 18–19.
112 Soekarno, *Perkundjungan Presiden Soekarno ke Atjeh* (Koetaradja: Semangat Merdeka Bahagian Pustaka, 1948), p. 26.
113 The other regions include East Sumatra, Pekalongan, Pemalang and Tegal (the so-called "Tiga Daerah" affair) in Central Java, Banten in West Java, and South Sulawesi. For an overview of these social revolutions, see Audrey Kahin, *Regional Dynamics of the Indonesian Revolution: Unity From Diversity* (Honolulu: University of Hawaii Press, 1985).
114 For an account of the social revolution in Aceh see, Anthony Reid, *The Blood of the People*, pp. 185–217; Eric Morris, 'Aceh: Social Revolution and the Islamic Vision', in Audrey R. Kahin (ed.), *Regional Dynamics of the Indonesian Revolution*, pp. 82–111; Insider, *Atjeh Sepintas Lalu*; and, S.M. Amin, *Sekitar Peristiwa Berdarah di Atjeh* (Djakarta: Penerbit Soeroengan, 1958). An account of the social revolution in East Sumatra can be found in Anthony Reid, *The Blood of the People*, pp. 218–245.
115 Anthony Reid, *The Blood of the People*, p. 205.
116 Insider, *Atjeh Sepintas Lalu*, pp. 94–99; also, Falita Alam, 'Teungku Amir Husin Almudjahid Dalam Perang Kemerdekaan di Aceh', Departemen Pendidikan dan Kebudayaan, Universitas Syiah Kuala, Fakultas Keguruan, Imu Pendidikan, Banda Aceh, 1984.
117 Insider, *Atjeh Sepintas Lalu*, pp. 94–99.
118 Anthony Reid, *The Blood of the People*, pp. 208–210.
119 Insider, *Atjeh Sepintas Lalu*, pp. 94–95.
120 For a history of the Darul Islam rebellion in Aceh, see M. Nur El Ibrahimy, *Tgk. M. Daud Beureueh: Peranannya dalam pergolakan di Aceh* (Jakarta: P.T. Gunung Agung, 1982); also, Nazaruddin Sjamsuddin, *The Republican Revolt*.
121 Edward Aspinall, 'Violence and Identity Formation in Aceh Under Indonesian Rule', in Anthony Reid (ed.), *Verandah of Violence*, p. 158.
122 Eric Morris, 'Social Revolution and the Islamic Vision', in Audrey Kahin (ed.), *Regional Dynamics of the Indonesian Revolution: Unity From Diversity*, p. 104.
123 A discussion of grievances expressed by the Acehnese elite during this period can be found in Eric Morris, 'Islam and Politics in Aceh: A Study of Centre-Periphery Relations in Indonesia', PhD thesis, Cornell University, 1983, pp. 172–178.
124 Edward Aspinall, *Islam and Nation: Separatist Rebellion in Aceh, Indonesia* (Stanford, CA: Stanford University Press, 2009), p. 31.
125 Nazaruddin Sjamsuddin, *The Republican Revolt*, p. 208.
126 *Ibid.*
127 'Dewan Perwakilan Rakjat Atjeh: Dalam sedjarah pembentukan dan perkembangan Pemerintahan di Atjeh sedjak Proklemasi 1945 sampai awal tahun 1966 dan Produk-produk Legislatif', Sekretariat DPRD-GR Propinsi Daerah Istimewa Atjeh, 1965, p. 17.
128 *Ibid.*, p. 22.
129 For an example of dialogue within Aceh's provincial government at the time, see *Keputusan-keputusan dan Bahan-bahan dari Musjawarah Kerukunan Rakjat Atjeh jang Berlangsung dari Tanggal 18 s/d 21 Desember 1962* (Kutaradja: Musjawarah Kerukunan Rakjat Atjeh, 1962).
130 Interview with Teuku Ali Basyah, Banda Aceh, 28 December 2011, p. 3.
131 *Laporan Tahunan Lengkap*, p. 9.
132 *Ibid.*, p. 10.

133 A more detailed overview of the emergence and history of the PKI in Aceh can be found in Jess Melvin, *A Silent Massacre: The Indonesian Communist Party and the 1965 Mass Killings in Aceh*, Honours thesis, The University of Melbourne, 2009, pp. 19–31.

134 *Ibid.*, pp. 19–20.

135 John Bowen, *Sumatran Politics and Poetics: Gayo History, 1900–1989* (New Haven: Yale University Press, 1991), p. 102.

136 Interview with "Coan", Medan, North Sumatra, 26 December 2010.

137 M. Nafiah, 'Pemandangan Umum dari Golongan Nasionalis dalam DPRD- GR Daerah Istimewa Atjeh Dalam Sidang Pleno Ke II Tentang Pelaksanaan Unsur2 Sjari'at Islam Bagi Pemeluk2nja', in *Pelaksanaan Unsur-Unsur Sjari'at Agama Islam di Daerah Istimewa Atjeh* (Implementation of Elements of Islamic Religious Law in Aceh Special Region)', Sekretariat DPRD-GR Daerah Istimewa Atjeh, 10 November 1962, p. 101.

138 *Pelaksanaan Unsur-Unsur Sjari'at Agama Islam di Daerah Istimewa Atjeh*, pp. 94, 101.

139 For example, see, 'Mustafa Miga: Rituling Ali Hasjmy harus dipertjepat', *Harian Rakjat*, 27 February 1964, p. 1.

140 An account of this incident can be found in Jess Melvin, *A Silent Massacre*, pp. 27–29.

141 Airgram from James F. O'Connor, First Secretary of Embassy for the Ambassador, US Embassy Jakarta to US Department of State, 25 March 1964. My sincere thanks to Michael Leigh for bringing this airgram to my attention.

142 Djuarsa had gained notoriety in 1963 for a campaign against members of the Chinese community in Bandung, West Java, whom he suspected of being aligned with the PKI. David Jenkins, *Suharto and His Generals: Indonesia's Military Politics, 1975–1983* (Ithaca, NY: Cornell Modern Indonesia Project, Southeast Asia Program, Cornell University, 1984), p. 105.

143 'Bebaskan Thaib Adamy', Sidang Pleno ke-II CC PKI, Kongres Nasional PKI Ke-VII, in Thaib Adamy, *Atjeh Mendakwa* (Banda Aceh: Comite PKI Atjeh, 1964), p. 126. Adamy believed he was arrested out of revenge for Jasin's removal. An account of this incident can be found in Jess Melvin, *A Silent Massacre*, pp. 25–27.

144 Asan, the sole surviving member of the PKI's Provincial Secretariat in Aceh, for example, remarks that "Njak Adam Kamil gave his blessing to the PKI". Interview with Asan, Hong Kong, 31 October 2011, p. 12.

145 Afifah Sholihana, 'Perjuangan Polri di Tlogowaru-Malang 1945–1947', Prodi Pendidikan Sejarah, Universitas Negeri Malang. Available online: http://jurnal-online.um.ac.id/data/artikel/artikel3880284A08FE5DE02953C6577B54D1CA.pdf.

146 From August 1962, representatives within Aceh's provincial government are referred to as belonging to various 'groups' (*golongan*), including 'Nationalist', 'Technocrat', 'Islamic', 'Christian' and 'Communist' groups. See 'Rapat antara Pimpinan DPRD-GR dengan Ketua2 Golongan', *Pelaksanaan Unsur-Unsur Sjari'at Islam di Daerah Istimewa Aceh*, Secretariat DPRD-GR Daerah Istimewa Atjeh, 10 November 1962, p. 181.

147 'Berita Daerah: Pidie', *Harian Rakjat*, 1 September 1965, p. 2; 'Berita Daerah: Atjeh Utara', *Harian Rakjat*, 1 March 1965; and 'Berita Daerah: Atjeh Timur', *Harian Rakjat*, 1 March 1965, p. 2.

148 This included branches in Sigli and East Aceh, as well as three BTI subdistrict branches in Simpang Tiga, Batee and Ulim in Pidie. 'Berita Daerah: Sigli', *Harian Rakjat*, 6 April 1965, p. 2; 'Berita Daerah: Langsa', *Harian Rakjat*, 3 March 1965, p. 2; and 'Berita Daerah', *Harian Rakjat*, 3 April 1965, p. 2.

149 This included branches in Banda Aceh, Bireuen, North Aceh and Pase. 'Berita Daerah: Banda Atjeh', *Harian Rakjat*, 6 March 1965, p. 2; and 'Berita Daerah: Banda Atjeh', *Harian Rakjat*, 13 May 1965, p. 2.

150 This included branches in Banda Aceh, Sigli and regional Pidie. 'Berita Daerah: Banda Atjeh', *Harian Rakjat*, 17 July 1965, p. 2; 'Berita Daerah: Sigli', *Harian Rakjat*, 15 April 1965, p. 2; and 'Berita Daerah: Pidi [sic.]', *Harian Rakjat*, 4 May 1965, p. 2.

151 This included branches in Banda Aceh and Aceh Besar. 'Berita Daerah: Banda Atjeh', *Harian Rakjat*, 12 March 1965, p. 2; 'Berita Daerah: Banda Atjeh', 18 September 1965, p. 2.

152 An additional twelve affiliated branches existed throughout the province. 'Berita Daerah: Banda Atjeh', *Harian Rakjat*, 18 September 1965, p. 2.

153 'Berita Daerah: Atjeh Timur', *Harian Rakjat*, 1 March 1965, p. 2.

154 'Berita Daerah: Sigli', *Harian Rakjat*, 15 February 1965, p. 2.

155 (Instruksi No. 9/64 Mendaneg), 'Berita Daerah: Atjeh Timur', *Harian Rakjat*, 1 March 1965, p. 2.

156 'Berita Daerah: Atjeh Utara', *Harian Rakjat*, 1 March 1965, p. 2.

157 'Ultah ke-45 PKI di Atjeh', *Harian Rakjat*, 27 June 1965, p. 2.

158 'Rapat Umum Ultah ke-45 PKI di Atjeh', *Harian Rakjat*, 21 June 1965, p. 2.

159 'Daftar Riwayat Hidup', prepared by Dahlan Sulaiman, given to the author, 29 December 2011 in Banda Aceh, p. 1.

160 Interview with Dahlan Sulaiman, Banda Aceh, Aceh, 29 December 2011, p. 8.

161 Interview with Zainuddin Hamid, "Let Bugeh", Banda Aceh, Aceh, 17 December 2010, p. 3.

162 'Berita Daerah', *Harian Rakjat*, 6 March 1965, p. 2.

163 Asan is unsure of his exact date and place of birth, though he believes he was born in around 1932, most likely in Singapore. His father was killed fighting in Malaya against the Japanese and, at four or five years of age, Asan moved with his mother to Meulaboh, West Aceh. His mother worked as a teacher at an *Asosiasi Huakiau* (Ch. '*Hua Chiao Tsung Hui*', *or* 'Association of Overseas Chinese') affiliated middle school (discussed at length in chapter 7). Asan joined the PKI in Sigli, northern Aceh, in 1957. Prior to this time, he had served as secretary for the *Asosiasi* and was involved with Baperki. He joined the PKI for ideological reasons. As he has recalled, "I had read many books in Chinese about the Communist struggle . . . I thought, if I can't join the revolution in China, if I have the chance to join the struggle in Indonesia, that is also good." Interview with Asan, Hong Kong, 31 October 2011, pp. 1, 25; and, Written personal account by Asan, given to the author, Hong Kong, 30 October 2011, pp. 1, 3.

164 Interview with Zainuddin Hamid, "Let Bugeh", Banda Aceh, Aceh, 17 December 2010, p. 3.

165 Interview with Dahlan Sulaiman, Banda Aceh, Aceh, 29 December 2011, p. 25.

166 *Ibid.*, p. 26.

167 Interview with Dahlan Sulaiman, Banda Aceh, Aceh, 29 December 2011, p. 13.

168 Interview with Zainuddin Hamid, "Let Bugeh", Banda Aceh, Aceh, 17 December 2010, p. 1.

169 Interview with "Coan", Medan, North Sumatra, 26 December 2010, p. 9.

170 Harold Crouch, *The Army and Politics in Indonesia*, p. 142.

171 Ulf Sundhaussen, *The Road to Power*, pp. 218–219.

172 In 1965, the present-day districts of Bireuen, North Aceh and Lhokseumawe were grouped together as a single expanded 'North Aceh' district.

173 Anthony Reid, *An Indonesian Frontier: Acehnese and Other Histories of Sumatra* (Singapore: Singapore University Press, 2005), pp. 26–27.

174 The North Aceh oil and gas industry, which would come to dominate the district's economy, was not established until the 1970s.

175 Interview with "Hamid", Lhokseumawe, North Aceh, 19 December 2011, p. 1.

176 *Ibid.*, p. 6.

177 *Ibid.*, p. 7.

178 *Ibid.*, p. 2.

179 *Ibid.*, p. 4.
180 The name and location of "Kampung X" has been withheld to protect the identities of interviewees.
181 Interview with "Tjoet" (a pseudonym), Kampung X, North Aceh, 11 February 2009, p. 1.
182 *Ibid.*, p. 2.
183 "Hasan" is a pseudonym. *Ibid.*
184 *Ibid.*, p. 13.
185 Interview with "Tjoet", Kampung X, North Aceh, 11 February 2009, p. 17.
186 *Ibid.* An account of the PKI's national campaign to win village-based support can be found in Rex Mortimer, *Indonesian Communism Under Sukarno*, pp. 227–328.
187 *Ibid.*
188 Interview with "Tjoet", Kampung X, North Aceh, 11 February 2009, p. 14.
189 "Zahara" is a pseudonym. *Ibid.*, p. 14.
190 "Jamil" (a pseudonym) does not recall the exact year he was born. Interview with "Jamil", Kampung X, North Aceh, 11 February 2009, p. 4.
191 *Ibid.*, p. 5.
192 *Ibid.*, p. 9.
193 *Ibid.*
194 *Ibid.*, pp. 10–11.
195 *Ibid.*, pp. 12–13.
196 *Ibid.*, p. 26.
197 John Bowen, 'The Transformation of an Indonesian Property System: "Adat", Islam and Social Change in the Gayo Highlands', *American Ethnologist*, Vol. 15, No. 2 (May 1988), p. 278.
198 Interview with Ibrahim Kadir, Takengon, Central Aceh, 7 February 2009, p. 1.
199 *Ibid.*, pp. 6, 14.
200 *Ibid.*, p. 6.
201 *Ibid.*, p. 14.
202 *Ibid.*
203 The Batak are an ethnic group from North Sumatra.
204 The Minang are an ethnic group from West Sumatra.
205 Interview with Ibrahim Kadir, Takengon, Central Aceh, 7 February 2009, p. 14.
206 *Ibid.*, pp. 12–13.
207 It is not clear why Kadir gives the acronym 'WMD' when the full name for the group, according to his account, forms the acronym 'WDM'. Ishak Djuarsa refers to this militia group "mentioned by Ibrahim Kadir" (which Djuarsa denies existed) as the "Emergency Mandatory Military [Service?]" (WMD: *Wajib Militer Darurat*), which would seem to better fit the acronym. 'Ishak Djuarsa: Sejak 1967, Pak Harto Sudah Seperti Imam yang Batal Wudu", *Tempo*, 2 April 2000, p. 39. '*Darurat Militer*' is the usual term for 'martial law', while '*Wajib Militer*' can mean 'conscription'.
208 Interview with Ibrahim Kadir, Takengon, Central Aceh, 7 February 2009, p. 13.
209 *Ibid.*, p. 5.
210 *Ibid.*, p. 6.
211 *Ibid.*, p. 4.
212 Interview with "Latifah" (a pseudonym), Banda Aceh, 15 February 2009, p. 1.
213 Muhammadiyah, meaning "followers of Muhammad", was founded in 1912 in Yogyakarta as a modernist Islamic organisation. In 1945 it advocated an Islamic state for Indonesia and joined Masjumi but survived the banning of Masjumi in 1960.
214 "Said" is a pseudonym. *Ibid.*, p. 2.
215 *Ibid.*
216 *Ibid.*
217 *Ibid.*, p. 4.
218 Interview with "Abdullah", Takengon, Central Aceh, 9 February 2009, p. 1.

219 *Ibid.*, p. 4.
220 *Ibid.*, p. 3.
221 *Ibid.*
222 *Ibid.*, p. 11.
223 In 1818, thirty-five ships from Salem and Boston arrived on Aceh's west coast. Upon their departure, they took with them 4,500 tons of pepper. Anthony Reid, *A History of Southeast Asia: A Critical Crossroads* (West Sussex: Wiley Blackwell, 2015), p. 197.
224 'West Aceh Bans Tight Trousers', *BBC News*, 28 October 2009. Available online: http://news.bbc.co.uk/2/hi/asia-pacific/8329804.stm.
225 Interview with T.M. Yatim, Meulaboh, West Aceh, 3 December 2011, p. 23.
226 *Ibid.*, p. 1.
227 *Ibid.*, p. 23.
228 *Ibid.*, p. 15.
229 *Ibid.*, p. 3.
230 *Ibid.*, p. 5.
231 Grated coconut (*kelapa kukur*), often cooked with egg, is an extremely cheap and unpretentious meal.
232 *Ibid.*, p. 6.
233 *Ibid.*
234 *Ibid.*, p. 5.
235 *Ibid.*, p. 4.
236 See, for example, 'Legenda Tuan Tapa dan Putri Naga', 5 January 2014. Available online: https://dmilano.wordpress.com/aceh-selatan/legenda-tuan-tapa-dan-putri-naga/.
237 John Bowen, *Sumatran Politics and Poetics*, p. 61.
238 Interview with "Oesman", Tapaktuan, South Aceh, 6 December 2011, p. 16.
239 *Ibid.*, p. 2.
240 *Ibid.*, p. 19.
241 *Ibid.*, p. 2.
242 The PNI was established in Jakarta in 1927 under the leadership of Sukarno.
243 Interview with "Oesman", Tapaktuan, South Aceh, 6 December 2011, p. 2.
244 *Ibid.*, p. 3.
245 *Ibid.*
246 The 'Bandar Betsy affair' refers to an event that occurred on the Banda Betsy plantation in Simalungun, North Sumatra in May 1965. In 1963, land used by peasants since the Japanese occupation was ploughed up for the plantation's use but then replanted by the peasants. On 13 May 1965, the land was ploughed up again by the plantation. When the peasants returned the next day to replant it a pensioned Warrant Officer named Sudjono was killed while attempting to obstruct the peasants. The army claimed Sudjono had been unarmed and attacked by the peasants, while the PKI-affiliated BTI, which had supported the peasants, along with other witnesses, testified at the ensuing trial that Sudjono had a pistol and beat several peasants before he was attacked. The trial become a major event and was eventually forced to relocate to Jakarta after Sumatra's Inter-Regional Military Commander Mokoginta threatened to arrest its judge, who Mokoginta claimed appeared reluctant to rule against the PKI. Harold Crouch, *The Army and Politics in Indonesia*, pp. 87–88, n. 46–47.
247 Interview with "Oesman", Tapaktuan, South Aceh, 6 December 2011, p. 2.
248 Interview with "Hamzah" (a pseudonym), Tapaktuan, South Aceh, 5 November 2011, p. 1.
249 *Ibid.*, p. 2.
250 *Ibid.*
251 *Ibid.*
252 *Ibid.*, p. 3.
253 Interview with "Ali" (a pseudonym), Sama Dua, South Aceh, 6 December 2011, p. 2.
254 *Ibid.*, p. 3.

255 An account of the Bakongan Revolt can be found in Anthony Reid, *The Blood of the People*, pp. 10, 20.
256 Adding to this sense of competitiveness, the founding member of the PKI in neighbouring East Sumatra, Xarim M. S., who had helped lead East Sumatra's social revolution, had originally been a leader in the PNI. *Ibid.*, p. 173.
257 Interview with "Ali", Sama Dua, South Aceh, 6 December 2011, p. 6.
258 *Ibid.*, p. 3.
259 For an account of life on the plantations during the colonial period, see, Ann Laura Stoler, *Capitalism and Confrontation in Sumatra's Plantation Belt*, 2nd ed. (Ann Arbor, MI: University of Michigan Press, 1995, originally 1985).
260 Nazaruddin Sjamsuddin, *The Republican Revolt*, p. 38.
261 Interview with "Saifuddin", Idi, East Aceh, 11 December 2011, p. 1.
262 *Ibid.*, p. 2.
263 *Ibid.*, p. 13.
264 *Ibid.*, p. 14.
265 *Ibid.*, p. 16.
266 *Ibid.*, p. 17.
267 *Ibid.*, p. 18.
268 One of the oldest Chinese temples in Southeast Asia can be found in Idi. During colonial times, Chinese from the Malay Peninsula would travel to Idi to facilitate trade across the Strait. 'Menelusuri Jejak Cina di Idi', *Atjeh Times*, 20 September 2012.
269 The local population also felt a cultural affinity with the Malaysian leader Tengku Abdul Rahman. This was because, Saifuddin explained, "Tengku", a formal term of address for certain Malay nobility, is also used in Aceh. Interview with "Saifuddin", Idi, East Aceh, 11 December 2011, p. 18.
270 Interview with "Taufik" (a pseudonym), Village 1, Tamiang, East Aceh, 18 December 2011, p. 1.
271 The name and location of "Village 1" has been withheld to protect the identities of interviewees.
272 Interview with "Taufik", Village 1, Tamiang, East Aceh, 18 December 2011, p. 1.
273 *Ibid.*, p. 2.
274 The name and location of "Village 2" has been withheld to protect the identities of interviewees. Interview with "Taufik", Village 1, Tamiang, East Aceh, 18 December 2011, p. 2.
275 "Pak Rusdi" is a pseudonym. *Ibid.*, p. 18.
276 *Ibid.*, p. 4.
277 Interview with "Taufik", Village 1, Tamiang, East Aceh, 18 December 2011, p. 4.
278 *Ibid.*
279 Ann Laura Stoler, *Capitalism and Confrontation in Sumatra's Plantation Belt*, p. 179.
280 Interview with "Taufik", Village 1, Tamiang, East Aceh, 18 December 2011, p. 11.
281 *Ibid.*, p. 3.
282 *Ibid.*, p. 10.
283 *Ibid.*, pp. 7–8.
284 *Ibid.*, p. 8.
285 *Ibid.*, p. 14.
286 *Ibid.*, p. 15. Taufik cannot recall the date of this incident.
287 *Ibid.*
288 Interview with "Karim" (a pseudonym) and "Aminah" (a pseudonym), Village 2, Tamiang, East Aceh, 12 December 2011, p. 15.
289 *Ibid.* A study of LEKRA nationally can be found in, Keith Foulcher, *Social Commitment in Literature and the Arts: The Indonesian "Institute of People's Culture", 1950–1965* (Clayton, Victoria: Centre of Southeast Asian Studies, Monash University, 1986). This book includes a reproduction of a rare short story by a LEKRA member from Aceh, Teuku Iskandar, T. Iskandar, 'Komunis Pertama'. I interviewed

Teuku Iskandar and a second LEKRA member from Central Aceh, Permadi Liosta, during research for my honours thesis. Both men recalled how LEKRA had been popular in Aceh when they joined during the early 1950s. Both Iskandar and Liosta were in Jakarta at the time of the genocide. Interview with Teuku Iskandar, Jakarta, 1 February 2009; and, Interview with Permadi Liosta, Jakarta, 2 February 2009.

290 Interview with "Karim" and "Aminah", Village 2, Tamiang, East Aceh, 12 December 2011, p. 17.

291 *Ibid.*, p. 19.

292 "Pak Joesoef" is a pseudonym.

293 "Karim" is a pseudonym. *Ibid.*, p. 1.

294 *Ibid.*, p. 7.

295 *Ibid.*, p. 5. For an account of the PKI's educational campaigns and cadre schools nationally during this period, see Ruth McVey, 'Teaching Modernity: The PKI as an Educational Institution', *Indonesia*, Vol. 50 (October 1990), pp. 5–27.

296 "Pak Rusdi", "Pak Saleh" and "Djoened" are pseudonyms. Interview with "Karim" and "Aminah", Village 2, Tamiang, East Aceh, 12 December 2011, pp. 5, 10.

297 Gerry van Klinken, *The Making of Middle Indonesia: Middle Classes in Kupang Town, 1930s–1980s* (Leiden and Boston: Brill, 2014), p. 156.

298 Interview with "Karim" and "Aminah", Village 2, Tamiang, East Aceh, 12 December 2011, p. 7.

299 *Ibid.*, pp. 4–5.

300 *Ibid.*, p. 4.

301 *Ibid.*

302 *Ibid.*, p. 12.

303 For an account of political life on military-controlled plantations in North Sumatra, see, Ann Laura Stoler, *Capitalism and Confrontation in Sumatra's Plantation Belt*. For an account of the role of the Pemuda Pancasila in North Sumatra see, Loren Ryter, 'Pemuda Pancasila: The Last Loyalist Free Men of Suharto's New Order?', *Indonesia*, Vol. 66 (October 1998), pp. 45–73.

304 Interview with "Karim" and "Aminah", Village 2, Tamiang, East Aceh, 12 December 2011, p. 12.

305 *Ibid.*, p. 3.

3 The order to annihilate
1–6 October

Aceh's military leadership was uniquely positioned on the morning of 1 October 1965 to respond to news of the actions of the 30 September Movement with a concerted attack against the PKI that was aimed at seizing state power. As the previous chapter demonstrates, this unique position was a result of the extensive preparations the military had undertaken in the province to prime existing military commands, mobilise civilian militias and implement incursions into civilian government during the lead-up to 1 October. The military's position was greatly assisted by the chance occurrence that on the morning of 1 October, Aceh's military and political leadership, along with key members of Sumatra's regional military and political leadership, one of Indonesia's Deputy Prime Ministers and a national member of the PKI's Politbureau happened to be in Langsa, East Aceh, attending a routine government meeting.[1] This coincidence helped the military leadership present at this meeting to establish a coordinated interpretation of events, enabling the military to launch a swift and coordinated attack against the PKI in the province from day one.

As will be shown, this attack was led centrally from Jakarta through the insubordinate leadership of Suharto, down through Sumatra's Inter-Regional Military Commander for Sumatra, Ahmad Junus Mokoginta, and Aceh's Military Commander, Ishak Djuarsa, who utilised the KOTI chain of command throughout Sumatra to effectively paralyse civilian government in Aceh before launching its attack. This attack, named 'Operasi Berdikari',[2] was activated on 1 October and was conceived of from its inception as a military operation to physically destroy the PKI. The attack was consolidated over the next five days, as the military leadership imposed martial law over Aceh and paralysed civilian government in the province. This attack, led nationally by Suharto, brought the Indonesian military to power and set the scene for the horrific killings that would shortly follow.

The morning of 1 October

On the morning of 1 October, Aceh's military and political leadership, including members of Aceh's provincial government and members of Aceh's Pantja Tunggal body, comprising of: Aceh's Governor, Aceh's Chief Public Prosecutor, Police Commander, *Front Nasional* Representative and Aceh's Military Commander

Djuarsa (who would arrive at 2pm), were in Langsa, East Aceh to attend a routine "Mass Meeting". They were joined by Sumatra's Inter-Regional Military Commander Mokoginta, North Sumatra's Military Commander Darjatmo and North Sumatra's Governor Sitepu, along with Indonesia's Deputy Prime Minister Soebandrio and national PKI Politbureau member Njoto, both of whom were scheduled to speak as 'special guests' at the meeting.[3]

According to Teuku Ali Basyah, who attended the meeting in his capacity as Head Provincial Government Spokesperson, its purpose was "to discuss many issues, including the Dwikora campaign, safety and government".[4] As Basyah waited for the meeting to get underway, he sat out the front of the East Aceh Bupati's house as Djuarsa, Mokoginta, Darjatmo, Sitepu, Soebandrio and Njoto travelled up from the North Sumatran border. The night before he and his colleagues had attended the closing night celebrations of the Indonesian Islamic Union Party's (PSII: *Partai Sarekat Islam Indonesia*)[5] Regional Conference for Aceh Special Region in Langsa.[6] The PSII's national president Anwar Tjokroaminoto and Aceh's former Governor Ali Hasjmy[7] (who had been deposed by a concerted PKI-led "retooling" campaign in 1964) had flown in from Jakarta for the event, drawing a large crowd of supporters from around the province.[8] Aceh's political leadership was enjoying a honeymoon period with the central government. Aceh was once again a province. The Darul Islam had been saved a humiliating surrender and its fighters were being reintegrated into the national army. Sukarno was still widely disliked and mistrusted, but the Army's National Chief of Staff, General Nasution, had proven himself to be the Acehnese elite's closest ally. The imminent arrival of Soebandrio, who Sundhaussen has described as "Sukarno's closest protégé",[9] and Njoto, must have appeared less of a challenge than it might have the year before, when Sukarno had reprimanded and then removed Aceh's previous Military Commander, Muhammad Jasin, for attempting to override democratic decision-making processes in the province by implementing aspects of Islamic law by sidestepping Aceh's provincial government. It appears that delegates outside Djuarsa's immediate circle had yet to hear news of the actions of the 30 September Movement.[10] Djuarsa, meanwhile, who had remained in Langsa to await the arrival of Soebandrio, Njoto and Mokoginta, appears to have first heard news about the actions of the 30 September Movement during the morning, when he received and responded to telegrams from Suharto and Mokoginta, as well as through personal contact with Mokoginta after 1pm.

According to the national newspaper *Waspada*, Soebandrio had left for Sumatra on 27 September with twelve ministers on a week-long 'socialisation' tour to consolidate the *Ganyang Malaysia* campaign at the "front line against that English nation (Malaysia)".[11] The intended destinations for this tour included Medan, Aceh, Padang, Bengkulu and Lampung. On the morning of 1 October, Soebandrio and Njoto were still in Medan when they heard about events in Jakarta over the radio between 6 and 8am.[12] At this time Soebandrio grouped together his entourage to discuss whether they should proceed with their plan to travel on to Aceh later that morning.[13] Soebandrio claimed at his 1966 show trial that he was uncertain about the authenticity of broadcasts from Jakarta announcing the actions of the 30 September Movement and worried that they may be fake "psywar" broadcasts from Malaysia.[14] Anxious not to cause a "panic" and calculating that the group had the means of maintaining contact with Medan and Jakarta, Soebandrio decided to carry on, with Mokoginta, Darjatmo and Sitepu travelling in their convoy.[15] Such a prestigious convoy was consistent with the seniority of Soebandrio's office, though it can also be assumed that Mokoginta and Darjatmo, both ardent anti-communists, and Sitepu, one of Indonesia's two PKI-allied Governors,[16] would have had a keen interest in Soebandrio and Njoto's public announcements. The *Ganyang Malaysia* campaign had become a proxy for the struggle between the military leadership and the PKI, with very concrete ramifications for Aceh and North Sumatra due to the proximity of the two provinces to the Malay Peninsula. Of key concern to the military was the recently implemented program to train and mobilise civilian militia groups in Sumatra, particularly along coastal areas, under the auspices of preparing for a potential attack from across the Malacca Strait. As described in Chapter 2, this program had initially been proposed by the PKI, but, fearing that such training was intended to establish a 'Fifth Force', or people's army, it had been quickly brought under the direction of Mokoginta in Sumatra, who subsequently enthusiastically expanded the program to include large-scale military operations such as the Operasi Singgalang, to prepare the military to seize state power.

Orders from Jakarta and Medan

According to the Aceh Military's Command's official Chronology, the first order sent to Djuarsa on 1 October was sent from the "Men/Pangad" (Minister/ Commander of the Armed Forces) and conveyed "news" that "a Coup movement has occurred under the leadership of Lieut[enant] Col[onel] Untung".[17] Considering that Suharto had assumed the position of Minister and Commander of the Armed Forces between 6.30 and 7am on 1 October and then refused to surrender this position on Sukarno's request at 4pm,[18] it can be assumed that the "Men/ Pangad" in this order refers to Suharto himself. This order was sent during the morning and appears to be the earliest known record of such an order sent by Suharto on this day. His next known order was not sent until later that evening at 9pm.[19] Here I do not intend to propose that Suharto chose for some reason to inform Djuarsa first, rather that it is likely this order was sent to all regional military commanders at this time, though copies of this order have yet to be discovered elsewhere. This would make logistical sense. It also supports Suharto's claim later that evening that "now we are able to control the situation both in the centre and the regions".[20] The existence of this earlier order supports the notion that the military acted in a coordinated manner from the morning of 1 October and that the military under Suharto acted in a pre-emptive manner to claim that the 30 September Movement was a coup attempt. This is because the 30 September Movement itself, as we have seen, did not declare a challenge to Sukarno's power, and thus attempt to launch a "coup", until 2pm.[21] This order is thus highly significant and prompts the need for a reassessment of military coordination during the morning of 1 October. The military's actions in those hours were more pre-emptive than it has previously been possible to demonstrate.

A second order was subsequently received by Djuarsa, sent by Mokoginta acting in his capacity as Mandala Satu Commander for Sumatra (Panglatu). The contents of this order, which has been recorded in the Chronology (time unstated, though presumably shortly after Suharto's initial order) are as follows:

News has been received from the Panglatu regarding the Council of Generals affair in Jakarta, with the instructions to:

1   Remain calm in your various locations
2   Carry out your tasks as normally as you can
3   Guard the discipline of your troops as best you can
4   Await further orders/instructions from the Panglatu.[22]

This order establishes that Mokoginta was in contact with Suharto during the morning of 1 October, and that the military leadership in Sumatra was utilising the KOTI command structure, under which the position of Panglatu existed, at the national and inter-provincial levels to lead its offensive from the morning of 1 October. Moreover, it can be argued that by accepting Suharto's self-appointment as military commander and his interpretation of the 30 September Movement as a "coup", Mokoginta, like Suharto, acted in an insubordinate manner when he subsequently refused to obey Sukarno's order that Suharto step down from his position as temporary Commander of the Armed Forces.

That Djuarsa accepted Mokoginta's authority is demonstrated in the records of two orders that he subsequently sent, which the Chronology states were "based upon the aforementioned instructions" to "relay the orders of the Panglatu to the troops under Djuarsa's command".[23] Moreover, these two instructions ('*Notakilat: -5/Kes/65 10020100*' and '*TERANG/G-1/1001180/65*'), are identified in the Chronology as radiograms from the 'Pangdahan 'A'' – that is, Djuarsa acting is his capacity as Defence Region Commander 'A' (Pangdahan: *Panglima Komando Daerah Tahanan 'A'*), which, as we have seen, had been established in Aceh on 1 August 1965 and activated on 1 October under the Kohanda Command structure as part of Operasi Berdikari. These two instructions are the earliest examples of this new position being used and appear to corroborate the understanding that the Operasi Berdikari was indeed activated on 1 October to facilitate the military's attack against the PKI.[24]

9–10am: Soebandrio arrives in Pangkalan Brandan

Between 9 and 10am, Soebandrio's convoy made a stop at Pangkalan Brandan, a relatively obscure oil town 25 km within the North Sumatran side of the provincial border.[25] Soebandrio had planned to deliver a prepared speech to workers at the oil field.[26] Captain Rani Junus, Permina's (*Perusahaan Minyak Nasional: National Oil Company*) Acting Manager, however, objected, wishing to keep the tight rein on labour unrest that he and the oil field's "paramilitary company security force"[27] had rigidly maintained since the end of the PRRI rebellion in the area.[28] When Soebandrio insisted, Rani eventually allowed Soebandrio to address a group of eighty work supervisors and section heads in the Permina guesthouse, where he is said to have "exhorted the men to remain diligent in their work [and] be prepared for important developments in the near future".[29] There is no reason to read anything conspiratorial into these announcements.

Soebandrio's actions on 1 October have long been scrutinised by New Order officials and ideologues in an attempt to portray his complicity in the actions of the 30 September Movement. During his 1966 show trial, for example, Soebandrio, who became targeted by the New Order as "the chief official scapegoat for Sukarno's policies",[30] was quizzed at length about his whereabouts and actions on the morning of 1 October.[31] Soebandrio's absence from Jakarta on 1 October presented a particular challenge for those attempting to portray his guilt, with early attempts made to implicate him as the central "mastermind" behind the coup itself. Indeed, a confidential telegram sent at 5.06am on 1 October from the US Consulate in Medan to the US State Department went so far as to make the extraordinary claim that "[m]ilitary sources speculate . . . this [the actions of the 30 September Movement] is Subandrio coup against army".[32] Why Soebandrio would choose to launch a coup movement in Jakarta as he travelled between Medan and Aceh is not explained; nor is why he would choose to spend the first crucial hours following the actions of the 30 September Movement addressing staff at an obscure oil field. Soebandrio's speech in Pangkalan Brandan should be viewed with this in mind. Indeed, the overall account of Soebandrio and his convoy's presence in Pangkalang Brandan appears to indicate that a sense of confusion and cautiousness prevailed. "All conversations" between Soebandrio, his convoy, Rani and his staff as they sat down to eat breakfast together following Soebandrio's speech, Anderson Bartlett has explained in his 1972 company history of Pertamina (as Permina would come to be named),[33] "centred on the events of the night before in Djakarta."[34] "Nobody had any certain information," however.[35] Soebandrio, for his part, is said to have debated with the members of his convoy whether or not the group should proceed to Langsa, before eventually departing during "the early part of the afternoon" with the assurance that the group would be able to maintain radio contact with both Medan and Jakarta.[36]

1pm: Djuarsa joins the convoy

At 1pm, Soebandrio's convoy arrived at the provincial border, where it was joined by Djuarsa and members of the Aceh Pantja Tunggal.[37] According to Djuarsa, the group then stopped in Kualasimpang, 12 km inside Aceh, for fifteen minutes, where both Soebandrio and Mokoginta received radiograms from Jakarta.[38] Djuarsa has alleged that Mokoginta's radiogram was sent from Brigadier General Sobiran, who had assisted Suharto in persuading troops who had come out in support of the 30 September Movement in the capital to disband, and that Soebandrio's radiogram was from Air Marshal Omar Dhani, Commander of the Indonesian Air Force, who had assisted the 30 September Movement to find Sukarno earlier that morning, and who is said to have insisted that Soebandrio return immediately to Jakarta. Soebandrio himself makes no note of this stopover in his account of the day[39] and Djuarsa's account should be treated with caution. In a rare 2000 interview with *Tempo* magazine, Djuarsa denied knowing why Soebandrio and Njoto were travelling to Langsa, stating in an apparent attempt to portray Soebandrio and Njoto's actions as suspicious, and in complete contradiction to his sworn 1966 testimony that he "didn't know" what they were doing there.[40] Djuarsa's allegations and denials point to the significance that has been placed on the early hours of 1 October by New Order officials and ideologues, who, through this narrow focus, seek to both justify and overwrite the story of the genocide with such accounts. This obfuscation may also expose sensitivity about Djuarsa's own actions on this momentous day.

2pm: The convoy arrives in Langsa

Soebandrio, Njoto, Djuarsa, Mokoginta, Darjatmo and Sitepu arrived in Langsa at around 2pm. Mokoginta, Darjatmo and Sitepu immediately departed to return to Medan, while Soebandrio, Njoto and Djuarsa took their places at the mass meeting.[41]

According to Basyah, the government meeting had opened as planned during the morning, with discussion remaining focused on the programmed agenda of the "Dwikora [campaign], security and government"[42] until Djuarsa and Soebandrio's convoy arrived at the meeting. At this time Soebandrio addressed the meeting, delivering a ten-minute speech.[43] The content of Soebandrio's speech is unfortunately not known. Djuarsa then delivered his own explosive speech. Basyah has recalled that Djuarsa was suddenly "very angry" and halted proceedings, declaring, "I've closed the meeting. The meeting is over. Go home!" Djuarsa then ordered the delegates to return to their posts, "some along the road through the interior . . . and some along the coastal road"[44] to await further instruction whilst bolstering government leadership in Aceh's districts. Djuarsa's decision to divide up delegates to return to Banda Aceh via different routes may have reflected a real fear that the movement in the capital might spread to the province. It may have alternatively signalled an understanding within the military leadership that a serious military mobilisation was about to be launched.

Basyah has recalled that Djuarsa through his speech to delegates characterised the actions of the 30 September Movement as a coup and as a coup that could occur on a national scale if "order" was not promptly restored, reasoning:

> NKRI [*Negara Kesatuan Republik Indonesia*: the Unitary State of Indonesia] is now controlled by them [the 30 September Movement] . . . Banda Aceh is currently empty [without political leadership]. . . . If it can happen in the centre, it could happen easily in the regions, you must return![45]

This statement may be the first example of the 30 September Movement being publicly characterised as a coup ("NKRI is now controlled by them") and pre-empts the 30 September Movement's own statements regarding the decommissioning of Sukarno's cabinet at 2pm that afternoon, which is generally regarded as the earliest point at which the Movement could be characterised as a "coup movement".

Djuarsa then arranged for a meeting to occur the following day in Banda Aceh between the provincial military and government leaders, before promptly departing himself for Banda Aceh.[46] Soebandrio and Njoto, meanwhile, left for Medan on a speedboat, arriving at the Belawan port just outside Medan, where they were put under the "protective custody" of Mokoginta and Darjatmo.[47] Basyah, meanwhile, remained in Langsa to help provide leadership and "join in with whatever was declared by Kodim".[48]

In ordering those attending the meeting to return to their posts and stating that the Indonesian state was under the control of the 30 September Movement, Djuarsa acted without endorsement from the President. Where Djuarsa gained authority to do this is pertinent to our understandings of military coordination of the attack against the PKI from 1 October. Djuarsa himself has claimed that after "hearing that several generals had been kidnapped in Jakarta . . . [m]y thoughts were straight away directed to a war situation. In such a situation I quickly acted to protect myself before I could be attacked. That is military principle".[49]

That Djuarsa's reaction was swift and based on an assessment that a war-like reaction was necessary is undoubtable. Along with military actions in Jakarta, Central Java[50] and North Sumatra,[51] it appears that Aceh was one of the first regions to experience the outbreak of the military's attack against the PKI. Djuarsa's swift response was undoubtedly cemented by his ability to coordinate directly with Suharto, Mokoginta and Darjatmo during the morning, as well as by his ability to gauge Soebandrio and Njoto's responses, allowing him to grasp the seriousness of events as well as the potential they presented to the military leadership to launch its long anticipated offensive against the PKI. That Djaursa may have believed the threat in Jakarta to be genuine at this time does not negate his insubordination, or his genocidal overreaction later on. Indeed, as the following chapters show, Djuarsa continued to escalate his attack even once it was clear that the 30 September Movement in the capital had been crushed. That Djuarsa's response was coordinated at the national, inter-provincial and provincial levels is now beyond doubt, thanks to the records of the orders he received and sent during the morning of 1 October and over the next two months.

Aceh's Governor Njak Adam Kamil also issued his own 'Declaration' (*Pernjataan No: b-7/10/DPRD-GR/65*) on behalf of Aceh's provincial government during the afternoon of 1 October while "on board a special train", as he steamed towards the provincial capital after the close of the mass meeting.[52] The Declaration consisted of two one-sentence statements. The first states the Aceh provincial government's:

> Resoluteness to remain loyal towards and to continue the revolution up until and including the victory of the Indonesian Revolution in accordance with the foundation and teaching provided by the Great Leader of the Indonesian Revolution, BUNG KARNO.[53]

The second declares the Provincial Government's "Resoluteness to sharpen the Dagger (*Rentjong*[54]) of Vigilance and to continue to support the unity of National revolutionary progressivism centred around Nasakom".[55] Nowhere are the actions of the 30 September Movement or the actual reaction to these events by the Indonesian military noted, nor does the document establish a series of events or outline specific actions to be taken. Why Kamil issued such a statement at this time is unknown, though it is significant that he felt the need to make such an announcement at this highly sensitive juncture. As explained in chapter 2, there is a perception among surviving PKI members from Aceh and Medan that Kamil was sympathetic towards the PKI, or at least not openly hostile toward the organisation. It may be that he was alarmed by the intensity of Suharto, Mokoginta and Djuarsa's statements and was aware of the campaign they were planning to launch and, not yet knowing how events would unfold, was keen to portray himself as more neutral than Djuarsa and Mokoginta. Alternatively, he may have been signalling that he intended to use his position as Governor and head of Aceh's provincial government to take a leading role in the military's attack against the PKI. As will be demonstrated repeatedly in what follows, Kamil would come to play a leading role in the military's annihilation campaign.

12pm: Mokoginta's midnight speech

At midnight, Mokoginta delivered a speech over the radio from Medan that explicitly stated the intentions of the military leadership. This speech, entitled 'Remain calm and full of vigilance towards all elements which damage and seek to destroy the Pancasila-Revolution-State and Our Nation, both from without as well as from within', declared that "a COUP DE 'ETAT" had been carried out "by those who call themselves the Indonesian Revolution Council or the 30 September Movement".[56] This coup attempt, the speech explains, was "counter revolutionary" and an act of "treachery towards the national revolution and our nation", thus establishing that participants in this "coup attempt" were to be considered enemies of the state. Mokoginta then proceeded to express grief regarding the generals who had been murdered, and relief that the President "that we love" had survived. He also stated that "the situation in the capital was able to be restored by the Armed Forces under the leadership of Major General Suharto", thus crediting Suharto with saving the nation and publically recognising his leadership in direct contradiction to Sukarno's order at 4pm that Suharto stand down. The speech then went on to announce:

5 Based on the above explanations and in order to safeguard the State/Nation and revolution, it is ordered **that all members of the Armed Forces resolutely and completely annihilate this counter-revolution and all acts of treason down to the roots.**

6 We request that all layers of civil society in Sumatra remain calm and on alert to all elements that are destroying and wish to destroy the Pantjasila-revolution-nation and our people, from both without and within.

7   In Sumatra we have already experienced in the past many types of "Councils" such as the Gadjah Council, the Banteng Council, Garuda Council etc.[57]
It turns out that these Councils have been the attempt of counter revolutionaries, which result in many victims among the people.

8   In order to save our revolution and state, which we love, we only adhere
to the Decree, Command, instructions, and speeches [*amanat*] of [Sukarno]
and, especially for the Army, the direct Instructions of the Supreme Commander of ABRI [*Angkatan Bersenjata Republik Indonesia*: Indonesian
Armed Forces], or those [instructions] channelled via the Temporary Leader
of the Armed Forces, Major General Suharto. . . .

9   I appeal to members of the Armed Forces: "Remain obedient to your Soldier's Pledge, that is: be obedient, loyal and respectful to your superiors."

10   Finally, be on guard, movements such as this do not necessarily need to be
initiated by the agents of Subversion – enemies of the revolution to weaken
the strength of the people and the Armed Forces.

11   With the protection of God, we will hopefully prevail – in control and eternal.

12   Independence! Long Live Bung Karno! Long Live the Indonesian
revolution![58]

This speech provides a major insight into the thinking of the military leadership
on 1 October. It is also, as far as I am aware, the earliest document to be recovered from throughout Indonesia to order "all members of the Armed Forces [to]
resolutely and completely annihilate this counter-revolution and all acts of treason
down to the roots". This statement is evidence that from day one the military leadership launched an offensive military campaign aimed at physically exterminating
those who had been "involved" with the 30 September Movement. This military
campaign was directly ordered by the military and was launched despite the military leadership knowing that security had already been restored in the capital.

Mokoginta's speech is also an example of the "dual leadership" that existed in
Indonesia and specifically in Sumatra from 1 October. While giving lip service
to Sukarno, such as by demanding that "all layers of civil society" remain calm
and follow the contents of Sukarno's 'Order of the Day', Mokoginta acted in an
insubordinate manner by declaring that he, and those troops under him, recognised "only" the "direct Instructions of the Supreme Commander of ABRI, [and]
those [instructions] channelled via the Temporary Leader of the Armed Forces,
Major General Suharto". This tactic allowed the military to claim that it acted
in the name of the state, while also allowing it to make full use of existing state
structures to launch its attack.

By citing other 'Council' movements, a reference to the Revolution Council
declared by the 30 September Movement, Mokoginta presumably intended to establish a sense of continuity with past common enemies and to provide a reminder of
past military responses, which, in the case of the PRRI rebellion, had included fierce
strafing and bombing by government airplanes and the mobilisation of civilians to
support the military's campaign.[59] These 'Council' movements had been manifestations of regional discontent with the central government led by regional military

commanders during the 1950s and were of particular significance in Aceh and North and West Sumatra. The Revolution Council was thus depicted as an armed rebellion to be put down militarily.

That the PKI is not explicitly identified in this speech is consistent with scholarly understandings of the military's reaction to the actions of the 30 September Movement. As Roosa has observed, "[Suharto] knew from the start that [the 30 September Movement] was an action that could be blamed on the Communist Party."[60] Mokoginta and Djuarsa, if anything, were even more firmly entrenched in this mindset, having both publicly distinguished themselves prior to 1 October as ardent opponents of the PKI, as evidenced by Mokoginta's response to the Bandar Betsy affair and Djuarsa's consolidation of military dominance within Aceh's Pantja Tunggal body. With the PKI completely on the back foot, and the 30 September Movement in tatters, Suharto, Mokoginta and Djuarsa could now "launch the army's plan for attacking the PKI and overthrowing Sukarno".[61] In this context, Mokoginta's warning that those responsible for the "movement" may not necessarily be easily identified as "agents of Subversion" may be interpreted as an attempt to introduce the notion that civilians, or at least non-traditional or "internal" opponents, might be a legitimate target of the military's attack. It is now certain that this attack was much more highly coordinated than has previously been thought provable.

Civilian youth militias begin to mobilise

It was not only the military that was beginning to move. Dahlan Sulaiman, a member of the PII (*Pelajar Islam Indonesia*: Indonesian Islamic High School Students) in Banda Aceh, who, as has been discussed in chapter 2, had been given civilian militia training by the military, and whose organisation would become involved in the *Front Pembela Pantja Sila* (Pantja Sila Defence Front) state-sponsored death squad that would help spearhead the killings in the province, has recalled how when he first heard news about the actions of the 30 September Movement in Jakarta over the radio, he "instinctively knew" that the PKI was behind the 30 September Movement.[62] As he explains, "[a]s people who had already been trained to understand the national political situation at the time, we, from that day [1 October 1965] already suspected that it was the communists who had done it." It was apparent to Sulaiman, as it was to the military leadership, that the events in Jakarta on the morning of 1 October presented anti-communist forces with the opportunity that they had been waiting for, just as it would have presumably been equally obvious to the PKI had the actions of the 30 September Movement been successful that such an event could have been used to their own strategic advantage. Sulaiman's apparent speed and independence in coming to this conclusion, as well as his swift reaction as outlined below, is nevertheless quite remarkable. According to Sulaiman, not only did he and his comrades from the PII come to the conclusion on the evening of 1 October that the 30 September Movement was the work of the PKI, but they sensed that events presented them with an opportunity to go on the offensive against the PKI. This response is consistent with the idea that political preparation had been undertaken in the province by the military leadership to prepare anti-communist political forces for a confrontation with the PKI. As Sulaiman has recalled:

> During the evening of 1 October, I immediately gathered comrades together to find large sheets of paper, newspapers, paint and paintbrushes, at the time there were yet to be permanent markers, to find Chinese ink and use small paintbrushes to write on the paper or the walls that this movement was a communist movement . . . I was the leader.[63]

Sulaiman and his comrades then proceeded to work into the night to produce the anti-communist posters that they would stick up throughout Banda Aceh during the early hours of 2 October until his remarkable confrontation with the military, as detailed below. Sulaiman has denied receiving instructions from the military to begin this poster campaign.[64] It is possible that he was acting independently of the military at this early stage, though it is now beyond doubt (as discussed below and in chapters 5 and 6) that civilian youth group members in Aceh, including Sulaiman, would soon receive instructions, encouragement and assistance from the military to carry out the abductions and killings that would follow. This timing is consistent with what is known about the formation of death squads nationally during this period. In Jakarta, the military worked directly with civilian youth group members from the evening of 1 October,[65] while in North Sumatra this occurred from 2 October.[66] On that very night in Jakarta, for example, Sulaiman's organisation, the PII, was being courted by the military, along with students from HMI and Gasbindo (*Gabungan Serikat Buruh Indonesia*: Amalgamated Indonesian Islamic Labour Federation[67]) to form a Muslim Action Command Against the Communists – the group that on 4 October would re-name itself as the newly expanded KAP-Gestapu (*Komando Aksi Pengganyangan – Gerakan Tiga Puluh September*: Action Command for the Crushing of the 30 September Movement) military-sponsored student death squad that would spearhead the military's campaign against the PKI in the capital.[68] On 2 October in Medan, meanwhile, a group called the Youth Action Command (*Komando Aksi Pemuda*) was formed and held an anti-PKI demonstration, before marching around town armed with weapons it had received from the military.[69] It is difficult to generalise about the initial stages of the mobilisation of student militia groups and the formation of military-sponsored death squads during the immediate aftermath of 1 October, because a national study of events in this period has yet to be conducted. The speed with which the PII took action in Banda Aceh, however, appears quite remarkable, and on a par with developments in Jakarta and in neighbouring Medan.

2 October

During the early hours of 2 October, Sulaiman and his comrades were busy. "We made [the posters]," he explains:

then left on bikes, to stick [them] up. Then for the very last one, just as the sun was about to rise, I stuck it to the guardhouse of the Regional Military Commander (Kodam Commander), the house of the Kodam Commander Ishak Djuarsa.

Then, just as I was commanding my friends to stick it up, the guard from the commander's house came, pointing at me with his bayonet, the long barrel of his gun, with its knife at the end. I felt the cool of the edge of the bayonet as it split my clothes, touching my skin, leaving a mark [he demonstrates, drawing an imaginary blade with his fingers forward across his shoulder blade].[70]

When asked why Djuarsa's staff might have reacted in such a negative manner to Dahlan and his group's actions, Dahlan explains: "Because at the time not everyone knew, it was seen as an offence. . . . It was seen as disturbance of the peace, at a time when they didn't know who was behind the [30 September] Movement."[71]

The military leadership, however, would soon change its position. What follows is an intriguing account of Sulaiman's interrogation at the Banda Aceh Kodim office,[72] where, Sulaiman recalls, he was questioned by the District Military Command's Head of Intelligence Captain Edi Yusuf, and the District Military Commander (Kodim Commander) himself, who grew increasingly angry with him, until, just as dawn was about to break, the Commander received an important telephone call from a superior.

The case of Dahlan Sulaiman

"I was scratched [with the bayonet]," Sulaiman recounts:

Then we were all arrested. At the time there were six of us . . . nothing bad happened to us, we weren't beaten up, but we did get told off. The general gist was, 'Why, oh why, are you doing this?' It was almost dawn; I think about 4am or 3.30am. Then they left us [in the guard post outside the Kodam Commander's house].

After that . . . you could hear people starting to chant at the mosques . . . it was almost dawn and a car came from Kodim led by Captain Edi Yusuf. I remembered him well because of my previous military training,[73] I was close to him . . . he was Javanese, but he was a very good man and when he saw me he said,

'Oh, little brother, what's going on?'

So I answered, 'Yeah, nothing's going on, big brother, this is how our struggle is (*beginilah kita berjuang*).'

'Ok, get in the car,' [he replied].

So the six of us got into his car, an old Russian Jeep. It was a big car, driven by his driver with him and his adjunct. At the time Edi Ysuf was . . . commandant of intelligence at Kodim. We were picked up and taken to the Kodim office, taken into the auditorium, we weren't restrained. We were told to sit down . . . then, after a few minutes, the Kodim Commander came out, but we didn't know it was the Kodim Commander or who it was because we couldn't see the person, there was a spotlight shining on us, he was at a table behind the lamp, we were blinded by the light, but he could see us. He started to ask [us questions], he had already read everything, there were some [of our posters] that hadn't yet been stuck up, they had been confiscated and read.

He asked, 'who is the leader?'

'Me, sir,' I said. . . .

'Why is it that you accuse this of being the work of the PKI?'

'Firstly,' I repeated, 'it's my political instinct, sir, as well as my military instinct.'

'Who are you? How can you talk about having a military instinct?'

'I was trained by the military, sir.'

'Where are you from?'

'I am from the *Malem Dagang* regiment,[74] a platoon commander.'

'Ohhhhh . . .,' he said.

'If you were in the regular military, that would mean you were an officer,' [he continued], because he [now] knew that I had completed three groups of training, three levels of training, until I was already at the level of officer, to the point that I had been armed (*dipersenjatai*). As it turned out, that night I hadn't brought my gun.

He asked, 'What kind of gun do you use?'

'Letvol VN,' with what ever number it was, 'sir,' I said.

'Did you bring it?'

'No, sir, because this was not a military assignment.'

'Ok, well, good, if that's the case,' [he said,] 'but you're mistaken, this is not the Communists, not the PKI. The PKI supports the government. It's not possible for them to have done this.'

I said, 'Maybe, sir,' then [repeated my reasoning for why I thought they were responsible].

'No, you're mistaken [he said] and you will be brought to account (*dihukum*). This will certainly have repercussions.'

'That's OK, sir, it's a risk of becoming involved in struggle (*resiko dari sebuah perjuangan*).'

'You call it struggle? You call disturbing the peace of our nation struggle?'

'Maybe this is your opinion tonight, sir. But I think that you might change your mind.'

Because I was brave enough to say this he became angrier and slammed down the butt of his gun. But I still couldn't see him, I didn't know it was the Lieutenant Colonel. . . .

When the dawn call to prayers were over and people were about to go and pray, the telephone on his desk rang, I didn't know who was on the line. . . . [But] the Lieutenant Colonel began to say, 'Ready, sir, ready, sir, yes, sir.' This was definitely his superior, it may have been the Panglima [i.e. Djuarsa], it may have been the assistant from Kodam. Straight away the spotlight was switched off, right in the middle of this critical situation, for the first time, oh my goodness, [I could see it was] the Kodim Commander, he himself had interrogated us, joined by Edi Yusuf from before. It was then that he started to use a softer voice and asked me again,

'If I let you go now, what will you do?'

I said, 'I will continue to put up the posters until it gets too light.' . . .

'Ok, [he replied] if that's what you're going to do, please make use of the little remaining time there is, finish your job, then go home, have a rest. Have you already eaten?'

'Not yet.'

'If that's the case, when you've finished come back here and eat some *nasi bungkus*[75] here.'[76]

When asked why the Commander could change his response so dramatically, Sulaiman responded:

I think the person who called said that we were right. By this stage it was already the second [of October], by the second it was already becoming known [*sic*] that it was the PKI. By then, also, the central RRI [*Radio Republik Indonesia* broadcasting centre] in Jakarta had already been taken over by RPKAD [Indonesian Special forces].[77] . . . When the sun came up [and we had finished], we went back and ate there [at Kodim].[78]

The tide of modern Indonesian history in Aceh had turned. As Special Forces troops converged on the southern border of the Halim air base in Jakarta during the early morning of 2 October, about to launch their final rout of the incoherent and botched 30 September Movement, the Banda Aceh Kodim was coming to the conclusion that a pre-emptive offensive was to be launched against the PKI aimed at its physical annihilation, no doubt spurred on by news of Mokoginta's incendiary midnight speech. In youth militia members such as Sulaiman the military leadership found at its disposal a most enthusiastic ally. When later that day Suharto broadcast over the radio that "We have already managed to take control of the situation both in the centre and in the regions",[79] there was no doubt a sense of recognition in Banda Aceh that this was indeed the case. Suharto then proceeded to exhort that the Armed Forces "work together . . . to annihilate the counter revolutionary actions that have been carried out by those who call themselves the '30 September Movement'" and that "[w]e are certain that with the full assistance of the people . . . we will be able to completely destroy the counter revolutionary 30 September Movement".[80] It was clear that he intended to launch this offensive with the assistance of the civilian population. The military's attack against the PKI would involve the full mobilisation of the population, with the training gained through the *Ganyang Malaysia* campaign and the Operasi Singgalang about to be implemented throughout the province.

3 October

At 7.30am on 3 October, an 'unauthorised' demonstration was held in Idi, East Aceh.[81] This demonstration, the first to be recorded in the Chronology, it is reported, was able to be "stopped/dispersed" by military, but not before the demonstrators "were able to destroy several shops." The demands of the demonstrators have not been recorded, but it is interesting that the first post–1 October demonstration in the province, and indeed possibly nationally,[82] should be held so close to the site of Djuarsa's first public announcement regarding the 30 September Movement's alleged coup attempt in the capital and the military's intended hard-line response. Langsa itself and its surrounding plantation areas constituted one of the PKI's strongest bases in Aceh, while Idi, 74.5 km northwest from Langsa, has historically been considered as a final eastern frontier of Aceh's cultural heartland. It may be that the population in East Aceh was more politically polarised than in other areas and had been radicalised by the arrival of Soebandrio and Njoto and by Djuarsa's subsequent announcements. Equally, the population may have been spurred on by news that in neighbouring North Sumatra, PKI-alligned Governor Ulung Sitepu had been placed under house arrest.[83]

The political situation throughout Indonesia had reached a critical moment. At 1.33am, Sukarno had issued a radio announcement from Jakarta in which he "repeated his order" that he had appointed Major General Pranoto Reksosamudro as temporary national Military Commander, with Suharto appointed to "carry out the restoration of security and order", under Pranoto.[84] Suharto responded to this announcement by issuing one of his own, in which he acknowledged that "from this moment" he stood down from his self-appointed role as temporary national Military Commander and recognised Sukarno as the national Military Commander, without mentioning Pranoto, and while continuing to accept his "task" to restore order.[85] He did not, however, halt the offensive he had launched through the KOTI command in Sumatra, or RPKAD actions in Java. Indeed, he retained his other assumed positions of Kolaga Commander and RPKAD Commander, through which he continued to supervise the launching of the military's attack. Suharto thus relinquished only one public title without surrendering a crumb of the effective control he now commanded over the Indonesian armed forces and state apparatus.

Understanding this intricate power play, national Police Minister and Commander Sutjipto Judodihardjo issued an announcement following the two radio announcements in Jakarta pledging the Indonesian National Police Force's (AKRI: *Angkatan Kepolisian Republik Indonesia*) "complete support" for Suharto.[86] Jakarta and its surrounding areas, meanwhile, were placed under martial law by the Military Commander, now Regional War Commander (*Peperda: Penguasa Perang*

Daerah) for Greater Jakarta, Major General Umar Wirahadikusumah, with individuals who had "received weapons" from the 30 September Movement given 72 hours to surrender or be "sentenced to death".[87]

As Suharto spoke politely in public, placating Sukarno while maintaining the semblance of political continuity, he and the military leadership were on the offensive on the ground. There was no doubt in the minds of the military leadership that the balance of power had tilted toward Suharto.

4 October

At 8pm on 4 October, the day the bodies of the six generals and one lieutenant murdered by the 30 September Movement were exhumed from the disused well at Lubang Buaya in Jakarta, Aceh's Pantja Tunggal Level I body, "Kodahan 'A' staff",[88] and the Pantja Tunggal Level II body for Greater Aceh, met in the Governor's meeting hall (*pendopo*) in Banda Aceh.[89] The purpose of this meeting was to "discuss and establish [their] position as well as to carry out a situation analysis related to the 30 September movement". Several documents were produced at this meeting. The first, 'Declaration of the Pantja Tunggal for Aceh Special Region', consists of four declarations and was signed by the members of Aceh's Pantja Tunggal body.[90] It reads as follows:

> The Aceh Special Region Pantja Tunggal, in relation to that which calls itself the '30 September Movement' declares:
>
> > First: To remain obedient and loyal to the P.J.M. [*Paduka Jang Mulia*: His Excellency] President/Commander of the Armed Forces/Great Leader of the Revolution BUNG KARNO in the Struggle to continue and complete the revolution as well as for the victory of the Indonesian Revolution in accordance with the Five Talismans of the Revolution (*Pantja Azimat Revolusi*);[91]
> >
> > Second: **To determinedly completely annihilate** (*bertekad bulat menumpas habis*) **that which calls itself the '30 September Movement' along with its lackeys.**
> >
> > Third: To heighten Awareness and National Alertness and always build the unity of National Progressive Revolutionary forces that give spirit to Nasakom, especially in the field of increasing the implementation of Dwi Kora and the Anti-Nekolim Struggle.
> >
> > Fourth: We pray that God will forever protect His Excellency the President/Commander of the Armed Forces/Great Leader of the Revolution BUNG KARNO and bless the People and Indonesian Revolution.[92]

This is the second earliest incitement that has been discovered in Aceh, and indeed nationally, for the '30 September Movement' to be "completely annihilated" after Mokoginta's midnight order on 1 October that "all members of the

Armed Forces resolutely and completely annihilate this counter-revolution and all acts of treason down to the roots".[93] The military leadership's annihilation campaign was thus adopted by Aceh's Pantja Tunggal body, which now exercised control over Aceh's civilian government, extending the military's then still aspirational genocidal campaign into the arena of civilian politics, while maintaining the rhetoric of Sukarno's Dwikora and anti-Nekolim campaigns to provide both continuity and the legal and logistical framework and legitimacy for this attack.

The second document, meanwhile, also signed by the Aceh Pantja Tunggal, entitled 'Announcement: Peng. No. Istimewa P.T.', goes even further to explain that:

> It is hereby announced to all layers of Society in Aceh Special Region that:
>
> I   The THIRTIETH OF SEPTEMBER MOVEMENT is a Counter Revolutionary Movement;
> II **It is mandatory for the People to assist in every attempt to completely annihilate the Counter Revolutionary Thirtieth of September Movement along with its Lackeys**;
> III Maintain calm and an environment of orderliness while always building the unity and integrity of National Progressive Revolutionary forces that give spirit to NASAKOM, while increasing preparedness and National alertness in the field of increasing the implementation of Dwi Kora and the Confrontation with Nekolim and its lackeys;
>
> We pray that God will always protect the P.J.M. President/Commander of the Armed Forces/Great Leader of the Revolution BUNG KARNO and bless the People and Indonesian Revolution.[94]

This Announcement thus goes further than the earlier document to instruct, for the first time known on record, that "[i]t is mandatory for the People to assist in every attempt to completely annihilate the Counter Revolutionary Thirtieth of September Movement along with all its lackeys."[95] Within three short days the Pantja Tunggal body in Aceh was issuing instructions for civilians to murder other civilians. To add insult to injury, the body issued these instructions in the name of Sukarno. Sukarno was now little more than a figurehead in Aceh. His words and instructions could be manipulated at the whim of the military leadership, who now enjoyed *de facto* control over the executive functions of the state in the province, and possibly over large sections of Sumatra, thanks to the pre-emptive role played by Mokoginta.[96]

It is at least no longer possible for the Indonesian state to claim that the military did not directly incite the population to engage in the killings that would shortly erupt.[97] It is also clear that no matter how enthusiastic the support of some civilian groups may have been for this campaign, this relationship was ultimately coercive, as civilians had been ordered to participate.

A second meeting, meanwhile, was convened at 11pm in Banda Aceh, attended exclusively by Kodahan 'A' staff at the "Kuala Skodam-I" (*Staf Komando Daerah Militer*: Kodam Staff) headquarters.[98] This meeting produced two telegrams. The first of these was an "Instruction" sent by Djuarsa acting as Pepelrada[99] to his subordinates and the second a telegram of "condolence" for the deaths of the generals in Jakarta, sent by Djuarsa to Sukarno.[100] It is not clear why Djuarsa chose to shift between his two roles as Pepelrada and Pangdahan 'A', and thus their parallel command structures. This utilisation of "dual leadership" may have been a reaction to the fact that not all Pantja Tunggal bodies, which incorporated the provincial Military Commanders acting in their capacity of Pangdam, were as willing in other provinces to side with Suharto as they were in Aceh, necessitating overlapping use of the Kodam, KOTI and Kohanda command structures. The refusal of North Sumatra's Governor Ulung Sitepu to support the emerging military regime, for example, weakened at least symbolically the reach of the Pantja Tunggal body in that province. Provincial Pepelrada, meanwhile, had recourse to significant *de facto* martial law powers not enjoyed by Pangdam outside of the Kolaga command, as discussed in chapter 2. It is not yet known if Kohanda structures were "activated" outside of Aceh and North Sumatra[101] on or after 1 October, though the designation of the Aceh Kohanda as Kohanda 'A' would appear to suggest that Aceh and North Sumatra were not alone. The new military regime was still feeling its way into its new post–1 October form and proving itself to be highly adaptable in the process.

5 October

5 October, Armed Forces Day, was an important turning point nationally for the military's consolidation of power. Traditionally a day to parade the strength of the military, the 1965 Armed Forces Day rally in Jakarta was transformed into a state funeral for the murdered generals. It was used to demonstrate the military's new dominance nationally, with Nasution delivering an emotional speech condemning the "betrayal of the 30 September Movement" and recognising Suharto's leadership.[102] Sukarno, who refused to attend the event out of fear for his safety,[103] was now placed in a position where he had to either publicly support the military leadership or be portrayed as complicit with the 30 September Movement. He chose to send an aide to announce that the murdered generals had posthumously been promoted.

The situation in Banda Aceh was not quite as clear. Asan, the sole surviving member of the PKI's Provincial Secretariat in Aceh, has recalled Armed Forces Day in Banda Aceh went ahead "according to plan", and that he and his comrades "joined in the parade, carrying a flag with the hammer and sickle on it in front of the PKI contingent".[104] He has also recalled, however, that at this time he felt as if "a political storm was about to hit",[105] with the political situation in the province escalating quickly, though he added that "nothing happened" between 1 and 5 October.[106] It is unclear why he and his comrades were apparently so unconcerned about the declarations issued the day before by the Aceh Pantja Tunggal. It may be that the PKI leadership in Banda Aceh, feeling no guilt and unaware of any connection between the PKI and the 30 September Movement, felt a false sense of reassurance, believing that no matter how dire the situation looked, it would soon be resolved by Sukarno.[107] The PKI in Aceh was completely unprepared for an attack by the military and appeared confused in its response. As Asan has explained:

> I never heard of any instructions from the CDB [*Comite Daerah Besar*: Provincial Headquarters of the PKI]-Aceh as to how to protect the organisation in the face of the political storm that had erupted. What the G30S was I am still not clear. . . . What is clear, I felt that the leaders of the CDB were confused; no one knew what had to be done. . . . No one knew that the PKI would become the target of military repression.[108]

The PKI leadership in Aceh had no idea they were about to become the target of a brutal and violent attack. In Medan, meanwhile, the military's preparations for the attack continued. Mokoginta delivered a 'Daily Order' to troops under his command, through which he condemned the 30 September Movement as counter-revolutionary and issued ten orders. These included instructions that the armed forces should:

5   Strengthen safety measures throughout the region of the Mandala I [Sumatra] [and] **actively assist the annihilation of the Counter Revolution** that is currently being implemented in Djakarta and its surrounding areas at the present time.
6   Carry out tasks for physical safety, mental-ideological safety and spiritual safety within your units and within the surrounding [civilian] community.
7   You must all continue to strengthen and guard the unity between the Dwitunggal [Hind. Lit. 'Dual Single Entity'] of the People [and] ABRI, remembering that the source of ABRI is the People, and the shield of the People is ABRI.
8   Be conscious and remember that the situation at the moment will definitely be exploited by the Nekolim and their lackeys to sharpen conflict, splits and rivalries until we forget our primary task, because we are easily influenced.
9   **Immediately annihilate the Counter Revolution and all forms of its treachery down to the roots**.
10 Finally: do not forget, our primary task is to see the success of Dwikora to win the Revolution! It is not impossible that that which calls itself the "Revolution Council" is the tool of a foreign nation [China][109]/a tool of the Nekolim and its stooge [Malaysia][110] that wants to stab in the back the Revolutionary struggle of the People of Indonesia.[111]

Mokoginta thus reiterates the insubordinate speech he had made at midnight on 1 October, publicly calling once again for the annihilation of the "Counter

Revolution", an action that he explains should be carried out "immediately" and "down to the roots" under the leadership of the military. The military, Mokoginta repeats, should work closely with the civilian population to implement the campaign. Through this speech Mokoginta also escalated his public rhetoric to portray this campaign as a continuation of Indonesia's national revolution to be carried out through the framework of Dwikora, an action which served to portray the military as acting to secure the Indonesian state and allowing it to make full use of existing state and military command structures, while acting in a manner that was clearly insubordinate to Sukarno. That Sukarno and his allies were unable to counter such claims indicates the level of success the military leadership was able to achieve in implementing its coup. As we shall see in chapter 7, these instructions are also the first recorded instance nationally of the 'Revolution Council' being declared as a "tool of a foreign nation", in an attempt to implicate China as an international backer of the 30 September Movement.

Back in Banda Aceh, the Head of Staff of the Aceh Military Region Command (Kasdam-I: *Kepala Staf Komando Daerah Militer*) gave a special briefing to his staff at midday, in which he stressed the importance that "misunderstandings" did not occur about the 30 September Movement.[112] Exactly what "misunderstandings" were meant by this is not recorded. It was also reported that special prayers for the dead (*sembahjang gaib*) were being carried out throughout the province for the generals, with what the Military Chronology has described as "anti-PKI sentiment" becoming "extremely widespread" in the province from this date onwards, leading to the emergence of pamphlets, banners, graffiti and "screaming" (*teriakan2*), which was cited as evidence of public support for the military's radical crackdown against the PKI.[113]

6 October

At 9am the next morning, Mokoginta delivered a speech in Medan establishing strict new press censorship guidelines.[114] The printing of all editorials and comment pieces "in any form of publication" was banned, under threat of offending journalists having their property seized by the military.[115] Only news broadcasts by RRI Jakarta, the Antara News Agency, KOTI, the various Armed Forces branches, Police, Mandala I Command and Explanations from the Provincial Pepelrada/"Pendahan"[116] were allowed to be transmitted in Sumatra, with this news to be transmitted "in its original form . . . without elaboration or commentary". Meanwhile, Mokoginta explains, the three sources of authority to be acknowledged in Sumatra were "declarations in support of the President/Supreme Commander of the Armed Forces . . . /Great Leader of the Revolution [Sukarno]", "declarations related to Dwikora" and the "declarations/instructions issued by [Sukarno]". This order, which was declared to be in effect throughout Sumatra, officially removed press freedoms and reiterated that each of Sumatra's provinces were to acknowledge Dwikora legislation. This order also placed operational command in Sumatra in the hands of Mokoginta and the provincial military commanders, who were no longer required to seek formal approval from Sukarno for

Dwikora related operations, effectively shutting Sukarno out of these operations throughout Sumatra, despite continued rhetorical references to his authority.[117] Sukarno had become a silenced figurehead as the military began moving to seize state power for itself.

The PKI is removed from the *Front Nasional*

At 11am, representatives from eight of Aceh's main political parties, including the PKI, met in Banda Aceh.[118] Aceh's provincial-level Pantja Tunggal and *Front Nasional*, which had been established in the province in 1961 to facilitate the participation of political parties in the formal political process under Guided Democracy, also took part.[119] Records of this meeting can be found in two 'Joint Decisions' (*Keputusan Bersama No. I.st.I/Kpts/1965* and *Keputusan Bersama: No. Ist. II/Pol/Kpts/1965*).

According to the first Joint Decision, attendees at the meeting were informed of the "national situation" and the "situation and conditions in Aceh special Region as a result of the . . . treasonous/counter-revolutionary [30 September] movement".[120] They were also asked to keep in mind Sukarno's speeches (*Amanat*),[121] instructions, explanations, announcements and orders, and to "weigh up" eight points, including an understanding that "[this] counter-revolutionary movement has carried out barbaric terror outside the realm of what is humane", and that this "treachery . . . weakens the potential and National Unity of Revolutionary Progressivism to destroy the Nekolim and its lackeys", and "cannot be explained in any other way than as benefiting the Nekolim and [as being] in the service of foreign Subversives".[122] It was also explained that "Manipol firmly tells us that a clear dividing line must be drawn between friends and enemies of the Revolution". Attendees at the meeting were thus being asked to mobilise as if war had broken out.

Three "collective decisions" were then made, including:

1   To condemn as strongly as possible this treacherous Movement that calls itself the "THIRTIETH OF SEPTEMBER MOVEMENT"
2   Assist with full energy all attempts to **completely annihilate** the "THIRTIETH SEPTEMBER MOVEMENT"
3   Urge and call upon His Excellency, the President/Supreme Commander of the Armed Forces of the Republic of Indonesia/Great Leader of the Revolution Bung Karno to immediately disband the PKI and the Mass Organisations that are grouped beneath its banner and declare it an illegal Party/counter revolutionary due to it becoming the brain, puppet master and main support of the treacherous Movement that calls itself the "THIRTIETH SEPTEMBER MOVEMENT".[123]

This statement was signed by all five members of Aceh's Pantja Tunggal body, the Executive Committee of Aceh's *Front Nasional* and representatives from all attending political parties, except, unsurprisingly, the PKI.[124] Unlike the signatories, the PKI representatives, Thaib Adamy and Muhammad Samikidin,[125] are listed with the explanation that they "did not consent to sign".[126] Aceh's political parties were thus mobilised to assist the military to "annihilate" the PKI, while PKI delegates faced the unconscionable task of consenting to their own annihilation. This declaration also makes it clear that the military's intended target group was not just members of the PKI, but also anyone considered affiliated with like-minded 'Mass Organisations'. Exactly which mass organisations were meant by this classification would soon be announced. Not all of these organisations had actual organisational affiliation with the PKI.

A second Joint Decision was then prepared by Aceh's *Front Nasional* body without the Pantja Tunggal in an apparent attempt to demonstrate that Aceh's political leadership also independently supported these actions. This second Joint Decision stated that "while waiting for a Decision" from Sukarno, it called upon:

1   The PANGDAHAN/PANGLIMA KODAM I/ACEH [Djuarsa], acting as PEPELRADA for Aceh Province,
2   GOVERNOR/HEAD OF ACEH SPECIAL REGION [Kamil], acting as Head of the Pantja Tunggal for Aceh Special Region to:

   a   Freeze the PKI and the Organisations under its banner in Aceh Special Region,
   b   Take the necessary steps against PKI elements and those in its Mass Organisations to guard against undesired events/developments that place the Pantja Sila Nation, the Republic of Indonesia, in danger.
   c   Immediately make non-active all PKI representatives/those from its Mass Organisations from all State Organisations and Government Bodies in Aceh Special Region.[127]

Again, the need to "take steps" against the PKI and "its Mass Organisations" is portrayed as necessary to assure the survival of the nation. Aceh's "Pangdahan/Panglima Kodam/Pepelrada" and Pantja Tunggal, meanwhile, are called upon to lead this campaign, demonstrating the multiple chains of command used to implement the military's annihilation campaign in the province. This time, however, the PKI delegation is (again unsurprisingly) no longer listed as attending the meeting.[128] Zainal Abidin, the Subdistrict Head (*Camat*) of Seulimum, has explained that Adamy and Samikidin were subsequently placed under arrest and detained at his office.[129] As we shall see in chapter 5, Abidin recalls that Samikidin would shortly be placed on a train headed for Takengon, before the train was stopped and he was killed.

That this removal was to involve the mobilisation of community-level violence was made explicit when Aceh's Pantja Tunggal body subsequently re-joined the meeting to declare the establishment of Aceh's state-sponsored Pantja Sila Defence Front death squad.[130] The record of this decision is the earliest known documentary evidence that the Indonesian state not only supported but also actively partook in the formation of civilian death squads for the purpose of conducting its attack against the PKI. As discussed in chapter 4, within a matter of days the Pantja Sila Defence Front would be credited with carrying out its first brutal abductions and murders in the province, having evolved into a fully functioning state-sponsored death squad.[131] The stage was now set for the military to launch its annihilation campaign.

Notes

1 The timing of this meeting appears to have been a product of chance, for, even though, as explained in chapter 2, the military leadership in Sumatra had been actively preparing to launch an attack against the PKI, the exact timing of this attack was not known until the morning of 1 October 1965, when the actions of the 30 September Movement provided the pretext for this attack.

2 'Berdikari' was a term used by Sukarno to promote Indonesian self-reliance.

3 *G-30-S Dihadapan Mahmillub 3, Djilid I, Perkara Dr. Subandrio* (Jakarta: Pusat Pendidikan Kehakiman A.D., 1967), p. 219.

4 Written account produced by Teuku Ali Basyah, given to the author, Simpang Surabaya, Banda Aceh, 21 December 2010.

5 The PSII was an ardently anti-communist party that split from Masjumi in 1947. It claimed its political lineage from the original Sarekat Islam, which had been established as a pre-war organisation in the Dutch East Indies. In 1923, Sarekat Islam had split into 'red' and 'white' groups, with the PSII developing out of the 'white' group and the PKI developing out of the 'red' group. Herbert Feith, *The Decline of Constitutional Democracy in Indonesia* (Ithaca and New York: Cornell University Press, 1962), pp. 138–139. The PSII was popular in Aceh and had two representatives in Aceh's provincial government during the early 1960s, the same number as the PKI. *Dewan Perwakilan Rakjat Atjeh*, p. 22; and *Sidang DPRD-GR Daerah Istimewa Atjeh*, 26 Mei 1965, p. 3.

6 Ali Hasjmy, *Semangat Merdeka: 70 tahun menempuh jalan pergolakan & perjuangan kemerdekaan* (Jakarta: Bulan Bintang, 1985), pp. 702–703.

7 *Ibid.*, pp. 702–703.

8 Interview with "Shadia" (a pseudonym), Banda Aceh, 12 February 2009.

9 Ulf Sundhaussen, *The Road to Power: Indonesian Military Politics, 1945–1967* (Kuala Lumpur: Oxford University Press, 1982), p. 162.

10 Hasjmy, for example, who left Langsa for Medan that morning, has recalled not hearing news that "there had been a 'coup'" in Jakarta until midday when he arrived in Binjai, 25 km from Medan. Ali Hasjmy, *Semangat Merdeka*, p. 705.

11 'Dr Subandrio bersama 12 Ment. "Turba"', *Waspada*, 29 September 1965, p. 1.

12 Anderson G. Bartlett III et al., *Pertamina: Indonesian National Oil* (Singapore: Amerasian Ltd, 1972), p. 237.

13 *G-30-S Dihadapan Mahmillub 3, Djilid I, Perkara Dr. Subandrio* (Jakarta: Pusat Pendidikan Kehakiman A.D., 1967), p. 217; and 'Surat Pernjataan A.J. Mokoginta' in *G-30-S Dihadapan Mahmillub 3*, p. 242.

14 *G-30-S Dihadapan Mahmillub 3, Djilid I, Perkara Dr. Subandrio*, p. 219.

15 *Ibid.*, pp. 218–219.

16 The second PKI-allied Governor was Bali's Anak Agung Bagus Sutedja. Harold Crouch, *The Army and Politics in Indonesia* (Jakarta: Equinox Publishing, 2007, originally 1978), pp. 77–78.

17 'Chronologis Kedjadian2 jang Berhubungan dengan Gerakan 30 September di Daerah Kodam-I/Atjeh', in *Laporan Tahunan Lengkap Kodam-I/Kohanda Atjeh, Tahun 1965* (Banda Aceh: Kodam-I Banda Aceh, 1 February 1966), p. 92.

18 Harold Crouch, *The Army and Politics in Indonesia*, p. 129.

19 While the exact time the order was sent is not stated in the Chronology eyewitness accounts and other corroborating evidence (outlined below) indicate it was sent during the morning. *Ibid.*, p. 132.

20 'Pidato Radio Pimpinan Sementara Angkatan Darat Major Djendral Soeharto', Pimpinan Sementara AD Republik Indonesia, Major Jendral Soeharto, 1 October 1965, in Alex Dinuth (ed.), *Dokumen Terpilih Sekitar G.30.S/PKI* (Jakarta: Intermasa, 1997), pp. 59–60.

21 'Decree No. 1 on the Establishment of the Indonesian Revolution Council', 1 October 1965, in 'Selected Documents Relating to the "September 30th Movement" and Its Epilogue', *Indonesia*, Vol. 1 (April 1966), p. 136.

22 'Chronologis', p. 92.

23 *Ibid.*

24 I have yet to find any references to this position being used prior to 1 October 1965 or during the period after the conclusion of the genocide in Aceh, suggesting this position was utilised specifically for the implementation of the military's attack against the PKI.

25 The Pangkalan Brandan oil field had been established in 1892 and run by Royal Dutch until it was nationalised and placed under the control of the national Permina (as it was then known) oil company in 1958. At this time Indonesian military Captain Rani Junus was appointed as Permina's Acting Manager, with four platoons at his disposal to provide security for the facility. 'Surat Pernjataan A.J. Mokoginta', in *G-30-S Dihadapan Mahmillub 3, Djilid I, Perkara Dr. Subandrio*, p. 242; and Anderson G. Bartlett III et al., *Pertamina*, pp. 44, 130, 134 and 237.

26 Anderson G. Bartlett III et al., *Pertamina*, p. 237 and 'Surat Pernjataan A.J. Mokoginta', in *G-30-S Dihadapan Mahmillub 3, Djilid I, Perkara Dr. Subandrio*, p. 242.

27 This "paramilitary company security force" was made up of former members of the Sriwidjaja battalion who had been sent to secure North Sumatra's oil fields during the PRRI rebellion. At the cessation of the rebellion, although the battalion was officially returned, officers were given the option to remain and become full-time employees of Permina, an opportunity several of the soldiers decided to take up. During the early 1960s the company's paramilitary security force turned its attentions to opposing PKI-affiliated labour unrest, such as mobilisations by Perbum (*Persatuan Buruh Minyak*: Oil Workers Union). In early 1965, the 'Bandar Betsy Affair' occupied the thoughts of Rani and his paramilitaries. Anderson G. Bartlett III et al., *Pertamina*, p. 237; and 'Surat Pernjataan A.J. Mokoginta', in *G-30-S Dihadapan Mahmillub 3*, pp. 242, 228 and 237.

28 Anderson G. Bartlett III et al., *Pertamina*, p. 237; and 'Surat Pernjataan A.J. Mokoginta', in *G-30-S Dihadapan Mahmillub 3*, pp. 227 and 237.

29 Anderson G. Bartlett III et al., *Pertamina*, p. 238.

30 Rex Mortimer, *Indonesian Communism Under Sukarno: Ideology and Politics, 1959–1965* (Jakarta: Equinox Publishing, 2006, originally 1974), p. 423.

31 This was a recurring line of questioning at Soebandrio's show trial. See, *G-30-S Dihadapan Mahmillub 3*.

32 'Incoming telegram' to the US Department of State, 1 October 1965, p. 1, cited in US Department of State, *Foreign Relations of the United States, 1964–1968: Volume XXVI, Indonesia; Malaysia-Singapore; Philippines* (Washington DC: Government Printing Office, 2001).

33 Permina was re-named 'Pertamina' (*Perusahaan Pertambangan Minyak dan Gas Bumi Negara*: State Oil and Natural Gas Mining Company) in 1968 following a merger with Pertamin (*Perusahaan Negara Pertambangan Minyak Indonesia*: Indonesian State Oil Extraction Company).

34 Anderson G. Bartlett III et al., *Pertamina*, p. 238.

35 Bartlett has mused that the strangest occurrence that morning had been news from the local Kodim Commander that "military exercises" had been held at 5.45am that morning. As part of these exercises, Bartlett explains, "Pangkalan Brandan was considered to be occupied by hostile forces, and that *KODIM* troops would maneuver to liberate the area," This training occurred under the guise of the *Ganyang Malaysia*

campaign, as an apparent follow-up to the Operasi Singgalang campaign. This particular mobilisation, however, Bartlett claims, was different to usual mobilisations, as it was launched without the prior knowledge of Rani's security forces, who "were given no part in the operations". Although these claims can be neither proved nor disproved, Bartlett's comments hint at the heightened level of military mobilisation, suspicion and mistrust that existed in Sumatra during this period and may suggest the military in Pangkalan Brandan was told to mobilise specifically in response to news of developments in Jakarta. *Ibid.*, pp. 238–240.

36 *Ibid.*, p. 239.

37 'Surat-Pernjataan M. Ishak Djuarsa', in *G-30-S Dihadapan Mahmillub 3*, p. 244.

38 *Ibid.*, p. 245.

39 In 1966 Djuarsa had declared "I don't know [what they were doing in Langsa]." *G-30-S Dihadapan Mahmillub 3*, pp. 218–219.

40 'Ishak Djoearsa: "Sejak 1967, Pak Harto Sudah Seperti Imam yang Batal Wudu" ', p. 39. Ishak Djuarsa passed away in March 2011, while I was still attempting to arrange an interview with him.

41 'Surat-Pernjataan M. Ishak Djuarsa', in *G-30-S Dihadapan Mahmillub 3*, pp. 220, 245.

42 Interview with Teuku Ali Basyah, Simpang Surabaya, Banda Aceh, 17 February 2009; and, written interview with Teuku Ali Basyah, given to the author, Simpang Surabaya, Banda Aceh, 7 December 2010.

43 'Surat-Pernjataan M. Ishak Djuarsa', in *G-30-S Dihadapan Mahmillub 3, Djilid I, Perkara Dr. Subandrio*, p. 245.

44 *Ibid.*

45 Second interview with Teuku Ali Basyah, Simpang Surabaya, Banda Aceh, 28 December 2011, p. 16.

46 Interview with Teuku Ali Basyah, Simpang Surabaya, Banda Aceh, 17 February 2009.

47 Anderson G. Bartlett III et al., *Pertamina*, p. 240.

48 Second interview with Teuku Ali Basyah, Simpang Surabaya, Banda Aceh, 28 December 2011.

49 'Ishak Djoearsa: "Sejak 1967, Pak Harto Sudah Seperti Imam yang Batal Wudu" ', p. 39.

50 Suharto launched his campaign against the 30 September Movement in Central Java from 16 October 1965. For initial military actions in Jakarta and Central Java, see John Roosa, *Pretext for Mass Murder: The 30th September Movement & Suharto's Coup D'Etat in Indonesia* (Madison: The University of Wisconsin Press, 2006), pp. 54–60; and, David Jenkins and Douglas Kammen, 'The Army Para-commando Regiment in Central Java and Bali', in Douglas Kammen and Katharine McGregor (eds.), *The Contours of Mass Violence in Indonesia, 1965–68* (Singapore: NUS Press, 2012), pp. 76–99.

51 The first mass rally against the 30 September Movement in Medan was held on 6 October 1965. Arrests began from this date. The outbreak of violence in the province did not, however, begin until the first week of November. For initial military actions in North Sumatra, see, Audrey Kahin, *Rebellion to Integration: West Sumatra and the Indonesian Polity* (Amsterdam: Amsterdam University Press, 1999), p. 243; and, Yen-ling Tsai and Douglas Kammen, 'Anti-Communist Violence and the Ethnic Chinese in Medan, North Sumatra', in Douglas Kammen and Katharine McGregor (eds.), *The Contours of Mass Violence in Indonesia*, pp. 138–143.

52 Pernyataan N. B-7/10/DPRD-GR/65, Banda Aceh, 1 October 1965.

53 Emphasis in original. *Ibid.*

54 A *rencong* is a traditional Acehnese dagger used both ceremonially and historically during warfare.

55 Pernyataan N. B-7/10/DPRD-GR/65, Banda Aceh, 1 October 1965.

56 Emphasis in original. 'Tetap tenang dan penuh kewaspadaan terhadap setiap anasir jang merusak dan ingin menghantjurkan Pantjasila-Revolusi-Negara dan Bangsa Kita,

baik dari luar maupun dari dalam', in Letdjen A.J. Mokoginta, *Koleksi Pidato2/ Kebidjaksanaan Panglima Daerah Sumatra* (Medan: Koanda Sumatera, 1966), p. 152.

57 These 'Councils' were related to a series of regional coups in Sumatra during the 1950s led by disgruntled military leaders demanding greater regional autonomy. The Banteng Council was declared in Central Sumatra on 20 December 1965, the Gajah Council was declared in East Sumatra on 22 December 1956 and the Garuda Council was declared in South Sumatra on 15 January 1958. On 15 February 1958 Lietuenant Colonel Ahmad Hussein declared the Revolutionary Government of the Republic of Indonesia (PRRI: *Pemerintah Revolusioner Republik Indonesia*) in an attempt to link these regional rebellions in a direct challenge to Sukarno. Audrey Kahin, *Rebellion to Integration*, pp. 184–210.

58 'Tetap tenang dan penuh kewaspadaan', pp. 152–153.

59 Audrey R. Kahin and George McT. Kahin, *Subversion as Foreign Policy: The Secret Eisenhower and Dulles Debacle in Indonesia* (New York: The New Press, 1995), p. 165.

60 John Roosa, *Pretext for Mass Murder*, p. 221.

61 *Ibid.*

62 Interview with Dahlan Sulaiman, Banda Aceh, Aceh, 29 December 2011, p. 17.

63 *Ibid.*, p. 18.

64 *Ibid.*

65 Harold Crouch, 'The Indonesian Army in Politics: 1960–1971', PhD thesis, Monash University, 1975, pp. 254–255.

66 The earliest reference to the Komando Aksi Pemuda in North Sumatra can be found in 'Telegram 813, US Embassy Jakarta to State Department', 2 October 1965, cited in Yen-ling Tsai and Douglas Kammen, 'Anti-Communist Violence and the Ethnic Chinese in Medan, North Sumatra', in Douglas Kammen and Katharine McGregor (eds.), *The Contours of Mass Violence in Indonesia, 1965–68*, p. 138.

67 Gasbindo was created by Masjumi. It was banned along with its parent organisation in 1960 after it was implicated in the regional revolts of the 1950s.

68 Harold Crouch, 'The Indonesian Army in Politics: 1960–1971', pp. 254–256; Donald Hindley, 'Alirans and the Fall of the New Order', *Indonesia*, Vol. 9 (April 1970), pp. 23–66; and, John R. Maxwell, 'Soe Hok-Gie: A Biography of a Young Indonesian Intellectual', PhD thesis, Department of Political and Social Change, Research School of Pacific and Asian Studies, The Australian National University, 1997, p. 130.

69 'Telegram to the US State Department from the US Embassy in Jakarta', cited in Yen-ling Tsai and Douglas Kammen, 'Anti-Communist Violence and the Ethnic Chinese in Medan, North Sumatra', in Douglas Kammen and Katharine McGregor (eds.), *The Contours of Mass Violence in Indonesia*, p. 138; also, 'Telegram from the US Consulate in Medan to the US State Department', 2 October 1965, in US Department of State, *Foreign Relations of the United States*.

70 Interview with Dahlan Sulaiman, Banda Aceh, 29 December 2011, p. 19.

71 *Ibid.*, pp. 19–20.

72 The district military commands in Banda Aceh and Aceh Besar were jointly coordinated through Kodim 0101.

73 This training is discussed in chapter 2.

74 The *Malem Dagang* regiment was a student militia group that received training and arms from the military. Detail of this training is given in chapter 2.

75 Cooked rice prepared at a food stall wrapped in a banana leaf with a selection of accompaniments. The connotation is that the Commander would order a nice meal for them, a sign of his sudden new support for their actions.

76 Interview with Dahlan Sulaiman, Banda Aceh, 29 December 2011, pp. 20–21.

77 The RPKAD was under the command of Colonel Sarwo Edhie. During the morning of 1 October Suharto used the RPKAD to put down the 30 September Movement. John Roosa, *Pretext for Mass Murder*, p. 58. It would also lead the killings in Java and

Bali from 17 October 1965. David Jenkins and Douglas Kammen, 'The Army Para-commando Regiment and the Reign of Terror in Central Java and Bali', in Douglas Kammen and Katharine McGregor (eds.), *The Contours of Mass Violence in Indonesia*, p. 83.

78 Interview with Dahlan Sulaiman, Banda Aceh, 29 December 2011, p. 21.

79 'Pidato Pimpinan TNI-AD (Sementara) Mayjen TNI Soehato tentang Penculikan Jendral-Jendral', in Alex Dinuth (ed.), *Document Terpilih*, p. 72.

80 *Ibid.*, pp. 72–73.

81 'Chronologis', p. 92.

82 KAP-Gestapu held its first rally in Jakarta on 4 October. Harold Crouch, *The Army and Politics in Indonesia*, p. 141.

83 Anderson G. Bartlett III et al., *Pertamina*, 238.

84 'Amanat Presiden/Panglima Tertinggi ABRI/Pemimpin Besar Revolusi Bung Karno', in *Dokumen Terpilih*, p. 83.

85 'Pidato Radio Panglima Kostrad Mayor Jenderal TNI Soeharto', in *Dokumen Terpilih*, p. 85.

86 'Pengumuman Ym. Menteri/Panglima Angkatan Kepolisian Tentang Jendral-Jendral Polisi Yang Duduk Dalam Dewan Revolusi', in *Dokumen Terpilih*, p. 89.

87 'Maklumat Penguasa Perang Daerah No. 01/Drt/10/1965 Panglima Jakarta dan Sekitarnya', in *Dokumen Terpilih*, p. 88.

88 It is not known why this command continued to be identified as 'Kodahan', when it was renamed 'Kohanda' to coincide with the launch of Operasi Berdikari on 1 October 1965. For the purpose of simplicity, I will use the name Kodahan, along with the corresponding position of Pangdahan, when they appear in original documents and Kohanda and Pangkohanda when they are used in the original documents.

89 'Chronologis', p. 92.

90 It was "prepared and readied for circulation" by Marademanis, from the Aceh Provincial Government Secretariat. 'Pernjataan Pantja Tunggal Daerah Istimewa Atjeh', 4 October 1965, p. 1.

91 The concept of 'Pantja Azimat Revolusi' was proposed by Sukarno in June 1965. The five 'talismans' or 'charms' include the Indonesian ideological concepts of Nasakom, Pancasila, the Political Manifesto, Trisakti and Berdikari. See Sukarno's Independence Day Speech on 17 August 1965, *Antara*, 17 August 1965.

92 Capitalisation in original, other emphasis added. 'Pernjataan Pantja Tunggal Daerah Istimewa Atjeh', 4 October 1965, p. 1.

93 'Tetap tenang dan penuh kewaspadaan', in Letdjen A.J. Mokoginta, *Koleksi Pidato2*, pp. 152–153.

94 'Pengumuman: Peng. No. Istimewa P.T.', Banda Aceh, 4 October 1965.

95 *Ibid.*

96 Further research is required to produce detailed chronologies of the military's actions during this early phase in provinces outside of Aceh.

97 It may be that this document will hold particular importance for any legal actions aimed at seeking accountability for the Indonesian genocide.

98 'Chronologis', p. 92.

99 "[I]nstruksi Pepelrada nomor TSR-3/Kilat/1005000", in 'Chronologis', p. 92.

100 'Chronologis', p. 92.

101 The Aceh Military Command's Kohanda structure map indicates that a North Sumatra Kohanda Command also existed.

102 'Pidato YM Menko Hankam/Kasam Jenderal TNI Dr. A.H. Nasution Pada Upacara Pelepasan 7 Pahlawan Revolusi', 5 October 1965, in *Dokumen Terpilih*, pp. 96–97.

103 Harold Crouch, *The Army and Politics in Indonesia*, p. 139.

104 Interview with Asan, 31 October, Hong Kong, p. 30.

105 Written interview with Asan, Part Two, given to the author, Hong Kong, 30 October 2011.

106 Interview with Asan, 31 October 2011, Hong Kong, p. 1.

107 Asan claims not to have been part of the Party's decision-making discussions during this period. *Ibid.*

108 Written interview with Asan, Part Two, given to the author, Hong Kong, 30 October 2011, p. 2.

109 The manner in which China and the ethnic Chinese community became implicated in the military's attack against the PKI is discussed in chapter 7.

110 This is a reference to the *Ganyang Malaysia* campaign.

111 Emphasis added. 'Tindakan2 Kontra Revolusi', in Letdjen A.J. Mokoginta, *Koleksi Pidato2*, pp. 172–173.

112 'Chronology', p. 92.

113 *Ibid.*

114 'Dilarang membuat editorial dan podjok dalam bentuk apapun, dalam setiap penerbitan', in Letdjen A. J. Mokoginta, *Koleksi Pidato2*, pp. 177–178.

115 The speech cites 'Kep. Pres. No. 37 KOTI/1965' as the legal basis for this ban. *Ibid.*, pp. 177–178.

116 *Ibid.*, p. 178. It is not known if 'Pendahan' is a misspelling of 'Pangdahan', or if 'Pendahan' represents a previously uncited position. It might, for example, be an abbreviation for '*Penerangan Daerah Pertahanan*', Defence Region Information [unit or officer].

117 Further research is required to understand how this was achieved outside of Sumatra.

118 The other political parties represented were the PNI, PSII, Partindo (*Partai Indonesia*: Indonesia Party), NU (*Nahdlatul Ulama*: 'Revival of the Islamic Scholars'), PI Perti (*Partai Islam Persatuan Tarbyiah Islamiyah*: Islamic Education Association Islamic Party), Catholic Party (*Partai Katolik*) and Parkindo (*Partai Kristen Indonesia*: Indonesian Christian Party). 'Keputusan Bersama No. I.st-I/Kpts/1965', Banda Aceh, 6 October 1965. Partindo was a small left-wing party that succeeded from the PNI in July 1958. It was sympathetic to the PKI. NU, a traditionalist Islamic group, was founded in 1926 as a breakaway group from Masjumi. PI Perti was formed in West Sumatra in 1930 to combat the influence of modernist Islamic associations. It had a strong following amongst Islamic traditionalists in Aceh. It initially supported the regional unrest of 1957 before shifting to the government side in 1958 when the PRRI/Permesta was proclaimed. Under Guided Democracy it strongly supported Sukarno and was sometimes considered to be sympathetic to the PKI. Robert Cribb and Audrey Kahin, *Historical Dictionary of Indonesia*, 2nd ed. (Maryland: Scarecrow Press, 2004), p. 340. Partai Katolik was founded in 1923. Parkindo, a Protestant Christian party, was formed in November 1945.

119 'Chronologis', p. 92.

120 'Keputusan Bersama No. I.st-I/Kpts/1965', Banda Aceh, 6 October 1965, p. 1.

121 Sukarno's speeches were often treated as formulations of state policy. See, Muhono, *Ketetapan MPRS dan Peraturan Negara jang Penting bagi Anggauta Angkatan Bersendjata* (Jakarta: Tentara Nasional Indonesia, 1966).

122 'Keputusan Bersama No. I.st-I/Kpts/1965', Banda Aceh, 6 October 1965, p. 1.

123 Emphasis added. *Ibid.*, p. 2.

124 *Ibid.*

125 Samikidin was originally from Langkat, a North Sumatran district bordering East Aceh, made famous as one of the most profitable Dutch plantation areas. He is said to have been a member of Persindo with T.M. Yatim in Langkat before moving to Meulaboh. Interview with T.M. Yatim, Meulaboh, West Aceh, 3 December 2011, p. 5.

126 *Ibid.*

127 'Keputusan Bersama: No. Ist. II/Pol/Kpts/1965', Banda Aceh, 6 October 1965, p. 1.

128 'Keputusan Bersama: No. Ist. I/Kpts/1965', Banda Aceh, 6 October 1965.

129 Interview with Zainal Abidin, Banda Aceh, 14 February 2009, pp. 12–13.

130 'Chronologis', p. 92.

131 Further information about the formation and activities of state-sponsored death squads in the province can be found in chapters 5, 6 and 7.

4 Djuarsa's coordination tour
1–11 October

As the military leadership orchestrated its undeclared coup during the morning of 1 October, Aceh's civilian population was also listening in real time to events unfolding in Jakarta via the radio. This information was communicated through the same public radio broadcasts heard by Aceh's military and civilian leadership in Langsa. To begin with, these broadcasts appear to have caused some confusion, as different groups and individuals sought to understand their meaning. This confusion would be resolved in the days following 1 October, as the military leadership embarked on a campaign to actively involve Aceh's civilian population in its annihilation campaign. Djuarsa would play a central role in this crucial initiation phase.

1 October: civilian responses in Banda Aceh

On 1 October, Asan, the sole surviving member of the PKI Central Committee for Aceh, was at the PKI provincial headquarters in Neusu, Banda Aceh when he heard news about events in Jakarta over the radio.[1] "We only knew about the G30S after hearing about it on the radio," he has recalled.[2] The announcement that Asan remembers listening to was the 30 September Movement's 2pm radio announcement proclaiming the formation of the Revolution Council. At this time, Aceh's military and civilian leadership, including PKI Secretary Thaib Adamy, were still in Langsa and Asan recalls feeling unsure about what was happening. Walking out into the street, Asan remembers noticing "it looked like there was no effect [from the broadcasts] in Banda Aceh, activities in the city were going ahead as normal". Indeed, Asan explains, Chinese National Day[3] celebrations went ahead as planned.[4] This would suggest the general community did not yet feel that events in Jakarta presented an imminent threat to the political situation in Banda Aceh.

Later that evening, when Adamy returned to Banda Aceh around sunset, he met Asan and his comrades at PKI headquarters. Adamy, Asan recalls, also appeared confused and asked Asan to ride with him on their pushbikes to the *Front Nasional* office, where they hoped to gain a greater sense of the political situation in Jakarta.[5] The office, however, was empty and the two men decided to part ways and they returned home "empty-handed". Far from attempting to begin an uprising in the province, as was alleged by Djuarsa, Adamy appears to have been confused and seeking guidance. Asan has claimed he never received any instructions from the Party detailing how he should respond either to the actions of the 30 September Movement or to the military's subsequent attack.[6] This false sense of calm lasted for several days. "For the first few days of October", Asan explains, "the situation was still calm",[7] with nothing "unusual" occurring before 5 October.[8]

Let Bugeh, a member of HMI (an organisation described by Djuarsa in the Complete Yearly Report as being "in the front line of the annihilation" (*di garis depan dalam penumpasan*),[9] who had received military training during the pre–1 October period, claims not to have heard about events in Jakarta via national radio broadcast. Rather, Bugeh recalls, he and his comrades first heard news about these events through the "network" of "HMI leaders in Jakarta".[10] "We heard," Bugeh explains, "but . . . we didn't know what was true and what wasn't."[11] Bugeh is insistent, however, that "it wasn't the military that made this [anti-PKI] campaign" in Aceh:

> It's possible that they [the military] did [lead this campaign] in Jakarta, but the way to create this kind of agitation [in Aceh] was easy, it wasn't difficult. It was fitting, this is because before this we were already having run-ins with them [the PKI].

Like Sulaiman, Bugeh seems keen to demonstrate his organisation's independence from the military. The possible reasons for this insistence, despite the overwhelming evidence to the contrary, will be discussed in chapter 6.

Zainal Abidin, Subdistrict Head for Seulimum, 60 km from Banda Aceh in Aceh Besar, who was in Seulimum on 1 October, meanwhile, remembers hearing a radio broadcast during the day "asking us to establish Revolution Councils in the subdistricts; it wasn't until the [late] afternoon that we knew that Untung was a communist, so it didn't happen".[12] This broadcast, the 2pm radio announcement made by the 30 September Movement, appears to have been received quite neutrally until Abidin and other civilian leaders in Seulimum heard the military leadership's own radio announcements during the evening. After hearing these announcements, Abidin recalls, "We weren't pro [the 30 September Movement] anymore. In fact, we supported the central government."

An order was also issued at this time for a public mass meeting to be held in Banda Aceh, where the military leadership would present its case for its annihilation campaign against the PKI. "Everyone from the subdistrict," Abidin explains, "sent someone to the mass meeting to support the Republic of Indonesia and Bung Karno the Great Leader of the Revolution. I remember."[13]

5 October: mass meeting to condemn the PKI in Banda Aceh

This mass meeting was held on 5 October at Blang Padang,[14] a large field in the centre of the town owned by the Aceh Military Command. This meeting appears to have been inspired by events earlier that morning in Jakarta, where the national

Armed Forces Day Parade had been turned into a public funeral for the murdered generals. Abidin claims to have played a leading role at this meeting. "We performed a prayer for the dead (*sembahyang mayat*)," Abidin recalls:

> I called the *ulama* [to perform the prayers] . . . The *ulama* weren't brave enough to come out, but we protected them . . . After that, the people of Aceh were angry again with the PKI . . . The people began to move. . . . People were extreme, but only after they knew the G30S was communist.[15]

The purpose of this meeting, Abidin explains, was to publically "condemn" (*mengutuk*) the G30S.[16] Attendees were also warned that if they refused to assist the military to arrest members of the PKI, Banda Aceh would "burn". The mass meeting, Abidin has said, was led "by civilians, but I feel that it was being protected (*dilindungi*) by ABRI. We worked together with the District Military Command (*Kodim*)". Abidin has claimed the subsequent outbreak of violence was "spontaneous", suggesting the PKI was attacked because it was "not accepted" by "the people" and considered to be "atheist".[17] This claim of "spontaneity" can now be proven untrue. Indeed, Abidin, who admits to playing a personal role in the subsequent violence, contradicts his above statement by explaining the "finishing off" (*diselesaikan*) of the PKI in the province was achieved as a result of the civilian population "working together with ABRI". "We eliminated the movement," Abidin explains, "including me in Seulimum. . . ."[18]

This mass meeting, in conjunction with the Armed Forces Day parade that had been convened by Djuarsa on the same day (as described in chapter 3), was the first public event to be held in the province following the 4 October order for "the People" to assist the military to "completely annihilate" the 30 September Movement. It was a key turning point in the military's attempt to actively involve Aceh's civilian population in its annihilation campaign. Both the military's strengthened position nationally following Suharto's speech at Lubang Buaya on 4 October and the deliberate inducement of a state of emergency in the province appear to have encouraged this escalation. The use of mass meetings to incite civilian participation in the military's annihilation campaign would be repeated throughout the province.

1 October: civilian responses in North Aceh

News of events in Jakarta also appears to have been transmitted to Lhokseumawe, North Aceh, via radio and then spread to surrounding rural areas via word of mouth. Hamid, who in 1965 was working as a small-scale metal worker,[19] has recalled, "to begin with" news about events in Jakarta "spread from mouth to mouth. This is because at that time there was no radio in the *kampung*."[20] Sjam, who in 1965 worked as a peasant and prayer leader on the outskirts of Lhokseumawe,[21] has also recalled hearing about events in Jakarta via word of mouth from other residents in his *kampung*.[22] Sjam recalls this news being like an "explosion".

Upon hearing this news, Hamid remembers that he and the other residents of his *kampung* were "made to join in the night patrol (*jaga malam*)" by the "Sub-district Head (*Camat*), police and Military Precinct Command (*Koramil*)."[23] Sjam also remembers these night patrols.[24] As we saw in chapter 2, night patrols had been established in the subdistrict in 1964 as part of the *Ganyang Malaysia* campaign. Hamid has explained how the patrols were intensified after 1 October, especially along the coast, with twelve men rostered on to each post.[25] These posts were ordered by the Subdistrict Head, police and Subdistrict Military Command to form a 'fence of legs' (*pagar betis*: an encirclement strategy later made infamous by the Indonesian military in East Timor[26]) along the beaches "to stop enemies coming in from the ocean."[27] This strategy seems to have had little practical application for an internal military operation, other than fostering public fear in the absence of any actual local disturbances. Indeed, the Aceh Military Chronology's 'Intelligence Map' records twenty-two "black sail" operations, or illegal landings, occurring in North Aceh between 1 October and 22 December 1965, and 136 for the whole of Aceh,[28] though neither Hamid nor any of my other interviewees remember sighting a single suspicious boat landing during this period. The real purpose of the night patrols, Hamid explains, was "to arrest and to kill" any "communists" that they found.[29] This, Hamid continues, was an order "from Jakarta". As Sjam explains, "There [would be] many people who were killed" in and around Lhokseumawe as a result of this policy.[30]

On 1 October, Arief was in Lhoksukon, 55 km east of Lhokseumawe. Then aged sixteen, he was performing in a LEKRA-affiliated travelling theatre troupe 'Geulanggang Labu',[31] named after a subdistrict in Bireuen, which performed popular plays in Acehnese along Aceh's east coast.[32] Arief recalls "hear[ing] about the coup in Jakarta" while he was sitting in a meeting.[33] This news had come over the radio.[34] Upon hearing this news, Arief recalls, the meeting disbanded in a state of "confusion".

News, meanwhile, appears to have been slower to break in "Kampung X", a small traditional *kampung* near Bireuen. Jamil, a small-scale fisherman, who says he was drafted without his knowledge as a member of the PKI by his brother-in-law, Hasan, has explained he was not aware of events in Jakarta "for a long time", until "arrests" of people associated with the PKI had already begun in the subdistrict.[35] Tjoet, a new mother in 1965 and wife of Hasan, has also independently recalled that she was not aware of the military's plan to attack the PKI until she witnessed the military directly arresting PKI members off the street,[36] as detailed in chapter 5. Both Jamil and Tjoet have explained it was the military that led these arrests and the subsequent killings in Bireuen. It appears this initial period of calm did not last very long.

7 October: Djuarsa arrives in North Aceh

During the morning of 7 October, Djuarsa left Banda Aceh on what would become the first leg of his post–1 October coordination tour. Travelling east, Djuarsa made his first stop in Sigli, Pidie, where he met with former Darul Islam leader Teuku

Daud Beureu'eh.[37] This meeting, which Djuarsa recounted in a 2000 *Tempo* article, has been corroborated by Dahlan Sulaiman, who claims to have travelled with Djuarsa to Pidie and then on to Lhokseumawe, where a mass meeting was held to coordinate the military's annihilation campaign in the district.[38] Beureu'eh, Djuarsa claims, who had attended the Armed Forces Day parade in Banda Aceh two days earlier, used this meeting to pledge his support to Djuarsa, declaring: "General, I support what you are doing with all my heart. I will order the people of Aceh to help you, General."[39] "After this," Djuarsa claims, "the people of Aceh straight away moved to exterminate the PKI."

This meeting is not recorded in the Aceh Military Chronology, but we need to take this account seriously. Ultimately self-incriminating, Djuarsa's recollections corroborate the understanding that while Beureu'eh and sections of Aceh's civilian population were supportive of the military's annihilation campaign, this support was ultimately mediated by Djuarsa.

Details which are recorded in the Military Chronology also testify to military involvement in this initial phase of the campaign in North Aceh. On 7 October, the Military Chronology records, pamphlets had begun to appear at the Lhokseumawe train station.[40] They condemned the PKI, called for Aidit to be hanged and called for "kidnappings to be responded to with kidnappings and cutting up (*pertjentjangan*)[41] to be responded to with cutting up."[42] This is a reference to the since disproved claim the generals murdered by the 30 September Movement were tortured and disfigured with knives, including having their genitals cut off.[43] Two days later on 9 October, meanwhile, the Military Chronology records that a demonstration of 2,000 people took place at 11am in Lhokseumawe, attended by members from four of Aceh's major political parties, including the PNI, NU, Muhammadiyah[44] and IP-KI.[45] Veterans from the "Angkatan 45" ('45 Generation),[46] "private sector workers" and students from the PII are also said to have attended.[47] This wide-ranging attendance indicates that support for the military's attack in the district was broader than Beureu'eh's Darul Islam networks. These protesters, the Military Chronology continues, called for the "PKI, Gerwani, Pemuda Rakyat, BTI, Lekra and its lackeys to be disbanded" and for "all PKI members and their supporters to be dismissed from all government bodies and organisations." "Hang the Gestapo [sic]," the leaflet is said to have continued, "slander is worse than murder. . . . The PKI is the same as Gestapo [sic], chase (*usir*) all PKI members out of Indonesia." The protest was then "received" by the North Aceh Tjatur Tunggal, whose spokesperson proceeded to address the protest, demonstrating implicit state support for this campaign in North Aceh.

1 October: civilian responses in Central Aceh

News about events in Jakarta began to circulate in Takengon, Central Aceh, in the days after 1 October. Ibrahim Kadir, who in 1965 was a primary school teacher and *didong* performer,[48] has recalled hearing news about a "PKI rebellion in Jakarta" via word of mouth during this period.[49] Latifah, a young mother in 1965, and wife of Said, the policeman who would later be accused of being associated with the PKI, recalls first hearing news about events from her husband.[50] Kadir and Latifah have both independently recalled feeling at this time that events in Jakarta did not have much immediate relevance to the community in Takengon until arrests started in the district.[51] These arrests would begin very quickly after Djuarsa visited the district on 7 October.

7 October: Djuarsa arrives in Central Aceh

Djuarsa travelled to Central Aceh on 7 October, on what would be his third post–1 October coordination tour destination following Pidie and Lhokseumawe.[52] His first activity in the district was to attend a meeting of Central Aceh's military leadership.[53] Unfortunately no records have been recovered from this meeting. Djuarsa then proceeded to the Musara Alun sports field, in central Takengon, where he delivered a speech to impress his intentions upon the crowds that gathered to hear him speak.[54] "Jusuf", today a local politician, attended Djuarsa's speech as a primary school student with his father.[55] He recalls that the catch-cry of the meeting had been "crush the PKI (*ganyang PKI*)".[56] People chanted this slogan with raised fists, Jusuf explains, and had understood that they were being instructed to kill members of the PKI. Kadir has also recalled that Djuarsa used the address to order civilians to murder members of the PKI.[57] "The PKI are *kafir* [non-believers]," Kadir recalls Djuarsa announcing. "I [Djuarsa] will destroy them to their roots! If in the *kampung* you find members of the PKI but do not kill them, it will be you who we punish!"

Djuarsa thus told the civilian population in Takengon that if they did not assist the military to kill members of the PKI, they themselves could expect to be heavily punished or even killed. This threat is further evidence that civilian participation in the killings was ultimately coercive. The military does not seem to have wasted much time after this, launching arrests in the district almost immediately. These arrests were led by the military. As Kadir has explained, on 11 October fifteen "armed people" arrived at his classroom door as he was teaching the national anthem to his year five students.[58] Upon opening the door, these "armed people", under the command of Lieutenant Abdullatif, whom he recognised as members of the "WMD" civilian militia group that had originally been mobilised to "crush" the Darul Islam rebellion in the district, proceeded to train their weapons at his head and tell his students, "[y]our teacher is going to be taken to town."[59] Kadir's house was then searched before he was taken to a military-controlled prison near the centre of town, where, over the next twenty-five days, all prisoners, except for him, were taken out at night on the back of trucks to be murdered at military-controlled killing sites throughout the district.[60] As we shall see in chapter 6, Kadir was forced to witness many of these killings firsthand. Indeed, he is believed to be the only prisoner to escape alive from this systematic killing campaign in the district.[61] It is not clear why Kadir was released. It is possible that as a relatively high-profile member of his community he was vouched for by a friend or family member with a connection to the military. Other similar but rare cases of release have been recorded in the province.[62]

1 October: civilian responses in West Aceh

News of events in Jakarta also appears to have been transmitted to Meulaboh, West Aceh via radio on 1 October.[63] According to Teuku Muhammad Yatim, who in 1965 was a member of the PSII and Assistant District Chief for Johan Pahlawan subdistrict, 12 km from Meulaboh, this news arrived "very quickly" and was delivered by "the military . . . from Kutaradja [Banda Aceh]."[64] This news conveyed a sense of urgency, prompting Yatim to "return home straight away", from where he was working in the field. Soon after this, Yatim continues, "the arrests [of PKI members] began" with surprising speed. As he explains, "Even I [as a member of the district government] was shocked." These arrests did not begin spontaneously. As Yatim has explained, the arrests and killings did not begin until after Aceh's Military Commander Ishak Djuarsa arrived in the district on 8 October.

8 October: Djuarsa arrives in West Aceh

Djuarsa, acting in his capacity as Pangdahan 'A', arrived in Meulaboh on 8 October with Aceh's Police Commander, S. Samsuri Mertojoso, for Djuarsa's fourth post–1 October coordination tour destination. The trip, almost 400 km via Bireuen and through the interior, would have required many hours. Djuarsa and Martojoso's arrival in Meulaboh is described in the Chronology as an "inspection", where, it is reported, they happened to find themselves "in front" of a demonstration that "called upon" Djuarsa and Martojoso to dissolve the PKI and its affiliated organisations.[65]

Yatim, however, suggests the visit was more coordinated than this. According to Yatim, in an account backed up by documents recovered as part of the Chain of Command documents bundle, Djuarsa had travelled to Meulaboh to specifically discuss what actions should be taken following the events of 1 October, first holding a meeting with West Aceh's civilian government before addressing the demonstration.[66] The purpose of this meeting and public address was to spark the campaign against the PKI that would culminate in the mass killings that occurred later in the district. Through Djuarsa's announcements at this time the PKI was portrayed as having launched a coup that would soon spread to West Aceh if drastic action was not taken. "[W]hen the Panglima came here for the meeting," Yatim recalls:

> it became even clearer what steps had been taken by the PKI. After this meeting . . . [it was said] let's go into the field, there's no longer a need for meetings *wo, wo, wo* [the sound of being revved up].[67]

A meeting was then held at the Teuku Umar sports field by Djuarsa, who announced,"If you don't kill [the PKI], they will be the ones doing the killing (*kalau tidak bunuh, mereka yang membunuh*)."[68] It was these announcements, Yatim recalls, which he describes as an "order . . . to kill the PKI",[69] that sparked the beginning of a wave of abductions, "arrests" and killings in the district.

11 October: meeting of the West Aceh Level II Provincial Government

This coordination in West Aceh continued after Djuarsa's departure. On 11 October, a 'Special Session and Open Meeting' of the West Aceh Level II Provincial Government was held in the district's meeting hall.[70] The four-hour meeting was an important decision-making event for the district's political elite and was attended by twelve members of the West Aceh civilian government, including T.M. Yatim, who attended as Assistant District Chief for Johan Pahlawan.[71] The District Military Commander for West Aceh, a representative of the Subdistrict Military Commander, a representative of the West Aceh Bupati, the West Aceh Pantja Tunggal, heads of government offices, and leaders of political parties and mass organisations from West Aceh's *Front Nasional* also attended the meeting.[72] Meanwhile, six apologies are listed, including one from Saidul (head of the West Aceh PKI and representative for the 'Communist Group'[73] within the West Aceh civilian government).[74] Saidul, Yatim recalls, was killed after being arrested.[75]

The purpose of the meeting, the documents explain, was to discuss "the event that calls itself the 30 September Movement".[76]

To open discussion, Nja' Moesa, Deputy Head of West Aceh's civilian government, described the 30 September Movement as a "Counter Revolution" which had decommissioned the Dwikora Cabinet and placed "the state of our Nation in the most worrying situation, both in the Centre [Jakarta] and in the regions".[77] He had gathered this information, Moesa explained, from radio broadcasts from Jakarta and Banda Aceh and from the five documents that form the body of the Chain of Command documents bundle. These directives were referenced throughout the meeting, along with "clarifications" requested from Djuarsa in his capacity as Pangdahan 'A', and Aceh's Police Commander, Martojoso, who are noted as having just made a visit to Meulaboh.[78] 'Minutes' from the meeting of West Aceh's Level II Provincial Government also provide us with a glimpse into the thinking of political parties in the district at the time.

Representatives from the West Aceh *Front Nasional* speak

After this discussion, representatives from the West Aceh district government proceeded to produce a binding declaration. Each political group from the West Aceh *Front Nasional*, less the Communist Group (which had been formally expelled), was given a chance to deliberate before their proposals were shared and collated into a united course of action.[79] "Quorum", it is noted, had been reached, despite the absence of delegates from the Communist Group.[80] This process was overseen and directed by the West Aceh military leadership and the West Aceh Pantja Tunggal.

Representatives from the National Group (*Golongan Nasional*), Religious Group (*Golongan Agama*) and Functionaries Group (*Golongan Karya*)[81] were given the opportunity to speak. The National Group, through its representative, M. Sjam Sary, described the actions of the 30 September Movement as "counter revolutionary terror".[82] Sary then declared that the National Group "supported in full" the documents that now form the Chain of Command documents bundle. These documents, the Minutes record, included the 'Announcement' by the Pantja Tunggal in Banda Aceh on 4 October that "the people are mandated to assist in every effort to completely annihilate the counter-revolutionary 30 September Movement" and the two 'Joint Decisions' by the Pantja Tunggal, *Front Nasional* and eight political parties in Banda Aceh on 6 October to "assist with full energy attempts to completely annihilate the 30 September Movement" and to "take all necessary steps against the PKI".[83] Finally, the National Group called upon President Sukarno "via the Pangdahan A" (Djuarsa), to dissolve the PKI and to treat it as an "illegal party".

The Religious Group, through its representative, Abd. Karim, essentially repeated these points. It described the 30 September Movement as "counter revolutionary" and referenced documents within the Chain of Command documents bundle, mirroring orders found within those documents to declare in its own words the need to:

> Call upon all layers of Society to always be on guard and to **assist ABRI to annihilate and eliminate the 30 September Movement along with its affiliated organisations**.[84]

This is the second example of written evidence that we have from Aceh, and indeed from throughout Indonesia, in which civilians are called upon to "annihilate" the "30 September Movement". At the time, not everyone was comfortable with this dramatic escalation. The Functionaries Group spoke next, represented by T.M. Yatim, who is recorded as expressing a rare documented example of apprehension about supporting the slide towards state-sanctioned violence that was occurring in the district.[85] He is documented in the Minutes declaring:

> We are unable to make a detailed decision, such as has already been conveyed by the groups [that have already spoken], we are not really clear what is meant by the Leadership.[86]

Yatim explained to me in 2011 that other participants at the meeting also felt pressured and understood such orders to be more than abstract denunciations. Even as the meeting got underway, Yatim has recalled, "arrests were already occurring", carried out by a local branch of the Pancasila Defence Front,[87] the military-sponsored death squad that had been established in Banda Aceh on 6 October.

Yatim claims to have walked out of the meeting as a sign of protest but this protest is not recorded in the Minutes. In fact, Yatim is listed as a member of the five-person 'Editorial Committee', as the representative for the Working Group, which would produce the official account of the meeting that can be found in the Chain of Command documents bundle.[88] Although there are obvious reasons for Yatim to 'misremember' by exaggerating his opposition to a call to lend support to a campaign of state-sponsored extra-judicial killing, even if he is wrong about his own role, his testimony supports the notion that this is indeed what the members of West Aceh's civilian government were being asked to support – and that they knew it. Indeed, there is evidence that Yatim's group attempted to move away from the explicit call for violent action made by the Religious Group, by proposing the use of more legalistic measures against the 30 September Movement. The cautiousness of the wording in this section of the Minutes hints at the sensitivity of the issues discussed. This section records the Functionaries Group as saying:

> Because we understand the problem, we are able to accept [that something must be done]. We don't want to just tag along with these decisions, but the decision of the Working Group is as such:
>
> 1   The Pepelrada, with the authority that he has, should immediately freeze the PKI/its affiliate mass organisations.
> 2   All those who represent the PKI [and] its affiliated organisations should be de-activated from all Government Organisations [and] Bodies within Aceh's Provincial Government.
> 3   Our [the West Aceh Level II Provincial Government's] declarations should include:
>
> (a)   Congratulations to Bung Karno, A.N. Nasution.
> (b)   The harshest condemnation of the 30 September Movement.
> (c)   Urge (*mendesak*) that those who are involved be punished with Revolutionary Law.[89]

The Religious Group's speech thus falls short of calling for the annihilation of the 30 September Movement. The final point of the Group's speech, however, is quite ambiguous. What is meant by "Revolutionary Law" is not made clear. It may be that the term was considered to be more euphemistic than calls to "annihilate", for, while it also implied a suspension of the normal legal framework, it was more reminiscent of the high-flown rhetoric used by Sukarno. As Daniel Lev has suggested, the concept of 'Revolutionary Law' had arisen under Guided Democracy, and was used by Sukarno as an alternative to the written law, which he portrayed as outdated and attached to the colonial period.[90] The term was also used, Lev continues, as a means to provide political leaders with a "symbol of flexibility and freedom from constraint", allowing them to move beyond the set limits of the law in the name of the revolution. Sukarno articulated his concept as a series of principles through which his notion of revolution could be implemented. As Sukarno explained in his 1965 Independence Day speech, there were six major "revolutionary laws" (*hukum-hukum revolusi*) that should be pursued.[91] These laws included the principle that "the revolution has friends and enemies", with the elucidation:

> It is important to know who your enemies and friends are; as such it is important to draw a clear line and take appropriate measures for dealing with these friends and enemies of the revolution.[92]

Though provocative, this Maoist-inspired explanation was not a call for physical violence. Rather, it was understood at the time as a reinforcement of Sukarno's long held understanding that counter-revolutionary elements existed within Indonesian society and that such elements should be isolated and "retooled" – that is, removed from political office. In the past these "retooling" campaigns had led to considerable political persecution, but not state-sanctioned killings. Now, as shall be seen below, the concept of 'Revolutionary Law' would be adopted by the military and reframed to justify physical annihilation.

Declaration by the West Aceh Level II Provincial Government

The meeting then moved without further discussion to produce a Declaration (*Pernjataan No: 4/DPRDGR/AB/1965*), based on the input of the various ideological groups. The Declaration did not provide the de-escalation that the Functionaries Group had hoped for. Instead it named each of the earlier Chain of Command documents, before declaring the 30 September Movement to be a "counter revolutionary movement" that wished to "abolish the Nation Declared on 17 August 1945" (i.e. Indonesia).[93] It then stated that the 30 September Movement had "carried out barbaric terrors outside the realm of what was human" and announced explicitly, for the first time in a document from Aceh issued on behalf of a government body, that "[t]here is now proof . . . [that] the 30 September Movement's brain, puppet master and greatest supporter is the PKI and its affiliated organisations."

All references to the 30 September Movement from 11 October in the district should now be interpreted as referring explicitly to the PKI. This statement of PKI guilt preceded by five months the official banning of the PKI nationally on 12 March 1966, when the acronym 'G.30.S/PKI' first began to be adopted in official documents nationally.[94]

The Declaration then proceeded to outline eight resolutions, which appear to incorporate the Functionaries Group's reservations by simply inserting them alongside the more drastic measures which had been called for. Resolutions one to four of the Declaration are essentially statements of loyalty towards the Indonesian state and President Sukarno. They describe the 30 September Movement as a "traitorous movement" that must be "condemned as strongly as possible".[95] The final four resolutions read as such:

5   Support in full the declaration of the Joint Declaration of the *Front Nasional* and Political Parties and Mass Organisations in West Aceh on 8 October, No:001/Ist/1965, as well as all Decisions and Declarations that are initiated in Aceh Special Region which are "consistent" with points 1 to 5 above.

6   Call upon all layers of Society to increase their awareness and sharpen the *rentjong* of vigilance **while assisting ABRI to annihilate and completely eliminate the 30 September Movement** along with its affiliated organisations while supporting firm unity and integrity.

7   Urge the President and Supreme Commander of the Armed Forces/Great Leader of the Revolution, Bung Karno, to as quickly as possible dissolve the PKI along with its affiliated mass organisations and to consider it to be an illegal Party/organisation.

8   Call upon the Pangdahan A/Panglima Kodam I/Atjeh [Djuarsa], acting as the Pepelrada Aceh to . . . freeze the PKI and its affiliated organisations . . . make non-active all PKI representatives/all those affiliated with it from Government Bodies . . . [and] take stringent measures against the PKI/its affiliated mass organisations to guard against undesired outcomes and issues which bring into danger the safety of the Nation and Pantja Sila in line with Revolutionary law.[96]

Measures which were originally designed to lessen the severity of the government attack against the PKI and its affiliated organisations, such as calls for freezing the PKI and "de-activating" its members from government positions, are thus used here as a means to intensify this attack, with the term "Revolutionary Law" used interchangeably with the term "annihilate". "Members" of the 30 September Movement were to be treated as enemies outside the law. Meanwhile, the West Aceh civilian government gave itself the authority to support any action "consistent" with the "spirit" of the campaign to attack the 30 September Movement, while also providing support for the military to act likewise.

Significantly, this is the earliest official directive produced by a purely government body so far found either in Aceh or nationally to call upon "all layers of Society" to participate in the military's annihilation campaign. The Declaration, which recognised the military's multiple command structures in the province, also acknowledged Suharto's insubordinate leadership nationally, by referring to him in his capacity as Minister for the Armed Forces, a position he assumed during the morning of 1 October and refused to renounce, despite being ordered by Sukarno to do so.[97] Copies of the document were sent to Suharto acting in this position.[98] It was also sent to Sukarno, Mokoginta, Djuarsa and key political bodies in the province, plus Radio Republic Indonesia in Banda Aceh.[99] As with other declarations and statements sent during this time, the broad circulation of the document served the dual purpose of indicating the West Aceh civilian government's loyalty to Suharto's insubordinate leadership, while also inciting other government bodies to act in a similar manner. As Yatim's testimony attests, delegates at the meeting appear to have been under extraordinary pressure to denounce the 30 September Movement and support the military's attack, at the risk of being labelled traitors themselves. At a minimum, it is now impossible for the military command in Jakarta to claim it was ignorant of what was happening in the regions at this time, as the military's orders were now being sent back up the chain of command.

1 October: civilian responses in South Aceh

News of events in Jakarta also reached South Aceh via radio. Oesman, who in 1965 was a high school teacher in South Aceh's main town of Tapaktuan, has recalled hearing news about a "coup" in Jakarta via radio.[100] Ali, a peasant farmer from Samadua subdistrict, a PKI stronghold 12 km inland from Tapaktuan, remembers hearing over the radio that a PKI "rebellion" had occurred.[101] Meanwhile, Hamzah, who in 1965 was working in the Subdistrict Office in Labuanhaji, 28 km northwest along the coast from Tapaktuan, recalls some people in the subdistrict heard news about events in Jakarta via the one or two radios that existed in the subdistrict. He himself heard the news via word of mouth.[102]

As had occurred in Seulimum, the radio broadcast Oesman and Ali heard appears to have been the broadcast made by the 30 September Movement itself. Oesman, for example, has explained that it was not until "an official came" to Tapaktuan that he knew "that the PKI had carried out a coup", as before the official arrived, Oesman has explained, "we only knew about the Council of Generals coup."[103] Ali, meanwhile, has recalled how after hearing this radio broadcast, "I thought to myself, it's happening, it's time for the rebellion [led by the PKI] . . . [and] I wanted to join in at that time in my *kampung*."[104] There thus seems to have been confusion in the district as to what exactly was occurring. In Oesman's opinion, as a civilian, it "only became clear a few months later", once the killings were over, what exactly had occurred.[105] Before this time, Oesman has recalled:

> We were in a state of fear . . . afraid of becoming implicated, even though we felt that we weren't . . . the situation wasn't clear. Who should we support? Did we want to support [the 30 September Movement's] Revolution Council? That wasn't definite. Who did we want to support?[106]

The fact that Oesman, like Abidin in Seulimum, had even considered supporting the Revolution Council is remarkable as it is generally acknowledged in literature on the immediate post–1 October period that only die-hard supporters of the PKI in Central Java responded positively to the 30 September Movement's call to action.[107] Oesman attributes this confusion in South Aceh to the district's isolation. As he explains:

> There were no TVs here at the time, only radio broadcasts, and even the radio had to use a battery and the antenna had to be placed on a coconut tree [to get a signal], so the news wasn't clear.[108]

In the meantime, he and others like him awaited direction. "[W]e would support whoever . . ." he begins, before trailing off, seeming to correct himself:

> We were waiting [for leadership] . . . we went with the flow (*kemana arahnya ke situ ikut*). It took a while before it was clear and we knew, oh, yeah, it was the PKI. . . . It's true that Tapaktuan is not really that engaged with those sort of things . . . even [the district government] was just following orders at that time.[109]

This leadership would come from the military-controlled South Aceh Pantja Tunggal and the Defence Sector Command (*Kosekhan*). The proposed course of action would be disturbing. Oesman has recalled that a meeting was held on 8 October, where it was explained that "the nation was in trouble" and that it was the "PKI who had carried out the coup".[110] Then, "once it was clear that it was the PKI that [did it], we were taught how to crush the PKI" (*setelah jelas itu PKI yang [buat], [kami] diajarkan pengganyangan PKI*).[111] As shall be seen, the term "crush" was not used metaphorically. Hamzah in Labuanhaji has also described how this campaign was led by the "government" that was now "united" behind the military's campaign.[112]

8 October: "anti-PKI" demonstration in South Aceh

According to Oesman, the new military-dominated district leadership was consolidated a week after 1 October on or around 8 October, at an "anti-PKI" demonstration held in Tapaktuan attended by the *Front Nasional*.[113] At this demonstration, Oesman has recalled, the *Front Nasional* issued an "appeal" that "whoever felt themselves to be involved with the PKI [should] report themselves [to the *Front Nasional*]." This appeal, he has explained, "was a trap" (*suatu jebakan*):[114]

> Many of them didn't understand, because they were also scared. Eh, [they were told] you have to report to save yourselves . . . to be separated (*dapat pengasingan*) etc, so they wouldn't be intimidated, that's how the propaganda went, so many of those who reported didn't know [about the 30 September Movement], [they weren't members of the PKI] but had perhaps been involved with the [BTI], or . . . with LEKRA.[115]

The purpose of asking those who considered themselves to be associated with the PKI to report, Oesman asserts, was to "ascertain . . . how many PKI people there really were".[116] Those who reported themselves to the *Front Nasional* subsequently became targets of the military's attack. Individuals who were allowed to leave after reporting either became the targets of public violence (described in chapter 5), or were re-arrested and taken to military-controlled killing sites (described in chapter 6). As Oesman has explained, "There was no normalisation [after this]." Around this time, Oesman recalls, the South Aceh Kosekhan, which was stationed at the District Military Command base,[117] "gave an explanation" that the population should be on guard and that a "night watch" be established to help facilitate this campaign.[118] The government, Hamzah explains, "had already unified (*sudah menyatu*) the people with the military".[119]

1 October: civilian responses in East Aceh

As outlined in chapter 3, Djuarsa had been in Langsa on 1 October. News also reached East Aceh's subdistricts on this day. News reached East Aceh's plantation-based Tamiang subdistrict on 1 October via radio.[120] Taufik, from Village 1 in Tamiang, recalls hearing news about events in Jakarta over the radio at this time.[121] He has described how "news about [the actions of the 30 September Movement] was everywhere" at this time. Karim and Aminah, a married couple from neighbouring Village 2, who both had ties to the PKI (Aminah had joined LEKRA at the age of twelve due to her love of music, while Karim, originally from Village 1, had been invited to a PKI cadre school) also recall first hearing news about events in Jakarta over the radio.[122] There was only one radio in the village, Karim explains, with residents pooling their money to buy batteries.[123] News, however, spread quickly through the two villages, along with reports about Soebandrio's visit to Langsa on 1 October. Karim had wanted to travel to Langsa to hear Soebandrio speak, but it was too far for him to ride his pushbike.[124]

According to Taufik, Aruji Kartawinanta, a minister in Soebandrio's convoy, had made a "shocking" announcement at this meeting in response to news from Jakarta, which was also circulated throughout the district at this time.[125] At this meeting, Kartawinata reportedly declared, "I don't agree with the basis of the Nation of the Republic of Indonesia being NASAKOM!" This statement challenged Sukarno's ideological basis for the Indonesian state and drew into question the legitimacy of the continued coexistence of "nationalism", "religion" and "communism" as accepted political streams within the Indonesian polity. Unfortunately, this statement cannot be corroborated. If correct, it suggests the ideological basis of the Indonesian state was being publically called into question in East Aceh at this early stage.

The situation in the two villages during the immediate aftermath of 1 October, meanwhile, remained calm. Karim and Aminah have recalled that "nothing occurred" for the first few days.[126] Shortly after this, however, Karim has recalled, residents in Village 1 were ordered to establish "guard posts" and organise village youths into shifts to patrol the perimeters of the village, especially along the perimeter with Village 2,[127] which was considered to be a "PKI village" because the Village Head was an active PKI member. Not long after this the killings began. According to Taufik, Karim and Aminah, the killings were limited to Village 2. As Taufik explains, "It was our neighbours who were killed."[128] These killings, they insist, were led by the military.[129] Although Taufik, as a bystander, has reason to distance himself from this violence, his account is corroborated by the descriptions of this violence, presented over the next two chapters, which suggest the military may indeed have played a particularly direct role in the killings in Tamiang.

Saifuddin, from East Aceh's peasant-based Idi subdistrict, also heard news about events in Jakarta via radio.[130] This broadcast, he explains, attempted to portray the 30 September Movement as a national security threat, indicating that the broadcast he heard was from the military. Saifuddin explains he did "not understand" what this broadcast meant, because while it was announced that "the PKI was going on the attack in Jakarta", there was no indication that this was also happening "in the village [Idi]".[131]

The killings in Idi, Saifuddin explains, did not begin until news started to circulate that "the PKI in Aceh was to be isolated (*disingkirkan*)".[132] These orders came from the military. As Saifuddin explains, "What we heard was that they [those associated with the PKI] were to be taken to the plantations [to be killed], to be taken to the military, or it wouldn't be resolved."

5 October: meeting of the East Aceh Level II
Provincial Government

The military's attack against the PKI was also coordinated in East Aceh's districts and subdistricts through a series of military- and government-run meetings. On 5 October, a meeting was held in the East Aceh Level II Provincial Government building in Langsa.[133] This meeting, which was portrayed as a means of explaining that '30 September Movement Affair', was led by the East Aceh Pantja Tunggal.[134] The meeting was also attended by the leadership of the East Aceh civilian government and "all its members", "the Armed Forces", heads of government bodies in the district, leaders from "all mass organisations in East Aceh", "community leaders", and representatives from eight of the main political parties in the district.[135] These parties included the PKI, which was represented by Radjab Nurdin, in addition to the PNI, Partindo, IP-KI, NU, PSII, PI Perti and Parkindo.[136]

Those attending this meeting heard Sukarno's "first and second announcements",[137] which were apparently meant to legitimate Suharto's insubordinate leadership, and "suggestions" from the East Aceh Pantja Tunggal and the East Aceh civilian government.[138] Attendees were also presented with the "opinions" of the political parties and mass organisations present, before producing a document of their own. This document, similar to that produced in West Aceh, outlines a list of "decisions" made at the meeting. These decisions are remarkably moderate in tone. The first three decisions made at the meeting include a generic expression of relief that Sukarno's life had been spared, a pledge of loyalty towards him and an expression of sympathy for the military leaders killed by the 30 September Movement. The sixth decision contains an appeal to God to protect the Indonesian Revolution. Decisions four and five, however, provide the reader with a deeper insight into dynamics in the district. These points read:

IV Continue to protect the integration between the Armed Forces of the Republic of Indonesia and the People to guarantee safety/general security and remain alert/on guard to confront the Nekolim within the framework of DWIKORA.

V   Condemn and demand that immediate, decisive and proportionate action be taken against those that have clearly (*njata2*) been involved in treachery towards to the Nation and Revolution along with its ideology, the Panca Sila.[139]

Point four, with its appeal to Dwikora, mirrors decisions being made in Banda Aceh and suggests the district military command had similarly implemented *de facto* martial law conditions in East Aceh. Meanwhile, point five is remarkably moderate in tone. While the Banda Aceh Pantja Tunggal meeting held on 4 October contained a resolution to "completely annihilate that which is called the '30 September Movement' along with its lackeys",[140] the East Aceh Pantja Tunggal, in this 5 October document, demanded only that "proportionate" action be taken and only against those who could be "clearly" proven to have been involved in the 30 September Movement. Even more remarkably, the document was signed by Radjab Nurdin on behalf of the PKI.[141] The only comparable document recovered from Aceh during this period is the 'Joint Decision' prepared on 6 October in Banda Aceh, which the PKI had refused to sign. This begs the question of why a PKI representative felt comfortable signing a roughly similar document in East Aceh. It is possible the more moderate language used by the Pantja Tunggal in East Aceh reflected the greater esteem with which the PKI was held in the district, while this variation also supports the idea that the PKI in Aceh, caught by surprise, did not respond to the military's attack from 1 October with a coordinated plan. Alternatively, it may have been the early timing of this document that meant the East Aceh Pantja Tunggal was unwilling to be too provocative in its language.

The repetition found in this and other documents produced in Aceh's districts at this time demonstrates the coordinated nature of the military leadership's attempt to involve local military and civilian government structures in its attack against the PKI. This coordination was intended to spread complicity for this attack and to ensure the military's annihilation campaign was implemented through a full mobilisation of the resources available to these structures. The pattern of events that emerges from these documents is that news of events in Jakarta first spread to civilian populations via radio. In some cases, as in Seulimum and Takengon, it appears the first news local populations heard of events in Jakarta was the 30 September Movement's own broadcasts announcing that a military coup led by the Council of Generals had been thwarted by the 30 September Movement. More commonly, however, the first news that local civilian populations heard was the military's broadcasts, announcing that the 30 September Movement had launched a coup attempt in Jakarta and that the military had launched a national offensive to annihilate the Movement and all those associated with it.

The military's announcements, along with the initial orders and directives issued by the national military leadership, were disseminated down to the district level in a very effective manner. Beginning with Suharto's order to Mokoginta during the morning of 1 October, which was then passed on to Djuarsa and Aceh's Level I Provincial Government later on the same day, these orders were received at the district level, enabling the military to coordinate its campaign down to the subdistrict level within a matter of days.

These initial orders and directives were followed by coordinating meetings in each of Aceh's districts, facilitated by Djuarsa's coordination tour throughout the province. In each district, an internal meeting was held with members of the district military leadership, before meetings took place between the newly consolidated military leadership and civilian government leaderships in the districts and subdistricts. The military used these meetings to pass on national and interprovincial military orders and directives before resolutions were sought from Aceh's district and subdistrict governments pledging support for the military's campaign. These resolutions were used to bring Aceh's district governments into line with the military leadership, as well as to spread complicity for the violence that the declarations called for. Members of Aceh's Level II provincial governments, Pantja Tunggal and *Front Nasional* bodies are documented signing such declarations, along with representatives from local political parties and mass organisations, which pledge their support for the military's annihilation campaign and call on the local civilian population to assist the military to implement its attack against the PKI.

Great pressure was placed on local district governments to achieve these resolutions, including open and veiled threats of violence, such as in West Aceh, where state-sponsored death squads were established and activated even as these coordinating meetings were taking place. Indeed, three separate state-sponsored death squads were formed in the province during this period: the Pantja Sila Defence Front, formed in Banda Aceh on 6 October; the Pantjasila Defence Front, formed in West Aceh around 11 October; and the People's Defence, established in South Aceh during the first two weeks of October. Night patrols and arrest campaigns were also initiated at this time.

Following this consolidation of Aceh's district military and civilian leadership, public meetings were held to communicate these directives to local populations. In Pidie and Lhokseumawe, Takengon and Meulaboh, Aceh's Military Commander Ishak Djuarsa attended these meetings as part of his coordination tour. My interviewees reveal that Djuarsa used these meetings to demand that local populations "assist" the military by hunting down and killing members of the PKI, while warning those who did not participate in this campaign that they risked becoming targets of violence themselves. It would be in the immediate aftermath of these public mass meetings, and not before, that the first reported killings would occur.

At the national and provincial levels, great emphasis was placed on maintaining the appearance of legal continuity between the pre–1 October and emerging post–1 October regimes. The military's campaign was portrayed at every level in Aceh as an extension of the *Ganyang Malaysia* campaign, which was to be implemented through existing legislation and the activation of the Kohanda command. Meanwhile, the use of multiple command structures by the military to implement this campaign at the district level demonstrates the flexibility of the military leadership as it eased itself into its new position of power. Now that consensus had been imposed, the military's annihilation campaign could begin in earnest.

Notes

1 Written interview with Asan, given to the author, Hong Kong, 30 October 2011, p. 1.
2 *Ibid.*
3 Chinese National Day is celebrated on 1 October.
4 Interview with Asan, Hong Kong, 31 October 2011, p. 30.
5 *Ibid.*
6 Written interview with Asan, given to the author, Hong Kong, 30 October 2011, p. 5.
7 *Ibid.*, p. 1.
8 Interview with Asan, Hong Kong, 31 October 2011, p. 30.
9 *Laporan Tahunan Lengkap Kodam-I/Kohanda Atjeh, Tahun 1965* (Banda Aceh: Kodam-I Banda Aceh, 1 February 1966), p. 12.
10 Interview with Zainuddin Hamid, "Let Bugeh", Banda Aceh, 17 January 2010, p. 8.
11 *Ibid.*
12 Interview with Zainal Abidin, Banda Aceh, 14 February 2009, p. 8.
13 *Ibid.*

14 *Ibid.*, p. 9.
15 *Ibid.*
16 *Ibid.*
17 *Ibid.*, p. 11.
18 *Ibid.*, p. 8.
19 Interview with "Hamid", Lhokseumawe, North Aceh, 19 December 2011, p. 2.
20 *Ibid.*, p. 8.
21 Interview with "Sjam", Lhokseumawe, North Aceh, 19 December 2011, p. 1.
22 *Ibid.*, p. 4.
23 Interview with "Hamid", Lhokseumawe, North Aceh, 19 December 2011, p. 8.
24 Interview with "Sjam", Lhokseumawe, North Aceh, 19 December 2011, p. 5.
25 Interview with "Hamid", Lhokseumawe, North Aceh, 19 December 2011, p. 9.
26 The 'fence of legs' (*pagar betis*) strategy has been used by the Indonesian military since at least the 1950s, when it was adopted against the Darul Islam rebellion in West Java as a means of involving civilians in counter-insurgency actions. By using civilians to lead these patrols, civilians became human shields, a tactic intended to demoralise both insurgents and local civilian populations. In addition to its actions against the Darul Islam, the PKI and in East Timor, the Indonesian military has also used the strategy in Ambon [1999–2002] and during the recent separatist struggle in Aceh. Matt Davis, *Indonesia's War Over Aceh: Last Stand on Mecca's Porch* (Oxon: Routledge, 2006), p. 186. For an account of the use of the 'fence of legs' strategy in East Java during the period of the Indonesian genocide, see, Vannessa Hearman, 'Dismantling the "Fortress": East Java and the Transition to Suharto's New Order Regime (1965–68)', PhD thesis, The University of Melbourne, 2012, pp. 175–176.
27 Interview with "Hamid", Lhokseumawe, North Aceh, 19 December 2011, p. 9.
28 There are two "black sail" operations recorded for Banda Aceh, six for Sigli, twenty-two for North Aceh, ten for East Aceh and ninety-six for West Aceh. 'Lampiran: Peta Dibidang Intelidjen', in 'Chronologis Kedjadian2 jang Berhubungan dengan Gerakan 30 September Didaerah Kodam-I/Atjeh'.
29 Interview with "Hamid", Lhokseumawe, North Aceh, 19 December 2011, p. 10.
30 Interview with "Sjam", Lhokseumawe, North Aceh, 19 December 2011, p. 7.
31 Geulanggang Labu was active in Aceh during the Japanese occupation, when it was used to promote Japanese propaganda, such as the idea of Greater East Asia and hatred against Western colonialism. The group continued to tour following the Japanese occupation. Reza Idria, 'Two Stages of Performance in Aceh: From State Conflict to Syariah Politics', in Barbara Hatley and Brett Hough (eds.), *Performing Contemporary Indonesia: Celebrating Identity, Constructing Community* (Leiden: Brill, 2008), p. 175. The group, along with others like it, was very popular. See also, Sulaiman Juned, 'Sandiwara Gelenggang Lebu'. Available online: http://sjuned.blogspot.com.au/2009/01/sandiwara-gelanggang-labu.html.
32 Interview with "Arief", Banda Aceh, 5 February 2009, pp. 1, 4, 8.
33 *Ibid.*, p. 8.
34 *Ibid.*, p. 1.
35 *Ibid.* p. 37.
36 Interview with "Tjoet", Kampung X, Bireuen, North Aceh, 11 February 2009, pp. 4–5.
37 'Ishak Djuarsa: Sejak 1967, Pak Harto Sudah Seperti Imam yang Batal Wudu', p. 39.
38 Interview with Dahlan Sulaiman, Banda Aceh, p. 33.
39 'Ishak Djuarsa: Sejak 1967, Pak Harto Sudah Seperti Imam yang Batal Wudu', p. 39.
40 'Chronologis', p. 3.
41 '*Daging cincang*' or '*tjentjang*' means 'minced meat'.
42 'Chronologis', p. 3.
43 Autopsy reports of the murdered generals, viewed by Benedict Anderson, showed no signs of torture. The false reports of torture appear to have been a deliberate attempt

to fuel anger against the 30 September Movement. See Benedict Anderson, 'How Did the Generals Die?', *Indonesia*, Vol. 43 (April 1987), pp. 109–134.

44 Muhammadiyah, meaning 'followers of Muhammad', was founded in 1912 in Yogyakarta as a modernist Islamic organisation. In 1945 is advocated an Islamic state for Indonesia and joined Masjumi but survived the banning of Masjumi in 1960.

45 'Chronologis', p. 3 IP-KI (*Ikatan Pendukung Kemerdekaan Indonesia*: League of Supporters of Indonesian Independence) was founded in 1954 by supporters of Nasution. The League participated in the 1955 general elections, before supporting the implementation of Guided Democracy, which it claimed could end divisions between the political parties. It withdrew its support for Guided Democracy when it appeared that Sukarno intended to leave the group out of his DPR-GR (Guided Democracy era) cabinet. It had a large support base among military officers and their families.

46 "Angkatan 45" refers to the generation of Indonesians who fought during the national revolution.

47 'Chronologis', p. 3.

48 Interview with Ibrahim Kadir, Takengon, Central Aceh, 7 February 2009, p. 1.

49 Interview with Ibrahim Kadir, Takengon, Central Aceh, 7 February 2009, p. 1; Interview with "Latifah", Banda Aceh, 15 February 2009, p. 2.

50 Interview with "Latifah", Banda Aceh, 15 February 2009, p. 2.

51 Interview with Ibrahim Kadir, Takengon, Central Aceh, 7 February 2009, p. 1; Interview with "Latifah", Banda Aceh, 15 February 2009, p. 2.

52 Second interview with Ibrahim Kadir, Takengon, Central Aceh, 8 February 2009. As outlined above, Djuarsa claims to have been in Pidie and North Aceh, on 7 October, meeting with Daud Beureu'eh. Meanwhile, the Military Chronology records Djuarsa arriving in Meulaboh, West Aceh, on 8 October. It is possible he travelled the 200 km from Pidie to Takengon on the same day.

53 *Ibid.*

54 Interview with "Abdullah", Takengon, Central Aceh, 9 February 2009, p. 15; Interview with "Jusuf", Takengon, Central Aceh, 9 February 2009, p. 4. Interview with Ibrahim Kadir, Takengon, Central Aceh, 7 February 2009, p. 5.

55 Interview with "Jusuf" (a pseudonym), Takengon, Central Aceh, 9 February 2009, p. 2.

56 *Ibid.*, p. 4.

57 Interview with Ibrahim Kadir, Takengon, Central Aceh, 7 February 2009, p. 5.

58 *Ibid.*, p. 1.

59 The WMD militia group was initially associated with the PKI, when it had been formed by the military to hunt down members of the Darul Islam in the district. It is thus significant that it was now being used to assist the military in its attack against the PKI. It is not known how this came about. It is possible that its members were coerced to participate under the threat of becoming targeted themselves. *Ibid.*

60 *Ibid.*, pp. 2–3.

61 Ibrahim Kadir was released from the prison after twenty-five days, when he was summoned to the Military Police office at the district military command headquarters. There, Kadir was met by a judge who apologised to him for an "administrative error" that had seen him arrested and detained by mistake. Kadir was then asked to "assist" the military by not making a fuss. Kadir recalls feeling demoralised and traumatised by his experiences in prison. Interview with Ibrahim Kadir, Takengon, Central Aceh, 7 February 2009, p. 3.

62 See, for example, the case of "Jamil" from Kampung X, as recorded in chapter 6. It is also possible that Kadir's role in assisting to prepare detainees for execution may have won him favours with some of the military personnel at the jail. Whether this could have helped him win his release, however, is unknown and debatable. Other individuals who assisted the military carry out the executions were killed once they were no longer considered to be useful.

63 Interview with T.M. Yatim, Meulaboh, West Aceh, 3 December 2011, p. 8.

64 *Ibid.*

65 'Chronologis', p. 3.

66 Interview with T.M. Yatim, Meulaboh, West Aceh, 3 December 2011, pp. 8, 10; and, 'Risalah Singkat, Sidang Istimewa, Rapat terbuka, Dewan Perwakilan Rakjat Daerah Gotong Rojong Daerah Tingkat II Atjeh Barat, 11 October 1965', p. 2.

67 Interview with T.M. Yatim, Meulaboh, West Aceh, 3 December 2011, p. 10.

68 *Ibid.*

69 *Ibid.*, p. 9.

70 'Risalah Singkat, Sidang Istimewa, Rapat terbuka, Dewan Perwakilan Rakjat Daerah Gotong Rojong Daerah Tingkat II Atjeh Barat, 11 October 1965', Meulaboh, West Aceh, 11 October 1965, p. 1.

71 The other twelve delegates from the West Aceh Level II Provincial Government were Nja' Moesa, M. Koedoes Saheimy, Tubin Abdullah, Joenoes, Abd. Xarim, M. Sjam Sary, M. Djahaidin Oemar, Noertinah, T. Al Amin Kaan, Tgk. Abu Bakar and Tgk. Abbas Hamidy. *Ibid.*, p. 1.

72 Members of the "BTN" are also listed as attending. It is not known what 'BTN' stands for. *Ibid.*

73 The concept of 'political groups' (*golongan politik*) emerged during the period of Guided Democracy as a means for political parties to continue to participate in the national and province-level DRP-GR and DPRD-GR despite the halting of parliamentary elections. To begin with, each political party had its own 'group', which existed alongside 'functional groups' (*golongan karya*) representing various sectors, including the military, police, civilian defence units (*Hansip*), civil servants, women, youth, *ulama*, workers and peasants. 'Produk-produk Legislatif', *Dewan Perwakilan Rakjat Atjeh*, pp. 264–269. Later, these groups would be streamlined into four overarching groups: 'Nationalist', 'Religious', 'Communist' and 'Functional' groups, to better align with Sukarno's concept of Nasakom.

74 'Risalah Singkat, Sidang Istimewa, Rapat terbuka, Dewan Perwakilan Rakjat Daerah Gotong Rojong Daerah Tingkat II Atjeh Barat, 11 October 1965', Meulaboh, West Aceh, 11 October 1965, p. 1; Interview with T.M. Yatim, Meulaboh, West Aceh, Aceh, 3 December 2011, p. 7.

75 Interview with T.M. Yatim, Meulaboh, West Aceh, Aceh, 3 December 2011, p. 7.

76 'Risalah Singkat, Sidang Istimewa, Rapat terbuka, Dewan Perwakilan Rakjat Daerah Gotong Rojong Daerah Tingkat II Atjeh Barat, 11 October 1965', Meulaboh, West Aceh, 11 October, p. 1.

77 *Ibid.*, p. 2.

78 *Ibid.*, p. 3.

79 'Risalah Singkat, Sidang Istimewa, Rapat terbuka, Dewan Perwakilan Rakjat Daerah Gotong Rojong Daerah Tingkat II Atjeh Barat, 11 October 1965', Meulaboh, West Aceh, 11 October, p. 3.

80 *Ibid.*, p. 2.

81 The 'Functionaries Group' in West Aceh represented members of the district's civil service, such as its representative T.M. Yatim, and may have also included members of the military in the district. Following the banning of the Communist Group in the district, only three groups are listed as remaining in West Aceh: the National Group, Religious Group and Functionaries Group. 'Risalah Singkat, Sidang Istimewa, Rapat terbuka, Dewan Perwakilan Rakjat Daerah Gotong Rojong Daerah Tingkat II Atjeh Barat, 11 October 1965', p. 4.

82 *Ibid.*

83 The meeting also discussed a 'Declaration' produced by the West Aceh *Front Nasional* in conjunction with political parties and mass organisations in the district on 8 October, which has yet to be recovered. The title of this declaration is not given. It is cited in 'Risalah Singkat, Sidang Istimewa, Rapat terbuka, Dewan Perwakilan Rakjat

Daerah Gotong Rojong Daerah Tingkat II Atjeh Barat, 11 October 1965', Meulaboh, West Aceh, 11 October 1965, p. 3.

84 *Ibid.*, p. 4.
85 I have yet to come across another example.
86 *Ibid.*
87 Interview with T.M. Yatim, Meulaboh, West Aceh, 3 December 2011, p. 9.
88 'Risalah Singkat, Sidang Istimewa, Rapat Terbuka, Dewan Perwakilan Rakjat Daerah Gotong Rojong Daerah Tingkat II Atjeh Barat, 11 October 1965', Meulaboh, West Aceh, 11 October 1965, p. 5.
89 *Ibid.*, p. 4.
90 Daniel S. Lev, 'Judicial Institutions and Legal Culture', in Claire Holt (ed.), *Culture and Politics in Indonesia* (Jakarta: Equinox Publishing, 2007), p. 261.
91 The other five revolutionary laws include: "the revolution is a genuine revolution"; "the revolution is a symphony of destruction and construction"; "the revolution has stages"; "the revolution must have an appropriate program"; and "the revolution must have appropriate principles and leaders". Sukarno, 'Tahun "Vivere Pericoloso" (TAVIP): Garis-garis Besar Haluan Pembangunan', 17 August 1964, in Muhono (ed.), *Ketetapan MPRS dan Peraturan Negara jang Penting bagi Anggauta Angkatan Bersendjata* (Jakarta: Tentara Nasional Indonesia, 1966), p. 1141.
92 *Ibid.*
93 'Pernjataan, No. 4/Dprdgr/AB/1965', Meulaboh, West Aceh, 11 October 1965, p. 1.
94 'PKI Sebagai Organisasi Terlarang: Keputusan Presiden/Panglima Tertinggi Angkatan Bersenjata Republik Indonesia Mandataris MPRS/Pemimpin Besar Revolusi No. 1/3/1966', in Alex Dinuth (ed.), *Dokumen Terpilih Sekitar G.30.S/PKI* (Jakarta: Intermasa, 1997), pp. 168–169. On 4 October, Suharto had accused the PKI-affiliated organisations Pemuda Rakyat and Gerwani of being involved in the 30 September Movement, he stopped short, however, of blaming the PKI as an organisation. This convention would remain in place until 12 March 1966, despite mass organisations, political parties and other non-government groups, including military-sponsored militia groups, using this acronym from 8 October 1965. *Ibid.*, pp. 103, 168–169.
95 'Pernjataan, No. 4/Dprdgr/AB/1965', Meulaboh, West Aceh, 11 October 1965, p. 2.
96 Emphasis added. *Ibid.*
97 On 7 October, Sukarno, recognising that Suharto would not step down, issued a statement declaring he would officially appoint Suharto as Minister/Commander in Chief of the Armed Forces (Men/Pangad). 'Presiden Soekarno Menangkat Mayor Jenderal TNI Soeharto Sebagai Menteri/Panglima Angkatan Darat', in Alex Dinuth (ed.), *Dokumen Terpilih*, p. 101.
98 'Pernjataan, No: 4/Dprdgr/AB/1965', Meulaboh, West Aceh, 11 October 1965, p. 3.
99 It was sent to Mokoginta acting in his position as "Dejah Sumatra in Medan" (Dejah: Deputi MKN/KASAD Wilajah: *Deputi Menteri Keamanan Nasional/Kepala Staf Angkatan Darat Wilajah*). Mokoginta held this position in his capacity as Deputy Minister of National Defence/Regional Army Chief of Staff. It was also sent to Aceh's Pantja Tunggal, all regents and city mayors in Aceh and all government bodies in West Aceh. *Ibid.*
100 Interview with "Oesman", Tapaktuan, South Aceh, 6 December 2011, p. 1.
101 Interview with "Ali", Samadua, South Aceh, 6 December 2011, p. 4.
102 Interview with "Hamzah", Tapaktuan, South Aceh, 5 December 2011, p. 4.
103 Interview with "Oesman", Tapaktuan, South Aceh, 6 December 2011, p. 7.
104 *Ibid.*, p. 4.
105 *Ibid.*, p. 8.
106 *Ibid.*, p. 6.
107 For an account of support for the 30 September Movement in Central Java, see David Jenkins and Douglas Kammen, 'The Army Para-commando Regiment and the Reign of Terror in Central Java and Bali', in Douglas Kammen and Katharine McGregor

(eds.), *The Contours of Mass Violence in Indonesia, 1965–68* (Singapore: NUS Press, 2012), pp. 77–80; for an official account of these events prepared by the military, see *40 Hari Kegagalan 'G.30.S'*, pp. 85–102.

108 Interview with "Oesman", Tapaktuan, South Aceh, 6 December 2011, p. 7.
109 *Ibid.*, pp. 8–9.
110 *Ibid.*, p. 7.
111 *Ibid.*, p. 9.
112 Interview with "Hamzah", Tapaktuan, South Aceh, 5 December 2011, p. 3.
113 This date was given as an estimate. Interview with "Oesman", Tapaktuan, South Aceh, 6 December 2011, p. 3.
114 *Ibid.*, p. 4.
115 *Ibid.*
116 *Ibid.*
117 *Ibid.*, p. 10.
118 *Ibid.*, p. 9.
119 Interview with "Hamzah", Tapaktuan, South Aceh, 5 December 2011, p. 3.
120 Interview with "Taufik", Village 1, Tamiang, East Aceh, 18 December 2011, p. 4; and Interview with "Karim" and "Aminah", Village 1, Tamiang, East Aceh, 12 December 2011, p. 5.
121 Interview with "Taufik", Village 1, Tamiang, East Aceh, 18 December 2011, p. 4.
122 Interview with "Karim" and "Aminah", Village 1, Tamiang, East Aceh, 12 December 2011, p. 5.
123 *Ibid.*, p. 13.
124 *Ibid.*, p. 12.
125 Interview with "Taufik", Village 1, Tamiang, East Aceh, 18 December 2011, p. 5.
126 Interview with "Karim" and "Aminah", Village 1, Tamiang, East Aceh, 12 December 2011, pp. 5–6.
127 *Ibid.*
128 Interview with "Taufik", Village 1, Tamiang, East Aceh, 18 December 2011, p. 4.
129 Interview with "Taufik", Village 1, Tamiang, East Aceh, 18 December 2011, p. 4; Interview with "Karim" and "Aminah", Village 1, Tamiang, East Aceh, 12 December 2011, p. 10.
130 Interview with "Saifuddin", Idi, East Aceh, 11 December 2011, p. 19.
131 *Ibid.*, p. 20.
132 *Ibid.*
133 'Peristiwa Apa Jang Menamakan Dirinja "Gerakan 30 September"', Langsa, East Aceh, 5 October 1965, p. 1.
134 The members of East Aceh's Pantja Tunggal body are identified as: T. Djohan-sjah, Mayor and Head of District; Iljas Machmud, District Military Commander; Drs Slamet S. P., District Police Commander; Usman Wallad, District Attorney for Langsa; Njak Ismail, the branch coordinator of the East Aceh *Front Nasional*; and Panut Alfisah, a judge representing the Justice Department in Langsa. *Ibid.*, pp. 2–3.
135 *Ibid.*, pp. 1, 3.
136 The representatives of these parties are identified as: M. Dharnazoon from the PNI, Zahar from Partindo, T. Itam Muli from IP-KI, T. Dahlan from NU, Zainuddin Bey from PSII, Muchtar Djuned from PI Perti and T. Sitompul from Parkindo. *Ibid.*
137 *Ibid.*, p. 1. This is a reference to announcements made by Sukarno on 2 and 3 October. Through these announcements Sukarno confirmed that he was safe, called for calm and reiterated that he had appointed Pranoto Reksosamodra as temporary Commander of the Armed Forces, and that he had assigned Suharto the task of "restoring order" as Kostrad (*Komando Cadangan Strategis Angkatan Darat*: Army Strategic Reserve) Commander. See 'Amanat Presiden/Panglima Tertinggi Angkatan Bersenjata R.I/ Pemimpin Besar Revolusi Bung Karno', 2 October 1965; and, 'Amanat Presiden/

Panglima Tertinggi ABRI/Pemimpin Besar Revolusi Bung Karno', 3 October 1965, in Alex Dinuth (ed.), *Dokumen Terpilih*, pp. 64–65, 83–84.

138 'Peristiwa Apa Jang Menamakan Dirinja "Gerakan 30 September"', Langsa, East Aceh, 5 October 1965, p. 1.

139 *Ibid.*

140 'Pernjataan Pantja Tunggal Daerah Istimewa Atjeh', Banda Aceh, 4 October 1965.

141 'Peristiwa Apa Jang Menamakan Dirinja "Gerakan 30 September"', Langsa, East Aceh, 5 October 1965, p. 1.

5 Pogrom and public killings
7–13 October

The first week following Djuarsa's coordination tour was characterised by the outbreak of public violence throughout Aceh. In general, this first wave of violence began with anti-PKI demonstrations. These demonstrations quickly escalated into pogroms,[1] as large crowds marched on offices and houses belonging to individuals associated with the PKI, which were subsequently ransacked and burnt. Individuals identified with this target group were also routinely abducted during this first wave of violence. These abductions, described universally as "arrests", resulted in the disappearance of the abductees, or their induced "surrender" to the military. Many of these abductees were subsequently murdered and their bodies left on public display.

Military records of public killings

There are 1,941 cases of public killings recorded in the military's Complete Yearly Report and Death Map for Aceh.[2] The military has always publically claimed not to have known who performed these killings. An example of this official denial can be found in the military's Complete Yearly Report, which explains:

> Between 6 October 1965 and 2 November,[3] demonstrations were held by the people throughout the province, who, filled with anger towards the PKI/ its Mass Organisations, along with its lackeys Baperki and the RRT [People's Republic of China], issued demands based on great conviction that the Government should immediately disband the PKI/its Mass Organisations and its lackeys, as well as **sentence its leaders to death** (*menghukum mati gembong2nja*). . . .
>
> This extreme anger on the behalf of the people did not just stop at demonstrations, graffiti and "destruction actions" (*aksi pengrusakan2*), but extended to abductions/killings (*pentjulikan2/pembunuhan*) of leaders of the PKI, its Affiliated Organisations and Baperki, numbering:
>
> (a) Atjeh Besar/Banda Aceh Defence Sector Command (*Kosekhan*) = 121 people
> (b) Atjeh Pidie Defence Sector Command = 314 people

(c) North Aceh Defence Sector Command = 187 people
(d) East Aceh Defence Sector Command = 350 people
(e) West Aceh Defence Sector Command = 105 people
(f) Central Aceh Defence Sector Command = 517 people
(g) South Aceh Defence Sector Command = 143 people
(h) Southeast Aceh Defence Sector Command = 204 people
Total = 1,941 people[4]

The military, however, went further than simply recording these killings in great detail. As will be outlined below, in addition to ordering the "annihilation" of targeted individuals, the military openly encouraged the abductions and subsequent murder of abductees. It also continued to provide leadership to Aceh's civilian population throughout this period and brought together pogrom participants at critical moments to provide them with greater direction and to signal the military's ongoing support for the violence. In other cases, the military carried out targeted killings directly, while continuing to authorise the formation of military-sponsored death squads. These military-sponsored death squads and other civilian proxies appear to have been responsible for a large proportion of the public killings recorded during this period.

7 October: the outbreak of public violence in Banda Aceh

7 October was a day of escalating demonstrations in Banda Aceh. The Military Chronology records that at 9am a demonstration was held in Darussalam,[5] Banda Aceh's university town. There, 200 students are said to have "condemned the 30 September Movement and expressed their sympathy for the six murdered Army Generals" while "calling for [the PKI-affiliated] CGMI (*Consentrasi Gerakan Mahasiswa Indonesia*: Unified Movement of Indonesian Students) to be disbanded and for CGMI students to be expelled" from Syiah Kuala University.[6]

One hour later, a demonstration led by PNI members carried out a "raid" of the SOBSI office and the house of PKI Secretary Thaib Adamy, located next to each other in Neusu,[7] 1.5 km from the centre of Banda Aceh. According to the Military's Chronology, "rusty/old hand grenades", "one *geren* [machine gun] bullet" and nine "cold [colt] 38 [hand gun] bullet shells" were seized from Adamy's house at this time.[8]

"Ramli", the son of Adamy, who, at the time, was seven years old and in his second year of primary school, vividly remembers these events. From 5 October, Ramli has recalled, "people lined up in rows" and began screaming anti-PKI slogans in the streets.[9] "Crush the PKI, PKI . . . Crush!" they screamed. "One person led the chanting . . . PKI! . . . Crush them!, Long live PNI!" outside his house. Ramli remembers joining in some of the screaming, not understanding what it meant. "The next day", Ramli explains, his father left with Ramli's second eldest brother, Yasrun, fifteen, who was in his first year of high school, heading towards Takengon. Ramli never saw his father and brother again. Ramli's mother, who was pregnant at the time, also left, taking Ramli and his younger siblings to stay with her and Adamy's extended family in Pidie.[10] One of Thaib Adamy's relatives, Muhammad Thaib, who lived in Pidie, was Head of Internal Security (Laksus: *Pelaksana Khusus Daerah*; lit. 'Special Regional Director', military intelligence), and he protected them. Ramli believes they all would have been killed if not for this protection.

When the demonstrators converged on Adamy's home, Ramli's eldest brother, Yusni, seventeen, who was in his final year of high school, and who had remained in Banda Aceh alone, was guarding the family house. Yusni was subsequently "arrested by a group of people" who had been at the demonstration and "taken to the jail in Keudah [the Military Police headquarters are in Keudah, 1 km from the centre of Banda Aceh]",[11] from where he was later taken to be killed (as will be described in chapter 6).[12] Thaib Adamy and Yasrun, meanwhile, were "arrested as they travelled between Bireuen and Takengon".[13]

Ramli has a very different explanation for the grenades and bullet shells that were allegedly found at his house and touted as proof that his father and the PKI had been preparing for armed rebellion. "I often picked up empty grenades," explains Ramli. "Behind our house was the SI-AD (*Sekolah Inteligen-Angkatan Darat*: Military Intelligence School)" training complex.[14] "There were lots of houses here," Ramli recalls, drawing a picture of his house and the surrounding area:

> Here there was a market garden, there were crops growing, our house was here, here was the train line, this was the DKA [*Djawatan Kereta Api*: state-run Railway Bureau] complex [where Thaib Adamy had worked] . . . here was the SI-AD, at the SI-AD there were houses for the soldiers. This is where we found a lot of old things that had been discarded by the soldiers, we found old thermoses, aluminium thermoses for drinking, some were made out of green tin, I often picked them up, I brought them back to our house to play, sometimes we found old rusty grenades that had already been used.[15]

Ramli and his friends would play at the training complex.[16] "Maybe this is what they mean when they talk about the grenades they found," Ramli ponders. "It could have been the old grenades from SI-AD that we played with and threw around, it could also be that they put them there to try and set a scene, but my father never had any weapons, he didn't even have a pistol."[17] Ramli also does not know where the uniforms alleged to have been found might have come from. His father had a yellow uniform from when he worked on the trains, but Ramli never saw his father with any military-style uniform. They could have been planted in the house, Ramli proposes: "Our house had already been abandoned, my older brother had already been arrested, we had already gone. If someone went in there we don't know, but my father never wore soldier uniforms."[18]

Presumably it was obvious to the military that a few old rusty grenades and empty bullet shells presented no risk. Such "evidence" is reminiscent of the photograph 'Belongings seized from the 'G-30-S'' (*Barang2 jang disita dari*

"*G-30-S*") that can be found in the military's propaganda booklet *The Forty Day Failure of the 30 September Movement* (*40 Hari Kegagalan "G.30.S."*), which presents a collection of mundane items photographed by the military and purported to be proof of the PKI's diabolical plans. It is possible Thaib Adamy and Ramli's two older brothers were killed over the "evidence" of children's playthings.

At 4pm, the Chronology reports, a demonstration attended by members of Aceh's main Islamic parties and youth organisations marched around the town before marching towards Neusu, where the PKI's headquarters were "destroyed and ransacked".[19] The house of PKI member Tjut Husin Fatly, who was in Beijing at the time, was broken into and "his furniture was burnt". Husin's wife and preschool-age daughter were subsequently detained at a "concentration camp" (*kamp-konsentrasi*) at Mate Ie, where an "executioner" (*algojo*) killed Husin's wife upon her release.[20] The house of PKI member Sumbowo and a PKI "study house" were also ransacked and burnt to screams of "Hang Aidit/Samikidin" and "Cut up (*tjentjang*) Anas HC".[21] As the fires burnt, a second demonstration, attended by some 15,000 people, set about burning down the PKI's headquarters.[22] Rumours were also circulated that an "anonymous letter", allegedly written by the PKI, had been received by the *Front Nasional*, which read: "We will have revenge on the Islamic Youth." This letter was most certainly a forgery (if it even existed) considering what we know about the PKI's reaction of confusion in the province. It was said to be held by the head of the *Front Nasional*, and was used by the military to spark further anger and fear in the community. Other misinformation spread during this time included "rumours" that an Islamic boarding school, named after the Acehnese hero Tjut Njak Dien, a fearsome female leader of the Acehnese resistance during Aceh's holy war against the Dutch, had been "attacked by the 30 September Movement" in Yogyakarta and one of its teachers, Professor Hasbi Alsidigi, "murdered" along with "several students". It is also recorded that a "proclamation letter" had been received by the military claiming that the "30 September Movement along with the PKI has killed Acehnese students in Jogja [Yogyakarta] along with members of the Muslim community in Java." These events, which would have been major news at the time, had they occurred, are not recorded in military accounts of events in Yogyakarta.[23]

The violent outbursts sparked by such misinformation achieved their intended outcome. The Military Chronology notes:

> As a result of the people's overflowing anger towards the PKI/its Mass Organisations and lackeys, the PKI leadership no longer felt safe staying in their homes and on 7 October 1965 disappeared, they then reappeared and requested protection from the Government, except for M. Thaib Adamy, former PKI Vice Secretary for Aceh, now MPRS [*Majelis Permusyawaratan Rakyat Sementara*: Provisional People's Consultative Council] member, whose whereabouts is currently unknown. . . .

The Pepelrada responded to this situation by grouping them [the PKI leadership] together in the Military Police Command detention facility (*rumah tahanan Militer Pomdam-I*).[24]

These demonstrations legitimised the military's attack and served to drive the targets of the pogroms directly into the arms of the military.

8–13 October: pogrom actions and abductions

At 12pm on 8 October, the Railway Workers Union (SBKA: *Sarikat Buruh Kereta Api*) office was "destroyed" by a mob of "Marhaenist workers",[25] who are alleged to have come across "several pieces of evidence" in the destroyed office, including: "13 military insignia patches, one packet of new green 1½ × 1½ cm patches ranging in rank from Private to Major, a hand grenade that is suspected to have been used for training and several documents/notes."[26]

Again, these pieces of evidence are almost certainly linked to the legal militia training the PKI was involved in, as detailed in chapter 2. At 3pm, the Chronology reports, a "wild demonstration" (*demonstrasi liar*) was carried out by "HMI students and the people", who converged on the house of PKI leader and Chairman for Aceh, Muhammad Samikidin.[27] After allegedly finding no one at home, the mob proceeded to take books and a typewriter from the house, before "destroying/burning" them. At this time, the Chronology explains, Aceh's Police Commissioner M. Hutabarat, based at the Subregional Military Command Headquarters (*Dan Resort Militer*), is said to have received a letter from "unknown authors", urging that the "demonstration movement" not be "held back" and for PKI members and their families who had requested protection to be "released" into the arms of the demonstrators.

At 8pm, a 'giant meeting' (*Rapat Akbar*) was held in front of the Baiturrahman Mosque (Banda Aceh's Grand Mosque) allegedly attended by 10,000 people,[28] including representatives from Banda Aceh's "Pantja Tunggal, Political Parties/Mass Organisations [and] Islamic leaders".[29] This meeting was addressed by an unnamed authority, who presented an "explanation about the 30 September Movement and other matters relating to this movement". Zainal Abidin, who in 1965 was the Subdistrict Head of Seulimeum, has also described a similar process occurring in Seulimeum, on the border between Banda Aceh and Aceh Besar, where a "large assembly" was "held by the people, but . . . protected by ABRI".[30] "We worked together with the District Military Command (*Kodim*)," explains Abidin.[31] In the aftermath of this assembly, Abidin recalls, "almost all workers, including the train workers [who were historically associated with the PKI[32]] were 'taken' [abducted] (*diambil*). Some were released, some were finished off (*diselesaikan*). But," he explains, as if to justify this violence, "we were working together with ABRI."[33]

Two hours later, in Banda Aceh, "youth from the same *kampung*" kidnapped members of the Pemuda Rakyat in Laksana *kampung*.[34] The abductees were then reported to have been "surrendered" to the Subdistrict Military Command (*ABRI Resort*) "in a molested/beaten up state". Fifteen minutes later:

in accordance with an Official Order from the Chief Public Prosecutor Harif Harapan, based upon the decision by the Pantja Tunggal [i.e. the 'Joint Decision' signed on 6 October that had called for the "complete annihilation" of anyone deemed to be implicated with the 30 September Movement], POMDAM [Military Police] took and transported family members/members of the PKI, numbering seven people, from the prison in Banda Aceh. These seven people had been surrendered from the District Police Command, where they had requested protection.[35]

Where these seven detainees were taken is not known, nor is their ultimate fate. Considering the Military Police were acting upon a directive calling for the "complete annihilation" of such individuals, it can be assumed they were murdered. Unlike in Aceh's other districts, the details of the 121 people reported to have been killed in the Death Map for Banda Aceh (whose corpses were dumped in public places in the district) are not recorded in the Chronology. It is possible that these "abductees" helped to make up this figure. Alternatively, they may have been transported to be killed at Banda Aceh's military-controlled killing sites over the next few days or weeks.[36]

The abductions and public killings were assisted by the military-sponsored death squads. As Dahlan Sulaiman, the PII member and death squad leader who today works as a private travel agent, has explained:

> We . . . would find the communists, especially, because we were youths, their youth leaders, we would take (*ambil*) them and then we would surrender them to the military and police. If we gave them to the police, the next morning they would be on the street again, already brave enough to disturb us again. So we gave them to the military . . . to Kodim [the District Military Command]. Our orientation was already towards Kodim, much of our operational matters had already been surrendered to Kodim.[37]

"We only picked up people we knew were definitely PKI, those that we had already seen [as active PKI members]," Sulaiman continues. "We read their names from a list made by the leadership (*susunan pengurus*)."[38] "We watched them . . . then we picked them up, and surrendered them to the authorities (*yang berwadjib*)." This statement, beyond being an attempt by Sulaiman to justify his actions, points to the existence of death lists and reveals the systematic nature of the campaign.[39]

The detainees who were surrendered to the District Military Command (*Kodim*) were then taken to the military-controlled 'concentration camp' at Mata Ie.[40] This camp was located at a military training base in the foothills of Seulawah on the border with Aceh Besar. "Those who were taken there," Sulaiman explains:

> you couldn't say they were detained, they weren't detained, because they had not been sentenced (*dihukum*), they were allowed to stay at the military barracks [in the 'concentration camp'], given food to survive, nothing was

done to them . . . [there were also detainees] brought from Sabang [on Weh island, west from Banda Aceh] that were received there. Also from Pidie [and] Sigli. . . .

They were all brought to Mata Ie, what happened after they got to Mata Ie, what happened, we don't know. What we did know was that one night, with the reason that the government and especially the military no longer had the budget or the money to pay for them [to feed and house them], they were returned to the people, they were released and told to go home, go back to their houses, but when they got back to their houses, to be straight, there was what is called a revolution. Some were protected by their relatives. There were also others that were not protected. Now, those that weren't protected, yeah, this is what it was like at the time, the people took their revenge.[41]

Sulaiman is here describing the massacre of released detainees by civilians. He is at pains to explain that "it was not the military or the [civilian] organisations . . . that did the killings . . . that didn't happen".[42] The fact that the military announced the release of prisoners before allowing them to return home, at the same time that civilians were being ordered to "assist the military" to "completely annihilate" the PKI, makes it difficult to believe that this was not the outcome that was, in fact, desired. Again, the "spontaneous" actions of civilians were used as a means of masking the military's own involvement in the violence. Ramli, who has recounted that Husin Fatly's wife and preschool-aged daughter were released from this same concentration camp, has suggested the released detainees were not killed by ordinary civilians, but rather by '*algojo*': specially designated killers – often politically suspect individuals – who were tasked with the psychologically unpleasant task of killing unarmed civilians.

Let Bugeh, an HMI member who was involved in the activities of the death squads in the province and who, when I interviewed him in 2010 was Head of the National Sports Committee for Aceh, has described a similar situation in which he and his fellow death squad members assisted the military by tracking down and "surrendering" people accused of being associated with the PKI to the military:

They [the PKI youth leaders] had already run away, gone in to the jungle. But we were also students and knew where their *kampung* were. So we hunted them. If we got them, we would surrender them . . . we hunted them into the jungle. I would arrest them and surrender them to Kodim.[43]

Bugeh took pains to say that he did not participate directly in the killing. "We didn't kill them," he explained. The military would:

accept them, interrogate them, that was up to them! They were interrogated. Were they really a communist or not? It was the military that interrogated them, not us. [There were] thousands [that were detained and interrogated in this way], throughout Aceh there were thousands of people that this happened to.[44]

During our interview Bugeh broke into Acehnese at this point, thinking that I would not be able to understand him, to explain to the other guests in his government office where we were meeting, that he and his comrades were, in fact, involved in the killings, saying, "We can't say that we killed them . . . because she is writing a book and people will get angry."[45] In doing so he exposed just how shallow such public denials can be.

The military came to play an even clearer coordinating role in the abductions and public killings as the campaign wore on. As the Military Chronology notes, at 10am on 9 October, a "vehicle from the Mobile Police Brigade (*Brimob: Brigade Mobil*)" arrived at the Military Police (*Pomdam: Polisi Militer Daerah Militer*) barracks "carrying family members of PKI members . . . women and children, numbering 17 people".[46] A "Power Wagon" (an open-backed four-wheel drive light truck produced by Dodge) then arrived carrying:

> 5 PKI members, who had been beaten up and who were only wearing their underwear, including a man named Hasan Saleh (CGMI), who for the last few days had been on the run from Pomda[m]-I, it was requested by Pomdam-I to the Police that Hasan Saleh be left at the Pomdam Ba[rracks].[47]

"The other four PKI members," the Chronology reports, "were then taken to the District Police Command."[48] At 12.30pm, it was decided between the Police Commander and the Deputy Military Police Commandant-I, Military Police Captain (*Wakil Pomdam-I Capten CPM*) Martojo, that, "in the interests of public calm and safety", a "travelling public announcement" would be made throughout the town, in "conjunction" with the Province's information service. Presumably this entailed an official travelling around the town on the back of a truck equipped with a loudspeaker.[49] The content of these announcements is not known, but their purpose appears to have been to normalise the military abductions and transportations of abductees that were now occurring in broad daylight.

At 3pm it is reported the Aceh Besar District Military Command (*Kodim 1010*), had "come to surrender to Pomdam-I two PKI members named A. Rauf [a PKI leader in Aceh] and Samikidin [the Aceh PKI Chairman] for them to request protection (*untuk meminta perlindungan*)".[50] The notion of Rauf and Samikidin "requesting protection" at the same time they were under the custody of the military defies explanation but their detention can be independently corroborated. Asan recalls seeing Rauf in the Pomdam during his own stay there, while Zainal Abidin has recalled how Samikidin was "arrested" shortly after 1 October and held at his office in Seulimeum, before he was "taken" to be "finished off". "[W]e didn't use the term to be killed" at that time, he explained.[51] Samikidin had allegedly pleaded with him shortly before being taken, asking him, "Why must it be like this?" and claiming that he was "not a communist".[52] Abidin remembers hearing that Samikidin, who he describes as a "pious man", was killed after being "pulled off" a train as he was being transported to Takengon.[53]

At 4pm a demonstration attended by an estimated 1,000 students is reported to have assembled in front of the Banda Aceh Pendopo, where the "Pantja Tunggal explained to them" that "in accordance with an instruction that has already been issued by the Panglatu [Mokoginta]" it was "no longer permitted to hold demonstrations".[54] The content of this instruction is not known. The demonstration proceeded to "condemn the barbaric actions of the 30 September Movement and to stand behind the President/Supreme Leader of the Armed Forces/Great Leader of the Revolution Bung Karno", while pledging to assist ABRI in its efforts to "restore security and order".[55] It also called upon the Aceh Special Region Pantja Tunggal for "GWASMA to be installed". It is not known what "GWASMA" refers to. It would appear, however, that rather than genuinely attempting to limit public mobilisation against the PKI, the military was keen to publically distance itself from this mobilisation while unofficially encouraging it.

That night the District Military Commander for Banda Aceh and Aceh Besar (*Dan Dim 0101*) declared a curfew between 9pm and 5am.[56] This curfew was quickly broken, however, when at 3am youths from Sukaramai *kampung* are said to have carried out an attack against the PKI "Cooperative Centre" in the *kampung*, "seriously injuring" several Pemuda Rakyat members in the process. No disciplinary actions are recorded as being taken against the participants in this mob attack.

On 10 October, a radiogram was sent from the Pepelrada Atjeh declaring that "all meetings and demonstrations must have permission from the Pepelrada Atjeh".[57] This new regulation was not intended to stop the demonstrations, but rather to ensure that they were better coordinated. As the Aceh Military Command's Complete Yearly Report notes:

> Except for the PKI/its Mass Organisations and Baperki, the other Political Parties/Mass Organisations have already taken an active role in annihilating (*mengambil bahagian aktif dalam menumpas*) the PKI/its Mass Organisations. Within this, there have been signs that a third force, or irresponsible individuals, have been attempting to subvert the anger of the people towards and to misguide them. Because of this, the Level-I Pantja Tunggal, in its briefing on 12 October, provided guidance to all political parties and mass organisations, to, in all their actions and efforts collect facts about the treachery of the "G-30-S", to [remain] under leadership and restrained [and] not to be diverted or taken for a ride by a third force, the Nekolim and individuals who only wish to fulfil their own ambitions.[58]

The military was keen to retain complete control over all acts of public violence and communicated this intention to its allies on the ground. The Chronology provides no detail as to who the "third force" mentioned in this entry might refer to, or the real challenge, if any, that it may have presented to the military leadership. Such rhetoric may well have been designed to remind participants in the pogroms that such public violence was not spontaneous at all. The violence, after all, has a very specific purpose: it was intended to publicly identify individuals associated with the PKI, break down community solidarity and to drive these individuals into the arms of the military.

The pogroms seem to have achieved their goal. On 13 October, the military Chronology reports that fifty-six PKI members along with members of the PKI's affiliated organisations and their family members had "requested protection" from the Kodahan 'A' Commander [Djuarsa] at the Main Regiment for the Aceh Military Command (Rindam-I: *Resimen Induk Kodam-I*).[59] Asan, the sole surviving member of the PKI Central Committee for Aceh who is both an eyewitness and near fatality of this process, has recalled how the military placed enormous pressure on the community to encourage those associated with the PKI to "surrender" at this time.

"My feeling," Asan explains, "was that the population of Banda Aceh was calm enough to begin with, then abusive posters [began to appear in the streets]," perhaps referring to the posters produced by Dahlan Sulaiman during the evening of 1 October, which received the blessing of the military leadership early the next day.[60] These posters, Asan recalls, were "written roughly in pencil . . . they weren't printed" and "denounced the PKI". Shortly after the emergence of these posters the first pogrom actions began. The PKI leadership in Aceh, Asan has explained, was unsure how to react, and enjoyed a false sense of security, convinced that the campaign would not be allowed to get too out of hand. Seeking protection from the police, Asan explains, was initially seen as a means of attempting to de-escalate the growing public violence. This assessment, he quickly came to realise, was a grave mistake.

The case of Asan: part one

Asan related the following extract to me during our interview in Hong Kong in October 2011. Here he describes how he found himself in the custody of the Military Police in Banda Aceh, before miraculously escaping with his life:

> I never heard of any instructions from the CDB-Aceh [PKI Provincial Headquarters] as to how to protect the organisations or to face the political storm that had erupted. What the G30S was I am still not clear. Indeed, what was recommended was to go to the police to request protection. I have no idea whether that was the decision of an individual or the CDB-Aceh as an organisation. What is clear, I felt that the leaders of the CDB were confused; no one knew what had to be done to face the political storm that had erupted.
>
> No one knew that the PKI would become the target of military repression. Then, one afternoon [a day or two after 5 October, when] four or five comrades were talking at the CDB, suddenly a member of Pemuda Rakyat came running in all on edge to tell us, the PNI was calling its members together to create a "Crush the PKI" front. We immediately shut down the CDB and went home. On the way home we could hear them screaming, "Crush the PKI!"
>
> The next day I felt that the political storm was about to hit. I asked my wife to prepare what she would need and to take our two children to stay for a while at her parents' house in Sigli, so that it was just me who would face what would happen [in Banda Aceh]. At sunset, Bung Rauf, Secretary

General [of the PKI for Banda Aceh], together with Bung Samikidin, Secretary General of the CDB Banda Aceh (Samikidin was Rauf's brother-in-law), came to my house and said that Bung Samikidin would stay here to stay out of the way. Meanwhile, Samikidin's wife and child, who was about two or three years old, was taken . . . to Medan. . . .

That night, Thaib [Adamy] brought someone home that I did not recognise, who was said to be there on party business, from Medan, North Sumatra. The three of them [Adamy, the man from Medan and Samikidin] talked inside the house and I sat on the veranda to keep a watch on what was happening outside the house, so if anything strange happened I could tell my three comrades to make themselves scarce.

The next day, Bung Thaib got in a car to Takengon, Central Aceh, where he needed to organise (*mengatur*) the Gayo. But, it was clear that Bung Thaib's actions had already caught the attention of the military. Bung Thaib was arrested immediately [after leaving] and brought back to Banda Aceh. On their way back, when the driver of the Jeep carrying Bung Thaib stopped to eat in a Chinese shop, a comrade saw Bung Thaib with both of his hands and feet shackled.[61]

Meanwhile, during the early afternoon the next day, Samikidin was picked up by Bung Rauf from my house, leaving the [Aceh PKI] CDB stamp [used for certifying official documents] for me take care of. They said goodbye and I never saw them again.

When I was alone, a teacher from the Tjen Hua middle school, Bung Yi, came to my house to remind me to be careful, lots of Indonesian people where asking where I was in Chinatown [Peunayong]. Not long after this an organiser of P[emuda] R[akyat] from Sigli, a young woman called Li . . . came to my house to tell me that I was being looked for. . . .

It was at this point that I made the decision to leave . . . but first I collected all the books and special magazines from when I had joined Party School and put them in a sack. . . . I hid them in the toilet out [the back of] the house. I thought, if the house was burnt by enemies, at least the books in the sack might survive. Then I left, borrowing someone's pushbike.

On the way I met a driver from the Chinese school in Sigli where I had taught, who told me that KAMI-KAPPI people[62] and Islamic fanatics had mobilised and were looking for me. . . . When I was about twenty meters from my destination where I planned to hide at a Chinese-owned shop, I could see that the door of the shop was wide open. Without thinking I rode the pushbike right into the house . . . [and] asked Bang[63] Ling if I would be able to hide in his house. He told me to climb up into the roof above the front room. I hid there for three days. . . .

One night, Bang Ling said to me, "Lots of Party members and cadres are going to the police to 'report themselves' and to request 'protection', I think it would be best if you reported yourself, as he held out some money in his hand to me. . . . Outside the rain was bucketing down. . . . That night I wasn't frightened . . . as I made my way towards the police office in Banda Aceh, where the head of police was still on duty. I sat in front of him [the Head of Police] and examined his face, I saw his hand clasp a club and wave it near my head as he gave me the warning, "Tell me the truth, if you don't want your head to be smashed!" This didn't make me scared. I said, "I'm just a teacher in the Party." He wrote down what I said, then he said "Anas H.C. [a leader in the Party] has also reported himself", at the same time as pointing to a box containing Anas's belongings at the police station where he was said to have "surrendered himself".

The Head of Police didn't get an explanation of the Party's activities from me, so in the end I was thrown into a dark room with bars and a guard who was asked to keep an eye on me, before [the Head of Police] left.

In the middle of the night, the guard asked me if I had family in Banda Aceh so he could let them know [I had been arrested] and they could come and see me. From his accent I knew he was a Batak[64] . . . diplomatically I answered, "No, I've just moved from Meulaboh." . . .

The next morning, a police officer who was on picket came up and screamed abuse at me, "You used to often scream 'The blood of the people has already risen!' (*darah rakyat telah bangkit!*)[65] Now you must come to terms with the fact that 'the Blood of the People of Aceh has Risen! (*Darah Rakyat Aceh Bangkit!*)*" Then he turned his back and said to the guard, "We don't receive people like him here and we can't protect him. Take him to the Military Police!"

When we got to the Military Police, I met with one of my childhood Acehnese friends from Meulaboh, who I had also met when I was teaching in Sigli, when he told me he had joined the Islamic Army (Darul Islam) to fight the government. . . . Now he had already been rehabilitated [received an amnesty] and become an intelligence officer with the Military Police. . . . He said to me, "Asan, we (meaning Islamist fundamentalists) [*kami (maksudnya fundamentalis Islam)*]" are looking for you;[66] if you are killed, don't disappoint me." But I gave him no reaction. . . .

I was asked some questions, then, after assessing me, the officer said to the police who had brought me, "We don't accept PKI here who report themselves and request protection. Take him back [with you]!" So I got back into the vehicle and left the Military Police.

When I got back to the Police station, I was thrown into a cell out the back that had only a long bench, and the policeman left. The Police Commissioner . . . after reading my "problem" came to look at me in the dark and let out a "My goodness!" (*Assstaga!*) and said to me very slowly, "You can't go home now." I didn't reply.

I returned to [my cell] and sat on the bench, that night I had already become a human handball. . . . That night . . . after the Commissioner had gone home . . . a youth came to me and said, "The Commissioner has ordered us to take you home!" I went with him out of the Police Station in a Jeep that was waiting for me with a driver who told me to sit beside him. Under the light of the street lamps I could still see the bodies of two sturdy police men who sat behind us silently but whose eyes watched my every move as I sat as motionless as I could. The driver asked me where I lived. . . .

In the car I was thinking hard. Was the Police Commissioner really letting me go for "humanitarian" reasons? Why would he be that good to me? Was it possible? This was a difficult question for me to answer. . . .

The Jeep was almost at my house in Kebun Sayur, Peunayong, when I asked the driver to enter the car park next to the Youth League basketball court. I pointed to some house near where my house was. When I got down from the car and was walking towards my street . . . I thought maybe these people who had brought me home in the Jeep were *killers* (*algojo*)! If they knew where my house was, they could come and kill me in the night. Straight away I turned into a different laneway . . . and went towards the vegetable warehouse in the Chinese district and climbed up into the roof where I sat on some cardboard and tried to think.[67]

Asan would remain in hiding for several weeks before he was once again forced to flee for his life. His story is continued in chapter 7. His above account provides a unique insight into conditions within Banda Aceh's police and Military Police compounds at this time. It would appear, for example, that there was some initial friction between these organisations as to what should be done with detainees such as Asan who had turned themselves over for protection, with the Military Police playing a leading role in determining that a permanent solution was to be found. To begin with, at least, it would appear the use of executioners (*algojo*) may have been a real attempt by the military to distance itself from the killings that had begun to occur. It may be that once the detainee population reached a critical mass, making such "discreet" murders more difficult and placing stress on the military's capacity to feed and detain this population, wholesale and direct eliminationist-style killings were adopted as the easiest manner with which to 'process' the detainee population.

10 October: the outbreak of public violence in North Aceh

Patterns of public violence in North Aceh were similar to those in Banda Aceh. On 10 October at 9pm, three days after Djuarsa's public meeting in the district, a demonstration "aimed at members of the PKI and its affiliated organisations" was held in Lhokseumawe attended by thirty people from political parties and mass organisations in the district.[68] This demonstration marched on the family homes of PKI members, which were subsequently ransacked and the furniture destroyed and burnt. By the time the demonstration arrived at the houses, the Military Chronology reports, the occupants had "already fled". This demonstration lasted until two in the morning.

At midnight on the same day at the PU Complex[69] in Bireuen, the Chronology reports, another "wild demonstration" was held by "irresponsible people", with Thaib from Meunasah Blang, an anti-PKI demonstrator, dying in the process.[70] It is not explained how Thaib died. Interestingly, this is the only example of the term '*meninggal dunia*', the Indonesian equivalent of the English 'passed away', being used in the Chronology, and indeed in all of the documents I have seen, to describe a death that occurred in the province during the genocide. Such language may indicate Thaib's death was accidental or the result of a heart attack. In all other cases the impersonal term 'killed' (*terbunuh*) is used, or, even more euphemistically, it is stated that a "corpse was found" (*majat diketemukan*).

The next day, a night curfew from 10pm to 6am was imposed by the Tjatur Tunggal in Bireuen. Far from encouraging a de-escalation in the campaign the curfew was followed by a demonstration in Gandapura Subdistrict, North Aceh, led by members of "various political parties/mass organisations and Muslim youth".[71] This demonstration quickly escalated into a violent raid at a gold shop owned by a man named Madjur. "The occupants/owners of the shop," the Chronology states, "were told to leave with only the clothes on their backs. Everything in the shop was burnt while the occupants/owners of the shop requested protection from the police (*AKRI*) in Bireuen."[72]

It is not explained why this shop was targeted. Gold shops in the province, as throughout Indonesia, were often owned by Chinese traders and it is possible demonstrators used the occasion as an excuse to steal the shop's high-value merchandise.

The next day, on 12 October, in Ulim, Pidie, "the people" proceeded to burn down seven houses believed to belong to PKI members.[73] While in Meureudu, also in Pidie, "the people" burnt motorbikes belonging to PKI members. The burning of offices and houses belonging to "PKI people" also occurred in "several subdistricts" at this time. "The number of PKI people in Aceh Pidie now requesting protection," the Chronology reports, "is 45 people." As shown by the military's keen interest in recording these events, it would appear the military and state apparatus in North Aceh was keeping a close eye on developments.

13–15 October: direct military involvement in arrests

Demonstrations in the district began to intensify from 13 October. "Since 13 October," the Chronology explains, "there have been arrests of people caught up in the 30 September Movement, numbering 50 people made up of PKI people/its Mass Organisations who are now detained in jail in Sigli."[74]

These arrests and subsequent detention of those arrested in military-controlled jails signalled an escalation of the military's campaign and demonstrates the military's increasingly direct role in the arrest and detention cycle in the district. As in other districts during this period, it appears these detentions may initially have been explained as "protective", causing people facing rising public violence to literally hand themselves over to the military. On 14 October, for example, it was reported that twenty-three members of "PKI/Gerwani" from Kota Bakti in Pidie "requested protection" from Battalion 113 in the district.[75] Others appear to have been less convinced of the "protection" the military could provide, with some, including a thirty-year-old man named Akob, a member of the PKI sub-branch in Tiro/Trusop Aceh Pidie, choosing to commit suicide rather than face arrest by either the death squads or the military.[76]

There certainly appears to have been extraordinary pressure placed on members of the PKI in the district. On 15 October the remaining members of the PKI sub-branch in Tiro/Trusop, Pidie provided a "declaration" to the police (AKRI) in Kota Bakti, signed by forty-three people, stating that they had "left/separated themselves from the PKI, and were obedient/loyal to the Government/the President/Armed Forces Commander/PBR Bung Karno and were determined to completely annihilate the 30 September Movement to its roots."[77]

Members of the PKI in the subdistrict thus swore to the police that they would assist in their own annihilation and in the annihilation of their comrades. Such declarations would later be used by the military to hunt down those who had not yet "surrendered".[78]

11 October: the outbreak of public violence in Central Aceh

The military played a particularly direct role in the outbreak of public violence in Central Aceh. Djuarsa's public speech in Takengon on 7 October had made the military's intentions explicit and thus there was less need to disguise the military's role in the outbreak of violence in the district. Indeed, only one incident is recorded in the Chronology for Central Aceh during this first phase of violence that is not directly attributed to the military or police. In this entry, recorded on 11 October, the day of Ibrahim Kadir's arrest, it is reported that between 9 and 11am, "checkpoints were set up against PKI members along the main road between Bireuen [and] Takengon by youth from Bireuen".[79] Such an initiative would appear to be in line with the military's own campaign. It is curious, however, that after the youth "managed to kidnap/run off in a car a PKI person named Amiruddin bin Daud", they were "chased by ABRI [the military], who managed to locate Amiruddin, whose hands had been tied and who had been beaten up, meanwhile 3 other PKI people were also saved (*diselamatkan*) by ABRI."[80]

It is not clear why the military in Central Aceh acted to stop this attack. It may be that Amiruddin was a military informer or spy whom the military wished to protect. Alternatively, the military may have simply wished to retain control over the killing process. Latifah, for example, whose husband had been detained during the time of the genocide and transported to Java as a political prisoner, has described how people accused of being associated with the PKI were openly arrested and "taken away" by the military at this time, with the public understanding that these people were to be killed. In one case in early October, Latifah recalls an elderly Javanese woman selling corn at the local street market being taken by the military:

> I went shopping. There was an elderly Javanese woman whose husband had already passed away. She was selling corn, I don't remember the name of it, boiled corn mixed with sugar and coconut. My children really liked it. They said, Mum, please buy us some. I was buying the corn, three packets, and

I wanted to pay when they [the military] came for her . . . oh my god . . . I hadn't yet given her the money . . . but they still wanted to take her. "What should I do?" I asked [and someone answered] just take the money Ma'am, it doesn't matter. She's already been taken by the military . . . No, no, I couldn't take it, I left it and the packets at her stall.[81]

It is not known why this woman was arrested, beyond that she was accused of being in some way affiliated with the PKI. Such public arrests were common. The PKI, Latifah has explained, "were being chased everywhere" at this time.[82] The "military and police" were directly involved in this process, openly identifiable by the uniforms they felt no need to remove.[83]

Indeed, the military appears to have been keen to make its involvement in the killings in the district as explicit as possible. Latifah, for example, recalls seeing the decapitated head of a man named Rauf:

being stuck on a pole and attached to the front of a Jeep. . . . [and] paraded around town. . . . There were people on top of the car, military, all of them. . . . It was a big procession. . . . [My child] followed, parading around the town. I saw this with my own eyes. . . . A head on top of a car. Oh God, dear God! (*Ya Allah Subhanallah!*)[84]

Public killings carried out by civilians also occurred in Central Aceh at this time. In one case, some members of the PKI were "brought together" in front of a mosque "to be killed" by an angry mob.[85] It was "their friends" that allegedly betrayed them in an attempt to save their own lives.

In another case, a man named Islah, the son of an *ulama*, who was rumoured to secretly be "a communist" but who is alternatively described as being mentally unstable, was "arrested" and "processed" by the police after allegedly attempting to "burn down" Quba Mosque,[86] a small wooden mosque with a corrugated iron roof, 1.3 km from the centre of town.[87] After several days Islah was released back into the community, when an "announcement" was made for him to be brought to the mosque to be killed in front of a waiting crowd.[88] For reasons that remain unclear, this public execution did not occur, but the next day Islah's corpse was found dumped in an alley that ran near the mosque. His throat had been slit and he had been disembowelled, his intestines spilling onto the road, partially eaten by dogs. In neither case did the military act to end this violence or attempt to punish those responsible. Such violence, after all, was in complete accord with Djuarsa's explicit instructions that civilians in the district should "kill" people considered to be associated with the PKI, or risk being "punished" themselves.

9 October: the outbreak of public violence in West Aceh

The first specific post–1 October deaths reported in the Aceh Military Chronology with a specific date, name of victim and locality listed for Aceh, and indeed for the whole of Indonesia, are reported as occurring in Meulaboh on 9 October, one day after Djuarsa's tour to the district.[89] On this day, it was reported:

> At 6am, the body of a member of the Pemuda Rakyat, named Safe'i, was found in a gutter in Meulaboh and at 10am two more bodies of members of the Pemuda Rakyat were found outside the city of Meulaboh, the killers are unknown (*pembunuhnja tidak diketahui*).[90]

Three hours later in Sinabang, on Simeulu Island, 186 km southeast of Meulaboh, the SOBSI office was "destroyed" and its "documents burnt".[91] A "small struggle" is subsequently said to have broken out "without victims".

Two days later, two more bodies were "found . . . by the side of the road" in Pulo Oe.[92] The victims are identified as Pang Ben, from Tjot Ting *kampung* and Waki Abbas from Muko *kampung*. Again, "the killer" is listed as "unknown".[93] On 12 October, "six corpses" were "found" in Rantau Kepala Gadjah, Kuala Tripa, 53 km southeast from Meulaboh.[94] All victims are listed as being "from the PKI group" in Djeuram. The military, these records suggest, was keeping a close eye on developments while demonstrating its implicit support for the violence by not acting to stop it. Indeed, these records show the military was even more involved than this. The Chronology reports:

> Beginning with a string of demonstrations between 9–12 [October], 9 people were kidnapped and brought by truck to Rantau Kepala Gadja K[ual]a Tripa, where the killings were to be carried out (*dilakukan pembunuhan disana*), however 3 people among them didn't die, [and] were able to run away badly injured to K[ual]a Tripa, where they reported to Hansip [Civilian Defence paramilitary units] that 6 of their friends had been killed, while asking for medical assistance, but they were not given the assistance they had asked for by Hansip, and in a state of fear the 3 people returned to Rantau Kepala Gadjah, where one of them died on the way back, meanwhile the fate of the other two is not known, neither where they went nor if they survived.[95]

This entry makes clear the military was aware of the existence of killing sites and the occurrence of mass killings in the district during this early period. The entry also implies the involvement of the state in these killings though the involvement of the military-trained and coordinated Civilian Defence (*Hansip*) paramilitary units in this violence (if not directly participating in the killing, then in refusing to help survivors). If the military did not directly coordinate these killings, it was aware they were occurring and was complicit in allowing these killings to continue. Indeed, the question must be asked how the compiler of the Chronology knew the fate of the unfortunate individual who escaped and "died on the way back", unless there was some mechanism by which the military was monitoring, if not actively assisting, such killings. The entry also provides an example of public demonstrations being used as a prelude for more organised violence and of trucks being used to transport groups of detainees to killings sites, as would become common during the second wave of violence in the province.

On 13 October, in Darul Makmur subdistrict, meanwhile, a further six people, who are listed as members of the PKI, are reported as being "killed" by "local people".[96] The next day, Leman, the PKI Secretary for Pulo Ie, 34.8 km southeast of Tapaktuan in South Aceh, "along with 8 other people whose identities are unknown" were "killed" by "the people" in West Aceh.[97]

14 October: the Pantjasila Defence Front "public awareness" campaign

The military-sponsored Pantja Sila Defence Front death squad had been operating in West Aceh since at least 11 October, when T.M. Yatim, the former Assistant District Chief for Johan Pahlawan who had attempted to protest the military's annihilation campaign in the district, has explained, the death squad had threatened members of the West Aceh district government. On 14 October, the death squad intensified its activities. On this day, the Chronology reports, a Pantjasila Defence Front[98] "Information Team" (*Team Penerangan*) "carried out information sessions" in Seunangan subdistrict "in the form of controlling the situation so there are not deviations/misuse of measures in the annihilation of that which calls itself the 30 September Movement."[99]

"In regards to this matter," the Chronology continues, "the attention of the people in each place visited by this team has been satisfactory."[100] Exactly what is meant by "satisfactory" is not elaborated upon. From this entry it would appear that the Pantjasila Defence Front Information Team was engaged in a "public awareness" campaign on behalf of the military, ensuring that the violence that was being encouraged was channelled correctly. If this account is correct, the Pantja Sila Defence Front, which Yatim describes as an "arrest-kill movement" (*gerakan tangkap-bunuh*),[101] had moved from being a clandestine killing unit, to serving a visible public role with quasi-governmental duties.

From its formation, the Front had been visible in the district and explicit in its purpose. Yatim has explained: "The Pancasila [Defence Front] organisation was formed to confront the [30 September] Movement, you know, before this time we'd never seen it."[102] "After [the 1 October] Affair, the arrests began, direct arrests . . ." carried out by the Pantjasila Defence Front in the district. These arrests appear to have served the purpose of terrorising the population and of placing pressure on the West Aceh district government. The Front also appears to have escalated its role in the killings during the days following this meeting. "The [Pantjasila Defence Front] protested against the members of the [district-level] Provincial Government that were close with and pro-Left," Yatim explains, while "since that morning" its members publicly arrested PKI members, presumably as a form of intimidation. Yatim has recalled:

> We didn't agree with these anarchic actions, it wasn't right, to exterminate the PKI, to directly arrest and kill, or to arrest them and take them to their

[the Pantjasila Defence Front's] office . . . arrest-kill, arrest-kill, these were the conditions.[103]

Yatim believes the Pantjasila Defence Front was being "led" by the "instruction to kill the PKI" that had been issued by Djuarsa on 8 October.[104] Yatim's reference to the use of "offices" by the Front in connection to this "arrest-kill" campaign, meanwhile, appears to allude to the use of death houses by death squads during the genocide in the district.[105]

12 October: the outbreak of public violence in South Aceh

The first record of public violence in the Chronology for South Aceh is dated 12 October. On this day at 1.30am, three days after the *Front Nasional* had called upon members of the PKI to "report themselves" at the first anti-PKI demonstration in the district, it is reported that Zulkifli Duty, the head of the PKI for Samadua Subdistrict, had been "kidnapped" by "various youths from six political parties".[106] Two days later, in Blang Pidie, it was reported that "5 people, including 4 Chinese people and one Indonesian" had been "killed by the people" and their property seized.[107] Later that day in Samadua, it was reported that ten people had been killed.[108] Their killers are not identified. It is not known why members of Aceh's Chinese community appear to be overrepresented within these first two groups of victims.[109] The next day in Blang Pidie, two more unidentified corpses were "found".[110] "The killer," the Chronology remarks, "is not known."[111]

Two days later, on 17 October, it is reported that the district-level military Defence Sector Command (*Kosekhan*) intervened directly to "take control" and seize the property of a fisherman named Asan. The property seized included "21,250 litres of patchouli oil, 1,240 litres of coconut oil and goods from his warehouse, goods from his shop and a BSA Type Fiat (a kind of truck)".[112] Why these items were taken is not known. The Fiat may have been seized to transport detainees to killing sites. Meanwhile, the patchouli oil, a perfumery oil used in traditional medicine, was of high economic value.[113] Such seizures were consistent with the military's inauguration of the Kohanda command during the morning of 1 October, as codified through Dwikora legislation. This legislation gave the military the right to seize property from civilians, as well as the right to mandate civilians to "implement Dwikora" in the provinces. The seizure of the patchouli oil, however, appears to have been more punitive, and may have been intended as punishment. Possibly, as with the above case of the raid on the gold shop in North Aceh on 11 October, the owner may have been seen in some way as politically disloyal.

Detentions of men and women who had reported themselves to the *Front Nasional* also began during this period. One of the detention sites used, Ali, the peasant farmer from Samadua subdistrict, recounts, was the Samadua primary school.[114] Oesman, who in 1965 was a high school teacher in Tapaktuan, who described the military's reporting process as a "trap", has explained how these individuals were not immediately detained after reporting:

After reporting they were allowed to return home, then they were summoned to come together, and then they didn't go home again. During the cleansing (*pembersihannya*) . . . [some] were taken from their homes, taken from here, taken from there. They weren't detained when they reported, no, they just reported, and only after that there was a separate team (*tim tersendiri*) that got involved.[115]

The purpose of this process seems to have been to identify targeted individuals while distancing the military from the killings that occurred during this period. Ali has claimed that the first "arrests" of those who had reported themselves to the *Front Nasional* were carried out by members of the PNI, under the leadership of local PNI leader Tengku Hasyim.[116] "People were angry once they found out it was the PKI," Ali explains, and the PNI leadership "went looking for the PKI at that time", "arresting" the members that they could find.[117] Ali has suggested the PNI led this attack because the PNI and PKI were rivals, and because there had been competition between the two organisations in the past.[118] Competition between the PNI and PKI had also occurred in other provinces, such as in Bali, where the PNI was also involved in attacking the PKI after 1 October 1965. The violence seen from 1 October 1965, however, was unique and cannot be understood in isolation from the military's annihilation campaign. Ali has explained that it was the *Front Nasional* which "gave instructions" for the arrests in South Aceh.[119] Oesman, meanwhile, has recalled how the South Aceh military Defence Sector Command (*Kosekhan*), which was stationed at the District Military Command (*Kodim*) base, "gave an explanation" during this period that the population should be on guard and a "night watch" established,[120] mirroring developments that had taken place earlier in North Aceh.

20 October: formation of the Pantja Sila Defence Front "Executive Board"

At 8pm on 20 October, the Chronology reports, an "Executive Board" was established for the "Level II South Aceh Pantja Sila Defence Front" death squad.[121] The Executive Board "consisted of the Pantja Tunggal, 'pious Islamic leaders' (*Alim-Ulama*), Political Parties/Mass Organisations, Intellectuals and individuals". This development not only indicates that a Pantja Sila Defence Front death squad had been established in South Aceh, joining its sister organisations in Banda Aceh, East Aceh and West Aceh, but that its activities received the explicit support of the military and civilian leadership in the district, as evidenced by the South Aceh Pantja Tunggal's membership of this body. The designation of this group as a 'Level II' organisation, meanwhile, supports the understanding that the various Pantja Sila Defence Front groups that existed throughout the province at this time existed as part of a centrally coordinated network.

Oesman also refers to a death squad named the 'People's Defence' (*Pembela Rakyat*) that he asserts operated in the district at this time. The *Pembela Rakyat* death squad, Oesman explains, "worked together" with the Pantja Tunggal to pursue the military's annihilation campaign in South Aceh. Oesman has related:

> The *Pembela Rakyat* was a spontaneous form of defence, [but] to contain this, to keep this in check, it was coordinated at the top level [by the *Front Nasional* and the Pantja Tunggal] . . . Of course it couldn't just be spontaneous, of course there was something.[122]

The use of multiple military-sponsored death squads in a single district has also been reported in East Aceh. It is impossible to verify the existence of these specific organisations without further corroborating evidence. It is apparent, however, that military-sponsored death squads played a key role in spearheading the public violence, and especially the public killings, that occurred in the province during this period.

13 October: the outbreak of public violence in East Aceh

The first anti-PKI demonstration in East Aceh following the "unauthorised" anti-PKI demonstration on 3 October, which occurred two days after Mokoginta and Djuarsa's presence in the district, is recorded as occurring on 13 October. On this day at 8am, the Military Chronology reports, a demonstration was held in Langsa.[123] This demonstration was attended by members of the anti-PKI Islamist youth organisations HMI and Ansor,[124] Indonesia's scouting organisation Pramuka,[125] other anti-PKI organisations[126] and "students".[127] The protesters called for the disbanding of the PKI and "screamed" (*berteriak-teriak*) for Aidit and "his lackeys" to be "hanged" (*gantung*) and for the "Gestapo 30 September Movement" to be buried (*kubur*). This provocative demonstration received the blessing of the military, which notes how it ran "smoothly".[128]

The next day at 6am, an anti-PKI demonstration was held in the border town of Kuala Simpang. Some 15,000 people are reported to have attended this demonstration, including members of political parties from the district,[129] youth organisations[130] and members of two women's organisations: Daughters of Alwasliyah (*Putri Alwasliyah*)[131] and Daughters of Muhammadiyah (*Putri Muhammadiyah*).[132] Why women appear to have played a particularly prominent role in this demonstration is not known. The demonstration then marched on a "PKI Baperki office",[133] which was destroyed and burnt, along with several houses "belonging to the BTI".[134]

Following these arson attacks, the demonstrators marched to the local sports field. After praying for the dead generals in Jakarta, the demonstrators were read a declaration by one of the protest leaders stating that the PKI and its affiliated organisations should be disbanded.[135] The local Infantry Battalion Commander (Dan Jonif III: *Komandan Bataljon Infantri*), Captain Said Zakaria, then directly addressed the demonstrators to "provide an explanation that it was necessary for the demonstration to disperse". This statement shows the military not only openly encouraged such violent demonstrations; it also provided explicit direction to demonstrators and had sufficient control over the actions to bring them to a close once they had served their purpose. The military was additionally involved in issuing other public announcements. Saifuddin, from Idi subdistrict, for example, has recalled how "[w]e heard news" that the PKI was to be disbanded directly from the "central [military] command and youth".[136]

Direct arrests were also conducted by the military at this time. Later the same day, it is reported in the Chronology that "Battalion 122" (*Jon 112*) was joined by Puterpra 401 and 402,[137] two local Territorial Affairs and People's Resistance Units responsible for the coordination of village-level Civilian Defence (*Hansip*) and People's Defence (*Hanra*) paramilitary groups in the area,[138] who carried out a "search/raid" in Suka-rachmad Village.[139] Four people were arrested as part of this "search/raid", including "the Head of the BTI, a courier from Java who was also a member of the Pemuda Rakyat, along with two others, whose identities are still unknown".

13 October: formation of the Pantja Sila Youth Defence Front

Multiple military-sponsored death squads were also established in the district at this time. On 13 October, a group called the East Aceh Pantja Sila Youth Defence Front (*Front Pemuda Pembela Pantja Sila*) was established in Langsa.[140] This group, which consisted exclusively of high school and university students, was established as a united front organisation with members from seven youth groups in the district, including Ansor Youth (*Pemuda Ansor*)[141] and Pemuda Pancas-ila.[142] The founding document of the Front reads, in part, as follows:

3   [We] strongly condemn that group that calls itself the "30 September Movement", and **insist that the Government sentence to death** those who were involved in this affair.

4   Insist that the PJM President/PBR/Commander of the Armed Forces/ Hero of Islam and Independence, Bung Karno, dissolve the Indonesian Communist Party and its mass organisations.

5   Insist that the Government *immediately purge (segera membersihkan)* PKI personnel from all Government Bodies.

6   Continue to stand behind Bung Karno and the Armed Forces to completely **annihilate those who are involved in the 30 September Movement** in this district.

7   Insist that the Government immediately take control of private enterprises that directly or indirectly provide assistance to the PKI and its lackeys.

8   Insist that the Aceh Pepelrada/Level I Pantja Tunggal and East Aceh Level II Pantja Tunggal freeze the activities of the PKI, Baperki, Partindo, PPI and IPPI (*Ikatan Pemuda Peladjar Indonesia*: Association of Indonesian High School Students)[143] in this region.[144]

This document clearly signals the group's intention to become involved in the military's annihilation campaign and explicitly indicates that it understood this campaign to mean that targeted individuals should be "sentenced to death". By referring to Sukarno as the "Hero of Islam", meanwhile, this document appears to appeal to the notion that the military's annihilation campaign should be promoted as a religious struggle, a characterisation which does not exist in internal military and government documents, but which was promoted by the military at public demonstrations throughout the district during the time of the genocide.[145] The document also makes reference to the notion that "PKI personnel" should be "purged" from government bodies, in apparent reference to the purge campaign that would sweep the province from 18 October. This purge campaign, which, at times, ran parallel to the killings, had its own dynamic and purpose.

That the Pantja Sila Youth Defence Front sent a copy of these documents to Suharto in Jakarta, Mokoginta in Medan and Djuarsa in Banda Aceh indicates that the Front recognised the leadership of these men and sought their endorsement for their actions. Likewise, that a copy of these documents was also sent to the provincial government in Banda Aceh[146] further indicates that these intentions were widely known. Meanwhile, the group's reference to itself as a 'Level II' branch once again indicates that the Pantja Sila Defence Front groups existed as part of a larger, centrally coordinated network of branches. Indeed, it would appear that a variety of military-sponsored death squads were operating in East Aceh during this period.

14 October: formation of the East Aceh Pantja Sila Defence Front

On 14 October, a group named the East Aceh Level II Pantja Sila Defence Front (*Front Pembela Pantja Sila Daerah Tk II*) was formed in Langsa.[147] This group was not aimed solely at youths and was established as a district branch (Level II) of the Front Pantjasila death squad that had been formed in Banda Aceh on 6 October.[148] An inauguration ceremony for the East Aceh Level II Pantja Sila Defence Front was held at Merdeka Square in front of the East Aceh District Military Command (*Kodim*) headquarters, following the holding of special prayers for the dead generals.[149] At this ceremony, members of the Front are said to have listened to "radio broadcasts" from Radio Republik Indonesia in Jakarta and to have "read newspapers printed in Medan between 1 and 13 October" before pledging their support for the military's annihilation campaign.

The founding document of the East Aceh Level II Pantja Sila Defence Front followed an almost identical formulation to the document produced by the East Aceh Pantja Sila Youth Defence Front the day before. After condemning the 30 September Movement, which it claimed had "carried out a Coup D'état" under the control of "PKI devils" (*iblis PKI*), the Front called for Sukarno to "completely annihilate down to its roots the '30 September Movement'", for the PKI to be "disbanded" and for "all government bodies" to be "cleansed".[150]

Like its sister organisations, the primary function of this group was to support the military's annihilation campaign. It also signalled its support for the purge of government bodies that would shortly commence. By referring to the PKI as "devils", the document also uses religious language to justify the dehumanisation and ultimate murder of the military's target group. On 28 October, as will be outlined below, the East Aceh Level II Pantja Sila Defence Front would receive the official support and assistance of the East Aceh district government to carry-out this genocidal campaign.

14 October: formation of the Movement of Believers for the Defence of Pantjasila

A third military-sponsored death squad, the Movement of Believers for the Defence of Pantja Sila (*Gerakan Massa Ummat Jang Bertuhan Untuk Memper-tahankan Pantjasila*), was established in the district in Idi on 14 October.[151] In its founding document, the Movement of Believers for the Defence of Pantja Sila pledged to "Assist ABRI with full capacity to completely annihilate the counter-revolutionaries".[152] It also claimed to have sponsored a mass meeting of 10,000 civilians, including members of the PNI, NU, PSII and Perti in Idi.

It would appear the Movement of Believers was involved in a public media campaign at this time. In addition to forwarding copies of its founding document to Suharto in Jakarta, Mokoginta in Medan and Djuarsa in Banda Aceh, it also sent copies to Radio Republik Indonesia in Banda Aceh and the "press/and daily [newspapers]" in Medan and Banda Aceh.[153]

The reason for the variation in the names of military-sponsored death squads in the district is not known. While the East Aceh Pantja Sila Youth Defence Front appears to have been a youth wing of the East Aceh Level II Pantja Sila Defence Front, it may be that the Pantja Sila Defence Front and the Movement of Believers for the Defence of Pantjasila represented slightly different political alliances, as these groups, at least in the case of East Aceh, do not have an overlapping organ-isational membership. Their creation may equally have been an attempt to present the impression that the death squads were spontaneous local creations, despite clear evidence to the contrary.

28 October: government support for the Pantja Sila Defence Front

The most damning evidence that cements the Pantja Sila Defence Front's status as a state-sponsored and coordinated death squad can be found in a 'Declaration' produced on 28 October in Langsa by the East Aceh district government. This Dec-laration (*Pernjataan: No. 12/Pernj/Dprd/1965*), references both the above quoted document prepared by the 'Action Committee' of the East Aceh Level II Pantja Sila Defence (*Pembela Pantja Sila Daerah Tk II*) and the Pantja Sila Youth Defence Front's founding document, before listing eight resolutions.[154] This government-produced Declaration opened with an expression of relief that the President's life had been spared and sympathy for the murdered generals, before pledging to:

3   Condemn as strongly as possible the barbaric and viciousness of the counterrevolutionary group (*kaum*) the "30 September Movement" and **call for the sentencing to death of those who were involved in this affair.**

4   To pledge obedience and loyalty towards [Sukarno] and **annihilate down to the roots this counter revolutionary group**.

5   Support as well as **provide as much assistance as possible** to the East Aceh Level II "Pantja Sila Defence [Front] Action Committee" **to annihilate the "30 September Movement" down to its roots**.

6   Support the policies of the East Aceh Level II Pantja Tunggal **for the annihilation of this counter revolution** (*Mendukung kebidjaksanaan Pentja Tunggal Tingkat II Atjeh Timur dalam penumpasan kontra revolusi tsb*) and express an intention to work as closely as possible with all Political Parties and Mass Organisations in accordance with the Command of the President in front of the Level I Pantja Tunggal for the whole of Indonesia in the Presidential Palace on Saturday 23 October 1965.

7   Call upon all layers of society to increase their awareness and preparedness to assist ABRI to annihilate and **completely eliminate the "30 September Movement" along with its lackeys** while supporting strong unity and integrity [of the state].

8   Hope that [Sukarno] disband the PKI and its Mass Organisations along with the other parties and organisations that have been involved in the "30 September Movement" affair.[155]

This document is the most explicit document that has yet to be found produced by a district-level provincial government in support of the activities of a military-sponsored death squad. It is evidence that the military's annihilation campaign – which is explained here to explicitly mean the "sentencing to death" of identified individuals – was pursued as state policy in East Aceh. Moreover, by introducing the term "group" (*kaum*) to describe this target group this document signals that it was not just the organisational leadership of the PKI and its affiliated organisations that were to be targeted for attack: the military's annihilation campaign was intended to result in the physical annihilation of an entire human group, named here as the "counter revolutionary group".

This document is also evidence the East Aceh district government pledged to actively provide "as much assistance as possible" to the East Aceh Level II Pantja Sila Defenders Front death squad to carryout this campaign. This extraordinary admission demonstrates that the East Aceh district government considered the provision of material assistance to the military's annihilation campaign to be consistent with government policy. The document also shows that the East Aceh district government actively incited civilians to participate in this campaign, by using the district government as a platform to "call upon all layers of society" to "assist" the military to implement the killings.

The Declaration was then forwarded to Sukarno and other key leaders of the military and civilian government in Jakarta; all Level II provincial governments throughout Indonesia; Mokoginta in Medan, Djarsa and the Pantja Tunggal in Banda Aceh; all Bupati and Mayors throughout Aceh; and all key military and civilian government leaders in East Aceh.[156] For good measure, it was also sent to the Radio Republic Indonesia studio in Banda Aceh and the "press/and daily [newspapers]" in Medan. There is thus no level of the state throughout Indonesia, either military or civilian, that could claim ignorance of what was occurring in East Aceh. Moreover, as there is no reason to think that East Aceh was in any way special, it is highly likely that this process was replicating itself throughout Indonesia at this time. A national network of state-sponsored death squads was being established at this time with the active assistance of provincial and district-level governments and the military in the provinces.[157]

Arief, the LEKRA-affiliated travelling theatre troupe performer, has described how these death squads operated "death houses" in Langsa during this period, where groups of people accused of being associated with the PKI were detained, interrogated and tortured before being killed.[158] One of these death houses, Arief recalls, was located in the Veteran's Building, near the mosque in Langsa. "People were tortured there every night," Arief explains. "It was extremely horrifying. From the street I would hear the noise, wooooop [the noise of people being tortured] . . . the sound [of what went on in that room] could be heard from outside."[159]

***

It is inescapable to conclude that there was coordination behind this first phase of violence in Aceh and that it was the military that provided the leadership behind this coordination. Distinct patterns can be seen in the outbreak and escalation of public violence throughout the province. Such patterns can be seen in the uniformity of the occurrence of anti-PKI demonstrations that were held in each district within days of the military's public coordinating meetings described in the previous chapter. In no district did public violence begin before these public meetings were held.

These anti-PKI demonstrations quickly evolved into destructive pogrom actions in which demonstrators marched on PKI offices and houses, which were subsequently ransacked and burnt under the watchful eye of the military. Abductions of targeted individuals also began to occur, frequently coinciding with the first pogrom action in a district. Many individuals abducted during this initial period were killed and their bodies left on public display. The primary purpose of these initial killings was to terrorise. Initially, these killings were carried out by ideological youth, members of the Civilian Defence (*Hansip*) and People's Defence (*Hanra*) paramilitary groups and other civilian proxies who were instructed to "assist" the military to "annihilate" all individuals considered to be associated with the PKI. As the violence wore on, however, special military-sponsored death squads were formed to spearhead the public violence campaign. By 20 October, a network of military-sponsored death squads existed throughout the province. These branches, with known branches in Banda Aceh (established on 6 October), West Aceh (11 October), East Aceh (14 October) and South Aceh (20 October), received the blessing, leadership and material assistance of the military and civilian governments.

An effect of these demonstrations, abductions and public killings was to drive targeted individuals into the arms of the military as they sought protection from the violence on the streets. Combined with an increase in systematic attacks carried out directly by the military and an increase in the numbers of abductees being "surrendered" to the military, the military was now faced with the question of what to do with this now large, growing prison population. After experimenting with releasing small groups of prisoners to be killed by its civilian proxies, it would choose, from 14 October, to systematically exterminate them.

Notes

1 Here I define a 'pogrom' as an organised violent attack against a civilian population.
2 See, 'Death Map'; also, *Laporan Tahunan Lengkap Kodam-I/Kohanda Atjeh, Tahun 1965* (Banda Aceh: Kodam-I Banda Aceh, 1 February 1966), pp. 6–7.
3 The first death is recorded as occurring on 9 October.
4 Emphasis added. *Laporan Tahunan Lengkap*, pp. 6–7.
5 'Chronologis Kedjadian2 jang Berhubungan dengan Gerakan 30 September Didaerah Kodam-I/Atjeh', p. 2.
6 *Ibid.*
7 *Ibid*; Interview with "Ramli" (a pseudonym), West Sumatra, 15 December 2011, p. 37.
8 'Chronologis', p. 2.
9 Interview with "Ramli", West Sumatra, 15 December 2011, p. 14.
10 *Ibid.*, p. 13.
11 *Ibid.*, p. 12.
12 An account of Yusni's arrest and murder can be found in chapter 6.
13 *Ibid.*, p. 14.
14 *Ibid.*, p. 37.
15 *Ibid.*, pp. 37–38. Ramli's hand-drawn picture can be found in Notebook 2, Aceh 2011/2012.
16 Interview with "Ramli", West Sumatra, 15 December 2011, p. 38.
17 Adamy also recalls finding discarded bullet shells at SI-AD.
18 *Ibid.*, p. 39.
19 The political parties listed as attending are: the PSII, Perti, NU and Muhammadijah. The student organisations listed as attending included HMI and GMNI. The GMNI, established 1 June 1945, was affiliated with the PNI. 'Chronologis', p. 2.
20 Written interview with Asan, given to the author, Hong Kong, 30 October 2011, p. 29.
21 'Chronologis', p. 2. It is not known what 'HC' stand for. Anas, originally from Meulaboh, West Aceh, was a member of the Aceh PKI's Operations Council (*Dewan Harian*) and head of LEKRA in the province. Interview with Asan, Hong Kong, 31 October 2011, p. 28.
22 'Chronologis', p. 2.
23 For example, see, *40 Hari Kegagalan*, pp. 94–102. This document records other alleged PKI atrocities committed during this period. Should the killings recorded in the Aceh Military's Complete Yearly Report have occurred, they would have provided the military in Yogyakarta with a propaganda coup. The absence of these events in this report suggests they were manufactured specifically for propaganda use in Aceh.
24 'Chronologis', p. 2.
25 'Marhaen' is a term coined by Sukarno to refer to a category of poor Indonesians who were oppressed by capitalism and imperialism, but who were not part of the traditional peasant or proletarian classes, as they were small land owners and owned a few tools. Sukarno is believed to have formulated this concept after meeting with a

man named Marhaen, a poor peasant who lived in such conditions. 'Marhaenism' was presented by Sukarno as a particularly 'Indonesian' form of Marxism.

26 'Chronologis', p. 3.
27 *Ibid.*
28 The citation of such a round number suggests this figure is an estimate.
29 'Chronologis', p. 3.
30 Interview with Zainal Abidin, Banda Aceh, 14 February 2009, p. 9.
31 *Ibid.*, p. 8.
32 John Bowen, *Sumatran Politics and Poetics: Gayo History, 1900–1989* (New Haven: Yale University Press, 1991), p. 102.
33 Interview with Zainal Abidin, Banda Aceh, 14 February 2009, p. 11.
34 'Chronologis', p. 3.
35 *Ibid.*
36 See chapter 6 for an overview of how this process of transportation and systematic killings occurred.
37 Interview with Dahlan Sulaiman, Banda Aceh, 29 December 2011, p. 10.
38 *Ibid.*, p. 32.
39 For an example of a death list used in North Sumatra, see, 'Daft[a]r Kader (CC) PKI Yang Diamankan', signed by Amir Hasan Nast BA, Simpang Matapao, North Sumatra, 1 Mai 1966, in Amir Hasan Nast BA, *Embun Berdarah* (self published, undated manuscript, in author's possession).
40 *Ibid.*, p. 10.
41 *Ibid.*
42 *Ibid.*
43 Interview with Zainuddin Hamid, "Let Bugeh", Banda Aceh, 17 January 2010, pp. 2, 4.
44 *Ibid.*
45 *Ibid.*
46 'Chronologis', p. 4.
47 *Ibid.*
48 *Ibid.*
49 This practice is still followed by community health clinics (Puskesmas: *Pusat Kesehatan Masyarakat*) and the Syariat Police (WH: *Wilayatul Hisbah*) in the province to this day. During fieldwork in Aceh in 2011 I witnessed the use of this technique to promote government immunisation programs and "jilbab raids".
50 'Chronologis', p. 4.
51 Interview with Zainal Abidin, Banda Aceh, 14 February 2009, p. 11.
52 *Ibid.*, p. 12.
53 *Ibid.*, pp. 11–12.
54 'Chronologis', p. 4.
55 It also called upon the Aceh Special Region Pantja Tunggal for "GWASMA" to be "installed." It is not known what "GWASMA" refers to. *Ibid.*
56 *Ibid.*
57 *Laporan Tahunan Lengkap*, p. 8.
58 *Ibid.*, p. 6.
59 'Chronologis', p. 7.
60 Written interview with Asan, given to the author, Hong Kong, 30 October 2011, p. 5.
61 The story of Thaib Adamy's death is detailed in chapter 6.
62 This is the earliest reference to the activities of the state-sponsored KAMI (Indonesian Student Action Front) and KAPPI (Indonesian School Student and Youth Action Front) death squads in Aceh during the time of the genocide. According to Dahlan Sulaiman, a former student death squad leader, KAMI was first formed in Aceh in late January 1966, while KAPPI was not officially formed nationally until 9 February 1966. Many students who would later join KAMI and KAPPI in Aceh were active prior to this time in different student militia groups and death squads. It is possible

Asan is using 'KAMI-KAPPI people' as a shorthand way of referring to these pro-military student militia and death squad groups. See chapter 7 for further discussion.

63 "Bang", short for "Abang", literally meaning 'older brother', is a common respectful term in Aceh for men older than the speaker but not yet old enough to be referred to as "Uncle" [in Acehnese: *Cek*] or "Father", "*Bapak*".

64 The Batak are an ethnic group from North Sumatra.

65 This is a reference to the type of revolutionary slogans that were used by the PKI during the 1946 social revolution in East Sumatra, today North Sumatra. Anthony Reid, *The Blood of the People: Revolution and the End of Traditional Rule in Northern Sumatra* (Kuala Lumpur and New York: Oxford University Press, 1979), p. 242.

66 That former Darul Islam members might have been "looking" for PKI members as a form of revenge during this period indicates that resentment continued between these groups. It is significant to note, however, that this former childhood friend pursued this revenge through the framework of the military's campaign. It was the military's national campaign that allowed such localised feelings of revenge to be acted upon, not feelings of localised revenge that caused the genocide.

67 Written interview with Asan, Part Two, given to the author, Hong Kong, 30 October 2011.

68 'Chronologis', p. 5.

69 It is not known what 'PU' refers to.

70 'Chronologis', p. 5.

71 *Ibid.*

72 *Ibid.*

73 *Ibid.*, p. 6.

74 *Ibid.*

75 *Ibid.*, p. 7.

76 *Ibid.*

77 Emphasis added. Unfortunately, the names of these forty-three individuals are not listed in the Chronology. *Ibid.*, p. 8.

78 An example of a membership list produced in Aceh during the time of the genocide with names attached is discussed in chapter 7.

79 'Chronologis', p. 5.

80 *Ibid.*

81 Interview with "Latifah", Banda Aceh, 15 February 2009, p. 5.

82 *Ibid.*, p. 6.

83 *Ibid.*

84 *Ibid.*, p. 4.

85 Interview with Mustawalad Blang, Takengon, 9 February 2009, p. 4. Blang is a human rights activist and member of the NGO Commission for the Disappeared and Victims of Violence (Kontras: *Komisi untuk Orang Hilang dan Korban Tindak Kekerasan*) in Takengon. He has conducted interviews with survivors of the genocide in Central Aceh.

86 *Ibid.*

87 To this day, it is reported in local media that the mosque was "burnt down by the PKI". 'Sejarah Masjid Quba Takengon', *Detik Aceh.com*, 4 December 2014.

88 Interview with Mustawalad Blang, Takengon, 9 February 2009, p. 4.

89 Prior to this, the earliest deaths reported in the literature are listed, without specifics or corroborating evidence, as occurring in West Java "from 4 October". "[O]n the day of the exhumation of Yani and his colleagues . . .," Sundhausen writes, "Muslim and supporters of the banned PSI started to kill communist cadres and members." Ulf Sundhaussen, *The Road to Power: Indonesian Military Politics, 1945–1967* (Kuala Lumpur: Oxford University Press, 1982), p. 217. Meanwhile, the earliest deaths recorded for Aceh are said to have begun "on 5 October" without corroborating

information. Said Abubakar, *Berjuang untuk Daerah: Otonomi Hak Azazi Insani* (Banda Aceh: Yayasan Nagasakti, 1995), p. 98.

90 'Chronologis', p. 4.
91 *Ibid.*, p. 3.
92 *Ibid.*, p. 5.
93 *Ibid.*
94 The names of the victims are listed as Saleh Djururawat, from Seunangan; Rezali, from Djeuram; Dollah, from Pulo Oe; and Daud Tgk Blad, Makmudan and Mak Dja-far, place of residence unknown. *Ibid.*, p. 6.
95 *Ibid.*
96 The names of the victims are listed as Gimin, from Serbadjari *kampung*; Djiul from Serbabangun *kampung*; Timbul and Warman from Alukota *kampung*; and Karidjan and Sali from Sukaramai *kampung*. *Ibid.*
97 *Ibid.*, p. 8.
98 It is not known why some of the Front Pantja Sila death squad organisations spell "Pantja Sila" (Five Principles) as two words, and others as one (i.e. "Pantjasila"). There does not appear to be any particular significance behind this decision.
99 *Ibid.*, p. 7.
100 *Ibid.*
101 Interview with T.M. Yatim, Meulaboh, West Aceh, 3 December 2011, p. 9.
102 *Ibid.*
103 *Ibid.*
104 *Ibid.*
105 The most detailed account of the internal workings of such death houses can be found in *The Act of Killing* transcripts [some of which did not make it into the final cut of the film]: MM Disc 1: 0–5; MM Disc 3: 8–11; CJ Disc 4: 0–5; CJ Disc 4: 2–1. A further reference to the use of death houses in Aceh during the time of the genocide can be found below in the section on East Aceh.
106 'Chronologis', p. 5.
107 *Ibid.*, p. 8.
108 The names of six of the victims are listed as Sukarno Imam Safe'i from Samadua; Majuni from Blang Padang; and Hap Tjok, Min On, Bun Tok Seng and Sio Nam from Blang Pidie. The remaining victims' identities are listed as unknown. *Ibid.*
109 For further discussion of anti-Chinese violence during the genocide in Aceh, see chapter 7.
110 'Chronologis', p. 8.
111 *Ibid.*
112 *Ibid.*
113 Indonesian patchouli oil is considered to be particularly high in quality. It sells for a high price on the world market.
114 Interview with "Ali", Sama Dua, South Aceh, 6 December 2011, p. 412.
115 Interview with "Oesman", Tapaktuan, South Aceh, 6 December 2011, p. 5.
116 Interview with "Ali", Sama Dua, South Aceh, 6 December 2011, p. 6.
117 *Ibid.*, p. 5.
118 *Ibid.*, p. 6.
119 Interview with "Ali", Sama Dua, South Aceh, 6 December 2011, p. 9.
120 Interview with "Oesman", Tapaktuan, South Aceh, 6 December 2011, p. 9.
121 'Chronologis', p. 9.
122 Interview with "Oesman", Tapaktuan, South Aceh, 6 December 2011, p. 12.
123 'Chronologis', p. 7.
124 Ansor, from the Arabic '*al-ansar*', "followers of the Prophet", was founded in 1934. Affiliated with the Nahdlatul Ulama (NU), it became infamous for its involvement in the killings. A history of Ansor, including an account of its role in the genocide, can be found in Erwien Kusuma, *Yang Muda Yang Berkiprah: Gerakan Pemuda Ansor*

Politik Indonesia Masa Demokrasi Liberal Hingga Masa Reformasi (1950–2010) (Bogor: Kekal Press, 2010). See also, Greg Fealy and Greg Barton, *Nahdlatul Ulama, Traditional Islam and Modernity in Indonesia* (Clayton, Victoria: Monash Asia Institute, Monash University, 1986).

125 Pramuka ([*Gerakan*] *Praja Muda Karana*: Indonesia's Scouting Organisation). Pramuka was first established in 1912. 'Pramuka Pantjasila' is also recorded as attending this demonstration. It is not known what organisation 'Pramuka Pantjasila' refers to, or what its relationship might have been with either Pramuka or the Pemuda Pancasila.

126 These organisations included Gasbindo, Perti and "GPKI". It is not known what organisation 'GKPI' refers to.

127 'Chronologis', p. 7.

128 *Ibid.*

129 These political parties are listed as including the NU, PNI and IP-KI.

130 These youth organisations are listed as including the 'Marhaenist Youth' (*Pemuda Marhaenis*), otherwise known as the 'Marhaenist Youth Movement' (*Gerakan Pemuda Marhaenis*). This socialist youth organisations was associated with Sukarno.

131 Daughters of Alwasliyah is the women's group of 'Al Wasliyah', a traditionalist Islamic organisation headquartered in Medan.

132 Putri Muhammadiyah was a women's group affiliated to Muhammadiyah.

133 This conflation between the PKI and Baperki was not based on organisational ties. As will be discussed in chapter 7, the use of this and other formulations was aimed at depicting the PKI as a "tool" of communist China.

134 'Chronologis', p. 7.

135 *Ibid.*

136 Interview with "Saifuddin", Idi, East Aceh, 11 December 2011, p. 21.

137 'Puterpra 401' was a position held at this time by Second Lieutenant Adam Jayja, based in Kuala Simpang. 'Puterpra 402' was a position held at this time by Second Lieutenant Madang St., based on Karang Baru. 'Puterpra 'Daftar Dislokasi Pasukan Oktober/ Nopember/Deseber '65', p. 3, in *Laporan Tahunan Lengkap Kodam-I/Kohanda Atjeh, Tahun 1965* (Banda Aceh: Kodam-I Banda Aceh, 1 February 1966).

138 Kuala Simpang, the first city on the Aceh side of the Aceh–North Sumatra border, is 10.3 km from Suka Rahmat. Karang Baru subdistrict is 18.8 km from Suka Rahmat.

139 'Chronologis', p. 7.

140 Untitled document, signed by the Front Pemuda Pembela Pantja Sila, Langsa, East Aceh, 13 October 1965.

141 Pemuda Ansor was a youth wing of Ansor.

142 The other five youth organisations included Indonesian Muslim Youth (*Pemuda Muslimin Indonesia*), Pemuda Marhaenis, PI Perti, Muhammadijah Youth (*Pemuda Muhammadijah*) and Alwaslijah Youth (*Pemuda Alwaslijah*). The Front also claims to have been supported by Indonesian Christian Youth (*Pemuda Kristen Indonesia*). Untitled document, signed by the Front Pemuda Pembela Pantja Sila, Langsa, East Aceh, 13 October 1965. Pemuda Muslimin Indonesia was formed in 1928 as a youth wing of the Syarikat Islam. Pemuda Muhammadijah was a youth group affiliated to Muhammadijah.

143 IPPI was formed in 1948. Its leadership consisted of socialists and communists and was sympathetic to the PKI.

144 Emphasis added. Untitled document, signed by the Front Pemuda Pembela Pantja Sila, Langsa, 13 October 1965, attached to 'Panitia Aksi Pembela Pantja Sila Daerah Tk II Atjeh Timur', Langsa, 14 October 1965.

145 Sukarno was first bestowed with the title 'Hero of Islam and Freedom' at the Africa-Asia Islamic Conference in Bandung, West Java, in March 1965. This conference, not to be confused with the Africa-Asia Conference held in Bandung in 1955, was held with the aim of countering perceived 'PKI/communist domination'. Choirotun

Chisaan, 'In Search of an Indonesian Islamic Cultural Identity, 1956–1965', in Jennifer Lindsey and Maya H.T. Liem (eds.), *Heirs to World Culture: Being Indonesian 1950–1965* (Leiden: KITLV Press, 2012), pp. 289, 311. The use of the title here appears intended to appeal to a 'non-communist' vision of Indonesia.

146 Untitled document, signed by the Front Pemuda Pembela Pantja Sila, Langsa, 13 October 1965, attached to 'Panitia Aksi Pembela Pantja Sila Daerah Tk II Atjeh Timur', Langsa, 14 October 1965.

147 'Panitia Aksi Pembela Pantja Sila Daerah Tk II Atjeh Timur', Langsa, East Aceh, 14 October 1965.

148 *Ibid*; 'Chronologis', p. 1.

149 'Panitia Aksi Pembela Pantja Sila Daerah Tk II Atjeh Timur', Langsa, East Aceh, 14 October 1965, p. 4.

150 *Ibid*.

151 'Panitia Aksi Gerakan Massa Ummat Jang Bertuhan Untuk Mempertahankan Pantjasila', Idi, East Aceh, 14 October 1965, pp. 1–2.

152 *Ibid*., p. 2.

153 *Ibid*.

154 'Pernjataan: No. 12/Pernj/Dprd/1965', Langsa, East Aceh, 28 October 1965, p. 1.

155 Emphasis added. *Ibid*., pp. 1–2.

156 The full list of recipients of this Declaration included: Sukarno; various ministers in Jakarta; the head of the *Front Nasional* in Jakarta; the Military Police Headquarters in Jakarta; Mokoginta, acting as Panglatu in Medan; Djuarsa, acting as Pangdahan 'A' in Banda Aceh; Aceh's Governor, Njak Adam Kamil; the head of the *Front Nasional* in Banda Aceh; a Substitute Judge; Banda Aceh's Provincial Police Commander; all Level II provincial governments throughout Indonesia; all bupati and mayors throughout Aceh; the Defence Sector Commander (Dan Sekhan: *Komandan Sektor Pertahanan*) in East Aceh; the *Front Nasional* in East Aceh; the Military Resort Commander (Danres: *Komandan Resort*); the Public Prosecutor; all government heads and all political parties and mass organisations in East Aceh. Pernjataan: No. 12/Pernj/Dprd/1965', Langsa, East Aceh, 28 October 1965, p. 2.

157 Further pointing to the national coordination of these groups, a national 'Front Pancasila' was established in Jakarta on 23 October 1965, made up of "anti-communist mass organizations", including the NU, Partai Katolik, PSII, Parkindo, IP-KI, Perti, PNI, Muhammadijah, SOKSI (*Swadiri Organisasi Karya Sosialis Indonesia*: Indonesian Socialist Union of Career Organisations) and Gasbindo, making this group similar in composition to the Front Pemuda Pantjasila and Pantjasila Defence Front death squads in Aceh, the Komando Aksi death squads in North Sumatra and the original KAP-Gestapu death squad in Jakarta.

158 Interview with "Arief", Banda Aceh, 5 February 2009, p. 5.

159 *Ibid*. Arief's account of death houses in Langsa mirrors accounts of the use of death squad operated death houses in Medan. The most comprehensive account of the activities of death squads in Medan can be found in, *The Act of Killing*, directed by Joshua Oppenheimer (Denmark: Final Cut for Real, 2012); *The Act of Killing* transcripts; *Snake River*, directed by Joshua Oppenheimer, 2004; and *The Look of Silence*, directed by Joshua Oppenheimer (Denmark: Final Cut for Real, 2014).

6 Killing to destroy
14 October–23 December

The military's annihilation campaign dramatically escalated after 14 October, when Djuarsa announced the Aceh Military Command's intention to launch a "war" against the PKI. Faced with a large prison population as a result of the arrests carried out during the first phase of the violence, the military leadership set about initiating systematic mass killings at military-controlled killing sites throughout the province. Key documents recovered from this period identify the role of the military in inciting and facilitating this violence, while eyewitness testimony reveals the direct role the military played in implementing the killings. The military, this chapter will demonstrate, was now killing to destroy.

14 October: formation of the 'War Room'

On 14 October, Djuarsa, acting in the capacity of Pangdahan 'A', issued an 'Instruction' (*Instr-1/10/1965*) "establishing the creation of a RUANG YUDHA (War Room) for all [military] units".[1] Evidence that such a body was established indicates that the military leadership conceived of its attack against the PKI as an internal armed conflict, and was actively establishing coordinating bodies to facilitate its campaign. In his introduction to the 'Complete Yearly Report', the establishment of the War Room, Djuarsa explains further:

> enabled KODAM I to carryout NON-CONVENTIONAL war in accordance with the Concept of Territorial Warfare . . . [and enabled the military to] succeed in **annihilating them ["GESTOK"] together with the people**.[2]

There was no attempt made in internal military documents at this time to disguise the role the military played in launching its attack against the PKI, which it explicitly conceived of as a war aimed at physically exterminating this target group, or to disguise its role in mobilising the civilian population to help it wage this war. As Djuarsa continues:

> [A]s a result of technical difficulties, the implementation of [the War Room] is not yet perfect. The aspects that can be said to be running [are] its communications function, which already allows the operation of communications

between both subordinate units and superiors (*kesatuan2 bawahan maupun atasan*).[3]

The War Room was a military-led body that coordinated the implementation of the genocide in the province. It was a twenty-four-hour operation. From 2 November, Djuarsa reports, the War Room had established an out-of-hours task force consisting of 'Assigned Defence Region Command Officers' (*Perwira Konsinjir Kodahan*) and 'Alert Officers' (*Perwira Siaga*), who were stationed at the War Room and rostered on to duty on a rotational basis.[4] The military in Aceh, Djuarsa explains, was placed on "highest alert" during this period.[5]

That the military leadership should escalate its involvement in this manner at a time when it was clear the PKI presented no real threat to anyone demonstrates the genocidal nature of the military's attack.[6] Such evidence also reveals the highly organised and coordinated nature of the attack. Indeed, I will argue, it was with the establishment of the War Room and the commencement of systematic mass killings in the province that the genocide proper in Aceh began.

Direct military involvement in the killings in Banda Aceh

The military would quickly come to play a direct role in the killings in Banda Aceh. Ramli, the son of Thaib Adamy, who was seven years old in 1965, has recalled how his father was killed at a military-controlled killing site at Lhoknga, a surf beach 15 km outside of Banda Aceh. Thaib Adamy and his second eldest son, Yasrun, 15, had fled Banda Aceh, headed towards Takengon by bus, on 6 October. "Right in the middle of their journey," Ramli explains, "my father was recognised, my brother wasn't recognised, but they were both arrested."[7] The story of how Adamy was killed was told to Ramli by "Ismail",[8] a relative of Adamy and member of the Military Police Corps, who claims he was ordered to kill Adamy.

After being pulled off the bus, Adamy and Yusni were brought back to Banda Aceh.[9] Ramli continues:

[H]e [Adamy] was taken in the direction of Meulaboh [along Aceh's west coast], [to] Lhoknga. There were lots of people that had been brought there on trucks, they were killed, decapitated (*dipenggal*) one by one, but when it was my father's turn, there was someone from CPM [the Military Police; Ismail, the CPM man who narrated this account to Ramli] who was guarding him, this CPM knew my father well, there was a family connection, he was related to one of my father's cousins . . . he had proof [that this account was true], I remember that my father used to have a watch that he had brought from Moscow, made out of gold. He always wore that watch. When he was about to be executed, this CPM man said, "Brother Thaib, you should run for it, we are close to the jungle, run for it." He was told to run away by the CPM man because he was the one guarding him, but my father said, "Perhaps this is my fate, if this is what is to become of me, yes, I must accept it, but if it must be you [that is to kill me], shoot me, don't decapitate me, and do it somewhere quiet [not at the mass killing site]." In the end, the CPM man took him, but he was unable to shoot him, [so] he asked someone else to do it, and the watch was given to me.[10]

Ismail clearly had motivation to possibly manipulate this account to portray Adamy as acquiescing to his death in this manner and to deny directly killing him. There is less reason, however, for Ismail to falsely admit to being present when Adamy was killed at a military-controlled killing site. According to Ramli, Thaib Adamy was subsequently buried at Lhoknga, just off the beach.[11] Ramli has chosen not to visit this site, though he says his relatives have shown him photographs of its location. To this day, Ramli does not know what happened to his brother Yasrun, though he is believed to have been murdered at this time, possibly alongside his father, despite still being only a teenager.[12] As Ramli has explained, the instruction to annihilate the PKI "down to the roots" (*sampai ke akar-akarnya*) was understood at the time as an instruction that even "children and grandchildren had to be killed", in order to physically exterminate entire families.[13]

Ramli has also explained how the military was directly involved in the death of his eldest brother, Yusni, 17, who had been abducted on 7 October when demonstrators had converged on the Adamy family home. After his abduction, Ramli recalls, Yusni was detained at the Military Police headquarters in Banda Aceh, from where he disappeared before being murdered.

One of Ramli's uncles, "*Pak Cik*",[14] went to the jail to check on the boy.[15] It was explained to Pak Cik, however, that the key to the cell "wasn't there" and that "perhaps it had been taken home by one of the guards", so Pak Cik went home briefly to eat.[16] When he returned, he learned that Yusni "had been taken by someone". Pak Cik tried to find the boy until he came to understand that Yusni had already been killed. Someone at the military jail with a key to the cell had given permission for Yusni to be taken off and murdered while Pak Cik was away. It is not known if Yusni was killed at a military-controlled killing site or if he was killed by members of the death squads that were assigned truckloads of detainees by the military to be murdered. In neighbouring North Sumatra this process was recorded by the military through a process known as "lending" (*dibon*), whereby a "receipt" of the number of detainees as well as the places where they were picked up and the locations where they were taken to be killed, was prepared and signed by death squad leaders, to help the military keep track of the annihilation of its prison population.[17] Ramli's account provides a vivid example of a military-controlled detention centre being used as a halfway house en-route to execution.[18]

Zainal Abidin, the Subdistrict Head for Seulimum, in a separate interview, has shed light on the manner in which detainees such as Thaib Adamy and Aceh PKI Chairman Muhammad Samikidin were treated during the period between their arrest and their murder at mass grave sites. According to Abidin, after Adamy was taken off the bus, he was brought to Abidin's government office in Seulimum,[19] 50 km from Banda Aceh along the main road between Takengon and North Sumatra. "Thaib Adamy was with me for a long time in Seulimum," Abidin explains, "but then he was taken to Takengon, he was put on a train. . . . Everyone who was detained there [at his office in Seulimum] was taken to Takengon. But what happened when they got there I don't know."[20] Why Adamy would be placed on a train travelling in the direction of Takengon, when he was ultimately brought back to Banda Aceh to be killed at Lhoknga, is not clear.

As we have seen, Abidin had also held Samikidin in his office before he too was placed on a train heading in the direction of Takengon, before being "pulled off" the train and "taken" (*diambil*) to be "finished off" (*diselesaikan*).[21] It may be that the process of placing detainees on a train headed for "Takengon", a destination they would never reach, but which, since the time of the national revolution, had been synonymous in Aceh with political exile,[22] provided a psychological comfort for government officials such as Abidin, allowing them to believe that they were not involved in transporting detainees to their deaths. Adidin, for example, attempts to describe the detention process as a means of limiting violence, explaining how "[t]he people were really very angry",[23] but the detention of detainees prevented "wild actions" (*gerakan-gerakan liar*).[24] "If we'd just released them," Abidin continues, "Banda Aceh would have exploded."[25]

This does not, however, explain the military's "inability" to stop detainees being "pulled off" the trains to be killed. Nor does it explain how some of these detainees, such as Adamy, ended up at military-controlled killing sites. Abidin contradicts himself further by revealing that he knew where these detainees were taken to be killed, adding, "but we don't need to talk about this".[26] "The majority of them," Abidin continues, "were killed at the beach [not in highland, landlocked, Takengon], there was also a place . . . at Indrapuri,"[27] a small inland town along Aceh's main road, half-way between Seulimum and Banda Aceh. Abidin also names Ujung Batee, a beach 30 km outside of Banda Aceh along the north coast, and Laweung, a coastal area 95 km along the north coast, as popular killing sites.

Moreover, in addition to admitting to "working together with the military" to "finish off" the PKI, Abidin admits to receiving instructions from the military at this time. This detention and killing campaign, he explains, was coordinated from Banda Aceh by the military, where he would "sometimes . . . be called to a meeting" to receive further instructions.[28] Despite his denials, it would appear that Abidin had a very clear idea of what was occurring in the district at this time and that the military was indisputably in control of the killing process.

20 October: Djuarsa "freezes" the PKI in Aceh

The military's control over the killing process would only increase. On 20 October, Ishak Djuarsa, in his capacity as Pangdahan 'A', gave a "briefing" to representatives from Aceh's political parties and mass organisations, the Banda Aceh Pantja Tunggal and heads of the civil service in the province at the Governor's Pendopo, where he provided an "explanation of the situation related to G-30-S".[29] This explanation was based on a 'Decision' (*Surat- Keputusan No: KEP/PEPELRADA 29/10/1965*) signed by Djuarsa that same day, acting in his capacity as Pepelrada for Aceh Special Region.[30]

This Decision claimed to draw its legitimacy from the two 'Joint Decisions' signed by the Pantja Tunggal, *Front Nasional* and representatives from Aceh's political parties in Banda Aceh on 6 October, along with the raft of KOTI-related legislation that had been activated on 1 October.[31] It included a decree to "freeze and temporarily halt all activities within the Legal Jurisdiction of the Pepelrada Atjeh" connected to the PKI,[32] as well as "any other Mass Org[anisations] beneath or connected to the PKI".[33] It also expelled all members of these organisations from "all government bodies", forbade members of these organisations from "leaving their places [of residence]" and, most forebodingly, declared, it "mandatory for all leaders of these Pol[itical] Part[ies]/Mass Org[anisations] to report themselves (*melaporkan diri*) to the Pepelrada/Military Police (*CPM*)/Police Force in their area by no later than 25 October 1965".

The timing of this 'Decision' to "freeze" (*membekukan*) the PKI and its "affiliated" organisations, some of which, like Baperki, had no formal relationship to the PKI, was very swift. The PKI would not be declared illegal nationally until 12 March 1966, when Suharto formally banned the Party "throughout every region of the Republic of Indonesia".[34] What would happen to those individuals who refused to report themselves by 25 October is not stated. It is likely, however, that such individuals were targeted for arrest and eventual murder. Those who reported themselves did not fare any better. As described below, such reporting was used by the military to identify targeted individuals. In general, those who were kept in detention upon reporting themselves were killed at military-controlled killing sites, while those who were released were recaptured by the military's civilian proxies and added to the number of public killings.

This Decision was then forwarded to the KOTI Commander and Commander of the Armed Forces in Jakarta (both positions held by Suharto),[35] Mokoginta in Medan, the Pantja Tunggal and provincial government bodies in Banda Aceh and Aceh's districts, as well as district and subdistrict military commanders.[36] Later that day in Banda Aceh, the military intensified its efforts to arrest people accused of "being involved in the G30S issue".[37]

26 October: formation of the "Indoctrination Team"

On 26 October, the day after the deadline for people deemed to be affiliated with the PKI to "surrender" themselves to the military, preparations were made, based on the "direction" of Suharto, to begin to establish an "Indoctrination Team" (*Team Indoktrinasi*) in Aceh to turn military officers in the province into "Political Commissars" (*Komisaris Politik*).[38] The role of these Political Commissars was to:

> prepare the Mental [state] of members of the Aceh Military Command [*Dam-I/Atjeh*] to become true Pantjasilaists, with the purpose of confronting Nekolim/G-30-S and strengthen/secure Pantjasila and prepare Indoctrination for Kodam-I/Atjeh personnel.[39]

This position appears to have been modelled on the PKI's own announcement, made on 2 September 1965, for Political Commissars to be appointed and deployed within the military to support Sukarno's 'Nasakomisation' campaign,[40] a development that had been vehemently opposed by the military at the time.[41]

Such a tactic may have been one of the ways in which the military leadership used "grand narrative" to desensitise its members to the violence they were being ordered to participate in. It also allowed the military to use the structures it had established during the *Ganyang Malaysia* campaign to launch its own annihilation campaign, without needing to establish a new ideological basis for the state. Instead, the military leadership adopted and subverted Sukarno's concept of the Pancasila state – a largely meaningless concept when taken at face value – while allowing it to present its own seizure of state power as a defensive and protective measure. The irony of the 30 September Movement being labelled as "Nekolim" ('Neo-Colonialist, Colonialist, Imperialist') served only to heighten the Kafkaesque nature of the military's ideological campaign, while allowing it to make use of the powerful rhetoric developed by the PKI during the early 1960s that had advocated for radical social change, while positioning itself as defending the existing social order.

The relationship between the military, youth leaders and executioners

The military outsourced important aspects of its annihilation campaign to civilian proxies. An understanding of the relationship between the military, youth leaders and executioners is vital to understanding the internal dynamics of the killings. The manner in which former members of these organisations have described their relationship with the military has not always been uniform. Dahlan Sulaiman, who in 1965 was in his final year of high school and who had demonstrated his initiative during the morning of 1 October by plastering the provincial capital with anti-PKI posters, disputes the idea the military had complete control over the attack against the PKI. Meanwhile, Let Bugeh, who in 1965 was a university student and a member of HMI, is more forthcoming in explaining his close relationship with Djuarsa.

In the previous chapter, Sulaiman described how he and other members of civilian youth militias and death squads were involved in hunting down communists and "surrendering" them to the military during the first phase of the violence. Sulaiman is adamant, however, that he and his comrades were not simply following military orders in doing this, and that it would be incorrect to suggest that the military had "coordinated everything".[42] "No, it wasn't like that in Banda Aceh," he explains:

> There were mass meetings, but we initiated them; it was the youth that did this. We were then joined by the [political] parties. We didn't feel as if we were being ordered around or told what to do by the military. There were speeches [at the mass meetings] given by the military, but they didn't explicitly order us to arrest PKI people, or indeed, call on us to kill them, that really did not happen. I am not trying to defend the military.[43]

Putting aside Djuarsa's 'Decision' on 20 October which demonstrates that there were explicit orders coming from the military at this time ordering the civilian population to assist in the arrest of people considered to be associated with the PKI, along with the 'Announcement' on 4 October ordering civilians to assist the military in its "annihilation" campaign, Sulaiman's insistence upon this distinction would appear aimed at stressing his and his comrades' agency and independence during the campaign. As Sulaiman has explained, he and his comrades were not simply "used by the military".[44] "Sometimes it was the military that became our opponent and who attempted to thwart our activities," Sulaiman continues. This statement seems to refer to his differences with the military during the early morning of 2 October, and his future split with the military as a member of the KAPPI death squad, as will be described in chapter 7.

Sulaiman is also keen to highlight his own centrality to the campaign. He has explained, for example, how he joined Djuarsa for part of his coordination tour, travelling with him to Sigli and Lhokseumawe on 7 October.[45] This was because, he boasts, "I was an important leader at that time, sorry to say that myself. I was a young person who was feared and held in awe at that time in Banda Aceh." Despite the self-serving nature of this testimony, Sulaiman provides unique insight into the manner in which Djuarsa appealed for public participation in the military's annihilation campaign. At a series of meetings that were held "after the PKI people had already been grouped together at [the military base in] Mata Ie",[46] Sulaiman explains, Djuarsa had delivered a speech through which he had explained:

> The state of our nation was in a state of, the term at that time was "transition period" (*panca roba*: also translatable as "difficult period"). The communists wanted the state to follow communist precepts. That is what was said [by Djuarsa]. They [the Communists] were trying to take over and control the head of the state, Bung Karno. That was said. To the people, [it was said] be alert to this situation.[47]

Djuarsa "did not say 'you have to kill the PKI'" at these meetings, Sulaiman continues, "[r]ather, you must be alert, be on guard, because the PKI wish to do this and this and this. . . ."[48] The military's campaign was thus described as a struggle for the Indonesian state. Sulaiman clearly saw the opportunities that this situation presented him and his comrades. As he elaborates, this environment "gave us a big enough opportunity to kill at this time, especially me as a leader who had a gun", before adding defensively, "[b]ut I swear to you I never killed anyone. I only beat them up if they resisted, at most I would hit them once or twice." Sulaiman's denial of involvement in the killings cannot be taken seriously.

Bugeh, meanwhile, is much more explicit in explaining his relationship with the military leadership, explaining that he was close enough to Djuarsa to have been called to his house to receive personal direction. "We would usually meet at the Panglima's [Djuarsa's] house," Bugeh told me. The statement hints at the closeness of the relationship between Djuarsa and youth leaders such as Bugeh, and that this was not a one-off occurrence. "He called me over," Bugeh recalls, "I was demonstrating against the PKI, he called and I went in."[49]

Djuarsa had been explicit in explaining the military's support for the killings. The Military Commander, Bugeh says, told him "he [Djuarsa] would support the annihilation of the communists, and that if anyone was killed . . . I [Djuarsa] am responsible, you [Bugeh and his comrades] are not responsible, but we needn't talk about this."[50]

Bugeh then explains, perhaps to underline Djuarsa's promise, and perhaps to conjure the immunity that this promise has so far afforded him: "If the communists were disappeared, that was the mood, he [Djuarsa] [said that he] would take responsibility. It was not the people who did the killings who would take responsibility."[51]

"The military was very agitated at this time," Bugeh continues, perhaps as a means of explaining the explicitness of Djuarsa's promise.[52]

As the chain of command relationship between the military leadership and the civilian militia groups and death squads that Sulaiman and Bugeh participated in can now be established, it would appear that the divergence between Sulaiman and Bugeh's characterisations of their relationship with the military leadership at the time of the killings may be more of a reflection of their current relationships with the Indonesian state. Bugeh, at the time of our interview, was head of the National Sports Committee for Indonesia in Aceh, and, as a prominent senior government official, had no reason to expect anything other than continued protection and complete immunity so long as he did not draw attention to the role of the military leadership in the initiation and implementation of the genocide (hence his warning that "[w]e can't say that we killed them"),[53] while Sulaiman works as a private travel agent without any special guarantee of personal protection other than that which is generally afforded to civilian participants.

Sulaiman's insistence at his independence in participating in the violence may also be a result of his subsequent split with the military as a member of KAPPI in 1966 (described in chapter 7), as well as his determination to portray himself as an important leader during this period, who did not have to dirty himself by participating in the killings as an executioner (*algojo*). Sulaiman, for example, describes a sense of stigma attached to individuals who acted as executioners for the military during this period, as distinct from participants in the pogroms, public killings and arrest campaigns. "[O]ne of the executioners," Sulaiman remarked in a hushed voice, as if he was saying something scandalous, "was DI/TII (a member of the Darul Islam)."[54] This unnamed person, Sulaiman continues, whom he insists on not identifying so as not to "embarrass" any surviving relatives, was an opportunist who had joined the PNI, the "ideological opposite" of the Darul Islam, after the surrender of the rebellion. This man, Sulaiman explains, had been happy to do the military's bidding, along with members of the PNI, who, he claims, had formed the "leadership of the killing" in Banda Aceh at the time.[55] It was this former member of the Darul Islam and a "leader of the PNI", Sulaiman proposes, who became the "two" main "executioners" in Banda Aceh at this time.

It is possible that these two executioners felt intimidated into taking on this low-status task after being threatened themselves. "In the end," Sulaiman explains, "the two of them . . . were killed," allegedly after killing "too many people".[56] Sulaiman thus makes a distinction between "participation" in the campaign against the PKI (including hunting down people accused of being affiliated with the organisation and "surrendering" them to the military), and acting as an "executioner" for the military. It may be that the executioners used during the second phase of the killings were not the heroic "youth" (*pemuda*) of the first phase, like Sulaiman and Bugeh, who proudly recall their involvement in the violence, but rather politically suspect people who could be manipulated into doing the military's dirty work, until they themselves became expendable – hence Sulaiman's apparent need to distance himself from this task.

Direct military involvement in the killings in North Aceh

Evidence has been recovered of the military's direct role in killings in North Aceh. This evidence includes a remarkable document produced by the North Aceh Regent (*Bupati*), T. Ramly Angkasah on 15 June 1966, titled 'Civilian Defence/People's Defence', which details the activities of the military-coordinated and trained Civilian Defence (*Hansip*) and People's Defence (*Hanra*) paramilitary organisations in the district between "the middle of October 1965 and the end of October 1965".[57] This timing places the activities outlined in this document at the height of the second phase of killings in the district. Through its painstaking attention to organisational detail, this document provides unique insight into the activities of Hansip and Hanra in the district and documents the roles they played in establishing "Guard Posts" throughout the district as part of the military's annihilation campaign. It also, most explosively, records how the North Aceh Defence Sector Command (*Kosekhan*) distributed weapons to Hansip and Hanra to facilitate the "cleansing/extermination of the G30S" in North Aceh during this time. As far as I am aware, no comparable document has been found elsewhere in Indonesia.[58]

The military arms Hansip/Hanra paramilitaries in North Aceh

"As we know," the 'Civilian Defence/People's Defence' (*Hansip/Hanra*) document begins, "the Organisational Structure of Hansip/Hanra in North Aceh is 'headed' by the district's Regent, T. Ramly Angkasah."[59] The document then proceeds to explain how:

a   Under the Command of the [subdistrict-level] Defence Region Sub-Command (Subdahan: *Komando Sub-Daerah Pertahanan*) Commander [at] Subdistrict Military Base 011 (*Rem 011*)/[and the] [district-level] Defence Sector Commander (*Dan Sekhan*) for North Aceh District Military Command 0103 (*Kodim 0103*) and working together with the Armed Forces and with the assistance of all layers of society in the district, a compact defence front has been organised/arranged and activated, its achievements include:

1   The Armed Forces along with the people organised within the Civilian Defence/People's Defence (*Hansip/Hanra*) have so far remained on guard in the name of security and defence of the nation.

2   Safety Guard Posts and defence fortifications are already complete and have been placed at strategic locations throughout the region of Sector IV North Aceh.

3   Posts along the length of the coast (in strategic locations) between Samalanga [40 km west from Bireuen, on the district border with Pidie] and Tanah Djambo Aje [38 km east from Lhokseumawe, on the district border with East Aceh] are in complete order. . . .[60]

b   Since the middle of 1965 the Hansip/Hanra Organisations in Sector IV North Aceh have experienced many positive changes, including in the area of Organisation, logistics, personnel, training and activities in the area of regional defence and People's resistance that has progressed satisfactorily. **The annihilation of G30S has been active and achieved in conjunction with the Armed Forces.**[61]

This document thus explains that Hansip and Hanra worked together in a formal capacity with the military to "annihilate" those associated with the PKI as part of a "compact defence front" established specifically for this purpose. The complex infrastructure that this relationship enabled, including a highly organised system of guard posts and defence fortifications, would have made movement in the district difficult and highly regulated. Meanwhile, continued reference to the *Ganyang Malaysia* campaign in this context acted as a means to mobilise Hansip/Hanra units as if the state faced an invading enemy.

This mobilisation was extensive and mirrored a war situation. The document continues:

c   The strength of the membership of Hansip/Hanra in Sector IV North Aceh is as follows:

1   There are 23 Battalions, that is 1 Battalion per Subdistrict- Sub Sector (*Ketjamatan- Sub Sektor*).

2   There are 95 Companies, that is 1 Company per Residency (*Mukim*: a subdivision of a subdistrict) and 1 Battalion at the Sector (*Sektor*) Headquarters at the Regent's Office for North Aceh and 1 Special Battalion for Lhokseumawe City.

3   There are 14,182 members (23 Battalions) in total.

4   There are 986 members of Hansip/Hanra from the District/Division at the District/Residency Offices.

5   The unification of Hansip/Hanra, that has already been made official by the Head of the North Aceh IV the Civilian Defence/People's Defence Sector Headquarters occurred as follows:

• On 16 August 1965 for the Bireuen KIMIKAJU[62] employees Hansip/Hanra Company.

- On 29 November 1965 for the Battalion 416 TGK/KUTA GLE in Samalanga Sub-Sector.[63]

The scale of this mobilisation is far greater that what has previously been imagined. Hansip/Hanra at this time is best understood as an activated paramilitary organisation (it is described by an eyewitness as a "Hansip army") due to the extent of its mobilisation.[64] As the document explains:

40% of Hansip/Hanra members for Sector IV North Aceh, both in the towns and villages have received basic military training under the leadership of the Armed Forces in the region.[65]

The "implementation of this training", the document continues:

still requires some improvements as a result of a shortage of training, payments and other issues. Regardless, in the spirit of Berdikari separate from funding, it is thanks to the policy/wisdom of officials/leaders that the training of Hansip/Hanra has been able to continue running little by little, especially thanks to assistance from the North Aceh District Military Command (*Kodim-0103*).[66]

This training, the document explains, facilitated the establishment of twenty "observation posts" throughout "Sector IV North Aceh", twenty of which are listed as "Coastal Observation Posts",[67] which may have been an attempt to further link the military's annihilation campaign to Sukarno's *Ganyang Malaysia* campaign and its attention to security along the Malacca Strait. Most incriminating, however, is the final section of the document, entitled 'Weaponry', which explains how Hansip/Hanra members in the district were armed by the military with American- and British-made machine guns and rifles for the purpose of facilitating this annihilation campaign. As this section explains:

Within the framework of the cleansing/extermination of the G30S, the membership of Hansip/Hanra in Sector IV North Aceh was given weapons by the North Aceh Defence Sector Command (*Kosekhan*) for this purpose, [the weapons] that were considered necessary by the regional Hansip/Hanra Sub-Sectors include:

a   9 L.E.s [Lee Enfields, a British-made bolt-action rifle] and 1 Sten [an American-made machine gun] for Seunuddon Sub-Sector,
b   16 L.E.s [rifles] for Samalanga Sub Sektor
c   1 Garand [M1 Garand, an American-made semi-automatic rifle] and 1 L.E. [rifle] for Djeumpa, Bireuen Sub-Sector
d   9 L.E. [rifles] and 1 Sten [machine gun] for the District Government Office in Lhokseumawe

e   9 L.E. [rifles] and 1 Sten [machine gun] for Vital Offices (BNI Unit II, III [Indonesian National Bank (BNI: *Bank Nasional Indonesia*) branches]).[68]

Hansip/Hanra members in North Aceh were thus systematically organised and armed by the military to implement the genocide in the district. That these guns were used to carry out large-scale killings is supported by references elsewhere in the report that record how a "shortage" of ammunition for these types of weapons developed in the province.[69] However, the full extent of involvement by Hansip/ Hanra in the killings has yet to be systematically investigated.[70]

Some of the activities of Hansip/Hanra in Lhokseumawe have been described below by Hamid, the small-scale metal worker who received paramilitary training as a member of Hansip from the military as part of the *Ganyang Malaysia* campaign in Lhokseumawe.

Systematic killings at military-controlled killing sites in Lhokseumawe

As a member of Hansip in North Aceh's main town of Lhokseumawe, Hamid participated in night patrols and witnessed some of the killings at mass graves in the district. He has explained how those who were arrested by the night patrols were taken to state-run jails, where they were "held" until "those who had been sentenced to death were taken in the middle of the night to the place [where they were to be killed]".[71] This process was directly overseen by the military and involved members of Hansip and villagers in the killing process. As Hamid elaborates:

> The PKI prisoners who had been arrested and held in the jail, they were taken in the middle of the night to Meunasah Lhok [30 km west along the coast from Lhokseumawe]. Later there would be a few people from the community [civilians] that had been chosen by the Military Precinct Command (*Koramil*) to become executioners (*algojo*); that was when they were killed. After they were killed, a hole would be dug to put the bodies in.[72]

It was also "military people" who gave the order for the killings and the digging of mass graves.[73] "People . . . were ordered" to act as executioners, Hamid explains: "The people who became executioners were people from the villages, from the Hansip army. If we wanted to, go ahead, there was an opportunity available. . . . They weren't real [professional] executioners."[74]

The location of these killing sites and the fact that killings were occurring was an open secret. As Hamid recalls, "If we wanted to watch the killings, that was allowed, we were able to, it wasn't forbidden . . . anyone who wanted to could watch."[75] Sjam, who in 1965 worked as a peasant and prayer leader on the outskirts of Lhokseumawe, also independently recalls watching victims being buried at a mass grave site in the district. On one occasion, Sjam recalls, a woman named Ramullah, who, as we shall see, would become famous as a "ghost" that would later be reported to haunt the area, was buried, along with several victims, as members of the community looked on.[76] Sjam does not know how many people were buried in this mass grave, located at Blang Panyang in the mountains, though he recalls seeing two corpses that had not yet been buried. Ramullah's corpse, Sjam remembers, had been "hacked at" (*dibacok*).[77] Other victims, Sjam recalls, had been shot.[78]

The killings were extremely violent. "Once, at that time,"Hamid recalls:

> there was an order that there was a person that had just been arrested, and that if they[79] arrived, [they were] to be killed immediately. At that time there was also a person that had been brought here from Samalanga, who was also meant to be killed, but it turned out that this person was *kebal* (invulnerable), so, their hands had been tied up, everything had been tied, but when they were about to be cut (*dipotong*: to have their throat cut or be decapitated), they resisted, the rope was cut, but they were fine [hadn't been killed].[80]

"He was able to run, even though he had already been cut," elaborates "Basri",[81] Hamid's friend, who sat next to Hamid throughout the interview. "Cek Dun finished him off," explains Hamid, and the victim's invulnerability was broken when he was "thrown straight into the hole [the mass grave]" and killed by being buried alive.[82]

Such stories of invulnerability are quite common throughout Indonesia during the genocide.[83] The mythology surrounding invulnerability appears linked to the reality of the one-sided nature of the military's attack against the PKI, in which victims put up no systematic resistance, but who were depicted by the military as presenting an existential threat to the nation.[84] This myth of invulnerability was a means for perpetrators to dehumanise their victims by denying them even the instinctive right to resist in a situation in which perpetrators otherwise had total control over their victims. Anyone who did not submit fully to this fate was depicted as a kind of monster with superhuman powers who must be responded to with even more extreme force.

Contemporary stories about ghosts and spirit possession, meanwhile, appear to be a way to talk about the suppressed history of the genocide, while allowing the speaker to maintain a degree of distance from the story being told. As Sjam has explained, Ramullah's spirit and the spirits of other "PKI activists" "haunt and possess the bodies of people" in the area to speak through the voice of the person they have possessed to tell people who they are and how they were killed.[85] Ramullah's ghost is well known in the district. Another of my interviewees independently told me both about her death and her fondness for possessing people.[86] The particularly public nature of Ramullah's death and burial appear to have helped to transform her into a humanised face of the genocide in the district.

Direct military involvement in the killings in Kampung X

This section presents two overlapping accounts of direct military involvement in the killings in Kampung X. These accounts have been drawn from two separate and independent interviews. The first account provides the eyewitness testimony of Tjoet, who in 1965 was a new mother and wife to Hasan, the PKI member who worked in a small coffee shop. The second account has been drawn from the eyewitness testimony of Jamil, the poor fisherman and brother-in-law to Hasan, who had placed Jamil's name on a PKI membership list.

Tjoet recalls that she became aware of the military's campaign against the PKI in Kampung X during the second week of October. At this time, she witnessed "Mahmud", the head of the PKI for Bireuen, who was also originally from Kampung X, being arrested off the street by military personnel.[87] "His legs were tied and his hands were tied and then he was thrown into a truck," Tjoet told me.[88] Tjoet went home and told her husband Hasan about Mahmud's arrest.[89] It was then Hasan told her for the first time that he had been appointed PKI Treasurer for Kampung X.[90] Shortly after this, the same military personnel came to Tjoet and Hasan's house looking for Hasan.[91] Apparently they didn't find him, because Tjoet relates that he subsequently "ran away" but "he was chased by the military who came after him . . . he ran into the undergrowth, the jungle".[92] He was hidden there by villagers. Following Hasan's escape, the military came repeatedly to Tjoet's house to threaten her.[93] As a result of these threats, Tjoet moved back to her family home in "Kampung Y"[94] but the military harassed her there too, coming to her home at night and threatening her with a large knife.[95] In the end Tjoet, agreed to return to Kampung X and was made to report to the military. The military, who were still looking for Hasan, continued to harass her. After about a month, Hasan came out of the jungle and surrendered himself to the Subdistrict Head, who took him to the Police and the Military Precinct Command (*Koramil*).[96] He was then transported to Bireuen, where he was detained for one month. At the end of this time, Hasan was taken to a bridge in Teupin Manee,[97] 10 km inland from Bireuen, where the Manee River (*Krueng Manee*) flows down from the highlands to the sea. He was killed there with a machete, but reportedly buried and not thrown into the river.[98]

After Hasan had escaped, Jamil became increasingly apprehensive. This was because, he recalls, "They [the military] came every night to pick us all up."[99] "If they arrested us," he explains:

> they would straight away take us to [Bireuen to be killed], they would kill us straight away if they arrested us. Some were arrested in the night, then taken straight away to Cot Panglima [a steep cliff used as an execution site along the mountainous road into Central Aceh]. They were all killed. . . . There was a message from the Subdistrict Head, asking people to go to Bireuen [to surrender themselves]; when they got to Bireuen, they were forced into a crouching position and all put in prison. The next night, they [the military] would pick up those with red throats (*orang berleher merah*: a term which appears to imply 'those who were to have their throats slit') . . . . People from [Kampung X] were [released and] told to go back to their villages, then they were picked up [again to be killed], [it was said] "go and arrest the ones with red throats".[100]

"The prison commander, who had three stripes [an insignia which denotes the rank of Captain]," Jamil went on to say, would determine who would be taken to be killed directly, or released to be re-arrested.[101] The killings in Bireuen, Jamil believes, began at the same time as in Aceh's other districts.[102] When asked if it was the military that carried out the killings in North Aceh, Jamil replied, "Of course it was the military, who else? They were the ones with the guns."

Jamil has further explained how the military coordinated this second wave of violence in the subdistrict. At the time systematic mass killings began, Jamil has recalled, a "meeting was held" in Kampung X in the school building.[103] This meeting was convened by "Daoed", leader of the PKI in Kampung X, who, under intense pressure, called upon PKI members in the subdistrict to "surrender themselves to him".[104] Jamil does not know exactly what happened to those members who followed Daoed's instruction, only that at this time people associated with the PKI "were being taken from where ever they were found, arrested and taken" to be killed.[105]

Generally, Jamil has said, the military conducted the searches and arrests in the subdistrict directly. "They [the military] went from house to house searching for PKI; if they didn't find one they went to the next house, to wherever they were."[106] Civilian Defence (*Hansip*) members in Kampung X were also involved in helping the military to carry out the arrests and killings.[107] Those who had been arrested, Jamil has recalled, were transported by the military to Bireuen, before being taken on to military-controlled killing sites, such as at Cot Panglima, to be executed.[108] "The killers," explains Jamil, "were instruments of the state."[109]

Detainees were also transported *en masse* into the district from other areas to be killed. In one case, Jamil recalls that fifty people from Samalanga were transported to Bireuen, where "they were all slaughtered".[110] This transportation of victims appears to have served the triple function of reducing kill loads in particular districts; allowing executioners to retain their anonymity by not being forced to kill their neighbours; and by confusing the relatives of arrestees as to whether or not their loved ones had been killed. There was no attempt to process the detainees through the judicial system. As Jamil put it, "[t]here was no sweet talk."[111]

Jamil was able to survive by escaping into the jungle in the days after Hasan disappeared, where he hid during the worst of the killings.[112] After hearing about the first arrests in Kampung X, Jamil recalls:

> I ran by myself. I knew people in the mountains, so I asked to stay with them. They were wood cutters . . . there was nothing to do but hang around and save myself. . . . [The people in the mountains] knew [what was happening to the PKI] but they hadn't been scared of me. It was me who had been afraid . . . [the arrests lasted] for about a month. They happened quickly. . . .
>
> There wasn't [animosity between the people in [Kampung X] and the PKI. . . . It was all just [military] provocation. We didn't even know [what had happened in Jakarta], I only knew about that at the end . . . when it was publicised on the TV and everywhere. . . . They said the PKI had no religion. . . . [But when I came down from the mountains] there wasn't a

problem [in my village]. . . . We hadn't been chased by the people in my village.[113]

Upon his return, Jamil was "told to go to Bireuen" to "turn himself in"[114] by "Muchtar", the Village Head of Kampung X, who worked in the Subdistrict Office.[115] The Subdistrict Office, Jamil told me, had a list of PKI members that it had been compiling from people who had been interrogated and from internal Party documents that had been seized from Hasan, the PKI treasurer for Kampung X.[116] After Jamil reported to the Subdistrict Office, he has recalled how Muchtar questioned him, asking him why he had joined the PKI.[117] Jamil was then sent to Bireuen, which ordinarily would have meant certain death. He was extremely fortunate, however, as the worst of the killings were over by this time.[118] Tjoet has recalled that an "announcement" was made around the time of Ramadan, which began in 1965 on 24 December,[119] for the killings to stop.[120] It is not known how widely this announcement was disseminated, though its timing coincides with other records that suggest the military attempted to bring systematic mass killings in the province to an end around this time. A front-page article in the national newspaper *Kompas* on 23 December 1965, for example, announced: "The PKI and its affiliated organisations have been disbanded (*dibubarkan*) in Aceh."[121] As will be discussed below, this date also corresponds with the final entry in the military Chronology, which is recorded on 22 December.[122]

At this time Jamil was told that he "would be alright" as he was a "group 'c' prisoner, not a group 'a' or 'b'", in apparent reference to the national classification system for detainees, which, as we shall see in chapter 7, was not implemented nationally until May 1966, but which was implemented in Aceh in late December 1965.[123] "This meant I was really a small fry," Jamil explains, "I was the only one from [Kampung X] [who was taken to Bireuen] who was able go back to the village."[124] Systematic killings were still, however, occurring at this time. As Jamil explains: "There were others who weren't [allowed to return to their villages]. I was there for one night . . . I saw people from other villages being taken by truck to Cot Panglima [to be executed by the military]."[125]

These killings may have been some of the last mass killings to occur in the district until a third wave of violence, aimed specifically at Aceh's Chinese community, erupted in April 1966.

3–8 November: public killings continue

In addition to the deaths detailed above, six more cases of public killings appear in the Chronology. These include a case recorded as occurring at 2pm on 31 October, when it was reported that the corpse of a man named Ibrahim Sufi, a primary school teacher from Lhokseumawe, had washed onto the bank of the Mon Geudong River in Sakti Subdistrict, Lhokseumawe.[126] The body is said to have been "stabbed in the neck with a spear, leaving a hole". Hamid claims to remember this case.[127]

On 3 November, meanwhile, it is reported that Mardjan, the head of the 'RPD'[128] in Lhokseumawe was "captured and killed by locals", along with two others whose identities are not recorded, after allegedly attempting to run away.[129] At 2pm on 8 November, meanwhile, the corpse of a man named Supardjan, head of the Lhokseumawe Correctional Services, is reported to have been found in Mbang *kampung*, 30 km from Lhokseumawe, his killer "unknown".[130] The reason why this man was targeted is not stated, though it is possible, considering his position, that he had refused to comply with military orders regarding the running of state-run jails in the district. The next day, at 3pm, it is reported in the Chronology that Tjut Areh from the PKI Sub-Section Committee (CSS: *Comite Subseksi*) in Kuta Makmur subdistrict in North Aceh was killed by "the people in Keude Krung" and "buried on the same day".[131]

The claim that these killings occurred without the knowledge and assistance of the military leadership in the district defies the substantial evidence that is now available. As can be seen in the 'Civilian Defence/People's Defence' document, the military was actively arming civilians to hunt down people accused of being associated with the PKI in North Aceh during this period. Moreover, it is clear from the above testimony that the military was directly involved in leading the campaign of detentions, transportations and killings in the district.

Direct military involvement in the killings in Central Aceh

Direct military involvement in the killings has also been documented in Central Aceh. As detailed in chapters 4 and 5, the military played a particularly direct role in the violence in Central Aceh immediately following 1 October. From the remaining entries in the Chronology that record direct military involvement in arrests in Central Aceh during this period, it is possible to form a tentative picture of how the military led the arrest and detention cycle in the district. From 14 October the scale of military-led arrests appears to have increased. On this day, the Chronology reports ten PKI members were arrested in the district.[132] The fate of these individuals is not known. It is likely, however, that they, like Ibrahim Kadir, were detained in military jails before being transferred to military-controlled killings sites to be murdered.

Thirteen days later, on 27 October, meanwhile, it is noted in the final entry in the Chronology for Central Aceh that a further fourteen people had been arrested, this time by the Central Aceh Defence Sector Commander (Dan Sekhan: *Sektor Pertahanan*) at 6.50am.[133] Again, the specific fate of these individuals is not recorded. They were probably killed at military-controlled killing sites.

Systematic mass killings at military-controlled killing sites in Kenawat

Abdullah, a former Darul Islam fighter, who in 1965 was a school teacher in Kenawat, 9.5 km south of Takengon, has described how he was forced to participate in systematic mass killings at a military-controlled killing site in Kenawat. "I didn't agree, I was just a teacher," Abdullah told me:[134]

> Oh, there were some that screamed, those PKI [people] . . . I helped out [at one of the killing sites], I didn't want to. I saw some of them that copped it, oh my god . . . they were [decapitated] . . . it bled.[135]

Although civilians were forced to participate in the killings, it was the military, he recalls, who coordinated them: "It was not the people."[136] Those who were arrested had their names on a list, Abdullah recalls.[137] This list may have originally been a PKI membership or aid recipient list, or a list compiled during the first round of arrests. These people were subsequently "grouped together" at as many as six detention sites, before being loaded on to the back of trucks and transported to military-controlled killing sites. Abdullah remembers whole families being arrested and taken away during this period.[138] He estimates that over two months as many as 2,800 people were killed in Central Aceh. This number is significantly higher than the military's own estimate of 517 deaths that are recorded for the district in the military's Death Map (which recorded public killings and not those at secret, military-controlled killings sites). It is possible – even probable – considering the evidence presented in this chapter, that a greater number of people were killed as part of the systematic mass killings than during the public ones. It is not possible to evaluate the validity of these figures in the absence of forensic research. Both figures, nonetheless, support the notion that the killings were widespread in the district. Abdullah's account also has many similarities with Kadir's account of the killings in Central Aceh.

Ibrahim Kadir's account of systematic mass killings in Takengon

Ibrahim Kadir, the former high school teacher and *didong* performer, provides a unique insight into the running of military-controlled killing sites in Central Aceh. In his following account, which he told to me over two days in Takengon in 2009 as we travelled to the sites he mentions, Kadir bears witness to the time he was forced by the military to prepare victims for execution and to witness the killing process at multiple military-controlled killing sites throughout the province.

After his arrest on 11 October, Kadir was held in a military jail in Takengon where he remained for twenty-five days.[139] Shortly after his arrest he was summoned by a member of the Military Police, who told him that he had been wrongly arrested, but that he must first "assist" the military if he wished to survive. Over the course of the remainder of his detention Kadir was forced to prepare other detainees to be executed. He did this by helping to tie their hands together and placing hessian sacks over their heads, before being forced to witness several mass executions at military-run killing sites in the district.[140]

Old PKI lists, Kadir has explained, were sometimes used by the military to identify those who were to be killed.[141] These people were "taken straight away. [Their heads] [s]tuffed into sacks [and] put into the back [of trucks], like rubbish being thrown away (*macam membuang sampah*)".[142] There was also a "concentration camp" (*camp untuk mengumpulkan*), Kadir has recalled, near Gentala in Takengon, where some of these detainees were kept before being transported to the killing sites.[143] Kadir remembers seeing people being loaded onto the backs of military trucks, "They were all shaking," he has recalled. "They all knew they were going to be killed. It was a very disturbing sight for me to see."[144]

Kadir has made it clear that the killings were part of a sophisticated system. The military would bring the detainees with hessian sacks over their heads and their hands tied before them on the back of trucks to the killing sites at night, before villagers, who had been told to assemble, were asked, "How many do you want?" The victims were then handed over to be executed, in order to help spread complicity throughout the community.[145] In some cases civilians were made to carry out the killings themselves. After participating in the killings, Kadir has recalled, the civilian executioners would drink alcohol at local food stalls, attempting to numb themselves.

Kadir recalls that the largest military-controlled killing sites in Takengon were located along the mountain pass roads of Burlintang Mountain (*Bukit Burlintang*), where he was brought by the military on several occasions to witness the killings.[146] Here, victims who had been brought on the back of military trucks from the jail in central Takengon were shot or decapitated, largely by the military. The bodies were then pushed over the side of the mountain and left unburied. The section of road where the killings were carried out was changed when certain areas began to smell "too rotten" as the bodies began to decompose, with "hundreds" of people killed at certain sites.

It was at one of these mountain pass sites, Kadir recalls, that he was forced to watch the execution of Sambami, the wife of Nain, a well respected doctor in Takengon, who was shot as she held her newborn child that had been born in detention. The bullet passed through the body of the child and then into Sambami.[147] They died together, Sambami screaming for her child.[148] Latifah, whose husband had been detained during the time of the genocide and transported to Java as a political prisoner, has also independently corroborated this story, which she says was told in whispers throughout the town.[149]

According to Kadir, another popular killing site was located closer to the town in Karang Debar,[150] next to the start of the mountain pass road into Burlintang Mountain. Here, villagers were forced to dig a large hole to be used as a mass grave for victims, who had their throats slit and were thrown into the hole.[151] Today a small coffee plantation partially covers the site, but stone markers are visible which allegedly indicate the perimeter of the mass grave. It is not known who placed these stones at the site.

Killings are also said to have occurred at Tritip Bridge (*Jembatan Tritip*), the final bridge into Takengon and only ten minutes' drive from the centre of town.[152] Here, recalls Kadir, victims were killed by the military with the assistance of villagers, before being buried in a mass grave close to the base of the bridge.[153] It is not clear why the victims were not thrown into the river. It may have been that the flow of the river at the time was not strong enough to carry the corpses away, and the riverside site was instead chosen because it was easier for the executioners to clean themselves afterwards. Stone markers are visible here too, which allegedly mark the perimeter of the mass grave site. Again, it is not known who placed the stones at the site. Their meaning, however, appears to be understood in the community. During our interview at the site, for example, Kadir asked a passer-by if he knew the significance of the site. This man confirmed, without collaborating with Kadir or knowing the topic of our discussion, that the riverbed contained a mass grave from the time of the killings. John Bowen has also mentioned this site, under the name "Iron Bridge", as a place where many people were killed during the genocide.[154]

Further along the road, Kadir has recalled that huts were built by a great stone cliff that intersects the road out of Takengon to act as checkpoints, with fires illuminating the location at night.[155] According to Kadir, the military brought victims to this site on the back of trucks and civilians were ordered to carry out the killings "to keep the nation clean" (*untuk menjaga kebersihan negara*),[156] a notion which seems critical to all purges and genocides. Kadir has suggested that killings also took place in the sugar cane plantations along the road out of Takengon, where victims were taken after being told they were being transported to Banda Aceh for processing – a ruse which, Kadir believes, meant relatives of the victims were often unsure whether their loved ones had been killed.[157]

The largest killing site in the district outside of Takengon, Kadir believes, was situated at the Ilang Bridge (*Totor Ilang*), near Bina'an Village.[158] Located high above a fast-flowing river, in a place that is also said to have been a favourite killing site for the Dutch during the colonial period, Kadir recalls that victims who were brought here were asked if they would prefer to be shot or decapitated before being thrown down the steep cliff embankments into the river. Bowen mentions this site, under the name "Red Bridge", as a place where many people were killed during the genocide.[159]

Direct military involvement in the killings in West Aceh

Details of direct military involvement in the killings in West Aceh have been recorded in the military Chronology. They have also been recalled by T.M. Yatim, who in 1965 was Assistant District Chief for Johan Pahlawan. These two accounts detail how the military was involved in arresting and detaining people accused of being associated with the PKI, as well as how military-sponsored civilian militia groups and death squads were used to carry out these tasks. Yatim's account details how civilians, including himself, were rostered onto shifts to witness or participate in the killings. "To begin with," he explains, when recounting how the killings started in Meulaboh:

> they [alleged PKI members and sympathisers] were arrested and detained in the District Military Command (*Kodim*) office, near that field [where Djuarsa made his public address on 8 October] they were grouped together there. They were the leaders. But they weren't killed straight away at the

time they were arrested. The next day they were released . . . then they were disappeared.[160]

Yatim recalls that "KAMI/KAPPI"[161] death squad members, who were "dressed in red", were then "sent out to kill".[162] These hunts were coordinated by the military. People were killed "in various ways", Yatim continues:

> There wasn't, you kill A, you kill B, it wasn't like that. . . . In general, it turned out that everyone connected to the PKI were traitors; we all knew who these people were. Sometimes we didn't know who the little ones were and it turned out they were big people in the PKI, the ones we knew were the head, the secretary. . . . For me in the government, things ran as normal; there weren't demonstrations [against the government].[163]

Here Yatim is describing the ease with which individuals could be accused of being associated with the PKI. Detainees who were not released back into to the community were retained in detention until they were transported to military-controlled killing sites.

Systematic mass killings at military-controlled killing sites in Meulaboh

Yatim recalls that he and other civilians in Meulaboh saw detainees being transported on the back of "pick-up trucks" from the neighbouring *kampung*.[164] Yatim knew the trucks were transporting detainees because "[e]veryone would say, 'oh look, that's a PKI truck . . . a truck carrying PKI people', but we didn't know where it was going; it was Gestapu, you know." Yatim subsequently claimed that he did not directly witness any arrests or killings, before recalling:

> [But] I did have some experiences, for example, we were asleep at home [one night], when we were called out, we were sleeping in our day clothes. It was said that there were some [detainees] that were about to be brought . . . there would be a vehicle, for what, I didn't know, when all of a sudden it was our turn, they [the detainees] were brought to the grave [Yatim mentions mass grave sites in Meulaboh both "near the sea" and "in the mountains"[165]], there was someone I knew, someone's child [who had been brought to the site to be killed] . . . "*Cut Bang* [respected older brother]," [the child asked,] "What is my fate? . . . It will be my turn to be taken to the vehicle, then I will be buried." What could I say? "I know you, your father, your mother is from here, you should run," [Yatim replied.] . . . [T]hat night, I couldn't sleep after that.[166]

In this account, Yatim describes how he was part of a roster system that helped to facilitate the transportation of detainees to the mass grave sites, while also reflecting on the mental strain he experienced participating in the campaign. He appears to have been particularly distressed by having to assist in the murder of individuals he knew from the community. Yatim also reflects on the central role played by the military in the killings. He says, for example, that he knew where these mass graves were located due to "orders" from the Subdistrict Office. These orders, Yatim adds, included an explanation that "this is the place, brothers, where we will dispose of the PKI".[167] "It was quite cheeky of them," Yatim continues. "We didn't like it, but what could we do about it?"[168]

Yatim appears to have witnessed some of the killings directly. "There was a woman," Yatim explains, recalling an incident that appears to have haunted him:

> who after being arrested, detained, [she was] not part of the mass extermination that I spoke about earlier, who was taken and brought briefly to my office, but she wasn't crying, she was very patient. It was all men, and she fought back, after she was let out of the vehicle. Wow, she was attacked, my goodness. . . . [She was attacked *en masse*],[169] there were some left [who hadn't yet been killed] but as they approached the grave, got down from the truck, all of a sudden, BANG, that's how they got into the grave [how they were killed] . . . [She] ran to the grave. That woman, she used to work in my in-laws' house [as a domestic servant] . . . we knew each other, so [when she was still in my office, before she was taken to be shot at the mass grave] I asked her, "How did you end up like this?" She didn't want to talk, "How did you get let out of detention?" [he asked again.] She still didn't want to talk, she also didn't want to drink, but she was very resolute, a true PKI *jihadi*. If Muslims were like that . . . wow, just the idea . . . she had put her hands up [was meeting her fate].[170]

Yatim's government office, like Zainal Abidin's in Banda Aceh, was used as a place to hold detainees before they were transported to the killing sites in the district. Not only was the military initiating and coordinating the implementation of the killings, it was also using government offices as temporary detention centres as part of its annihilation program. From Yatim's description of conditions at the killing sites, detainees disembarked from the truck that had transported them, before being made to approach a mass grave site where they were shot by a firing squad.

25 October – 8 November: public killings continue

Entries in the Chronology for West Aceh also depict the continuation and intensification of public killings in the district. The first of these entries resemble earlier entries which documented public killings in the district. On 25 October, for example, it is reported that three killings occurred in Seunangan, 34.5 km northeast of Meulaboh.[171] Two days later, two more killings are recorded.[172]

From 2 November, however, the number of recorded killings increased. On that day for example, twelve killings are recorded.[173] Six days later, the Chronology reported that "[f]our people who are members of the PKI in Meulaboh have been killed by the people".[174] A large number of these victims appear to have been Chinese.[175]

On 12 November, meanwhile, twenty-one people, including members of the PKI, BTI and Pemuda Rakjat, are reported as having been killed in the Laheun Ka Bubon and Peurembeu areas.[176]

Two days later, on 14 November, it is recorded that four corpses "have been found" in Alubilie, southeast of Meulaboh (in present-day Nagan Raya district), drifting in the water, after the victims apparently attempted to "run away" by crossing a river.[177] Meanwhile, on 27 November, an organiser of the BTI in Samatiga is reported to have been killed in Reusam, Samatiga.[178]

The scale of these killings is striking. Indeed, the two larger-scale killings, one of twelve individuals and the other of twenty-one individuals, do not follow the general pattern of public killings in the province due to their sheer scale. They are better understood as massacres. It is possible that these large-scale killings – the largest ones recorded in the Chronology (excluding mass killings at military-controlled killing sites) – represented a stage in which "public killings" began to take on the characteristics of the mass killings otherwise seen at military-controlled killing sites in the province.

Direct military involvement in the killings in South Aceh

Information about direct military involvement in the killings in South Aceh was recorded in the Chronology and in eyewitness testimony from Ali, the peasant farmer from Sama Dua and Oesman, who in 1965 worked as a junior high school teacher in Tapaktuan. Their testimony points towards the central role played by the military in coordinating and implementing the killings in the district.

According to Ali, orders to implement the killings in South Aceh came from the military, the Pantja Tunggal and the *Front Nasional*.[179] It was the *Front Nasional*, Ali says, which "carried out the killings".[180] These orders were understood as being part of a province-wide and, ultimately, national military-led campaign. As Oesman has explained:

> It's like this my child, whatever the orders were from Banda Aceh, they were followed in South Aceh. People in South Aceh were obedient to ideas from Banda Aceh. To deviate from this was frightening enough, the G30S affair was a deviation . . . whatever was said by Ishak Djuarsa, whatever was suggested by the [Governor], whatever was done through an explanation from the Military Command in Banda Aceh [Kodam I Iskandar Muda] that's what happened, what was implemented in Tapaktuan.[181]

Killings in the district began in mid-October and continued into November. A 17 November entry in the Chronology reports, "news has been received from the South Aceh Defence Sector Command (*Kosekhan*) that, since 11 October",[182] fifteen members of the PKI and its affiliated organisations "have been recorded . . . as being killed".[183] How these individuals met their deaths is not recorded.

Systematic mass killings at military-controlled killing sites in South Aceh

Systematic mass killings were also carried out at military-controlled killing sites in the district. According to Ali, those who had been arrested and detained by the military, after originally having been encouraged to report themselves to the *Front Nasional*, were systematically picked up from their places of military-controlled detention under the cover of darkness and transported by truck to killing sites. As Ali relates:

> We were on night watch [at the time]. I didn't see the actual killings, but I saw when they [those who had been held in detention] were brought on the back of a . . . truck. When they were killed I didn't see. . . . [But] I knew that they were brought on the trucks, one truck, two trucks. I [also] saw the graves, at Ujung Batu [12.3 km east of Tapaktuan] . . . there were three heaps, three [mass] graves.[184]

Ali also names Alu Bane, 76 km northwest along the west coast from Tapaktuan, as an area where killing sites and mass graves were located.[185]

It appears that member parties of the *Front Nasional* in the district were placed under pressure to "assist" the military during this period. An entry in the Chronology for 25 October, for example, records that the leadership of the South Aceh Partindo branch had been compelled to produce a "loyalty pledge" (a document written by a political party, through which the organisation pledged its allegiance to the military leadership while undertaking to assist the military to carryout the military's annihilation campaign). Similar "loyalty pledges" were also being produced in East Aceh during this time.

This document "informed the South Aceh Defence Sector Command (*Kosekhan*)" that the South Aceh Partindo branch along with its affiliated mass organisations had dissolved itself and pledged that it:

> denounced the actions of the G30S which was masterminded by the PKI and its lackeys, remained loyal to the PJM President/Commander in Chief of the Armed Forces/PBR Bung Karno and [was] **ready to assist ABRI to annihilate the G30S.**[186]

Meanwhile, the South Aceh Defence Sector Command was involved in carrying out arrests in the district into December. On 1 December, for example, the Chronology records that the South Aceh Defence Sector Command was involved in directly "carrying out [the] arrests" of six people accused of being "involved in the G30S".[187] On 9 December, the South Aceh Defence Sector Command is recorded as "detaining" seven "members of the PKI and its affiliated mass organisations", most of whom were women.[188] It can be assumed that these listed individuals were subsequently killed. As Ali explains, "They [the PKI] were completely scrubbed out."[189]

Direct military involvement in the killings in East Aceh

A large quantity of documents has been recovered from East Aceh that point to the direct involvement of the military in killings in the district. These documents include evidence the military's annihilation campaign was adopted as state policy down to the subdistrict level. They also show the systematic manner in which political parties were induced to pledge their loyalty to the military during this period and demonstrate the growing paranoia of military officers as a result of military interrogation practices.

28 October: the Djulok Tjatur Tunggal supports the annihilation campaign

On 28 October, the same day the East Aceh Level II Provincial Government in Langsa released its Declaration pledging "as much assistance as possible" to the East Aceh Level II Pantja Sila Defence Front death squad in Langsa, a meeting was held in Djulok, 25 km west of Idi Rajeuk.[190] This meeting was attended by the subdistrict's Tjatur Tunggal body,[191] five political parties and mass organisations,[192] four 'civilian leaders', four religious leaders (*alim ulama*), five village administrators and five mosque officials.[193] The large meeting expressed thanks that Suharto and Nasution had survived, condemned the actions of the 30 September Movement, which, it was said, had been "orchestrated by the PKI", and expressed sympathy for the generals killed. It is then noted that it would:

4   Strongly condemn the 30 September Movement and Revolution Council and sentence those involved as severely as possible in accordance with Revolutionary law.

5   Request His Excellency President/Commander of ABRI/Great Leader of the Revolution Bung Karno immediately disband the PKI/its Mass Org[anisations] and other Political Parties that have been involved in the 30 September Movement and **completely annihilate them to their roots**.

6   Pledge loyalty and faithfulness to [Bung Karno] and obedience to [Bung Karno's] decision regarding [his] latest explanation regarding the 30 September Movement.

7   **Be ready and prepared to assist the Armed Forces to annihilate the 30 September Movement.**[194]

This government-produced 'Declaration' represents a marked escalation from the statement released by the East Aceh Level II Provincial Government on 5 October, which only called for "decisive and proportionate action" to be taken against those who could "clearly" be demonstrated to have been involved in the 30 September Movement. Punishment was now to be "as severe as possible" and uninhibited by normal legal procedure, as the term "Revolutionary law" would appear to imply. The course to be requested and prepared for was "annihilation": an outcome that was to be pursued under the leadership of the military.

The reference in the Declaration to Sukarno's "latest explanation", meanwhile, may refer to Sukarno's press interview following the collapse of the 30 September Movement, which was published in the national *Sinar Harapan* newspaper on 14 October. Through this interview Sukarno called for calm and promised to formulate a "political solution for the problem that has arisen as a result of the so-called 'September 30th Movement'".[195] Sukarno wanted this speech to de-escalate the military's attacks against the PKI. Instead, his statement was twisted and used by the Djulok Tjatur Tunggal as a means to legitimise and intensify this attack. Sukarno's words had been similarly twisted on 20 October in Medan, when Mokoginta, while also referencing Sukarno's 14 October speech, had turned Sukarno's promise to formulate a political solution on its head to claim that, rather than calling for calm, Sukarno had "already instructed us to create calm (*mentjiptakan ketenangan*), so that there is a political solution . . . To do this we need a purging of our body . . . [we] need to intensify our activities to destroy the 30 September Movement to its roots".[196] Sukarno's "political solution" was thus re-interpreted to coincide with the military's annihilation campaign. In this context, the Declaration produced by the Djulok Tjatur Tunggal to pledge "obedience" to "Bung Karno's latest explanation" was clearly an attempt to harness the authority that such an announcement provided to pursue a campaign diametrically opposed to Sukarno's actual statement.

The Declaration by the Idi Rajeuk Tjatur Tunggal was subsequently forwarded to Sukarno, the national military leadership and the national parliament in Jakarta; Mokoginta in Medan; Djuarsa, Aceh's Governor; the Banda Aceh Pantja Tunggal and the provincial government in Banda Aceh; and the district military leadership, East Aceh Pantja Tunggal and the Level II Provincial Government in Langsa.[197] It was also sent to the national Radio Republic Indonesia radio station in Jakarta and the Radio Republic Indonesia station in Medan "to be broadcast". The Declaration was then disseminated down to the village level in the district through the village administrators and mosque officials, who attended the meeting as signatories.

30 October: the Idi Rajeuk Pantja Tunggal calls for public hangings

Two days later, on 30 October, the format of this meeting was replicated in neighbouring Idi Rajeuk by the local subdistrict Pantja Tunggal, which, along with representatives of four political parties, including the NU, PNI, PSII and PI Perti; representatives of "all mass organisations in Idi Rajeuk Subdistrict"; and local civilian leaders, produced a 'Declaration' subtitled "Determination of the people of Idi Rajeuk Subdistrict, East Aceh, in regards to the affair that calls itself the '30 September Movement'".[198] After repeating the opening sentiments expressed in the Declaration produced in Djulok on 28 October, the Idi Rajeuk Declaration called for the increased integration of the military with "the people" and "condemned as strongly as possible" the 30 September Movement.[199] It then proceeded to call upon Sukarno to:

V. 1   Immediately disband the Indonesian Communist Party along with all its Mass Org[anisations] that share its principles, while also removing all PKI elements and those of its mass organisations from Government Bodies and from Government, as they have truly carried out treason against the Republic of Indonesia and the Indonesian Revolution as well as against the ideology of the Republic of Indonesia, that is PANT-JASILA, and **they are not to be given the right to live on Indonesian soil**

2   to take strong action and join in and **assist ABRI in the annihilation down to the roots** of the counter-revolutionary "30 September Movement" and those elements (*oknum*)[200] who are part of or involved in Gestapu

3   for elements (*oknum*) who are involved in the "30 September Movement" to be ***sentenced to be hanged in public.***[201]

The language used in this Declaration made it as clear as possible that the word "annihilate" (*menumpas*) should be taken literally. People accused of being associated with the PKI were to be treated as traitors and enemies of the state who were not to be afforded even the "right to live", for even if a denial of the "right to live on Indonesian soil" is understood to mean deportation rather than immediate extermination, one is confronted with the logical conclusion that in a context in which "annihilation" of this target group is being actively pursued by the state, the withdrawal of the "right to live on Indonesian soil" in the absence of a plan to transfer this target group outside of Indonesian territory refers to the physical destruction of this group. This concept resembles the way that the term "deportation" was used during the Nazi Holocaust to mean transportation for the purpose of systematic mass murder.[202] Likewise, the call for this target group to be "sentenced to be hanged in public" has a literalness that the common slogan painted on banners or screamed at rallies to "hang Aidit" does not possess.

It is impossible without further investigation to know whether hangings were carried out in Idi Rajeuk as a result of this Declaration. Testimonial evidence in the film *The Act of Killing*, however, suggests that hanging certainly took place in North Sumatra.[203] Oppenheimer has also interviewed survivors of the genocide from Aceh who recall hangings there.[204] Acehnese historians Sufi and Aziz, meanwhile, suggest in their book *Peristiwa PKI di Aceh*, that hangings occurred in Aceh at the time of the genocide, describing how "[t]hey all [PKI, Gerwani, Pemuda Rakyat, CGMI and Baperki members] died on the gallows".[205] Sufi, however, distanced himself from this claim when I interviewed him in 2010.[206]

As the Pantja Tunggal was not an executive or judicial body, these calls do not possess the weight of a formal order or law. They do, however, signal the intentions of Idi Rajeuk's judicial and executive bodies, which are represented through the Pantja Tunggal, to work together to pursue these intentions and to encourage civilian participation. Moreover, this Declaration provides evidence that the military's annihilation campaign was understood as military "policy" (*kebijaksa-naan*) that was being implemented by the Mandala Satu Command, Pantja Tunggal bodies and Defence Sector Command (*Kosekhan*) structures at this time.[207]

The production of such documents appears to have been routine in East Aceh during this period. On 2 November, a third document was produced in Darul Aman, 6 km southwest of Idi Rajeuk, as the result of a meeting between the Darul Aman Tjatur Tunggal and representatives from five political parties in the Iditjut state primary school building.[208] This document is so similar to the two cited above that it may well have been produced from a template, or have been copied with minimal variation.

A fourth document, signed on 30 November by the Darul Aman subdistrict government, has also been found amongst the archive documents. This one is a verbatim copy of the document signed on 2 November by the Darul Aman Tjatur Tunggal.[209] Meanwhile, a fifth nearly identical document was produced on 1 December in Kotabinjai, the final town within the Acehnese side of the border with North Sumatra, by the Kotabinjai subdistrict government.[210]

These documents attest to the high level of coordination behind the military's annihilation campaign in East Aceh, as elsewhere in the province. They are also evidence that the military's annihilation campaign was being actively pursued down to the subdistrict level. Moreover, as reports of the implementation of this campaign were sent back up the chain of the command, the national and provincial military leadership cannot claim that it was unaware that this is how its orders and directives were being interpreted at the local level in East Aceh.

14 October–9 November: the use of "loyalty pledges"

Political parties and mass organisations in East Aceh were placed under extreme pressure by the military to support its annihilation campaign. This support was coordinated through the use of signed documents, through which signatory organisations pledged their allegiance to the military leadership and pledged to assist the military to implement its annihilation campaign. Interestingly, these "loyalty pledges" were produced both by organisations that were considered to be sympathetic to the PKI and by organisations that were not.

The first loyalty pledge produced by an organisation considered to be loyal to the PKI was produced on 14 October by Partindo in Langsa.[211] It condemned the 30 September Movement and pledged its support for the military's annihilation campaign before disassociating itself from the national Partindo organisation.[212]

The second loyalty pledge was produced on 20 October, signed by both the Marhaenist Youth and the National Indonesian Farmers Union in Idi. It condemned the 30 September Movement before pledging that the two organisations were "[r]eady to assist the military (*ABRI*) in the annihilation of the 'G.30.S'/ Revolution Council, in line with the order of the Minister/Supreme Commander of the Armed Forces [Suharto] as issued on 16 October 1965".[213] It also pledged its support for the state-sponsored Movement of Believers for the Defence of

Pantja Sila death squad that, as has been discussed above, had been established in Idi six days earlier. This pledge was then forwarded to the military leadership in Jakarta, Medan, Banda Aceh and East Aceh.

Nine days later, on 20 October, this pledge was followed by a formal 'Declaration', also signed by both the Marhaenist Youth and the National Indonesian Farmers Union in Idi. This Declaration pledged the two organisations were "[r]eady to assist ABRI to completely annihilate the G30S counter-revolution regardless of the sacrifices necessary".[214]

On 9 November, meanwhile, the Marhaenist Women's Movement in Langsa produced a very similar document, through which it pledged its "full support to ABRI, which has been given the task of securing security . . . by annihilating the 30 September Movement" and to "fight to the last drop of blood to save the national ideology of Pantjasila".[215] This document recognised the leadership of Mokoginta in his position as "Dejah Sumatra/Panglatu" and ordered all members of the Marheinist Women's Movement in East Aceh to follow its pledge to fight to the "last drop of blood", an order which is described as an "Instruction".[216]

The pressure these organisations must have felt would have been immense. Should they have refused to produce such documents, they would have risked becoming targeted. Meanwhile, in pledging to assist the military to implement its annihilation campaign, members of these organisations were, in effect, offering to participate in the murder of their former political allies. That these pledges were forwarded widely to the media and to all levels of the military and civilian leadership suggests that the documents also performed a propagandistic purpose. Specifically, it would appear, these documents were intended to signal the military's success in crushing any potential opposition in the district. They also served as a warning to the national leaderships of these organisations.

The loyalty pledges produced by organisations that were not considered to be sympathetic to the PKI also promised to support the military's annihilation campaign, but placed less emphasis on denouncing the 30 September Movement, presumably because these groups were already seen by the military as political allies.[217] The first of these documents, produced by the PSII on 14 October, explained that the PSII in Langsa was "still able to be trusted", before pledging that it "completely supported" the military's campaign, "as is being demonstrated in the field",[218] suggesting the PSII was already actively engaged in assisting the military in its annihilation campaign in the district.

The second document, a 'Declaration' produced by the NU on 27 October in Sungai Raja, Rantau Selamat Subdistrict, located between Langsa and Tamiang, meanwhile, condemned the 30 September Movement and the PKI before pledging "to assist ABRI throughout each step to annihilate the Movement that is being led by the damned Communists (*Komunis keparat*), who do not accept God or humanitarian values".[219]

While the third document, a 'Declaration' was produced on 29 November by the head of Muhammadijah in Langsa, East Aceh.[220] This pledge also "call[ed] upon" Sukarno to "sentence to death . . . all those involved" with the 30 September Movement".[221] It then proceeded to announce that the NU in East Aceh was "ready to assist ABRI to annihilate the counter revolutionary 30 September Movement to its roots and fully support all policies that are decided upon by ABRI".

These documents recognised the military as being ultimately responsible for the annihilation campaign in East Aceh. They also indicate that the military leadership provided "suggestions" and "instructions" as to how the annihilation campaign should be implemented. The involvement of these political parties in the military's annihilation campaign was both intended and coordinated by the military.

Direct military involvement in the killings in Idi Rajeuk

Saifuddin, the son of peasants, was fifteen years old in 1965. He was visibly anxious when he spoke about the military's role in the implementation of the killings in Idi Rajeuk, where the local Pantja Tunggal had called for public hangings on 30 October and where two of the above loyalty pledges were produced. During our interview he stopped himself on several occasions to say, "That's political, I really don't know."[222] He did confirm, however, that he had "heard of the names" of the Pantja Tunggal and the government-sponsored Pantjasila Defence Front death squad (established in Langsa on 14 October), "but [I] didn't monitor their actions or get involved with these bodies".[223] He confirmed that the military was in control of the arrests and killings in the subdistrict. Saifuddin had previously explained that people in the community were told that people associated with the PKI "were to be taken to the plantations [to be killed], to be taken to the military, or it wouldn't be resolved". Saifuddin claims, however that he "didn't see this directly, I don't know exactly how it happened".[224]

Many of the victims killed in Idi Rayeuk, Saifuddin continues, "were people from outside [the subdistrict]".[225] Saifuddin doesn't know how many people were killed in Idi Rayeuk at this time, though he does recall "[i]t was a lot, yeah".[226] One of the locations in the subdistrict where victims were buried, Saifuddin has recalled, was on "Seunudok Mountain", which he explains is now known as "PKI Mountain", and which is said to be "haunted" (*angker*) due to the large number of PKI graves there.[227]

Direct military involvement in the killings in Tamiang

Documents of the type produced in western East Aceh have not been recovered from eastern East Aceh. This absence may be a matter of chance relating to the storage of such documents. Alternatively, or perhaps additionally, the increased political polarisation in eastern East Aceh due to the different political composition of the area, characterised by its plantation-based economy and unionised workforce, including its large PKI membership, may have resulted in distinct patterns of violence in the area. Karim and Aminah, the married couple from Village 2 in Tamiang, who had been involved with the PKI through Aminah's membership of LEKRA, for example, suggest the military played a direct role in coordinating and implementing its annihilation campaign in Tamiang and its surrounding areas.

The military, they both explain, was the driving force behind the killings in Tamiang and was responsible for "taking" those who were to be killed.[228] "If we say it was the military," Karim continues:

> it's a fact that the people were not mobilised. Those who were considered to be involved [with the 30 September Movement], they [the military] took themselves. . . . It was not [the people]. The people did not do anything [were not involved] here.[229]

After the establishment of guard posts in the district following 1 October, Karim has recalled, military personnel were sent directly into Village 2, where they met with Pak Rusdi, Village 2's PKI Village Head, who was asked to identify members of the PKI and people associated with the party to the military.[230] Karim remembers one particular incident from this time, when Pak Rusdi came up to him in the company of military personnel and proceeded to ask him to identify PKI "cadres" in the village to the military personnel – a request that Karim says he declined. Individuals who were identified as being associated with the PKI were then asked to report to the guard posts.[231] After reporting, Karim explains, these individuals were sent home and required to report once a week to the local Territorial Affairs and People's Resistance Officer (*Puterpra*).[232] Karim and Aminah can recall ten people from Village 2 who were arrested and released in this manner, including Pak Rusdi himself.[233]

One day, Karim continues, this group of identified individuals was suddenly called to a "meeting" in Bukitrata.[234] "They were then taken from [the meeting] [by military personnel] and never returned." "To this day," Aminah explains, "they have yet to return. I was also scared at this time because I heard this is what happened if you were taken." It is not known what happened to this group, but it is assumed they were killed by the military on "X Mountain"[235] and dumped in a mass grave.[236] Karim explains that people became very scared of the military during this period.[237] Taufik, the young law graduate and son of a former coolie transport agent, meanwhile, has also independently estimated the number of people killed in Village 2 as nine. He also remembers another two individuals who were killed, one in neighbouring "Village 3"[238] and the other in Village 1.[239] He refuses to be drawn on the detail of these deaths, explaining only that "[t]hey were taken away, where they were killed we don't know, it was like that".[240] These accounts corroborate information found in the military's Chronology for eastern East Aceh, while also shedding light on the role of the military in facilitating arrests and detentions during this period.

16 October–2 November: public killings continue

On 16 October, the military Chronology reported that eight members of the PKI in Pulo Tiga, close to the border with North Sumatra, had "surrendered" to the Defence Sector Commander (*Dan Sekhan*) in East Aceh to "request protection".[241] These eight people, "after being given an explanation" by the Defence Sector Commander, were then "returned to their various *kampung*".

On 19 October, meanwhile, it is reported in the Chronology that eight members of the PKI were arrested and detained as the result of a "raid" in Sukadjadi, Suka-rachmad, Pulo Tiga, Batangara, Bundar *kampung* and the Kaula Simpang areas.[242] Two days later, on 21 October, the Central Committee of the PKI for Tamiang, Hulu, Pulo Tiga and Kuala Simpang is reported to have signed a declaration that "condemned as strongly as possible the 30 September Movement and implored the Government to eradicate down to the roots the G.30.S. and [declared that the signatories of these documents] were ready to assist the military (*ABRI*) to carry out its annihilation of the G.30.S.".[243] The intimidation that these signatories felt must have been immense.

These military arrests were accompanied by interrogations, carried out to elicit intelligence from the detainees. In an entry for 26 October, for example, a man named Sawondo was "arrested" in Langsa, accused of being a member of the PKI and subsequently interrogated.[244] This interrogation was said to reveal that the PKI in Langsa, under the leadership of a man named as Amir Hamzah, had formed a "troop" of 120 men based in Alue Sileumek that was preparing to fight back against the military's attack. It was also "revealed" that on 30 September, the day before the outbreak of the 30 September Movement, Amir Hamzah had "received instructions" from Radjab Nurdin, a PKI cadre in Langsa, to "prepare 100 Pemuda Rakjat members" in preparation of Njoto's visit to Langsa. Evidence of this resistance has yet to be found.

On 2 November, meanwhile, the East Aceh Defence Sector Command, was directly involved in the arrest and interrogation of a man named Untung who is said to have confessed to having been sent on assignment to Aceh from Pang-kalan Brandan, 35 km from the border with Aceh in North Sumatra, by a North Sumatran leader of the PKI, whose name is unclear in the document.[245] As a result of this assignment, Untung allegedly confessed he had sixty firearms and was preparing a force of sixty PKI members from Sarangdjaja Hilir/Tangkahandurian, in Pangkalan Brandan, North Sumatra, to "advance" on East Aceh. While, on 8 November it is recorded that a man named J. Pranoto was detained at a Guard Post in Rantau and accused of attempting to flee to Medan, and who "upon inspection" was discovered to have pictures of a "mother ship, fighters, [word unclear] and a submarine in his bag" (*kapal induk, pemburu,* [unclear] *dan kaapal selam*).[246]

Such intelligence is highly suspect, with no evidence existing beyond the mili-tary's own records to suggest that such 'resistance' was mobilised.[247] None of my interviewees, for example, ever reported being aware of planned PKI resistance at any time during the period of the genocide in Aceh. The idea that an underground resistance movement was being assembled and that "submarines" were being used in Aceh, though preposterous in hindsight, undoubtedly stoked fears that, despite no serious resistance being visible, such resistance may have been "invis-ible", either hidden in the jungles or out at sea. James Siegel, for example, has recorded how during this period people in the province "reported seeing lights at sea imagined to be Communist signals".[248] It is not known whether such "discov-eries" were cynical fabrications, such as the propaganda that was being pumped out of Jakarta during this time regarding the mutilation of the generals murdered by the 30 September Movement, or whether they were the genuine suspicions of interrogating officers.[249] As David Chandler and John Roosa have observed in their research into the practice of eliciting intelligence through torture during the Cambodian genocide and in Indonesia, it is easy for interrogating officers to fall into a kind of paranoia, in which continued denials are routinely taken to be confirmation of the information being sought.[250] Such "discoveries" may have also played an important psychological role in convincing those involved in the violence that they were responding with reasonable force to an aggressor and that they were not themselves the aggressors, despite their personal interactions with detainees indicating that their adversary was disorganised and defenceless.[251]

Military-sponsored mass demonstrations were also held in Langsa during this period. These demonstrations played an important role in helping to orchestrate civilian participation in the military's annihilation campaign. An entry in the Chronology for 12 November for example, records a demonstration that was held in the district's main town at 8am by 10,000 women "who had been co-ordinated by the *Front Nasional* [and the] Pantja Sila Defence [Front] [death squad] for the purpose of annihilating the G-30-S".[252] This demonstration was said to have finished at 11.15am in an "orderly fashion".[253] It is not elaborated upon in the entry whether the stated "purpose" of this demonstration to participate in the military's annihilation campaign was literally fulfilled at this time, such as through a resurgence of pogrom-type actions in the town. It would appear, however, that the timing of the demonstration was intended to coincide with the arrival of Djuarsa in the district six days later.

11–18 November: Djuarsa's second coordination tour

Djuarsa departed Banda Aceh at 2pm on 11 November to conduct a second coordination tour of the province in his capacity as Pangdahan A.[254] The focus of this tour was to be Aceh's east coast and Central Aceh, with planned stops in North Aceh, East Aceh and Central Aceh. The exact purpose of this tour is not stated in the Chronology. It would appear, however, that Djuarsa used this trip to assess the implementation of the military's annihilation campaign in the districts he visited.

Details of Djuarsa's movements on the tour remain sketchy. Only his activities in Aceh Pidie and East Aceh are recorded in the Chronology, albeit briefly. It is known, for example, that Djuarsa was in Aceh Pidie on 12 November.[255] During this time he inaugurated a Lieutenant Colonel named Abdullah Hanafiah as Commander of the District Barracks Veterans Legion. No further information is given about Djuarsa's activities in the district. The next morning, however, it is recorded that killings continued in the district, when, at 9am, a man named Sjamsuddin, who was alleged to be a member of the PKI, was murdered by an "unknown killer".[256] Such killings would continue in the district until 21 November.[257]

More detail is known about Djuarsa's activities in East Aceh. Djuarsa arrived in Tamiang on 18 November.[258] His visit was marked by a demonstration of 6,000 women from Tamiang, who "held a Demonstration within the framework of the annihilation of the PKI/its lackeys in K[ual]a Simpang" in his honour. While this demonstration was underway, a "Kima-112 patrol" (*Kima, Kompi Markas*: lit. Barracks Company, a patrol of the '112' military company tied to the local military barracks) and members of a group of 156 armed military personnel under the command of the East Aceh Defence Sector Command[259] "carried out the arrest of five PKI people at the Liput river and surrendered them to the East Aceh Defence Sector Command (*Kosekhan*)".[260] The following day, a second patrol was carried out by the Kima-112 patrol in the Batang Are region, during which time seven "PKI people" were arrested before being "surrendered to the [Military Police] POM-I/21 Post" in Kuala Simpang.[261]

Although the Chronology remains cryptic about the purpose of Duarsa's second tour, stating only that he "happened to be there" (*jang berkebetulan berada disana*),[262] it seems that the purpose of Djuarsa's visits was not to criticise local leaders for their zealous implementation of the military's annihilation campaign, or to bring the violence to an end. Indeed, arrests and killings continued during Djuarsa's tour, and may even have intensified in East Aceh at this time. It would appear that Djuarsa used this visit as a means to assess the extent and "success" of the killings in order to report this information to Mokoginta, who visited Banda Aceh in his capacity as Mandala Satu Commander (*Panglatu*) less than one week later.

24 November–13 December: Mokoginta and Djuarsa call for reflection

Mokoginta arrived in Banda Aceh on 24 November where, at 4pm, he addressed a mass meeting attended by an estimated 100,000 people.[263] This extremely large meeting, the largest of its kind to be held in the province during the time of the genocide, was "organised and used" by Djuarsa to "explain developments and the current national situation" to attendees. The purpose of the meeting thus appears to have been for the military leadership to consolidate its position and to maintain control over the public narrative of events. The sheer scale of the attendance underscores the importance that the local military leadership placed in this event as an organising tool. Further information about this meeting is unfortunately not available. It does appear, however, that coordination between Mokoginta and Djuarsa intensified from this time.

Six days later, on 30 November, the Chronology reports that Djuarsa, acting in his capacity as Pangdahan A, travelled to Medan with the head of Aceh's Allied Intelligence Staff (*G1*)[264] for the purpose of carrying out an "inspection" (*inspeksi*).[265] The result of this inspection, where Djuarsa once again would have had the chance to meet with Mokoginta, is not recorded.

Six days later, on 6 December, a meeting of the Aceh provincial government was convened.[266] At this meeting, the Aceh provincial government presented a resolution to Djuarsa as Pepelrada. This resolution, the Chronology reports, called upon Djuarsa to "wait" for a declaration from Sukarno calling for the immediate disbanding of the PKI and its affiliated organisations. Considering that Djuarsa had issued a decree declaring the PKI and its affiliated organisations had been "frozen" on 20 October, it is not immediately clear what the Aceh provincial government was asking Djuarsa to "wait" for. The timing of this meeting did, however, coincide with a meeting held by Sukarno in Jakarta on the same day. Through this meeting the President – who was now no more than a figurehead – formalised the establishment of the Operational Command for the Restoration of Security and Order (Kopkamtib: *Komando Operasi Pemulihan dan Ketertiban*).[267] This new body allowed the military to implement *de facto* martial law at the national level and would become the new military regime's chief instrument of political control before Suharto's official assumption of the position of President in March 1966 (see chapter 7).[268]

It is my opinion, based on the available evidence, that a decision was reached between Mokoginta and Djuarsa around this time that the military's annihilation campaign had achieved its purpose and that the widespread public killings and systematic mass killings which had wracked the province for the last two months should be brought to a close. Having physically exterminated its political enemies in Aceh and bolstered by the military's continued consolidation of power nationally, the military leadership in the province was now turning its thoughts to governing.

On 13 December a "Commander's Call" (*Commonderscall*) was held at the Krueng Daroy Hotel in Banda Aceh between Djuarasa and the province's Inter-District Military Resort Commanders (*Dan Rem*), District Military Commanders (*Dan Dim*) and Battalion Commanders (*Dan Jon*).[269] A Commander's Call is an opportunity for a Command to come together and to recognise the Command's achievements. Djuarsa, in his capacity as Pangdahan A, used this event to reflect on the success of the military's annihilation campaign in the province and to "face the follow up to G30S".[270]

19–24 December: systematic mass killings are brought to a close

Four days later, on 19 December, Mokoginta, acting in his position as Inter-Regional Defence Region Commander for Sumatra (*Pangandahan Sum*) once again returned to Banda Aceh.[271] At 11am he held a "Briefing" at the Garuda Cinema in Banda Aceh with Djuarsa and "the various heads of the Armed Forces with a ranking of Second Lieutenant Assistant or above" in order to provide them with an "explanation of the situation".

Later that evening, this "Briefing" was followed by a second mass meeting which was held in front of Banda Aceh's Grand Mosque between 8.30 and 11.30pm.[272] How many people attended this meeting is not recorded. Mokoginta, the Chronology explains, used the meeting to announce various "decisions" that had been reached at the earlier meeting. This included an "explanation" that "the activities of the PKI [and] its affiliated organisations have already been declared to have been disbanded/brought to an end". This announcement appears to have been intended to state that the military's annihilation campaign had been successful. Six days later, on 25 December, Mokoginta would tell the American Consul in Medan: "there are only 120 PKI left in Atjeh . . . 6,000 have been killed there".[273]

The mass meeting was then addressed by the Secretary of the Consultative Council of Ulama (*Musyawarah Alim-Ulama*) for Aceh, Aceh's peak Islamic body, who used the opportunity to communicate a series of "decisions" to Mokoginta and the waiting crowd.[274] These decisions were based on a controversial document issued by the organisation one day earlier. This document, described as a *fatwa*, proclaimed that "the teachings of communism are atheistic (*kufur*) and are forbidden (*haram*) to all followers of Islam" and that "perpetrators/those behind G.30.S are "*kafir harbi*" [an enemy whom it is permitted to kill] [and] whom it is mandatory to completely annihilate (*wajib ditumpas habis*)".[275]

These "decisions", delivered in front of Aceh's Grand Mosque, were intended to provide religious sanction for the military's annihilation campaign and to portray the genocide as a righteous battle of good versus evil. By "receiving" these decisions, the military was already actively promoting a narrative that minimised its own agency behind the violence and instead portrayed the genocide as an ideological and religious struggle. The genocide was not to be understood as a struggle between the military and the PKI, but as a struggle between the PKI and Islam.

Indeed, it appears the military played a direct role in the production of these decisions. The original document from which these decisions had been drawn had been produced after the Council listened to a series of "introductory speeches" by none other than Djuarsa in his position as Aceh's Defence Region Commander and Njak Adam Kamil in his position of Governor.[276] Shortly afterwards, the Council had declared: "*Ulama* are advisors to rulers (*penguasa*) and tools of the government (*alat-alat pemerintah*)." In addition to condemning the PKI and portraying the military's annihilation campaign as a kind of holy war, the point of the meeting appears to have been to establish the Consultative Council of Ulama as a mouthpiece of the new military regime.

The worst of the mass killings came to an end over the next few days. This development was reported on the front pages of *Kompas* on 23 December and coincided with the start of Ramadan the following day. The military Chronology, meanwhile, would run cold from 22 December, when it was reported the Aceh Military Command celebrated its anniversary at the Gajah sports field.[277] The mood at this celebration can only be imagined. In less than three months the Aceh Military Command had physically obliterated its major political rival and had placed Aceh's civilian government under *de facto* martial law.

***

There was, of course, nothing spontaneous about this second wave of violence. The military deliberately chose to begin transporting detainees to military-controlled killing sites, where they were systematically murdered. The purpose of these killings was to physically destroy the military's target group. Evidence of this intent can be found in the military's description of this wave of killings as an internal "war", which, it explained, was intended to "annihilate" the PKI and all those considered to be associated with it.

The systematic and intentional nature of this campaign can be seen in the patterns and similarities that emerged throughout Aceh's districts and sub-districts.

Indeed, not only is it clear that the military and civilian leadership in Aceh's districts and subdistricts received a coordinated set of orders and directives passed down from the national to the inter-provincial to the provincial military leadership at this time; district and subdistrict civilian leaderships in the province were also compelled to produce their own directives, which were then passed back up the chain of command. These directives aimed to secure support for the military's annihilation campaign at the local level. The military further ensured this support by distributing machine guns and rifles to members of the Hansip and Hanra paramilitary organisations. Government records explain that this was done with the explicit intention that recipients would assist the military in its "cleansing [and] extermination of the G30S".

The identity of the executioners at military-controlled killing sites varied slightly across districts. In Banda Aceh the military and military police carried out the killings directly. In North Aceh, members of the civilian militias and paramilitary organisations carried out the executions alongside members of the military. In Central Aceh, political prisoners were themselves forced to assist in the execution process alongside the military. In West Aceh and South Aceh, it appears that members of the district government were present and assisted the military in carrying out the killings at military-controlled killing sites. In East Aceh, meanwhile, the military appears to have played a particularly visible role in facilitating the killings. In some cases the role of executioner may have been assigned to individuals the military considered to be politically suspect. In all cases, it was the military that was ultimately responsible for the killings that occurred.

By December 1965, as we will see further in the following chapter, the military began to turn its attention toward governing. The jails had been emptied of political prisoners. The military and population, the military insisted, should be proud of their achievements. They could also, it was implied, draw comfort from the understanding that the killings had been religiously sanctioned.

This was not, however, to be the end of the violence. A new wave of violence targeted specifically at Aceh's Chinese community would erupt in April 1966, while the military would continue its purge of Aceh's civil service until as late as March 1967.

Notes

1 Capitalisation and translation of 'Ruang Yudha' as 'War Room' in the original. Other emphasis added. *Laporan Tahunan Lengkap Kodam-I/Kohanda Atjeh, Tahun 1965* (Banda Aceh: Kodam-I Banda Aceh, 1 February 1966), p. 17.
2 *Ibid.*, p. 85.
3 *Ibid.*, p. 17.
4 *Ibid.*
5 *Ibid.*, p. 18.
6 The 30 September Movement had been decisively crushed by the evening of 1 October 1965.
7 Interview with "Ramli", West Sumatra, 15 December 2011, p. 14.
8 "Ismail" is a pseudonym. Ramli does not give Ismail's name in order to protect Ismail's identity.

9 *Ibid.*
10 *Ibid.*, pp. 14–15.
11 *Ibid.*, p. 15.
12 *Ibid.*, p. 1.
13 *Ibid.*, p. 7.
14 'Pak Cik' is Acehnese for 'uncle'. Ramli does not give Pak Cik's real name.
15 Interview with "Ramli", West Sumatra, 15 December 2011, p. 12.
16 *Ibid.*
17 See, 'Daft[a]r Kader PKI Yang Diamankan' in Amir Hasan Nast BA, *Embun Berdarah* (self published, undated manuscript, in author's possession).
18 After fleeing to Pidie, Ramli, his mother and surviving siblings travelled to North Sumatra, where Ramli's mother was imprisoned for seven years due to her connection with the PKI. After the worst of the killings were over, Ramli returned to Aceh to live with Pak Cik, who defended Ramli against the persecution he faced as the son of a PKI leader. Ramli was originally banned from attending school, but was eventually accepted after Pak Cik appealed directly to Ishak Djuarsa, who he knew personally through a family connection. Interview with "Ramli", West Sumatra, 15 December 2011, p. 11.
19 Interview with Zainal Abidin, Banda Aceh, 14 February 2009, p. 13.
20 *Ibid.*
21 *Ibid.*, p. 11.
22 Teuku Njak Arif, Aceh's first post-independence governor, had, for example, been exiled to Takengon during Aceh's social revolution in April 1946 along with "all the ruling *uleebalang* families from Aceh Besar". Arif died in Takengon two months later due to complications from diabetes. Anthony Reid, *The Blood of the People: Revolution and the End of Traditional Rule in Northern Sumatra* (Kuala Lumpur and New York: Oxford University Press, 1979), pp. 209–210.
23 Interview with Zainal Abidin, Banda Aceh, 14 February 2009, p. 11.
24 *Ibid.*, p. 12.
25 *Ibid.*
26 *Ibid.*, p. 20.
27 *Ibid.*
28 *Ibid.*, p. 12.
29 'Chronologis Kedjadian2 jang Berhubungan dengan Gerakan 30 September Didaerah Kodam-I/Atjeh' in *Laporan Tahunan Lengkap Kodam-I/Kohanda Atjeh, Tahun 1965* (Banda Aceh: Kodam-I Banda Aceh, 1 February 1966), p. 9.
30 'Surat-Keputusan No: KEP/PEPELRADA 29/10/1965', Banda Aceh, 20 October 1965.
31 *Ibid.*, p. 1.
32 These organisations are listed as including Pemuda Rakjat, Gerwani, BTI, SOBSI, Lekra, CGMI, PPI, IPPI, Perhimi (*Perhimpunan Mahasiswa Indonesia*: Indonesian University Students' Association) and HSI (*Himpunan Sardjana Indonesia*: Association of Indonesian Scholars). Perhimi was an organisation for Chinese Indonesian university students. It became officially affiliated to Baperki in 1965. HSI was affiliated with the PKI.
33 'Surat-Keputusan No: KEP/PEPELRADA 29/10/1965', Banda Aceh, 20 October 1965, p. 2.
34 'PKI Sebagai Organisasi Terlarang: Keputusan Presiden/Panglima Tertinggi Angkatan Bersendjata Republik Indonesia/Mandataris MPRS/Pemimpin Besar Revolusi No. 1/3/1966', in Alex Dinuth (ed.), *Dokumen Terpilih Sekitar G.30.S/PKI* (Jakarta: Intermasa, 1997), pp. 168–169.
35 On 15 October, Suharto presented a speech to the *Front Nasional* in Jakarta in the capacity of 'Minister/Commander of the Armed Forces'. 'Presiden Soekarno Mengangkat Mayor Jenderal TNI Soeharto Sebagai Menteri/Panglima Angkatan Darat' and 'Pidato Sambutan Men/Pangad Mayor Jenderal TNI Soeharto di Depan PB. Front Nasional, 15 October 1965', in Alex Dinuth (ed.), *Dokumen Terpilih*, pp. 101, 105–118.

36 'Surat-Keputusan No: KEP/PEPELRADA 29/10/1965', Banda Aceh, 20 October 1965, p. 3.
37 'Chronologis', p. 9.
38 *Laporan Tahunan Lengkap*, p. 71.
39 *Ibid.*
40 Julius Pour, *Gerakan 30 September: pelaku, pahlawan & petualang* (Jakarta: Kompas, 2010), p. 85.
41 Ulf Sundhaussen, *The Road to Power: Indonesian Military Politics, 1945–1967* (Kuala Lumpur: Oxford University Press, 1982), p. 193.
42 Interview with Dahlan Sulaiman, Banda Aceh, 29 December 2011, p. 28.
43 *Ibid.*, p. 33.
44 *Ibid.*, p. 32.
45 *Ibid.*, p. 33.
46 *Ibid.*, p. 34.
47 *Ibid.*, p. 33.
48 *Ibid.*, p. 13.
49 Interview with Zainuddin Hamid, "Let Bugeh", Banda Aceh, 17 January 2010, p. 9.
50 *Ibid.*, p. 8.
51 *Ibid.*
52 *Ibid.*
53 That Bugeh told me so much may appear to contradict this, but it should be recalled that the only time Bugeh explicitly mentioned that he participated in the killings was when he thought I could not understand him (i.e. when he broke into Acehnese). As Oppenheimer has explained, perpetrators of the genocide have historically used partial admissions to enhance their prestige and power over the community. The process of making explicit what had previously only been partially alluded to acts to 'short-circuit' official propaganda accounts of the genocide. Joshua Oppenheimer, 'Show of Force: Film, Ghosts and Genres of Historical Performance in the Indonesian Genocide', PhD thesis, University of the Arts London, 2004, pp. 63, 196.
54 Interview with Dahlan Sulaiman, Banda Aceh, 29 December 2011, p. 29. As explained in chapter 2, the Darul Islam is still treated with great reverence in Aceh and links between the Darul Islam and the military leadership are studiously avoided.
55 *Ibid.*, pp. 29–30.
56 *Ibid.*, p. 30.
57 'Pertahanan Sipil/HANRA', in *Laporan Bupati Kepala Daerah T. Ramli Angkasah dalam memimpin Pemerintahan Kabupaten Aceh Utara mulai April 1965 s/d Mei 1966 disampaikan dalam Sidang Paripurna ke 1/1966 DPRD-GR Kabupaten Aceh Utara di Lhokseumawe tanggal*, 15 Juni 196[6].
58 There has yet to be a systematic study of the role of Hansip/Hanra in the Indonesian genocide. Hansip/Hanra also appear to have played a key role in the killings in North Sumatra, including participating in the transportation of detainees to military-controlled killings sites and guarding these killing sites. Members of Hansip/Hanra were also involved in the execution process. Amir Hasan Nast BA, *Embun Berdah* (self published, undated manuscript, in author's possession), pp. 38–56; and, Interview with Joshua Oppenheimer, Sydney, Australia, 7 June 2013.
59 'Pertahanan Sipil/HANRA', p. 1.
60 A 'touring information campaign' was also carried out at this time, apparently as part of a public relations effort. Point a(5) of the document explains: "Since the middle of October 1965 until the end of October 1965, a touring information campaign by officials has already been carried out under a single Command [including both] the Sub-Region Defence Command/[district-level] Defence Sector Command (*Subdahan/Kosekhan*) to provide a meaningful explanation to the entire population in the district of North Aceh in relation to the annihilation of G30S and Confrontation against Neo-Col[onialist]-Im[perialist] British Malaysia."

61 Emphasis added. *Ibid.*
62 It is not known that 'Kimikaju' stands for.
63 *Ibid.*, pp. 1–2.
64 As detailed in chapter 2, the Aceh Military Command calculated 18.7% of North Aceh's population were active Hansip/Hanra members or members of active student militia groups during the time of the genocide.
65 'Pertahanan Sipil/HANRA', p. 2.
66 *Ibid.*, pp. 1–2.
67 These 'Coastal Observation Posts' were located in Kuala Samalanga, Udjong Radja Samalanga, Tjalok Samalanga, Kuala Peudada, Kuala Djeumpa Bireuen, Kuala Radja Bireuen, Kuala Djangka Peusangan, Kuala Tjeurape Mon Keulaju Gandapura, Kuala Blang Lantjang Tjunda, Kuala Mamplam Tjunda, Kuala Keureutue Tanah Pasir, Kuala Ulee Rubek Seunuddon, Kuala Pase Geudong, Kuala Udjong Blang Lhokseumawe, Teupin Mane Bireuen, Tjot Girek Lhosukon, Blang Pulo Tjunda, Geulanggang Labu Mtg.Glp.dua, Tjot Gapu Bireuen and Tambue Samalanga. *Ibid.*, p. 2. The location of these posts suggests the military command in North Aceh was also involved in operations in neighbouring Bireuen.
68 Emphasis added. *Ibid.*
69 *Ibid.*, p. 32.
70 Considering the large number of active Hansip/Hanra personnel present in the district and throughout Aceh at the time of the genocide (for figures, see chapter 2), it would appear the role of the military trained and coordinated paramilitaries has so far been underestimated.
71 Interview with "Hamid", Lhokseumawe, 19 December 2011, pp. 12, 17.
72 *Ibid.*, p. 13.
73 *Ibid.*
74 *Ibid.*, p. 14.
75 *Ibid.*, p. 17.
76 Interview with "Sjam", Lhokseumawe, 19 December 2011, p. 5.
77 *Ibid.*, p. 6.
78 *Ibid.*, p. 5.
79 The Indonesian (*orang yang dibawa*) is gender-neutral.
80 Interview with "Hamid", Lhokseumawe, 19 December 2011, p. 14.
81 Interview with "Basri" (a pseudonym), Lhokseumawe, 19 December 2011, p. 14.
82 Interview with "Hamid", Lhokseumawe, 19 December 2011, p. 15.
83 Examples of "invulnerability", as retold by perpetrators, can be found in Amir Hasan Nast BA, *Embun Berdarah*, p. 56; 'Mochamad Samsi: Haram Membunuh Cicak Jika Belum Membunuh Kafir', *Tempo*, 1–7 October 2012, p. 66; and Joshua Oppenheimer, 'Show of Force', pp. 145–146.
84 Joshua Oppenheimer, 'Show of Force', pp. 147–148.
85 Interview with "Sjam", Lhokseumawe, 19 December 2011, p. 6.
86 Interview with Mun, Lhokseumawe, 19 December 2011, p. 1.
87 "Mahmud" is a pseudonym. Interview with "Tjoet", Kampung X, Bireuen, 11 February 2009, p. 4.
88 *Ibid.*, p. 5.
89 *Ibid.*, p. 4.
90 *Ibid.*, p. 5.
91 *Ibid.*, p. 8.
92 *Ibid.*, p. 6.
93 *Ibid.*, p. 8.
94 The name and location of "Kampung Y" has been withheld to protect the identities of interviewees.
95 *Ibid.*
96 *Ibid.*, p. 24.

97 *Ibid.*, p. 25.
98 *Ibid.*, p. 8. "Tjoet" was told this information by villagers.
99 Interview with "Jamil", Kampung X, Bireuen, 11 February 2009, p. 5.
100 *Ibid.*, p. 6.
101 *Ibid.*
102 *Ibid.*, p. 15.
103 *Ibid.*, pp. 15–16.
104 "Daoed" is a pseudonym. *Ibid.*, pp. 16–17.
105 *Ibid.*, p. 18.
106 *Ibid.*, p. 19.
107 *Ibid.*, p. 27.
108 *Ibid.*, p. 19.
109 *Ibid.*, p. 26.
110 *Ibid.*, p. 29.
111 *Ibid.*, p. 30.
112 *Ibid.*, pp. 5–6.
113 *Ibid.*, pp. 31–39.
114 *Ibid.*, p. 40.
115 "Muchtar's" identity has been withheld to protect "Jamil". Interview with "Jamil", Kampung X, Bireuen, 11 February 2009, pp. 47, 49.
116 *Ibid.*, p. 48.
117 *Ibid.*, p. 49.
118 *Ibid.*, p. 12.
119 Due to the lunar cycle upon which the Islamic calendar is based, there were two months of Ramadan in 1965, the first between 4 January and 4 February 1965 and the second beginning on 24 December and running for a lunar month. The final date, in late January 1966, is not given. 'Almenak "Waspada" 1965' (Ngajogyakarta: Jajasan Penerbitan Pesat, n.d.), p. 11.
120 Interview with "Jamil", Kampung X, Bireuen, 11 February 2009, p. 12.
121 'PKI dan seluruh ormasnja dibubarkan di Atjeh', *Kompas*, 23 December 1965.
122 'Chronologis', p. 21.
123 Interview with "Jamil", Kampung X, Bireuen, 11 February 2009, p. 12.
124 *Ibid.*, p. 13.
125 *Ibid.*
126 'Chronologis', p. 12.
127 Interview with "Hamid", Lhokseumawe, North Aceh, 19 December 2011, p. 33.
128 It is not known what 'RPD' stands for.
129 'Chronologis', p. 14.
130 *Ibid.*, p. 15.
131 *Ibid.*, p. 16.
132 The names of those detained are listed as: "Rama, Gayo PKI Secretary; M. Daud, Leadership Council; Sedjak, Leadership Council; M. Jacob, Leadership Council; Idris Lekra; Aman Siti Aisjah, PKI Leader for Lampahan [27km from Takengon]; Misman, Pemuda Rakjat; Suwandy, Pemuda Rakjat; Daud Helmy, Pemuda Rakjat; and Achmad Banra alias Aman Labu". 'Chronologis', p. 7.
133 The names of those detained are listed as: "Kasim, an advisor to the PKI; Chaliddin, Chief Judge for Central Aceh; BTI members Mangun, Bonai and Kaiman; Dasimin from Pemuda Rakjat; and Abd. Karim, Djaharuddin, Sukirman, Abu[unclear], M. Junus, Skardo, Ramelan and Untung from the PKI". *Ibid.*, p. 12.
134 Interview with "Abdullah", Takengon, Central Aceh, 9 February 2009, p. 11.
135 *Ibid.*
136 *Ibid.*, p. 10.
137 *Ibid.*, p. 15.
138 *Ibid.*, p. 12.

139 Interview with Ibrahim Kadir, Takengon, Central Aceh, 7 February 2009, p. 3.
140 Second interview with Ibrahim Kadir, Takengon, Central Aceh, 8 February 2009, p. 1.
141 Interview with Ibrahim Kadir, Takengon, Central Aceh, 7 February 2009, p. 6.
142 *Ibid.*, p. 8. The use of the term "rubbish being thrown away" has parallels with language used by death squad members in Medan during the genocide. *The Act of Killing* extended transcripts, MM Disc 1: 0 and MM Disc 3: 6.
143 Interview with Ibrahim Kadir, Takengon, 7 February 2009, p. 8.
144 *Ibid.*, p. 9.
145 Second interview with Ibrahim Kadir, Takengon, Central Aceh, 8 February 2009, p. 2.
146 *Ibid.*
147 *Ibid.*
148 *Ibid.*
149 Interview with "Latifah", Banda Aceh, 15 February 2009, pp. 3, 8.
150 Second interview with Ibrahim Kadir, Takengon, Central Aceh, 8 February 2009, p. 2.
151 *Ibid.*
152 *Ibid.*
153 *Ibid.*
154 James R. Bowen, *Sumatran Politics and Poetics: Gayo History, 1900–1989* (New Haven: Yale University Press, 1991), p. 120.
155 Second Interview with Ibrahim Kadir, Takengon, Central Aceh, 8 February 2009, p. 2.
156 *Ibid.*
157 *Ibid.*, p. 3.
158 *Ibid.*
159 James R. Bowen, *Sumatran Politics and Poetics*, p. 120.
160 Interview with T.M. Yatim, Meulaboh, West Aceh, Aceh, 3 December 2011, p. 10.
161 The formation and activities of KAMI/KAPPI in Aceh are discussed in chapter 7.
162 Interview with T.M. Yatim, Meulaboh, West Aceh, Aceh, 3 December 2011, pp. 13–14.
163 *Ibid.*, p. 12.
164 *Ibid.*, p. 13.
165 *Ibid.*, pp. 11, 16.
166 *Ibid.*, p. 14.
167 *Ibid.*, p. 16.
168 *Ibid.*, p. 13.
169 Here Yatim appears to be describing a group sexual attack against the woman that preceded her murder.
170 *Ibid.*, p. 16.
171 The names of those killed are listed as: "Paiman (Sabupri/Lekra); Marikam (PKI Seumajam); and Anwar (PKI Meulaboh)". 'Chronologis', p. 11.
172 The names of those killed are listed as Tgk. Mak Piah and Usman, both from the BTI in Teunom. *Ibid.*, p. 12.
173 The Chronology explains: "There have been killings (*telah terdjadi pembunuhan*) of members of the PKI/its mass or[ganisations] in the region of the T. Umar Subdahan . . . the names [of those killed] include . . . Mak Isa, PKI Teunom; Ahmad, Pemuda Rakjat; Ponijem, Gerwani; Sampir Amir Jusuf and Marikun, Pemuda Rakjat; Sulaiman Pd. Head of the BTI; Paimin, Sarbupri; Ngadiman, Head of Gerwani; Badai, a sympathiser of the PKI/Head from Pula Ie Residency; Ali, PKI Sinabang; Imam Sjafie Sjamsudin, Pemuda Rakjat Sinabang; Rakimsjidin, Pemuda Rakjat Meulaboh and several other people whose [identities] are unknown." *Ibid.*, p. 13.
174 *Ibid.*, p. 15.
175 The names of those killed are listed as: "Li Lion Su, alias Lukman, 'an Indonesian citizen' (WNI: *Warga Negara Indonesia*, the implication being that Li Lion Su was an Indonesian-born member of Aceh's Chinese community, or a naturalized Indonesian

citizen), Lio Kok Men, an Indonesian citizen (*WNI*), Noi Jie Nam, WNI and Phan Kin Fat, alias Adek".

176 The entry in the Chronology reads: "There has been a killing by the people (*telah ter-djadi pembunuhan oleh massa rakjat*) in West Aceh of members of the PKI/its mass org[anisations]/PKI sympathisers of 21 people in the Laheun Ka Bubon and Peu-rembeu area including: Jusuf Tjut, Petua Adji, M. Jusuf, Tjin Ie Sub, alias Atok, an Indonesian Citizen (*WNI*).[and member of] Pemuda Rakjat; Njak Man, BTI, and Tai Waw, alias Tani Pin, an Indonesian Citizen (*WNI*) [and member of] Pemuda Rakjat; Abd. [name unclear], Si Noh, Hasan, Razali Djunet, T. Kader, T. Zainal Abidin, BTI; Muhammad Ali, Pemuda Rakjat; Senen, Sarbupri; Paiman, Sarbupri; Atma Dimodjo, Sarbupri; Najak Husin and Sjamsari, Head of Partindo/the illegal PKI."

177 *Ibid.*

178 The victim is identified as "Lampau". *Ibid.*, p. 18.

179 Interview with "Ali", Sama Dua, South Aceh, 6 December 2011, pp. 9, 11.

180 *Ibid.*, p. 10.

181 Interview with "Oesman", Tapaktuan, South Aceh, 6 December 2011, p. 13.

182 No specific incident is recorded in the Military Chronology as occurring on 11 Octo-ber in South Aceh. The first deaths in the district are recorded as occurring on 14 October. 'Chronologis', pp. 5, 8.

183 The names of those killed include the five people listed as killed on 14 October, as well as: "Tgk. Chalidin, 45, Head of the South Aceh BTI; H. Nur Akbar, 35, Secretary of the PKI's South Aceh District Committee (*Sie Komite: Propinsie Komite*); Ach-maddjahbuddin, 45, a member of the PKI's Subdistrict Committee (*Sub Sie Komite: Sub Provinsie Komite*) in Samadua; S.K. Hasjim, 30, a member of the PKI's Subdis-trict Committee in Klut Utara; Anji, 40, a 'financial source' for the PKI and its affili-ated mass organisations; Sutan Damar, 50, the 'Ka Sub Sie Komite PKI' (presumably, *Kepala Sub Provinsie PKI*: PKI Subdistrict Level Committee Head) in Batee, Blang Pidie; and Rahman, Nanjan and T. Zainal Abidin, all 40, and members of the PKI's Subdistrict Committee in Batee, Blang Pidie". 'Chronologis', p. 17.

184 Interview with "Ali", Sama Dua, South Aceh, 6 December 2011, pp. 10–11.

185 *Ibid.*, pp. 9–10.

186 'Chronologis', p. 11.

187 The names of those arrested include: "Hasan Abady, 48, from Hilir *kampung*; Djoha-nis, 25, from Padang *kampung*; Amiruddin, a post office worker, 30, from Kampung Lho'Bengkuang; M. Hatta, 48, from Gunung Kerambil *kampung*; A. Gafar, 40, from Lho'Bengkuang; and Ganjong, 20, from Paras *kampung*, Tapa'tuan". *Ibid.*, p. 19.

188 The names of those listed as detained include: "Fatimah Zahara, 22, from Tapaktuan; Darsinah 22 and Zulbaidah, 22, both from Kampung Hulu Tapaktuan; Ratna, 18, and Aminah, 40, both from Kampung Kotafadjar; Nurlela, 25, Head of Gerwani in Kam-pung Terbangan; and M. Ladjur, 22, from the 'CSI PKI' (it is not known what 'CSI PKI' stands for) in Klut Utara". *Ibid.*

189 Interview with "Ali", Sama Dua, South Aceh, 6 December 2011, p. 18.

190 'Pernjataan', Djulok, East Aceh, 28 October 1965.

191 It is not clear why a Tjatur Tunggal body, the predecessor of the Pantja Tunggal, was retained at the subdistrict level in Djulok. The members of the Djulok Tjatur Tung-gal are listed as comprising of the Wedana (District Chief), a Puterpra Officer, a Police Commander and the Periodic Head of the *Front Nasional*. Under the original Tjatur Tunggal structure a representative of the *Front Nasional* would not have been included. Instead, the fourth place would have been taken by a representative of the judiciary, who is not included here. It is possible that this body in Djulok was still called the Tjatur Tunggal because for some anomalous reason it did not have a rep-resentative from the judiciary and thus had *four* (i.e. 'Tjatur', four, not 'Pantja', five) members, although it more closely resembled the Pantja Tunggal due to inclusion of a *Front Nasional* representative. This is odd, however, as the military was trying phase

out Tjatur Tunggal bodies in favour of Pantja Tunggal bodies during this period. Tjutur Tunggal bodies are also recorded as operating in Pidie, Bireuen and Djeumpa in North Aceh during the time of the genocide.

192 The five political parties represented are NU, PSII, PNI, Ansor, PMI (*Pemuda Muslim Indonesia*: Indonesian Muslim Youth) and a 'peasant' representative. 'Pernjataan', Djulok, East Aceh, 28 October 1965, p. 2.

193 *Ibid.*, pp. 1–2.

194 Emphasis added. *Ibid.*, p. 1.

195 'President Sukarno's First Press Interview After the Collapse of the September 30th Movement', 14 October 1965, in 'Selected Documents Relating to the "September 30th Movement" and Its Epilogue', *Indonesia*, Vol. 1 (April 1966), p. 154.

196 'Nekolim: Membangun projek Nekolim Malaysia, sebagai pangkalan militer asing jang dengan langsung ditundjukan kepada rakjat si Malaysia, Brunai, Serawak dan Sabah, disamping tudjuannja untuk mengepung langsung Indonesia', Medan, 20 October 1965, in Letdjen A.J. Mokoginta, *Koleksi Pidato2/Kebidjaksanaan Panglima Daerah Sumatra* (Medan: Koanda Sumatera, 1966), p. 181.

197 'Pernjataan', Djulok, East Aceh, 28 October 1965, p. 3.

198 'Pernjataan Kebulatan Tekad Rakjat Ketjamatan Idi Rajeuk, Kabupaten Atjeh Timur, tentang peristiwa apa jg menamakan dirinja "Gerakan 30 September"', Idi, East Aceh, 30 October 1965, pp. 1–2.

199 *Ibid.*, p. 1.

200 'Oknum', lit. 'element' is a dehumanising term to describe a member of an organisation or movement. For a discussion of the use of this term by the military, see Loren Ryter, 'Pemuda Pancasila: The Last Loyalist Free Men of Suharto's Order?', in Benedict Anderson (ed.), *Violence and the State in Suharto's Indonesia* (Ithaca, New York: Cornell Southeast Asia Program Publications, 2002, originally 2001), p. 126.

201 The phrase in italics is underlined in the original, other emphasis added. 'Pernjataan Kebulatan Tekad Rakjat Ketjamatan Idi Rajeuk, Kabupaten Atjeh Timur, tentang peristiwa apa jg menamakan dirinja "Gerakan 30 September"', Idi, East Aceh, 30 October 1965, pp. 1–2.

202 Hannah Arendt, *Eichmann in Jerusalem: A Report on the Banality of Evil* (New York: Penguin Books, 2006, originally 1963), p. 157.

203 *The Act of Killing*, Adi Zulkadry's voice-over during his family trip to the mall; Also, *The Act of Killing* extended transcripts, MM Disc 4, 1.

204 Interview with Joshua Oppenheimer, Sydney, Australia, 7 June 2013.

205 Rusdi Sufi and M. Munir Aziz, *Peristiwa PKI di Aceh: Sejarah Kelam Konflik Ideologis di Serambi Mekkah* (Banda Aceh: C.V. Boebon Jaya, 2008, originally 2006), p. 127.

206 Interview with Rusdi Sufi, Banda Aceh, 16 December 2010.

207 The document includes the pledge to: "Completely support the policies (*Mendukung sepenuhnja kebidjaksanaan*) of: 1) The Mandala Satu Commander (*PANGLATU*): 2) PANGDAHAN A/The Level I Pantja Tunggal I for Aceh Special Region: 3) Defence Sector Command (*KOSEKHAN*)/The Level II Pantja Tunggal for East Aceh: to completely annihilate the "30 September Movement." 'Pernjataan Kebulatan Tekad Rakjat Ketjamatan Idi Rajeuk, Kabupaten Atjeh Timur, tentang peristiwa apa jg menamakan dirinja "Gerakan 30 September"', Idi, East Aceh, 30 October 1965, p. 2.

208 The five political parties represented are PNI, IP-KI, NU, PSII and PI Perti. '[The first line of the title of the document is missing as a result of previous photocopying] Darul Aman tentang peristiwa apa jang menamakan dirinja Gerakan 30 September', Darul Aman, East Aceh, 2 November 1965, p. 1.

209 The only difference between the two documents is that the second document was signed by the Assistant Subdistrict Chief (*Wedana*) rather than by the Darul Aman Tjatur Tunggal, and is presented as a 'Declaration from the Darul Aman Subdistrict Office'. 'Pernjataan dari Kantor Ketjamatan Darul Aman', Darul Aman, East Aceh, 30 November 1965, p. 1.

210 This document has been heavily distorted through poor photocopying and is illegible in parts. It includes the pledge that "we [the Kotabinjai subdistrict government] are ready to assist the military to annihilate the 30 September Movement". '[Title unclear]', Kotabinjai, East Aceh, 1 December 1965.

211 'Pernjataan No. 068/1965', Partai Indonesia, Langsa, East Aceh, 14 October 1965.

212 This pledge was forwarded to the national Partindo leadership in Jakarta, Mokoginta and Djuarsa, Aceh's Governor and members of the provincial and East Aceh military and civilian leadership. It was also sent to Radio Republik Indonesia in Banda Aceh and Medan and the "press/daily newspapers" in Banda Aceh and Medan. *Ibid.*

213 Untitled document, signed by Gerakan Pemuda Marhaenis and Persatuan Tani Nasional Indonesia, Idi, East Aceh, 20 October 1965.

214 'Pernjataan No. 97/J/PAT/1965', Gerakan Pemuda Marhaenis and Persatuan Tani Nasional, Idi, East Aceh, 29 November 1965.

215 'Pernjataan No. 001/Pol/D.P.T./1965', Dewan Pemimpin Tjabang Gerakan Wanita Marhaenis Atjeh Timur, Langsa, East Aceh, 9 November 1965, pp. 1–2.

216 This document was forwarded to Sukarno, Suharto, Mokoginta and Djuarsa. It was also sent to the national leadership of the Marhaenist Women's Movement and the PNI in Jakarta. *Ibid.*, p. 2.

217 See, 'Partai Sjarikat Islam Indonesia Anak Tjabang Ketj. Seunagan, No. 15/AT/1965', Pempimpin Anak Tjabang Partai Sjarikat Islam Indonesia Ketjamatan Seunagan, East Aceh, 14 October 1965; 'Pemimpin Daerah Al Djamiatul Washlijah [Alwaslijah] Daerah Tingkat II, Langsa, Atjeh Timur, No. 31/PD/AW/1965', Langsa, East Aceh, 22 October 1965; 'Pemimpin Daerah Al Djamiatul Washlijah Daerah Tk. II Aceh Timur dan Pimpinan Fakultas Tarbijah Fakultas Ekonomi Malikussaleh Universitas Langsa', Langsa, East Aceh, 22 October 1965; 'Pernjataan', Pengurus Partai Nahdatul Ulama, Sungai Raja, East Aceh, 27 October 1965; and, 'Pernjataan No. J-161/1965', Pimpinan Muhammadijah Daerah I, Langsa, East Aceh, 29 November 1965.

218 'Partai Sjarikat Islam Indonesia Anak Tjabang Ketj. Seunagan, No. 15/AT/1965', Pempimpin Anak Tjabang Partai Sjarikat Islam Indonesia Ketjamatan Seunagan, East Aceh, 14 October 1965.

219 'Pernjataan', Pengurus Partai Nahdatul Ulama, Madjelis wakil Tjabang Simpang Raja, Sungai Raja, East Aceh, 27 October. This is an example of religious identity (or lack of religious identity, i.e. perceived atheism) being used to define the target group and as a justification for the annihilation of this target group.

220 'Pernjataan: No. J-161[?]/1965', Pimpinan Muhammadijah Daerah I Atjeh Timur, Langsa, East Aceh, 29 November 1965, p. 1.

221 *Ibid.*, p. 2.

222 Interview with "Saifuddin", Idi, East Aceh, 18 December 2011, pp. 23, 28–29.

223 *Ibid.*, p. 22.

224 *Ibid.*, p. 20.

225 *Ibid.*, p. 29.

226 *Ibid.*, p. 28.

227 *Ibid.* The idea of former killing sites and grave sites associated with the genocide being "haunted" (*angker*) is quite common throughout Indonesia. Annie Pohlman has observed that the term '*angker*', which is also used to describe sacred sites, or sites that are 'eerie' or 'terrible', "implies an ambiguous state of being both known/remembered and purposefully avoided/forgotten . . .". Annie Pohlman, 'Telling Stories about Torture in Indonesia: Managing Risk in a Culture of Impunity', *Oral History Forum d'histoire orale*, Vol. 33 (2013), Special Issue "Confronting Mass Atrocities", p. 8. Examples of sites associated with the genocide being described as "*angker*" can also be found in Joshua Oppenheimer, 'Show of Force', pp. 218–219.

228 Interview with "Karim" and "Aminah", Village 2, Tamiang, East Aceh, 12 December 2011, p. 16.

229 *Ibid.*

230 *Ibid.*, p. 7.
231 *Ibid.*, pp. 20–21.
232 *Ibid.*, p. 10.
233 *Ibid.*, pp. 20–21.
234 *Ibid.*, p. 22.
235 The name and location of "X Mountain" has been withheld to protect the identities of interviewees.
236 *Ibid.*, p. 23.
237 *Ibid.*, p. 17.
238 The name and location of "Village 3" has been withheld to protect the identities of interviewees.
239 Interview with "Taufik", Village 1, Tamiang, East Aceh, 18 December 2011, p. 2.
240 *Ibid.*, p. 2.
241 'Chronologis', p. 8.
242 Those arrested are named as D. M. Jamil, Dulsalam, Jatimo, M. Nur Siregar, M. Nur Achmadi, M. Kasim, Miskam and Tukiran. *Ibid.*, pp. 7, 9.
243 *Ibid.*, p. 10.
244 'Chronologis', p. 12.
245 The name appears to have four letters, ending in 'li'. 'Chronologis', p. 13.
246 *Ibid.*, p. 15.
247 There is other evidence presented of such "resistance" throughout the Chronology. Commonly this resistance is recorded as a sighting of an "armed group" of PKI members. For example, see 'Chronologis', pp. 8, 12, 13, 14, 16, 17, 21.
248 James T. Siegel, *The Rope of God* (Ann Arbor: University of Michigan Press, 2000, originally 1969), p. 414.
249 The military recorded "illegal flights" (*blackflight*), "illegal boat arrivals" (*blacksail*) and "infiltration" (*infiltrasi*) operations in the province for the whole of 1965. It also kept a table of individuals who had been arrested for "subversive actions" and alleged breaches of the 1963 Subversion Act (*PenPres11/1963*), beginning in December 1964, suggesting that such information was originally linked to pre–1 October military campaigns in the province and was largely propagandistic in nature, as there is no evidence that there were any major military operations in Aceh in 1965 prior to 1 October, with the exception of the military's own training mobilisations. 'Grafiek: Kedjadian Selama Tahun-1965 Didaerah Kodam-I Atjeh' and 'Daftar: Oknum2 Jang Melanggar Pen. Pres. NR.-11/1965 Didaerah Kodam-I Atjeh dan Dikenakan Tahanan Dalam Tahun 1965', pp. 1–6, in *Laporan Tahunan Lengkap Kodam-I/Kohanda Atjeh, Tahun 1965* (Banda Aceh: Kodam-I Banda Aceh, 1 February 1966).
250 See, David Chandler, *Voices From S-21: Terror and History in Pol Pot's Secret Prison* (Berkeley and Los Angeles: University of California Press, 1999), pp. 127–137; and John Roosa, 'The Truths of Torture: Victims' Memories and State Histories in Indonesia', *Indonesia* (April 2008), pp. 31–49.
251 An interesting study of how individuals psychologically adapt to the role of "guard" or "interrogator" can be found in Phillip Zimbardo, *The Lucifer Effect: Understanding How Good People Turn Evil* (New York: Random House, 2008). For a discussion of the process of dehumanisation, see David Livingstone Smith, *Less Than Human: Why We Demean, Enslave, and Exterminate Others* (New York: St. Martin's Press, 2011).
252 'Chronologis', p. 15.
253 *Ibid.* The cited (estimate) figure of 10,000 attendees is comparable with earlier cited demonstration attendee numbers in Banda Aceh (see chapter 4).
254 'Chronologis', p. 15.
255 *Ibid.*
256 *Ibid.*, p. 16.
257 *Ibid.*, p. 17.

258 *Ibid.*
259 'Daftar: Kekuatan ABRI Hansip/Hanra/Sukwan di Kohanda Atjeh', in *Laporan Tahunan Lengkap Kodam-I/Kohanda Atjeh, Tahun 1965* (Banda Aceh: Kodam-I Banda Aceh, 1 February 1966), p. 2.
260 'Chronologis', p. 17.
261 *Ibid.*
262 *Ibid.*
263 'Chronologis', p. 18.
264 G1 was the supreme intelligence coordinating body and the intelligence/covert operations arm of KOTI.
265 *Ibid.*
266 'Chronologis', p. 19.
267 'Keputusan Presiden/Panglima Tertinggi Angkatan Bersenjata Republik Indonesia/ Panglima Besar Komando Operasi Tertinggi No. 179/KOTI/165 tentang Pembentukan Kopkamtib', in Alex Dinuth (ed.), *Dokumen Terpilih*, pp. 145–147.
268 The body was first announced unilaterally by Suharto on 10 October. Harold Crouch, *The Army and Politics in Indonesia* (Jakarta: Equinox Publishing, 2007, originally 1978), p. 223.
269 'Chronologis', p. 20.
270 *Ibid.*
271 *Ibid.*
272 *Ibid.*
273 Cited in, Yen-ling Tsai and Douglas Kammen, 'Anti-communist Violence and the Ethnic Chinese in Medan, North Sumatra', in Douglas Kammen and Katharine McGregor (eds.), *The Contours of Mass Violence in Indonesia, 1965–68* (Singapore: NUS Press, 2012), p. 139.
274 Chronologis', p. 20.
275 'Keputusan-keputusan Musyawarah Alim-Ulama Sedaerah Istimwea Aceh', Majelis Permusyawaratan Ulama Daerah Istimewa Aceh, Krueng Daroy, Banda Aceh, 18 December 1965.
276 *Ibid.*
277 'Chronologis', p. 21.

7 Consolidation of the new regime

Anti-Chinese violence and purge of Aceh's civil service

How was the genocide brought to an end? Unlike the Nazi and Khmer Rouge regimes, which scrambled, unsuccessfully, during their final days to eliminate any remaining documentary and human evidence, the Indonesian regime was under no external or internal pressure to bring its genocidal activities to an end. As a result, the Indonesian regime was able to bring the genocide to an end through a political consolidation period that would last many years.

This chapter will focus on two distinct campaigns that took place in Aceh that were both concurrent with and in the immediate aftermath of the killings already described in the previous chapters. It will deal with anti-Chinese violence in the province and the military's purge of Aceh's civil service.

But first, we need to consider how the military leadership itself understood this consolidation period.

A four-stage campaign

Speaking in Medan on 11 April 1966,[1] four months after he announced the end to the military's annihilation campaign in Banda Aceh, Mokoginta identified four distinct phases in the annihilation campaign. He would describe these phases with uncanny clarity. The first three phases he depicted as such:

1 THE FIRST PERIOD, from 1 October 1965 until December 1965 was the **period of physical destruction of the G-30-S movement** (*periode penghantjuran gerakan G-30-S setjara fisik*) as an organisation, its leadership and activists.

2 THE SECOND PERIOD, from December 1965 until the beginning of March 1966 was the period of the epilogue phase to G-30-S in the areas of political, social and economic life, during which time the various events that occurred in Jakarta caused struggle between [the people and the] remnants of the PKI and its supporters. . . . The results of this reverberation were felt in the regions, including in Sumatra.

3 THE THIRD PERIOD, 11 March until 17 March [1966], was the period in which politics was determined and the height of the socio-political crisis in this country of ours, during which [time], with the President's

Letter of Instruction to the Commander of the Armed Forces [the *Super-semar*: *Surat Perintah Sebelas Maret*, Order of March Eleventh], steps were taken to guarantee safety and order and the stability of the government, along with the personal safety and authority of the President and his teachings, which was subsequently followed up with Presidential Decree No. 1/3/1966 on 12 March 1966, which dissolved the PKI and its Mass Org[anisations], declaring it to be an illegal party.[2]

Here Mokoginta not only confirms the "physical destruction" of the "G-30-S movement", but explains that this phase of killings was but the first stage of a larger campaign by the military to seize and then consolidate state power.

The second period within Mokoginta's schematisation, the so-called "epilogue phase", between December 1965 and March 1966, meanwhile, saw a consolidation of the military's position. This period witnessed the formation of the military-sponsored Indonesian Student Action Front (KAMI: Indonesian Student Action Front) and Indonesian High School Student and Youth Action Front (KAPPI: *Kesatuan Aksi Pemuda Pelajar*) death squads. It also saw the launch of the of the 'Tritura' (*Tri Tuntutan Rakyat*: Three Demands of the People) campaign. Initially led by KAMI in Jakarta, the Tritura campaign called for the lowering of prices, the formal banning of the PKI and a purge of the cabinet. It was instrumental in strengthening the military leadership's position vis à vis Sukarno.

This period also saw the outbreak of ethnic-based killings of members of the Chinese community in Aceh.

The third period, which began on 11 March 1966, meanwhile, is identified by Mokoginta as "the period in which politics was determined". It covers the first week following Sukarno's effective transfer of power to Suharto through 'Supersemar', the '11 March Order', which formalised Suharto's effective seizure of state power. It is this Order, produced five months after the launch of the military's annihilation campaign, that is commonly referred to as evidence that the military launched a coup against Sukarno.[3]

The 11 March Order was secured by the military after a concerted pressure campaign led by KAMI and KAPPI demonstrations and overt military action in the capital.[4] Exactly how this Order was extracted remains a matter of profound sensitivity to the post-Sukarno Indonesian state. Soekardjo Wilardjito, a former Lieutenant who had guarded the Presidential Palace in Bogor, West Java, on the night of 11 March when the Order was obtained, has persuasively argued the Order was obtained by force.

During the morning of 11 March, Sukarno, in Jakarta, addressed his cabinet and reaffirmed his commitment to Marxism in an attempt to appear firm in the face of escalating demonstrations by KAMI and KAPPI.[5] As this address was underway, pro-Suharto Brigadier General Kemal Idris and Colonel Sarwo Edhie stationed three companies of Indonesian Special Forces (RPKAD) troops in front of the Presidential Palace. The troops subsequently removed their insignia and identifications, while signalling that they were prepared to use force to strip Sukarno of what remained of his authority. This act of intimidation caused Sukarno to panic and flee the capital by helicopter for his residence in Bogor.

At midnight that night, Wilardjito has recalled, four high-ranking military officers arrived at Bogor and demanded to see the President.[6] The army officers then handed Sukarno, who was wearing his pyjamas, a pink folder containing a document.[7] Sukarno responded to seeing this document with shock, asking why the document had been issued in the name of the Military High Command instead of in the name of the President.[8] One of the officers pointed his pistol at Sukarno, telling him, "There is no time for amendments, just sign it, Sir. *Bismillah*. In the name of God, just sign it!"[9] Sukarno acquiesced and the army officers returned triumphantly to Jakarta.

Despite Sukarno's insistence that the '11 March Order' gave Suharto only limited additional powers to "restore order", Suharto used the order to consolidate his seizure of power by arresting fifteen unsympathetic ministers and effectively taking control of the Cabinet.[10]

The fourth period identified by Mokoginta, meanwhile, referred to the shift from physical annihilation to bureaucratic purges that would come to affect all levels of government and the civil service in Indonesia. It was during this period that the military leadership was able to consolidate control over the government. As he explains:

4 THE FOURTH PERIOD (the period that we are in now [April 1966]), began on 18 March 1966, when 18 Ministers[11] who were no longer trusted by the people . . . were isolated from the Cabinet and removed from the leadership of the Nation.

> It was then that the New Cabinet was formed, the perfected DWIKORA Cabinet, or what is better known as the AMPERA (*Amanat Penderitaan Rakyat*: Mandate of the People's Suffering) Cabinet. . . . This new cabinet was sworn in by the President/Sup[reme] Com[mander of the Armed Forces/Great Leader of the Revolution as mandated by the MPRS on 30 March [1966], 12 days ago.[12]

The military leadership was now in a position to consolidate its gains. It did this by creating a "New Cabinet" and removing ministers who were seen as unsympathetic to the new regime. The 30 March 1966 MPRS session, which occurred during this phase, has been described by Sundhaussen as a "major victory for Suharto", who was "confirmed as the prime policy-maker".[13] This process made official the control Suharto now enjoyed over both the executive and legislative functions of the state. Although Sukarno would retain the official title of President until 12 March 1967, the swearing-in of the new cabinet on 30 March 1966, nineteen days after the '11 March Order', formalised the military's seizure of state power that had been launched on 1 October 1965, when Suharto had assumed control over the executive functions of the Indonesian state.

Bearing in mind that the genocide had a slightly different timeline in each of Sumatra's eight provinces, it is striking how the dates given by Mokoginta (based in Medan) correspond with the waves of killings in Aceh outlined in previous chapters. Such synchronised timing points to the campaign's coordinated, inter-provincial scope. Moreover, the candid way in which Mokoginta describes the "physical destruction" of the '30 September Movement' confirms once again that the military knew perfectly well that its "annihilation campaign" meant, and was explicitly communicated to mean, the murder of the military's political opponents as part of a state-sponsored campaign of genocide.

January 1966: formation of KAMI/KAPPI in Aceh

The exact date of the formation of KAMI and KAPPI in Aceh is not known. Dahlan Sulaiman, the former death squad leader, believes that a provincial KAMI branch was formed in Banda Aceh approximately "three months" after KAMI was formed in Jakarta.[14] KAMI had been established in Jakarta in late October 1965 by anti-communist youth organisations under the direction of the national Minister for Higher Education, Brigadier General Sjarif Thajeb.[15] There the movement had close contact with the military leadership, including Kemal Idris, Sarwo Edhie and the Chief of Staff of the Jakarta Military Command, Colonel A.J. Witono, from whom it received backing and coordination.[16] On 10 January 1966, KAMI Jakarta was involved in the declaration of the 'Tritura' (Three Demands of the People) campaign launched at the University of Indonesia, where, after listening to an address by Edhie, students marched on government buildings to demand the lowering of prices, the formal banning of the PKI and a purge of the cabinet.[17] This campaign was supported by Suharto and the military leadership, and rapidly became a vehicle for criticising Sukarno and the remaining power that he possessed.[18]

From this time KAMI became increasingly radical, culminating in a mass rally on 23 January in Jakarta that broke into the State Secretariat next to the Presidential Palace.[19] Alarmed by the rising confidence and the challenge to authority that such an action presented, members of the Presidential Guard fired on the protesters, killing a student named Arief Rahman Hakim. This action inflamed the protesters and their military backers, with soldiers loyal to Suharto firing a last salute over Hakim's grave at his funeral on 25 January. The next day Sukarno dissolved KAMI, but KAMI members continued to protest in defiance of the order, formally renaming their organisation 'KAPPI' (*Kesatuan Aksi Pemuda Pelajar Indonesia*: Indonesian High School Student and Youth Action Front).[20] Combined 'KAMI/KAPPI' demonstrations continued throughout February, culminating in their support for the 11 March 1966 Order.[21] The demonstrations were an important factor in the military's consolidation of power in the capital. They were also important in Aceh, where local branches of the two organisations would play a similar role.

Dahlan Sulaiman, the former death squad leader who today works as a travel agent, has recalled that he joined KAPPI when it was first formed in Banda Aceh, when he also became involved in the Tritura campaign in the province.[22] The intention of KAMI and KAPPI in Aceh, he has said, was to achieve further systemic change than had been achieved through the violence of the killings. Sulaiman explains:

> KAPPI was formed [in Banda Aceh] because of [the political situation], because of conditions before it was formed. There'd been G30S PKI, the PKI rebellion, and then the people, especially youth and university students and high school students, they took actions against the PKI, and then, after that, the situation required that there was a more systematic change, a change that touched on all aspects of our nation at that time. Because of this, to continue the struggle to eradicate the PKI's rebellion . . . university students formed KAMI . . . which then joined with KAPPI. [KAPPI] embraced various non-communist student organisations . . . I joined KAPPI because at that time I was at university. I joined and I became one of its leaders.[23]

Sulaiman added that KAPPI in Banda Aceh was made up of "leaders of the student movement [and] youth organisations" that had "already been trained" by the military during the lead-up to the military's seizure of state power on 1 October 1965.[24] Sulaiman claims he does "not know" where KAPPI received its orders from, "but what is clear [is that] sometimes we used the masses [to attack] victims". He thus explains how KAPPI mobilised the population in a similar manner to the death squads during the periods of public killings and systematic mass killings in the province. Sulaiman then corrects himself to explain: "But this didn't happen in Aceh, that only happened in Jakarta." The purpose of KAPPI, Sulaiman says, was to do more than assist the military to implement violence. KAPPI also played an important role in advocating for structural political change. "What we did," Sulaiman continues:

> when we formed KAPPI, we had three demands, what was called Tritura. The first was to disband the PKI, but it wasn't only the PKI that was disbanded and finished off; what we wanted to do was to restructure the Indonesian political system. This meant the disbanding of the PKI had to be accompanied with a restructuring of the party and political system in Indonesia. That was first. The second [demand] was to dissolve the cabinet . . . because the cabinet . . . was no longer objective anymore, it was being made up as it went along, it was all only to do with the needs of the President at that time, to handle and accommodate the forces that existed, until the political forces . . . [that remained were only] the people that he [Sukarno] liked. It [the political system] was no longer well, that was second. We didn't only want to dissolve the cabinet . . . we wanted to restructure the bureaucracy of government.[25]

As in Jakarta, KAPPI was used in Aceh as a means of consolidating the military's seizure of power by spearheading the campaign for the systematic structural change that would see the official emergence of the New Order. In addition to campaigning to restructure the cabinet, KAMI/KAPPI would also play a prominent role in anti-Chinese violence in the province before splitting with the military over the question of leadership. This split occurred during the third and final phase of violence in the province, when Aceh's Chinese community became the target of attack.

Anti-Chinese violence in Aceh 7 October 1965–17 August 1966

Aceh's Chinese community became the target of violence in 1965–66 in two distinct ways. From 7 October, ethnic Chinese members of the PKI and other PKI-affiliated organisations, including the Consultative Body for Indonesian Citizenship (Baperki: *Badan Permusjawaratan Kewarganegaraan Indonesia*, the mass organisation for Chinese Indonesians with close informal links to the PKI), were targeted alongside "indigenous" (*pribumi*) Indonesians as part of the military's annihilation campaign against the PKI. By April 1966, indiscriminate violence against Aceh's Chinese community broke out, led by KAMI/KAPPI members who saw no reason to differentiate between the various political factions within the community. This distinct phase of violence culminated in Djuarsa issuing an order on 21 April for all "alien" Chinese to leave the province by 17 August 1966 under threat of facing violence if they remained.[26]

Research into violence against Indonesia's Chinese community during the time of the genocide has been limited. To date, this research has uncovered reports of targeted killings of ethnic Chinese in North Sumatra, Central Java, Lombok,[27] Sumbawa, South Kalimantan, West Kalimantan[28] and Aceh.[29] Despite the limited nature of this research, questions related to the nature of anti-Chinese violence in 1965–66 are controversial. Robert Cribb and Charles Coppel, for example, have argued that "there is simply no evidence for a special targeting of Chinese for murder during this period".[30] Instead, they argue, ethnic Chinese targeted during this time were targeted primarily because of their political identity, as defined by their relationship, either real or imagined, with the PKI and its affiliated organisations, including Baperki, rather than because of their ethnic identity *per se*. This argument is tied to their assertion that it is incorrect to characterise these killings as racially motivated and that, as a consequence, in their opinion, the Indonesian killings should not be described as a genocide.[31] Here I will argue that while I agree ethnic Chinese who were murdered in Aceh during the time of public and systematic mass killings (7 October–23 December 1965) were killed primarily because of their alleged relationship with the PKI, this does not mean race was absent as a motivating factor behind this violence. Moreover, evidence uncovered during my fieldwork suggests that from April 1966 ethnic Chinese in Aceh were targeted as a group. Below I will outline the contours of anti-Chinese violence in Aceh between 7 October 1965–17 August 1966. But first, I need to introduce Ho Fui Yen, Xie Jie Fang and Wak Tin Chaw, whom I met in Hong Kong in November 2011, where I had travelled to meet Asan, the sole surviving member of the Aceh PKI Secretariat.[32]

Ho Fui Yen was born in 1946 in Banda Aceh. She grew up in Peunayong, Banda Aceh's Chinatown. After finishing school, she travelled to Medan to train as a teacher. Upon completing her training, Ho returned to Banda Aceh and taught at a Chinese-language school for one year until the events of 1 October 1965 caused the school to be closed and forced Ho's family to flee the province.[33]

Xie Jie Fang was born in 1946 in Banda Aceh. He grew up in Peunayong. Xie's father had travelled to Aceh from Guandong in southern China when he was thirteen. He had travelled with a friend who often travelled between Malaya, Indonesia and China, and who had taught him the art of furniture making. After finishing school, Xie travelled to Medan to train as a teacher and graduated from training with Ho. Xie then returned to Banda Aceh to teach at the same Chinese-language school as Ho, where he taught for one year before the events of 1 October 1965 intervened and he and his family were forced to flee.[34]

Wak Tin Chaw was also born in 1946 in Banda Aceh, and grew up in Peunayong. Her father, Wang, was originally from Shandong, between Beijing and Shanghai. Wang had been a cloth merchant, but during the Japanese occupation of Aceh he and two of his close friends opened a restaurant in Peunayong, the Hap Seng Hing (Ind. *Kemenangan dan Kesenangan*, or 'Happy Victory'), which served barbecued pork. Her father was a leader of the local Chinese community and had been a member of the anti-Japanese underground. Wak has explained that the restaurant was used as venue for the clandestine anti-Japanese underground to hold meetings.[35] Wang would later play a leading role in helping to evacuate members of Aceh's Chinese community from the province following Djuarsa's 21 April expulsion order.

Importance of political identity within the Chinese community in Aceh

Ho, Xie and Wak do not describe the Chinese community in Aceh as homogenous. On the contrary, they have argued it was deeply fragmented along ideological lines. According to Ho, "[t]he Chinese community [in Aceh] was divided into two groups, one that was Kuomintang [Chinese National Party] and one that was Kunchantang [Chinese Communist Party]. One was pro-Taiwan, the other pro-Beijing."[36]

Ho, Xie and Wak were members of the pro-Beijing group. They expressed this sentiment through their membership of the Association of Overseas Chinese (the *Asosiasi Huakiao*, Ch. *Hua Chio Tsung Hui*), which had first been established in Jakarta following the establishment of diplomatic ties between Indonesia and the People's Republic of China in April 1950.[37] As part of this group they followed developments in Chinese politics and felt an affinity with the People's Republic of China. Members of Baperki were similarly part of the pro-Beijing group. They tended, however, to be more focused on domestic Indonesian politics, and were strong supporters of Sukarno's political program.[38] Chinese Indonesian members of the PKI, such as Asan, the sole surviving member of the PKI's Provincial Secretariat in Aceh, whose story will be continued later in this chapter, were primarily involved in the PKI's national campaigns and supported the Chinese Revolution through this framework, while continuing to retain close links with the broader pro-Beijing group.

On the other side of this ideological divide was the pro-Kuomintang group. This group was less influential nationally than the pro-Beijing group as a result of Indonesia's recognition of the People's Republic of China.[39] This, however, had not always been the case[40] and the pro-Kuomintang group maintained a significant presence in the country. Unfortunately, no figures are available for the early 1960s, or for Aceh specifically, but Kuomintang membership in Indonesia during the 1950s is believed to have been the largest in the world outside of Taiwan, with approximately 30% of Chinese residents in Indonesia reportedly pro-Kuomintang.[41]

The animosity between the two groups had its roots in Chinese politics, but this animosity also had manifestations within Indonesia. From February to August 1958, for example, the pro-Kuomintang group supported the Revolutionary Government of the Republic of Indonesia (PRRI: *Pemerintah Revolusioner Republik Indonesia*) rebellion, led by dissident military generals in West Sumatra, with Taiwan funnelling weapons to the rebels through Aceh.[42] Their support for the rebellion, driven by Sukarno's increasingly close relationship with the People's Republic of China, demonstrated that the pro-Kuomintang group was willing to side with the regional military leadership against Sukarno. Once the rebellion was put down, members of the group lost their places in Sukarno's government and pro-Kuomintang schools were shut down.[43] These bans fostered resentment within the group.

It is not clear how this rivalry played out in Aceh. The religious character of the Darul Islam rebellion, which was courted by the PRRI leadership,[44] may have tempered this alliance in the province. Meanwhile, universal Chinese opposition to the Japanese occupation during the Second World War, which had been enthusiastically supported by the leadership around Daud Beureu'eh, who would later lead the the Darul Islam rebellion in the province, may have tempered this alliance even further. It is clear, nonetheless, that the pro-Kuomintang group had little sympathy for Sukarno and was ideologically opposed to the PKI.

Despite this clear ideological division within Aceh's Chinese community, however, it is unlikely the average *pribumi* Indonesian citizen would have been able to differentiate between these two groups without some form of guidance or previous interaction with the community. Indeed, to members of the military-sponsored death squads – who were only too keen to blame Aceh's Chinese community for the province's political and economic problems – such a distinction may have been considered irrelevant.

Anti-Chinese racism has been a recurring theme within Indonesian politics. During the colonial period Indies society was classified by the Dutch in terms of racial divisions. Europeans, 'Foreign Orientals' (mainly Chinese and also Arabs) and 'natives' (*Inlanders*) were governed by separate laws and had different rights. Under this system local Chinese were considered to be 'native' for legal purposes by the Dutch and subject to native courts, while, at the same time, banned from owning farmland as 'non-natives'.[45] As a consequence of this restriction, local Chinese often settled in towns and became concentrated in trade-related livelihoods.

After Independence, citizenship was extended to non-*pribumi* Indonesians, including local Chinese, who had been born in Indonesia. Indonesia's Chinese community continued to be subject to discrimination however. In 1950, a government program known as the 'Benteng System' was established with the stated intention of encouraging the growth of an indigenous entrepreneurial class, in part to counter the dominance of Chinese in trade that had been promoted by previous Dutch policies. As a result of this program, *pribumi* Indonesian importers were given privileges, including the special granting of credit, licenses and the right to import certain goods.[46] These privileges were not afforded to ethnic Chinese Indonesian citizens. Despite coming under heavy criticism from Indonesia's Chinese community, these special privileges were reaffirmed in 1956, while the transfer of *pribumi*-owned enterprises to non-*pribumi* groups was also prohibited.[47] These discriminatory measures helped to legitimise feelings of resentment against Chinese people, who were blamed for Indonesia's faltering economy.[48]

In November 1959, the restrictions were extended further when a new regulation (Presidential Decree No. 10) banned non-citizen "aliens" from engaging in retail trade and mandated that they transfer their businesses to Indonesian nationals no later than 1 January 1960. This regulation is estimated to have caused an exodus of more than 100,000 Chinese Indonesians to China, while also seriously disrupting the Indonesian economy, as indigenous business owners were ill prepared to fill this gap.[49] The Presidential Decree also signified a new approach of legally differentiating between local Chinese who had become citizens and those who remained non-citizens. Many Indonesians of Chinese descent chose to support the implementation of the regulation in order to "save their own skin".[50] Unsurprisingly this caused further tensions within the community. Baperki in particular was criticised for failing to better protect the Chinese community despite its close relationship to Sukarno.[51]

Anti-Chinese sentiment, meanwhile, was encouraged by the military. In March–May 1963 a series of anti-Chinese riots broke out in West Java led by "gangs of youths", including members of the PSI and HMI, who smashed and burnt Chinese-owned shops and cars.[52] In addition to terrorising the local Chinese community, these riots were intended to embarrass Sukarno, who was seeking to establish closer relations with China, a relationship which Sukarno explained was based on the two countries' joint struggle "against imperialism and neo-colonialism".[53] General Ishak Djuarsa, then of the Siliwangi Division's "civic action" organisation, is said to have had foreknowledge of the students' plans and to have allowed the riots to grow out of hand.[54] Djuarsa had no personal aversion to encouraging racist violence. Indeed, Peter Dale Scott has drawn a direct link between these anti-Chinese riots, which were the most serious to occurr under Guided Democracy and anti-Chinese violence during the time of the genocide.[55]

Implication of China and the Chinese community in the military's attack

The implication of "China" and "Chinese people" in the events of 1 October 1965 occurred within the first few days of the military's campaign. The drawing of links between members of Indonesia's Chinese community and these events was not, however, an automatic process. After all, the PKI itself had to be retrospectively implicated. Communist China and, later, members of Indonesia's Chinese community more generally, were implicated in a similar manner. This process of implication occurred in three distinct waves that gradually extended to larger sections of the Chinese community in Aceh.

When news of the 30 September Movement broke during the morning of 1 October 1965, the military leadership and its Western allies were caught off-guard and unsure of exactly who was behind the movement. The confusing nature of the Movement meant that it was not immediately apparent how the military leadership could blame the PKI, let alone explain the PKI's motivation for involvement in such an action.[56] It was within this climate that China first began to enter the discussion.

As an anonymous US State Department official mused in their assessment of the events of 1 October in a telegram sent to the US embassy in Jakarta on 2 October 1965:

> Like Indo Army, we have long assumed that at what it considered [an] appropriate time the PKI would make overt bid for power. We were surprised that PKI chose present period for open assault re Army . . . Only tenable conclusion we have been able [to] reach . . . is that Aidit and PKI were under heavy pressure from Chicoms [Chinese Communists] to produce abrupt and prompt victory for Chicom interests in Asia.[57]

The "proof" that the US presented of China's alleged involvement in the actions of the 30 September Movement included the Movement's timing to allegedly coincide with China's National Day, held on 1 October.[58] This did not explain, however, why the Movement was named the 30 September Movement, the date it was apparently meant to be launched. Further "proof" was provided by two additional equally weak claims. The first of these claims, that "2,000 Chinese weapons" had been distributed "to communist youth and women's groups on October 1, 1965",[59] was later denied by the head of KOTI's political section, Brigadier General Soetjipto.[60] The second claim, meanwhile, that "the only embassy in Jakarta that was not flying its flag at half-mast" on 5 October, the day of the state funeral for the assassinated Generals "was the Chinese",[61] was qualified on 16 October by the US Ambassador to Indonesia Marshall Green, when he explained to US State Department officials that "most missions, including the Soviets" and Thailand did not fly their flags at half-mast or send representatives to the funerals, as the "FonOff [Foreign Office] failed to notify missions here".[62]

The manufactured nature of the US's attempt to implicate China in the actions of the 30 September Movement is perhaps best captured in Green's observation to the US State Department on 19 October 1965. As Green explained: "We have bonanza chance to nail [C]hicoms [Chinese Communists] on disastrous events in Indonesia" with a "continuation [of] covert propaganda" recommended as the "best means of spreading [the] idea of [C]hicom complicity".[63] The US hoped to implicate China and the PKI in one hit. However, the Indonesian military leadership, for the time being, took a more tentative approach. In a report sent to the US State Department on 17 October, an unidentified Indonesian military general is said to have told Green: "We already have enough enemies. We can't take on Communist China as well."[64]

Explicitly accusing China of involvement in the actions of the 30 September Movement could have exposed the new military regime to actual Chinese intervention. Such intervention might have included a severing of diplomatic ties, the withdrawal of much-needed development funds, or the actual arming of a communist insurgency movement – a situation that would have been a realisation of the military's worst nightmare. Likewise, overt Chinese support for the 30 September Movement's "coup attempt" may have exposed the Chinese government to US-led intervention. Indeed, it may have been this apparent deadlock that prevented the "1965 Affair" from escalating into an international stoush.

Recognising the volatility of the situation, the Indonesian military leadership's response was cautious. On 4 October, Suharto delivered a speech in Jakarta in which he implicated the Air Force, Pemuda Rakyat and Gerwani in the actions of the 30 September Movement, but made no mention of China.[65] On 5 October in Medan, however, Mokoginta, acting in his capacity as Inter-Regional Military Commander, had delivered his speech condemning the 30 September Movement, through which he described the Movement as a "tool of a foreign nation", in reference to China.[66]

Mokoginta's more aggressive stance appears to have been adopted in Aceh. On 6 October, the Aceh Pantja Tunggal and eight of the province's political parties would issue their 'Joint Statement', in which the 30 September Movement was described as being "in the service of Foreign Subversives".[67] While it could be argued Mokoginta and the Aceh Pantja Tunggal's claim that China was somehow behind the 30 September Movement was meant to condemn the PKI rather than the ethnic Chinese community *per se*, Aceh's Chinese community was nonetheless placed under a cloud of suspicion from this time.

7–13 October: public killings

Anti-Chinese sentiment travelled quickly throughout the province. As detailed briefly in chapter 4, posters allegedly appeared at the Lhokseumawe train station on 7 October that read:

> The PKI is replaying its old story/Madiun, attempting to change 17 August 1965 [the anniversary of Indonesian Independence] with a Peking proclamation. Aidit is the puppet master: Kidnapping is to be responded to with kidnapping, chopping up (*pertjentjangan*) [mincing] is to be responded to with chopping up (*pertjentjangan*). Destroy the PKI, *Allahu Akbar*.[68]

The reference to a "Peking proclamation" raised the spectre of Chinese sovereignty over Indonesia and alluded to the idea that China was behind the actions of the 30 September Movement.

On the same day, an anti-PKI rally had been held in Banda Aceh, which called for the PKI to be disbanded. This rally transformed into an attack against the Chinese community when, at 4pm, the Military's Chronology reports:

> a riotous demonstration by the people attacked the Pelangi shop,[69] Baperki office, Chung Hua Chung Hui (Ch. '*Hua Chiao Tsung Hui*', *Asosiasi Huakiao*: Association of Overseas Chinese) office, IPETI Stadium[70] and the houses of several Baperki leaders.[71]

This is the first attack against Baperki and the pro-Beijing Chinese community recorded in the Chronology. From this entry it appears that no difference was made between Baperki and the *Asosiasi*, or between the business and private lives of these individuals. Indeed, the targets of the attacks seem to have been targeted as part of the same initial mobilisation against the PKI.[72]

The next attack against Baperki recorded in the Chronology occurred on 9 Ocotber in Sigli, when, at 3.00pm, the Chronology reports, a demonstration was held by "members of political parties/organisations and the people" in the town who:

> demanded that the PKI and its affiliated organisations be disbanded, before continuing with the destruction of shops, including the Pah On, Ping Ping, Kim Kie, Rimbaraja shops,[73] the GPTP [*Gabubungan Perkumpulan Tionghoa Perantauan*: Federation of Overseas Chinese] office, the Baperki office, PKI office, Lekra, Pemuda Rakyat office and Gerwani office, a KBM car[74] . . . was also burnt.[75]

Baperki and *Asosiasi* members seem to have been targeted because of their perceived connection with the PKI. The specific focus on destroying Chinese-owned businesses during these early attacks, meanwhile, echoed earlier anti-Chinese violence in Indonesia. There is no way of knowing from these entries whether the targeted shops belonged to members of targeted groups, such as the PKI or Baperki, or whether they were attacked simply for being owned by "Chinese".

Meanwhile, the treatment of local Chinese members of the PKI in Aceh does not appear to have been significantly different to that experienced by Indonesian members of the PKI in the province.

The following section continues the story of Asan, the sole surviving member of the Aceh PKI leadership team. He was an active member of Aceh's pro-Beijing Chinese community. As documented in chapter 5, Asan had been targeted by the military because of his leadership position within the PKI. His close and ongoing connections with the pro-Beijing community, however, appear to have been a major factor behind his survival.

The case of Asan: part two

After cheating death on the night of his release from the police station during the second week of October 1965, Asan made his way to the Hap Seng Hing

(Ind. '*Kemenangan dan Kesenangan*' or 'Victory and Happiness') Restaurant in Peuanyong, Banda Aceh's Chinatown, which was run by Wak Tin Chaw's father, Wang.[76] Asan recalls: "I knew the owner of the restaurant was sympathetic to *Tiongkok Baru* [lit. 'New China'; a statement which implies the owner was a supporter of Mao and the People's Republic of China] and I also often ate there."[77]

After spending the night under the roof of the vegetable warehouse in Peunayong, where he had hidden after his escape from the Military Police and their executioners, Asan has recalled:

> I got down from [the roof of the vegetable warehouse] and knocked on the restaurant's door. Wang opened the door, and before he gave me permission to enter I went in. Seeing me like this he immediately reclosed the door and I openly explained I had come to ask for protection. . . . Of course, Wang found it hard to refuse, but he was also scared to agree. I am certain he understood the seriousness and dangerousness of the situation. If found out by the armed forces who were in charge it could be a disaster for his whole family. . . . He looked at me for a long time and then said, "We are both Chinese!" This really made my heart swell and I have never forgotten Wang's big-heartedness. He asked me if I had eaten, and after I told him I had, he asked me to follow him. We went out a door at the back of the restaurant, then down a small alleyway that connected to the back door of the house where he lived. I followed him upstairs into a room and he told me I could sleep there with his son that night. . . .
>
> In the morning, Wang brought me some biscuit-bread and a bottle of water . . . [he] showed me how in front of the window there was a gutter that connected to the next door's window and told me to go across and hide in there. After having the biscuit-bread and the bottle of water, I crawled along the gutter to the next-door window. I became aware it was the *Asosiasi Huakiao* office building that had been destroyed by rioters.[78] From a gap I could see down, the glass of the windows was smashed, the cupboards were also smashed with documents scattered about everywhere, the steps were also broken. . . . The building had been brutally wrecked just a few days earlier by KAMI/KAPPI[79] and that was what made this building the safest. I hid up there feeling calm all day long.
>
> In the evening Wang quietly called to me to crawl back to his house, and suggested I go down to the restaurant. As I got to the door he told me, "[w]alk straight ahead, when you get to the intersection, over the other side of the main road is a small shop with its light still on and its door wide open, go in there and there will be someone who will receive you. I went as Wang showed me, but after taking just four to five steps out onto the street two men appeared from the darkness looking right and left as if they were inspecting me and making me worry they were Islamic fundamentalist executioners[80] who were looking for and chasing me. This feeling of alarm made me begin to walk faster as I crossed the main road and looked for the shop. . . . As I went into the shop I saw the two men sit down, I did not address them and

walked quickly past them and made my way to the back [of the restaurant] and sat on a step near the toilet to catch my breath and calm myself down.

A young man [who worked at the restaurant] came over to me who was very tense and quite angrily said to me in Chinese, "Argh, nothing's happened yet you've lunged in here nervous like that. Now there are people who've seen you come in here. That Chinese man definitely knows who you are, he owns the medicine shop on the other side of the road and has a Kuomintang passport, he's a blue."[81] . . . What should I do? I looked at this young man who looked so impatient and like he wanted me to go back out and leave the place . . . I thought in my heart, if I leave now, the situation can only get more dangerous, the government armed forces who were everywhere at that time could follow me. . . . Suddenly I thought of a tactic . . . I told the young man to go to the back door and slam it as hard as he could and to scream loudly in Chinese and Indonesian for me to leave . . . let his voice be heard in the neighbouring houses so they'd think their neighbour had just thrown Asan out. . . .

I waited on the step until the neighbours had gone back into their houses . . . then the young man shut the door and took me upstairs to rest. He then told me that he was also from [the same name clan as Asan] and had gone to school in Medan. . . . [Then] a young man of about thirty emerged . . . who came over to me to talk. From what he said I could tell that he had read Mao Tse-Tung, and this made me be able to relax a bit more about staying there. After speaking for a moment he asked me to "rest well" and went into his own room. . . .

The next day, a young man who lived next door came up to meet me. He discussed how he had contacted his brother-in-law who regularly hired a truck [for his business]. [This young man, who was a friend of Wang] asked [his brother] to come to Banda Aceh to take me to Medan.[82] A few days later the truck came to the house and I got up into it without being seen because I was hidden inside a wooden box that was lifted up onto the truck. . . . Because the truck was being guarded by a soldier in uniform we were able to pass through the guard substation into Medan.[83]

After cheating death for a second time and arriving safely in Medan, Asan met with his wife and sons, who would shortly leave on board a boat, the *Kuang Hua*, for China. Asan, however, would spend many years on the run in Indonesia before finally being reunited with his family in Hong Kong.[84]

Asan's account demonstrates the strength and importance of group identity within the pro-Beijing Chinese community in Aceh. Members of this community placed their own lives, and those of their families, at risk in order to shelter Asan. Regardless of this group's thoughts about the 30 September Movement, the military's attack against the PKI, Baperki and the pro-Beijing group acted to increasingly polarise Aceh's Chinese community to either support the military's attack, or, through covert means, to attempt to support friends, comrades and family members who had already come under attack from the military.

11–18 October: intimidation of the Baperki leadership in Langsa

A rare insight into the kind of pressure Baperki members in Aceh were facing at this time can be found in a declaration signed by the Baperki leadership in Langsa, East Aceh, on 18 October 1965. This declaration explains how during the early evening of 11 October 1965, the Baperki leadership in Langsa received:

> explanations from the East Aceh District Military (*Kodim-0104*) Commander, acting as Defence Sector Commander (*Dan Sekhan*) for East Aceh, Major Iljas Mahmud . . . in the Kodim-0104 Canteen . . . [about] the coup attempt by ex-Lieut. Col. Untung . . . which was masterminded by the godless PKI and its cover [groups] and also, it keeps being mentioned, Baperki, which has become involved with these barbaric actions.[85]

The declaration also refers to a radio broadcast from Jakarta allegedly made by Sukarno, which called for:

> the **complete annihilation down to the roots** of that which calls itself the '30th September Movement' and members of the PKI and its cover [groups] which have carried out barbaric deeds, **until [they are] wiped from the face of the earth of Indonesia.**[86]

Such a broadcast, of course, was never made.[87] The purpose of this fake broadcast, or "interpretation", perhaps by Major Iljas Mahmud at the 11 October meeting, was intimidation. Someone who dared to speak on behalf of the President was calling for the extermination of the PKI and all those associated with it, including Baperki; this was a clear incitement to murder members of this group.

It is not known whether the Baperki leadership in Langsa believed in the authenticity of this broadcast, but this may have been irrelevant. Under threat of being "wiped from the face of the earth" and under the baleful eye of Mahmud, the Baperki leadership quickly produced eight resolutions based on its acceptance "of the involvement of the Baperki Organisation" in the 30 September Movement.[88] These resolutions included the following:

1. That we do not want to be implicated and do not know anything about [the actions of the group] calling itself the 30 September Movement . . . we demand that they are treated resolutely and firmly in accordance with Revolutionary law. . . .
5. We call upon [Sukarno] that the PKI and its covers be disbanded and **not be given the right to live** (*djangan diberi hak hidup lagi*) **in this Nation of the Republic of Indonesia** which is based on the "PANTJASILA" and punish those involved in G30S [the 30 September Movement] in accordance with Revolutionary law.

6   We urge the East Aceh District Military (*Kodim-0104*) Commander as the Defence Sector Commander (*Dan Sekhan*) for East Aceh and the East Aceh Pantja Tunggal to freeze all activities of the PKI and its cover [organisations] in East Aceh including punishing those [word unclear] who are involved in the G30S.

7   As a result of the act of barbaric terror which calls itself the G30S which was masterminded by the PKI and its cover [organisations], "We the members of BAPERKI Langsa" which number . . . one hundred and forty-eight people, declare that we have left the BAPERKI Langsa Organisation, and declare the that the BAPERKI Langsa Organisation is dissolved as of 18 October 1965, anything involving the BAPERKI Organisation from the date of this declaration is not our responsibility, in connection with this we have attached a list of the names of the members of BAPERKI [in Langsa] which is already dissolved.[89]

8   We stand behind [Sukarno] and are prepared to carry out various tasks to help ABRI [the Indonesian Armed Forces] . . . .[90]

The Baperki leadership in Langsa clearly wanted to distance itself from Baperki as a national organisation. This statement also suggests that Baperki in Langsa was under significant pressure to condemn the national organisation, with any wavering in this regard open to be interpreted as support for the "barbaric actions of the 30 September Movement". Meanwhile, points one and five support the idea that those allegedly involved in the 30 September Movement be dealt with "in accordance with Revolutionary law", a concept which meant the PKI and "its cover [organisations]", a term that referred to organisations deemed to be affiliated with the PKI, should "not be given the right to live in this Nation". As with similar earlier threats against the PKI and its affiliated organisations, in a context in which no deportation of such individuals was being actively pursued, such a statement must be interpreted to mean the PKI and "its cover [organisations]" should "not be given the right to live" as such.

This intimidation did not end with verbal threats. Attached to the 'Declaration' is a two-page list of 148 Baperki members in Langsa.[91] Considering the timing of this document's production, it is likely that this part of the document was used as a death list by the military. As we have seen, the military and its civilian proxies often used lists like this to identify targeted individuals for arrest and execution. At the very least, the military knew the identity of Baperki members in the district and could use this information to threaten them if they did not fulfil the document's pledge to "help" the military.

14 October–23 December: public killings continue

As this declaration was being prepared, the Baperki leadership in the district was subjected to two physical attacks. According to the Chronology, the first occurred at 6am on 14 October in Kuala Simpang, the first town on the Acehnese side of the border with North Sumatra, when:

15,000 people from NU, Perti, IP-KI, Marhaenist Youth, Daughters of Alwaslijah [*Putri Alwaslijah*], Marhaenist Daughters [*Putri Marhaenis*] and Muhammadijah Women's group [*Wanita Muhammadijah*] carried out a demonstration and destruction/burning of the equipment/furniture in the PKI, Baperki office.[92]

The second recorded attack against Baperki occurred "simultaneously" on Pulo Tiga, 60 km south of Langsa, when:

> a demonstration [was] carried out by the Pemuda Pantjasila[93] to destroy the office of the Baperki PKI office and several BTI owned houses. ABRI immediately carried out prevention because the demonstration went so far as to attack foreign-owned shops.[94]

In both cases, the destruction of Baperki offices is portrayed as part of the attack against the PKI itself, as evidenced in the conjoining of the terms PKI and Baperki in these two records, a practice that was not followed by either the PKI or Baperki, but rather appears intended to portray the two organisations as indistinguishable targets for attack. These attacks may have been directly linked to the military's discussions with the Baperki leadership, with the intention of showing the group that force would be used if the leadership refused to comply. The interesting intervention of the military in the protest in Pulo Tiga, portrayed as an attempt to "prevent" attacks against Chinese-owned shops, may, for example, have been intended to demonstrate that it was within the military's power to call off the attacks should Baperki decide to comply. This intervention may, equally, have been a sincere effort to save shops belonging to members of the pro-Kuomintang Chinese community in the province. The indiscriminate nature of civilian attacks against Chinese-owned property at this time suggests that civilians were unable, or unwilling, to differentiate between pro-Beijing and pro-Kuomintang Chinese, with the result that the Chinese population in general became subject to attack when the military did not directly intervene to stop this from occurring.

The first recorded public killings of Chinese Indonesians are said to have occurred in two separate cases on 14 October in South Aceh.[95] In the first case, in Blang Pidie, 76 km northwest of Tapaktuan, five people were reported killed by "the people", four of whom were identified as "Chinese people . . . whose belongings were also seized".[96] In the second case in Sama Dua, 12 km northwest of Tapaktuan, ten people were killed, of whom four were identified as Chinese Indonesians.[97] Further information about why and how these fatal attacks may have occurred is not detailed. It would appear, however, that these victims were killed alongside non-Chinese Indonesians as part of a single target group.

This joint targeting was consistent with Djuarsa's 29 October 'Decree', said to have been retrospectively active since 20 October, to "freeze and temporarily halt" the activities of "PKI political organisations and mass organisations", including Baperki.[98] This Decree had also expelled the members of these organisations from "all government bodies" in Aceh and forbade their members from "leaving their place" (presumably their homes), while announcing that it was "mandatory for all leaders of these Political Parties/Mass Organisations . . . to report themselves to the Pepelrada/Military Police/local Police by 25 October 1965 at the latest".[99] This subsequent reporting was used by the military and its civilian proxies to identify members of these organisations, either for immediate attack or for detention and eventual murder.

In total, twenty-one individuals from Aceh's Chinese community are recorded in the Chronology as having been killed in public in the province between 1 October and 23 December 1965.[100] This figure does not include Chinese Indonesians who did not use Chinese names. It also does not include victims killed at military-controlled killing sites, nor does it include the following cases of public violence directed against Baperki members as recalled by Ho Fui Yen, Xie Jie Fang and Wak Tin Chaw.

Ho, Xie and Wak have explained that Baperki members were specifically targeted for murder during this period. Ho, for example, recalls:

> The head of Baperki in Banda [Aceh], Jan Sun Ming, was beaten on the beach until he was badly injured. He was taken to hospital, and I was able to see him in the hospital. He was completely covered [in bandages], only his eyes were visible . . . On the second day, he was taken away . . . he disappeared. I don't know where he was taken [it was assumed he was murdered], his corpse was also not found.[101]

Jan had been attacked because he was a leader of Baperki. Ho does not know who took Jan. She believes, however, that whoever took him did so with the blessing of the military. Xie, meanwhile, has recalled how one of his friends, a former classmate and member of Baperki, was killed during this period along with three of his associates. As he recalled, "One was pushed out to sea [where he died], one was burnt, dead, and one was stabbed."[102] Furthermore, one of his students was:

> arrested and then . . . thrown out to sea; he wasn't dead yet, but he was tied up and then thrown out at sea, "feeding the fish" is what was said. He was taken out in a small boat.[103]

Another friend, who had come from Simeulue to "study from Baperki" at a school in Banda Aceh, was having a singing lesson with Xie when he was arrested and "taken home", before being killed due to his perceived affiliation with Baperki.[104] As Xie has remarked, being friends with a Baperki person was sufficient "for you to be thought to be a Baperki person" and to be targeted.[105] Such violence was apparently widespread. Similar attacks occurred in other districts in Aceh, including Meulaboh, Tapaktuan and Blangpidie, as well as in other "small towns" in the province.[106]

This violence against Baperki members, however, constituted only one stage in an escalation of violence against Aceh's Chinese community. As Xie elaborates, "after people arrested [the] PKI, [they] arrested Baperki; after that they began to arrest Chinese people (*orang Tionghoa*)" in general.[107] This third wave of violence, which began in December 1965, was aimed at Aceh's Chinese community as a group, with its members targeted based on their shared ethnic identity.

A new wave of anti-Chinese violence

My interviewees told me that one night in "early 1966", the houses of members of the pro-Beijing Chinese community in Banda Aceh were marked with signs with red paint.[108] Although Ho, Xie and Wak did not know who made these marks, they believed they had the blessing of the military, based on information given to the military from the pro-Kuomintang group.[109] The following day, the marked houses were targeted by violent demonstrators led by students involved with the "KAMI/KAPPI" youth militias, "who created chaos by throwing rocks at the houses that had been marked with this code".[110] The demonstrators then broke into the houses, including Ho's family home, where her parents were threatened and her father beaten.[111]

According to Xie, this type of intimidation continued over the next month or two, increasing in severity until, in the days before the 8 May announcement, "it started to happen every day, at night time [and] those whose houses had been marked were arrested. My father and my older brother were beaten until they bled".[112] Xie's family was also told to flee the province and threatened that they would be killed if they did not leave. The pro-Beijing Chinese community became "scared and not brave enough to go outside".[113] These arrests were allegedly conducted by KAMI/KAPPI members, with those who were arrested taken to KAMI/KAPPI offices, which were used as interrogation centres with the blessing of the military.[114]

Xie also recalls a "death car" that would circle the neighbourhood at the time, which was used to arrest members of the pro-Beijing group off the street. Xie described his own disturbing encounter with this car as he walked along the street early one morning at the beginning of 1966:

> [O]ne of my friends told me not to go out, [but] my clothes were filthy; I only went home every five to six days to bathe. There may have been someone who had seen [me return] from the Taiwan Kuomintang side who told the military. When I arrived at my house at almost two in the morning there was a car that stopped at the side of the road. I was scared and startled; I became on guard [and] I immediately started to flee, [to] run. The reason was that car. Before Chinese were killed, crushed . . . one of my friends who was a teacher told me when we had come home from school riding together on a bike. . . . He asked me, "Do you know what this car is for? This is the one that arrests people, cuts them up. Have a look, inside there's a long box, do you know what's in it?" He said, "A spear, a knife, to cut people up with." That's why I ran that night when the car came. If I hadn't run, I may have disappeared.[115]

Meanwhile, Zainal Abidin, the Subdistrict Head of Seulimum, has explained how during this time Chinese people began to be targeted indiscriminately.[116] "The people began to move," Abidin recalls:

> They took Chinese who weren't PKI. Some [of these people] were punished, such as in Bireuen, where those Chinese (*Cina-Cina itu*) were laid

out on the asphalt (*dijemur di aspal*) [under the hot sun]. The reason [that was given] was they were all Communists. In my opinion they weren't all Communists. The people [attacking them] were extreme, but that was because they had just found out that the 30 September Movement was Communist.[117]

15–18 April 1966: escalation of violence in North Aceh

The intensification of violence and intimidation of the pro-Beijing Chinese community in Aceh was related to a national upswing in violence against Indonesia's Chinese community. In Jakarta, on 15 April 1966, approximately 50,000 "WNI Chinese" (Chinese Indonesians with Indonesian citizenship) were called together to pledge their loyalty to the Indonesian state.[118] On the same day, a rally was held at the Reuleut sports field in Bireuen, North Aceh, where "Indonesian citizens of Chinese descent" pledged their loyalty to the Indonesian state in front of military and government representatives.[119] Following this rally, an "anti-RRT" (anti-People's Republic of China) rally was held by demonstrators who marched around the town holding banners reading, "Cut Relations with RRT", "Seize RRT property", "Long live ABRI", "Long Live Lieut[enant] [sic.] Gen. Soeharto", "Crush the RRT", "Crush those Wrecking the Economy", "Crush those Stealing the Economy" and "Lower Prices".[120] This demonstration then marched to the Subdistrict Office in Djeumpa to "report to the Tjatur Tunggal", where it was "welcomed and given advice" by the Deputy Commander of the Third Infantry Battalion "on behalf of the Bireuen Tjatur Tunggal". "China" was now being made a scapegoat for the failing Indonesian economy, and this rising anti-Chinese sentiment and violence was officially sanctioned by the local military command. The pro-Beijing community was terrified and many started making arrangements to travel in groups by road to Medan, where they were told a ship from China would come to meet them.[121]

On 18 April, student activists in Bireuen held another "anti-RRT demonstration", which escalated into a pogrom when an unspecified number of "RRT Chinese" were "arrested" by the students, before being "brought together and surrendered" to the Bireuen Pantja Tunggal.[122]

During this action, the Military Chronology reports, a Chinese man named Jun Sin, who had been seized and beaten by the students, "screamed that all the members of the Bireuen P[antja] T[unggal] were taking bribes". Jun Sin's outburst is a rare example of a victim being depicted as possessing agency and rebelling against his situation in an official document from this period.

The next day, the demonstrations spread to Samalanga, Matang Glumpang Dua and Geurugok, where students seized control of forty Chinese-owned shops and "assembled" an unspecified number of "RRT Chinese" who were subsequently "surrendered" by the students to the Bireuen Pantja Tunggal.[123] These accounts show that the target of the demonstrations had broadened to include "RRT Chinese" in general. They also show the increasing geographical spread of these demonstrations and the manner in which they were oriented towards requesting further action from the Bireuen Pantja Tunggal, a pattern which can also be observed in earlier military-orchestrated demonstrations and pogrom-type actions against the PKI.

On the same day, a "loyalty rally" was held in Lhokseumawe, where three hundred "Indonesian citizens of Chinese descent" pledged their loyalty to the state in front of the North Aceh Military Commander, Lieutenant Colonel Mohd. Sjakur.[124] As in Bireuen, the ceremony was followed by "citizens and students" marching around the town, carrying banners with anti-Chinese slogans.[125] When the demonstrators attempted to destroy Chinese-owned shops, however, the military stepped in to "guard the whole town".[126] The document fails to explain why the military acted in this manner. It may have been that these shops belonged to members of the pro-Kuomintang group who were considered an ally by the military leadership. This unexpected rebuke upset the protesters. The next day, students who had attended the rally attempted to hold a new one, but were held back by the military.[127] The ensuing scuffle climaxed when Sjakur struck a student named Rusli A.D. on the head with his baton, drawing blood. This enraged the students, prompting the military to fire warning shots.[128]

After rushing their comrade to hospital, the demonstrators renewed their attacks on Chinese-owned shops in the town.[129] In response, the military fired a second round of shots allegedly "above the students", that fatally wounded a junior high school student named Iskandar and further enraged the crowd. After a second trip to the hospital, the demonstrators marched on the North Aceh Military Command's headquarters, where some demonstrators called for the shooter, a soldier, to be hanged, while others continued to destroy Chinese-owned shops "without making a distinction if the shop belonged to a Chinese [citizen] or an Indonesian citizen of Chinese descent". The demonstration then spilled over into the neighbouring subdistrict of Muara Dua, with non-students joining in.[130] Although the demonstration was outwardly anti-Chinese, demonstrators also appear to have been frustrated with the military itself, and expressed this frustration by refusing to accept the military's demands that they stop their indiscriminate destruction. In this deteriorating situation, the military leadership decided it was more important to retain control over the protestors than to protect its ally the pro-Kuomintang group.

On 18 April 1966, a delegation of KAPPI students from Bireuen was detained by the North Aceh Pantja Tunggal as it attempted to enter Lhokseumawe to join the demonstrations.[131] An all-night meeting was held to determine whether the students should be allowed to "gather together RRT people and surrender them to the [North Aceh] Defence Sector Commander (*Dan Sekhan*)" and "visit their comrade . . . at the Lhokseumawe Hospital". This permission was granted and, immediately following the meeting "the students began to carry out the detention of RRT Chinese who were brought together on the front yard of the Bupati [Regent]'s office . . . with their faces beaten [and] naked except for their underpants."[132]

The fate of these individuals, who are recorded as numbering 304 people, is not known, beyond that they were reportedly "surrendered to the North Aceh Military Commander to be given supervision and what was needed".[133] Such actions are eerily reminiscent of what happened to members and sympathisers of the PKI during the earlier phases of violence in the province.

This indiscriminate violence against the Chinese community in North Aceh has been independently corroborated by Zainal Abidin, who has explained how following a series of "large meetings":

> the people began to move and to take Chinese (*ambil Cina*) who weren't PKI. There were those who were punished (*dihukum*). This occurred in Bireuen where Chinese were laid out [under the hot sun] on the asphalt (*dijemur di aspal*). The reason was that they were communist. In my opinion they weren't all communists [but] people were extreme, but only after they knew the G30S was communist.[134]

The Chinese community in North Aceh was now being targeted as a whole.[135]

KAMI/KAPPI splits with the military leadership

On 22 April 1966, anti-Chinese violence, combined with anti-military sentiment, spread to the neighbouring town of Lhoksukon and was considered serious enough for Djuarsa to travel to Lhokseumawe the following day to "see up close" what had been happening.[136] Djuarsa was disturbed by developments and, at a meeting held in North Aceh on 24 April, ordered officials to "take serious action and investigate what has happed including those who are believed to be involved". Subsequently, several of the students who had been involved in the demonstrations and "arrests" were arrested themselves and taken to Banda Aceh for further questioning.

KAPPI would later complain bitterly in a letter to the head of the North Aceh Level II Provincial Government, North Aceh's Bupati, T. Ramli Angkasah, that KAPPI members had been treated unfairly during this process.[137] Not only had KAPPI members been "beaten up" in jail, KAPPI's General Secretary for Lhokseumawe, Sofjan Ibrahim, explained, they had also been "lectured to" by Angkasah, even though the demonstrations and "raids" (*gerebek*) carried out by KAPPI had been "in line with orders" that had come "directly from the Head of the Province" (Djuarsa).[138] It is not clear how this misunderstanding developed. It appears that Angkasah was concerned KAPPI was becoming uncontrollable. In his official response to KAPPI, Angkasah chastised it for behaving in a disrespectful manner towards the local military command and civilian leadership and for becoming too fond of "beating [people] up [and] stealing".[139] Angkasah followed up this accusation by explaining that all belongings seized by KAPPI from "RRT shops" rightfully belonged to the North Aceh Defence Sector Commander (*Dan Sekhan*).[140] It thus appears that the argument between KAMI/KAPPI and the local military and civilian leadership in North Aceh was, at least in part, an argument over control of the spoils of the military's annihilation campaign. It was in this context that Djuarsa issued his expulsion order on 8 May.[141]

Flight from Banda Aceh

The Chinese community in Banda Aceh was initially concerned that the military and its civilian militia groups would exploit any attempt on their part to flee the province as an opportunity to attack them as they made the long, exposed trip towards safety in Medan.[142] In an attempt to ascertain the risk of such a trip, the pro-Beijing group under the leadership of Wak Tin Chaw's father Wang, asked that a soldier accompany the first convoy of several families. This request was granted and a group of soldiers were assigned to travel ahead of the convoy that consisted of three trucks. As the convoy reached Meureudu, between Sigli and Bireuen, a group of "bandits" appeared and attempted to attack the convoy. The soldiers, however, kept their word and protected the convoy until it reached Medan. When news reached Banda Aceh that the first convoy had arrived safely in Medan and had indeed received military protection, further convoys of Chinese Indonesians began to leave the province. The community was warned, however, that this protection would only be afforded until 17 August.[143] At least 10,000 members of Aceh's Chinese community would flee the province during this time, including both "alien" Chinese (WNA: *Warga Negara Asing*, individuals with foreign citizenship status) and "non alien" Chinese (WNI: *Warga Negara Indonesia*, individuals with Indonesian citizenship), despite Djuarsa's announcement that only "alien" Chinese would be affected by the expulsion order.[144]

Ho, Xie and Wak have recalled that all members of the pro-Beijing group were forced to leave the province during this time.[145] Some members of the pro-Kuomintang group were, however, permitted to remain in the province, while others were forced to flee. The pro-Kuomintang families that Ho, Xie and Wak identify as being permitted to remain in the province owned shops in Banda Aceh.[146] The military leadership offered protection to these families in return for their loyalty to the new regime. These exceptions, however, do not negate the racist nature of the military's expulsion campaign, which targeted Aceh's Chinese community as a group based on ethnic identity and by reason of guilt by association.

Upon their arrival in Medan, the refugees faced further intimidation and violence, as North Sumatra's Military Commander Brigadier General Sobiran "did nothing to subdue the anti-Chinese militancy of the students" in the province.[147] Approximately 4,000 of the refugees from Aceh, including Ho, Xie, Wak and Asan's wife and children, were able to board the Chinese ship the *Kuang Hua*, which made four trips to the port in Belawan, just outside of Medan, carrying approximately 1,000 refugees each time it departed.[148] The arrival of the *Kuang Hua* in port sparked violent attacks by KAMI and KAPPI members in Medan, prompting Mokoginta to announce on 13 November that stern measures would be taken against "actions aimed at disturbing society" and that the attempts of "Chinese desiring to be repatriated should not be hampered".

Mokoginta may not have approved of Djuarsa's decision to order the expulsion of "alien Chinese" from Aceh. In a speech delivered in Medan on 21 April, three days after the North Aceh military fired on student protesters ransacking Chinese-owned shops in Lhokseumawe, he had declared that "actions which are racialist (*rasialis*)" should be avoided.[149] Why Mokoginta would appear to be so concerned about "racialist" actions in unclear. It is known, for example, that he had backed violent actions against Baperki in North Sumatra in November 1965.[150] It is likely that Mokoginta meant that he wished to maintain a distinction between members of the pro-Beijing group and the pro-Kuomintang group, similar to the military leadership's position in Aceh prior to Djuarsa's issuance of the expulsion order. Historians Yen-ling Tsai and Douglas Kammen, for example, have argued the military leadership in North Sumatra attempted to "confine" violence against the Chinese community "to attacks of Baperki and Hua Zhong (*Asosiasi*)[151] schools".[152] Mokoginta was nonetheless unable or unwilling to stop Djuarsa following through with the expulsion. It is possible that Djuarsa, in the face of escalating violence in the province, felt that he had no choice but to attempt to remove the focus of this violence, which threatened to destabilise the new military regime. In doing so, he may have helped avoid a new wave of mass killings in the province. This was not done out of concern for the victims of this violence, but rather to protect the gains achieved through the military's earlier waves of genocidal violence.

The patterns of violence perpetrated against Aceh's Chinese community in late 1965 and 1966 suggest the military leadership's primary motivation was to physically destroy its major political opponent, the PKI. This included the targeting of ethnic Chinese members of the PKI and the large-scale murder of members of Baperki who were alleged to be associated with the PKI. From April 1966, however, Aceh's Chinese community as a whole became the focus of violence in the province. This indiscriminate violence was tolerated by the military until it became counterproductive by threatening to destabilise the new regime. That the military was able to bring this third wave of violence under control so quickly demonstrates the ultimate authority the military had over this violence. Not even KAMI/KAPPI would be permitted to upset the military's new grip on power. This control and desire to establish stability can also be seen in the military's purge of the civil service.

***

The purge of Aceh's civil service 18 October 1965–31 March 1967

The following section documents the purge of Aceh's civil service. The purge occurred as a discreet process within the genocide. An analysis of this process is able to perhaps uniquely illustrate that the genocide was not purely a *destructive* process, but also a process designed to cleanse and capture the Indonesian state – to bring into being Suharto's so-called "New Order" – while retaining the bureaucratic contours of the pre-genocidal state.

In Aceh, the earliest documentation of the military's purge of the province's civil service is from mid-October 1965. Described as a campaign to "cleanse the body" (*membersihkan tubuh*) of the government services,[153] this purge was province-wide.[154] It was part of the nationally coordinated military campaign, with its instructions emanating from the same national, inter-provincial and pro-vincial commands that implemented the genocide, as we shall see. The purge was an extension, or alternative expression, of the genocide. Some individuals targeted as part of this campaign were killed. Others were interrogated and impris-oned. The purge was a bureaucratisation of the impulse to annihilate the PKI, as well as an attempt to preserve the apparatus of the Indonesian state, in order to consolidate the military's new regime.

At the local level the purge was implemented by high- to mid-level government employees, with each of the purge documents cited in this chapter signed either by Aceh's Governor, Brigadier General Njak Adam Kamil,[155] a bupati,[156] a Regional Secretary[157] or a head of the variety of government services represented in the documents.[158]

Documentation of the purge recovered during my research comprises eighty-two individual documents, which denounce some one hundred and eleven peo-ple who are said to have been "dismissed", "made non-active" or "suspended" from their place of employment or study.[159] Dated between 18 October 1965 and 31 March 1967, the documents in question fall into two main batches. The first consists of thirty-six documents produced during the period 18 October 1965–28 January 1966, at the height of the genocide and early consolidation period (see Table 7.1). The second consists of forty documents produced on 24 December 1966, at a time when systematic mass killings in Aceh had ceased (see Table 7.2). Table 7.1 demonstrates how the purge was conducted simultaneously through-out the province in a methodical and standardised manner. Table 7.2 provides a glimpse of the sheer scale of the campaign.

Table 7.1 Early purge documents: 18 October 1965–5 February 1966

No.	Purge document date	Name	Region	Occupation	Document signed by
1	18 October 1965	Ibnu Sjakur	Banda Aceh	Head of the Forestry Department	Governor
2	18 October 1965	Ir Gani Abu	Banda Aceh	Forestry Department	Governor
3	20 October 1965	S.M. Lahat	Takengon	Bupati's office	Bupati
4	20 October 1965	Sedjuk	Takengon	Agriculture Department	Bupati
5	21 October 1965	M. Yusuf	Banda Aceh	Forestry Department	Head of Administration
6	27 October 1965	Chalidin Hakim	Takengon	Technical worker	Bupati

(*Continued*)

Table 7.1 (Continued)

No.	Purge document date	Name	Region	Occupation	Document signed by
7	27 October 1965	Achmad Banta	Takengon	Natural Resources Department	Bupati
8	27 October 1965	Sampe Ganti	Takengon	Livestock Department	Bupati
9	28 October 1965	Tjut Radja	Banda Aceh	Fisheries worker	Provincial Secretary on behalf of the Governor
10	31 October 1965	M. Ali	North Aceh	Medicine Board	Bupati
11	31 October 1965	Latif	North Aceh	Government worker	Bupati
12	31 October 1965	Supranoto	North Aceh	Government worker	Bupati
13	31 October 1965	Ismail Ruddin	North Aceh	Agricultural educator	Bupati
14	31 October 1965	Al Wahab	North Aceh	Agricultural expert	Bupati
15	31 October 1965	Parsan Samanurdy	North Aceh	Fish pond security guard	Bupati
16	31 October 1965	T. Sulaiman	North Aceh	Agriculture Department	Bupati
17	6 November 1965	Musa St	Takengon	Agriculture Department	Bupati
18	6 November 1965	Kamal Pasja	Takengon	Agriculture Department	Bupati
19	9 November 1965	Baramsjah	Central Aceh	Fisheries Department	Bupati
20	11 November 1965	D.S. Naksir Tarigan	Banda Aceh	Forestry technician	Provincial Secretary
21	11 November 1965	Ngadimin	Banda Aceh	Forestry supervisor	Provincial Secretary
22	11 November 1965	Arif Mustafa	Banda Aceh	Forestry technician	Provincial Secretary
23	12 November 1965	Abd. Chalik	Banda Aceh	Administrative worker	Provincial Secretary
24	12 November 1965	M. Natsir	Banda Aceh	Administrative worker	Provincial Secretary
25	12 November 1965	Togar Z.A. Situmeang	Banda Aceh	Administrative worker	Provincial Secretary
26	13 November 1965	Abbas	Tapaktuan	Livestock supervisor	Bupati
27	13 November 1965	Umar Tahir	Tapaktuan	Livestock educator	Bupati
28	13 November 1965	M. Junan	Tapaktuan	Courier	Bupati

No.	Purge document date	Name	Region	Occupation	Document signed by
29	13 November 1965	Anwar Djamil	Tapaktuan	Livestock educator	Bupati
30	16 November 1965	Murito	Banda Aceh	Fishing	Provincial Secretary on behalf of the Governor
31	18 November 1965	T. Natsjah	Banda Aceh	Forestry Department	Head of Civil Service Bureau
32	20 November 1965	M. Junan B	Banda Aceh	Student	Governor
33	20 November 1965	Agus Hc	Banda Aceh	Forestry Department	Head of Administration
34	22 November 1965	M. Husin	Banda Aceh	Student	Governor
35	22 November 1965	M. Saleh Djali	Banda Aceh	Student	Governor
36	22 November 1965	T.R. Kahar	Tapaktuan	Bupati's office	Bupati
37	22 November 1965	Abd. Rachman	Tapaktuan	Government worker	Bupati
38	23 November 1965	Hasan	West Aceh	Agricultural educator	Bupati
39	23 November 1965	S.T. Mubahar	West Aceh	Agricultural educator	Bupati
40	23 November 1965	T. Usman Mus	West Aceh	Fisheries Department	Bupati
41	23 November 1965	Sulaiman Pd	West Aceh	Fisheries Department	Bupati
42	27 November 1965	Bahruddin	Greater Aceh	Fisheries Department	Bupati
43	8 December 1965	Anas Rahim	South Aceh	Education Department	Education Department
44	8 December 1965	Abd. Samad	South Aceh	Education Department	Education Department
45	8 December 1965	Nurlaili	South Aceh	Education Department	Education Department
46	9 December 1965	Zahar	Langsa	Unclear	Bupati
47	9 December 1965	Name unclear	Langsa	Unclear	Bupati
48	9 December 1965	Name unclear	Langsa	Unclear	Bupati
49	23 December 1965	T. Radja Adilan B.A.	South Aceh	District Secretary	Police Commissioner
50	31 December 1965	T. Radja Kahar	South Aceh	Bupati's office	Police Commissioner

(*Continued*)

Table 7.1 (Continued)

No.	Purge document date	Name	Region	Occupation	Document signed by
51	13 January 1966	Usman Banta	Greater Aceh	Agricultural educator	Head of Agricultural Department
52	28 January 1966	T. Husin	South Aceh	Inland Fisheries Department	Bupati
53	5 February 1966	Bahri	Aceh	Civil servant	Inland Fisheries
54	5 February 1966	Abd. Hamid	Aceh	Civil servant	Inland Fisheries
55	5 February 1966	Ismail	Aceh	Civil servant	Inland Fisheries
56	5 February 1966	Murito	Greater Aceh	Civil servant	Inland Fisheries
57	5 February 1966	Bahruddin	Greater Aceh	Civil servant	Inland Fisheries
58	5 February 1965	Mohammad Jusuf	Meulaboh	Civil servant	Inland Fisheries
59	5 February 1966	Baramsjah	Takengon	Civil servant	Inland Fisheries
60	5 February 1966	Mawardi Hasan	Takengon	Civil servant	Inland Fisheries
61	5 February 1966	Mariana	Pidie	Civil servant	Inland Fisheries
62	5 February 1966	T. Husin	Tapaktuan	Civil servant	Inland Fisheries
63	5 February 1966	Parsan	Lhokseumawe	Civil servant	Inland Fisheries[i]

[i] Purge documents file

Sources of authority for the purge campaign

The highly coordinated nature of the purge campaign is evident in the instructions cited at the top of each document. Appearing as single- or double-sided pages of typescript, the purge documents, like others produced during this period, typically open with a catalogue of military and government instructions with which they claim to comply, before recording the name or names of those individuals who are to be dismissed, with up to eleven people named in a single document.[160] In eleven cases the names of these individuals also appear in an attached "list", in which the names, occupations and other pertinent information of the accused is clearly displayed. The purge documents then proceed to identify the multiple authorities to whom the documents were to be forwarded.

The earliest purge document, signed by Governor Kamil on 18 October 1965 in Banda Aceh, during the height of systematic mass killings in the province, lists the provenance of the purge campaign as stemming from multiple sources, including a Joint Decision of the "Pantja Tunggal/*Front Nasional* and Political Parties", issued in 6 October 1965. This Joint Decision "urged" "the Regional War Authority (*Peperda*: *Penguasa Perang Daerah*) and Governor/Head of Aceh Special Region to immediately freeze (*membekukan*) the PKI and its affiliated organisations."[161]

The purge document also refers to an "Instruction from the Mandala-I Siaga Commander [Mokoginta]" issued on 6 October 1965,[162] "clarifications" from the Aceh Special Region Pantja Tunggal and an:

> Instruction from the Head of KOTI's political section (*KOTI G-V*)[163] as released by all Departments/[word unclear] in the centre [Jakarta] as well as in the Regions via the Peperda throughout Indonesia for an assembly (*apel*, with a roll call) to be held every morning to check which government employees have not come to work since 30 September 1965.[164]

It can thus been seen that the purge campaign drew its authority from the same sources as the genocide itself, that is, from the national military leadership, as coordinated through the KOTI chain of command, including Suharto acting in his position as KOTI Commander and Commander of the Armed Forces in Jakarta; Mokoginta acting it his capacity as the 'Mandala-I Siaga Commander' (*Panglatu*) in Medan; and Djuarsa acting in his capacity as Regional Authority for the Implementation of Dwikora (*Pepelrada*). The Aceh Pantja Tunggal also played a key role in this campaign by acting as a bridge between the military and Aceh's civilian leadership.

The use of the position of 'Regional War Authority' (Peperda: *Penguasa Perang Daerah*), a position that this document indicates was also held by Djuarsa at this time, meanwhile, indicates that the purge campaign was intended to be understood as a military-led operation that was to be implemented as if a state of war had been declared. This is the first reference to the use of the Peperda chain of command in Aceh, a task that had otherwise been performed through the activation of the Kohanda Command on 1 October, which had placed the province under effective martial law from this date. This reference to the activation of the position of Peperda in Aceh (a position that had been activated in other provinces that did not have access to Sumatra's extensive Mandala Satu Command since the earliest days of the military's attack[165]) indicates the growing homogenisation and centralisation of the military's national campaign. The military's attack had been centrally coordinated from 1 October 1965, but the military leadership had relied on existing provincial and inter-provincial military commands to implement the early stages of its campaign while providing these existing commands with centralised leadership and directives. It thus appears that the national military leadership had now consolidated these chains of command and was able to issue instructions that it could expect to be implemented on a national scale.

The purpose of this document was to mandate the holding of special assemblies for government employees, to be held daily, to identify anyone who did not show up for work, as well as to presumably communicate to all employees that the state was closely scrutinising their activities. Such a tactic allowed government departments to maintain strict control over their employees during this period, while also generating an environment in which anyone who did not comply would be treated as an enemy. The stakes were high. A dispatch from the Australian embassy in Jakarta, sent on 19 November 1965, records that the military was routinely holding "assemblies" in front of workplaces, where attendees were asked "whether they wish[ed] to continue to work as usual or not", with those who declined "summarily shot".[166]

Purge documents dating from November 1965, when direct military involvement in the killings was still underway, also refer to additional sources of authority to those outlined above. An example of the additional sources cited in these documents include a 'Decision' issued by Djuarsa on 20 October 1965;[167] a "secret" letter produced by the head of the Aceh Forestry Department (*No.01/rahasia/ G.30.S./1965*), dated 26 October 1965;[168] and a "top secret" letter (*23–11–1965 No. 15/Sangat Rahasia*) issued by the Governor of Aceh on 23 November 1965.[169]

The content of these decisions and additional instructions is unfortunately unknown. We know about them only because they are referenced in the purge documents. The existence of such decisions issued by Djuarsa and "secret" and "top secret" letters issued from heads of government departments and Aceh's Governor during this period, however, indicate that not only was the purge campaign highly coordinated and overseen by the military, but that the content of such directives may have been quite explicit in order to have been classified in this manner. It is not clear, for example, why the leaders of the genocide considered it unproblematic to issue official documents during this time declaring that it was "mandatory . . . to assist the military to completely annihilate the 30 September Movement" and for people associated with the PKI to be "hanged in public", while it did not feel comfortable making its plans for the purge campaign public.

A linguistic example of this apparent moderation can be seen in the manner in which individuals identified in the purge documents as having been "dismissed", "made non-active" or "suspended" from their placed of employment are curiously described as having been done so on a "temporary basis", with the individuals identified in these documents said to have been placed on "half wages".[170] This language is also mirrored in the two entries in the Chronology that reference the purge campaign in the province. On 18 October 1965, for example, it is noted in the Chronology that: "The Head of Region XI Director General for Customs has temporarily suspended 4 of its members for being involved in the 30 September movement."[171]

No reason is given for why these people were "temporarily suspended". Meanwhile, on 24 October, it is reported that six individuals "have already been suspended/temporarily fired from their positions/duties as a result of being involved in the G30S."[172] Two PKI leaders, Muhammad Samikidin and Anas HC, are included in the list of individuals affected by this document.[173]

The mild language used in these documents is striking. It is known that at least some of the individuals targeted by the purge campaign were killed. Both Samiki-din and Anas were murdered during the early stages of the military's annihilation campaign in the province.[174] Meanwhile, it is known that others were imprisoned but survived, while some even had their employment restored.[175] The fate of the majority of such individuals remains unknown.[176]

On the one hand, such coyness may have been simple hypocrisy. The purge documents, with their attached lists of names, could well have been used as one form of the membership lists that were used as death lists by the military and those acting on its behalf. Such a fate may be hinted at in ten cases in the early purge documents where it is reported that the individuals named are "missing", or "not at their posts" (*tidak berada diposnja*),[177] a status which implied guilt, as it could now "be presumed that the accused has a relationship and is working closely with the political parties/mass organisations involved in the '30 September Movement'".[178]

Meanwhile, in seven other cases, individuals are reported euphemistically as "under the arrest of those who have the authority",[179] and in a further seven cases, as "under house arrest",[180] with the requirement of "reporting every day to their Departmental Head".[181] Such individuals may well have supplied the quotas of those who would be transported to Aceh's military-controlled killing sites.

This deliberately euphemistic use of language was, it seems, used to disguise the true nature of these actions from both victims and perpetrators alike in a similar way to which terms such as "collateral damage" and "enhanced interrogation" are used today. In addition to providing a psychological comfort, however, such language may have also reflected the legalistic nature of the purge, which required that the military present its attack against the PKI as a preservation of the existing state bureaucracy.

Legal justification of the purge campaign

In addition to the above quoted sources of authority, the purge campaign was bolstered by a raft of Guided Democracy–era laws dating from the 1950s to mid-1960s, the most common of which refer to the hiring and firing of civil servants. These laws include Presidential Regulation No. 8, 1952, which authorised the temporary stepping down and termination of employment of civil servants "awaiting a final decision" regarding their employment;[182] Law No. 21, 1952, which outlined the chain of command within the civil service;[183] and Law No. 18, 1961, which stipulated the requirements of membership of the government service, including personal loyalty to the state and the Pancasila.[184] Three other commonly cited laws and regulations in the dismissal letters include Law No. 24, 1956, which authorised the establishment of Aceh as a region separate from North Sumatra;[185] Law No. 1, 1957, which recognised the right of "Autonomous Regions" and "Special Regions", such as Aceh, to limited autonomy;[186] and Government Regulation No. 6, 1959, a regulation that related to the devaluing of the Rupiah.[187] This final regulation was related to the military's attempt to limit inflation during the immediate post–1 October period.[188]

More than being a simple legalistic "cover" for the purges, the citation of these laws, along with the systematic compilation and storage of the purge documents, appears to point to the notion that the recording of the purges was, in fact, an integral part of their purpose. Unlike the killings, for which official documents appear to be missing or unforthcoming, the purges were a legal action, aimed not just at removing the military's political enemy, but also at preserving the legal framework of the civil service for use by the new regime, while replacing those within the system who were deemed undesirable. It was essential to document the purges in order to legitimate the positions of those who replaced those who had been purged.

As can be seen in the strengthening of the military's existing military command structures during the period of the genocide, the repression and violence that stemmed from 1 October 1965 was not aimed at the destruction of the Indonesian state, but at its reorientation. Despite the horrific violence that accompanied this reorientation, the legal basis of the Indonesian state was retained. This is because the military wanted to preserve and extend the economic and political gains it had made since the early 1950s. To do this, the leadership decided to annihilate the major threat to these gains, while retaining the structures of the pre–1 October state. The genocide and subsequent purge campaign settled, as it were, the struggle for the Indonesian state that had been fought since at least the early 1950s.

Later purge documents

The systematic and extensive nature of the purge campaign can also be seen in the collection of purge documents produced between 17 May 1966 and 31 March 1967. This collection includes a cluster of thirty-eight documents produced on 24 December 1966, which are signed by a representative of Aceh's Forestry Department. Like the earlier purge documents, these documents are almost identical in their presentation and "released from [their] positions" employees of the Forestry Department throughout the province.[189] The production of these documents certainly appears to have been industrial in scale.

All thirty-eight documents produced on 24 December 1966 claim to have been written in response to a 'Letter from the Head of the Indonesian Forestry [Department]', dated 17 October 1966, on the topic of 'Secrets about the membership of the Aceh *Sarbuksi* (*Sarekat Buruh Kehutanan Seluruh Indonesia*: All Indonesia Forest Workers Union)'.[190] They also claim to be based on multiple sources of authority, including a Presidential Decree issued by Suharto;[191] an Instruction from the President;[192] a letter from the Deputy Minister for Forestry;[193] a secret letter from the Forestry Department (*No. 797/Rahasia, 1 September 1966*); a letter from the 'Special Team (*Team Chusus*) for the Cleansing of Personnel (*Pembersihan Personil*) from the Forestry Department';[194] and a Decision from the 'Screening Team' (*Team Screening*) at the Governor's Office.[195]

It is clear these documents were intended to target members of the Sarbuksi union in Langsa, East Aceh, as part of a highly coordinated and centralised campaign. This campaign drew its authority from the highest powers in the country including Suharto (now 'Acting President')[196] and a 'Special Team for the Cleansing of Personnel' from the Forestry Department that appears to have been established specifically to oversee the purge. Unfortunately the content of these instructions is not known, as the original documents cited in the purge documents have yet to be recovered. The internal workings of this campaign, it seems, were not intended to be public knowledge.

These purge documents were then sent back up the chain of command, including to the Department of Internal Affairs and Regional Autonomy in Jakarta; a special commission, 'Komisi A', that appears to have been established in Banda Aceh to facilitate the purge campaign at the provincial level; Djuarsa acting as Pangdahan 'A' in Banda Aceh; and an additional seven government bodies in Banda Aceh and East Aceh, including the Finance Bureau and Government Treasury in Banda Aceh. This comprehensive list of recipients points to the important role these documents played in consolidating the new regime by legitimating the new civil service.[197]

As there is no particular reason for the Forestry Department in Langsa to be singled out as the main focus of this campaign it is likely that similarly comprehensive purge campaigns were carried out in other Departments and districts during this period. As can be seen from the records of the purge documents presented in this chapter, many departments, including the Agriculture Department, Education Department, Fisheries Department, Inland Fisheries Department, Livestock Department, Natural Resources Department and Medicine board were involved in this purge. Civil servants working in local government offices were also targeted.[198] These later purge documents were produced in a radically different climate to the earlier purge documents, during a time when public killings and systematic mass killings had ostensibly ceased, suggesting that the later purge documents performed a role other than inciting physical violence, namely to consolidate the military's new regime.

Classification of the accused

The specific fate of the individuals listed in these purge documents is not known. It does appear, however, that those listed in these documents were classified according to the national prisoner classification system, which came into effect in May 1966.[199] This classification system, based on Presidential Instruction No. 9/KOGAM/5/1966 (*Instruksi Presiden No. Inst/09/Kogam/5/66*), divided accused individuals into three major categories.[200] "A" category individuals were alleged to be "hard-core" PKI functionaries and members accused of being directly involved in the actions of the 30 September Movement; "B" category individuals were alleged PKI functionaries, or members or sympathisers of the PKI's affiliated mass organisations; while "C" category individuals were considered to have been only minimally involved with the PKI or the 30 September Movement.[201]

Table 7.2 Later purge documents: 17 May 1966–31 March 1967

No.	Purge document date	Name	Region	Occupation	Document signed by
64	17 May 1966	Nur Amal	East Aceh	Unclear	Bupati
65	17 May 1966	Unclear	East Aceh	Unclear	Bupati
66	29 June 1966	Mohd Ali	Meulaboh	Subdistrict office	Bupati
67	17 October 1966	Djumain	Rantau	Assistant	Forestry Department
68	26 October 1966	Alimuddin	Tapaktuan	Justice office	Bupati
69	21 December 1966	Armansjah	Meulaboh	Civil servant	Head of Administration
70	21 December 1965	Mohd. Amir	Meulaboh	Civil servant	Head of Administration
71	23 December 1966	Sidi Muchtar	Kualasimpang	Forestry police	Forestry Department
72	24 December 1966	Effendi Pd	Meulaboh	Head of Forestry Police	Forestry Department
73	24 December 1966	Zainab	Meulaboh	Civil servant	Forestry Department
74	24 December 1966	Ramli	Kualasimpang	Assistant to Head of Local Forestry Police	Forestry Department
75	24 December 1966	Abd Rahman	Rantau	Assistant to Head of Local Forestry Police	Forestry Department
76	24 December 1966	Ham Onang	Unclear	Administration	Forestry Department
77	24 December 1966	Abdul Manaf	Rantau	Assistant to Head of Local Forestry Police	Forestry Department
78	24 December 1966	Budiman	Kutacane	Assistant to Head of Local Forestry Police	Forestry Department
79	24 December 1966	Jusli Hakim	Lhokseumawe	Forestry Police	Forestry Department
80	24 December 1966	Solamat	Kutacane	Forestry Police	Forestry Department
81	24 December 1966	M.D. Tulod	Idi	Assistant	Forestry Department
82	24 December 1966	Djumain	Rantau	Assistant	Forestry Department
83	24 December 1966	Areman	Kualasimpang	Unclear	Forestry Department
84	24 December 1966	Djailani	Kutacane	Assistant	Forestry Department
85	24 December 1966	Parluhutan Dongoran	Simpang Jernih	Forestry Police	Forestry Department
86	24 December 1966	Urip Santoso	Simpang Jernih	Forestry Police	Forestry Department

Table 7.1 (Continued)

87	24 December 1966	Diapari Pulungan	Kualasimpang	Forestry Police	Forestry Department
88	24 December 1966	Sjahrial	Langsa	Forestry Police	Forestry Department
89	24 December 1966	Ader Siregar	Kualasimpang	Forestry Police	Forestry Department
90	24 December 1966	H. Batubara	Kualasimpang	Forestry Police	Forestry Department
91	24 December 1966	Abdullah	Meulaboh	Forestry Police	Forestry Department
92	24 December 1966	Muhammad	Simpang Ulim	Forestry Police	Forestry Department
93	24 December 1966	Hasballah	Lhokseumawe	Forestry Police	Forestry Department
94	24 December 1966	Sjahminan	Lhokseumawe	Forestry Police	Forestry Department
95	24 December 1966	Njak Ni Achmady	Unclear	Forestry Police	Forestry Department
96	24 December 1966	Suardi	Unclear	Forestry Police	Forestry Department
97	24 December 1966	Darwis	Unclear	Forestry Police	Forestry Department
98	24 December 1966	T.R. Kamil	Unclear	Forestry Police	Forestry Department
99	24 December 1966	Sulaiman	Banda Aceh	Forestry Department	Forestry Department
100	24 December 1966	Sulaiman Achmad	Banda Aceh	Forestry Department	Forestry Department
101	24 December 1966	Zainal Abidin	Banda Aceh	Forestry Department	Forestry Department
102	24 December 1966	Osuhandi	Banda Aceh	Forestry Department	Forestry Department
103	24 December 1966	Mahja bin Eed	Banda Aceh	Forestry Department	Forestry Department
104	24 December 1966	Sjamsuddin Aly	Banda Aceh	Forestry Department	Forestry Department
105	24 December 1966	Abdul	Banda Aceh	Forestry Department	Forestry Department
106	24 December 1966	Helmy	Banda Aceh	Forestry expert	Forestry Department
107	24 December 1966	M. Junus	Banda Aceh	Forestry expert	Forestry Department
108	24 December 1966	BA Haruddin	Banda Aceh	Forestry Department	Forestry Department
109	24 December 1966	Saodah	Banda Aceh	Forestry Department	Forestry Department
110	31 March 1967	T. Sjamsuddin	Tapaktuan	Justice office	Bupati
111	31 March 1967	Unclear	South Aceh	Agriculture Department	Bupati[i]

[i] Purge documents file

The purge documents produced on 24 December 1966 all cite Presidential Instruction No. 9/KOGAM/5/1966,[202] which had been issued on 13 May 1966 by Suharto on behalf of Sukarno, who was still nominally President.[203] They also classify all individuals named as "C" category prisoners and extend this classification further to include two additional subcategories. B.A. Haruddin and Helmy, both from Banda Aceh, for example, are classified as "C.1" category prisoners, while the remaining thirty-six individuals are classified as "C.2" category prisoners. These subcategories are unusual. "C" prisoners were by far the largest group to be identified nationally, because the majority of individuals considered to be directly associated with the PKI and its affiliated organisations had been murdered by this stage. Despite this, subcategorisation did not begin nationally until 1975.[204] It appears this process began earlier in Aceh. References to these subcategories can be found in the original Presidential Instruction issued on 13 May 1966, which divided accused individuals into "A", "B" and "C" categories while foreshadowing the subcategorisation of "C" prisoners by identifying "C.1" individuals as "members of the illegal PKI party or leaders of its mass organisations" and "C.2" individuals as "normal members of illegal mass organisations that had been . . . protected by the PKI", but who had "not been directly involved in 'G-30-S'".[205]

The purge documents furthermore stipulate that categorised individuals were to be "treated according to paragraph 5, clause 3" of Presidential Instruction No. 9, which explains that individuals classified as "C.1" are to be "dismissed without honour", while those classified as "C.2" are "not to be granted promotion . . . [but must] receive indoctrination".[206] It thus appears that these individuals were not necessarily imprisoned, but were either dismissed or subjected to "re-education". What such indoctrination entailed is not stated. It is possible that long-term political prisons, known nationally as 'Political Re-indoctrination Centres', were established in Aceh, as they were throughout Indonesia during the national purge campaign.[207] I have yet, however, to come across evidence of such centres in the province. Latifah, for example, who was in Takengon at the time of the genocide, and whose husband, Said, a policeman, was accused of being a member of the PKI, has explained that her husband was sent to a jail "on Java" following the cessation of killings in the province, where he died after being severely tortured.[208] Clearly at least some political prisoners who survived the genocide may have been sent outside the province during the purge campaign. Another of my interviewees, "Shadia", recalls how her husband, "Nurdin", who was not a member of the PKI or its affiliated organisations, was dismissed from the Tax Department in Banda Aceh during the purge because he had been absent from his workplace on 1 October 1965, as he had been on his honeymoon with Shadia in Jakarta.[209] Nurdin was not detained and was eventually re-employed without any further penalty.

From entries in the military's Complete Yearly Report it appears a special 'Mental Operation Commando Team' (*Team Komando Operasi Mental*) was established by the military for the purpose of carrying out such indoctrination. As an 'Annex' to the Complete Yearly Report explains: "As follow up to the annihilation of Gestapu, indoctrination for the restoration of the Revolutionary spirit (*jiwa Revolusi*) was launched by the Aceh Special Region National Front Mental Operation Commando Team."[210]

"Indoctrination material", the Report notes in relation to earlier post–1 October indoctrination campaigns carried out by the Mental Operation Commando Team in the province, included the distribution of key military texts, such as Nasution's *Fundamentals of Guerrilla Warfare* and copies of the "Tri Ubaya Sakti" doctrine that had been produced by the military leadership in August 1965 to justify its intention to seize state power, as discussed in chapter 2.[211] The distribution of such material shows that the military leadership intended to form, as Mokoginta had explained in his 11 April 1966 speech, a "perfected Dwikora Cabinet" – a "New Order" through which to consolidate its post-genocide regime.[212]

Mokoginta's vision for the future

Mokoginta was not shy in his praise of the effects of the military's annihilation campaign. On 11 April 1966, he went so far as to describe the "Gestapu Affair" as a "blessing in disguise" (*'rachmat jang tersembunji', suatu 'blessing in disguise'*).[213] This was because, he explained, prior to 1 October 1965 the Indonesian nation had been heading in the wrong direction. Not only was the Indonesian economy faltering, its people had been fooled by leaders who were "[o]nly good at making speeches . . . slogans and mottos" and who insisted on living in a way that was "foreign to the people",[214] a criticism which he aimed at both Sukarno and the PKI alike.

Mokoginta, however, did not only aim his criticism at Sukarno and the PKI. He also took aim at "Liberal Democracy" and "Western political thought" in general. "We cannot forget," he explains, that:

> both Liberal Democracy and Communism are products of Western political thought and norms. Both of these are foreign to the norms and mentality of Eastern people, especially Indonesians . . . [B]oth must be obliterated from our political life (*dilenjapkan dari kehidupan politik kita*).[215]

In doing so, Mokoginta portrayed the genocide as an unavoidable clash of civilisations in which the military had been forced to act to preserve the nation's genuine character.

Mokoginta was especially critical of the role played by political parties and mass organisations within the "Western democracy" (*demokrasi barat*) model that had been allowed to develop in Indonesia.[216] Under this model, he argued, political parties and mass organisations had been given too much power, which in turn drove these groups to "seek political domination". Meanwhile, these excessive freedoms had allowed conflicts to develop, leading to "cliques or interests that went against the national interest".[217] In short, Mokoginta sought to blame Indonesia's political upheavals on an excess of democracy and blamed the victims of the military's annihilation campaign for bringing the killings upon themselves.

The solution, Mokoginta argued, was for the military to continue to implement martial law throughout Sumatra through the retention of the island's Pepelrada, while Sumatra's "political class" was instructed to "cleanse" itself of all "foreign" political influence and to instead focus its energies on re-building the economy.[218] Democratic space in Indonesia was to be eliminated, while the military was to emerge as the dominant political force.

***

The two campaigns of anti-Chinese violence and the purge of Aceh's civil service demonstrate the systematic nature of the military's involvement in the genocide and its consolidation period. Not only did the military encourage and facilitate violence against members of Aceh's Chinese community when such violence served its purposes, it also ended this violence when the military feared it was moving beyond its control. That the military was able to bring this violence under control so quickly demonstrates the controlled and calculated nature of the violence unleashed by the military during this time. The purpose of the military's annihilation campaign, after all, was to achieve the very specific political aim of bringing the military to power.

Meanwhile, by insisting on sticking to the letter, if not the spirit, of the law to purge Aceh's civil service, the military managed to maintain the integrity of the civil service as an operating arm of the state, while subverting its activities to its own purposes. Far from descending into the type of chaos described in the military's propaganda accounts of the violence, the genocide was highly coordinated and calibrated to be responsive to the operational objectives of the military leadership. The intent of the military was to capture the Indonesian state and recreate it in its own image. This led to a situation in which the military promoted a campaign of unchecked physical violence while adopting a "nation building" stance during the consolidation phase. It is perhaps this consolidation phase that, more than any other, illuminates the highly calibrated nature of this campaign.

Notes

1 The published version of this speech is not dated. During the course of this speech Mokoginta declares, "Today is the second day of Easter." 'Kebidjaksanaan Pembangunan di Wilayah Sumatera', in Letdjen A.J. Mokoginta, *Koleksi Pidato2/Kebidjaksanaan Panglima Daerah Sumatra* (Medan: Koanda Sumatera, 1966), p. 267.

2 Capitalisation in original, other emphasis added. 'Kebidjaksanaan Pembangunan di Wilayah Sumatera', in Letdjen A.J. Mokoginta, *Koleksi Pidato2*, pp. 264–265.

3 Harold Crouch, *The Army and Politics in Indonesia* (Jakarta: Equinox Publishing, 2007, originally 1978), pp. 179–192; and, Ulf Sundhaussen, *The Road to Power: Indonesian Military Politics, 1945–1967* (Kuala Lumpur: Oxford University Press, 1982), p. 236.

4 Harold Crouch, *The Army and Politics in Indonesia*, p. 187.

5 Ulf Sundhaussen, *The Road to Power*, pp. 234–235.

6 Soekardjo Wilardjito, *Mereka Mendorong Bung Karno: Kesaksian Seorang Pengawal Presiden* (Yogyakarta: Penerbit Galangpress, 2009), p. 341.

7 *Ibid.*, p. 342.

8 *Ibid.*, p. 331.

9 *Ibid.*

10 Ulf Sundhaussen, *The Road to Power*, p. 236.

11 Crouch lists fifteen ministers who were identified by the military to be arrested on this day in Jakarta. The arrests were performed by Sarwo Edhie and the RPKAD as well as, in one case, by KAPPI. Harold Crouch, *The Army and Politics in Indonesia*, p. 195.

12 'Kebidjaksanaan Pembangunan di Wilayah Sumatera', in Letdjen A.J. Mokoginta, *Koleksi Pidato2*, pp. 264–265.

13 *Ibid.*, p. 239.

14 Interview with Dahlan Sulaiman, Banda Aceh, 29 December 2011, p. 4.

15 Harold Crouch, *The Army and Politics in Indonesia*, p. 165.

16 *Ibid.*, pp. 165, 167.

17 John R. Maxwell, 'Soe Hok-Gie: A Biography of a Young Indonesian Intellectual', PhD thesis, Department of Political and Social Change, Research School of Pacific and Asian Studies, The Australian National University, 1997, p. 139.

18 Ulf Sundhaussen, *The Road to Power*, pp. 230–231.

19 *Ibid.*, p. 233.

20 Crouch argues KAPPI was officially formed on 9 February 1966, *Ibid.* Harold Crouch, *The Army and Politics in Indonesia*, p. 184.

21 Ulf Sundhaussen, *The Road to Power*, pp. 235–236.

22 Interview with Dahlan Sulaiman, Banda Aceh, 29 December 2011, p. 2.

23 A separate organisation named 'KAPI' (*Kesatuan Aksi Pelajar Indonesia*: Indonesian [High School] Student Action Front) was also formed at this time, specifically for middle and senior high school students. It subsequently joined with KAPPI, which embraced students and youth of all ages. *Ibid.*

24 *Ibid.*

25 *Ibid.*

26 Charles Coppel, *Indonesian Chinese in Crisis* (Kuala Lumpur: Oxford University Press, 1983), p. 69.

27 Robert Cribb and Charles Coppel, 'A genocide that never was: explaining the myth of anti-Chinese massacres in Indonesia, 1965-66', *Journal of Genocide Research*, Vol. 11, Issue 4, p. 450; also, Charles Coppel, *Indonesian Chinese in Crisis*, pp. 59–61.

28 Jamie S. Davidson, *From Rebellion to Riots: Collective Violence on Indonesian Borneo* (Wisconsin: University of Wisconsin Press, 2008), pp. 56–84. West Kalimantan is home to Indonesia's largest Chinese population. According to Davidson, anti-PKI violence "failed to materialise" in West Kalimantan during the immediate aftermath of 1 October due to the relatively small size of the organisation in the province. Allegations of Chinese complicity in the actions of the 30 September Movement did, however, gain traction. From March 1966, as anti-Chinese sentiment spread nationally, new restrictive policies aimed at West Kalimantan's Chinese population were introduced in the province, while Chinese people accused of being associated with the PKI were ordered to leave the province by Brigadier General Ryacudu, Head of West Kalimantan's 'G30S PKI Annihilation Operation'. Key PKI cadre managed to escape arrest and built an extensive underground organisation in Bengkayang district, from where they launched an armed resistance movement under the name of the West Kalimantan Communist Army (TKKB: *Tentara Komunis Kalimantan Barat*). In early 1967, the local military launched a series of operations to crush the resistance movement,

whose members were described as a "band of Chinese communists". Anti-Chinese massacres broke out in the province in November 1967. The number of Chinese believed to have been killed in West Kalimantan at this time range from 2,000 to 5,000. *Ibid.* These killings are not generally included in discussions of anti-Chinese violence resulting from the military's annihilation campaign against the PKI.

29 Charles Coppel, *Indonesian Chinese in Crisis*, p. 69; also, Eric Morris, 'Islam and Politics in Aceh: A Study of Centre-Periphery Relations in Indonesia', PhD thesis, Cornell University, 1983,', pp. 247–248.

30 *Ibid.*, p. 448.

31 *Ibid.*, pp. 458–461.

32 My sincere thanks to Chan Chung Tak for making this meeting possible. The following interview with Ho, Xie and Wak was conducted as a multilingual group interview, with Chan kindly acting as translator.

33 Interview with Ho Fui Yen, Xie Jie Fang and Wak Tin Chaw, Hong Kong, 1 November, 2011, pp. 3, 12, 31, 33.

34 *Ibid.*, pp. 3, 29, 30–31.

35 *Ibid.*, pp. 31, 36–37, 40.

36 *Ibid.*, p. 9.

37 The Association of Overseas Chinese (*Asosiasi Huakiao*) should not be confused with the term 'overseas Chinese' (*Huakiao*), which can be used to describe ethnic Chinese communities living outside China without regard to political orientation. Leo Suryadinata (ed.), *Ethnic Chinese in Contemporary Indonesia* (Singapore: Institute of Southeast Asian Studies, 2008), pp. 3; also, Song Zhongquan, 'Ten Years of the Qiao Zong (1962)', in Leo Suryadinata (ed.), *Political Thinking of the Indonesian Chinese, 1900–1995: A Sourcebook* (Singapore: Singapore University Press, 1999), p. 87. The local Chinese-language school where Ho and Xie taught was run by *Asosiasi*-affiliated teachers. Meanwhile, Wak's father, who had been politically active before the formation of the *Asosiasi*, was both a leader within the 'overseas Chinese community' and the *Asosiasi*. Interview with Ho Fui Yen, Xie Jie Fang and Wak Tin Chaw, Hong Kong, 1 November, 2011, pp. 14, 21. Ho, Xie and Wak refer to the ethnic Chinese community in Aceh collectively as "*orang Tionghoa*" (lit. Chinese people).

38 Siauw Tiong Djin, *Siauw Giok Tjhan: riwayat perjuangan seorang patriot membangun nasion Indonesia dan masyarakat Bhineka Tunggal Ika* (Jakarta: Hastra Mitra, 1999), p. 386.

39 Aimee Dawis, 'Chinese Education in Indonesia: Developments in Chinese Education in Post-1998 Era', in Leo Suryadinata (ed.), *Ethnic Chinese in Contemporary Indonesia*, p. 79.

40 In 1927 the Dutch colonial government had launched a crackdown against communist forces in the Indies. This crackdown resulted in the loss of direct contact between Chinese communists in China and Indonesia. The pro-Kuomintang group, meanwhile, continued to grow in size and influence. George McT. Kahin, 'The Chinese in Indonesia', *Far Eastern Survey*, Vol. 15, No. 21 (23 October 1946), p. 328.

41 Hong Liu, *China and the Shaping of Indonesia, 1949–1965* (Japan: Kyoto University Press, 2011), p. 157.

42 Audrey Kahin and George McT. Kahin, *Subversion as Foreign Policy: The Secret Eisenhower and Dulles Debacle in Indonesia* (New York: The New Press, 1995), p. 121.

43 Discussion with Chan Chung Tak, Hong Kong, 1 November 2011.

44 Nazaruddin Sjamsuddin, *The Republican Revolt: A Study of Acehnese Rebellion* (Singapore: Institute of Southeast Asian Studies, 1985), pp. 296–297.

45 Leo Suryadinata, *Pribumi Indonesians, the Chinese Minority and China* (Singapore: Heinemann Asia, 1992), p. 12.

46 *Ibid.*, pp. 130–132.

47 *Ibid.*, p. 134.

48 Indonesia's productive capacity had been destroyed during the Japanese occupation and the subsequent armed struggle against the Dutch. The country also had little industry. As the ethnic Chinese minority had run important economic activities since colonial times, discriminatory actions against Chinese businesses during the 1950s were popularly seen as an extension as the righting of colonial-era injustices. Thee Kian Wie, *Indonesia's Economy Since Independence* (Singapore: Institute of Southeast Asian Studies, 2012), p. 20.

49 Charles Coppel, *Indonesian Chinese in Crisis*, pp. 37–38.

50 Leo Suryadinata, *Pribumi Indonesians*, pp. 135–136.

51 Daniel Lev, *No Concessions: The Life of Yap Thiam Hien, Indonesian Human Rights Lawyer* (Washington: University of Washington Press, 2011), p. 173.

52 Ulf Sundhaussen, *The Road to Power*, p. 179.

53 This alliance was known as the 'Jakarta-Peking Axis' during the closing years of Guided Democracy (1963–1965). Liu Hong, 'Chinese Overseas and a Rising China', in Zheng Yongnian (ed.), *China and International Relations: The Chinese View and Contribution of Wang Gungwu* (Oxon: Routledge, 2010), p. 186.

54 Ulf Sundhaussen, *The Road to Power*, p. 179.

55 Peter Dale Scott, 'The United States and the Overthrow of Sukarno, 1965–1976', *Pacific Affairs*, Vol. 58 (Summer 1985), pp. 239–264.

56 John Roosa, *Prextext for Mass Murder: The September 30th Movement and Suharto's coup d'etat in Indonesia* (Wisconsin: University of Wisconsin Press, 2006), pp. 61–81.

57 'Telegram From the Department of State to the Embassy in Indonesia', Washington, 22 October 1965, cited in, US Department of State, *Foreign Relations of the United States, 1964–1968: Volume XXVI, Indonesia; Malaysia- Singapore; Philippines* (Washington DC: Government Printing Office, 2001), p. 332.

58 Marshall Green, *Indonesia, Crisis and Transformation, 1965–1968* (Washington, DC: The Compass Press, 1990), p. 52.

59 *Ibid.*, p. 59.

60 Charles Coppel, *Indonesian Chinese in Crisis*, p. 55. Brigadier General Soetjipto would also initiate the formation of KAP-Gestapu, the state-sponsored death squad, in Jakarta on 3 October 1965. Harold Crouch, 'The Indonesian Army in Politics: 1960-1971', PhD thesis, Monash University, 1975, p. 255.

61 Marshall Green, *Indonesia, Crisis and Transformation*, p. 56.

62 'Telegram From Marshall Green, US Embassy in Jakarta to US Department of State', 16 October 1965, p. 2, in US Department of State.

63 'Telegram 1086 From US Embassy in Jakarta to State Department', 19 October 1965', cited in, Bradley Simpson, *Economists With Guns: Authoritarian Development and U.S.-Indonesian Relations, 1960–1968* (Stanford, CA: Stanford University Press, 2008), p. 180.

64 'Telegram From the Embassy in Indonesia to the Department of State', Jakarta, 17 October 1965, cited in, US Department of State, *Foreign Relations of the United States*, p. 325.

65 'Army Commander Suharto's Charge of Air Force Involvement in His Statement Made Upon Discovery of the Bodies of the Generals on October 4', in 'Relating to the "September 30th Movement" and Its Epilogue', *Indonesia*, Vol. 1 (April 1966), p. 159.

66 Letdjen A.J. Mokoginta, *Koleksi Pidato2*, p. 172.

67 *Keputusan Bersama No. Ist-I/Kpts/1965*, Banda Aceh, 6 October 1965, p. 1.

68 'Chronologis Kedjadian2 jang Berhubungan dengan Gerakan 30 September Didaerah Kodam-I/Atjeh', p. 3.

69 It is not known which shop this refers to, though is it is likely it was attacked because of its known or perceived ownership by members of Aceh's ethnic Chinese community.

70 It is not known what 'IPETI' stands for.

71 'Chronologis', p. 3.

72 It was also on this day, for example, that Tjut Husin Fatly, a non-ethnic Chinese Indonesian from Tangerang and head of the PKI's Provincial Secretariat in Aceh, was singled out by protesters because he had travelled to Beijing for medical treatment. As has been discussed in chapter 5, Fatly's house was ransacked and burnt. His wife and preschool-aged daughter were subsequently detained at a "concentration camp" at Mata Ie, where an "executioner" killed his wife upon her release.

73 It is not known which shops these refer to. It is likely they were attacked because of their known or perceived ownership by members of Aceh's Chinese community.

74 It is not known what 'KBM' stands for.

75 'Chronologis', p. 4.

76 Written personal account by Asan, given to the author, 30 October 2011, in Hong Kong, p. 4; Interview with Ho Fui Yen, Xie Jie Fang and Wak Tin Chaw, Hong Kong, 1 November 2011, p. 36.

77 Written personal account by Asan, given to the author, 30 October 2011, in Hong Kong, p. 4.

78 The Military Chronology reports that the "Chung Hua Chung Hui" (*Asosiasi Hua-kiau*) office was destroyed by demonstrators during the afternoon of 8 October. 'Chronologis', p. 3.

79 As outlined above, KAMI was not established in Banda Aceh until January 1966. Considering the timing of Asan's escape, it is possible that Asan is referring to members of the youth organisations involved in the first phase of public killings that later joined KAMI and KAPPI in the province.

80 When asked to clarify this statement, Asan explained, "Islamic fundamentalists" did not initiate the violence against the PKI, but "Islamic executioners" (*algojo Islam*) had been "secretly given weapons" by Ishak Djuarsa "to kill the PKI". Written interview with Asan, given to the author, Hong Kong, 30 October 2011, p. 6.

81 'Blue' is a reference to the Taiwanese (pro-Kuomintang) national emblem, which is depicted as a white sun on a blue background.

82 Wak has recalled how her mother smuggled food to Asan during this period. The food was wrapped in banana leaves and hidden under her clothes. Interview with Ho Fui Yen, Xie Jie Fang and Wak Tin Chaw, Hong Kong, 1 November 2011, p. 38.

83 Written personal account by Asan, given to the author, Hong Kong, 30 October 2011, pp. 4–5.

84 Asan does not say why he did not board the *Kuang Hua* with his family. *Ibid.*, p. 5.

85 '*Pernjataan*', Pengurus Baperki Tjabang Langsa, Langsa, East Aceh, 18 October 1965, p. 1.

86 Emphasis in original. *Ibid.*

87 Sukarno made three announcements between 1 and 18 October 1965, two on 3 October, when he urged the population to remain calm and avoid jumping to conclusions, and the third on 14 October, when he announced he would "formulate a political solution" to the crisis. Cited in, 'Selected Documents', pp. 152–155.

88 '*Pernjataan*', Pengurus Baperki Tjabang Langsa, Langsa, East Aceh 18 October 1965, p. 1.

89 This list remains attached to Baperki's declaration. The fate of these 148 individuals is not known. It is possible that this list, as occurred elsewhere in the province at the time of the genocide, was used as a death list by the military or military-sponsored death squads to identify these individuals for arrest, detention and murder.

90 Emphasis added. '*Pernjataan*', Pengurus Baperki Tjabang Langsa, Langsa, East Aceh, 18 October 1965, pp. 1–'DE2.

91 *Ibid.*, pp. 4–5.

92 'Chronologis', p. 7.

93 The Pemuda Pantjasila was a military-affiliated civilian militia group that was particularly active during the genocide in neighbouring North Sumatra, where it operated

under the direction of the North Aceh Military Command through the framework of the Komando Aksi. Joshua Oppenheimer, 'Show of Force: Film, Ghosts and Genres of Historical Performance in the Indonesian Genocide', PhD thesis, University of the Arts London, 2004, p. 35.

94 'Chronologis', p. 7.
95 *Ibid.*, p. 8.
96 The names of these victims are not listed. *Ibid.*
97 The names of these Chinese victims are listed as Hap Tjok, Min On, Bun Tok Seng and Sio Nam, all from Blang Pidie. *Ibid.*
98 See chapter 6.
99 '*Surat Keputusan No: Kep/Pepelrada-29/10/1965*', Banda Aceh, 20 October 1965, p. 2. As discussed in chapters 5 and 6, the subsequent reporting by members of these organisations was used by the military to identify members of these organisations, some of whom were detained directly before being transported to military-controlled killing sites to be murdered, while others were subsequently "released" (like Asan) before being rearrested by the military or military-sponsored death squads to be murdered.
100 'Chronologis', pp. 1–21.
101 Interview with Ho Fui Yen, Xie Jie Fang and Wak Tin Chaw, Hong Kong, 1 November 2011, p. 5.
102 *Ibid.*, p. 22.
103 *Ibid.*, p. 13.
104 *Ibid.*, p. 22.
105 *Ibid.*, p. 13.
106 *Ibid.*, p. 6.
107 *Ibid.*, p. 4.
108 The houses whose doors were marked were the same houses that had flown the Chinese flag to mark China's National Day on 1 October 1965. *Ibid.*, p. 9.
109 *Ibid.*, pp. 7–9.
110 *Ibid.*, p. 7.
111 *Ibid.*, p. 8.
112 *Ibid.*, p. 10.
113 *Ibid.*
114 *Ibid.*, p. 25.
115 *Ibid.*, p. 23.
116 Interview with Zainal Abidin, 14 February 2009, Banda Aceh, p. 9.
117 *Ibid.*
118 Charles Coppel, *Indonesian Chinese in Crisis*, p. 67.
119 'Perkembangan di Bidang Politik/Keamanan: Mengenai Apel Setia WNI Keturunan Tionghoa dan Demonstrasi Para Peladjar/KAPPI Jang Terdjadi di Dalam Kabupaten Aceh Utara mulai April 1966', in *Laporan Bupati Kepala Daerah T. Ramli Angkasah dalam memimpin Pemerintahan Kabupaten Aceh Utara mulai April 1965 s/d Mai 1966, disampaikan dalam Sidang Paripurnake 1/1966 DPRD-GR Kapbupaten Aceh Utara di Lhokseumawe*, 15 June 196[6], p. 1.
120 *Ibid.*
121 *Ibid.*, pp. 10, 12.
122 *Ibid.*
123 *Ibid.*
124 *Ibid.*, p. 2.
125 *Ibid.*
126 *Ibid.*
127 *Ibid.*
128 *Ibid.*, p. 3.
129 *Ibid.*

130 *Ibid.*
131 *Ibid.*, p. 4.
132 *Ibid.*, p. 5.
133 *Ibid.*
134 Interview with Zainal Abidin, 14 February 2009, Banda Aceh, p. 9.
135 This event, or another similar event in the district, was also recorded by the *Peking Review*, which reported how after 15 April 1966 Chinese families in North Aceh were driven from their homes and forced to stand in the sun for more than five hours: "The hooligans [civilian attackers] forced the men to take off their clothes, poured various coloured paint over them, daubed their bodies with anti-China slogans and beat them up." Cited in, Charles Coppel, *Indonesian Chinese in Crisis*, p. 69.
136 'Perkembangan di Bidang Politik/Keamanan', p. 5.
137 'Kesatuan Aksi Pemuda Peladjar Indonesia (KAPPI) Lhokseumawe, Sekretaris Umum Dewan Pengurus Harian Kesatuan Aksi Pemuda Peladjar Indonesia', Sofjan Ibr., Lhokseumawe, North Aceh, 15 June 1966, p. 1.
138 *Ibid.*
139 'Bupati/Kepala Daeah Kab. Atjeh Utara Tentang Pertanjaan2 Dari KAPPI Lhokseumawe', Bupati/Kepala Daerah Kabupaten A. Utara T. Ramli Angkasah, Lhokseumawe, North Aceh, 16 June 1966, p. 1.
140 *Ibid.*, p. 2.
141 Charles Coppel, *Indonesian Chinese in Crisis*, p. 69.
142 Interview with Ho Fui Yen, Xie Jie Fang and Wak Tin Chaw, Hong Kong, 1 November 2011, p. 10, 12.
143 *Ibid.*, pp. 10, 13.
144 *Ibid.* Charles Coppel argues all 10,000 refugees who fled Aceh at this time were "alien" Chinese. This assessment is drawn from Djuarsa's 8 May 1966 announcement that only "alien" Chinese were required to leave the province by 17 August 1966 and a report produced by the Indonesian government's 'Special Staff for Chinese Affairs', produced in 1968. Charles Coppel, *Indonesian Chinese in Crisis*, pp. 69, 194. Eric Morris, an Aceh specialist, meanwhile, argues Chinese with Indonesian citizenship were also forced to flee the province at this time. Eric Morris, 'Islam and Politics in Aceh', p. 248. The evidence presented in this chapter supports Morris' finding that both "alien" and "non alien" Chinese made up this figure. The Indonesian state had little incentive to admit that Indonesian citizens of Chinese descent were forced to leave Aceh province at this time as part of a military-sponsored campaign as such a campaign was clearly racist in character.
145 Interview with Ho Fui Yen, Xie Jie Fang and Wak Tin Chaw, Hong Kong, 1 November 2011, p. 11.
146 *Ibid.*
147 Charles Coppel, *Indonesian Chinese in Crisis*, p. 92.
148 *Ibid.*, p. 93.
149 Letdjen A.J. Mokoginta, *Koleksi Pidato2*, p. 243.
150 Yen-ling Tsai and Douglas Kammen, 'Anti-Communist Violence and the Ethnic Chinese in Medan, North Sumatra', in Douglas Kammen and Katharine McGregor (eds.), *The Contours of Mass Violence in Indonesia, 1965–68* (Singapore: NUS Press, 2012), p. 142.
151 'Hua Zhong' is an alternate typography for '*Hua Chiao Tsung Hui*', referred to throughout this book as the '*Asosiasi Huakiao*'. *Ibid.*, p. 137.
152 *Ibid.*, p. 142.
153 For example, 'No: 591/UPO/1965, Kutipan dari daftar surat keputusan Gubernur/ Kepala Daerah Istimewa Atjeh', Banda Aceh, 18 October 1965.
154 Purge documents have been recovered from Banda Aceh, Aceh Besar, Pidie, North Aceh, East Aceh, Central Aceh, West Aceh, South Aceh and Southeast Aceh.
155 Five of the documents have been signed by, or on behalf of, Kamil.

156 Thirty-four of the documents have been signed by a bupati.

157 Five of the documents have been signed by Regional Secretaries.

158 These heads of government services included Aceh's Head of Administration (*Kepala Tata Usaha*), C. Silitonga (forty-four documents); the head of Aceh's Government Staffing Bureau, Teuku Pakeh (one document); the head of Aceh's Department of Peasantry, Abad Wiradinata (one document); the head of Aceh's Department of Inland Fisheries, Husin Ali B. (eleven documents); and the head of Aceh's Department of Education and Culture, Idris Adamy (four documents).

159 Three of the documents refer to students: M. Junan B., who is referred to as studying in Tegal, Central Java (dated 20 November 1965) and M. Husin and M. Saleh Djalil, studying in Bandung, West Java (both dated 22 November 1965).

160 The eleven people named in this document are: Bahri, Abd. Hamid and Ismail from Banda Aceh; Murito and Baharuddin from Aceh Besar; Mariana from Sigli; Parsan from Lhokseumawe; Baramsjah and Mawardi Hasan from Takengon; Mohammad Jusuf from Meulaboh; and T. Husin from Tapak Tuan. 'No: [?]/Pbh/SK/1966', Salinan [words unclear], Banda Aceh, 5 February 1966.

161 'Kutipan dari daftar surat keputusan Gubernur/Kepala Daerah Istimewa Atjeh, No. 591/UPO/1965', signed by Gubernur/Kepala Daerah Istimwea Atjeh Njak Adam Kamil, Banda Aceh, 18 October 1965.

162 "*No.TR.072/OPU/1965*", *Ibid.*

163 KOTI G-V, KOTI's political section, was headed by Brigadier General Sucipto, who had formed the Action Front for the Crushing of the 30 September Movement (KAP-Gestapu: *Komando Aksi Pengganyangan-Gerakan Tiga Puluh September*) in Jakarta on 4 October 1965.

164 The document additionally refers to the "Loyalty Pledges" (Declaration Letters) discussed in chapter 6 which "called for the immediate disbanding/freezing of the PKI and its mass org[anisations]". 'Kutipan dari daftar surat keputusan Gubernur/Kepala Daerah Istimewa Atjeh, No. 591/UPO/1965', signed by Gubernur/Kepala Daerah Istimwea Atjeh Njak Adam Kamil, Banda Aceh, 18 October 1965.

165 A 'State of War' (*Keadaan Perang*) was declared in Jakarta on 2 October. A directive issued on 4 October 1965, sent from the Minister of Information, Major General Achmadi, is addressed to the Military Commander for Greater Jakarta "acting as Pepelrada/Peperda". 'No. 155/M/65', Meneteri Penerangan Republik Indonesia, Major Djendral Achmadi, Djakarta, 4 October 1965, reproduced in, *Fakta2 Persoalan Sekitar 'Gerakan 30 September'* (Jakarta: Pusat Penerangan Angkatan Darat, 1965), pp. 160–162.

166 'Political Savingram No. 58', Australian Embassy, Jakarta, 19 November 1965, p. 6, cited in David Jenkins and Douglas Kammen, 'The Army Para-commando Regiment and the Reign of Terror in Central Java and Bali', in Douglas Kammen and Katharine McGregor (eds.), *The Contours of Mass Violence in Indonesia, 1965–68* (Singapore: NUS Press, 2012), p. 85. It is not explained why anyone would state they did not wish to work under such circumstances.

167 This Decision (*Surat Keputusan No.Kep/Peplrada-29/10/1965*) was issued by Djuarsa acting in his capacity as Pepelrada. See, for example, 'Salinan dari daftar surat2-keputusan Kepala Dinas Kehutanan Daerah Swatantra Tingkat I Daerah Istimewa Atjeh', signed by Kepala Tata Usaha, C. Silitonga, Banda Aceh, 20 November 1965.

168 For example, 'Kutipan daftar surat keputusan Gubernur Kepala Daerah Istimewa Atjeh Nomor: 621/UPO/1965', signed by Sekretaris Daerah [name unclear], Banda Aceh, 11 November 1965.

169 For example, 'No: 28/Rhs/A', Pengawai2/Guru2 S.D. jang terlibat dalam "G.30.S.", Kepala Dinas P.D. dan K. Daerah Istimewa Atjeh, Banda Aceh, 6 December 1965.

170 For example, 'Kutipan dari daftar surat keputusan Kepala Daeah Tgk. II Atjeh Tengah', signed by Bupati/Kepala Daerah Tk. II Atjeh Tengah, Takengon, Central Aceh, 20 October 1965.

171 These targeted individuals are identified as: "Moefizar Jusuf, from the Customs Office; Nurwan Nanil, a skilled worker from the Customs Office; Salomo S, a skilled worker from the Customs Office and M. Nur a skilled worker from the Customs Office". 'Chronologis', p. 9.

172 These suspensions are said to have been "[b]ased on a decree issued by the Governor, *No. 195/Sk/Per/26*". *Ibid.*, pp. 10–11.

173 These targeted individuals are identified as: "Ibnu Sjakur, Head of the Forestry Department for Aceh Special Region; R. Pontjeresi K.D., Head of the Agriculture Department for Aceh Special Region; Mohd Samikidin, Second Deputy Head of the Periodic Work Group for Baproda (*Badan Produksi Desa*: Village Production Body)/ Deputy Head of the *Front Nasional*; Buchari Jusif, member of the Baproda Mass Movement (*Gerakan Massa Baproda*); Dasar . . . and Anas HC". *Ibid.*

174 Asan was shown a box of Anas' belongings at the police station where Asan is said to have "surrendered himself", while Samikidin was killed after being "pulled off a train" following his "surrender" to the Banda Aceh Kodim and his detention at Zainal Abidin's government office in Seulimuem. (See chapter 5.)

175 Interview with "Latifah", Banda Aceh, 15 February 2009; Interview with "Shadia", Banda Aceh, 12 February 2009.

176 Further research is required to locate the individuals named in these documents, or, should this prove impossible, their surviving relatives.

177 The ten people identified as "missing" or "not at their posts" are listed as: S.M. Lahat, Takengon (20 October 1965), Chalidin Hakim, Takengon (27 October 1965), Achmad Banta, Takengon (27 October 1965), Sampe Ganti, Takengon (27 October 1965), Tjut Radja, Sigli (28 October 1965), T. Natsjah, Banda Aceh (18 November 1965) and Alimuddin, Tapaktuan (27 October 1966).

178 For example, see 'dismissal letter' dated 11 November 1965.

179 The seven people identified as being "under the arrest of those who have the authority" are listed as: S.M. Lahat, Takengon (20 October 1965), Chalidin Hakim, Takengon (27 October 1965), Achmad Banta, Takengon (27 October 1965), Sampe Ganti, Takengon (27 October 1965), Tjut Radja, Sigli (28 October 1965), T. Natsjah, Banda Aceh (18 November 1965) and Alimuddin, Tapaktuan (27 October 1966).

180 The seven people listed as being "under house arrest" are listed as: Latif, Lhokseumawe (31 October 1965); Supranoto, Bireuen (31 October 1965); Ismail Ruddin, Bireuen (31 October 1965); Al Wahab Penggabean, Muara Dua Juanda (31 October 1965); Parsan Samanurdy, Lhokseumawe (31 October 1965); T. Sulaiman, Lhoksukon (31 October 1965); and Nur Amal, Aceh Timur (17 May 1966).

181 For example, see 'dismissal letter' dated 31 October 1965.

182 '*Peraturan Pemerintah No. 8, 1952*'. Available online: https://ropeg-kemenkes.or.id/documents/pp_08_1952.pdf. This Presidential Regulation is cited in the purge documents thirty-six times.

183 '*Undang-undang No. 21, 1952*'. Available online: www.ropeg-depkes.or.id/documents/uu_17_1961.pdf. This Law is cited in the purge documents forty-seven times.

184 '*Undang-undang No. 18, 1961*'. Available online: www.ropeg-depkes.or.id/documents/uu_18_1961.pdf. This Law is cited in the purge documents thirty-seven times.

185 '*Undang-undang No. 24, 1956.*' Available online: http://dapp.bappenas.go.id/website/peraturan/file/pdf/UU_1956_024.pdf. This Law is cited in the purge documents forty-nine times.

186 '*Undang-undang No. 1, 1957*'. Available online: www.bpn.go.id/Publikasi/Peraturan-Perundangan/Undang-Undang/undang-undang-nomor-1-tahun-1957-927. This Law is cited in the purge documents forty-nine times.

187 '*Peraturan Pemerintan No. 6, 1959*'.Available online: www.hukumonline.com/pusatdata/detail/lt50405e58742da/node/951/pp-no-6-tahun-1959-pendirian-institut-teknologi. This Regulation is cited in the purge documents fifty-six times.

188 By late 1965 the Indonesian economy was in crisis. Production was in decline, communication networks were on the brink of collapse and electricity supply was

breaking down. On 13 December 1965, the Rupiah was devalued, with Rp. 1,000 becoming Rp. 1. Ulf Sundhaussen, *The Road to Power*, pp. 229–230.

189 The minor differences in these documents appear to be the product of typing multiple versions of the same document in a short space of time. See purge documents file.

190 For example, 'Salinan dari surat keputusan Kepala Dinas Kehutanan Propinsi Daerah Isimewa Atjeh, signed by C. Silitonga, Kepala Tata Usaha, Banda Aceh, 24 December 1966, No. 285/1966'.

191 *Keppres No. 85/Kogam/66.*

192 *Instruksi Pesiden No. Inst/09/Kogam/5/66.*

193 *No. 290/XV/10/KD.*

194 *No. 5/Team/Ch/1966, 10 October 1966.*

195 The documents also claim to draw authority from a radiogram from the *Kas Kogam* (*Kepala Staff Kogam*: Kogam Head of Staff) (*No. T-724/DA/8/1966*).

196 Suharto began to sign orders "in the name of" (*atas nama*) "President/Supreme Commander of the Armed Forces" from 12 March 1966, the day following the 11 March Order. See, 'Presiden Republik Indonesia Pengumuman No. 1', Pemimpin/Panglima Tertinggi/Pemimpin Besar Revolusi/Mandataris MPRS atas nama beliau ttd Letnan Jendral Soeharto, Jakarta, 12 March 1966, in Alex Dinuth (ed.), *Dokumen Terpilih Sekitar G.30.S/PKI* (Jakarta: Intermasa, 1997), pp. 166–167. Suharto was officially appointed President on 12 May 1967. 'Ketetapan Majelis Permusyawaratan Rakyat Sementara Republik Indonesia No: XXXIII/MPRS/1967', Ketua Majelis Permusyawaratan Rakyat Sementara Republik Indonesia, Jenderal A.H. Nasution, Jakarta, 12 March 1967, in *Ibid.*, pp. 286–289.

197 The full list of recipients includes: Department of Internal Affairs and Regional Autonomy in Jakarta; DPRD-GR for Aceh Special Region (Komisi A) in Banda Aceh; Governor/Head of Aceh Special Region in Banda Aceh; Governor/Head of Aceh Special Region (Staff Bureau) Banda Aceh; Governor/Head of Aceh Special Region (Finance Bureau) Banda Aceh; Head of Legal Department, Governor's Office/Head of Aceh Special Region, Banda Aceh; Head of Ministry of Forestry, 9 Djuanda St, Bogor; The Government Treasury (*Kas Negara*) in Banda Aceh [possibly the provincial body responsible for the civil service pay roll]; Pangdahan 'A' Acting as Head of Pepelrada in Banda Aceh; Bupati/Head Level II Provincial Government East Aceh in Langsa; Head of Forestry Level II, in Langsa. *Ibid.*

198 Interview with "Shadia", Banda Aceh, 12 February 2009.

199 Justus M. Van der Kroef, 'Indonesia's Political Prisoners', *Pacific Affairs*, Vol. 49, No. 4 (Winter 1976–1977), p. 628.

200 *Ibid.*

201 *Ibid.*, pp. 628–629.

202 For example, 'Salinan dari surat keputusan Kepala Dinas Kehutanan Propinsi Daerah Isimewa Atjeh No. 285/1966', signed by C. Silitonga, Kepala Tata Usaha, Banda Aceh, 24 December 1966.

203 'Instruksi Presiden/Panglima Tertinggi Angkatan Bersendjata Republik Indonesia/ Panglima Besar Komando Ganjang Malaysia No. Inst-09/Kogam/5/66', [title unclear in the document] Suharto, 13 May 1966.

204 Justus M. Van der Kroef, 'Indonesia's Political Prisoners', p. 633.

205 'Instruksi Presiden/Panglima Tertinggi Angkatan Bersendjata Republik Indonesia/ Panglima Besar Komando Ganjang Malaysia No. Inst-09/Kogam/5/66', [title unclear in the document] Suharto, 13 May 1966, p. 2.

206 *Ibid.*, p. 3.

207 Justus M. Van der Kroef, 'Indonesia's Political Prisoners', p. 631. A 'Map of detention centres across Indonesia', produced by Tapol (1976), does not show prisons, labour camps, detention centres and interrogation centres in Aceh. Available online: http://intersections.anu.edu.au/issue10/pohlman.html. It is not clear if this absence is

because such centres were not established in the province, or because research has yet to be conducted in the province. I have yet to come across references to such centres through my research.

208 Interview with "Latifah", Banda Aceh, 15 February 2009.
209 "Shadia" and "Nurdin" are pseudonyms. Interview with "Shadia", Banda Aceh, 12 February 2009.
210 'Annex: Territorial Kodam-I/Atjeh', p. 2.
211 *Laporan Tahunan Lengkap Kodam-I/Kohanda Atjeh, Tahun 1965* (Banda Aceh: Kodam-I Banda Aceh, 1 February 1966), p. 72.
212 'Bupati/Kepala Daeah Kab. Atjeh Utara Tentang Pertanjaan2 Dari KAPPI Lhokseumawe', Bupati/Kepala Daerah Kabupaten A. Utara T. Ramli Angkasah, Lhokseumawe, North Aceh, 16 June 1966, p. 1.
213 English in the original. Letdjen A.J. Mokoginta, *Koleksi Pidato2*, p. 263.
214 *Ibid.*, p. 264.
215 *Ibid.*, p. 270.
216 *Ibid.*, p. 269.
217 *Ibid.*
218 *Ibid.*

Conclusion
Anatomy of a genocide

This book has presented a new narrative of the Indonesian genocide in Aceh. It has demonstrated that the military did not initially attempt to deny its role in this campaign. Instead, this book has shown that the military openly coordinated its initiation, before mobilising civilian government and society to participate in its implementation – all the while meticulously documenting its progression. The genocide was pursued as official policy and the documents and records presented in these pages were produced to help better coordinate this policy, enabling the genocide to be simultaneously coordinated at the national, inter-provincial, provincial, subdistrict and village levels. This new narrative, though limited to one province (Aceh) and one inter-regional chain of command (Sumatra), presents new opportunities to understand the Indonesian genocide as a national event and raises new questions, in particular, as regards the question of how we approach the question of accountability.

Why genocide?

We have already examined why the killings constitute a case of genocide under the 1948 Genocide Convention. As I have argued, there is strong evidence the military leadership both possessed and acted upon an intent to destroy Indonesia's communist group. This intent was first stated on 1 October 1965, when the military leadership announced it was mandatory for soldiers to "completely annihilate" the 30 September Movement. It would then evolve on 4 October to include the order for civilians to participate in this annihilation campaign. By 14 October, the military had established a "War Room" to oversee its implementation.

I have also argued the military's target group constitutes a protected group under the Convention. The military's attack did not only target card-carrying members of the PKI, but rather a much larger group that can be understood in part as a religious group (identified by the military as "atheists", while by its members as "Red Muslims"); in part as an ethnic or racial group (in the case of ethnic Chinese victims); and, as per Robert Cribb's argumentation, as an ideologically constituted national or subnational group (Indonesia's communist group).

But why did the military decide to pursue genocide? The genocide was not inevitable. It was the result of a series of conscious decisions and orders. Indeed, it was the result of a one-sided war.

During the months leading up to 1 October 1965, both the military and PKI were involved in a rapidly escalating struggle for the Indonesian state. Unable to compete openly through elections, the PKI pursued a mass mobilisation strategy while the military leadership attempted to expand its martial law powers. This competition was sent into hyper-drive by the *Ganyang Malaysia* campaign. Sukarno called upon Indonesian society to mobilise in order to defeat Western imperialism and complete the Indonesian revolution while the PKI called for the crushing of "*Nekolim*" ('Neo-Colonialist, Colonialist, Imperialist') forces within the country. The military leadership began to fear the PKI intended to use this campaign to bring itself to power. This fear appeared to be confirmed on 17 August 1965, when Sukarno announced his support for the PKI's proposal to establish a 'Fifth Force' or people's army, which directly threatened the military's monopoly over armed force.

The military leadership believed the PKI was readying itself for a confrontation. It expected a civil war. It is possible the military truly believed the 30 September Movement was the opening salvo of a PKI-led uprising. It would have become quickly apparent, however, that this was not the case. The PKI may have talked tough but its members were unarmed and caught off-guard both by the 30 September Movement and by the military's aggressive response. The military, after all, had been preparing to launch its own bid for state power on the back of just such a pretext event.

The Movement's murder of the generals enabled the military to launch a much more forceful attack than otherwise would have been possible. As Sukarno dithered, a vacuum of power developed in the capital. The military seized this initiative and began to operate autonomously while seizing control over the media and placing civilian government under *de facto* martial law conditions. Then, when it became clear that a PKI uprising was not occurring, the military chose to intensify its attack. It deliberately pursued a one-sided war against an unarmed segment of the population that was unable to offer any meaningful resistance. As the military explained on 11 October, the PKI and all those alleged to be associated with it were to be "wiped from the face of the earth".[1]

Identifying phases in the genocide

This book has identified four phases within the genocide in Aceh: an initiation phase, a phase of public violence, a phase of systematic mass killings and a consolidation phase. During the initiation phase, the military presented an essentially "aspirational program", wherein the military leadership communicated its intent to launch a violent campaign to physically annihilate the PKI and anyone considered to be associated with it. It is not possible to flick a switch and have genocide running at full swing. Mass violence needs to be coordinated and there needs to be consensus over what sort of a campaign is to be carried out. Coordinating consensus was the function of the key orders outlined in chapters 3 and 4.

On the morning of 1 October 1965, orders were sent out by Suharto in Jakarta that there had been a coup, said to have been launched by the 30 September Movement. It was also communicated that those loyal to the military leadership should await and then follow his orders. At 9pm, Suharto then announced that the military leadership had "already managed to take control of the situation" and that both "the centre" and "the regions" were now under the military leadership's control.

Records of the military's internal communications from 1 October on, documented in chapter 3, indicate that it was the military leadership's intention to act independently of President Sukarno from the beginning. The military leadership did not declare their activities as a coup because their plan was premised on retaining existing state structures and chains of command. The military leadership made it equally clear that it would ignore instructions from Sukarno that it did not wish to obey, acting in an explicitly insubordinate manner on at least two occasions.

The first recorded act of insubordination, as observed by John Roosa, occurred at 4pm on 1 October, when Suharto refused to accept Sukarno's order that he step down from his self-appointed position as temporary Commander of the Armed Forces.[2] The second occurred at midnight when Mokoginta in Medan declared that he and those troops under him recognised "only" the "direct Instructions of the Supreme Commander of ABRI, [and] those [instructions] channelled via the Temporary Leader of the Armed Forces, Major General Suharto". These two acts of insubordination confirm that the military leadership under Suharto acted independently from Sukarno from 1 October 1965, constituting an effective seizure of as much state power as the military needed for its purposes. This did not mean the military had direct control over every aspect of the operation of the Indonesian state from this time. This was never the national military leadership's intention.

These acts of insubordination received no significant challenge from Sukarno, who was only able to repeatedly request that the military leadership comply with his instructions; nor did they face a significant challenge from unsympathetic military units in Central Java and East Java, who had initially signalled their support for the 30 September Movement.[3] The military also faced only minimal resistance from unsympathetic PKI-aligned provincial governors in North Sumatra and Bali, who were, at most, only able to momentarily put the brakes on the military's campaign in their respective areas of operation before they were isolated and arrested.[4] The military leadership was able to contain and override these pockets of resistance. Indeed, at no point did these pockets of resistance represent a serious threat to the military's stated objectives. The military leadership exercised effective control over the repressive and ideological functions of the state from at least 9pm on 1 October, when Suharto announced that he had the regions under his control. This amounted to an undeclared coup, which was launched during the morning of 1 October, hours before the 30 September Movement announced the formation of its Revolution Council at 2pm.

In Aceh, the military leadership named this operation Operasi Berdikari. That this operation was pursued in order to block the PKI from gaining further power, rather than for the purpose of radically restructuring the state, explains why the military leadership felt no compulsion to divest Sukarno of his position as President, unless he attempted to organise a counter-challenge, which he did not.

The military's campaign to seize state power became genocidal when the military leadership announced its intention to physically annihilate the PKI. The earliest record of such a stated intention dates from midnight on 1 October 1965. The swiftness with which these genocidal intentions were announced suggests that large-scale physical confrontation had always been part of the military's original plan to seize control of the state.

By 4 October, the military leadership had announced it was mandatory for civilians to participate in its annihilation campaign, with those who refused to comply liable to become a target of this campaign themselves. The military explained the campaign as justifiable self-defence. This justification, however, lost its legitimacy when it became apparent that the 30 September Movement did not present an ongoing threat. At no stage after the early hours of 1 October was the military's control challenged by the 30 September Movement, and yet its stated intentions to physically annihilate the PKI would only grow from this time. Indeed, by 14 October, the military leadership in Aceh actively conceived of its attack against the PKI as an armed conflict for which the state was to be fully mobilised.

The military also attempted to justify its attack by promoting the idea that it should be understood as a kind of holy war. It did this by propagating false propaganda accounts of PKI attacks against Muslims, which sought to portray the PKI as being responsible for the violence. It also encouraged Aceh's peak Islamic body, the Consultative Council of Ulama, to issue a *fatwa* against the PKI, which described the PKI as an enemy so depraved it was to be assigned the status of "*kafir harbi*", an enemy whom it is permitted to kill and "whom it is mandatory to completely annihilate". The military leadership then publicly legitimised this declaration by having this *fatwa* read in the presence of Mokoginta in front of Banda Aceh's Grand Mosque.

The military's as-yet aspirational genocidal program was, however, unable to move to implementation until several local and national thresholds had been met. The first was met nationally on 5 October, when the military leadership mobilised and rallied behind Suharto on Armed Forces Day in Jakarta. This was a show of force by the military leadership under Suharto, to demonstrate he was serious about his stated objective of annihilating the PKI and all those accused of being associated with it. This intention was then communicated to Indonesia's regional military commands, before being communicated to down to the provincial and district levels.

Asan has testified that the period 1–5 October in Banda Aceh felt like a "gathering storm". Asan and his comrades in the PKI leadership however, miscalculated the military's intentions. Confident that Sukarno would protect them if the military attempted to attack the Party, he and his comrades felt that although the situation looked bad, the violence that was being threatened would not eventuate.

What Asan and his comrades did not realise, but what Mokoginta and Djuarsa understood very well, was that the military leadership, despite retaining the command structures and other organisational trappings of the pre–1 October state, no longer recognised Sukarno's authority, having effectively seized state power on the morning of 1 October.

Once consensus had been established within the military leadership on 5 October that physical annihilation was indeed intended, and once this intention had been consolidated at the national, inter-provincial, provincial and district levels, the genocide was able to shift into its first phase of violence. While the genocide was a nationally coordinated campaign, if the relative local balance of political forces, as in Aceh, was favourable to the military leadership, this first threshold could be reached swiftly. If the local balance of political forces was less favourable to the military leadership, as it was in Central Java and Bali, reaching this first threshold was delayed.[5] This variation did not, however, weaken the centralised nature of the campaign in these areas or lessen military accountability for the violence once it had broken out. Rather, this variation demonstrates the force of the military's campaign, which was always able to override these examples of hesitation to initiate and implement the genocide on a national scale.

I will argue below that the evidence that the Indonesian genocide was initiated and implemented as a centralised and national campaign is overwhelming and beyond any reasonable doubt.

The violence began with military-orchestrated demonstrations and the use of inflammatory slogans and posters. When local forces, such as Dahlan Sulaiman and his comrades in the PII in Banda Aceh, took initiatives to support this campaign, the military provided support when it was in the military's interest to do so. It must be recalled that the pogroms that occurred took place within a context in which the civilian population was being told that it was "mandatory" for them to assist the military in its campaign, thus making all civilian participation, no matter how enthusiastic, coerced to some extent. The pattern that emerges from these pogrom actions in Aceh is of an initial march upon PKI offices carried out with the support, if not open encouragement and direction, of the military, which then progressed to the burning down of offices and other buildings and houses considered associated with the PKI and Indonesia's communist group more broadly. Shortly after this, "arrests" and the "surrender" of people accused of being associated with the PKI commenced. These arrests and surrenders had a pseudo-legal character and received sanction and coordination from the military, with individuals either arrested without charge or legal process before being taken to the military, or "surrendering" themselves directly to the military.

It was at this point that the killings in Aceh began. In some cases individuals or small groups of people were killed directly on the streets, or taken, commonly under the cover of darkness, to death houses or other unidentified locations. There they were murdered, perhaps after being tortured, and their bodies were sometimes left in public places to induce terror and to act as warnings.

The pogroms and public killings broke down normal social bonds and established violence as the manner in which the military's campaign was to be pursued.

Individuals who only days before had been accepted within their communities were now identified as targets to be "annihilated". These actions grew increasingly violent in character and drove the target group of the military's attack into its arms, as members of the targeted organisations sought to escape the violence on the streets – often believing they would be protected if they acquiesced to being taken into custody. It was at this stage that members of the PKI and its affiliated organisations began surrendering themselves *en masse* to the military in Aceh.

The next threshold would be reached around 14 October in Aceh, when the military's annihilation campaign progressed to its next phase of open military involvement in the killings. The similarities in the timing of this progression throughout Aceh's districts again points to the high level of coordination that existed behind this campaign. The reasons for this progression were probably largely practical in nature. Faced with a large new prison population, a critical decision needed to be made as to what should be done with the detainees. A decision was made to exterminate them. Within the space of just over a week, individual killings in Aceh were becoming impractical. It is not known exactly how the decision was made nationally to begin transporting detainee populations to military-controlled killing sites to be murdered, though the similarities in this stage of the campaign throughout Aceh's districts, and throughout Indonesia on a national scale,[6] indicate that this progression was coordinated. The phrase "completely annihilate" was no longer to be taken as figurative or aspirational.

In this phase, we can see certain patterns develop throughout the province related to the treatment of detainees, such as the manner in which detainees were transported to mass grave sites, as well as in the methods adopted at the killing sites to perform the murders.

In relation to the treatment of detainees, it was common for the military to initiate an arrest campaign in which it either participated directly, or directed members of civilian militia groups, death squads or the political parties to search for people considered to be associated with the PKI, or to initiate campaigns whereby people associated with the PKI felt pressured to report themselves. Upon capture, these men and women were not afforded the normal processes of legal incarceration. They were held without formal charge or trial at military-controlled prisons or other holding sites, including military-controlled concentration camps and government offices. Some detainees were released back into the community during this phase, and were required to report themselves regularly. Most of these people were later hunted down for recapture by the military and its civilian proxies. This process was intended to formally distance the military from the killings, while spreading terror through the community as it became apparent that the perpetrators of the violence enjoyed complete impunity for their actions.

From 14 October, detainees in Aceh began to be transported to military-controlled killing sites, often in locations close to their place of residence. In other cases it was common for detainees to be transported to killing sites outside their local district. In many cases the military carried out these transportations, using military or government vehicles, or trucks confiscated from the local population. These transportations generally happened under the cover of darkness, but ample eyewitness evidence suggests their existence was widely known in local communities. The killings were never meant to be completely hidden, but rather, knowledge and half-knowledge of them was used as a means of inducing fear and compliance in the community.

Upon arriving at the designated killing sites, detainees were killed by members of the military, or by people the military appointed as executioners. Victims were often shot or decapitated in a group before being buried in mass graves that were often dug by members of the local community. In other cases, civilian militia groups or death squads carried out the killings, while in still others, special "executioners" were designated, often from among sections of the community whose loyalty was considered to be suspect, including former Darul Islam fighters and members of the PNI. While members of the civilian militias and death squads were often proud to take part in the military's campaign, the act of killing itself was considered to be an unsavoury and often psychologically disturbing process. Where possible, the actual act of killing would be delegated as far down the chain of command as possible.

An economy of violence emerged. Just as questions of efficiency and resources influenced the manner in which people were killed, many of these variations appear to be based on the practicality of logistics. This makes good sense when the genocide is understood as a systematic program that was simultaneously initiated at various levels as a nation-wide campaign. Practicality and efficiency were key determinants behind the selection of detention, transportation and killing methods used. Such considerations were also behind the military's decision to mobilise civilian populations to participate in this campaign.

By viewing the genocide through a detailed, documented and layered chronology, it is now possible to pinpoint to within a matter of days the dates at which each phase in the violence progressed to the next in Aceh province. This chronology, which has been drawn from the Indonesian genocide files and corroborated by my interviewees in the province, provides insight into how the military's campaign was able to spread from the national to the local level. It is also apparent that the progression between these phases cannot purely be explained by the simple existence of the original orders or directives that had first declared the military's genocidal intentions. These orders were passed down through various chains of command and required the full mobilisation of the state apparatus, civil institutions and society at all levels in order to fully succeed. The documentation of genocide that has been cited in this book is thus the documentation of the mobilisation of a society into a mechanism calibrated to dispense mass murder as it might otherwise dispense an immunisation or irrigation campaign.

Identifying the universal in the Indonesian genocide

Hannah Arendt, in her classic study *Eichmann in Jerusalem*, has identified several key factors she sees as critical for the initiation and implementation of the Holocaust. Many of these factors can also be identified in the case of the Indonesian genocide in Aceh. By identifying the specific manifestations of these factors, it may be possible to glimpse the commonality of some of these patterns, and thus what may be universal about genocidal states.

The first of Arendt's factors, the use of legal frameworks to normalise the actions of a criminal state, can be seen in the use of existing military commands by the military leadership (especially the Kodam, KOTI and Kohanda commands, as well as the use of Dwikora legislation) to initiate and implement its campaign. During later stages of the military's campaign, the military leadership also relied upon the formal dismissal of members of the civil service to provide the purge with a legal basis and to preserve these structures for the new regime.

The second of Arendt's factors, the mobilisation of the state and its resources to implement its genocidal policies, can also be seen in the use of existing military commands. Likewise, it can be seen in the mobilisation of civilian government and the Pantja Tunggal, Tjatur Tunggal and *Front Nasional* bodies to coordinate civilian participation in the genocide. The genocide in Aceh, as in Nazi Germany, was implemented as official state policy.

The third of Arendt's factors is the compartmentalisation of steps related to the implementation of this campaign in order to reduce feelings of individual responsibility among perpetrators and the graduation of violence used in the pursuance of these policies. Such graduation can be seen in the manner in which first-wave violence, including demonstrations and pogrom actions, escalated into public killings before the emergence of direct military involvement in the violence. During the second wave of violence, violence also escalated from military-led arrests, to mass detention at military-controlled detention sites, to transportation and murder at military-controlled killing sites. These phases in the violence echo Arendt's observation that the violence of the Holocaust passed through three major phases, beginning with expulsion, before escalating to concentration and finally mass killing. As discussed above, the escalation between phases appears to have been responsive to practical considerations. This escalation may have also assisted in the normalisation of each phase. As in Nazi Germany, where the systematic concentration and transportation of the Jewish population to mass killing sites was described as a process of "deportation",[7] the destruction of those who became identified with the PKI was depicted as a graduated "removal from the public space".

Compartmentalisation of these phases can be seen in the manner in which individuals involved in arrests appear to have been separated from individuals involved in detentions, who were in turn separated from those involved in transportations, and again from those involved in the physical killings. Generally this compartmentalisation was not necessarily based on an individual's broader understanding of what was occurring, hence Let Bugeh's claims that he, as a member of a state-sponsored death squad, was "only" involved in hunting down suspects and surrendering them to the military after brutalising them, and Zainal Abidin's claim that he, as a Subdistrict Head, "didn't know" what happened to the individuals he had detained in his government office once they were taken away.[8] Both clearly did know – and were able to describe the broader killings in considerable detail. Their initial denials, however, hint at the importance denying responsibility for involvement in the genocide (both legal and psychological) appears to have held for participants in it.

The fourth of Arendt's factors, the use of "winged words" to shield individuals from the reality of the violence perpetrated, can be seen in the avoidance in the Indonesian genocide files and in testimonial accounts of the genocide of direct words like "murder", and the avoidance of references to agency behind the killings. "Corpses" are "found" and people accused of being associated with the PKI are referred to as "*oknum*" (a dehumanising term that translates literally as "element"), not people or civilians. These "*oknum*" are "crushed", "annihilated" and "cleansed".[9]

There is plenty of violence within these words but, as Arendt tells us, the avoidance of usual terms to describe murder may act to distance perpetrators from previously accepted legal norms relating to murder and justice. Similarly, terms such as "being transported", "placed on trucks" or "placed on trains" in Aceh appear to have acted to provide a buffer between an acknowledgement that individuals were systematically being taken to killing sites to be murdered. Likewise, by describing the abduction and forcible disappearance of individuals as "arrests", an illusion of legal process was maintained, allowing participants in the violence to maintain the facade – if only to themselves – that the individuals whom they abducted and handed over to the military to be murdered were afforded access to due (legal) processes, a situation which parallels the concept of "deportation to the East" employed during the Holocaust.

Meanwhile, the fifth of Arendt's factors, the use of grand narrative to allow perpetrators to feel as if they are part of something "heroic", can be seen in the manner in which the genocide was framed as an historic and heroic showdown against a mortal enemy ("our enemy since 1948") and as a continuation of the great national revolution, a crushing of "counter revolutionaries" and "imperialists" (originally communist concepts that had been popularised by Sukarno during the early 1960s) and even as a "war". In reality the killings of 1965–66 were a one-sided slaughter. That the Indonesian military may have conceived of the genocide as a war, and mobilised and launched its attack accordingly, does not diminish the parallel symbolic nature of the use of this term, which allowed the military to portray its aggressive attack as a struggle against an armed opponent. Meanwhile, the military attempted to frame the killings as a holy war, a tactic that was intended not only to present the killings as civilian-led, but to also provide religious justification and blessing for the killings. Heroic narratives thus appear to have been used to shield perpetrators and onlookers from the reality of what they were doing and seeing.

The documents cited in this book suggest that an understanding existed that the actual act of murder could not be written about explicitly, despite the same documents recording the formation of death squads, distribution of arms and other actions that facilitated the murders. Not once in the documents that I have seen is it explicitly stated that the military murdered members of the PKI. The reality of the genocide was, as had been described by Heinrich Himmler in the case of Nazi Germany, "a page of glory in our history which has never been written and is never to be written".[10] Yet, while Germany lost the war and the story of the Holocaust has since been told innumerable times, the New Order canonised the dead generals and prohibited research into the killings.

It may be that the very act of writing and telling this suppressed history of the genocide, told as it was experienced by those who lived through it, may be one of the most powerful means through which to shatter the legitimacy of previously hegemonic propaganda versions of this history. Moreover, by identifying these factors as reflective of a deeper logic inherent within the genocidal state, it may be possible to expose the truly systematic nature of this campaign and to glimpse, as it were, the mechanics of mass murder that lie not so far from the surface of all modern nation states.

Understanding the genocide as a centralised and national campaign

The major question for those interested in understanding the 1965–66 killings when I began research for this book was whether the military was responsible for the killings. The Indonesian genocide files have proven that the military was, indeed, responsible for the killings and that it made no secret of this fact in its internal communications. A question I have often been asked since I first began to present the information contained within this book is whether the situation in Aceh was somehow unique, such that my findings might apply only to that province. At heart, this question has asked if it is possible to prove the genocide was implemented as a centralised and national campaign.[11]

This question must be answered in two parts. I do not argue against the proposal that Aceh may, in some ways, have been unique. As a province that had recently experienced armed conflict during the Darul Islam rebellion, Aceh remained prepared to launch a new military offensive. Meanwhile, as a province described as the "citadel of opposition" to the PKI,[12] Aceh was susceptible to the military's propaganda offensive against the PKI. Specific socio-political factors that may have helped contribute to the speed and intensity of the killings in Aceh already discussed in this book include: the military's control over Aceh's Pantja Tunggal body as a result of the PKI's short-sighted 1964 campaign to "retool" Aceh's provincial government; the desire of recently pardoned former Darul Islam fighters who had been incorporated into the provincial military command to demonstrate their loyalty to the new military regime; and the history of ideological conflict in the province between the PKI and members of modernist Islamist organisations, such as PII and HMI, that had been aligned with Masjumi – Aceh's most popular political party until it was outlawed following a PKI-led ban in 1960. These factors alone, however, do not account for the scale or intensity of the violence in the province. To provide a useful contrast, West Java, which had also recently experienced armed conflict during the Darul Islam rebellion, experienced a relatively "low" death toll during the genocide.[13] West Java's population, at close to 22 million, was almost eleven times larger than Aceh's population of 2 million. Yet, it is believed 10,000 people were killed in West Java during the time of the genocide – roughly the same number of people estimated to have been killed in Aceh. By contrast, in Central Java, which also had a population of close to 22 million, it is believed approximately 100,000 were killed during the time of the genocide.[14] Adjusted for population size, the scale of the killings in Aceh was closer to that seen in Central Java. It has been proposed that the smaller death toll in West Java was caused by the military's unwillingness to extensively arm civilian militia groups in the province for fear that they might begin to operate outside the military's control.[15] Considering that both Aceh and West Java shared a history of recent involvement in the Darul Islam rebellion and local ideological opposition to the PKI, this comparison suggests that the role of the military was decisive in determining the scale of the killings in the two provinces. Moreover, while it is possible that these socio-political factors may have increased the speed and intensity of the killings in Aceh, it is clear the killings did not occur without the direction and direct intervention of the military. As this book has shown, the killings were not spontaneous. They were the deliberate outcome of military policy.

This leads us to the second part of the question. If the killings in Aceh were the result of a deliberate military campaign, is it possible to prove that this campaign was part of a larger, national campaign? Let us begin with what is already known. It has been known since the time of the genocide that Suharto assumed the position of Commander in Chief of the Armed Forces during the early hours of 1 October 1965. This position had been held by General Ahmad Yani until he was kidnapped and murdered by the 30 September Movement. Suharto would repeatedly refuse to surrender this position when ordered to by Sukarno. It is now also known that Suharto seized control over the Supreme Operations (KOTI) Command, which had also been under the command of Yani until the early hours of 1 October (chapter 1). In addition to granting Suharto control over the KOTI Command, this position gave Suharto direct control over the two Mandala Commands that controlled special military operations in Sumatra and Kalimantan. Suharto would use both of these positions to not only coordinate the military's attack in Jakarta, but also in Indonesia's regions.

In Sumatra, this book has shown, this chain of command continued down through Mokoginta, who jointly held the positions of Inter-Regional Military Commander (under the Kodam structure) and First Mandala (*Mandala Satu*) Commander (under the KOTI structure). At the provincial level in Aceh, this chain of command then extended down through Djuarsa, who held the positions of Aceh Military Commander (under the Kodam structure), Regional Authority to Implement Dwikora (under the KOTI structure) and Defence Region Commander (also under the KOTI structure). This final chain of command (the Kodahan/Kohanda Command) was activated on 1 October in direct response to the national military leadership's declared intention to move against the PKI (chapter 2).

In addition to demonstrating centralized command responsibility during the time of the genocide in Aceh, the Indonesian genocide files show these national chains of command were utilised to coordinate the genocide from 1 October. It is now known, for example, that during the morning of 1 October, Suharto, Mokoginta and Djuarsa communicated with each other via telegram to discuss the "coup" in Jakarta. At midnight that night, Mokoginta acknowledged the insubordinate leadership of Suharto and ordered all troops under his command, throughout Sumatra, to "resolutely and completely annihilate" individuals accused of being associated with the 30 September Movement. At some point during the day, 'Operasi Berdikari' was launched by Djuarsa, acting in his position as Defence Region Commander, to coordinate the military's 'annihilation campaign' against the PKI in Aceh. This campaign was conducted with the full knowledge and support of the national military command.

Suharto's direct command over the military's attack against the PKI can also be seen in Kalimantan and Eastern Indonesia. A Second Mandala Command had been in place in Kalimantan on 1 October. This command was led by Brigadier General M. Panggabean, who had been close to Ahmad Yani and who would prove himself loyal to Suharto.[16] Violence, however, did not erupt in Kalimantan until October 1967, when the military mobilised the Dayak militia to kill 5,000 ethnic Chinese in the territory.[17] By this stage, the military's attack against the PKI in the territory was coordinated by the Kopkamtib (Operational Command for the Restoration of Security and Order) Command, which had been established under Suharto's command on 6 December 1965.[18] This new command would coordinate the military's attack against the PKI from this date in Kalimantan, under the leadership of Major Genderal D. Sumartono and in Eastern Indonesia,[19] under the leadership of Major General Askari.[20]

Suharto also had direct control over the military's attack against the PKI in Java and Bali, which was coordinated by the RPKAD Special Forces under the leadership of Sarwo Edhie.[21] The RPKAD began its attack against the PKI in Central and East Java from mid-October 1965, while it began its attack against the PKI in Bali in December 1965. These campaigns, which occurred in the PKI's major membership centres, have been extensively documented by researchers.[22] It is thus possible to see that the military, under the leadership of Suharto, controlled its attack against the PKI through three major command structures: the KOTI Command (Sumatra), the Kopkamtib (Kalimantan and Eastern Indonesia)[23] and the RPKAD (Java and Bali). Each of these command structures operated autonomously from each other until the national rollout of the Kopkamtib in December 1965, but acknowledged the same national military command. It was through these command structures that Suharto was able to coordinate the genocide as a centralised, national campaign. The fact that multiple command structures were used to coordinate a nationwide genocide is not unique to Indonesia. Multiple command structures were also used during the Nazi Holocaust, with different killing techniques seen in different territories.[24]

Centralised coordination of this campaign can also be seen in the organisation of death squads on Sumatra, Java and Bali, which were apparently jointly coordinated by RPKAD Special Forces Commander Sarwo Edhie.[25] It is yet to be known if this centralised coordination of military-sponsored death squads also extended to Kalimantan and Eastern Indonesia. Similarly, centralised coordination can be seen in the national rollout of the prisoner classification system from May 1966 (chapter 7). From this time, all political prisoners accused of being associated with the PKI throughout the archipelago were given a standard label, either 'a', 'b' or 'c', which determined how they were to be processed by the rapidly crystallising New Order bureaucracy.

Meanwhile, centralised coordination of the genocide can be seen in the military's internal communications. An examination of the military's own internal communications relating to its role in initiating and implementing the genocide in Aceh and Sumatra more generally shows that the military understood very clearly that its actions were part of a centralised and coordinated national campaign. Mokoginta and Djuarsa continually received and acted upon directives from Jakarta throughout the duration of the genocide. They also sent copies of their own orders and directives back up this chain of command to their superiors in the national military leadership as well as to Sukarno, the national government and the national radio station in Jakarta. There is no reason to believe Sumatra was unique in this respect.

Finally, it is now clear that the military, in its internal communications, described its campaign to crush the PKI as a national campaign. In the more than 3,000 pages of documents that have been recovered and analysed for this book, there is not a single argument made by the military or government that Aceh or Sumatra was in any way unique in its need to launch an attack against the PKI. The military's attack was always framed as 'saving' the Indonesian state, as a national entity, from an existential threat that had arisen in Jakarta. This attack was subsequently launched in each of Indonesia's provinces more or less concurrently, as part of a national campaign.

The evidence in this book demonstrates that the coordination and intention behind this campaign was much greater than it has previously been possible to prove. In doing so, it challenges the idea that the 1965–66 killings should be seen as a series of autonomous or semi-autonomous province-wide campaigns, as has long been a feature of analysis of this event. In 1991 Robert Cribb observed that there did not appear to be a single national pattern behind the killings.[26] As he explained: "The central difficulty for historians has been the problem of reconciling their national and local dimensions." This was because, although the killings were clearly "precipitated by a national event, the attempted coup in Jakarta" and involved "avowedly national actors – the army, the PKI [and] organized Islam", it appeared that "the relatively scant information we possess suggests that a host of local factors in each region determined the scope and scale of each bout of killing".

This argument was originally aimed at suggesting that even if it could not yet be proven that the national military leadership had ordered the killings as part of a single, centralised, national campaign, it was possible to argue that local military commanders might have ordered the killings in their various areas of operation. This approach was a response to the serious lack of evidence then available, and enabled researchers to present evidence they had of military involvement in the killings in their specific locations of research without having to constantly defend why they could not prove military agency behind the killings as a national event. As outlined in chapter 1, while it has long been suspected by Indonesia researchers and genocide scholars that the killings were centrally coordinated by the military, the inability of Indonesia researchers to prove this centralized coordination presented a "evidence problem" that has severely hampered research into the killings since they occurred. In presenting "each bout of killing" as occurring autonomously from a national pattern, this argument unfortunately dovetailed with military reports of the killings, which presented the killings as the result of local factors in each of Indonesia's provinces.[27] The discovery of the Indonesian genocide files has fundamentally altered what is now knowable regarding military agency behind the killings.

It is now clear that the military played a far more active role in the killings. Indeed, it is now possible to prove that the military acted with intent to destroy its target group, as evidenced by its sustained orders to "annihilate down to the roots" Indonesia's communist group. Likewise, it is now possible to prove that the national military leadership fully mobilised the military and civilian state apparatuses, along with the civilian population more generally, to initiate and implement the killings, using clearly identifiable chains of command to do so. In short, it is now possible to prove that the military perpetrated genocide as part of a centralised, national campaign.

Further research is required to demonstrate the specific manner in which aspects of this campaign were initiated and implemented in areas of Indonesia outside of Aceh, and to build upon current understanding of military involvement in these areas, especially in areas outside those that have been studied so far in North Sumatra, Jakarta, East Java and Bali. It can nonetheless be reasonably extrapolated that similar patterns and use of existing military command structures, mobilisation of state apparatuses and mobilisation of the civilian population occurred throughout Indonesia during the period of the genocide, producing similar patterns in how the genocide was initiated and implemented in these areas. It is likely that the discovery of military- and government-produced documents from other regions will build upon the general patterns outlined in this book. The burden of proof to demonstrate that the Indonesian genocide should not be understood as a national and centralised campaign now lies with those who wish to maintain the military's version of events. As this book has shown, the Indonesian military, for its part, never had any question about its own role in the killings.

What next?

The question of accountability for the Indonesian genocide is no longer a matter of attempting to establish whether or not the Indonesian military and state should ultimately be held accountable for the crimes of the Indonesian genocide, but rather a question of what is to be done with this knowledge.

For almost half a century those responsible for one of the twentieth century's worst atrocities have enjoyed complete impunity for their actions. The allies of the military's New Order regime in Washington, London and Canberra have, meanwhile, been able to escape scrutiny for their own roles in this atrocity. It is farcical to believe the Indonesian state will spontaneously initiate a meaningful truth-seeking, let alone justice-seeking, investigation into these dark events without serious pressure being applied. As shown by Komnas HAM's current inability to convince Indonesia's Attorney General of the need to initiate a legally binding investigation into the events of 1965–66, despite the clear legal mandate for such an investigation, refusal to come to terms with the Indonesian genocide is firmly rooted within the Indonesian state. This continued impunity has deep and practical consequences for contemporary Indonesian society, and indeed the international community. It fosters impunity and the understanding that in order to get away with mass murder, one simply has to do it on a large enough scale and with the correct backing.

The Indonesian genocide has recently been thrust into the international spotlight to a degree perhaps unprecedented since it was first perpetrated as a result of the runaway success of and critical acclaim for Joshua Oppenheimer's two films *The Act of Killing* (2012) and *The Look of Silence* (2014).[28] This attention has, in turn, helped to spur on many new initiatives and reinvigorate a previously small and relatively obscure field of research. In Indonesia, in January 2014, presidential spokesman Teuku Faizasyah conceded that the killings constituted "violations against humanity", before warning that Indonesia should not "be pushed by outside parties" to rush "reconciliation".[29] This was a reference to growing calls for the Indonesian government to publically acknowledge the genocide and to implement Komnas HAM's recommendation for a legally binding investigation. Beyond the obvious question of what reconciliation Faizasyah is speaking about when the Indonesian government is actively blocking Komnas HAM's recommendation, this comment represented a major admission from the government.

A similar positive step can be seen in the holding of the government-sponsored 'National Symposium on the 1965 Tragedy' in April 2016. In attempting to downplay the scale of the killings by insisting that the government does not have evidence that "a [large] number of people got killed back in 1965", Minister Luhut Pandjaitan has issued an irresistible challenge. Though, as this book has demonstrated, it is clear that it is not a lack of evidence, but rather, a lack of political will, that is holding back investigation into the genocide in Indonesia.

Local NGOs throughout the country have also stepped up their activities to document the genocide. Following Pandjaitan's comments, multiple activist groups, including Kontras and YPKP, came forward with lists of mass grave sites from the 1965–66 period.[30] In response, in May 2016, President Jokowi announced the formation of a special team to investigate this growing list of reported mass grave sites.[31] No further news has been heard about this special investigation team.

Meanwhile, internationally, the 'International People's Tribunal for 1965' (IPT-65) was held in The Hague in November 2015 to mark the fiftieth anniversary of the genocide.[32] Calls have even been made in the US Senate for the US government to apologise for its own involvement in the genocide.[33]

The most significant outcome of this new attention on the killings has been that the Indonesian genocide is no longer spoken of as an agentless mystery and "spontaneous" orgy of mass violence, but as a deliberate campaign of state-sponsored violence. Such an understanding demands that, beyond the urgent need for further public admissions from the Indonesian government and its Western backers, and the need for survivors and their families to be fully rehabilitated,[34] there must be some form of legal accountability for the Indonesian genocide if the international laws that are held as the binding fabric of the international community are to retain meaning as a means of holding perpetrators of human rights atrocities to account. The pursuit of punitive justice for individual perpetrators might have little benefit at this point, considering that most high-level leaders of the genocide (including Suharto, Mokoginta and Djuarsa) are now dead. As the case of Duch (Kaing Guek Eav) in Cambodia and Eichmann himself in Israel demonstrates, the incarceration or execution of one old man – especially if this individual can only be proven to have played a mid-level role in the genocide – will not atone for the sins of the past. This is especially the case if such an individual effectively becomes a scapegoat for the regime, allowing the current government to escape tricky questions about its own connections with the past regime and dodge ongoing questions of impunity.

This does not mean, however, that perpetrators should continue to enjoy complete impunity for their actions. Justice can take many forms and it may well be considered that a process of truth-telling accompanied by an official investigation into the genocide empowered to identify the individuals and institutions responsible for the violence may well be the most realistic and practical alternative. Such a process would remain a ground-breaking achievement after half a century of blatant impunity. Indeed, if such a process is delayed much longer there will simply no longer be any eyewitnesses to testify and add critical details to our understanding of the genocide. Such an outcome would be a tragedy, considering the current level of international awareness and interest in the genocide. The answer to the question 'what next?' must be a clear and emphatic demand for truth and justice.

Notes

1 Cited in, '*Pernjataan*', Pengurus Baperki Tjabang Langsa, Langsa, East Aceh, 18 October 1965, p. 1.
2 John Roosa, *Pretext for Mass Murder: The 30th September Movement & Suharto's Coup D'Etat in Indonesia* (Madison: The University of Wisconsin Press, 2006), p. 58.
3 In Central Java, officers in the Diponogoro division had initially shown their support for the 30 September Movement. The deputy governor of Central Java, Sujono Atmo, was also considered to be closely allied to the PKI. Harold Crouch, *The Army and Politics in Indonesia* (Jakarta: Equinox Publishing, 2007, originally 1978), p. 143. In East Java, officers in the Brawijaya division were reluctant to take action against Sukarno's wishes. The Deputy Governor of East Java, Satrio Sastrodiredjo, was also considered to be closely allied to the PKI. *Ibid.*
4 As explained in chapter 3, in North Sumatra, Governor Brigadier General Ulung Sitepu was placed under house arrest after returning to Medan from the meeting in Langsa on 1 October 1965. Sitepu would later die in jail, while Suteja was "disappeared". Arief Ikhsanudin, 'Dituduh Komunis, Gubernur Bali Dihilangkan', *Historia*, 1 October 2015. Available online: http://historia.id/modern/dituduh-komunis-gubernur-bali-dihilangkan. In Bali, Governor Anak Agung Bagus Suteja made virtually no public statements and appeared only rarely at public ceremonies and gatherings during October 1965. He also imposed a ban on local military coverage of "G-30-S developments" in "an apparent attempt to create

some political breathing space" in Bali. See, Geoffrey Robinson, *The Dark Side of Paradise: Political Violence in Bali* (Ithaca and New York: Cornell University, 1995), p. 228.

5 In Central Java, the killings reached their peak in mid-November. In Bali, killings began in December. Harold Crouch, *The Army and Politics*, p. 152.

6 For Java, see, David Jenkin and Douglas Kammen, 'The Army Para-commando Regiment and the Reign of Terror in Central Java and Bali', in Douglas Kammen and Katharine McGregor (eds.), *The Contours of Mass Violence in Indonesia, 1965–68* (Singapore: NUS Press, 2012); also, Vannessa Hearman, 'Dismantling the "Fortress": East Java and the Transition to Suharto's New Order Regime (1965–68)', PhD thesis, The University of Melbourne, 2012; for Bali, Geoffrey Robinson, *The Dark Side of Paradise*; for North Sumatra, Joshua Oppenheimer, 'Show of Force: Film, Ghosts and Genres of Historical Performance in the Indonesian Genocide', PhD thesis, University of the Arts London, 2004; for South Sulawesi, Taufik Ahmad, 'South Sulawesi: The Military, Prison Camps and Forced Labour', in Douglas Kammen and Katharine McGregor (eds.), *The Contours of Mass Violence in Indonesia*.

7 Hannah Arendt, *Eichmann in Jerusalem: A Report on the Banality of Evil* (New York: Penguin Books, 2006, originally 1963), p. 82.

8 See chapters 5 and 6.

9 These are words commonly used in communist purges. The Khmer Rouge in Cambodia used the terms "smash" and "sweep clean". David Chandler, *Voices From S-21: Terror and History in Pol Pot's Secret Prison* (Berkeley and Los Angeles: University of California Press, 1999), pp. 41, 51.

10 Heinrich Himmler, 'Speech given to SS Group Leaders in Posen'. Available online:www.historyplace.com/worldwar2/holocaust/h-posen.htm.

11 I was, for example, asked this question at the Association of Asian Studies Annual Conference in Toronto, where I presented a paper as part of the panel, 'Still Unresolved Problems in the Indonesian Killings, 1965–68', 18 March 2017. I was also asked this question at the 'Critical Perspectives on US-Southeast Asia Relations', Workshop, Columbia University, New York, 21 April 2017.

12 Airgram from James F. O'Connor, First Secretary of Embassy for the Ambassador, US Embassy Jakarta to US Department of State, 25 March 1964.

13 Douglas Kammen and Katharine McGregor, 'Introduction: The Contours of Mass Violence in Indonesia, 1965–68', in Douglas Kammen and Katharine McGregor (eds.), *The Contours of Mass Violence in Indonesia*, pp. 17–18.

14 *Ibid.* Population figures are drawn from Indonesia's 1971 census. See, 'Penduduk Indonesia menurut Provinsi, 1971, 1980, 1990, 1995, 2000 dan 2010', *Badan Pusat Statistik*. Available online: www.bps.go.id/linkTabelStatis/view/id/1267.

15 *Ibid.*

16 Harold Crouch, *The Army and Politics*, pp. 73, 223.

17 Jamie S. Davidson, *From Rebellion to Riots: Collective Violence on Indonesian Borneo* (Wisconsin: University of Wisconsin Press, 2008), pp. 60–80; also, 'Tim Ad Hoc Penyelidikan Pelanggaran HAM yang Berat Peristiwa 1965–1966', *Laporan Akhir Tim Ad Hoc Penyelidikan Pelanggaran HAM yang Berat Peristiwa 1965–1966* ('*Laporan Akir '65*'), Komnas HAM, Jakarta, 5 May 2012, p. 185.

18 '*Laporan Akhir '65*', p. 163. Suharto first announced his intention to establish the Kopkamtib on 10 October 1965.

19 Public violence began in Kupang on 28 October 1965. Mass meetings were held in the town on 20 November 1965 and 17 January 1966. Steve Farram, 'The PKI in West Timor and Nusa Tenggara Timur: 1965 and beyond', *Bijdragen tot de Taal-, Land- en Volkenkunde*, Vol. 166, No. 4 (2010), p. 387.

20 '*Laporan Akhir '65*', p. 163. The Kopkamtib structure was also replicated in Sumatra under the command of Mokoginta. As this occurred after the worst of the killings in Aceh (December 1965), the establishment of this structure is of limited relevance in

that province. It may have played a more central role in other provinces in Sumatra. Kopkamtib would eventually come to coordinate the military's campaign nationally.

21 *Ibid.*, p. 165.

22 See, for example, John Roosa, *Pretext for Mass Murder*, pp. 29–30; also Geoffrey Robinson, *The Dark Side of Paradise*, pp. 281, 284–285, 295–297.

23 The Kopkamtib was established in Sumatra on 21 December 1965.

24 Four battalion-sized (*Einsatzgruppen*) killing units, for example, were deployed from 1941 in the occupied Soviet Union. Each of these units reported directly to the Reich Main Office in Berlin. These units were not used outside of this territory. Robert Rozett and Shmuel Spector, *Encyclopedia of the Holocaust* (New York: Routledge, 2013), pp. 201–202.

25 Ibrahim Sinik, a prominent journalist in Medan, on a talk show shown in *The Act of Killing*, directed by Joshua Oppenheimer (Denmark: Final Cut for Real, 2012), in a scene that did not make it into the final cut of the film, explains he was appointed head of the *Kasatuan Aksi* (the network of death squads that operated throughout North Sumatra during the time of the genocide) by Sarwo Edhie (*The Act of Killing*, extended transcripts, AFVM Disc 1:3). Edhie, in addition to leading the killings in Java and Bali, also played a role in coordinating the KAMI/KAPPI death squads in Jakarta (Harold Crouch, *The Army and Politics in Indonesia*, p. 166). If Sinik's admissions are correct, this would appear to confirm that death squads in Sumatra were not only coordinated by the military at the provincial level, but also coordinated nationally and centrally from Jakarta, where they were receiving money from the United States ('Telegram From US Ambassador Green to US State Department, 2 December 1965', *Foreign Relations of the United State, 1964–1968: Volume XXVI, Indonesia; Malaysia- Singapore; Philippines* [Washington: Government Printing Office, 2001]).

26 Robert Cribb, 'Introduction', in Robert Cribb (ed.), *The Indonesian Killings of 1965–1966: Studies From Java and Bali* (Clayton, Victoria: Central of Southeast Asian Studies, Monash University, 1991), p. 21.

27 A more recent formulation of this position can be found in Douglas Kammen and Katharine McGregor, 'Introduction: The Contours of Mass Violence in Indonesia, 1965–68', in Douglas Kammen and Katharine McGregor (eds.), *The Contours of Mass Violence in Indonesia*, pp. 8–10.

28 *The Act of Killing* has, to date, won sixty-two awards. *The Look of Silence* has, to date, won thirty-six awards. Links to international press coverage of the two films can be found at www.theactofkilling.com and www.thelookofsilence.com.

29 Josua Gantan, 'Indonesia Reacts to 'Act of Killing' Academy Nomination', *The Jakarta Globe*, 23 January 2014.

30 See, for example, 'Kontras Temukan 16 Lokasi Kuburan Massal Korban 1965', *Kompas*, 26 April 2016.

31 Human Rights Watch, 'Indonesia: Protect Mass Graves of 1965–66 Massacres', 22 May 2016. Available online: www.hrw.org/news/2016/05/22/indonesia-protect-mass-graves-1965–66-massacres.

32 The Final Report of the IPT 65 was announced in July 2016. 'Final Report of the IPT 1965: Findings and Documents of the IPT 1965', 20 July 2016. Available online: www.tribunal1965.org/final-report-of-the-ipt-1965/.

33 Tierney Sneed, 'Between Indonesia and the Oscars, "The Act of Killing" Makes a Stop in D.C.', U.S. News, 18 February 2014. Available online: www.usnews.com/news/articles/2014/02/17/between-indonesia-and-the-oscars-the-act-of-killing-makes-a-stop-in-washington.

34 Survivors continue to face social stigmatisation despite the formal abolition of their status as "ex-tapol" (former political prisoners). Legal restrictions against this group were maintained until 2011. Today, survivors continue to face restrictions on their freedom of speech and suffer the effects of fifty years of economic marginalisation. See Adriaan Bedner, 'Citizenship Restored', *Inside Indonesia*, Edition 122, Oct– Dec 2015. Available online: http://www.insideindonesia.org/citizenship-restored-3

Index

Studies of the Weatherhead East Asian Institute
Columbia University

Selected titles

(Complete list at: http://weai.columbia.edu/publications/studies-weai/)

Making Time: Astronomical Time Measurement in Tokugawa Japan, by Yulia Frumer. University of Chicago Press, 2018.

Resurrecting Nagasaki: Reconstruction and the Formation of Atomic Narratives, by Chad Diehl. Cornell University Press, 2018.

Promiscuous Media: Film and Visual Culture in Imperial Japan, 1926–1945, by Hikari Hori. Cornell University Press, 2018.

The End of Japanese Cinema: Industrial Genres, National Times, and Media Ecologies, by Alexander Zahlten. Duke University Press, 2017.

The Chinese Typewriter: A History, by Thomas S. Mullaney. The MIT Press, 2017.

Food of Sinful Demons: Meat, Vegetarianism, and the Limits of Buddhism in Tibet, by Geoffrey Barstow. Columbia University Press, 2017

Mobilizing Without the Masses: Control and Contention in China, by Diana Fu. Cambridge University Press, 2017.

Forgotten Disease: Illnesses Transformed in Chinese Medicine, by Hilary A. Smith. Stanford University Press, 2017.

Aesthetic Life: Beauty and Art in Modern Japan, by Miya Mizuta Lippit. Harvard University Asia Center, 2017.

Youth For Nation: Culture and Protest in Cold War South Korea, by Charles R. Kim. University of Hawaii Press, 2017.

Socialist Cosmopolitanism: The Chinese Literary Universe, 1945–1965, by Nicolai Volland. Columbia University Press, 2017.

Yokohama and the Silk Trade: How Eastern Japan Became the Primary Economic Region of Japan, 1843–1893, by Yasuhiro Makimura. Lexington Books, 2017.

The Social Life of Inkstones: Artisans and Scholars in Early Qing China, by Dorothy Ko. University of Washington Press, 2017.

Darwin, Dharma, and the Divine: Evolutionary Theory and Religion in Modern Japan, by G. Clinton Godart. University of Hawaii Press, 2017.

Dictators and Their Secret Police: Coercive Institutions and State Violence, by Sheena Chestnut Greitens. Cambridge University Press, 2016.

The Cultural Revolution on Trial: Mao and the Gang of Four, by Alexander C. Cook. Cambridge University Press, 2016.

Inheritance of Loss: China, Japan, and the Political Economy of Redemption After Empire, by Yukiko Koga. University of Chicago Press, 2016.

Homecomings: The Belated Return of Japan's Lost Soldiers, by Yoshikuni Igarashi. Columbia University Press, 2016.

Samurai to Soldier: Remaking Military Service in Nineteenth-Century Japan, by D. Colin Jaundrill. Cornell University Press, 2016.

The Red Guard Generation and Political Activism in China, by Guobin Yang. Columbia University Press, 2016.

Accidental Activists: Victim Movements and Government Accountability in Japan and South Korea, by Celeste L. Arrington. Cornell University Press, 2016.

Ming China and Vietnam: Negotiating Borders in Early Modern Asia, by Kathlene Baldanza. Cambridge University Press, 2016.

Ethnic Conflict and Protest in Tibet and Xinjiang: Unrest in China's West, coedited, by Ben Hillman and Gray Tuttle. Columbia University Press, 2016.

One Hundred Million Philosophers: Science of Thought and the Culture of Democracy in Postwar Japan, by Adam Bronson. University of Hawaii Press, 2016.

Conflict and Commerce in Maritime East Asia: The Zheng Family and the Shaping of the Modern World, c. 1620–1720, by Xing Hang. Cambridge University Press, 2016.

Chinese Law in Imperial Eyes: Sovereignty, Justice, and Transcultural Politics, by Li Chen. Columbia University Press, 2016.

Imperial Genus: The Formation and Limits of the Human in Modern Korea and Japan, by Travis Workman. University of California Press, 2015.

Yasukuni Shrine: History, Memory, and Japan's Unending Postwar, by Akiko Takenaka. University of Hawaii Press, 2015

The Age of Irreverence: A New History of Laughter in China, by Christopher Rea. University of California Press, 2015

The Knowledge of Nature and the Nature of Knowledge in Early Modern Japan, by Federico Marcon. University of Chicago Press, 2015

The Fascist Effect: Japan and Italy, 1915–1952, by Reto Hofmann. Cornell University Press, 2015

Empires of Coal: Fueling China's Entry into the Modern World Order, 1860–1920, by Shellen Xiao Wu. Stanford University Press, 2015